Keep this book. You will need it and use it throughout your career.

About the American Hotel & Lodging Association (AH&LA)

Founded in 1910, AH&LA is the trade association representing the lodging industry in the United States. AH&LA is a federation of state lodging associations throughout the United States with 11,000 lodging properties worldwide as members. The association offers its members assistance with governmental affairs representation, communications, marketing, hospitality operations, training and education, technology issues, and more. For information, call 202-289-3100.

LODGING, the management magazine of AH&LA, is a "living textbook" for hospitality students that provides timely features, industry news, and vital lodging information.

About the American Hotel & Lodging Educational Institute (EI)

An affiliate of AH&LA, the Educational Institute is the world's largest source of quality training and educational materials for the lodging industry. EI develops textbooks and courses that are used in more than 1,200 colleges and universities worldwide, and also offers courses to individuals through its Distance Learning program. Hotels worldwide rely on EI for training resources that focus on every aspect of lodging operations. Industry-tested videos, CD-ROMs, seminars, and skills guides prepare employees at every skill level. EI also offers professional certification for the industry's top performers. For information about EI's products and services, call 800-349-0299 or 407-999-8100.

About the American Hotel & Lodging Educational Foundation (AH&LEF)

An affiliate of AH&LA, the American Hotel & Lodging Educational Foundation provides financial support that enhances the stability, prosperity, and growth of the lodging industry through educational and research programs. AH&LEF has awarded millions of dollars in scholarship funds for students pursuing higher education in hospitality management. AH&LEF has also funded research projects on topics important to the industry, including occupational safety and health, turnover and diversity, and best practices in the U.S. lodging industry. For more information, go to www.ahlef.org.

MANAGING FRONT OFFICE OPERATIONS

Educational Institute Books

MANAGING FRONT OFFICE OPERATIONS

Ninth Edition

Michael L. Kasavana, Ph.D.

**American
Hotel & Lodging
Educational Institute**

Disclaimer

This publication is designed to provide accurate and authoritative information in regard to the subject matter covered. It is sold with the understanding that the publisher is not engaged in rendering legal, accounting, or other professional service. If legal advice or other expert assistance is required, the services of a competent professional person should be sought.

—From the Declaration of Principles jointly adopted by the American Bar Association and a Committee of Publishers and Associations

The author, Michael L. Kasavana, is solely responsible for the contents of this publication. All views expressed herein are solely those of the author and do not necessarily reflect the views of the American Hotel & Lodging Educational Institute (the Institute) or the American Hotel & Lodging Association (AH&LA).

Nothing contained in this publication shall constitute a standard, an endorsement, or a recommendation of AH&LA or the Institute. AH&LA and the Institute disclaim any liability with respect to the use of any information, procedure, or product, or reliance thereon by any member of the hospitality industry.

Contents

Preface

FROM THE TIME a guest makes a reservation and arrives at a hotel through the time he or she departs, front office personnel play a central role in coordinating resources and services designed to meet the guest's needs. Guests generally have more contact with front office staff than with any other hotel department staff; as a result, to many guests, the front office *is* the hotel. Guests will contact front office staff with questions, requests, comments, and complaints. Front office staff members who effectively anticipate, respond, and address these challenges help exceed the expectations that hotel guests have.

A capable, courteous, and professional front office staff member can contribute to making each guest's stay a pleasant experience and, in the process, encourage the guest to return. In so doing, front office staff members strive to meet guest needs while also ensuring smooth and profitable hotel operations. This may not always be an easy task. Poorly trained front office employees can do great harm to a hotel's reputation, reduce or eliminate profitability, and antagonize guests.

This ninth edition of *Managing Front Office Operations* will help you—whether you are a front office manager or staff member or a hospitality student—to understand, organize, perform, and evaluate the front office functions that are critical to a hotel's success. This book details information about numerous aspects of front office operations and management. It examines complex relationships between hotel departments, technological advances, and unique front office strategies. All topics are presented in an easy-to-read and easy-to-understand format. Although the book concentrates on the many technical aspects of front office management, it also emphasizes the importance of guest service. Indeed, the quality of guest services often separates a great hotel experience from an average one. This edition's many discussions on guest service provide the reader with appropriate insight into this important area.

Model job descriptions for selected front office positions are in various sections of the book. The text also touches on such important industry concerns as multicultural workforce management, employee recruitment and retention, and compliance with the Americans with Disabilities Act. Review questions and definitions of key terms appear at the end of each chapter, followed by a section providing relevant website addresses for those seeking more in-depth information on a broad range of topics mentioned in the text.

In addition to preserving the strengths of the eighth edition, this edition incorporates many improvements. New material describes the potential impact of automated information technologies on a variety of front office functions. Also included in this edition are sections on the revenue manager, the ways in which blogging and social networking affect hotels, manual backup procedures in case of automated system failure, identity theft prevention, payment card security standards, the green hotel, and Internet concepts and protocols (in the extensive appendix at the end of the book). These topics have become critical to front office operations, and front office managers must be knowledgeable of and fluent in the capabilities and language of a revised front office toolbox. In addition, important discussions of front office operations have been expanded throughout the text, especially with respect to human resources management, business forecasting, revenue management, budget planning, and front office staff interaction with sales, housekeeping, and security personnel. I am confident these revisions and innovations will provide each reader with a clear, systematic view of front office operations and management.

Michael L. Kasavana, Ph.D.
East Lansing, Michigan

About the Author

Michael L. Kasavana, Ph.D., is the NAMA (National Automatic Merchandising Association) Endowed Professor in Hospitality Business in *The* School of Hospitality Business at Michigan State University. He is considered the School's resident technology expert. Dr. Kasavana completed his undergraduate and graduate work at the University of Massachusetts—Amherst. He received a bachelor's degree in hotel, restaurant, and travel administration; a master of business administration in finance; and a doctorate in management information systems. He has written several books, instructional software packages, and a host of research journal and trade industry magazine articles.

Dr. Kasavana's teaching and research efforts have been sharply focused on IT applications for hotels, restaurants, casinos, and private membership clubs, with a special emphasis on self-service technology. He is an active consultant and a recipient of the MSU Distinguished Faculty Award, the MSU Teacher-Scholar Award, and the Eli Broad College of Business Withrow Teacher/Scholar Award. He has presented numerous seminars on a variety of topics in the United States, Canada, Rome, Hong Kong, and other areas of the world. Dr. Kasavana is a member of the International Technology Hall of Fame sponsored by Hospitality Financial and Technology Professionals (HFTP) and a recipient of the Distinguished Achievements Award from the Food Service Technology Consortium (FS/TEC). He is credited with creating the terms "Menu Engineering" and "V-Commerce."

In addition to his responsibilities at the MSU hospitality business school, Dr. Kasavana serves as the university's Faculty Athletic Representative to the NCAA, Big Ten, and CCHA athletic conferences. He also chairs the MSU Athletic Council.

Chapter 1 Outline

Competencies

1. Explain how the travel and tourism industry can be categorized, and classify hotels in terms of their size and target markets. (pp. 3–13)

2. Classify hotels in terms of their levels of service, and ownership and affiliation. (pp. 13–20)

3. Describe characteristics of business, pleasure/leisure, group, and international travelers. (pp. 20–22)

4. Identify factors that influence travelers' buying decisions. (pp. 22–25)

5. Describe how hotels can become more ecologically responsible and the incentives they have to do so. (pp. 25–29)

1

The Lodging Industry

Eᴌᴌsᴡᴏʀᴛʜ M. sᴛᴀᴛʟᴇʀ—the Henry Ford of the modern hotel—once said, "The guest is *always* right."[1] Some might counter this turn-of-the-century hotelier by saying, "Guests are *not* always right—but they are always *guests*." Either way, these statements reflect the ultimate challenge hospitality professionals face: to provide service that meets the ever-changing needs and demands of guests.

For many, the hospitality industry holds a certain glamour and sophistication. This is partly due to the image most hotels choose, refine, and project to the public. Much of this image is created through architecture and design. Yet a building is really only bricks, mortar, steel, glass, and furnishings. The property's architecture and style may be important in setting the theme, but other factors are also important in differentiating one hotel from another. These factors can include the property location, variety and quality of food service, special features and amenities, and, perhaps most important, a staff that puts all of this together with service to create the overall image and competitive position.

Front office personnel are literally on the front line in creating that image. Reservations agents are often the first to have contact with the guest, while front desk agents, concierges, bell attendants, and door attendants are among the first employees guests see upon arriving at a hotel. The variety of talents and skills needed to satisfy guest needs makes front office work interesting and rewarding. And since no two guests, two hotels, or two days are ever the same, front office work can't help being exciting and challenging.

This chapter outlines some basics about the hospitality industry, and describes how hotels can be classified by size, target markets, level of service, and ownership and affiliation. It also discusses the reasons people travel. The chapter touches on some of the challenges the industry faces when accommodating the increasing number of guests from different cultures and nations, and discusses influences on travelers to buy. Finally, the chapter concludes with a section about "green" hotels.

The Hospitality Industry

The hospitality industry is part of a larger enterprise known as the travel and tourism industry. The travel and tourism industry is a vast group of businesses with one common goal: providing necessary or desired products and services to travelers.

Exhibit 1 divides the travel and tourism industry into five parts, and shows some of the components of each part. The hospitality industry consists of lodging and food and beverage operations, as well as institutional food and beverage

Exhibit 1   Overview of the Travel and Tourism Industry

Travel and Tourism Industry				
Lodging Operations	**Transportation Services**	**Food and Beverage Operations**	**Retail Stores**	**Activities**
Hotels	Ships	Restaurants	Gift Shops	Recreation
Motels	Airplanes	Lodging Properties	Souvenir Shops	Business
Resorts	Autos	Retail Stores	Arts/Crafts Shops	Entertainment
Timeshare Hotels	Buses	Vending	Shopping Malls	Meetings
Condominiums	Trains	Catering	Markets	Study Trips
Conference Centers	Bikes	Snack Bars	Miscellaneous Stores	Sporting Events
Camps	Limousines	Cruise Ships		Ethnic Festivals
Parks		Bars/Taverns		Cultural Events
Extended Stay		Banquets		Seasonal Festivals
Bed and Breakfast		Contract Food Services		Gaming
Casinos				
Convention Hotels				
Cruise Ships				

services, which do not cater to the traveling public. Lodging operations stand apart from other travel and tourism businesses, since they offer overnight accommodations to their guests. Many lodging properties provide food and beverage service, recreational activities, and more.

An organization that addresses travel and tourism issues in the United States—particularly those affecting the hospitality industry—is the *American Hotel & Lodging Association (AH&LA)*. As the trade association of the American lodging industry, AH&LA is a federation of hotel and lodging associations located in the fifty states, the District of Columbia, Puerto Rico, and the U.S. Virgin Islands. Canada and most other countries with many lodging establishments have similar national organizations. These national trade associations normally work together through the International Hotel and Restaurant Association (IHRA) for common purposes. IHRA is based in Paris, France.

A leading service of AH&LA is its Educational Institute. Since its founding in 1952, more than two million individuals have benefited from its programs and services—making it one of the largest hospitality industry educational centers in the world. This non-profit organization provides essential educational and training resources for the expanding hospitality industry, and helps prepare dedicated individuals for careers and career advancement within the industry.

Classifying Hotels

With so many properties offering so many services in such a huge industry, it is easy to understand how people might get confused about the differences between hotels, motels, inns, and other lodging establishments. The fact is that the distinctions are not always clear. The confusion is compounded because owners can classify their properties as they deem appropriate, making it even more apparent why universally agreed-upon definitions are difficult to implement. Still, despite the numerous exceptions, some general property distinctions exist and are widely accepted.

A **hotel** or inn may be defined as an establishment whose primary business is providing lodging facilities for the general public, and that furnishes one or more of the following services: food and beverage service, room attendant (housekeeping) service, concierge, bell and door attendant service (sometimes called uniformed service), laundry or dry cleaning, and use of furniture and fixtures. Hotels have 50 to 2,000 rooms, and sometimes more; very large hotels may have more than 5,000 guestrooms. Inns usually average 5 to 50 rooms and provide a higher level of personalized service.

The term *motel* is a contraction of *motor hotel*. It is a lodging facility that caters primarily to guests traveling by automobile. Early motels often provided parking spaces near guestrooms, but that has changed in recent years as motel owners and franchisors have become more aware of guest security. Motels may be located in any setting, but are usually found in suburban or roadside areas. They became especially successful in the 1950s and 1960s with the development of the interstate highway system in the United States. Many motels are two-story or low-rise buildings located near major highways. Pool areas with shrubbery, trees, and children's playgrounds are familiar "trademarks" for many motels. In most cases, motels do not offer the full range of services and facilities available in a hotel.

Unless otherwise indicated, this chapter will use the term *hotel* as a general term for hotels, motels, inns, suite hotels, conference centers, resorts, and other lodging properties.

There are many ways to classify hotels. The categories discussed in this chapter are based on hotel size, target markets, levels of service, and ownership and affiliation. It is important to note, however, that some properties defy easy classification, and a particular property may fit into several categories.

Size

Size—or the number of guestrooms in a property—provides a common way to categorize hotels. Hotels are typically grouped in four size categories:

- Under 150 rooms
- 150 to 299 rooms
- 300 to 600 rooms
- More than 600 rooms

These categories enable hotels of similar size to compare operating procedures and statistical results. Unless otherwise specified, hotels in the classifications discussed in the remainder of this chapter may be of any size.

Target Markets

Two of the most important marketing challenges a hospitality property encounters are: "Who stays at our property?" and "Who else can we attract?" Through marketing research, tools, and strategies, lodging properties seek to identify **target markets.** Target markets are distinctly defined groups of travelers that the hotel seeks to retain or attract as guests.

A popular trend in the hospitality industry is to define or identify smaller, distinct groups or "segments" within larger target markets, and to develop products and services aimed specifically at satisfying these segments. This process of **market segmentation** has contributed to substantial growth, particularly within hotel chains. For example, Marriott Hotels and Resorts now has many different brand names: J. W. Marriott, Marriott Marquis, Marriott Hotels, Marriott Inns, Courtyard by Marriott, and Fairfield Inn by Marriott. Marriott also owns the Ritz-Carlton and Renaissance brands, and people can reserve rooms at any of its locations through the same reservation system. Even Marriott's extended-stay segment has been divided into sub-markets, with Residence Inn by Marriott, TownePlace Suites by Marriott, and SpringHill Suites by Marriott. Each brand is directed toward a type of guest, or *market segment,* that Marriott identified as distinct. Many other major lodging companies have taken the same segmentation approach. InterContinental Hotels Group, Starwood Hotels & Resorts Worldwide, and Hilton Hotels Corporation employ market segmentation through various products to attract more customers. The advantage to this approach is that a variety of properties can be located in a particular geographic market, thereby attracting a variety of guests. The disadvantage is that guests may become confused when trying to differentiate between the facilities and services of each brand within a chain.

Hotels target many markets and can be classified according to the markets they attempt to attract and serve. The most common types of properties based on target markets include commercial, airport, suite, extended-stay, residential, resort, lifestyle, bed-and-breakfast, vacation ownership/condominium, casino, conference center, and convention hotels. There are also several alternative types of lodging properties that directly compete with hotels; these are discussed at the end of this section.

Commercial Hotels. The very first inns and hotels were usually located in the towns and villages they primarily served. It was not until the age of railroads that the hotel business began to expand in the United States. Traveling by railroad was faster, easier, and safer than traveling by horse-drawn carriage or even by the first automobiles. Railroads connected the country, and railroad stations were generally located near the center of each town. Travelers getting off trains usually needed a place to stay. As more people traveled, the demand for hotels grew. In turn, more hotels were built, many conveniently located near railroad stations. The Waldorf=Astoria Hotel in New York City was constructed above a below-ground railroad platform, which it occasionally used as an entrance for important persons arriving by rail. (The original Waldorf=Astoria was on the site of what is now the Empire State Building.) In time, hotels located in the city center not only catered to travelers but also became the social centers of the community.

Like their historic counterparts, commercial hotels continue to be located in downtown or business districts, areas that are convenient and of interest to their target markets. Commercial hotels form the largest group of hotel types. Although they primarily cater to business travelers, many tour groups, individual tourists, and small conference groups also find these hotels attractive. In the past, commercial hotels were referred to as *transient hotels* because of the relatively short length of time guests stayed in them compared with other hotels.

Guest amenities at commercial hotels may include complimentary newspapers, in-room coffee makers, free local telephone calls, cable television, access to DVD players and DVDs, video games, personal computers, high-speed Internet access, ergonomic desks and chairs, and fax machines. Car rental arrangements, airport pick-up services, 24-hour food service, semi-formal dining rooms, and cocktail lounges are usually available. Most commercial hotels have conference rooms, guestroom suites, room service, and banquet meal service. Commercial hotels may offer laundry-valet service, uniformed services including concierge service, in-room refreshment centers, complimentary local transportation, and retail stores. Swimming pools, health clubs, tennis courts, saunas, and running areas may also be among a commercial hotel's offerings.

Airport Hotels. Just as railroads spurred the first expansion of hotels in the United States in the late 1800s and early 1900s, air travel encouraged a distinct type of hotel growth in the 1950s through the 1970s. Air travel did not really exist in its current form until modern commercial jet aircraft were introduced in the late 1950s. These jets traveled much faster and were much larger than earlier aircraft, and prompted dramatic economic growth in the United States. Demand skyrocketed for lodging facilities located near airports, especially international airports. Similar to the way hotels appeared near downtown railroad stations, hotels appeared near airports across the United States.

Airport hotels are popular because of their proximity to major travel centers. More than any other type of hotel, airport hotels vary widely in size and level of services. Typical target markets include business clientele, airline passengers with overnight travel layovers or canceled flights, and airline personnel. Hotel-owned limousines or courtesy vans often transport guests between the hotel and the airport. Signs announcing direct telephone service to nearby hotels for reservations and pick-up service are common in most airports. Many airport hotels feature conference rooms to attract a particular market: those guests who travel to a meeting by air and wish to minimize ground travel. Guests who stay at airport hotels and hold their meetings there often enjoy greater convenience and significant overall cost savings with such arrangements.

Suite Hotels. Suite hotels are among the fastest-growing segments of the lodging industry. These hotels feature guestrooms with a living room or parlor area and a separate bedroom. Some guest suites include a compact kitchenette with a refrigerator and in-room self-service hot beverage setup. In exchange for more complete living quarters, suite hotels generally have fewer and more limited public areas and guest services than other hotels. This helps keep suite hotels' guestroom prices competitive.

Suite hotels appeal to several different market segments: people who are relocating transform suites into temporary living quarters; frequent travelers enjoy the comforts of a "home away from home"; and vacationing families discover the privacy and convenience of non-standard hotel accommodations designed with families in mind. Professionals such as accountants, lawyers, and executives find suite hotels particularly attractive, since they can work or entertain in an area outside the bedroom. Some suite hotels offer complimentary evening receptions, breakfasts, or hors d'oeuvre or snack service. Such gatherings give guests opportunities to socialize, which may be important for those staying at the property for extended periods.

Extended-Stay Hotels. Extended-stay hotels are similar to suite hotels, but usually offer more complete kitchen amenities in the guestroom. Extended-stay hotels are designed for travelers who intend to stay five nights or longer and require reduced hotel services. These hotels usually do not provide food, beverage, uniformed services, or valet services. In addition, housekeeping services may not be provided on a daily basis. Like suite hotels, extended-stay hotels attempt to establish a homelike feeling through their interior and exterior designs. In addition, unlike for most types of hotels, room rates in extended-stay hotels are often determined by the length of a guest's stay. Popular extended-stay brands include Extended StayAmerica, Homewood Suites, and Staybridge Suites.

Residential Hotels. Residential hotels provide long-term or permanent accommodations for people in urban or suburban areas. Located primarily in the United States, these properties house residents who want and can afford daily, limited hotel services. Residential hotels are not nearly as popular or prevalent as they once were. They have been replaced in part by suite and condominium hotel properties.

The layout of a residential guest unit may closely resemble a suite hotel guestroom. Guest quarters generally include a sitting room, bedroom, and small kitchenette. Sometimes people who contract to live in residential hotels may be considered tenants by law. Residents may choose to contract for some or all of the services provided to guests in a commercial hotel. A residential hotel may provide daily housekeeping, telephone, front desk, and uniformed services. A restaurant and lounge may also be located on the premises.

Many other types of hotels also house semi-permanent or permanent guests, despite their emphasis on other markets. Likewise, residential hotels may also offer short-term, or transient, guest accommodations.

Resort Hotels. Guests often choose resort hotels as their planned destination or vacation spot, setting resorts apart from other types of lodging operations. A resort may be located in the mountains, on an island, or in some other exotic location away from crowded residential areas. The recreational facilities and breathtaking scenery typical of most resorts are not typical of most other hotels. Most resort hotels provide extensive food and beverage, valet, and room services for vacationers. Many also provide special recreational activities for guests, such as dancing, golf, tennis, horseback riding, nature hikes, sailing, skiing, and swimming. Most resort hotels try to be positioned as a "destination within a destination" by providing a wide range of facilities and activities, giving guests many choices and fewer reasons to the leave the property.

A more leisurely, relaxed atmosphere distinguishes most resort hotels from their commercial counterparts. Resort hotels strive to provide enjoyable guest experiences that encourage repeat business and word-of-mouth recommendations. Recreational activities are frequently arranged for groups of guests. Resort hotels often employ social directors who plan, organize, and direct a range of guest programs.

Resort hotel communities are an expanding area of resort development. These communities may be developed from existing hotel facilities sold as timeshare units or condominiums, or as new destination properties developed specifically as resort communities.

Lifestyle Hotels. Lifestyle hotels are an additional lodging industry classification designed to further segment the marketplace. Lifestyle hotels are intended to appeal to specific travelers who enjoy certain architecture, art, culture, special interests, and amenities. Guests appreciate these aspects of a lifestyle property and consider them important to their overall experience. Most major lodging companies have entered this market segment with new lifestyle brands, or are converting existing brands to lifestyle choices. In addition, many independently owned and operated lifestyle hotels are popular destination attractions.

Lifestyle brands reflect the interests of their guests. For example, some promote eco-friendly environments, while others promote healthful living or social interactivity. Some brands are directed at the interests of a specific age group, offering amenities specifically designed for those guests. Lifestyle hotels tend to be constructed with 100 to 250 guestrooms and have limited or no meeting space. Food service offerings at lifestyle hotels vary, depending upon the brand design and market tier (for example, world-class or mid-range). The interior décor, building and guestroom design, and many other ambient details (such as background music and artwork) contribute to the success of a lifestyle hotel guest experience.

Bed-and-Breakfast Hotels. Bed-and-breakfast hotels, sometimes called "B&Bs," are an often overlooked group of lodging properties. B&Bs range from houses with a few rooms converted to overnight facilities, to small commercial buildings with twenty to thirty guestrooms. The owner of a B&B, the host or hostess, usually lives on the premises and is typically the property manager. Breakfast service may range from a simple continental breakfast to a full-course meal. Thousands of B&Bs exist today, deriving popularity from intimate, personal service for leisure travelers. Some B&Bs provide such fine accommodations and service that they have earned some of the best ratings from highly respected hotel rating services. Most B&Bs offer only lodging and limited food service or, as the name implies, breakfast only. Meeting rooms, laundry and dry-cleaning services, lunch and dinner, and recreational facilities are usually not offered. Due to limited services, the price for a room at a B&B tends to be lower than at a full-service hotel.

Vacation Ownership and Condominium Hotels. Another expanding segment of the hospitality industry is the *vacation ownership hotel*, sometimes referred to as *timeshare* or *vacation-interval* hotels. Vacation ownership properties typically attract individuals who purchase the ownership of accommodations for a specific period of time—usually one or two weeks a year. These owners then occupy the unit, usually a condominium, during that time. Owners who cannot or choose not to occupy the unit during their time period may have the unit rented or brokered by the management company that operates the hotel. Since the property functions as a hotel in many respects, travelers renting the unit may not realize it is actually part of a vacation ownership hotel. These hotels have become especially popular in resort areas, but some are also located in commercial areas and may be owned by area companies that need to house visiting executives or consultants. Owners may not be able to afford owning a condominium year-round, but can afford fractional ownership (ownership of a unit for a few weeks a year). One popular feature of vacation ownership hotels is the ability to trade ownership time with another owner in another location. For example, an owner of a beach-front vacation ownership unit may want to trade time in the unit for time in a winter ski unit. Often, the management company can work with the owner to find someone willing to trade. This allows owners the opportunity to vary their vacations each year, without giving up the benefits of ownership. Two major vacation ownership exchange companies are Interval International and Resort Condominiums International. Several major hotel companies are also represented in this market, including Marriott, Hilton, and Disney. The American Resort Development Association provides educational and representational services to this market.

Condominium hotels are similar to vacation ownership hotels. The difference between the two lies in the type of ownership involved. Units in condominium hotels have only one owner instead of the multiple owners typical of vacation ownership hotel units. In a condominium hotel, an owner informs the management company of when he or she wants to occupy the unit. That way, the management company is free to rent the unit for the remainder of the year. When the management company rents the unit, a portion of the revenue goes to the owner.

Vacation ownership and condominium owners receive the revenue from the rental of their units and pay the management company a fee for advertising, rental, housekeeping, and maintenance services. Vacation ownership and condominium owners are also responsible for furnishing and paying for the general maintenance of their units. In many cases, condominium and vacation ownership hotels were actually built as apartment or condominium buildings and converted to lodging use. Normally, these units consist of a living room, dining area, kitchen, bathroom, and one or more bedrooms. Guest laundry facilities are often provided in the unit, but may be provided in a common area of the building as well. Guests of condominium hotels usually rent a unit for at least one week. Guests often contract for a specific unit at a specific time each year.

Casino Hotels. Hotels with gambling facilities may be categorized as a distinct group: *casino hotels*. Although the guestrooms and food and beverage operations in casino hotels may be quite luxurious, their function is secondary to, and supportive of, casino operations. As with resort hotels, casino hotels tend to cater to leisure and vacation travelers.

Casino hotels attract guests by promoting gaming and headliner entertainment. Most casino hotels provide a broad range of entertainment opportunities, including golf courses, tennis courts, spas, and theme recreational activities. Casino hotels may also provide specialty restaurants and extravagant entertainment, and may offer charter flights for guests planning to participate in casino activities. Gambling activities at casino hotels may operate 24 hours a day, 365 days a year; this may significantly affect the operation of the rooms and food and beverage divisions. Some casino hotels are very large, with several thousand guestrooms.

A special hotel format involves riverboat gambling. Since most riverboats do not provide lodging accommodations, hotels are often located where the riverboats dock, in order to accommodate gamblers. These hotels are not considered casino hotels because they do not have gaming as part of their facilities.

Conference Centers. While many hotels provide meeting space, conference centers are specifically designed to handle group meetings. Most full-service conference centers offer overnight accommodations for meeting attendees. Because meetings are their focal point, conference centers typically place great emphasis on providing all the services and equipment necessary to ensure a meeting's success—for example, technical production assistance, high-quality audiovisual equipment, business service centers, flexible seating arrangements, flip charts and display screens, and so forth.

Conference centers are often located outside metropolitan areas and may provide extensive leisure facilities: golf courses, indoor and outdoor swimming pools, tennis courts, fitness centers, spas, running and hiking trails, and more. Conference centers typically charge meeting planners a single price, which includes attendee guestrooms, meals, meeting rooms, audiovisual equipment, and related services. Guest amenities may not be as plentiful at conference centers, since these centers concentrate more on meeting the needs of conference planners and organizers than on meeting the needs of program attendees. Conference centers may also accept transient business, but this is usually done to fill vacant guestrooms and is not a large portion of the business.

Convention Hotels. Convention hotels form another segment of the lodging industry that has grown significantly in recent years; demand for the convention market has nearly doubled in the past twenty years. While most commercial hotels have fewer than 600 rooms, convention hotels—designed to accommodate large conventions—often offer as many as 2,000 rooms or more.

Convention hotels have a sufficient number of guestrooms to house a significant majority of attendees at most conventions. Convention hotels often have 50,000 square feet or more of exhibit hall space, plus ballrooms and an assortment of meeting rooms. Most convention properties offer dining facilities ranging from self-serve restaurants or cafeterias to elaborate formal dining rooms. Convention hotels are primarily directed toward business travelers with a common interest. A full line of business services is generally available, including teleconferencing, secretarial assistance, language translation, high-speed Internet access, and facsimile (fax) machines. Examples of convention hotels are the Gaylord Opryland Resort & Convention Center in Nashville, the Wyndham Anatole Hotel in Dallas, and the Hyatt Regency in Chicago. Some casino hotels, like the Mandalay Bay and MGM Grand in Las Vegas, offer similar facilities.

Convention hotels usually attract the convention market for state, regional, national, and international meetings. While most hotels book the majority of their group business within two years of the meeting date, convention hotels may book their business up to ten years in advance. Many groups are so large that they have to book space that far in advance to ensure adequate facilities and housing for their attendees.

In some cases, convention hotels do not offer all the facilities necessary, but are affiliated with a local *convention center*. The local community usually owns the convention center, which often has its own sales force. Convention centers not only have space for meetings and conferences, they also have more than adequate space for exhibits and private booths. Some convention centers have more than one million square feet of floor space in a single building. Convention centers normally coordinate efforts with nearby hotels to ensure that guestrooms are available for convention attendees. Hotels, in turn, sell the convention center to appropriate markets to garner guestroom business.

Alternative Lodging Properties. Besides the types of hotels just described, there are several other types of lodging establishments that compete for business and leisure travelers. Recreational vehicle parks, campgrounds, and mobile home parks are somewhat like hotels, since they involve the rental of space for overnight accommodations. But although similarities exist, these alternatives stand apart from other lodging facilities. In some resort areas, parks and campgrounds strongly compete with traditional lodging operations because they appeal to a broader range of travelers. For example, many state and national parks offer campgrounds and lodges that compete directly with hotels. These facilities may have an advantage over local hotels, since they are located on park land, are usually competitively priced, and may be subsidized. Unlike hotels, however, campgrounds and recreational vehicle parks require that guests bring their accommodations with them.

Still another form of alternative lodging is the corporate lodging business. Corporate lodging is designed for guests wishing to stay for very long periods of time, often up to six months or longer. While hotels are usually designed for guests staying one to ten nights, corporate lodging is better suited to guests with very long stay requirements. Guests often include business executives moving from one city to another, consultants on temporary assignments, corporate trainers, professional athletes, and personnel connected to special projects such as movie shoots. Instead of guestrooms, corporate lodging usually provides fully furnished apartments for guests. In many cases, the building owners provide the apartments. In other cases, a service provider supplies the apartment to the guest. The service provider rents the apartment, and provides the furniture and housewares, as well as housekeeping and other services, to guests. Since apartments are used instead of hotel buildings, a single provider in a community can provide corporate lodging in many community locations, allowing guests greater flexibility. Corporate lodging is usually cost-competitive with hotels, since apartments can be rented and furnished by the owner or service provider for a lower daily cost than that incurred by hotels. Corporate lodging has been a major growth industry recently, expanding well beyond North America to Europe and Asia. Some hotel companies have corporate lodging divisions, including ExecuStay by Marriott and BridgeStreet Worldwide by Interstate Hotels & Resorts. Other corporate lodging companies are divisions of residential real estate companies, such as Equity Residential and Charles E. Smith.

The cruise ship industry is another example of alternative lodging. Cruise ships have become major competition for resorts, especially in the Caribbean region, and are primary competitors of resort hotels. They have many amenities similar to those offered at island resorts, while offering the unique advantage of moving from island to island as part of the experience. Modern cruise ships have all of the advantages of resort hotels. Cruise ships come equipped with many modern conveniences, such as fitness centers, movie theaters, multiple dining and cocktail lounge facilities, spas, casinos, shops, and ship-to-shore communications, including satellite television and Internet access. Cruise ships may be small, offering as few as two dozen cabins, or large, with several hundred cabins or more. Some cruise ships even offer small conference facilities for corporate or association meetings.

Levels of Service

Another way to classify lodging properties is by level of guest service, which is a measure of the benefits provided to the guest. The level of guest service offered in a hotel varies without regard to hotel size or type, and some hotels offer more than one level of service. The level of service is usually reflected in a guest's room rate. Before discussing specific levels of service, this section will look at some basic issues pertaining to service, including the intangibility of service, quality assurance, and rating services

The Intangibility of Service. Hotels are not simply in the business of selling tangible products such as comfortable beds and wholesome food. In fact, it is the *intangible* services a hotel provides that contribute most to the guest's hospitality experience. These services are not physical things, but rather actions, deeds, performances, or efforts. For example, a meal served in a hotel dining room is certainly a tangible element of a guest's experience. However, hospitality means more than just a good meal: it means surrounding the meal with a particular ambience, including the dining room's décor and the attitude of its staff. These intangible elements can be just as important to the guest as the tangible elements.

The difficulty is that after a service has been delivered, the purchaser generally has nothing tangible to show for it. Services cannot be touched, tasted, or tried on for size, and are virtually impossible to "return." For the most part, guests leave a hotel with only the memories of their experiences. To counteract this, many hotels try to create an image of their services that is powerful, clear, and precise. The hotel's service becomes an instantly recognizable standard, signature, or trademark of the hotel, almost like a tangible product. The hotel's employees must then sustain that image through their commitment to service.

Every service provided by a hotel must be appropriate to the market the property wishes to attract and satisfy. For example, guests at a small roadside lodging property probably would be surprised if someone attempted to escort them to their rooms after registration. However, in larger hotels with an appropriately defined market and level of service, escorting guests to rooms is an expected, important part of the hotel's image.

Quality Assurance. The intangible services that a hotel delivers tend to be less standardized than the tangible objects produced by a manufacturer. One of the greatest challenges the hospitality industry faces today is controlling service variability. The consistent delivery of services is the result of a program of **quality assurance.**

The traditional quality control techniques of manufacturing industries may not be appropriate for the hospitality industry. In manufacturing industries, consumers are normally isolated from the production processes, and products are tested and inspected before they are sold. In hotels, some quality control techniques used in manufacturing industries may apply: guestrooms are inspected after they are cleaned, and the recipes of menu items are tested before the items appear on a restaurant's menu. However, in many instances, guests are not isolated from the hotel's production processes. For example, registration is a service that is produced and delivered by hotel employees and consumed by guests simultaneously.

Consistency is the key to quality service. The ingredients of consistency are the standards that a lodging property develops. But, while standards establish and define quality, only the hotel's staff can make quality a reality. It is the consistency of a particular hotel or chain of hotels that often creates or sustains guest loyalty and preferences, as well as a unique market niche.

Rating Services. Several groups in the United States provide hotel evaluation and rating services for travelers. The American Automobile Association (AAA) and the *Mobil Travel Guide* provide the best known of these services. The finest hotels rated by AAA have earned either a five- or four-diamond rating. *Mobil Travel Guide* awards either five or four stars to the hotels earning its highest ratings.

It is extremely difficult for a hotel to earn either five diamonds or five stars. Standards are very strict and include consistency in the quality of facilities and services from year to year. While there are hundreds of four-diamond and four-star hotels in the United States, there are fewer than fifty five-diamond or five-star hotels.

In other parts of the world, similar rating services are provided by private organizations and by governments. For example, the Mexican government provides ratings of hotels from one star to five stars, plus an additional category of Gran Turismo for the finest hotels. In Europe, one of the best-known and respected rating services is *The Red Guide* provided by Michelin. *The Red Guide* provides up to three stars for the finest hotels and restaurants, and has been published for over 100 years.

For the sake of simplicity, lodging properties can be discussed in terms of four different levels of service: world-class, upscale, mid-range, and economy/limited service. In many cases, a subclass of world-class hotels—first class—refers to hotels earning either four diamonds or four stars under the AAA or *Mobil Travel Guide* rating services.

World-Class Service. Hotels offering **world-class service**—sometimes called luxury service—target top business executives, entertainment celebrities, high-ranking political figures, and wealthy clientele as their primary markets. World-class hotels provide upscale restaurants and lounges, exquisite décor, concierge service, and opulent meeting and private dining facilities. Guests may find oversized guest-rooms, heated and plush bath towels, large bars of soap, oversized in-room safes, sophisticated entertainment centers, multiple television sets, and upgraded fur-nishings, décor, and artwork. Housekeeping services are typically provided twice daily, including a nightly bedroom turn-down service. Complimentary local and international newspapers may be delivered daily to each guestroom. World-class hotels seldom have more than 400 guestrooms, given the level of service they pro-vide, and in many cases have fewer than 200 guestrooms. In North America, these hotels are often classified as five-star or five-diamond hotels, referring to the rating services discussed previously. Other rating systems may apply around the world. As one might expect, world-class service hotels are usually the most expensive, but also provide the highest value for the price paid.

The public spaces of a world-class hotel (for example, the lobby, hallways, and entryways) may be large and elaborately decorated and furnished. Several food and beverage outlets are frequently available to cater to the diverse tastes of the hotel's guests and visitors. The hotel may also offer a variety of retail outlets, such as gift shops, clothing and jewelry stores, specialty retail shops, and international newsstands.

Above all, world-class hotels stress personalized, sometimes customized guest services, and maintain a relatively high ratio of staff members to guests. This ratio enables the hotel to offer an extensive variety of amenities and unique services and to respond quickly to guest requests. For example, some of the finest hotels in Asia boast a ratio of two or more employees per guest. Many world-class hotels in North America have more than one employee per guest. World-class hotels fre-quently employ a multilingual concierge in an effort to provide special assistance to international guests. Among their many services, concierges may help guests register, obtain tickets for transportation and entertainment, provide travel direc-tions and sightseeing information, or arrange for secretarial or business services. Additionally, some world-class hotels may provide private butler service on des-ignated floors. Private butlers may be asked to arrange room service meals and cleaning services for clothing, to unpack and pack luggage, and to provide many other customized services.

Executive floors. In some hotels, certain floors are designated to provide some of the hotel's guests with world-class attention. Properties offering *executive floors* (sometimes known as *tower, concierge,* or *club floors*) provide non-standard guest-room furnishings and additional guest services in these areas of the hotel. Execu-tive floors usually are designed with larger, deluxe guestrooms that may contain a number of unique amenities. Recent trends for these floors include in-room fax machines, DVD players, large televisions, and even computers. Executive-level guestrooms or suites might also feature an in-room refreshment center and may be stocked with signature bathrobes, fresh fruit, and fresh-cut flowers.

Usually, the luxury services offered on executive floors are not confined to the guestroom. A concierge, or personal butler, may be stationed on each executive floor. Access to these floors may be restricted by the use of special elevator keys that allow only authorized guests to enter. In many cases, the executive or tower floors offer a private lounge. Special complimentary food and beverage services may be offered in the evening, and a continental breakfast may be served in the morning. Conveniences such as secretarial services or special check-in and check-out arrangements may also be available.

Upscale Service. Upscale service hotels are patronized by travelers seeking exceptional service and accommodations, but not at the level of world-class hotels. The primary clients are business executives, high-level industry meeting attendees, and leisure travelers interested in the extra comforts and amenities these hotels provide. Upscale hotels tend to provide multiple food service and dining experiences and often have several food and beverage outlets, each offering a different cuisine. Guests are provided modern guestroom amenities, including flat-panel televisions, luxurious bedding, choice of pillows, in-room coffee stations, ergonomic work environments, and other features. Housekeeping services are often scheduled twice daily, including evening turndown service upon request.

Although upscale service hotels do not provide the unusual staff-to-guest ratio provided in world-class hotels, upscale properties are nevertheless known for providing excellent service. Upscale service hotels appeal to select travelers by providing executive floors, valet parking, door and bell service, concierge services, business centers, shopping outlets, and more. These hotels can range in size from 100 to 2,000 guestrooms, depending on target market and location. In addition, some upscale service hotels offer large meeting facilities that can host 500 or more attendees for a meeting or banquet. In North America, these hotels are often classified as four-star or four-diamond hotels; around the world, other rating systems may apply. In any case, upscale service hotels are generally less expensive than world-class service hotels.

Mid-Range Service. Hotels offering **mid-range service** appeal to the largest segment of the traveling public. Mid-range service is often modest but sufficient. Although the staffing level is adequate, the mid-range property does not try to provide elaborate services. A mid-range property may offer uniformed guest services, airport limousine service, and food and beverage room service. Like world-class and upscale hotels, mid-range properties range in size from small to large. The typical hotel offering mid-range service is of medium size, roughly 150 to 299 rooms.

A mid-range property may offer a specialty restaurant or all-day dining room and a lounge catering to visitors as well as hotel guests. The lounge may feature entertainment on the evenings the hotel is expected to be most busy. Guests likely to stay at a mid-range hotel include businesspeople, individual travelers, and families. Rates are lower than world-class or upscale hotels, since the properties offer fewer services, smaller rooms, and a smaller range of facilities and recreational activities. Such factors often make mid-range hotel properties appealing to those travelers desiring some hotel services, but not the full range of luxuries offered at world-class or upscale properties. Since meeting rooms are usually available at mid-range hotels, people planning small conferences, group meetings, and conventions also may find mid-range hotels attractive.

Economy/Limited Service. Economy/limited service hotels also are a growing segment of the hospitality industry. These properties provide clean, comfortable, inexpensive rooms and meet the basic needs of guests. Economy hotels appeal primarily to budget-minded travelers who want rooms with the minimal amenities required for a comfortable stay, without unnecessary, often costly, extra services. Since a large proportion of the population travels on limited funds, economy properties have a potentially large market from which to attract clientele. The clientele may include families with children, bus tour groups, traveling businesspeople, vacationers, retirees, and groups of conventioneers.

Initially, the only amenities offered at many economy properties were an in-room telephone, a bar of soap, towels, and a television set with local channels. Most economy properties now offer cable or satellite television, swimming pools, playgrounds, small meeting rooms, and other special features. What most economy properties *do not* offer is room service, uniformed guest services, large group meeting rooms, laundry or dry-cleaning services, banquet rooms, health clubs, or any of the more elaborate amenities found at mid-range and world-class properties.

An economy property generally does not provide full food and beverage service, which means guests may need to eat at a nearby restaurant. However, many economy hotels provide a free continental breakfast in the lobby area.

Ownership and Affiliation

Ownership and affiliation provide another means of classifying hotel properties. Two basic equity structures exist: independent hotels and chain hotels. An **independent hotel** has no affiliation with other properties. **Chain hotel** ownership may take a number of forms, depending on the association that the chain organization has with each property. This chapter points out several distinct forms of chain ownership, including management contracts, franchises, and referral groups. Many chain hotel companies tend to be a mixture of several types of ownership.

Independent Hotels. Independent hotels have no identifiable ownership or management affiliation with other properties. In other words, independent hotels have no relationship to other hotels regarding policies, procedures, marketing, or financial obligations. A typical example of an independent property is a family-owned-and-operated hotel that is not required to conform to any corporate policy or procedure. From a business perspective, some independent properties are organized as sole proprietorships or partnerships, while others are incorporated to restrict insurance risk and personal liability.

The unique advantage of an independent hotel is its autonomy. Since there is no need to adhere to a particular image, an independent operator can offer a level of service geared toward attracting a specific target market. Moreover, the flexibility inherent in a smaller organization often allows the independent hotel to quickly adapt to changing market conditions. An independent hotel, however, may not enjoy the broad advertising exposure or management insight and consultancy of an affiliated property, and is unable to take advantage of the volume purchasing power of a chain hotel. Examples of well-known independent hotels include The Breakers in Palm Beach, Florida; The New York Palace Hotel in New York; and the Del Coronado in San Diego.

Chain Hotels. Chain ownership usually imposes certain minimum standards, rules, policies, and procedures to restrict affiliate activities. In general, the more centralized the organization, the stronger the control over the individual property. Chains with less dominant central organizations typically allow individual hotel managers to exercise more creativity and decision-making autonomy.

Several different structures exist for chain hotels. Some chains own affiliated properties, but many do not. Some chains exert strong control over the architecture, management, and standards of affiliate properties. Other chains only concentrate on advertising, marketing, and purchasing. Some chains may have only a small corporate structure and minimum membership standards, and therefore would not be equipped to provide a high level of assistance to local ownership.

A chain is usually classified as operating under a management contract or as a franchise or referral group. The following discussion highlights how each type of chain operates, and how each type differs from the other.

Management contracts. Management companies are organizations that operate properties owned by other entities. These entities range from individual businesspeople and partnerships to large insurance companies. Here's an example of how a management company might be hired to run a hotel. A group of businesspeople may decide that a hotel would enhance local business conditions. If the group's preliminary business feasibility study is favorable, the group might attempt to obtain financing to build the hotel. Many lending institutions, however, would require professional hotel management, and possibly chain affiliation, before they would approve a loan. At this point, the group could contract with a professional hotel management company to operate the proposed property, probably on a long-term basis. Assuming the hotel management company is acceptable to the lenders, a **management contract** would be signed by the developers and the management company.

Under this type of contract, the owner or developer usually retains the financial and legal responsibility for the property. The management company usually operates the hotel, hires its employees, pays its expenses, and, in turn, receives an agreed-upon fee from the owner or developer. After operating expenses and management fees have been paid, any remaining cash usually goes to the owners, who may use this cash to pay debts, insurance, taxes, and so forth.

Management contracts have proven successful for many major hotel chains. Some management contract companies do not have a brand name. These companies usually operate franchises or independents for property owners. The franchising company provides the purchasing power, advertising, and central reservation system, while the management company provides the management expertise.

Management contracting is usually a means of rapidly expanding a hotel company's operations with far less investment per property than direct ownership requires. Hotel management companies are sometimes established just to manage hotels for other investors. These companies appear to offer a unique advantage to property owners and managers because of their expertise in operations, financial management, staffing, marketing and sales, and reservation services. Some of these companies have grown quite large. For example, Interstate Hotels & Resorts Worldwide manages approximately 400 hotels around the world for various owners, and works with almost every franchise brand available.

Franchise and referral groups. Some of the best-known U.S. hotels belong to franchise and referral groups. These properties are located in most cities and towns, along interstate highways, and in resort areas. Franchise and referral groups have enjoyed the most growth in the worldwide lodging business in recent years because travelers prefer to stay with brands they recognize, and owners trust in brand names to attract business. There is, however, an organizational distinction between franchise and referral group chain hotels.

Franchising is simply a method of distribution whereby one entity that has developed a particular pattern or format for doing business—the *franchisor*—grants to other entities—*franchisees*—the right to conduct such a business, provided the franchisee follows the established pattern. In the lodging industry, most organizations offering franchises have first established the quality of their product and expertise in operations by developing parent-company (franchisor-owned) hotels. Franchise organizations typically have established standards for design, décor, equipment, and operating procedures, to which all franchised properties must adhere. This standardization is what enables franchise chains to expand while maintaining a consistent, established product and level of service.

The franchisor usually provides the franchisee with other reasons for purchasing a franchise aside from a strong brand name. These include national or international central reservation networking, national advertising campaigns, management training programs, advanced technology, and central purchasing services. Some franchisors also provide architectural, construction, and interior design consulting services. Some of the better-known franchising companies are InterContinental Hotels Group (Crowne Plaza, Holiday Inn, Staybridge Suites, and Candlewood Suites), Choice International (Quality Hotels and Inns), Wyndham Worldwide (Ramada Inns, Howard Johnson, Wingate, and Days Inn), and Starwood Hotels & Resorts Worldwide (Sheraton and Westin). In some cases, a company may provide management contract services as well as sell franchises. For example, most Four Points Hotels by Sheraton are franchises, while most Sheraton brand hotels are either owned by Sheraton or have Sheraton management contracts.

A franchise arrangement is not necessarily right for all lodging properties. Some operations are so distinct that belonging to a franchise system and conforming to a set of standards may be perceived as harmful. For these operations, a referral group might be more appropriate. **Referral groups** (sometimes called membership groups) consist of independent hotels that have banded together for some common purpose. While each property in a referral system is not an exact replica of the others, there is sufficient consistency in the quality of service to consistently satisfy guest expectations. Hotels within the group refer their guests to other affiliated properties. Through this approach, an independent hotel may gain a much broader level of exposure. Best Western International, one of the largest hotel systems in the world, is an example of a referral group. The owners of Best Western International are the individual property owners. Preferred Hotels & Resorts Worldwide, The Leading Hotels of the World, and ALHI are referral groups serving generally upscale hotels.

Belonging to a franchise or referral group provides several benefits, the most obvious being a more extensive reservation system and expanded advertising through pooled resources. These advantages are so important that lending institutions may often be reluctant to lend money to potential investors unless the investors have established an affiliation with a franchise group or referral organization.

As with franchise organizations, referral groups provide central purchasing services. These services reduce expenses to the individual hotels, since items are purchased in larger quantities. Owners can purchase interior furnishings, bath amenities, linens and towels, and restaurant items at quantity prices. Referral groups require members to maintain certain operating standards, so that guests can enjoy consistent quality.

Classifying Guests

Guests, like hotels, can be categorized. These categories, some quite elaborate, are typically most useful to a property's marketing function. Classifying guests by their reasons for traveling offers some useful general insights into the different wants and needs of guests. The market for the lodging industry can be segmented into three major categories, based on reasons for travel: business, pleasure/leisure, and group. A fourth category is made up of international travelers.

Business Travelers

The business travel market is important to many lodging properties. Historically, business travelers were the first and primary market for hotels, dating back to the railroad age. In the United States, more than 35 million people take business trips each year. Business travelers average about five trips per year, and, because business travelers are less likely to share rooms or stay with friends or relatives, they account for a significant portion of lodging demand. Regular business travel is that segment of the business travel market not related to meetings and conventions.

Regular business travel is an important source of business for many lodging properties. Within the last few years, hotels and airlines have designed specific products and services for the traveling business executive. Increased attention has also been given to traveling businesswomen. A special segment of business travelers is predisposed to stay at luxury hotels. Frequent business travelers generally provide their travel agents with broad parameters outlining the type of hotel in which they wish to stay. The growing number of suite hotels directed specifically toward the business traveler has influenced growth within this market segment. Business hotels usually have amenities and facilities specifically directed at business travelers. Examples include meeting space, offices in the building that travelers can rent, secretarial or computer services, in-room safes, and 24-hour room service. In addition, one of the latest trends is to provide Internet access, either through computers or the guestroom television.

Pleasure/Leisure Travelers

While business travel generally rates as an important source of business for hotels, pleasure/leisure travel is also very important. Although downturns in economic cycles tend to reduce travel, it is generally true over time that more and more people are experiencing an increase in discretionary income and leisure time; as a result, more and more people are traveling.

The segments of the pleasure travel market often overlap. The specific segmentation of this market often depends on the attractions, products, and services offered in the destination area of a lodging property. Typical market segments include specialized resort travel (for example, those seeking health spa facilities or instruction in such sports as tennis and golf), family pleasure travel, travel by the elderly, and travel by singles or couples.

Of all the travel industry market segments, pleasure/leisure travelers are among the most difficult to understand. In contrast with business travelers, who consider the cost of travel a necessary expense, pleasure travelers are generally price-sensitive. Income is an important factor in shaping the demand for pleasure travel. Vacation activities and lodging accommodations compete for the traveler's discretionary income as well as leisure time. The amount of discretionary income directly affects pleasure travel because it is the source for supporting leisure-related activities.

There are two hybrids of business and pleasure travel. One hybrid results when a business finances an employee's pleasure travel as an incentive. Another hybrid form results when a business traveler adds vacation travel to the end or beginning of a scheduled business trip.

Group Travelers

Group travel is different from business travel because some groups, such as organized tour groups, travel for pleasure.

Business travel related to meetings and conventions is commonly classified into two markets: *institutional* and *corporate/government.* Gatherings held by the institutional market are usually open to the public. Examples of institutional gatherings include national conventions held by various trade associations. Gatherings held by the corporate/government market are usually closed to the public because they often deal with private corporate or government business matters. Examples of corporate gatherings include management meetings, sales meetings, new product introductions, training seminars, professional and technical meetings, and stockholder meetings.

Conventions and smaller meetings are critically important to much of the lodging industry. They result in the sale of guestrooms as well as banquet and meeting room facilities. Meetings and conventions can attract hundreds or thousands of people, but a single meeting planner typically decides where and when to have a meeting. Therefore, a hotel's sales and marketing department often focuses its efforts on meeting planners. In some cases, a hotel's sales and marketing personnel can persuade meeting planners to hold meetings at the hotel during the off season, thereby generating revenue during a slow time.

International Travelers

Hotels face an interesting and enormous challenge as international travel continues to expand. International guests bring a different set of needs and expectations, and of course language barriers can be an issue. Hotels lacking translation services may be severely disadvantaged in a city where a Japanese company has just opened a manufacturing plant, for example. Multicultural factors are also important considerations in staffing, interior design, food and beverage services, and recreational facilities. To meet this multicultural challenge, hotel managers must decide what international markets they want to serve, and establish a program to accommodate those markets.

Consider how Japanese guests would appreciate a traditional Japanese breakfast of miso soup, fish, and rice, while guests from Great Britain would enjoy a familiar breakfast of fried eggs and breakfast meats. An international guest would also appreciate a hotel staff that could say "hello," "thank you," and other simple words and phrases in his or her native language.

A large portion of the labor force in U.S. hotels today is foreign-born. People from Mexico, the Caribbean, India, Pakistan, Japan, China, and Africa are among the employees working in the hospitality industry. While many of these employees hold unskilled or semi-skilled positions, many possess multilingual skills and an understanding of the customs and cultures of international guests. Enlightened hotel managers look to these foreign-born employees for additional proficiency and versatility in serving international guests. Hotels may find themselves establishing training programs for foreign-born employees. These training programs may include English language lessons as well as classes in the customs of various other countries. On the other hand, foreign-born employees may teach classes to improve the skills of native-born employees in serving international guests.

Buying Influences on Travelers

Many things affect a traveler's selection of overnight accommodations. Buying influences may include satisfactory experiences with a hotel, advertisements by a hotel or a chain organization, recommendations by family members or friends, the location of a hotel, and preconceptions of a hotel based on its name or affiliation. To persuade guests to choose one hotel over others, many hotels develop marketing plans that may include the use of billboards, newspaper and radio advertisements, printed publications, the Internet, personal and telephone sales efforts, public relations activities, and direct mail pieces.

Until recently, travel agents had a significant impact on consumer hotel selections. Consumers often depended on travel agents to select a hotel appropriate to their needs. However, within the past few years the Internet has played a much larger role in directing, and even attracting, personal travel. There are now dozens of Internet travel sites with varying business models and different ways of attracting customers and pricing travel products. These electronic distribution channels have reduced the role of travel agents and have emerged as mainstream marketing and sales opportunities for hotels.

At the same time, more businesses are relying on **travel management companies** (large travel agencies with significant room rate negotiating power) to control travel expenses. Travel management companies are contracted by client companies and may receive a commission payment for travel booked. In turn, the travel management companies provide cost savings for their clients by consolidating the travel of all their clients and using that bundled buying power to negotiate discounted pricing for hotel rooms, plane tickets, car rentals, and other travel products. American Express, WorldTravel BTI, Navigant, and Carlson Wagonlit are some of the better-known travel management companies, all of which provide travel services through websites as well as traditional offices.

A potential guest's buying decision may also be influenced by the ease of making reservations (whether via the front desk, the reservations department, or the hotel's website) or an employee's description of the hotel and its accommodations and facilities. The website's navigational tools or the reservationist's tone of voice, helpfulness, efficiency, and knowledge are all factors that may contribute to a guest's decision to stay at a particular hotel. More and more, potential guests search the Internet or contact several hotels in the destination area to compare room rates, services, and amenities before purchasing.

What influences repeat business? Many guests say that the most important factors that bring them back to a hotel are the quality of service and the property's overall cleanliness and appearance. Good service is good business. Front office staff members are among the most visible hotel representatives in this regard. The front office's challenge is to obtain repeat business by providing a level of service that meets and exceeds guest expectations.

Business travelers offer a tremendous opportunity for attracting repeat business. Satisfied business travelers may not only return for the same business purposes, but may also bring other business acquaintances, family members, and guests, or even revisit the property for a personal vacation.

Guests often become loyal to particular chains or properties. Chain or brand loyalty can be a matter of habit, maximization of value to price, or satisfaction with the hotel's products or services. Since it is difficult to obtain reliable pre-purchase information about services, consumers may be reluctant to change hotels because they are unsure whether the change will actually increase their satisfaction. In order to "comparison shop" for services, consumers must visit various hotel properties in person. Also, consumers often perceive greater risks in purchasing services than they do in purchasing manufactured products. This increases the likelihood of brand loyalty when a lodging property succeeds in satisfying its guests.

Frequent traveler and electronic marketing programs are directed toward creating and sustaining brand loyalty for hotels, restaurants, and airlines. Programs such as Marriott Rewards, Starwood Preferred Guest, Hyatt Gold Passport, and Holiday Inn Priority Club are designed to give guests an added incentive to stay at one brand of hotel over another. Many such programs are affiliated with airline and car rental programs and offer rewards for flying a specific airline, staying at a specific hotel chain, and renting a specific company's car. Rewards can be free airline trips, free hotel stays, free car rentals, free amenities, discounted food and beverage services, guestroom upgrades, and even entire vacations for those who accumulate a large number of points or credits.

Since many hotel companies offer similar frequent traveler programs, the original intention of these programs to increase brand loyalty has been somewhat diluted. Many frequent travelers have actually come to expect frequent guest programs, thereby devaluing such programs and making them less enticing. Although frequent guest programs are expensive to operate, most hotel companies perceive them as worthwhile in retaining some valued repeat guests whose business might otherwise be lost.

Another reason guests may become brand-loyal is their own recognition that repeat patronage may lead to greater satisfaction of their needs. This can be especially important in the luxury sector of the lodging industry. The hotel staff and management may learn the tastes and preferences of regular guests and therefore be better able to provide the services these guests expect. The Ritz-Carlton chain has developed an extensive guest history system to communicate guest preferences to each of its hotels, even if a guest has never stayed at a particular property before.

One factor affecting brand loyalty in the lodging industry is the unavailability of some brands in certain locations. If a consumer prefers to stay in hotels belonging to a specific chain but is unable to locate an affiliate at a particular destination, he or she may decide to stay at a property belonging to a different chain. This is one way the consumer learns about competing brands. If the competing brand offers roughly the same quality level or higher, loyalty to the former hotel chain may diminish.

Among the most interesting recent influences on travelers are website design, site navigation, and specific websites that serve as reference guides for travelers. Hotel brands spend a lot of time and money designing and redesigning websites to attract and retain clientele. Internet search engines such as Google.com, Yahoo.com, and Ask.com also are becoming significant influences on travelers. Search engines index websites based on key words or references embedded in the websites and match them to words that travelers enter when using the search engine. The closer the match between the searched item and the indexed site, the higher the site is listed in the search engine response.

Recently, websites have been specifically designed to let travelers write about their experiences at hotels, restaurants, casinos, clubs, theme parks, and other travel operations. Travelers peruse these sites when deciding whether to stay at a particular property, turning to reviews written by others who have stayed there. These features are part of the online technology applications called *blogging* and *social networking*.

Blogging and Social Networking

A web log or *blog* is a web page that serves as a publicly accessible chronicle or personal diary. It is similar in functioning to a discussion board. Blog posts are typically listed or logged in chronological order and displayed on the blog in reverse order to the reader, with the newest posts appearing at the top. The posts are a series of topical discussions written by a *blogger*. The general neutrality of a blog provides an anonymous platform for all interested readers. Blog content, similar in force to word-of-mouth power, can influence purchasing decisions, affect marketing strategies, and affect corporate image.

A blog that is dedicated to a specific business or business segment is often termed a *b-blog*. Several b-blogs are dedicated to the hospitality industry. A guest who has had an outstanding experience at a lodging property may be inclined to write about it on a public blog, wherein the guest is the blogger. Accounts of great experiences can enhance a property's image and appeal, while negative accounts tend to have the opposite effect. A quick index to blogs can be found by searching tagged blog site contents. Tags can be created from key words or meaningful acronyms. Online media, such as discussion forums and e-mail exchanges, are examples of alternate forms of blogs.

Social networking services, also called social networking sites, are designed to build upon interaction within an online or virtual community. Web-based social networking sites offer a setting for individuals or groups to create a profile to share with fellow members of the site. The website provides a variety of communication formats, including instant messaging, chat rooms, e-mail, blogs, and discussion groups. Many social networking sites offer privacy to members by allowing them to create restricted profiles and to maintain control over how much information is viewable to other members. For example, on some sites, users must agree to be friends before they can see each others' private profiles. Social networking sites can be created for personal reasons (such as communicating with family and friends), for business purposes (discussing news, promotions, discounts, or job hunting), or for finding individuals with similar interests (such as dating or searching for friends). Two widely subscribed social sites for connecting community members are MySpace (launched in 2003) and Facebook (launched in 2004).

The Green Hotel

What does *being green* mean? Although *green* has become a popular descriptor, it has no standard definition beyond its application to an eco-friendly business. Given the many building industry guidelines and the proprietary systems some hotel companies have developed, *being green* can range from encouraging guests to reuse towels, to recycling waste, to using wind electricity, to cooking with organic foods, to reducing carbon emissions, to installing rooftop solar panels. Complying with various benchmarks can result in earning a green label from an association such as the U.S. Green Building Council.

While a newly constructed property can more easily establish environmentally friendly systems, as opposed to older properties that require retrofit products to achieve success, a significant majority of the hotel industry is seeking compliance. The traveling public appears to be increasingly interested in patronizing hotels that invest in environmentally friendly buildings, equipment, processes, and techniques. In fact, some hotel companies have adopted environmental checklists that must be adhered to by both company-operated properties and franchised locations. Similarly, U.S. government agencies have a policy guideline that requires hotels and convention centers to file environmental performance data with the U.S. Environmental Protection Agency (EPA) if they wish to earn the agencies' business. In addition, the Association of Corporate Travel Executives (ACTE) values environmental performance when choosing hotels to host its meetings; the ACTE, active in more than fifty countries, prefers to conduct its events at venues with strong environmental programs. In fact, the group requires candidate hotels to include an environmental considerations addendum indicating their green practices before it will consider their business.

Striving for reductions in greenhouse gas emissions, carbon neutrality, recycling, and organic gardening might be among the environmental goals of a **green hotel** property. Capturing waste heat from power generators, using renewable energy sources, and educating guests about environmental issues affected through lodging-related processes are also important elements in a comprehensive eco-friendly campaign. Several websites list green and/or certified hotel properties, including *Travel + Leisure*, LEED, and the Energy Star program. Green hospitality operations can generate both economic (cost savings) and environmental (recycling and reusing) advantages. The appendix to this chapter presents an extended case study describing one hotel's efforts to implement green practices.

Green initiatives are in place worldwide, not just in the United States and North America. Perhaps one of the best known initiatives is The Prince's Foundation for the Built Environment, headquartered in London, England, and founded by Prince Charles. Its purpose is to create an educational foundation to improve the quality of life through the teaching and practice of timeless and ecological ways of planning, designing, and building. The foundation promotes ecological principles for improving building designs through environmentally friendly considerations. The foundation is associated with architects, engineers, manufacturers, and other organizations, including hotel companies.

LEED Certification and the Energy Star Program

Hotels are increasingly earning eco-certification through a variety of industry programs designed to recognize commitment to ecological responsibility. The hotel industry plays a major role in the successful implementation of ecotourism. Perhaps best known among a host of domestic classifications that hotel companies support are the Leadership in Energy and Environmental Design (LEED) rating system and the Energy Star Award program.

LEED Certification. The LEED program was created by the U.S. Green Building Council (USGBC) to certify that buildings meet standards of energy efficiency, conservation, and community sensitivity. The LEED certification was developed to encourage and accelerate global adoption of sustainable green building and development practices through the implementation of universally accepted tools and effective performance criteria. LEED is a nationally accepted benchmark for the design, construction, and operation of high-performance green buildings. It promotes a unique approach to construction that recognizes performance in five important areas of environmental health: sustainable site development, water savings, energy efficiency, materials selection, and indoor environmental air quality. The LEED program operates under the auspices of the USGBC, which estimates the advantages of building green to be reflected in decreased operating expenses and increased occupancy value over the life of the building. The four levels of LEED certification are, from highest to lowest, Platinum, Gold, Silver, and Certified. The USGBC estimates that, in the near future, nearly two-thirds of all consumers will elect to do business with companies that are LEED certified.

The LEED Rating System was developed through a consensus-based process led by various LEED committees of the building and construction industry. Architects, facility managers, engineers, interior designers, landscape architects, and construction managers use LEED standards. Eco-construction is increasing in popularity, and LEED benchmarks are in place in more than 40 countries, including Canada, Brazil, Mexico, and India.

Energy Star Program. The EPA's Energy Star program focuses on energy efficiency in various pieces of equipment and appliances. Hotel properties may be recognized with an Energy Star Award for increased energy efficiency. The Energy Star rating process requires hoteliers to enter energy performance metrics (such as monthly utility bills) into an automated benchmarking system that determines changes in energy conservation. The American Hotel & Lodging Association is a partner and strong supporter of the Energy Star program for the hospitality industry. The Energy Star award is presented yearly by the EPA and the U.S. Department of Energy (DOE) to honor organizations that have made outstanding contributions to protecting the environment through energy efficiency.

Nearly 100 hospitality companies have received industry recognition, including Accor North America (for increased energy efficiency), Carlson Companies, Inc. (for constrained consumption), Marriott International, Inc. (for superior energy performance), Hilton Hotels Corporation (for energy-efficient buildings), Hyatt Corporation (for energy-centric design), Ritz-Carlton Hotel Company (energy-sensitive operations), and Starwood Hotels and Resorts Worldwide, Inc. (for energy performance enhancement). The hospitality industry slogan for the Energy Star Award is: "Make strong energy performance your competitive advantage!" The goal of a strategic energy management program should focus on reduced costs and increased guest satisfaction. Energy Star estimates that a 10-percent reduction in energy consumption can have a financial impact equal to raising the hotel's average daily rate by $1.35 for full-service properties, and by 60 cents for limited-service properties.

Hotel Compliance. Hotels have engaged in a variety of architectural, electrical, mechanical, and natural-process improvements to establish compliance within LEED and/or Energy Star rating systems. Such areas as energy management, water management, biodiversity management, and waste management are receiving attention. The objective of a green program is to minimize waste and maximize efficiency.

Energy management. Improved technology can make gains in energy efficiency more easily attainable. Lodging properties can establish credit toward LEED certification in the use of electricity by implementing a renewable energy program through the use of wind power, run-of-river power, solar power, window tinting, and other techniques designed to contain and/or reduce energy consumption and related expenditures. Some hotels have sought benefits in this area by interconnecting their energy management systems with their property management systems to ensure consumption reduction when a room is unoccupied. The linking of energy use and room occupancy presents a natural synergy for conservation. At the time of check-out, all non-critical equipment in a guestroom can be automatically controlled or turned off. Items such as alarm clocks and refrigerators would not be affected, while thermostatic controls, television sets, select room lighting, and related components might all be subject to a power-down condition.

Related areas of compliance involve replacing incandescent light bulbs with fluorescent lighting, resulting in a possible 75 percent savings; installing energy-efficient laundry equipment and digital thermostats; and reducing clear air circulating equipment through adoption of a smoke-free policy. Hotels can also reduce energy consumption by replacing air filters in in-room heating/cooling systems more frequently. Clogged filters cause fans to work longer; clean filters also mean cleaner rooms. Energy-efficient guestrooms are also important. Furthermore, some properties are drying laundered items in the sun. Capturing waste heat from power generators, using geothermal energy, transitioning to renewable energy sources, and applying solar energy when appropriate will significantly contribute to overall energy efficiency.

Water management. Water conservation and recycling are key components of an effective water management program. Among hospitality industry practices are collecting rain water for use, placing water meters in guestrooms so guests can track usage, and grinding guest soaps to use as laundry detergent for hotel uniforms.

Biodiversity management. Hotel companies can participate in biodiversity management by sharing their land with wildlife, embarking on an ecological restoration program to transform scarred and misused land into increased levels of diversity and use, and installing and maintaining hiking trails. Hotels can provide staff training in plant identification and wildlife conservation. They can further demonstrate commitment to the local community by promoting organic produce and gardens, controlling carbon emissions, and installing a hydro-plant. In addition, hotels can use recycled paper products, and utilize organic produce and gardens.

Waste management. Hotels can greatly reduce waste by recycling. For example, hotel restaurants can compost food waste or donate wholesome, unused food to charity. Hotels can also purchase items that are not packaged in individual servings, and can purchase supplies from green vendors. Hotel meeting facilities can serve water in pitchers and glasses instead of in individual servings of bottled water, and can use recyclable cutlery and napkins in food service. Reducing the amount of garbage the hotel generates, combined with donating realized savings to community and school projects, can also lead to increased goodwill within the local community.

Green Meetings

Green meetings, green hotels, green convention centers, green suppliers, and international awards for being green affect all aspects of the hospitality industry. As mentioned earlier, many companies and associations now require that hotels meet certain green requirements before they consider giving them their meeting business. The organizations communicate these requirements to the hotels along with their meeting specifications, and the hotels must address their ability to meet the requirements in their bids for the business.

Environmentally conscious meetings are a growing trend. With a growing number of resources becoming rare and expensive, organizations today increasingly support eco-friendly meetings. The greening of a meeting can be accomplished in many ways, including not pre-filling water glasses at banquet tables, collecting name tags and badge-holders for reuse when meetings end, providing recycling areas inside exhibit areas, and using compostable cups instead of water bottles. Some meeting planners insist that meeting facilities use biodegradable and recyclable materials before they will consider booking meetings there. Research indicates that more than 60 percent of meeting planners deliberately avoid a destination or venue with a poor environmental record. Many industry observers do not consider green considerations a fad, but rather a long-term trend.

By definition, a green meeting incorporates environmental awareness throughout all stages of the meeting to minimize negative impacts on the environment. Basically, a green meeting supports a green initiative and is expected to save money while improving the environment. The Convention Industry Council's Green Meetings Report is the reference for the meeting planning industry, while the EPA's *"It's Easy Being Green!"* publication stipulates mandatory requirements for green meetings. Sustainable Travel International works with such industry leaders as Continental, Marriott, and Leading Hotels of the World to reduce their carbon footprint. Recently, Virginia, California, Michigan, Florida, and Vermont initiated their own certification programs for green hotels. The bottom line is that people are more environmentally aware and are basing business decisions on environmental factors as well as on logistics.

In 2003, IMEX introduced the Green Meeting Award and recently partnered with the Green Meeting Industry Council to launch the Green Exhibitor Award and Green Supplier Award. Green meeting leaders claim that being green is not only right for the environment, it actually saves businesses money.

Summary

The lodging industry is part of the larger travel and tourism industry. One of the world's largest industries, the travel and tourism industry is composed of a vast group of businesses oriented toward providing necessary or desired products and services to travelers. This industry can be segmented into five parts: lodging operations, transportation services, food and beverage operations, retail stores, and travel-related activities. The lodging operations classification consists of hotels, motels, inns, suite hotels, conference centers, lifestyle hotels, upscale service hotels, and other lodging establishments. Although the distinction between these property types is not always clear, properties can be grouped by size, target market, level of service, and ownership and affiliation.

As with hotels, guests can be divided into categories. Guests are typically grouped according to their reasons for travel: business, pleasure/leisure, or group. A fourth category consists of international guests. Hotel managers serving a large international guest market may rely on their foreign-born employees for added proficiency in serving international guests. The more information a hotel has about its guests, the better it can anticipate and satisfy their needs.

Many things affect a traveler's selection of overnight accommodations. Buying influences may include satisfactory experiences with a hotel, advertisements, recommendations by family members and friends, a hotel's location, and preconceptions of a hotel based on its name or affiliation. Until recently, travel agents had a significant impact on consumer hotel selections, but now the Internet plays a much larger role in directing, and even attracting, personal travel. Hotel brands spend a lot of time and money designing and redesigning websites to attract and retain clientele. Internet search engines such as Google.com, Yahoo.com, and Ask.com also significantly influence travelers. Several b-blogs are dedicated to the hospitality industry. Guests may write about their experiences at a lodging property; what they write can enhance or diminish a property's image and appeal. Businesses are relying on travel management companies to control their travel expenses. Travel management companies consolidate the travel needs of all their clients and use that bundled buying power to negotiate discounted pricing for travel products.

What influences repeat business? Many guests say that the most important factors that bring them back to a hotel are the quality of service and the property's overall cleanliness and appearance. Frequent traveler and electronic marketing programs also help create and sustain repeat business.

The traveling public is increasingly interested in patronizing hotels that invest in environmentally friendly buildings, equipment, processes, and techniques. Hotels have engaged in a variety of architectural, electrical, mechanical, and natural-process improvements to establish compliance within LEED and/or Energy Star rating systems. The goal of a strategic energy management program should be to reduce costs and increase guest satisfaction. Green meeting leaders claim that being green is not only right for the environment, it actually saves businesses money.

While a hotel property's architecture and style may be important in setting its theme, front office personnel play an integral role in defining its image. The variety of talents and skills required to satisfy guest needs makes front office work interesting and rewarding.

Endnote

1. Floyd Miller, *Statler—America's Extraordinary Hotelman* (New York: Statler Foundation, 1968), p. 36.

Key Terms

chain hotel—A hotel owned by or affiliated with other properties.

economy/limited service—A level of service emphasizing clean, comfortable, inexpensive rooms that meet the most basic needs of guests. Economy or limited service hotels appeal primarily to budget-minded travelers.

franchising—A method of distribution whereby one entity that has developed a particular pattern or format for doing business (the franchisor) grants to other entities (franchisees) the right to conduct such a business provided they follow the established pattern.

green hotel—An eco-friendly hotel that strives to reduce greenhouse gas emissions, recycle, save water and energy, and support organic gardening, among other environmentally friendly activities.

hotel—A general term used to describe hotels, motels, motor hotels, inns, suite hotels, conference centers, resorts, and other operations providing lodging facilities, various services, and conveniences to the traveling public.

independent hotel—A hotel with no ownership or management affiliation with other properties.

management contract—An agreement between the owner/developer of a property and a professional hotel management company. The owner/developer usually retains the financial and legal responsibility for the property, and the management company receives an agreed-upon fee for operating the hotel.

market segmentation—The practice of defining or identifying smaller, distinct groups or *segments* within larger markets; *corporate business travelers*, for instance, is a segment of *business travelers*.

mid-range service—A modest but sufficient level of service that appeals to the largest segment of the traveling public. A mid-range property may offer uniformed service, airport van service, and food and beverage room service; a specialty restaurant, coffee shop, and lounge; and special rates for certain guests.

quality assurance—An approach to ensuring the consistent delivery of services.

referral group—A group of independent hotels that have banded together for their common good. Hotels within the group refer departing guests or those guests they cannot accommodate to other properties in the referral group.

target markets—Distinctly defined groupings of potential buyers (market segments) at which sellers aim or "target" their marketing efforts.

travel management company—A large travel agency with significant room rate negotiating power.

upscale service hotel—A hotel that appeals to business executives, high-level industry meeting attendees, and leisure travelers interested in extra comforts. Upscale hotels tend to have multiple food service outlets, each with a different cuisine. Guests enjoy such amenities as flat-panel televisions and luxurious bedding. Housekeeping services are often scheduled twice daily, including evening turndown service upon request.

world-class service—A level of guest service that stresses personal attention. Hotels offering world-class service provide upscale restaurants and lounges, exquisite décor, concierge services, opulent rooms, and abundant amenities.

Review Questions

1. What do all travel and tourism businesses have in common? How does the hospitality industry relate to the travel and tourism industry?

2. What are four general ways of classifying hotels? Why can hotels fit into more than one category?

3. What are some distinctions between resort hotels and commercial hotels?

4. For what purpose are conference centers specifically designed? How do they serve their target market?

5. What are some basic issues surrounding the concept of service? How can a hotel help ensure consistency in an intangible product?

6. What is world-class service? What personnel are employed in a world-class hotel? What is an executive floor?

7. What is a unique advantage of an independent hotel? How might independent hotels be at a disadvantage?

8. How might a management contract be involved in the development of a hotel? What are the differences between a franchise and a referral group?

9. What are three chief categories of travelers, in terms of the purpose for traveling? How can a hotel influence a traveler's decision to visit or return to the hotel?

10. Why is international travel becoming so important to the hospitality industry? What major challenges do hotel managers face in this area?

11. Why are Internet blogging and social networks of interest to the hospitality industry?

12. What is a "green" hotel? Why are hotels interested in being green?

Internet Sites

For more information, visit the following Internet sites. Remember that Internet addresses can change without notice. If the site is no longer there, you can use a search engine to look for additional sites.

Travel and Lodging Associations

American Hotel & Lodging
Association (AH&LA)
www.ahla.com

American Hotel & Lodging
Educational Institute
www.ahlei.org

Hospitality Financial & Technology
Professionals
www.hftp.org

Hospitality Sales and Marketing
Association International (HSMAI)
www.hsmai.org

International Council on Hotel,
Restaurant and Institutional Education
(CHRIE)
www.chrie.org

International Hotel & Restaurant
Association (IHRA)
www.ih-ra.com

Travel and Tourism Research
Association (TTRA)
www.ttra.com

World Tourism Organization (UNWTO)
http://www2.unwto.org/en

Hotels and Hotel Companies

Associated Luxury Hotels
International (ALHI)
www.alhi.com

Best Western
www.bestwestern.com

Choice Hotels International
www.hotelchoice.com

Days Inn of America, Inc.
www.daysinn.com

Extended Stay Hotels
www.extendedstayhotels.com

Fairmont Hotels & Resorts
www.fairmont.com

Gaylord Opryland Resort &
  Convention Center
www.gaylordhotels.com

Hilton
www.hilton.com

Homewood Suites by Hilton Hotels
http://homewoodsuites.hilton.com

Hotel Del Coronado
www.hoteldel.com

Hyatt Hotels Corporation
http://goldpassport.hyatt.com

InterContinental Hotels Group
www.ichotelsgroup.com

Interstate Hotels & Resorts
www.interstatehotels.com

Knights Inn
www.knightsinn.com

Marriott
www.marriott.com

Oakwood Corporate Housing
www.oakwood.com

Preferred Hotels & Resorts
www.preferredhotels.com

Radisson Hotels & Resorts
www.radisson.com

The Ritz-Carlton Company
www.ritzcarlton.com

Sheraton Hotels & Resorts
www.starwoodhotels.com/sheraton

Walt Disney World
www.disneyworld.disney.go.com

Westin Hotels and Resorts
www.starwoodhotels.com/westin

Condominium and Timeshare Organizations

American Resort Development
  Association
www.arda.org

Community Associations Institute
www.caionline.org

Disney Vacation Club
www.dvc.disney.go.com/dvc/index

Hilton Grand Vacations Company
www.hiltongrandvacations.com

Interval International
www.intervalworld.com

Marriott Vacation Club
www.marriottvacations.com

Resort Condominiums International
www.rci.com/RCI

Casino Hotels

Caesars Entertainment
www.caesars.com

Harrah's
www.harrahs.com

Pechanga Resort & Casino
www.pechanga.com

Travel Management Companies

American Express
https://travel.americanexpress.com/
home

Carlson Wagonlit Travel
www.carlsonwagonlit.com

BCD Travel
www.worldtravel.com

"Green" Hotels

AH&LA's Green Resource Center
www.ahla.com/green.aspx

Travel + Leisure magazine
www.travelandleisure.com

Green Globe International
www.greenglobeint.com

U.S. Green Building Council (USGBC)
www.usgbc.org

"Green" Hotels Association
www.greenhotels.com

U.S. Environmental Protection Agency
Energy Star program
www.energystar.gov

Green Lodging News
www.greenlodgingnews.com/
waste-management

🔍 Case Studies ──────────────────────────────────

A Big Fish in a Small Pond Flounders in the Great Lakes

Jeff Marlin took down his hospitality management diploma from his office wall and packed it on top of a nearly full box of books and papers. It was Jeff's last day as assistant general manager of the Fairmeadows Inn in suburban Lake Zurich, Illinois. Tomorrow he started a new job as front office manager at the Merrimack, an 800-room convention hotel in downtown Chicago.

Not bad for someone just three years out of school, he thought to himself as he finished packing. *After this job, there's nothing I can't handle.* It was true, the assistant GM's job had taught him to be a jack-of-all-trades. He had hired many of the property's twenty employees and knew them all by name. He had a good relationship with the head of housekeeping; he knew he could count on a quick response to special requests like readying a handicap-accessible room on short notice. He was proud that, during his tenure at the Fairmeadows Inn, his property had consistently had the highest average daily rate and highest occupancy of all the Fairmeadows properties in his region.

With no full-time sales department, Jeff had become quite skilled at drumming up business among local groups. The Chamber of Commerce and the Kiwanis held monthly luncheon meetings (catered by the restaurant across the street) at the Fairmeadows and always put up visiting guests at the property. During the summer softball season, the 124-room property was hopping as softball teams of fifteen to twenty players from neighboring regions stayed overnight at the Fairmeadows when they played the Lake Zurich team. Even then, Jeff was pleased with the front desk's ability to handle check-in and check-out procedures smoothly. At other times of the year, front desk traffic was easier, with only two or three people checking in or out at any given time.

Jeff knew that he could handle anything his new job would throw at him. Hadn't he learned the Fairmeadows's new computer system faster than anyone on staff—and trained the front desk staff how to use the programs? Reservations, sales, check-in/check-out, training, daily reports—*yeah, I'm ready to move up,* Jeff thought.

Jeff's confidence got its first jolt as he strolled through the front doors of the Merrimack the next morning at eight o'clock. Over 200 people jostled one another in the lobby as four front desk agents worked non-stop to get them checked out. *What's going on here?* Jeff wondered. A bell attendant asked the somewhat dazed Jeff if he could be of assistance, then gave Jeff directions to the general manager's office.

"Welcome aboard, Jeff," said Al Grayling, as Jeff entered the GM's office. "Hope you didn't have any trouble finding me."

"Who are all those people in the lobby?" Jeff asked. "I've never seen such a crowd before."

Al laughed. "Get used to it, Jeff. That's actually one of our smaller groups checking out this morning. There'll be lots of days when you and your staff will be checking out one group of 400 people and checking in another 400."

"Of course," Jeff laughed weakly. "It's a convention hotel. I knew that. Well, where do I start?"

Al took Jeff out to the front desk, where he was introduced to the morning shift—Carole, Franklin, Ashari, and Dean. They greeted him briefly, then turned their attention back to the guests who were checking out. At the Fairmeadows Inn, Jeff often pulled a shift at the front desk when things got busy. Glancing over Franklin's shoulder, though, Jeff realized that the computer system the Merrimack used was completely different from the one he was used to, and that the check-out methods performed so efficiently by his new staff were also unfamiliar. *Better let them do what they do best until I pick up the routines,* he decided.

The phone rang. Jeff knew he could handle that. "Merrimack Hotel, Jeff Marlin. How may I help you?"

"Jeff? This is Nancy Troutman, director of sales. You're the new front office manager, right? Al Grayling said you'd be starting today," said the voice on the other end of the line. "Jeff, I need you to let me know when the cosmetics sales convention group checks in. I want to meet with Sheila Watkins as soon as she arrives to go over plans for their awards banquet. I'm at extension 805. Got it? The information should be in the group résumé book at the front desk. Bye."

Jeff had to ask Ashari for the group résumé book; they didn't even have one at the Fairmeadows Inn. She also showed him the daily report, which was three pages longer than the reports he was used to. He tried to figure out the different set-up and the unfamiliar items—F&B, banquets, groups in and out, VIP list, out of order rooms. *I need a report to explain this report,* Jeff thought.

As long as he was looking at reports, he decided to ask Ashari for a copy of the night audit.

"Oh, that goes right to accounting," she explained.

"Not to me?" he asked. She shook her head, then pointed out the number for accounting on the staff phone list.

The list itself overwhelmed Jeff. So many departments, so many managers. PBX, reservations, sales, front office—he'd handled all of that at his last job. Here at the Merrimack, there was a separate department for each function. Would he ever find his way around this organization?

Maybe I'd have been better off as a big fish in my small pond, he thought.

After lunch, Jeff was back at the front desk. Working with Dean, he was getting oriented to the Merrimack's room management software and feeling his confidence rebound a little. It was still a couple of hours until the cosmetics convention group came in, so traffic at the front desk was fairly slow.

A couple, the woman in a wheelchair, came to the front desk. The Armbrusters had reservations for a handicap-accessible room, but when Jeff checked the room status, he discovered that no such rooms were clean and ready for occupancy. He asked Dean to continue taking the Armbrusters' registration information while he attempted to resolve the problem with their room.

Jeff searched the phone list until he found the housekeeping manager, Dolores Manta. "Dolores, this is Jeff at the front desk. I need a handicap-accessible room prepared for immediate occupancy. How quickly do you think you could have one ready?"

"Just who are you?" asked Dolores. "We do have procedures around here. Don't you know you can't order a room like you order a pizza? No one informed me that an accessible room was a priority. Why did you wait until 1:30 to tell me this? Didn't you know they were coming in? Isn't it in the log?"

The head housekeeper at the Fairmeadows Inn had never responded to any of Jeff's requests like this; he was taken aback. What was the big deal, anyway?

"I'm the new front office manager; it's my first day," he explained. "No, I didn't know they were coming in. The log? Uh, I don't know about … oh, wait, here it is. I guess I didn't know.…" He tried to recover. "I apologize for not following the right procedure, but I still have two guests here who need a room. Do you have any suggestions for me?"

"Well, my staff is pretty tied up getting rooms ready for those 500 cosmetics salespeople coming in at 4 p.m., but I'll see if I can take someone away from that and prepare Room 167 for you," said Dolores. "But, Jeff, don't let it happen again."

The cosmetics convention group was late arriving, but Jeff stayed on to make sure that Nancy Troutman, the sales director, was notified about their arrival. He didn't want to start that relationship off as badly as he had with the housekeeping manager. She was surprised, though, when he called.

"Why didn't you just assign the task to one of the front desk agents?" she asked. "I didn't mean that you personally needed to take care of this, just as long as I got the word. Thanks, though."

By the end of his first long day, Jeff wasn't at all certain he wanted to come back for a second day. This was supposed to be a career move up, but it sure didn't feel that way. He decided to call Gavin Albacore, a college buddy who was reservations manager at a convention hotel in St. Louis. *Maybe he would have some good advice,* Jeff thought.

Discussion Questions

1. How could the general manager at the Merrimack have made Jeff's transition into his new job easier?

2. What steps could Jeff have taken to make a smoother transition to the new job?

3. What advice might Jeff's friend have to help him make this a successful career move?

Case Number: 3321CA

The following industry experts helped generate and develop this case: Richard M. Brooks, CHA, Vice President, TWE Group; and S. Kenneth Hiller, CHA, General Manager, Holiday Inn, Beachwood, Ohio.

Choosing the Right Person for the Job

Alan Christoff looked up from the report on his desk as his assistant brought in the morning mail. He flipped through the stack until he came to a large envelope bearing the unmistakable logo of the prominent hotel chain for which he was senior vice president of development. Christoff was in the process of finding someone to head up the hotel company's new interval ownership business unit. Construction was already underway on phase one of the company's first venture—a 200-unit timeshare resort on the South Carolina coast. The plan called for the resort to be built in phases with an anticipated five-year sellout and a twelve-month building cycle—two buildings a year for five years. When it was finished, the resort would feature twenty two-bedroom units in each building, along with tennis courts, swimming pools, and a central facilities building. Selling one-week intervals per unit and closing a sale with one out of every ten prospects making site visits, the sales effort might have to attract over 100,000 prospects to reach the sellout goal.

Christoff's immediate concern was finding a manager for the hotel chain's interval ownership business unit. The human resources manager had forwarded him the résumés of the three applicants she felt were best qualified for the position. Christoff slid the résumés out of the envelope and sat back to review them.

The first résumé was that of Micah Thompson. Christoff recognized the name as one of the hotel chain's rising stars. He held a hospitality degree from Cornell and had earned his CHA designation. His career had begun in operations; his résumé listed experience with reservations and yield management. Currently the general manager of the company's Daytona Beach hotel, Thompson, with his impressive sales and marketing skills, had earned a reputation for success in opening new properties and turning around troubled ones.

In his cover letter, Thompson cited his pre-opening experience, marketing skills, familiarity with resort destinations, and his desire to grow with the company. "I am certain that being general manager of this timeshare operation will not be significantly different from managing a hotel," he wrote.

Christoff chuckled at that statement. He wondered if Thompson had ever tried to run a property as it was being built around him, or deal with the logistics of conducting site inspections for literally tens of thousands of prospective time-share customers. Still, Thompson did have a strong track record with the hotel company and was well-regarded by the hotel company's executive team. With the company's history of internal promotions, Thompson ought to be a shoo-in for the job, thought Christoff.

Christoff turned to the next résumé. Elena Ramirez was currently the assistant general manager at a 400-unit resort condominium property in Colorado. She had formerly been an owners' relations manager with another resort condominium. Ramirez had strong knowledge of the real estate product and a proven track record in dealing with a rental program and property resales. From her job descriptions, it appeared that all of her experience had been with whole owner-ship condominiums, rather than with interval ownership.

"In addition to my experience with onsite sales and condominium rental pro-grams, I have developed a strong working relationship with our owners' asso-ciation and feel confident in dealing with individual owners and understanding their unique needs," Ramirez wrote in her cover letter. She also made a point of noting that her current property had twice the number of units as the hotel chain's planned 200-unit resort, so she felt confident of her abilities to succeed in the new environment.

Let's see, mused Christoff. Four hundred units; that's 400 owners. I wonder if she realizes she would be managing 10,000 owners? Still, she probably had a bet-ter idea of what she would be facing than someone who had never worked in the condominium business before.

The final résumé was from Earl Jackson. He was a timeshare industry vet-eran with nearly ten years of experience at interval ownership properties. Before that, he had been in the real estate industry for twelve years. Christoff noted that Jackson had even included his real estate license number on his résumé. Jackson's timeshare experience included operations, marketing, and sales. Christoff looked for evidence of hotel experience, but found none.

"I look forward to the opportunity to work with a branded chain," Jackson wrote. "I believe my experience in vacation-ownership management will enable me to work effectively with the sales staff to sell inventory and to communicate with both owners and hotel company management."

Discussion Questions

1. What criteria should Christoff consider when selecting a manager to head up the interval ownership business unit?

2. Based on criteria developed in Discussion Question #1, what are the strengths and weaknesses of each applicant?

3. Which applicant should Christoff hire? Why?

Case Number: 604CJ

The following industry experts helped generate and develop this case: Jerry Hewey, CHA, Condominium Consultant, Aspen, Colorado; Larry B. Gildersleeve, Executive Vice President, MeriStar Hotels and Resorts, Inc.; Pedro Mandoki, CHA, President, Plantation Resort Management, Inc., Gulf Shores, Alabama; and Jack

Rush, CHA, General Manager and Managing Agent of the Port Royal Ocean Resort Condominium Association in Port Aransas, Texas.

Tub for Two

Mary, the front desk agent who had been with the Boden Oceanside Resort and Lodge for nearly six months now, was trying her best to persuade the Wade party to take a look at one of the stylish executive suites in the lodge. Mary had that southern hospitality and didn't like to see guests leave dissatisfied without having done her utmost to show them the opportunities at the resort. Mr. and Mrs. Wade were celebrating their twentieth anniversary and had looked forward to a romantic get-away in a quaint lodge. The brochure for the Boden had described the Romance Package, which included a two-night stay, champagne, carriage ride, dinner for two overlooking the ocean sunset, and a beautifully appointed room. They had phoned reservations to be sure everything they wanted would be available.

When they first saw the room that they had been assigned, the bottle of champagne, two fluted glasses, and a bouquet of fresh-cut flowers adorned the coffee table. Mrs. Wade wandered over to the bathroom to see what it was like. As she returned to the main room she told the bellperson who was delivering the luggage that the bathtub wasn't fit for two. He looked somewhat puzzled and then replied that it did appear to be a single-person tub but that it did have Jacuzzi fittings. Mrs. Wade asked the bellperson if there were any rooms with tubs fit for two in the lodge. He didn't think so, but they could go check.

Mary was hoping that the executive suite would so impress the Wades that they would accept its single-size tub and decide that a tub for two was an unnecessary amenity. They consented to let her escort them to the suite. As the Manager on Duty (MOD) watched them ascend the staircase, he commented to no one in particular that they would be back. He decided to anticipate the next step in hopes of satisfying the Wades even if they chose to move to another hotel in the area. He knew that Mrs. Wade was counting on that tub! He picked up the phone book to find the number for two of the upscale, yet small resorts in the area. The second one had just what he was looking for. A nice suite with an ocean view and a large Jacuzzi tub that could fit up to five people comfortably. He also checked on availability in the main dining room to be sure that the Wades would have a table with a view. He knew that they had reserved seating at the Boden for 7:30 P.M. He made the reservation at the new location for this same time.

Mary and the Wades arrived back at the front desk and Mary asked the MOD if she should refund the Wades' deposit. Of course they had made the decision to leave and so it was up to the resort to decide whether or not to give the deposit back. Mrs. Wade insisted that she had been led by the reservations agent to expect a Jacuzzi tub for two and that she never would have made the reservation if she had known it would be different. In addition, Mrs. Wade had expected a more quaint style of lodge. This was just another typical hotel. And it wasn't anywhere near downtown as she had expected.

The MOD told Mary that the Boden would be happy to return the deposit and that they were very sorry that the Wades had felt misled by reservations.

The MOD went on to tell the Wades that he had phoned another resort in the area that they might really like and that a nice suite with a large Jacuzzi tub and an ocean view had been reserved in their name. In addition, the new resort was located closer to town, was smaller in size than the Boden Oceanside Resort and Lodge, and the very elegant main dining room had a table reserved in their name for 7:30 p.m.

The Wades left feeling satisfied and yet a little disappointed. The MOD commented to Mary that they may even have seemed a little embarrassed about making a fuss, because they said they might return to the Boden on another occasion. They just really wanted that tub for two.

Discussion Questions

1. What were the main expectations of Mr. and Mrs. Wade?

2. When and how were these expectations formed?

3. If you were the MOD, would you have gone to all that trouble to help the Wades?

4. Was Mary right in trying to find the Wades a substitute room in the resort?

5. Should the MOD have refunded the deposit in this case?

Case number: 608C01

This case also appears in Todd Comen, *Case Studies in Front Office Management* (Lansing, Mich.: of the American Hotel & Lodging Educational Institute, 2003).

Chapter Appendix: Case Study for Green Hotel Practices

Comfort Inn & Suites Boston/Airport

Property	The Comfort Inn & Suites Boston/Airport
	85 American Legion Highway, Revere, Massachusetts 02151
Contact Information	http://www.comfortinn.com/hotel-revere-massachusetts-MA051?amp;promo=gglocal
	(781) 485-3600
Hotel Category	Branded, Mid-Rate (Select Service)
	Comfort Inn & Suites by Choice Hotels
Property Oversight	Developer: Old Bayside Partners LLC
	Owner: Saunders Hotel Group (SHG)
	Management Company: Saunders Hotel Group
Gross Square Feet (GSF)	Eight stories above grade; no basement
Number of Guestrooms	208 rooms
Construction Type	New construction
Date Completed	September 2000
High Performance	• Site
	• Materials and Waste Management
	• Energy
	• Water
	• Indoor Environmental Quality
	• Education
	• Performance Measurement
Awards and Certifications	AH&LA Environmental Hotel of the Year
	Boston Green Tourism, Charter Member
	British Airways Tourism for Tomorrow Prize
	Choice Hotels Exceptional Environmental Awareness Award, 2002
	Ceres Company
	Climate Neutral accommodations (Cool Rooms) certified
	Co-op America, member
	Energy Star Partner of the Year
	Green Hotel Association, member
	Skal International Ecotourism Award
	NWF (National Wildlife Foundation) Corporate Excellence Award

Opened in September 2000, the Comfort Inn & Suites Boston/Airport is located near Boston Logan International Airport and is managed by the Saunders Hotel Group (SHG). SHG was an early pioneer of high-performance operations, starting

---

Excerpted from Michele L. Diener, Amisha Parekh, and Jaclyn Pitera, *High Performance Hospitality: Sustainable Hotel Case Studies* (Lansing, Mich.: American Hotel & Lodging Educational Institute, 2008).

from innovations implemented at the Park Plaza in 1989. SHG has been able to take the lessons learned at the Park Plaza, and later at The Lenox, and apply them to the Comfort Inn & Suites franchise in Revere, Massachusetts. SHG built the Revere property from the ground up over an abandoned municipal landfill. The hotel has deftly been able to balance high-performance operational practices with Comfort Inn & Suites' corporate brand standards. The Comfort Inn & Suites Boston/Airport is an excellent case study in effective team collaboration, high-performance operations, performance measurement, education, and outreach.

Background

As just mentioned, the Comfort Inn & Suites Boston/Airport is located near Boston Logan International Airport and is managed by SHG. Tedd Saunders leads EcoLogical Solutions, a sustainable consulting practice that he created as an outgrowth of environmental work with SHG. While growing up, Mr. Saunders enjoyed going on family camping trips and had developed a broad appreciation for the natural world. His mother was a holocaust survivor and raised her family with a "no waste" mentality. Mr. Saunders' father has a genuine "sense of wonder" as described by Rachel Carson in her book of the same name. This parental combination strongly influenced Mr. Saunders' commitment to corporate social responsibility.

The idea for sustainable operations took shape at the Park Plaza Hotel in Boston, which SHG managed from 1976 to 1996. At one million square feet, the Park Plaza was the largest family-owned-and-operated hotel in the United States. The Park Plaza also had the largest private laundry in the city. Tedd Saunders evaluated their operational practices and found ways to cut their operating expenses by reducing energy and water consumption as well as the waste stream. SHG has been able to take the lessons learned at the Park Plaza property and apply them at other hotels in the company's portfolio, including The Lenox and the Comfort Inn & Suites franchise in Revere, Massachusetts. The Revere property opened in September 2000.

The lessons learned at other portfolio hotels heavily influenced SHG's approach to the construction of its eight-story Comfort Inn & Suites. An energy management system with infrared motion sensors, cooling towers, an ozone laundry system, low-flow hardware for plumbing fixtures, and efficient window glazing all were specified in the construction documents. They were cost effective, and they helped to reduce SHG's impact on the environment while lowering operational expenses. In addition, SHG built the Revere property from the ground up, constructing a steel-and-concrete edifice over an abandoned municipal landfill. According to the United States Green Building Council (USGBC), rehabilitating environmentally damaged sites reduces pressure on undeveloped land. This also has created a rapport between SHG and the local municipality.

Comfort Inn & Suites Boston/Airport meets both SHG's mission and Choice Hotels' branding criteria (with some operational waivers granted). It meets and exceeds guest expectations, as demonstrated by having won Choice Hotels' gold medal for excellence in every year the hotel has been in operation. At the same time, the hotel offers guests an opportunity to learn about environmentally sustainable practices, both at the hotel and in their own homes. Not only has the Comfort Inn & Suites Boston/Airport avoided sprawl by undertaking construction on previously underdeveloped land, it has also reduced energy and water consumption and takes pride in a sustainable education program that reaches out to staff, guests, the local community, and many businesses and educational groups. The hotel's Green Team, an interdisciplinary group comprising various staff, meets monthly to measure sustainability progress and identify new areas for improvement.

Organization

Project Team

The project team consists of the property oversight group—the developer, owner, and management company. In this case, the property oversight group members were all from the same parent company, although they represented different subsidiaries.

Contact Information. Below is contact information for the project team.

Developer	Old Bayside Partners LLC http://www.old-bayside.com
Owner	Saunders Hotel Group http://www.saundershotelgroup.net
Management Company/ General Manager	John Mitchell Saunders Hotel Group http://www.saundershotelgroup.net JMitchell@ComfortInnBoston.com
Environmental Sustainability Consultant	Tedd Saunders EcoLogical Solutions http://www.ecological-solutions.net tsaunders@ecological-solutions.net

Developer:

- Old Bayside Partners LLC; Jeff Saunders, Gary Saunders, and Steve Bodi.

- High-Performance Qualifications: Old Bayside had no specific requirements for high-performance development, but did look for properties that other developers usually overlook. For example, brownfields are not typical acquisition candidates because remediation is often costly and time-consuming. However, development on brownfields conserves undeveloped land and this is better for the environment.

Owner:

- Saunders Hotel Group; the Saunders family.

- High-Performance Qualifications: SHG specialized in high-performance hotel operations primarily because of its long relationship with EcoLogical Solutions.

Management Company/General Manager:

- John Mitchell, Regional Manager for the Saunders Hotel Group.

- High-Performance Qualifications: Mr. Mitchell had no prior high-performance construction or operations background.

Managerial Structure

The Comfort Inn & Suites Boston/Airport has a relatively flat organizational structure and minimal hierarchy. The Saunders family is very much involved and is on site regularly. This access to top management makes it easier to promote new ideas and implement changes. While the focus on environmental sustainability at the Comfort Inn & Suites Boston/Airport seems to be driven from the top down, the hotel's management team actually makes sure staff from all business areas serve on the Green Team. This is part of an overall approach which encourages employee involvement and appears to improve morale, increase the quality of operations, and reduce employee turnover.

Figure 1 represents the reporting structure at the Comfort Inn and Suites Boston/Airport for the administrative and managerial positions only.

Green Team. The hotel has an active Green Team that meets monthly to discuss fifteen to twenty items that relate to the progress of its sustainability initiatives as well as opportunities for improvement. The team has representatives from each of the hotel's key groups. Tedd Saunders from EcoLogical Solutions helps lead the meeting and brings in external knowledge as needed.

Staff Training and Compensation

The Comfort Inn & Suites Boston/Airport requires minimal sustainability training but, when it is needed, management focuses on employees in housekeeping, sales, and reservations, as well as on front desk and reception staff, so they can respond to guest questions and concerns. Management personnel at the hotel do not have to transition existing housekeeping staff to work with new products, because Green Seal–certified products have been used since the hotel opened. According to Omar Zenon, the operations manager, "The staff is not reluctant, primarily due to the fact that the hotel has been around for five years. So, it is no longer a new concept and it is not an issue. Also, it is easier, safer, and better for cleaning."

The front desk staff, receptionists, and reservationists have been trained to answer guest questions regarding the hotel's high-performance program. If front

Figure 1: Managerial Structure

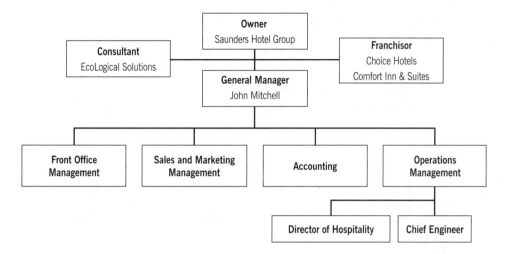

desk staff members do not have the answer to the guest's concern, they take the question to the right person and then get back to the guest. The hotel also has an "eco" bulletin board in the back-of-house office space to help employees learn how to reduce their environmental footprints, both at the office and at home.

At the Comfort Inn & Suites Boston/Airport, the general manager's compensation is based in part on gross operating margin—a significant incentive to keep costs low. Environmentally sustainable operations help to achieve this goal and have helped motivate all management staff. Guests also motivate staff through the Choice Hotels' staff recognition program. Choice Hotels offers Platinum, Gold, and Silver employee awards that are based on guest scores for service (with a rating of 60 percent or above).

The Comfort Inn & Suites Boston/Airport is a relatively flat organization and employees stay with the family business over the long-term. For example, there are members of the housekeeping staff who have been there since the opening of the hotel in 2000. According to one staff member,

> Everyone is willing to go above and beyond. We are all motivated to help with the hotel because this is our second home, or maybe it is our first home—because we spend so many hours here.

The hotel's management recognizes the needs of each staff member and assigns roles appropriately to keep individuals motivated regarding their high-performance efforts. The most eco-friendly staff member receives the annual Shining Star award. Another incentive includes the monthly housekeeping award for a staff member who goes above and beyond his or her job responsibilities. The award is a day off with full compensation. The Saunders family also offers the opportunity for a four-year scholarship at Newbury College for the children and grandchildren of Comfort Inn & Suites Boston/Airport employees.

Community Outreach and Education

The Comfort Inn & Suites Boston/Airport encourages staff members to volunteer with community greening efforts outside of work, as well as during in-house staff volunteer days. A number of managers and staff members volunteered at the Revere Beach and Franklin Park cleanup projects.

Construction and Operations

Table 1 summarizes the most prominent among the high-performance features of the Comfort Inn & Suites Boston/Airport construction and operations.

Table 1 HIGH-PERFORMANCE CONSTRUCTION AND OPERATIONS HIGHLIGHTS	
1. Site	• The hotel has three compressed natural gas (CNG) airport shuttle vans, and participates in a carbon offset program.
2. Material and Resources, and Waste Management	• The hotel was built on a brownfield site that required environmental remediation. • The hotel uses biodegradable hot cups for take-out coffee and tea. • Housekeeping staff use Green Seal–certified cleaning supplies throughout the hotel. • Pool cleaning employs an ionization process, dramatically reducing chlorine use. • Bulk amenities and refillable dispensers are located in all guest bathrooms. • The hallway renovation used recycled content carpeting. • Food sorting for composting takes place in both the kitchen and dining area. • The Comfort Inn & Suites Boston/Airport recycles paper, rigid containers, printer toner cartridges, batteries, and cell phones.
3. Energy	• The hotel has installed Vendor Miser's motion sensors for vending machines that save 57% of the vending machine's energy use. • Motion sensors in the guest rooms control thermostat settings. • There is compact fluorescent lighting throughout the hotel. • The HVAC cooling towers, fans, LED signs, and efficient windows help to decrease the hotel's overall energy use.
4. Water	• The ozone laundry system uses cold water and environmentally friendly disinfectants. • Low-flow bathroom fixtures include toilets, showers, and faucets.
5. Indoor Environmental Quality	• Recent renovation: All hallways have been painted with low volatile organic compound (VOC) paint and Rug Institute-certified carpet and padding. • Recent renovation: All hallways have been upgraded with new carpet and wall coverings made with low VOC adhesives.

1. Site

The Comfort Inn & Suites Boston/Airport is an airport hotel built in the suburban setting of Revere, Massachusetts. The hotel is not accessible by public transportation and can only be reached by private automobile or a hotel shuttle. From an environmental standpoint, this is a limitation, because it does not promote mass transportation. However, three of the hotel shuttle vans run on compressed natural gas (CNG) and only one van runs on petroleum. Additionally, the Saunders Hotel Group is considering the purchase of carbon credits through TerraPass to offset the carbon emitted by the thirty-minute shuttle service cycle between the hotel and the airport. This would cost the hotel approximately $2,800 annually to offset 300 tons of CO_2.

It is important to note that the Saunders Hotel Group preserved greenfields by building on a brownfield site that was originally zoned for industry. This is a significant sustainability feature, because building the hotel did not consume natural spaces and SHG made the land useful—land that would have been otherwise less valuable. The site was previously a municipal landfill. In order to develop the land for constructing a hotel, the site had to be capped. This ensured that previous contaminants would not harm human beings or the atmosphere.

2. Materials and Resources, and Waste Management

Comfort Inn & Suites Boston/Airport's interior design and operational practices help minimize use of new resources and materials and also reduce the waste stream from the hotel.

Interior Design. Although vinyl wall covering is used throughout the hotel, it has been installed with low volatile organic compound (VOC) adhesives. In addition, the rolled Origins carpets, manufactured by the Shaw Carpet company with recycled content, also have been installed with low VOC adhesives. The majority of the wood throughout the hotel is a laminate.

Choice Hotels recently required the Comfort Inn & Suites Boston/Airport to meet the parent company's standards by upgrading the bed sheets to a 200-thread-count fabric. The hotel found that the higher thread count actually lasts longer. The hotel typically replaces the bed sheets every six months to a year and uses the retired sheets as cleaning rags before discarding them.

Operations. From a materials and resources standpoint, most of the sustainable initiatives affect the day-to-day operations of the Comfort Inn & Suites Boston/Airport. The hotel composts food scraps from the buffet breakfast, uses biodegradable hot cups instead of Choice Hotels' standard Styrofoam, and is in the process of getting a waiver from Choice Hotels to use organic fair trade coffee. The hotel intends to source this coffee from Earth Share, a company that donates the proceeds of its sales to environmental causes.

For cleaning the swimming pool, the hotel has implemented an ionization process that uses electric ions instead of chlorine to take pollutants out of the water. The hotel uses Rochester Midland cleaning supplies and Enviro-Care products for daily guestroom cleaning. These cleaning products are purchased in bulk (one to five gallons) and are Green Seal certified to extend the life of fabrics and reduce health hazards for employees.

Signage in the hallways encourages guests to use the wicker recycling baskets. The hotel also recycles paper, rigid containers, printer toner cartridges, batteries, and cell phones from its back-of-house operations. In addition, to reduce waste, the hotel sought and received special permission from Choice Hotels to purchase refillable dispensers for bulk soap, shampoo, conditioner, and lotion. This has eliminated the cost of 220,000 individual amenity bottles each year.

To measure its performance, the Comfort Inn & Suites Boston/Airport solicits comments from guests specifically about environmental initiatives, using comment cards made from 100% post-consumer recycled paper. Hotel staff members post their responses to guest comments, showing that they actually pay attention to guest suggestions. Every time the hotel orders a ream of paper, the paper company plants a tree.

3. Energy

At the Comfort Inn & Suites Boston/Airport, energy efficiency is primarily the result of operational equipment and technology that was installed when the hotel was built and during subsequent ongoing renovations. As mentioned earlier, in the Background section, SHG's approach to the Comfort Inn & Suites Boston/Airport construction was influenced by lessons learned at other hotels. SHG had years of operating experience with the hotels in its portfolio and was able to apply that experience because the Comfort Inn & Suites Boston/Airport was SHG's first ground-up construction project.

Operations. The Comfort Inn & Suites Boston/Airport helps guests conserve energy by using occupancy sensors installed in the guestrooms. These sensors activate or deactivate the thermostat by detecting the presence or absence of the guest. Each room is individually zoned and has its own thermostat for the guest to control within a range of 65–85°F. Almost all of the light bulbs throughout the property are compact fluorescent, which also contributes to energy savings.

SHG has installed an innovative energy-efficient feature, known as Vendor Miser, for the soda vending machines. The system controls the display lighting with motion sensors while keeping the beverages refrigerated. The decision to install this system was not difficult to make, because the payback time frame for energy savings was only two years, with an annual 67% reduction of energy consumption over traditional machines.

Although the Comfort Inn & Suites Boston/Airport was not built according to specific high-performance building standards, such as USGBC LEED (Leadership in Energy and Environmental Design) criteria, SHG incorporated features in both the building's core and shell to make the hotel highly efficient. In the building's core, the HVAC system uses roof cooling towers that inherently consume less energy than compressors do while cooling air. In the shell of the building, SHG installed rigid insulation efficient windows, compact fluorescent light bulbs, LED exit signs, and fans to reduce energy consumption. The roof is a white reflective rubber membrane that also contributes to the building's energy conservation program by reflecting the sun's heat away from the building. However, the roof requires cleaning for maximum efficiency.

4. Water

The hotel's design allowed for water-saving innovations.

Construction. SHG added low-flow water fixtures to the guestrooms and public restrooms in the initial design phase of the project to reduce water consumption. The equipment rates are: toilets at 1.6 gallons per minute, showers at 2.5 gallons per minute, and faucets at 1.5 gallons per minute.

The hotel achieves most of its water conservation through the ozone laundry equipment and the bathroom low-flow water fixtures. SHG has installed an ozone laundry system by Ozotech Inc. to conserve both energy and water. The machine is operated with cold water and the ozone acts as a disinfectant.

As a result, SHG saves heat energy (by using cold water) and conserves water (by reusing it). The hotel washes guestroom linens and towels with this system. However, the hotel also provides coin-operated machines for washing personal items. Dry cleaning typically is sent off site.

5. Indoor Air Quality

At the time of the building's construction, the indoor environmental quality-enhancing features at Comfort Inn & Suites Boston/Airport were operational. Since then, additional steps have been taken to improve the indoor air quality, specifically during a recent hallway renovation project.

Operations. In order to improve the air quality in the hallways, the hotel used paints and adhesives with low VOC emissions. The adhesives included those in the carpet and in the wall covering. The renovation improved the indoor air quality and became a good marketing tool for SHG.

Business Case

Market Positioning and Consumer Response

The hotel is a Comfort Inn & Suites franchise, and the brand's parent company, Choice Hotels International, creates the standards for brand positioning and communication. Examples of the standards set by Choice Hotels include website content, guestroom layout, coffee brand, mattress quality, and online guest satisfaction surveys. Choice Hotels sets these standards to create a consistent brand image across all Comfort Inn & Suites hotels.

The Comfort Inn & Suites Boston/Airport attracts a variety of guests. A significant amount of the hotel's traffic is the result of its proximity to Boston Logan International Airport. The hotel has contracts with major airlines to house flight crews during layovers, as well as passengers from cancelled flights. The hotel offers a park-and-fly program for guests flying in and out of Logan Airport. Tour groups and leisure travelers visiting Boston on a more modest budget also tend to stay at this hotel. The hospitality business in this area is highly competitive, with a number of full-service hotels nearby (Courtyard, Hampton Inn, and Hilton). The Comfort Inn & Suites Boston/Airport must be able to maintain contracts and ensure repeat business through excellent customer service.

Few of the hotel's guests overtly seek out an environmentally sustainable hotel, but the Comfort Inn & Suites Boston/Airport is finding that Northern European and British consumers and travel agencies are more aware of environmental issues and appreciate the hotel's efforts. Upon their arrival, the majority of the guests are unaware of the hotel's commitment to sustainability. In order to keep the format and information consistent with other hotels in the chain, the Choice Hotels' website does not allow the Revere hotel to advertise its environmentally sustainable features. However, the hotel staff promotes a number of programs to educate guests once they are in the hotel. There are several environmental conservation posters and educational signs displayed throughout the hotel. For example, the men's restroom on the first floor has a sign stating that urinals consume 40 percent less water than is consumed by low-flow toilets. The hotel also places educational cards in guest cars that offer environmental tips on how to reduce gas usage on the road.

The "Tread Lightly" box placed at the front of the hotel lobby encourages guests to recycle old athletic shoes and offers a room discount based on the size of the shoe donated. This recycling box was designed by local art school students and helps communicate the hotel's commitment to sustainability. The sneakers are recycled by Nike into safe turf for playgrounds. There is an eco-suggestion box by the elevators that encourages guests to suggest ideas for improving the hotel's environmental performance. The bulk soap and lotion dispensers in the bathrooms are the environmentally sustainable features most noticed by guests, and they are often complimented in the remarks found on the guest comment cards.

The hotel's greening efforts do not seem to have resulted in a price premium, nor have they attracted major new business. However, the hotel has received a large amount of publicity; the hotel handles an average of three calls per week from journalists. The hotel's efforts also have resulted in awards from Energy Star, NWF, and British Airways, among others. The hotel is currently helping lead Boston Green Tourism, which is working with the Massachusetts Lodging Association, the mayor's office, the convention bureau, and others to make Boston a green destination known worldwide for its urban ecotourism leadership.

Why High-Performance Construction?

LEED certification was not as popular at the time of Comfort Inn & Suites Boston/Airport's construction and the hotel was not built to any specific green construction standards. SHG did, however, install equipment that would result in energy and water savings. Since the developer, owner, and management company are all the same entity, all of those involved had a shared vision of creating a hotel that would run efficiently and be a green model.

The decision to build on a brownfield site requiring minimal clean-up helped the hotel save money on construction costs. Since it was a brownfield site, SHG was able to purchase the land for less than they would have spent on a non-brownfield site. Additionally, SHG obtained an Alternative Use License (AUL) that allowed them to build a hotel on the site as long as they capped the land. This saved time in the construction schedule, because they did not have to remove the soil and treat it, or perform an in situ remediation. We are unable to quantify the exact benefits due to confidentiality issues.

Why High-Performance Operations?

The Comfort Inn & Suites Boston/Airport operations are considered high performance because they result in cost savings and because they benefit the hotel's employees and guests. Environmentally friendly operations are very important to SHG and are manifested in every aspect of the facility, including the formation of a Green Team and the educational signage throughout the hotel.

The hotel's operations incorporate both innovative operational practices as well as common industry practices. Leading innovative examples include the bulk amenity dispensers in the guestrooms (instead of single amenity containers) and the ionization pool-cleaning system instead of a chlorine system. The bulk dispensers save the hotel almost 220,000 individual amenity bottles annually. The ionizing pool-cleaning system had a two-year payback by replacing cleaning chemicals with a one-time purchase of electrodes.

Common industry practices at the hotel include the use of washable linens and curtains (washing is cheaper than dry cleaning) and the use of recycled paper for office printing.

In addition to the bulk amenity dispensers and the ionization pool cleaning system, the hotel has a few other practices with obvious benefits for hotel guests and staff. For example, environmentally sustainable cleaning products are much nicer for hotel staff because they are less abrasive and do not pollute the air. Recycled-content toilet paper and napkins are items that guests can see. These products are cost neutral.

Advantages of High-Performance Construction and Operations

The Comfort Inn & Suites Boston/Airport has implemented high-performance operations and has installed equipment to save money through reduced product costs and operating expenses. The Saunders family also believes it is important to run the hotel this way for the benefit of guests and employees.

The hotel's decision to install water conservation technologies in the construction phase of the project saves the hotel money during the operations phase. For example, the ozone laundry system has capital costs of $36,000 with a payback of two years. The utility costs savings include a 25 percent reduction in water consumption, chemicals, sewage output, and electricity. There is an 86 percent reduction in hot water usage.

More cost savings occur with efficient energy equipment. Vendor Miser, the vending machine lighting sensor, cuts energy costs by $189 annually and only cost $165 to install.

Less tangible but nonetheless important advantages are guest comfort and awareness, and employee comfort and productivity. By installing efficient equipment and by employing high-performance operational practices, the hotel benefits guests and employees with a comfortable and healthy environment where they can identify with environmental responsibility. This has significant potential for increasing both employee retention and customer satisfaction.

Table 2 highlights the financial benefits of high-performance construction and operations at the Comfort Inn & Suites Boston/Airport.

Table 2 FINANCIAL BENEFITS OF HIGH-PERFORMANCE CONSTRUCTION AND OPERATIONS FEATURES			
High-Performance Feature	**Capital Cost**	**Payback Period**	**Benefits**
Ozone laundry system	$36,000	Two years	A 25% reduction in water consumption, chemicals, sewage output, and electricity consumption; an 86% reduction in hot water usage.
Vendor Miser	$165	Less than 1 year	Saves electricity usage by $189 annually.

Table 3 is a summary of high-performance hotel construction and operation advantages realized by the property oversight stakeholders—developer, owner, and management company.

Best Practices and Conclusions

As mentioned earlier, the Comfort Inn & Suites Boston/Airport is an excellent case study in effective team collaboration, high-performance operations, performance measurement, and education and outreach.

The following best practices implemented at the Comfort Inn & Suites Boston/Airport have been identified as industry best practices for environmentally high-performance construction and operations:

- Food composting
- Compressed natural gas shuttle vans
- Ozone laundry system
- Vendor Miser
- Green Team
- Sharing best practices with overall brand

The hotel's management team believes that sustainability cannot be accomplished without the assistance and guidance of others. Successful sustainable design depends on the commitment of all members of the team, including the guests. The hotel's Green Team continues to monitor operational practices to identify environmentally sustainable initiatives that offer a return on investment to the hotel. The Green Team continues to be a leader in the industry as well as in the community, educating guests and working closely with the Boston Chamber of Commerce to improve Boston's record of environmental responsibility.

Table 3 STAKEHOLDER ADVANTAGES SUMMARY		
Developer	**Owner**	**Management Company**
The developers had lower project land costs because they acquired a brownfield site that was originally designated for industrial use. They built the hotel by obtaining an Alternative Use License (AUL). The site did not require major cleanup and there was no adverse impact on the construction schedule.	The owners have created an environment where staff at all levels are encouraged to contribute ideas to the high-performance program. The program's success and international visibility creates higher staff retention and morale.	The management team has created an environment where staff at all levels are encouraged to contribute ideas to the high-performance program. The program's success and international visibility helps create higher staff retention and morale.
	Energy Star certification and environmental awards are third-party verifications that the Comfort Inn & Suites Boston/ Airport has high operating efficiency and quality environmental programs. These credentials help to promote the hotel to guests and staff.	Energy Star certification and environmental awards are third-party verifications that the Comfort Inn & Suites Boston/ Airport has high operating efficiency and quality environmental programs. These credentials help to promote the hotel to guests and staff.
	Reduced operating expenses equate to higher profits. Innovations include: • Vendor Miser vending machine motion sensors reduce energy consumption by 67%. • In-room occupancy sensors cut heating and cooling costs. • Bulk toiletry dispensers for soap, shampoo, and lotion save 220,000 individual amenity bottles annually. • Low-flow bathroom fixtures reduce water costs. • Cooling towers reduce heating, ventilating, and air conditioning (HVAC) costs. • An ozone laundry system has a payback of two years, has saved on hot water consumption and sewage bills, and has dramatically reduced usage of chemicals.	Reduced operating expenses equate to higher profits. Innovations include: • Vendor Miser vending machine motion sensors reduce energy consumption by 67%. • In-room occupancy sensors cut heating and cooling costs. • Bulk toiletry dispensers for soap, shampoo, and lotion save 220,000 individual amenity bottles annually. • Low-flow bathroom fixtures reduce water costs. • Cooling towers reduce heating, ventilating, and air conditioning (HVAC) costs. • An ozone laundry system has a payback of two years, has saved on hot water consumption and sewage bills, and has dramatically reduced usage of chemicals.

Walking Tour

Building Exterior/Entrance

- Notice the airport shuttle van—three out of the four vans use compressed natural gas to run the engines. In addition, the Comfort Inn & Suites Boston/Airport purchases carbon offset credits from TerraPass to offset the emissions from van travel.

Lobby

- Notice the "Tread Lightly" box placed at the front of the hotel to collect sneakers that will be recycled into flooring for playgrounds. The hotel offers a discount based on the size of the shoe donated (size 8 = $8 nightly discount). The container was designed in the shape of a running shoe by local Boston art school students. This recycling box demonstrates the depth of the company's commitment to sustainability.

- Now look up. Wow, that is a big fan! The lobby seating-area ceiling reaches up to the second floor, and this area is directly across from the entrance. As a result, this design has led to loss of heat in the central lobby (heat rising and escaping) during the winter months. The large fan circulates the warm air downward and remedies this problem.

Breakfast Buffet Area

- In this area, tent cards on each table explain how to separate food waste properly so that the Comfort Inn & Suites Boston/Airport can compost scraps appropriately.

- In addition, the hotel received special approval from its parent company, Choice Hotels, to purchase biodegradable disposable hot cups (in addition to reusable glasses and ceramic mugs) instead of the standard Styrofoam cups.

- Also, notice all the awards and recognition plaques the Comfort Inn & Suites Boston/Airport has received since its opening. These awards and plaques are displayed throughout the lobby. Additional educational materials can be found in the elevator as well as in every guestroom.

- Take a look at the vending machines behind the buffet area. Are the lights on or off? Each vending machine has been equipped with a Vendor Miser to control the machine's energy use. If the motion detector senses movement, the machine turns its lights on. When no guest accesses it for several minutes, it "powers down" to conserve energy. Whether the machine's lights are on or off, it continues to keep beverages refrigerated.

Pool

- Just before you put on your swim trunks, check out the guest comment station and let the hotel know what you think about their environmental initiatives.

It is worth noting that the comment cards are printed on 100% post-consumer recycled paper.

- Rest assured that when you do go swimming, the Comfort Inn & Suites Boston/Airport uses a non-toxic pool cleaning process. The ionization process employs electric ions instead of chlorine to clean the water.

Guestrooms

- On the way to your room, check out the wicker recycling bins in the hallway. Signs just above the bins tell guests what they can and cannot recycle.

- The hotel washes linens on site, using an ozone laundry system for disinfecting. Ozone uses only cold water and has no toxic side effects. In addition, the ozone system eliminates some water consumption.

- Next, turn on your television and find the EcoChannel. The owners of the hotel produced a five-minute educational video communicating the mission, objectives, and future of green hotels. This and other entertainment videos run 24/7 for free.

- Finally, step into your bathroom. There you will notice bulk amenities for soap, shampoo, conditioner, and lotion. Using bulk containers eliminates the need to purchase and dispose of 220,000 individually packaged amenities each year. It also allows the hotel to improve the quality of the actual amenity products with the saved purchasing and disposal costs.

Chapter 2 Outline

Competencies

1. Explain what a mission is, and describe how goals, strategies, and tactics are used to accomplish a hotel's mission. (pp. 57–60)

2. Describe how hotels are organized and explain how functional areas within hotels are classified. (pp. 60–64)

3. Describe the functions performed by departments and positions within the rooms division. (pp. 64–73)

4. Identify the functions performed by other divisions and departments within a full-service hotel. (pp. 73–76)

5. Describe the organization of the front office, including traditional work shifts, alternative scheduling practices, and the purpose of job descriptions and job specifications. (pp. 77–80)

Hotel Organization

$\mathbf{A}$ PERSON ENTERING A HOTEL LOBBY for the first time might never guess the complexities underlying the day-to-day operation of the property. He or she might not recognize that the courtesy of the door attendant, the competent and friendly manner of the front desk agent, and the tidiness of the guestroom reflect hours of planning, extensive communications, ongoing training, and a coordinated effort to create the workings of an efficient organization. The actual network of a hotel's divisions, departments, and personnel in a smoothly operating hotel should be invisible to the casual observer. But the services that result from a hotel's smooth operations are highly visible. Providing those services presents hotels with a unique challenge.

For a hotel to run effectively and efficiently, every employee must understand the property's mission and work to achieve it. Every employee must ensure that guests are so impressed by the property's facilities and services that they will want to come back and will enthusiastically recommend the property to others.

Teamwork is the key to success. All employees must have a spirit of cooperation both within and between their departmental areas. While every department and division should strive to offer and improve quality guest service, it is especially important that good service be emphasized in high-profile locations like the front office. The ability of front office employees to answer questions, coordinate services, offer choices, and satisfy guest requests is critical to the hotel's mission.

This chapter examines the relationship of hotel employees, departments, and divisions, as well as how each of these components contributes to achieving the property's mission. Several sample job descriptions for front office staff positions are shown in the appendix to this chapter.

Organizational Missions

Every organization has a reason or purpose for existing. Its purpose forms the basis for the organization's mission. An organization's mission can be expressed in a **mission statement,** which defines the unique purpose that sets one hotel or hotel company apart from others. The mission statement expresses the underlying philosophy that gives meaning and direction to hotel policies. While employees learn the tasks involved in their jobs—or the *what to do* of the job—the mission statement communicates the *why we are doing it* of the job. Hotel employees may derive a sense of purpose from a well-conceived mission statement. For example, a hotel's mission may be to provide the finest facilities and services in the market while providing a good place for its employees to work and a reasonable return on investment to its owners. From such a mission statement, employees know what is expected of them (providing the finest facilities and services in the market, thus helping the owners to earn a reasonable return on their investment), as well as what they can expect (a good place to work).

A hotel's mission statement often addresses the interests of its three main constituent groups: guests, managers, and employees. First, a hotel's mission statement can address the basic needs and expectations of the hotel's guests. Regardless of a hotel's size or service level, it is safe to assume all guests have the following basic expectations:

- Safe, secure accommodations
- A clean, comfortable guestroom
- Courteous, professional, knowledgeable, and friendly service
- Well-maintained facilities and equipment

Hotel guests generally anticipate a particular level of service at a given property type. If a hotel clearly defines its markets and consistently delivers the level of service those markets expect, it can satisfy its guests, encourage repeat business, and improve its reputation.

Second, a hotel's mission statement can reflect its management philosophy. Since styles of operation differ, mission statements often vary from property to property. In fact, a hotel's mission is one of the principal means it uses to distinguish itself from other hotels. A mission statement guides managers in their jobs by identifying the property's basic values.

Third, the mission statement can help the hotel's employees meet or exceed both guest and management expectations. A mission statement can also serve as a basis for job descriptions and performance standards and as an introduction to the property for new employees. The property's mission statement should appear in employee handbooks and training manuals, and should accompany job descriptions.

Consider this example of a hotel mission statement:

> The mission of our hotel is to provide outstanding lodging facilities and services to our guests. Our hotel focuses on individual business and leisure travel, as well as travel associated with group meetings. We emphasize high quality standards in our rooms and food and beverage divisions, as well as the finest service available in our market. We provide a fair return on investment for our owners and recognize that this cannot be done without well-trained, motivated, and enthusiastic employees.

Goals

Once the hotel has defined and formulated its mission statement, the next step is to set goals. **Goals** are those activities and standards an organization must successfully perform or achieve to effectively carry out its mission. A goal is more specific than a mission; it requires a certain level of achievement that can be observed and measured. Measurable goals encourage hotel employees to perform effectively while enabling management to monitor employee progress. Many organizations evaluate their goals frequently. Yearly goal planning is common, and sometimes these goals are broken down by month or quarter. Some goals are financial and are linked to the hotel's budget and forecasting cycle. Other goals may deal with the quality of guest service, frequency of guest or employee accidents, property security, or the number of new corporate clients the hotel has obtained. Even more important, goals often become part of the management team's evaluation process. Salary increases, bonuses, awards, and other forms of recognition are often linked to specific goals. Management and staff should be periodically evaluated on their progress toward meeting the hotel's goals. Management can determine whether goals are being achieved or whether corrective action is necessary. A properly written goal includes an action verb followed by a specific form of measurement such as a time interval or a level of quality, quantity, or cost.

The following are examples of measurable front office goals:

- Increase the hotel's average occupancy level by 2 percent above the previous year's level.

- Increase the volume of repeat guest business by 10 percent.

- Reduce average check-in and check-out times by two minutes.

- Reduce the number of guest complaints by 20 percent.

- Respond to all guest maintenance requests within one half hour.

It is very common for more than one department to be involved in achieving a goal. For example, in order for the front desk to achieve a goal of checking every guest in within a two-minute period, it is necessary for the housekeeping department to keep the inventory of clean and vacant rooms current. For this reason, some hotel goals are stated as property-wide goals, not simply as departmental or divisional goals. Achieving goals is often the result of close coordination between departments. The goals of various departments can be tied together, and the success of one department often leads to the success of others. Joint goal-setting also fosters cooperation and *esprit de corps* among departments.

Strategies and Tactics

By establishing property-wide, measurable goals, a hotel enables its managers and employees to concentrate on specific strategies that will help the property achieve its goals. Goals define the purpose of a department or division; they direct the actions of managers and employees and the functions of the department or division toward fulfilling the hotel's mission. To achieve its goals, a department or division establishes **strategies**—the methods a department or division uses to achieve its goals. **Tactics** further define how goals will be achieved. Tactics are the day-to-day operating procedures that implement successful strategies. It is important that goals and strategies set at the departmental and divisional levels complement and support the property's mission and its property-wide goals.

Examples of goals, strategies, and tactics involving areas within the front office are:

- Registration—*Goal:* Operate the front desk efficiently and courteously so that guests may register within two minutes of arrival. *Strategy:* Preregister all expected guests with reservation guarantees as rooms become available from the housekeeping department. *Tactic:* Preprint registration cards for arriving guests and separate the cards of all guests with a reservation guarantee.

- Guest Cashiering—*Goal:* Post all charges reaching the front desk within thirty minutes (for properties using a non-automated system). *Strategy:* Provide sufficient staffing to enable rapid and accurate posting of guest charges when they are received. *Tactic:* Review occupancy forecasts weekly to develop proper staffing guidelines.

- Bell Stand—*Goal:* Respond to every check-out luggage request within ten minutes. *Strategy:* Keep a log of when bell attendants are dispatched and when they return from each guest call. *Tactic:* Enter guest name, room number, bell attendant assigned, and time out and time in for each luggage request.

- Telecommunications Department—*Goal:* Answer every telephone call within three rings of the telephone, regardless of whether it is an inside call or an outside call. *Strategy:* Perform telephone traffic studies periodically, reviewing the number of calls received, to ensure that the proper number of telephone lines are available for both incoming and outgoing telephone calls. *Tactic:* Print a daily traffic report from the telephone switchboard and record volume by time on a spreadsheet.

Hotel Organization

The people authorized by a hotel's owner to represent his or her interests are called hotel management. In small properties, hotel management may consist of just one person. Management guides the operation of the hotel and regularly reports the general state of the hotel's financial health to its owner. The major duties of a hotel management team include planning, organizing, coordinating, staffing, directing, controlling, and evaluating hotel activities and/or personnel. Management performs its duties to reach specific objectives and goals. These duties involve the activities of various hotel divisions and departments.

The top executive of a property is usually called the managing director, general manager, or innkeeper. For discussion purposes, this chapter refers to the top executive as the general manager. The general manager of an independent hotel normally reports directly to the owner or the owner's representative. The general manager is ultimately responsible for the success of the hotel and supervises all hotel divisions, either through a resident or assistant manager or through division heads. Chain organizations usually have a district, area, or regional executive who supervises the general managers located at the properties within his or her jurisdiction.

While the general manager is responsible for supervising all hotel divisions, he or she may delegate responsibility for specific divisions or departments to an assistant general manager, resident manager, or director of operations. When the general manager is absent, the assistant general manager, resident manager, or director of operations usually serves as the acting general manager. When these four managers are all off the premises, a manager-on-duty (MOD) is often appointed to assume overall managerial responsibility. Front office managers are often called upon to be the MOD when more senior managers are not on the property.

Historically, resident managers actually *lived* in the hotel. Essentially, it was the resident manager's job to be available twenty-four hours a day, seven days a week. Over time, more authority has been delegated to other managers. While many resident managers are still responsible for the rooms division, it is rare for a property to require its resident manager to live on the premises.

To qualify for a department head position, an individual must thoroughly understand the functions, goals, and practices of a particular department. Front office managers are usually considered department heads.

Organization Charts

An organization requires a formal structure to carry out its mission and goals. A common way to represent that structure is the **organization chart.** An organization chart is a schematic representation of the relationships between positions within an organization. It shows where each position fits in the overall organization, as well as where divisions of responsibility and lines of authority lie. Solid lines on the chart indicate direct-line accountability; dotted lines indicate relationships that involve a high degree of cooperation and communication, but not a direct reporting relationship.

An organization chart should be flexible. It should be reviewed and revised yearly, or more often if business conditions significantly change. Employee responsibilities may change as individuals assume more duties, depending on their qualifications and strengths. Some organizations list each employee's name on the chart along with his or her title. A copy of the property's organization chart should be included in the employee handbook distributed to all employees.

Since no two hotels are exactly alike, organizational structures must be tailored to fit the needs of each individual property. The charts in this chapter illustrate several organizational possibilities: a full-service property, a property with separately owned food and beverage operations, and a rooms-only hotel.

A full-service property that offers both lodging and food and beverage service will probably have an extensive organizational structure. Exhibit 1 shows an organization chart outlining the management-level positions in a large full-service property. All but two of the lines on the chart are solid, indicating reporting relationships. The dotted lines connecting the sales director to the catering director and the reservations manager represent the close working relationships among these positions.

Some hotels may lease food and beverage outlets to another company. This means that food and beverage operations and guestroom operations are separately owned and managed. When another company operates food and beverage, it is essential that both companies communicate closely, as their goals may not be shared at all times. Exhibit 2 shows a typical organization chart for a hotel with leased food and beverage operations. In this example, informal consulting relationships exist between the managers and owners of the two businesses. The restaurant manager and the hotel's sales department manager must also work closely together. These relationships are indicated by dotted lines.

Exhibit 1   Organization Chart: Management Positions in a Full-Service Hotel

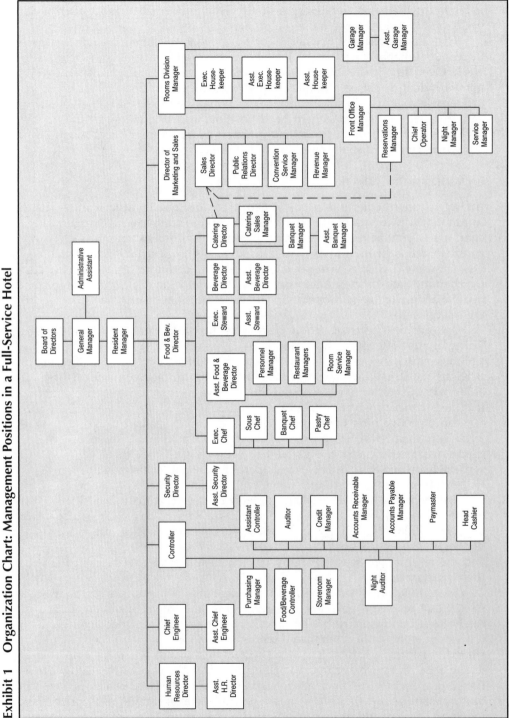

Exhibit 2 Organization Chart: Hotel with a Leased Food and Beverage Operation

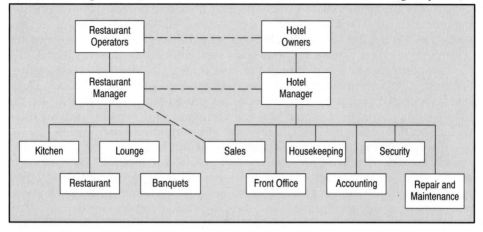

Exhibit 3 Organization Chart: Rooms-Only Hotel

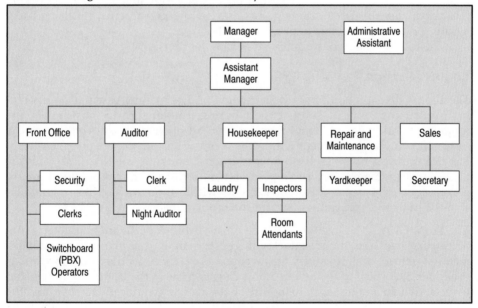

Exhibit 3 presents a possible organizational structure for a hotel without a restaurant. The charts in Exhibits 1–3 illustrate some of the many organizational variations possible among lodging properties.

Classifying Functional Areas

A hotel's divisions and departments (its *functional areas*) can be classified in almost as many ways as the hotel itself. One method involves classifying an operating division or department as either a **revenue center** or **support center.** A revenue center sells goods or services to guests, thereby generating revenue for the hotel. Typical revenue centers include the front office, food and beverage outlets (including room service), and catering. Even if the hotel itself does not operate a revenue center (as is often the case with retail stores or full-service spas), the money the revenue center pays to lease the hotel space contributes to the hotel's income.

Support centers, also referred to as cost centers, include the housekeeping, accounting, engineering and maintenance, and human resources divisions. These divisions do not generate direct revenue, but provide important support for the hotel's revenue centers. Designers of accounting and information systems often find it useful to segment a hotel by revenue and support centers.

The terms **front of the house** and **back of the house** may also be used to classify hotel departments, divisions, and personnel. Front-of-the-house areas are areas where guests interact with employees. Such areas include the front office, restaurants, and lounges. In back-of-the-house areas, interaction between guests and employees is less common. Housekeeping staff members occasionally interact with guests, but it is not part of their primary duties as it is for front desk and bell staff. Although back-of-the-house employees may not *directly* serve guests by taking an order, assisting with registration, or delivering luggage to a guestroom, these employees *indirectly* serve guests by cleaning guestrooms, repairing leaky faucets, or correcting errors in guest accounts.

The following sections examine typical hotel divisions.

Rooms Division

The rooms division comprises departments and personnel essential to providing the lodging services guests expect during a hotel stay. In most hotels, the rooms division generates more revenue than all other divisions combined. The front office is one department within the rooms division. Others are housekeeping, uniformed services (bell attendants, door attendants, valet parkers), and the concierge. In some properties, the reservations and switchboard or telecommunications functions are separate departments within the rooms division. Exhibit 4 shows a sample organization chart for the rooms division of a large hotel.

The Front Office. The front office is the most visible department in a hotel. Front office personnel have more contact with guests than do staff in most other departments. The front desk is usually the focal point of activity for the front office and is prominently located in the hotel's lobby. Guests come to the front desk to register; to receive room assignments; to inquire about available services, facilities, and the city or surrounding area; and to check out. The front desk often serves as the hotel control center for guest requests concerning housekeeping or engineering issues. International guests use the front desk to exchange currency, find a translator, or request other special assistance. In addition, it may also be a base of operations during an emergency, such as a fire or a guest injury.

Other front office functions include receiving and distributing mail, messages, and facsimiles (faxes), as well as guest cashiering. Cashiers post charges and payments to guest accounts, all of which are later verified during an account auditing procedure (often called the *night audit*). Front desk personnel also may verify outstanding accounts receivable, and produce daily reports for management. Some

Exhibit 4 Organization Chart: Rooms Division of a Large Hotel

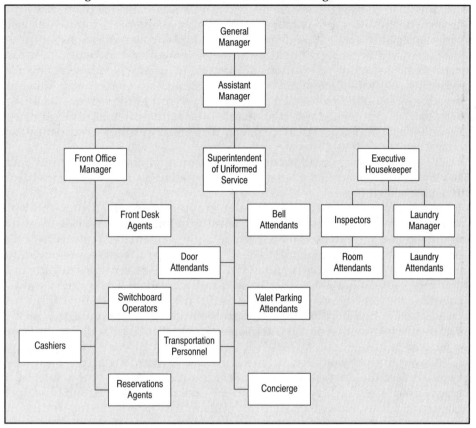

hotels have added concierge services to their list of front office functions. In a sense, concierge services are simply an extension of the guest services provided by front office personnel.

The functions of the front office are to:

- Sell guestrooms, register guests, and assign guestrooms.

- Process future room reservations, when there is no reservations department or when the reservations department is closed.

- Coordinate guest services.

- Provide information about the hotel, the surrounding community, and any attractions or events of interest to guests.

- Maintain accurate room status information.

- Maintain guest accounts and monitor credit limits.

- Produce guest account statements and complete proper financial settlement.

Reservations. More than half of all hotel guests make reservations for hotel accommodations through toll-free telephone numbers, direct telephone lines, the Internet, hotel sales representatives, travel agencies, property-to-property networks, postal delivery, telex and fax, e-mail, and other communications services.

Every lodging property has its own way of monitoring and managing its reservations function. The reservations department is responsible for receiving and processing reservation requests for future overnight accommodations. Although procedures may differ from hotel to hotel with regard to reservations handling, maintenance, processing, and confirmation, the purpose remains the same: to accommodate guest requests in a manner that maximizes hotel occupancy and room revenue.

In the past, the reservations department merely captured reservations data. Potential guests contacted the hotel, which accepted or denied reservations based on room availability.

Reservations systems can be programmed to provide reservations agents with information on the types of rooms available (including room rate, view, furnishings, amenities, and bed size) for a given day. Many automated systems can even provide agents with the exact room number if necessary. Such technology shifts responsibility for room sales from the front desk to the reservations department. More recent technology automatically alerts the reservations agent when the guest requesting the reservation has already stayed at the hotel, or even if he or she has stayed at other hotels in the chain. Reservations systems provide agents with a great deal of information on the hotel, some of which can be provided to the guest on request.

Advanced technology has helped transform reservations agents into salespeople. In fact, the reservations department is a great place to start a hotel sales career. Reservations agents should convey the desirability, features, and benefits of staying at the hotel, rather than simply process an accommodation request. It is no longer satisfactory for a reservations agent to defer to the front desk to determine a room's rate at registration. This shift in responsibility away from the front desk to the reservations department is important because it allows management to accurately forecast not only occupancy but revenue as well. Whenever possible, reservations agents should confirm the rate at the time the guest makes the reservation. In fact, most guests requesting a reservation will not book a room without receiving a confirmed rate. The reservations system should reinforce the guest's decision to stay at the property and provide sufficient information to satisfy guest inquiries.

It is essential for reservations department personnel to work closely with the hotel's sales and marketing division when group reservations are being solicited or processed. In fact, some hotel companies now place the reservations functions under the direction of the sales department instead of the front office. In any case, sales department representatives must be kept informed of room availability to ensure they know how many rooms are available in the reservations system on any given day. On a day-to-day basis, reservation managers must review reservations system reports and room availabilities to avoid *overbooking*. Overbooking can create bad feelings and contribute to lost business in the future. The management of reservations is further complicated by the fact that several states have enacted legislation prohibiting overbooking.

An additional dimension of reservations is the reservations department's coordination with the chain or referral group's reservation center, sometimes termed a *call center*. In most cases, reservation centers provide a significant portion of a hotel's occupancy. This is one of the most important reasons hotel owners affiliate with a chain or referral group. Reservation centers do much more than provide a convenient and inexpensive way for potential guests to make reservations. They have become communications hubs for the company, coordinating room availability and rates for airline reservation systems, Internet reservation sites, and other reservation channels.

Telecommunications. The telecommunications switchboard area or department maintains a complex communications network similar to that of any large company. The telecommunications department may also be called a **private branch exchange (PBX).** Hotel switchboard or PBX operators may have responsibilities that extend beyond answering and distributing calls to the appropriate extension. Switchboard operators may also place wake-up calls, answer questions about the hotel, monitor automated systems (such as door alarms and fire alarms), and coordinate emergency communications. Operators also protect guests' privacy, thereby contributing to the hotel's security program by not divulging guestroom numbers. Some hotels now instruct guests to call the hotel operator or a special guest service department for all service requests, including housekeeping, room service, and even bell service. Another recent trend involving guest safety with telephone systems is to have all house phones (telephones in public areas of the hotel used for calling within the hotel) ring the operator for call processing. This reduces the risk of unwanted or mistaken guestroom telephone calls. Many hotels also provide guest paging services over a public address system.

Recent technological advances have considerably decreased the responsibilities and workloads of telephone switchboard operators. Hotels have installed technology that allows guests to place their own room-to-room or outgoing phone calls. Most guestroom phones offer touchtone convenience and may feature call waiting or caller ID. Also available is guest voice mail, which reduces the reliance on hotel operators to record messages for guests and turn on message waiting lights in guestrooms. Call accounting systems can place direct-dialed calls over the least costly route available. Call accounting systems, which automatically price calls, also enable hotels to add surcharges and access charges to local and long-distance calls. Call accounting systems communicate with a front desk system to automatically post telephone charges to a guest's account. This reduces disputes at the front desk over charges for calls that were not actually completed.

Some hotels have installed answering devices for calls coming from outside the hotel. These automated answering devices, or AADs, direct callers to guest reservations, dining reservations, group sales, or other departments without the intervention of an operator. Voice messaging technology also can help improve the efficiency and effectiveness of incoming telephone traffic. In addition, voice messaging can allow callers to leave guest messages in their own voice, a service many guests appreciate.

Technology can also automatically place wake-up calls to guestrooms at preprogrammed times. With an automated system, when a front desk agent or switchboard operator receives a request for a wake-up call, he or she enters the room number and the desired time into the auto wake-up system. Some hotels have systems that allow guests to program the telephone to wake them up—without the assistance of a hotel employee. The system then places the wake-up call as specified, and plays a recorded message when the guest answers the phone. This can be especially helpful in large hotels where hundreds of wake-up calls for the same time may be requested. In world-class hotels, the system may alert the hotel operator to make the wake-up call at the requested time.

Uniformed Service. Employees in the hotel's uniformed service department generally provide the most personalized guest service. Given the high degree of attention this department pays to guests, some properties refer to uniformed service simply as *guest service.* Among the primary positions within the uniformed service department are:

- *Bell attendants,* who provide baggage service between the lobby area and the guestroom.

- *Door attendants,* who provide curb-side baggage service and traffic control at the hotel entrance.

- *Valet parking attendants,* who provide parking service for guests' vehicles.

- *Transportation personnel,* who provide transportation services for guests.

- *Concierges,* who are very knowledgeable about the local area and assist guests by making restaurant reservations; arranging for transportation; getting tickets for theater, sporting, or other special events; and so on.

While personnel in reservations, front desk, and communications areas affect guest perceptions, it is often employees in uniformed service who make a lasting impression. This is especially true in world-class or luxury hotels that offer a broad range of guest services. Uniformed service employees are usually classified as tipped employees, since a portion of their income is derived from guests' gratuities. To some degree, uniformed service personnel can affect their income through the quality and frequency of service they provide. While uniformed service jobs may not appear complex, they are critical to the smooth operation of a hotel. Quite often it is the ability of uniformed service staff to properly anticipate guest needs and communicate effectively with guests that makes the difference in the hotel's service quality.

Among the major challenges the manager of the uniformed service department faces are: setting the proper service standards, recruiting and training employees, and ensuring that employees successfully provide quality service. Since uniformed service employees generally receive among the lowest hotel wages, keeping them trained and motivated can be an enormous job. Without a doubt, well-motivated uniformed service employees can enhance the hotel's image while earning a good income through a combination of wages and tips. Providing excellent service can be personally rewarding as well.

Bell attendants. Many guests arrive at a hotel with heavy baggage or several pieces of luggage. Guests receive help handling this luggage from probably the best-known employee on the uniformed service staff: the bell attendant.

Bell attendants should be carefully selected. Since most hotels have carts for transporting baggage, the physical ability to actually *carry* the baggage is not a critical job qualification, although heavy lifting is often involved. More important, bell attendants should have strong oral communication skills and should display genuine interest in each guest. Depending on the size and complexity of the hotel, bell attendants may be counted on to:

- Transport guest luggage to and from guestrooms.

- Familiarize guests with the hotel's facilities, services, and safety features, as well as the guestroom and any in-room amenities.

- Provide a secure area for guests requiring temporary luggage storage.

- Provide information on hotel services and facilities, as well as group functions.

- Deliver mail, packages, messages, and special amenities to guestrooms.

- Pick up and deliver guest laundry and dry cleaning.

- Perform light housekeeping services in lobby and entry areas.

- Help guests load and unload their luggage in the absence of a door attendant.

- Notify other departments of guest needs, such as informing the housekeeping department if a guest requests a crib or extra towels.

While many of these tasks appear simple, they all require a degree of professionalism. For example, to assist a guest with his or her luggage, the bell attendant must know how to properly load a luggage cart. Fragile items must not be placed below heavy items. The cart must also be properly balanced so that it does not tip over or become difficult to steer.

Due to their direct contact with guests, bell attendants have an opportunity to communicate vital information to them and help them feel welcome at the hotel. A bell attendant who consistently and clearly conveys a warm welcome and proper information to each guest is a very valuable employee. One of a hotel's best marketing opportunities arises when the bell attendant escorts the guest to his or her room. Familiarity with the area outside the hotel, as well as with the hotel's restaurants, entertainment lounges, recreational activities, meeting rooms, and safety and security measures, is an important part of the job. It is through informal conversation that bell attendants become key players in the hotel's sales and marketing efforts. Bell attendants should make an extra effort to learn guests' names and perhaps the purpose of their stay. This makes guests feel especially welcome and allows bell attendants to provide more personal service.

Door attendants. Door attendants play a role similar to bell attendants: they are dedicated to welcoming guests to the hotel. Door attendants are generally employed in hotels offering world-class or luxury service. Some of the duties door attendants perform include:

- Opening hotel doors and assisting guests upon arrival.

- Helping guests load and unload luggage from vehicles.

- Escorting guests to the hotel registration area.
- Controlling vehicle traffic flow and safety at the hotel entrance.
- Hailing taxis, upon request.
- Assisting with valet parking services.
- Performing light housekeeping services in the lobby and entry areas.

Like bell attendants, door attendants must be well informed about hotel facilities and the local community. Guests frequently ask door attendants for directions to businesses, government offices, transportation centers, restaurants, and local landmarks and attractions. One of the most challenging responsibilities for a door attendant is controlling vehicle traffic at the hotel entrance. Controlling vehicle traffic can be a very demanding job, especially when the hotel is busy.

Experienced door attendants are capable of handling all these tasks with aplomb. A skilled, experienced door attendant learns the names of frequent guests. When these guests return to the hotel, the door attendant is able to greet them *by name* and can introduce them to other front office staff. Such personal service enhances the reputation of the hotel and provides the guest with a unique experience.

Valet parking attendants. Valet parking is generally available at hotels offering world-class or luxury service. Specially trained employees park guest and visitor automobiles. The personal attention and security of valet parking service is considered both a luxury and a convenience. Guests do not have to worry about finding a parking space, walking to the hotel in inclement weather, or finding their vehicles in the parking lot. Hotels generally charge a higher fee for valet parking than for self-service parking. In addition to paying the higher fee for valet parking, guests are also likely to tip the valet parking attendant.

Valet parking attendants are also responsible for the security of vehicles being moved to and from the hotel entrance. Attendants should not take a car into their care without issuing a receipt to the guest or visitor, usually in the form of a ticket. On the hotel portion of the ticket, the attendant should note any existing damage to the vehicle. Vehicle keys must be kept in a secure area and issued only by qualified personnel. Cars should not be issued to guests or visitors without proper documentation; in most cases, guests or visitors must return the receipt or ticket issued by the attendant before they can receive their keys. If a key is lost or given to the wrong person, the vehicle can be rendered inoperable or considered stolen and the hotel may be held financially responsible.

The uniformed service department is responsible for all vehicles under its care, and reports information to the front desk each night so that parking charges can be posted to guest accounts. In addition, when the vehicle entrance to the hotel is busy, valet parking attendants should help keep the area running smoothly by providing traffic control assistance.

Transportation personnel. Already common at most airport hotels, transportation services and departments are gaining in popularity at other types of properties. Many airport hotels offer complimentary bus service between the airport and the hotel on a regular schedule. In some cases, a guest can simply step from an airport's baggage claim section to a conveniently located courtesy van area. In other cases, the guest must telephone the hotel before being picked up. Some hotels provide direct-connect phone lines through a courtesy board at the airport for guest convenience.

Bus or courtesy van drivers must be well trained and properly licensed to operate hotel vehicles. Since these drivers are sometimes the first contact the guest will have with the hotel, it is important that they be polite, efficient, and knowledgeable about the property. It is generally customary for drivers to provide some information about the hotel while in transit, either through a live spoken presentation or a pre-recorded audiotape. Drivers should also help guests entering and exiting the vehicle. An experienced driver efficiently and carefully loads guest luggage into the van. As a result of such assistance, guests won't have to wrestle with heavy bags while entering and exiting the vehicle. Many hotels have equipped vans with two-way radios. While these radios are provided primarily for safety and scheduling reasons, drivers may ask guests for their names and relay the information to the hotel. This allows the hotel to prepare for guests before their actual arrival.

Another recent addition at many hotels is providing courtesy transportation service to local business, shopping, entertainment, sporting, and dining establishments. At some properties, limousines may be made available to VIP guests. Transportation personnel may be classified as either tipped or non-tipped employees.

In all cases, drivers must present the proper image of the hotel. Guest privacy must be maintained, especially in limousines. Any conversations among guests must be considered confidential and should not be discussed with hotel employees, family, or friends. Also, traffic safety is a critical concern. Drivers must be licensed according to state and federal laws. They must know how to check their vehicles to ensure that all equipment is working correctly. Safety equipment, such as flares and fire extinguishers, must be checked regularly, and drivers must be familiar with their use.

Concierges. Even though this guest service position has existed for quite some time, the concierge is perhaps the least understood position in the uniformed service area. In the distant past, the concierge was the castle doorkeeper. The concierge's job was to ensure that all the castle occupants were secure in their rooms at night. The concierge often accompanied traveling royalty to provide security and to travel ahead of the royal party to finalize food and lodging arrangements. As hotels became more common in Europe, the concierge eventually became part of the staff that provided personalized guest services. It is common to find a concierge at a world-class or luxury hotel.

Certified concierges may display prominent crossed gold keys on their jacket lapel. To earn these keys, a concierge must be certified by the international association of concierges, known as **Les Clefs d'Or** (Golden Keys). This concierge association has established high standards for its members. While many hotels employ experienced staff to assist guests with special needs, the title concierge technically applies only to members of Les Clefs d'Or.

Concierges may provide custom services to hotel guests. Duties include making reservations for dining, securing tickets for theater and sporting events, arranging for transportation, and providing information on cultural events and local attractions. Concierges are known for their resourcefulness. Getting tickets to sold-out concerts or successfully making last-minute dinner reservations at a crowded restaurant are expected of a good concierge. Most successful concierges have developed an extensive network of local, regional, and national contacts for a variety of services. Especially important, however, are the local contacts the concierge has established at restaurants, box offices, car rental offices, airlines, printers, and other businesses. Some hotels actually encourage concierges to visit appropriate businesses and organizations to establish and strengthen such relationships. Finally, a highly successful concierge should speak several languages.

With the implementation of advanced technology throughout the hotel, guests may require assistance in accessing and using such devices, networks, or systems. For this reason, some hotels employ a *technology concierge,* a staff member who specializes in assisting guests with technology issues. For example, if the hotel offers in-room high-speed Internet access and the guest is unable to access the network, the technology concierge may be dispatched to help resolve the issue.

The concierge position is generally a salaried position, but gratuities from guests are common expressions of gratitude for exemplary service. In some hotels, the head concierge is the manager of the uniformed service department. When this is the case, the head concierge assumes additional responsibilities for supervising all uniformed service personnel. In large hotels, the head concierge is often too busy to undertake such tasks and supervises employees in the concierge department only.

As mentioned in the introduction to this chapter, service is becoming more important in attracting guests and maintaining their ongoing loyalty. In many hotels offering world-class and mid-range accommodations and services, the role of the full-service concierge or guest-service staff is becoming a key to establishing the reputation of the hotel.

Housekeeping. Housekeeping is perhaps the most important support department for the front office. Like the front office, housekeeping usually is part of the rooms division of the hotel. In some hotels, however, the housekeeping function is considered an independent hotel division. This is especially true in very large or convention hotels, where the housekeeping staff may number several hundred employees. Effective communication among housekeeping and front office personnel can contribute to guest satisfaction while helping the front office to effectively monitor guestroom status. Housekeeping employees clean occupied and vacated rooms, inspect rooms before releasing them for sale, and communicate the status of guestrooms to the front office. At most properties, a front desk agent cannot assign a guestroom until the room has been cleaned, inspected, and released by the housekeeping department.

The housekeeping department often employs a larger staff than other departments in the rooms division. Normally, an executive housekeeper is in charge of the department, aided by an assistant housekeeper. In large hotels there can be several assistant housekeepers, each responsible for specific floors, sections, or, in very large hotels, entire buildings. The department also includes inspectors, room attendants, housepersons, lobby and general cleaners, and laundry personnel. Room attendants are assigned to specific sections of the hotel. Depending on the hotel's service level, average guestroom size, and cleaning tasks, room attendants may clean eight to eighteen rooms per shift. If the hotel has its own laundry, house-keeping department staff may clean and press the property's linens, towels, and uniforms, and may also launder guest clothing.

Housekeeping personnel (usually executive housekeepers) are responsible for maintaining two types of inventories: recycled and non-recycled. Recycled inventories are those items that have a relatively limited useful life but are used repeatedly in housekeeping operations. These inventories include such items as linens, uniforms, and guest amenities like irons and hair dryers. Non-recycled inventories are items that are consumed or worn out during the course of routine housekeeping operations. Non-recycled inventories include cleaning supplies, small equipment items, and guest supplies and personal grooming items. Guest amenities and linens are among the items and conveniences most often requested by guests.

To ensure the speedy, efficient rooming of guests in vacant and inspected rooms, the housekeeping and front office departments must promptly inform each other of any change in a room's status or availability. Teamwork between housekeeping and the front office is essential to effective hotel operations. The more familiar housekeeping and front office personnel are with each other's departmental procedures, the smoother the relationship.

Food and Beverage Division

The hotel's food and beverage division generally ranks second to the rooms division in terms of total revenue. Many hotels support more than one food and beverage outlet. There are almost as many varieties of hotel food and beverage operations as there are hotels. Possible outlets include quick-service, table-service, and specialty restaurants, coffee shops, bars, lounges, and clubs. The food and beverage division also typically supports other hotel functions such as room service, catering, and banquet planning. Banquets, normally held in the hotel's function rooms, may represent tremendous sales and profit opportunities for the food and beverage division. Hotels that appeal to group and convention business typically generate large amounts of banquet and catering revenues. In group hotels, catering opportunities may extend to the guestrooms, where suites often serve as settings for special hospitality parties given by companies. These are often upscale events, providing good opportunities for creativity on the part of the catering department. Catered functions, such as weddings and anniversaries, may also provide significant revenue opportunities for the food and beverage division.

Sales and Marketing Division

The size of a hotel's sales and marketing staff can vary from one part-time employee to more than a dozen full-time employees. In small properties, the general manager often fulfills all of the sales and marketing roles. In large hotels, the sales and marketing responsibilities are typically divided into five functions: sales, **revenue management,** convention services, advertising, and public relations. The primary goal of the division is to promote the sale of hotel products and services. To this end, sales and marketing staff members need to coordinate their efforts with the front office and other hotel divisions to effectively assess and communicate guest needs.

Marketing employees strive to attract guests to the hotel. They research the marketplace, competing products, guest needs and expectations, and future demand. Based on their findings, they then develop advertising and public relations programs for the hotel. Sales staff, on the other hand, strive to create revenue through the direct sale of hotel products to guests and groups. Front desk agents also may act as salespersons, especially when negotiating with and registering **walk-in** guests. In many hotels, the reservations office works very closely with the sales department, and serves in a sales role when guests call the hotel to make reservations.

Revenue Management. The revenue manager is responsible for ensuring that the hotel is maximizing its revenue by balancing the room rates guests pay with hotel occupancy. The challenge the manager faces is to secure the highest possible room rate for each potential guest, while not turning away any potential guests simply because room rates are too high. The revenue manager works cooperatively with the sales department, the reservations department, and often other departments to determine which room rate strategies should be applied to ensure that the hotel achieves its room revenue goals. Hotel sales team members often check with the revenue manager before quoting room rates for groups or local business associates. The revenue manager also establishes room rates for the reservation office and works with the hotel's many distribution channels, which include the hotel's website, corporate Internet sites, third-party websites, airline reservation systems, visitors' bureaus, and others. Revenue management often extends beyond room rates, and considers non-room revenues in order to optimize the property's total revenue opportunities. In small hotels, the front office manager, the reservations manager, or the general manager may also serve as the revenue manager. Often hotels of the same brand are "clustered" geographically and assigned to a single revenue management department designed to effectively serve multiple hotels.

Accounting Division

A hotel's accounting division monitors the financial activities of the property. Some hotels use off-premises accounting services to complement the work of their internal accounting division. In this case, the hotel's staff collects and transmits data to a service bureau or chain headquarters. A hotel that performs its accounting work on the premises will employ a larger accounting staff with a higher level of responsibility.

Accounting activities include paying outstanding invoices, distributing unpaid statements, collecting amounts owed, processing payroll, accumulating operating data, and compiling financial reports. In addition, the accounting staff may be responsible for making bank deposits, securing cash loans, and performing other control and processing functions as required by hotel management. In many hotels, the night audit and the food and beverage audit are considered accounting division activities.

The accounting division's success depends on close coordination with the front office. The front office cashiering and guest accounting functions include monitoring cash, checks, payment cards, and other methods of guest account settlement. The most common financial transactions handled by front office staff members are receiving cash payments, verifying personal checks, processing payment cards, tendering change, and monitoring guest account statements. In small hotels, the front office is also responsible for monitoring the credit status of registered guests.

Engineering and Maintenance Division

A hotel's engineering and maintenance division is responsible for maintaining the property's structure and grounds, as well as its electrical and mechanical equipment. This division may also be charged with swimming pool sanitation, parking lot cleanliness, and fountain operations (some hotels, however, may have a separate grounds department or an outdoor and recreation department for these tasks). Quite often, the operation of the hotel's safety equipment comes under the engineering and maintenance division as well.

Not all engineering and maintenance work is handled by the hotel's staff. Often, problems or projects require outside contracting. For example, special skills may be needed to calibrate building controls, charge fire extinguishers, and test and adjust building fire alarms. The special equipment that cleans kitchen duct work, disposes of grease and other refuse, or removes snow from parking lots may require that these tasks be contracted. Since some of the work of the engineering and maintenance division must be done in cooperation with the housekeeping department, some hotels have combined housekeeping and engineering into a single unit called the Operations Department.

The front office must efficiently exchange information with a representative of the engineering and maintenance division to ensure guest satisfaction. A guest complaint about a leaky faucet, malfunctioning lamp, or sticking lock shouldn't rest with a front desk agent but should be written up and quickly relayed to engineering and maintenance staff for corrective action. Conversely, front desk staff must be informed quickly about maintenance problems that render a room unsuitable for sale. They also must be informed when the room becomes ready for sale again.

Security Division

While all employees at every hotel should be concerned about the safety and security of hotel guests, visitors, and employees, many properties have a security division that is dedicated to these responsibilities. Security staff may include in-house personnel, contract security officers, and off-duty or retired police officers. Security responsibilities may include patrolling the property; monitoring surveillance equipment; and, in general, ensuring that guests, visitors, and employees are safe and secure. Critical to the effectiveness of the security division is the cooperation and assistance of local law enforcement officials.

A hotel's security program is strongest when employees outside the security division participate in security efforts. For example, front desk agents play a critical part in key control by issuing guestroom keys to registered guests *only*. Room attendants practice security when they verify a guest's room key *before* allowing that guest to enter a room they are cleaning. All employees should be wary of suspicious activities anywhere on the premises, and report such activities to the security staff. A key role of the security division is to ascertain that the hotel staff is strongly aware of safety issues through training and enforcement of standards. Hotel management should maintain strong, positive relationships with the local safety agencies as part of its ongoing safety and security program.

Human Resources Division

Hotels have increased their investment in and dependence on human resources management. The size and budgets of human resources divisions have grown steadily, along with their responsibility and influence. This expanded role is mirrored by the growing preference for the broader term *human resources management* over *personnel management.* In properties that are not large enough to justify a separate human resources office or division, the hotel's general manager often supervises the human resources function. When a hotel company has several properties in an area, it may choose to "cluster" the human resources function. With this arrangement, the hotel company has one main office and a skilled human resources manager to serve all the properties in the area. This reduces the cost for each hotel and brings a higher level of knowledge to all of the hotels.

Recently, the scope of the human resources division has changed in response to new government legislation, a shrinking labor pool, and growing pressures from competition. Although techniques have changed, the basic functions of the human resources division remain the same: employment (including external recruiting and internal reassignment), training, employee relations (including quality assurance), compensation, benefits, administration (including employee policies), labor relations, and safety.

Other Divisions

Many hotels staff a variety of other divisions to serve their guests. The range of possibilities reflects the diversity of hotels.

Retail Outlets. Lodging properties often establish gift shops, newsstands, or other retail outlets in their lobbies or other public areas. These outlets generate revenue for the hotel based on a percentage of sales or a fixed space rental fee.

Recreation. Some hotels—primarily resorts—staff a division dedicated to providing group and individual recreational activities for guests. Some recreation divisions also undertake landscaping the property's grounds and maintaining the swimming pool. Golf, tennis, bowling, snorkeling, sailing, walking tours, bicycle trips, horseback riding, hikes, and other activities may be arranged by recreation division staff. The division may also plan and direct activities such as arts and crafts shows or children's programs. Typically, recreation employees collect fees for organized activities or arrange for charges to be posted to guest accounts.

Casino. Casino hotels have a casino division that operates games of chance for guests and protects the property's gambling interests. The casino division may offer various forms of entertainment and other attractions to draw customers into the property and its gambling facilities. For casino hotels, revenues derived from gambling are usually larger than revenues from hotel operations. Therefore, casino priorities may take precedence over hotel priorities.

Front Office Operations

Traditional front office functions include reservations, registration, room and rate assignment, guest services, room status, maintenance and settlement of guest accounts, and creation of guest history records. The front office develops and maintains a comprehensive database of guest information, coordinates guest services, and ensures guest satisfaction. Employees in diverse areas of the front office perform these functions.

While no industry standards exist for front office positions, front office organization charts can help to define departmental reporting and working relationships. The highest level of employee and guest satisfaction can be ensured through a carefully designed front office organization, together with comprehensive and well-planned goals and strategies, work shifts, job descriptions, and job specifications.

Organization of the Front Office

Large hotels often organize the front office according to functions, with different employees handling separate areas. This division of duties can enhance the control the front office has over its own operations. Front office personnel can provide more specialized attention if each area is responsible for only one segment of the guest's stay. Such a separation of duties may not be practical in a small hotel, where it is common for one or two individuals to handle all front desk operations.

The front office in a large hotel supports many positions with a considerable separation of duties. These positions typically include, but are not limited to:

- *Front desk agents*, who register guests and maintain room availability information.

- *Cashiers*, who handle money, post charges, and oversee guest account settlement.

- *Information clerks*, who take messages, provide directions to guests, and handle facsimiles (faxes) and packages.

- *Telephone operators*, who manage the switchboard and coordinate wake-up calls.

- *Reservations agents*, who respond to reservation requests and create reservation records.

- *Uniformed service agents*, who handle guest luggage and escort guests to their rooms.

If a hotel is automated, each employee may be restricted to accessing only those electronic records pertinent to his or her function.

The front office of a mid-size hotel performs the same functions, but with fewer employees. Staff members are often cross-trained, and job duties are typically combined. For example, a front desk agent may also serve as a cashier and information clerk. He or she may also be trained to assume the duties of a switchboard operator and a reservations agent in their absence. During busy periods, several agents may work at the same time. Although each agent may be assigned identical duties, the agents may informally divide the functions among themselves. For example, one agent may register guests and handle the switchboard, another may function as a cashier, and a third may handle reservations and information requests.

Small hotels may have a single front desk agent who performs nearly all the functions with little assistance. If the front desk agent becomes overwhelmed by the workload, the general manager or accountant, if properly trained, can help relieve the burden. In a small property, the general manager and accountant often become more directly involved with front office operations.

Work Shifts

A forty-hour workweek is the typical workload for front office employees in most hotels. Federal and state wage and hour laws apply to the front office, and, in addition, some properties may be bound by union contracts and rules. A front office employee may work any one of the property's work shifts, depending on the front office's needs and the staff member's availability. Traditional front office work shifts are:

- Day shift   7 A.M.–3 P.M.
- Evening shift   3 P.M.–11 P.M.
- Night shift   11 P.M.–7 A.M.

A recent trend in front office operations is to provide a limited level of guest service during late night hours, thereby reducing the number of employees required on the night shift. In mid-size and smaller hotels, the night auditor also serves as the front desk agent.

Front office work shifts may vary with guest business patterns. A program of flexible work hours, or **flextime,** allows employees to vary the time they start and end work. Certain busy hours during a work shift, however, may require the presence of a majority of the staff. For example, one front desk agent may work from 6 A.M. to 2 P.M. so that wake-up calls and check-outs can be handled more efficiently through the 7 A.M. shift change. On the other hand, scheduling a front desk agent to work from 10 A.M. to 6 P.M. may allow for smooth processing of late-morning check-outs and guest arrivals during the time when evening shift personnel are scheduled for a meal break.

Other types of alternative scheduling include variations on the traditional workweek of five 8-hour days. A **compressed work schedule** occurs when an employee works 40 hours in fewer than five days (for instance, four 10-hour days). **Job sharing** is an arrangement in which two or more part-time employees share the responsibilities of one full-time position. Each worker may perform all aspects of the position on alternate days, or divide the duties while the employees work simultaneously.

Part-time employees are an increasingly important source of labor for the hospitality industry. Many potential workers, such as students, parents of young children, and retirees, may not be available to work full time. Part-time workers give the front office the flexibility to respond to fluctuating guest demands while reducing overall labor costs. Alternative scheduling programs, however, require careful planning and evaluation before implementation.

Job Descriptions

A **job description** lists all the tasks that are required of a work position. A job description may also outline reporting relationships, additional responsibilities, working conditions, necessary equipment and materials, and other important information specific to the place of employment. To be most effective, job descriptions should be customized to the operational procedures of a specific lodging property. Job descriptions should be task-oriented; they should be written for a position, not for a particular employee. Job descriptions will become dated and inappropriate as work assignments change, so they should be reviewed at least once a year for possible revision. Typically, front office managers write job descriptions. Employees should also be involved in writing and revising their job descriptions. Properly written job descriptions can minimize employee anxiety by specifying the chain of command and the responsibilities of the job.

Well-written job descriptions can also be used:

- In evaluating job performance.
- As an aid in training or retraining employees.
- To prevent unnecessary duplication of duties.
- To help ensure that each job task is performed.
- To help determine appropriate staffing levels.

Each front office employee should receive a copy of the job description for his or her position. Final job candidates may also receive a copy of a job description, even before receiving a job offer. This is better than having someone accept a job offer and then decline it because he or she was unaware of the job's requirements.

A word of caution about job descriptions is appropriate. In the United States, job qualifications, and, therefore, job descriptions, are subject to certain federal laws. The Americans with Disabilities Act (ADA) states that people with disabilities are considered qualified for a position if they can perform the position's **essential functions** with or without **reasonable accommodation.** Job descriptions should be created before an open position is advertised, and they should list essential functions. Management must not discriminate against an applicant with a disability merely because the applicant cannot perform a non-essential function. Improper job descriptions may not only lead to improper hiring decisions, they may also expose the hotel to liability for illegal discrimination. At the same time, proper job descriptions may open opportunities for qualified applicants who have disabilities covered under the ADA.

Job descriptions play many roles in an organization. They should be used in the job interview, so that the person applying for a position understands what is expected of him or her. Job descriptions can also be used for promotion, transfer, or — in certain cases — disciplinary action. Therefore, having complete and accurate job descriptions is an essential part of managing front office operations, as well as any other hotel department. (The appendix at the end of this chapter presents a sampling of front office job descriptions.)

Job Specifications

Job specifications list the personal qualities, skills, and traits an employee needs in order to successfully perform the tasks outlined in a job description. Basically, front office job specifications spell out front office management's expectations for current and prospective employees; they are typically prepared by the front office manager with input from front office employees. Job specifications are usually developed after job descriptions, since a particular job may require special skills and traits. Factors considered for a job specification are: formal education, work experience, general knowledge, previous training, physical requirements, communication ability, and equipment skills. Job specifications often form the basis for advertising job opportunities and identifying eligible applicants; they may also help to identify current employees for promotion. A sample job specification for a generic front office staff member is shown in Exhibit 5.

Although standardized job specifications do not exist throughout the industry, certain traits and skills likely appear in job specifications in most hotels. Because of their high degree of guest and visitor contact, front office employees often must possess extraordinary interpersonal skills. Evaluating an applicant on the basis of these traits may be highly subjective. Nonetheless, traits important to front office work include:

- Professional demeanor
- Congenial, outgoing personality
- Helpful attitude
- Good diction, grammar, and speaking voice
- Flexibility
- Well-groomed appearance
- Willingness to learn
- Orientation to detail

Successful performance of front office procedures usually requires general skills acquired through education and experience. Valuable employees possess practical skills, knowledge, and aptitude. Mathematical abilities (for cashiering and accounting tasks) and keyboarding (for recordkeeping and computer operation) are often necessary in front office work. Some hotels may find it beneficial to have employees in the front office who speak more than one language, to better serve international guests.

Front office personnel must be team players. They must be willing to work together for the benefit of the entire operation.

Summary ───────────────────────────

The services that result from a hotel's smooth operation are highly visible to guests. Guests are more likely to return to or recommend a lodging property if they enjoy their stay. For a hotel to run effectively and efficiently, every employee must understand and work to achieve the property's mission. The hotel's mission

Exhibit 5   Sample Job Specification: Front Office Positions

Job Specification
Front Office Personnel

Our property considers the following traits important for the successful perfor-mance of front office work.

1. *Professional Demeanor*
    - Reports to work on time
    - Has a positive attitude toward the job and the hotel
    - Recognizes positive and negative aspects of the job
    - Possesses maturity in judgment
    - Appears businesslike
    - Maintains control and composure in difficult situations

2. *Congenial Nature*
    - Smiles readily
    - Exhibits cordial and pleasant behavior
    - Is a people person

3. *Helpful Attitude*
    - Is sensitive to the guests' needs
    - Possesses a sense of humor
    - Responds and speaks intelligently
    - Demonstrates creativity
    - Practices good listening skills

4. *Flexibility*
    - Willing and able to accept a different workshift if necessary
    - Understands others' points of view
    - Willing to try new ways of doing things; innovative
    - Works well with guests and hotel staff; a team player

5. *Well-Groomed Appearance*
    - Dresses appropriately; meets property standards for personal grooming, wearing jewelry, and the wearing of and caring for his or her employee uniform (if applicable)

statement expresses the underlying philosophy that gives meaning and direc-tion to hotel policies. The mission statement should address the interests of three diverse groups: guests, management, and employees. A sound mission statement should address guests' expectations, reflect management's philosophy, and pro-vide hotel employees with a sense of purpose.

The front office is typically responsible for developing and maintaining a comprehensive database of guest information, coordinating guest services, and ensuring guest satisfaction. Large hotels tend to organize the front office by func-tional areas in order to enhance control over operations. In a computerized prop-erty, each employee may be restricted to accessing only those electronic records pertinent to his or her function.

A hotel operating department can be classified as either a revenue center or a support center. By definition, a revenue center sells goods or services to guests, thereby generating revenues. A support center does not generate direct revenue, but instead provides important backing for the hotel's revenue centers. The terms *front of the house* and *back of the house* also refer to hotel operational areas. Areas in the front of the house are those in which guests and employees directly interact. In back-of-the-house areas, there is little direct contact between guests and staff members. Although back-of-the-house employees may not directly serve guests (by, for example, taking an order, assisting with registration, or delivering luggage to guestrooms), they indirectly serve guests by cleaning guestrooms, repairing leaky faucets, or correcting errors in guest accounts. Typical hotel operating divisions and departments include rooms, reservations, food and beverage, sales and marketing, accounting, engineering and maintenance, security, and human resources.

A job description lists a majority of the tasks assigned to the position. A job description may also outline reporting relationships, additional responsibilities, working conditions, equipment and materials to be used, expected standards of performance, and other important information specific to the property. To be most effective, job descriptions should be customized to the operational procedures of a specific lodging property. Job specifications list the personal qualities, skills, and traits a person needs to successfully perform the tasks outlined in a job description. They can be used in promotions, transfers, and disciplinary actions. Several sample front office job descriptions are presented in the chapter appendix.

🔑 Key Terms

back of the house—The functional areas of a hotel in which staff have little or no direct guest contact, such as the engineering, accounting, and human resources divisions.

compressed work schedule—An adaptation of full-time work hours that enables an employee to work the equivalent of a standard workweek in fewer than the traditional five days.

essential functions—A term used in the Americans with Disabilities Act; according to government guidelines, the essential functions of a job are those functions or fundamental job duties that the individual who holds the position must be able to perform unaided or with the assistance of a reasonable accommodation.

flextime—A program of flexible work hours that allows employees to vary their times of starting and ending work.

front of the house—The functional areas of a hotel in which staff have extensive guest contact, such as the food and beverage facilities and the front office.

goals—Those activities and standards an organization must successfully perform or achieve to effectively carry out its mission.

job description—A detailed list identifying all the key duties of a job as well as reporting relationships, additional responsibilities, working conditions, and any necessary equipment and materials.

job sharing—An arrangement in which two or more part-time employees share the responsibilities of one full-time position.

job specification—A list of the personal qualities, skills, and traits necessary to successfully perform the tasks outlined in a job description.

Les Clefs d'Or—The international association of concierges; the title "concierge" technically applies only to members of Les Clefs d'Or.

mission statement—A document that states the unique purpose that sets a hotel apart from other hotels, expresses the underlying philosophy that gives meaning and direction to the hotel's actions, and addresses the interests of guests, management, and employees.

organization chart—A schematic representation of the relationships among positions within an organization, showing where each position fits into the overall organization and illustrating the divisions of responsibility and lines of authority.

private branch exchange (PBX)—A hotel's telephone switchboard equipment.

reasonable accommodation—A change in the usual way of doing a job so that a qualified person with a disability can participate, but a change that does not impose "undue hardship" on the employer.

revenue center—A hotel division or department that sells products or services to guests and thereby directly generates revenue for the hotel; the front office, food and beverage outlets, room service, and retail stores are typical hotel revenue centers.

revenue management—The practice of maximizing revenue by balancing the room rates guests pay with hotel occupancy. The challenge is securing the highest possible room rate for each potential guest, while not turning away any potential guest simply because room rates are too high.

strategy—A plan of action a department or division uses to achieve its goals.

support center—A hotel division or department that does not generate revenue directly, but supports the hotel's revenue centers; includes the housekeeping, accounting, engineering and maintenance, and human resources divisions.

tactics—The day-to-day operating procedures that staff members use to implement strategies.

walk-in—A person who arrives at a hotel without a reservation and requests a room.

Review Questions

1. What is the purpose of a hotel's mission statement? What are the three groups of people whose interests should be addressed in a hotel mission statement?

2. How do a hotel's goals relate to its mission statement and to departmental and divisional goals and strategies?

3. How does an organization chart show employee reporting and consulting relationships? Why should an organization chart be flexible?

4. Which hotel departments and divisions are typically classified as revenue centers? Why?

5. Which hotel departments and divisions are typically classified as support centers? Why?

6. What main divisions are typically found in the organization of a full-service hotel?

7. How may a limited-service hotel differ in its organization from a full-service hotel?

8. How does the front office interact with the rest of the rooms division and the other main divisions in a full-service hotel?

9. Why is it impossible for some front offices to divide employee duties according to function?

10. What are the three traditional front office work shifts? What variations on the traditional workweek might a hotel adopt?

11. How are job descriptions typically used? How do they differ from job specifications?

Internet Sites

For more information, visit the following Internet sites. Remember that Internet addresses can change without notice. If the site is no longer there, you can use a search engine to look for additional sites.

Americans with Disabilities Act (ADA)   Les Clefs d'Or (USA)
www.ada.gov   www.lcdusa.org

Case Study

Dark Days at Sunnyvale: Can Teamwork Part the Clouds?

The Sunnyvale Resort is a 300-room luxury property with a lake on one side and a golf course, riding stables, and tennis courts on the other. Once considered the premier resort of the South, the rich (both old and new money) considered it fashionable to winter at Sunnyvale back in the twenties and thirties. However, by the sixties, its glory had begun to fade and so had its revenues. In 1978, the resort added fifty suites and 20,000 square feet of meeting space in an effort to attract group business. This helped for a time, but in the last five years both occupancy and room rates were caught in a seemingly unstoppable decline. Recently, the resort lost a star in the travel guides and was now listed as a three-star property.

Losing a star spurred Thomas Redgrave to take action. Mr. Redgrave was the resort's owner, and he was not happy that a property that should be making $15 to $16 million a year in revenue had grossed less than $12 million in each of the last two years. He gave the general manager, who had been with the resort since 1977, a nice farewell dinner and a gold watch, then hired Ken Richards, an experienced general manager from a convention hotel in Richmond, to come in and turn things around.

At a meeting with Ken, Mr. Redgrave summed up the situation as he saw it. "I'd like to renovate Sunnyvale and really bring it back to where it ought to be. As a businessman, I know sometimes you have to spend money to make money. But I'd have to put several million dollars into the place to do it right. The way things are going at Sunnyvale right now, I'm not sure I'd get the kind of return on investment that I should.

"The last general manager was here long before I bought the place and he didn't communicate with me very much. I try to be a 'hands-off' owner and I gave him plenty of room, but for the last few years the numbers have been bad and getting worse, and he didn't seem to know what to do about it. I'll be honest—I don't know that much about the hotel business. But that's why I hired you. I want you to find out what's wrong and get the revenues back up to where they should be. If I see signs that you've got Sunnyvale back on track, I'll open the purse strings. It'll take some time, but we'll make everything at Sunnyvale first-class again. That'll make me happy, and down the road it'll make your job a whole lot easier."

From his experience at other properties, Ken knew that low occupancy and low rates were not the resort's real problems, only the symptoms. His first inspections of the property revealed quite a few minor blemishes—walls that needed painting, leaky showerheads, thin carpets, and so on. In fact, the entire resort, even the relatively new suites and meeting spaces, had an air of genteel shabbiness. But, more importantly, Ken took time during his first week to meet one-on-one with all of Sunnyvale's managers. He especially wanted to learn all he could about his department heads before calling his first executive staff meeting next Monday morning.

Skip Keener, the resort's director of sales, had been with Sunnyvale for over forty years and fondly remembered the resort's glory days. "When I first got here, the property sold itself," he told Ken. "Never had a problem filling the place up. We were featured in *Southern Living* magazine practically every year. But all of a sudden we fell out of fashion, and then in the seventies they put in all that meeting space that I have to sell to groups like vacuum-cleaner salesmen, the Kentucky Aluminum Siding Association, and the North Carolina Association of Used Car Dealers. This is the kind of business that keeps us going now. I tell you, the place sure isn't what it used to be."

The resort's executive housekeeper, Ruth Harless, had been with the property for almost thirty years and she missed the glory days, too. "It was a slower pace back then," she said. "Guests stayed longer—ten days, two weeks, even a month or more. You got to know them and they got to know you. Now, most guests are here for a big meeting and are out in two or three nights. It's 'rush, rush, rush.'" Ken learned that Ruth's reputation for upholding cleaning standards was not what it used to be. The comments he heard were: "She used to be a real stickler for detail—every room was spotless, but there's no denying that the rooms just aren't as clean anymore." Ken also learned that Ruth had stopped attending executive staff meetings years ago. "I don't have time," was her excuse.

Bob Ruggles was the resort's chief engineer. Since he had been with the property for "only" eleven years, Skip and Ruth still considered him "the new guy." "I don't know why, but I just never hit it off with them," he lamented to Ken. He also lamented the fact that, because the resort was old, every day he faced a large number of minor maintenance problems. "If it's not the plumbing, it's the electrical. If it's not the electrical, it's the HVAC system acting up. It's always something. I run to put out one 'fire' and two more take its place. I can't catch up."

The reservations manager, Teresa Mansfield, had been with the resort for three years and she was also considered a "newcomer." No one on the executive staff went out of the way to talk to her. One assistant manager from another department told Ken that "she seems angry about something all the time, but she never says much." Her complaint was that she was left out of the decision-making at the resort and was expected to just do as she was told. Skip frequently sold more rooms than were allocated to group sales, for example, without telling her. "I don't know exactly what rooms I can sell from one day to the next," she lamented.

The last, and newest, member of the executive staff was Jon Younger, the resort's food and beverage director. He had arrived at the property just six months ago, after the previous F&B director of twenty-eight years, Abe Williams, had retired. Unfortunately, Abe had chosen to coast into retirement, and the department's performance had declined during the last three years of his tenure. Smart and ambitious, Jon had tried to whip the F&B staff back into shape and restore the resort's reputation for F&B excellence, but his opportunities to shine had been few. Skip, the director of sales, had received so many F&B complaints from clients during Abe's last years that he had begun to book most of the big F&B group functions off-site, and "comp" a lot of the minor ones he allowed the resort's F&B department to handle (a complimentary cocktail party for a group's first night was a favorite giveaway). Jon had asked Skip to book more F&B functions in-house and had lobbied the previous general manager for support, but had made no headway. In his early thirties and feeling the pressure of his first job as a department head, Jon had become defensive and abrasive in his dealings with Skip and the others.

By Friday of Ken's first week, Sunnyvale's major difficulties were coming into focus. The sales department was so busy bringing in business that it wasn't communicating with the rest of the staff like it should. The result was confusion, poor service, and dissatisfied guests. To entice dissatisfied guests back to the resort, the sales staff was constantly lowering room rates. It was a downward spiral that Ken had to find a way to stop.

Next Monday morning, Ken began his first staff meeting by reassuring his department heads that the owner was committed to the resort's long-term health. "Mr. Redgrave wants to put a lot of money into the place and make it a four-star property again, but first he wants to see that we can turn the rates and occupancy around and beef up the bottom line. I'm committed to taking action quickly and I know all of you want to makes things better, too." Ken picked up a pen and a legal pad and surveyed the managers gathered around the table. "I've looked at the reports," he nodded toward a stack of papers on the table in front of him, "but I'm interested in hearing what all of you think. Does anyone have any ideas about why the revenue's been down the past few years?"

Silence hung over the room while the department heads looked at the table or shot sidelong glances at each other. Finally, Jon Younger spoke up. "I think a big problem is that we're giving too much F&B business away." Another silence descended on the group.

"Yes," Ken agreed after a while, trying to prompt more comments, "I noticed in the financial statements that the F&B lines seem very low for a resort of this size. What's going on there?"

"Well, I hate to say it," Skip said, "but I got so many complaints from clients that I finally decided I'd better send them off-site for F&B. I've lined up a few outside caterers that do a good job for me, and just up the road there's the Mountainview Gourmet Steakhouse. I send groups up there and they get steaks bigger than their plates, servers in Wild West costumes, skits and 'gunfights' and other entertainment while they eat—they love it."

"The problem with that," Jon said sharply, "is that Skip's not giving me a chance to show what I can do. Those complaints he's talking about happened back when Abe was here. And we're getting killed with all the comps he's giving away. Every group that comes in gets a comp cocktail party the first night, which wipes out the restaurant's dinner sales because everybody goes to the party and scarfs down the heavy hors d'oeuvres and free booze. Why not a banquet the first night? That's high-profit business that we really need."

"What about that, Skip?" Ken asked.

"Well, all I can say is that it's hard when a client looks you in the eye and says, 'Last time we booked here, the banquet was terrible—eight of my people stood around embarrassed because you under-set by eight places, you forgot the ice sculpture, the soup was cold, the entrées were late and most of them were cold, too, and I had to listen to my people griping about it the entire time I was here. So if you want me back you're gonna have to do something different.' A lot of my clients come back every year or two, and they remember the things that went wrong the last time."

Ken made a note on his pad. "But the problems your clients refer to didn't happen on Jon's watch, is that right?"

"True," Skip said. "But I still have to fight the perception that we can't deliver quality F&B."

Another silence descended on the group. Ken turned to Teresa. "What problems do you see in the reservations area?"

Teresa swallowed hard. It wasn't her usual style to speak up, but this might be the best time to get things out in the open with the new general manager. "Well, one thing that could be better," she began, "is that I'm never sure how many rooms Skip has sold, so occasionally I've had to turn guests away because of overbookings. But much more often we've suffered from 'underbookings.' That's when Skip asks for more rooms than he really needs, rooms I could have sold, but they stand empty because he blocked them off and then didn't need them for his groups. That happens a lot more than it should.

"It's also hard to have to sell the less-desirable rooms all the time," Teresa continued. "Skip tends to use up the suites and the nicer guestrooms—even the ones allocated to me—with his groups. To make it worse, I'm under pressure to sell those less-desirable rooms at a premium. The budget calls for a group rate of $150, but a lot of the time Skip gives groups a $120 rate. This pressures me to sell my allotment of rooms at an even higher rate than my budgeted target of $170 per room. That's hard to do when all the rooms that are left are at the end of the hall, or next to the laundry, or the ones with no view."

Skip crossed his arms over his chest. "Groups should get a break, especially with the kind of service they usually get around here. And part of your paycheck isn't riding on how many rooms you sell, like mine is. If you think it's easy selling ten thousand rooms a year, try it sometime!"

Ken turned to Skip. "You had to meet a 'rooms sold' target, not a revenue target?"

"Correct. No bonus unless I sold ten thousand rooms. It's not easy, especially when there's problems—VIPs standing in the lobby because their suites aren't ready, for example. Do you have any idea how hard it is to sell somebody the next time, when the first thing that happens to Mr. Bigshot is that he has to cool his heels in the lobby while his room is cleaned? Instead of getting ushered up to his nice suite and feeling pampered, he gets ticked off."

"Wait a minute," Ruth interrupted. "Whenever that happens, I always pull room attendants off their regular rooms so they can blitz through the suites and get them ready."

"Ready?" Skip snorted. "They're never as 'ready' as they should be! If I had a nickel for every time the fresh flowers and fruit baskets weren't placed in the suites like they're supposed to be—"

"I get them in the rooms every time I'm notified," Jon interjected.

"You're right, Jon, sometimes I forget to tell you," Ruth said defensively, "but I have my hands full just trying to 'rush rush rush' to get everything clean and get my crew back on their regular duties. It disrupts the entire day."

"What about the cleaning problems?" Skip asked Ruth. "It's embarrassing when the president of a state association comes to me—this happened just two weeks ago—and tells me his wife found a hairball in the bathtub drain and is afraid to take a shower now."

"What do you expect when you tell people they can check in at noon, when check-out time is noon, too?" Ruth said. "We're not given time to do a proper job."

"Does that happen a lot?" Ken asked. "I mean, people wanting to check in to suites that people have just checked out of?"

"All the time," Ruth said.

"So you have to do these 'cleaning blitzes' pretty often?" Ken laid a hand on the reports in front of him. "I noticed that housekeeping's labor costs are pretty high—all those blitzes helps explain that."

"They certainly happen more often than they should," Ruth replied. "And you're right, it's costly, because my crew has to stay later to finish their regular assignments. The overtime adds up."

"The guest complaints add up, too," Teresa said. "When Ruth pulls her crew from their regular assignments to blitz the suites, the regular guestrooms aren't getting done. So they get cleaned late, and those guests end up inconvenienced and unhappy. So the guest dissatisfaction ripples down through the entire resort."

"Also," Ruth added, "when you have ten minutes to try to whip a room into shape, you intentionally skip over some things and miss others, so the constant blitzing doesn't do my housekeepers any good, either. They start to get sloppy even when they aren't rushed. Some of them figure if a quick touch-up is okay for a VIP suite, it's okay for a regular guestroom, too. I really have to fight that attitude with some of my crew."

"We've got to plan a little better in the future," Ken said, scribbling in his legal pad.

"It's hard to plan when you don't get much advance notice about groups coming in or what their needs are," Teresa said pointedly, looking at Skip.

"It's one of the reasons I can never catch up," Bob chimed in. "I never know what's going on, either. I just get calls all the time: 'Leaky toilet in Room 113.' 'The guest in Suite 27 turned on the air conditioning and nothing happened.' Fine. I ask for the rooms for five days, then suddenly they have to be sold because a big group's coming in. The repairs aren't made, guests complain, and I get chewed out."

"And I have to lower the rates next time for that group," Skip said. "I call the client and he says a bunch of my people were unhappy last time, why should I come back? So I give him a break on the rates, comp the coffee breaks, breakfasts, what have you, to try to get him to come back for another year. Sometimes it works, and sometimes I lose a group."

"And my housekeepers are unhappy because they keep reporting maintenance problems that never get fixed," Ruth said. "They ask me why, and I don't know what to tell them, because I'm never told why either."

"If you would talk to me once in a while, I'd be glad to tell you," Bob said. "It's not all my fault. I can't get any cooperation out of anybody."

"Do you really need five days every time?" Teresa asked. "Cooperation is a two-way street, you know. Sometimes it's hard to keep a room 'out of order' that long."

"I'd like to have five days. I don't see why it's such a big deal."

"One room out for five days is not a big deal," Skip said, "but you keep adding rooms to your list, so eventually it gets to be a big deal."

Ken held up his hands to halt the discussion, then surveyed the group over steepled fingers. "Obviously there's a lot of frustration in this room. You're frustrated because you want to get your jobs done, but your co-workers—instead of helping you—are sometimes getting in the way. This not only frustrates you, it frustrates our guests as well, because they're not receiving the service they should." Ken paused. "You're not getting in each other's way on purpose, or because you want to make someone else's life miserable," Ken smiled. "I just think you're all too focused on your own areas and aren't seeing the big picture.

"From what I've heard today, I'd say our biggest problem is that we're not talking to each other. We've got to learn to communicate better so we can serve each other and our guests better. More communication will help bring the bigger picture into focus for everybody.

"I want to show Mr. Redgrave some positive changes within ninety days," Ken continued. "With that in mind, I'd like all of you to come to next Monday's staff meeting with ideas on how you can improve communication and work together better as a team. I'll think about it as well, and come to the meeting prepared with recommendations for each of you. I think teamwork will be the key to doing a better job of satisfying our guests and moving revenues in a positive direction."

Discussion Questions

1. What are the problems that each department experiences because of poor communication among the executive staff?

2. What recommendations can Ken make to each of the resort's department heads to help them work together as a team?

3. What actions should Ken take if his department heads, after a suitable period of time, don't seem to be coming together as a team?

4. What can Ken show Sunnyvale's owner in the next ninety days to demonstrate that the resort is making progress?

Case Number: 3322CA

The following industry experts helped generate and develop this case: Richard M. Brooks, CHA, Vice President, TWE Group; and S. Kenneth Hiller, CHA, General Manager, Holiday Inn, Beachwood, Ohio.

Chapter Appendix

Selected Front Office Model Job Descriptions

Cross-training front office employees has helped standardize procedures in many hotels. In a small hotel, for instance, one employee may handle reservations, registration, switchboard, and check-out tasks. Lines of responsibility have also blurred, as more and more properties adopt computerized front office recordkeeping systems. These systems can combine information required for most front office tasks in a common database that can be accessed by many front office employees.

Many hotels refer to front office employees as *front office agents, guest service representatives,* or something similar. Even in hotels with a traditional division of duties, the titles for each position may change over time. These changes may reflect a reevaluation of the tasks involved or an attempt to avoid the negativity associated with certain titles. The position titles that were used in this chapter represent trends in the lodging industry. This appendix presents generic model job descriptions for typical front office positions found in a mid-size hotel.

JOB DESCRIPTION

POSITION TITLE: FRONT OFFICE MANAGER

REPORTS TO: Assistant Manager or General Manager

POSITION SUMMARY: Directly supervises all front office personnel and ensures proper completion of all front office duties. Directs and coordinates the activities of the front desk, reservations, guest services, and telephone areas.

DUTIES AND RESPONSIBILITIES:

1. Participates in the selection of front office personnel.
2. Trains, cross-trains, and retrains all front office personnel.
3. Schedules the front office staff.
4. Supervises workloads during shifts.
5. Evaluates the job performance of each front office employee.
6. Maintains working relationships and communicates with all departments.
7. Maintains master key control.
8. Verifies that accurate room status information is maintained and properly communicated.
9. Resolves guest problems quickly, efficiently, and courteously.
10. Updates group information. Maintains, monitors, and prepares group requirements. Relays information to appropriate personnel.
11. Reviews and completes credit limit report.
12. Works within the allotted budget for the front office.
13. Receives information from the previous shift manager and passes on pertinent details to the oncoming manager.
14. Checks cashiers in and out and verifies banks and deposits at the end of each shift.
15. Enforces all cash-handling, check-cashing, and credit policies.
16. Conducts regularly scheduled meetings of front office personnel.
17. Wears the proper uniform at all times. Requires all front office employees to wear proper uniforms at all times.
18. Upholds the hotel's commitment to hospitality.

PREREQUISITES:

Education: Minimum of two-year college degree. Must be able to speak, read, write, and understand the primary language(s) used in the workplace. Must be able to speak and understand the primary language(s) used by guests who visit the workplace.

Experience: Minimum of one year of hotel front-desk supervisory experience, experience handling cash, accounting procedures, and general administrative tasks.

Physical: Requires fingering, grasping, writing, standing, sitting, walking, repetitive motions, verbal communications, and visual acuity.

JOB DESCRIPTION

POSITION TITLE: FRONT DESK AGENT

REPORTS TO: Front Office Manager

POSITION SUMMARY: Represents the hotel to the guest throughout all stages of the guest's stay. Determines a guest's reservation status and identifies how long the guest will stay. Helps guests complete registration cards and then assigns rooms, accommodating special requests whenever possible. Verifies the guest's method of payment and follows established credit-checking procedures. Places guest and room information in the appropriate front desk racks and communicates this information to the appropriate hotel personnel. Works closely with the housekeeping department in keeping room status reports up to date and coordinates requests for maintenance and repair work. Maintains guest room key storage, and maintains and supervises access to safe deposit boxes. Must be sales-minded. Presents options and alternatives to guests and offers assistance in making choices. Knows the location and types of available rooms as well as the activities and services of the property.

DUTIES AND RESPONSIBILITIES:

1. Registers guests and assigns rooms. Accommodates special requests whenever possible.
2. Assists in preregistration and blocking of rooms for reservations.
3. Thoroughly understands and adheres to proper credit, check-cashing, and cash-handling policies and procedures.
4. Understands room status and room status tracking.
5. Knows room locations, types of rooms available, and room rates.
6. Uses suggestive selling techniques to sell rooms and to promote other services of the hotel.
7. Coordinates room status updates with the housekeeping department by notifying housekeeping of all check-outs, late check-outs, early check-ins, special requests, and part-day rooms.
8. Possesses a working knowledge of the reservations department. Takes same day reservations and future reservations when necessary. Knows cancellation procedures.
9. Files room keys.
10. Knows how to use front office equipment.
11. Processes guest check-outs.
12. Posts and files all charges to guest, master, and city ledger accounts.
13. Follows procedures for issuing and closing safe deposit boxes used by guests.
14. Uses proper telephone etiquette.
15. Uses proper mail, package, and message handling procedures.
16. Reads and initials the pass-on log and bulletin board daily. Is aware of daily activities and meetings taking place in the hotel.

(continued)

FRONT DESK AGENT *(continued)*

17. Attends department meetings.

18. Coordinates guest room maintenance work with the engineering and maintenance division.

19. Reports any unusual occurrences or requests to the manager or assistant manager.

20. Knows all safety and emergency procedures. Is aware of accident prevention policies.

21. Maintains the cleanliness and neatness of the front desk area.

22. Understands that business demands sometimes make it necessary to move employees from their accustomed shift to other shifts.

PREREQUISITES:

Education: High school graduate or equivalent. Must be able to speak, read, write, and understand the primary language(s) used in the workplace. Must be able to speak and understand the primary language(s) used by guests who visit the workplace.

Experience: Previous hotel-related experience desired.

Physical: Requires fingering, grasping, writing, standing, sitting, walking, repetitive motions, hearing, and visual acuity, and may on occasion have to lift and carry up to 40 pounds.

JOB DESCRIPTION

POSITION TITLE: RESERVATIONS AGENT

REPORTS TO: Front Office Manager

POSITION SUMMARY: Responds to communications from guests, travel agents, and referral networks concerning reservations arriving by mail, telephone, telex, cable, fax, or through a central reservation system. Creates and maintains reservation records—usually by date of arrival and alphabetical listing. Prepares letters of confirmation and promptly processes any cancellations and modifications. Tracks future room availabilities on the basis of reservations, and helps develop forecasts for room revenue and occupancy. Additional duties may include preparing the list of expected arrivals for the front office, assisting in preregistration activities when appropriate, and processing advance reservation deposits. Knows the types of rooms the hotel has as well as their location and layout. Knows of all hotel package plans—meaning status, rates, and benefits.

DUTIES AND RESPONSIBILITIES:

1. Processes reservations by mail, telephone, telex, cable, fax, or central reservation systems referral.
2. Processes reservations from the sales office, other hotel departments, and travel agents.
3. Knows the types of rooms available as well as their location and layout.
4. Knows the selling status, rates, and benefits of all package plans.
5. Knows the credit policy of the hotel and how to code each reservation.
6. Creates and maintains reservation records by date of arrival and alphabetical listing.
7. Determines room rates based on the selling tactics of the hotel.
8. Prepares letters of confirmation.
9. Communicates reservation information to the front desk.
10. Processes cancellations and modifications and promptly relays this information to the front desk.
11. Understands the hotel's policy on guaranteed reservations and no-shows.
12. Processes advance deposits on reservations.
13. Tracks future room availabilities on the basis of reservations.
14. Helps develop room revenue and occupancy forecasts.
15. Prepares expected arrival lists for front office use.
16. Assists in preregistration activities when appropriate.
17. Monitors advance deposit requirements.
18. Handles daily correspondence. Responds to inquiries and makes reservations as needed.
19. Makes sure that files are kept up to date.

(continued)

RESERVATIONS AGENT *(continued)*

20. Maintains a clean and neat appearance and work area at all times.
21. Promotes goodwill by being courteous, friendly, and helpful to guests, managers, and fellow employees.

PREREQUISITES:

Education: High school graduate or equivalent. Must be able to speak, read, write, and understand the primary language(s) used in the workplace. Must be able to speak and understand the primary language(s) used by guests who visit the workplace.

Experience: Previous hotel-related experience desirable.

Physical: Requires fingering, grasping, writing, standing, sitting, walking, repetitive motions, hearing, visual acuity, and good speaking skills.

JOB DESCRIPTION

POSITION TITLE: FRONT OFFICE CASHIER

REPORTS TO: Front Office Manager

POSITION SUMMARY: Posts revenue center charges to guest accounts. Receives payment from guests at check-out. Coordinates the billing of credit card and direct-billed guest accounts with the accounting division. All guest accounts are balanced by the cashier at the close of each shift. Front office cashiers assume responsibility for any cash used in processing front desk transactions. May also perform a variety of banking services for guests, such as check cashing and foreign currency exchange.

DUTIES AND RESPONSIBILITIES:

1. Operates front office posting equipment.
2. Obtains the house bank and keeps it balanced.
3. Completes cashier pre-shift supply checklist.
4. Takes departmental machine readings at the beginning of the shift.
5. Completes guest check-in procedures.
6. Posts charges to guest accounts.
7. Handles paid-outs.
8. Transfers guest balances to other accounts as required.
9. Cashes checks for guests following the approval policy.
10. Completes guest check-out procedures.
11. Settles guest accounts.
12. Handles cash, traveler's checks, personal checks, credit cards, and direct billing requests properly.
13. Posts non-guest ledger payments.
14. Makes account adjustments.
15. Disperses guest records upon check-out.
16. Transfers folios paid by credit card to each credit card's master file.
17. Transfers folios charged to the non-guest ledger to each company's master file.
18. Balances department totals at the close of the shift.
19. Balances cash at the close of the shift.
20. Manages safe deposit boxes.

PREREQUISITES:

Education: High school graduate or equivalent desired. Must be able to speak, read, write, and understand the primary language(s) used in the workplace.

Experience: Previous hotel-related experience beneficial.

Physical: Requires fingering, grasping, writing, standing, sitting, walking, repetitive motions, hearing, and visual acuity. Must possess basic computational ability.

JOB DESCRIPTION

POSITION TITLE: HOTEL SWITCHBOARD OPERATOR

REPORTS TO: Front Office Manager

POSITION SUMMARY: Speaks clearly, distinctly, and with a friendly, courteous tone. Uses listening skills to put callers at ease and obtains accurate, complete information. Answers incoming calls and directs them to guestrooms through the switchboard (PBX) system or to hotel personnel or departments. Takes and distributes messages for guests, provides information on guest services, and answers inquiries about public hotel events. Provides a paging service for hotel guests and employees. Processes guest wake-up calls.

DUTIES AND RESPONSIBILITIES:

1. Answers incoming calls.
2. Directs calls to guestrooms, staff, or departments through the switchboard or PBX system.
3. Places outgoing calls.
4. Receives telephone charges from the telephone company and forwards charges to the front desk for posting.
5. Takes and distributes messages for guests.
6. Logs all wake-up call requests and performs wake-up call services.
7. Provides information about guest services to guests.
8. Answers questions about hotel events and activities.
9. Understands PBX switchboard operations.
10. Provides paging services for hotel guests and employees.
11. Knows what action to take when an emergency call is requested or received.
12. Monitors automated systems including fire alarms and telephone equipment when the engineering and maintenance department is closed.

PREREQUISITES:

Education: High school graduate or equivalent. Must be able to speak and understand the primary language(s) used by guests who visit the workplace.

Experience: Previous hotel-related experience desirable.

Physical: Requires fingering, grasping, writing, standing, sitting, walking, repetitive motions, hearing, visual acuity, and good verbal skills.

JOB DESCRIPTION

POSITION TITLE: NIGHT AUDITOR

REPORTS TO: Front Office Manager or Accounting Department

POSITION SUMMARY: Checks front office accounting records for accuracy and, on a daily basis, summarizes and compiles information for the hotel's financial records. Tracks room revenues, occupancy percentages, and other front office operating statistics. Prepares a summary of cash, check, and credit card activities, reflecting the hotel's financial performance for the day. Posts room charges and room taxes to guest accounts including guest transactions not posted during the day by the front office cashier. Processes guest charge vouchers and credit card vouchers. Verifies all account postings and balances made during the day by front desk cashiers and agents. Monitors the current status of coupon, discount, and other promotional programs. Is able to function as a front desk agent especially in terms of check-in and check-out procedures.

DUTIES AND RESPONSIBILITIES:

1. Posts room charges and taxes to guest accounts.
2. Processes guest charge vouchers and credit card vouchers.
3. Posts guest charge purchase transactions not posted by the front office cashier.
4. Transfers charges and deposits to master accounts.
5. Verifies all account postings and balances.
6. Monitors the current status of coupon, discount, and other promotional programs.
7. Tracks room revenues, occupancy percentages, and other front office statistics.
8. Prepares a summary of cash, check, and credit card activities.
9. Summarizes results of operations for management.
10. Understands principles of auditing, balancing, and closing out accounts.
11. Knows how to operate posting machines, typewriters, and other front office equipment and computers.
12. Understands and knows how to perform check-in and check-out procedures.

PREREQUISITES:

Education: Minimum of a two-year college degree. Must be able to speak, read, write, and understand the primary language(s) used in the workplace. Must be able to speak and understand the primary language(s) used by guests who visit the workplace.

Experience: Minimum of one year of hotel front desk supervisory experience, experience handling cash, accounting procedures, and general administrative tasks.

Physical: Requires fingering, grasping, writing, standing, sitting, walking, repetitive motions, verbal communications, and visual acuity.

JOB DESCRIPTION

POSITION TITLE: GUEST SERVICES MANAGER

REPORTS TO: General Manager/Front Office Manager

POSITION SUMMARY: Oversees all guest services operations, including front desk, reservations, PBX, bell staff, and transportation services to ensure quality and guest satisfaction.

DUTIES AND RESPONSIBILITIES:

1. Answers letters of inquiry regarding rates and availability.
2. Trains new Guest Services department personnel.
3. Maintains a thorough knowledge of the room rack locations, types of rooms, room rack operations, package plans, and discounts.
4. Maintains a detailed knowledge about the hotel's services and hours of operations.
5. Oversees servicing and security of the safe deposit boxes.
6. Knows all safety and understands emergency procedures and how to act upon them. Understands accident prevention policies.
7. Knows cash handling procedures. Files and posts all changes to guest master and city ledger account.
8. Possesses a thorough knowledge of credit and check-cashing policies and procedures and adheres to them.
9. Anticipates and intervenes in all incidents of guest dissatisfaction and attempts to satisfy all such guests, within hotel policy.
10. Develops and maintains all aspects of the hotel's reservations system directed toward the maximization of profit.

PREREQUISITES:

Education: Minimum of a two year college degree. Ability to speak and understand the primary language(s) used by guests who visit the workplace. Ability to speak, read, write, and understand the primary language(s) used in the workplace.

Experience: Minimum one year of hotel front-desk supervisory experience, experience handling cash, account procedures, and general administrative tasks.

Physical: Requires fingering, grasping, writing, standing, sitting, walking, repetitive motions, verbal communications, and visual acuity.

JOB DESCRIPTION

POSITION TITLE: CONCIERGE

REPORTS TO: **Front Office Manager**

POSITION SUMMARY: Serves as the guest's liaison for both hotel and non-hotel services. Functions are an extension of front desk agent duties. Assists the guest, regardless of whether inquiries concern in-hotel or off-premises attractions, facilities, services, or activities. Knows how to provide concise and accurate directions. Makes reservations and obtains tickets for flights, the theater, or special events. Organizes special functions such as VIP cocktail receptions. Arranges for secretarial services.

DUTIES AND RESPONSIBILITIES:

1. Develops a strong knowledge of the hotel's facilities and services and of the surrounding community.
2. Provides guests with directions to attractions or facilities in or outside the property.
3. Provides guests with information about attractions, facilities, services, and activities in or outside the property.
4. Makes guest reservations for air or other forms of transportation when requested. Obtains necessary itinerary and tickets.
5. Makes guest reservations for the theater and other forms of entertainment when requested. Obtains necessary tickets and provides directions to facilities.
6. Organizes special functions as directed by management.
7. Arranges secretarial and other office services.
8. Coordinates guest requests for special services or equipment with the appropriate department.
9. Contacts roomed guests periodically to ascertain any special needs.
10. Handles guest complaints and solves problems to the degree possible.

PREREQUISITES:

Education: Minimum of two years college education with emphasis in business, sales, or marketing. Must be able to speak, read, write, and understand the primary language(s) used in the workplace and by guests who visit the workplace.

Experience: Minimum of two years sales experience with a minimum of one year supervisory experience.

Physical: Requires bending, stooping, climbing, standing, walking, sitting, fingering, reaching, grasping, lifting, carrying, repetitive motions, visual acuity, hearing, writing, and speaking. Must exert well-paced mobility to reach other departments of the hotel on a timely basis.

Chapter 3 Outline

Competencies

1. Summarize front office operations during the four stages of the guest cycle. (pp. 103–110)

2. Describe front office recordkeeping systems and front office documents. (pp. 110–115)

3. Describe the front desk and its support devices, and describe the services and equipment of a hotel's telecommunications area. (pp. 115–122)

4. Identify and describe property management systems used by the front office. (pp. 122–129)

3

Front Office Operations

$\mathbf{A}$LL THE FUNCTIONS, ACTIVITIES, AND AREAS of the front office are geared toward supporting guest transactions and services. Critical to the success of the department and the hotel are appropriately designed and used front office work areas, equipment, forms, and reports. Also paramount is the accurate planning and monitoring of front office transactions.

To many guests, the front office *is* the hotel. It is the main contact point for nearly every guest service the hotel provides. This chapter examines front office operations in terms of the various stages of a guest's stay, referred to as the guest cycle. Discussion focuses on the various forms, work space designs, equipment, related tasks, and automated applications appropriate to each stage.

The Guest Cycle

The financial transactions a guest makes while staying at a hotel determine the flow of business through the property. Traditionally, the flow of business can be divided into a four-stage **guest cycle.** Exhibit 1 diagrams these four stages: pre-arrival, arrival, occupancy, and departure. Within each stage, important tasks related to guest services and guest accounting can be identified and analyzed.

The guest cycle in Exhibit 1 is not an inflexible standard. Since activities and functions tend to overlap between stages, some properties have revised this traditional guest cycle into a sequence of pre-sale, point-of-sale, and post-sale events. For automated properties, this revised sequence significantly improves coordination among hotel operating departments. Regardless of the number of stages, the guest cycle identifies a logical sequence of hotel-guest interactions.

Front office employees need to be aware of guest services and guest accounting activities at all stages of the guest stay. Front office employees can efficiently serve guest needs when they clearly understand the flow of business through the hotel. Exhibit 2 indicates which front office personnel are most likely to serve the guest during each stage of the guest cycle. The guest cycle also suggests a systematic approach to managing front office operations.

Pre-Arrival

The guest chooses a hotel during the *pre-arrival stage* of the guest cycle. The guest's choice can be affected by many factors. The type of travel is often an important factor. People traveling on business may be more concerned about convenience than price. People traveling for vacation or personal reasons are more likely to be cost-conscious, since they are paying the bill. They also may be more flexible

Exhibit 1   The Guest Cycle and Related Front Office Functions

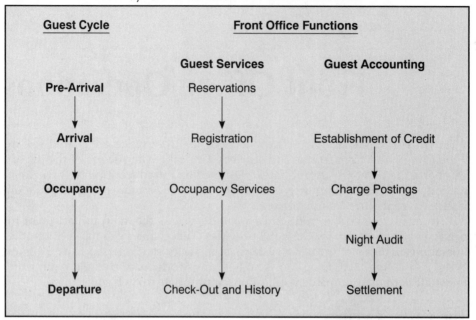

Exhibit 2   Interaction During the Guest Cycle

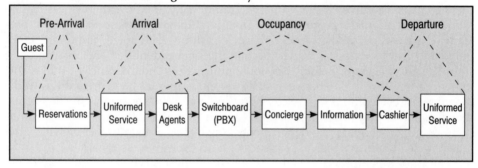

about where they travel and the hotels they stay in; the popularity of Internet sites offering deeply discounted hotel rooms for vacation travelers willing to be flexible about where and when they travel is certainly evidence of that. In addition to the type of travel, guests must consider such factors as previous experiences with the hotel; advertisements and promotions; company travel policy; recommendations from travel agents, friends, or business associates; the hotel's location and reputation; frequent traveler rewards programs; and preconceptions based upon the hotel's name or chain affiliation. The guest's decision may also be influenced by the ease of making reservations and how the hotel's reservations agent or website describes the hotel and its facilities, room rates, and amenities. In reality, the reservations department is the sales office for the hotel's non-group business.

Its employees must be sales-oriented and present a positive, strong image of the hotel. The front office staff's attitude, efficiency, and knowledge may influence a caller's decision to stay at a particular hotel. Similarly, the ease with which a guest can navigate the hotel's website can be a contributing factor in property selection.

A reservations agent must be able to respond quickly and accurately to requests for future accommodations. The proper handling of reservation information can be critical to the success of a lodging property. Efficient procedures allow more time for the reservations agent to capture needed information and to market hotel services.

If a reservation request matches room availability in the reservation system, the request can be accepted, and the reservations agent creates an electronic **reservation record.** The creation of a reservation record initiates the hotel guest cycle. This record enables the hotel to personalize guest service and appropriately schedule necessary staff and facilities. By confirming a reservation, the hotel verifies a guest's room request and personal information, and assures the guest that his or her lodging needs will be addressed. Using the information collected during the reservations process, a **property management system (PMS),** the term used for a hotel's main computer system (discussed in more detail later in the chapter), may be able to initiate pre-registration applications. Such pre-registration functions include automatically assigning a specific room and rate to guests who have not yet registered, and creating an electronic **guest folio.** A guest folio is a record of the charges incurred and credits acquired by the guest during the guest cycle.

An automated reservation system helps maximize room sales by accurately monitoring room availabilities and forecasting rooms revenue. (To further maximize room sales, some of these systems are supplemented by revenue management systems.) By analyzing reservation transaction reports, front office management can develop a better understanding of the hotel's reservation patterns. Data collected during the reservations process become especially useful in subsequent front office functions. But, without a doubt, the most important outcome of an effective reservations process is having a room available when the guest arrives.

Arrival

The *arrival stage* of the guest cycle includes registration and rooming functions. After the guest arrives, he or she establishes a business and legal relationship with the hotel through the front office. It is the front office staff's responsibility to clarify the nature of the guest-hotel relationship and to monitor the financial transactions between the hotel and its guests.

Many guests arrive at the hotel entrance by private automobile, taxicab, or shuttle bus. The entrance is often the first place guests directly interact with hotel staffers. It is for this reason that world-class, upscale, convention, casino, and resort hotels typically station attentive uniformed staff there. Door attendants direct traffic in the hotel entrance, help guests unload luggage, open doors for arriving and departing guests, and provide directions and information about both on-premises and nearby points of interest. Valet parking staff members are often available to provide automotive parking assistance to guests not using self-park. Bell attendants, who are often stationed near the front door, escort guests with luggage to the front desk for registration. While a mid-scale, economy, or limited-services hotel might employ a small number of staff members to provide similar service, most do not.

The front desk agent should determine the guest's reservation status before beginning the registration process. Persons with reservations may have already undergone pre-registration activities. Persons without reservations, known as "walk-ins," present an opportunity for front desk agents to sell guestrooms. To sell successfully, the front desk agent must be very familiar with the hotel's room types, rates, and guest services and be able to describe them in a positive manner. A walk-in is not likely to register if he or she is not convinced of the value of renting a particular hotel room. Once a person has registered, whether they have a reservation or are a walk-in, they legally become a guest. Often, the hotel's property management system can be used to quickly identify available rooms and amenities. An electronic reservation record, created during the pre-registration application or at the time of check-in, is essential to efficient front office operation. A registration record includes information about the guest's intended method of payment, the planned length of stay, and any special guest needs such as roll-away bed or a child's crib. It should also include the guest's billing address, e-mail address, and telephone number.

When the guest presents a form of identification, it serves as proof of intent to establish an innkeeper-guest relationship. Presenting a valid payment card during registration, for example, is deemed evidence of the traveler's intent to become a guest. The innkeeper-guest relationship has many legal benefits for both the hotel and the guest. For example, the hotel obtains legal assurance of payment for the room and services provided, while the guest obtains legal assurance of personal safety while on the premises.

Gathering all requisite information in detail at the time of reservation and registration enhances the front office's ability to satisfy special guest needs, forecast room occupancies, and settle guest accounts properly. At check-out, the guest's registration record may also become the primary data source for creating a guest history record. This record is a collection of personal and financial information about a guest that can help the hotel in its subsequent marketing and sales efforts. It also provides a basis for facilitating online reservation or registration at the time of a return stay. The hotel's property management system has a predetermined formula (algorithm) that applies registration information to automatically assign a room type and rate for each guest. Room and rate assignment depend on reservation information (long-run availability) and room status (short-run availability) information. The housekeeping status of a room must be communicated to the front desk as soon as possible so that the property management system can maximize room assignments. Some common room status terminology is defined in Exhibit 3.

Hotel room types may range from a standard single guestroom to a luxurious suite. Exhibit 4 defines some typical hotel room types. Furnishings, amenities, and location within the property will tend to differentiate room rates within the same room type.

Front desk agents must also be sensitive to accessibility issues for guests with physical impairments. The Americans with Disabilities Act requires new

Exhibit 3   Room Status Terminology

During the guest's stay, the housekeeping status of the guestroom changes several times. The various terms defined are typical of the room status terminology of the lodging industry. Not every room status will occur for each guestroom during every stay.

Occupied: A guest is currently registered to the room.

Complimentary: The room is occupied, but the guest is assessed no charge for its use.

Stayover: The guest is not expected to check out today and will remain at least one more night.

On-change: The guest has departed, but the room has not yet been cleaned and readied for resale.

Do not disturb: The guest has requested not to be disturbed.

Sleep-out: A guest is registered to the room, but the bed has not been used.

Skipper: The guest has left the hotel without making arrangements to settle his or her account.

Sleeper: The guest has settled his or her account and left the hotel, but the front office staff has failed to properly update the room's status.

Vacant and ready: The room has been cleaned and inspected and is ready for an arriving guest.

Out-of-order: The room cannot be assigned to a guest. A room may be out-of-order for a variety of reasons, including the need for maintenance, refurbishing, and extensive cleaning.

Lock-out: The room has been locked so that the guest cannot re-enter until he or she is cleared by a hotel official.

DNCO (did not check out): The guest made arrangements to settle his or her account (and thus is not a skipper), but has left without informing the front office.

Due out: The room is expected to become vacant after the following day's check-out time.

Check-out: The guest has settled his or her account, returned the room keys, and left the hotel.

Late check-out: The guest has requested and is being allowed to check out later than the hotel's standard check-out time.

and renovated properties to be barrier-free in design. The term *barrier-free* means that facilities and accommodations must be designed with the disabled guest and visitor in mind. Some of the more prevalent features of barrier-free guestrooms are extra-wide doorways for wheelchairs (both entry doors and bathroom doors), extra-large bathrooms, grab bars beside the toilet and inside the bathtub area, roll-in showers for wheelchairs, lowered vanity countertops and extra height (knee space) under the sink, handles on doors and bathroom fixtures instead of knobs, and strobe lights and pillow shakers as part of the smoke and fire detection systems (for the hearing impaired). Other aspects of barrier-free design are addressed later in the chapter.

Exhibit 4   Room Type Definitions

The following room type definitions are common throughout the lodging industry.

Single: A room assigned to one person. May have one or more beds.

Double: A room assigned to two people. May have one or more beds.

Triple: A room assigned to three people. May have two or more beds.

Quad: A room assigned to four people. May have two or more beds.

Queen: A room with a queen-size bed. May be occupied by one or more people.

King: A room with a king-size bed. May be occupied by one or more people.

Twin: A room with two twin beds. May be occupied by one or more people.

Double-double: A room with two double (or perhaps queen) beds. May be occupied by one or more persons.

Studio: A room with a studio bed—a couch that can be converted into a bed. May also have an additional bed.

Mini-suite or junior suite: A single room with a bed and a sitting area. Sometimes the sleeping area is in a bedroom separate from the parlor or living room.

Suite: A parlor or living room connected to one or more bedrooms.

Connecting rooms: Rooms with individual entrance doors from the outside and a connecting door between. Guests can move between rooms without going through the hallway.

Adjoining rooms: Rooms with a common wall but no connecting door.

Adjacent rooms: Rooms close to each other, perhaps across the hall.

Once a registration record is created, the front desk agent turns his or her attention to identifying the guest's method of payment. The hotel guest accounting cycle depends on captured information to ensure deferred payment for rendered services. Whether the guest uses cash, personal check, credit card, debit card, travel voucher, smart card, or some alternative method of payment, the front office must take measures to ensure eventual payment. A proper credit check at the outset of a transaction greatly reduces the potential for subsequent settlement problems. If a guest has not secured management approval of credit before arriving at the property, the hotel might deny the guest's request for credit at the time of check-in.

Registration is complete once the guest has established his or her method of payment and departure date. The guest is issued a room key and allowed to proceed to the room without assistance, or a uniformed service employee may escort the guest to the room. When the guest arrives at the room, the occupancy stage of the guest cycle begins.

Occupancy

The manner in which the front office staff represents the hotel is important throughout the guest cycle, particularly during the *occupancy stage*. As the center of hotel activity, the front desk is responsible for coordinating guest services.

Among many services, the front desk provides the guest with information and supplies. The front office should respond to requests in a timely and accurate way to maximize guest satisfaction. A concierge may also be on staff to provide special guest services.

A major front office objective throughout the guest cycle is to encourage repeat visits. Sound guest relations are essential to this objective. Guest relations depend on clear, constructive communications between the front office, other hotel departments and divisions, and guests. The hotel must be aware of a guest complaint in order to resolve it. Front desk agents should carefully attend to guest concerns and try to seek satisfactory resolutions as quickly as possible.

Security is a primary front office concern throughout all stages of the guest cycle, especially during occupancy. Security issues likely to apply to front office employees include verifying guest identify and other information, and protecting guest funds and valuables.

Various transactions during the occupancy stage affect guest and hotel financial accounts. Most of these transactions will be automatically processed through property management system interfaces to revenue centers according to established posting and auditing procedures.

The room rate of the guestroom is usually the largest single charge on the guest's folio. Additional expenses can be charged to a guest's account if he or she established acceptable credit at the front desk during registration. Goods or services purchased from the hotel's restaurant, lounge, room service department, telephone department, transportation areas, gift shop, spa, and other revenue outlets may be charged to guest accounts. Many hotels establish a maximum limit on the amount that guests can charge to their accounts without partial settlement. This amount is usually referred to as the **house limit** and can be automatically monitored by the property management system. Guest accounts must be continually monitored to ensure that the house limit is not exceeded.

Front desk accounting records must be periodically reviewed for accuracy and completeness through a system audit, which can be programmed to run automatically at any time during the day. Even though automated properties *can* perform the audit at any time, they almost invariably follow the hotel tradition of performing the audit at night, since transaction volumes tend to be lower then, and most transactions occur earlier in the day.

Regardless of when the system audit takes place, room charges (room rates and room tax) are automatically posted to guest accounts as part of the audit routine. Other system audit tasks usually include: online verification of account postings, monitoring of accounts and credit limits, identification of discrepancies in room status, and the production of operating reports.

Departure

Guest services and guest accounting aspects of the guest cycle are completed during the cycle's fourth phase: *departure*. Effective front office monitoring includes processing the guest out of the hotel and creating a guest history file. The final element of guest accounting is settlement of the guest's account (by bringing the account to a zero balance).

At check-out, the guest vacates the room, receives an accurate statement of the settled account, returns the room keys, and leaves the hotel. Once the guest has checked out, the front office system automatically updates the room's availability status and closes the account.

During check-out, the front office staff should determine whether the guest was satisfied with the stay and encourage the guest to return to the hotel (or another property in the chain). The more information the hotel has about its guests, the better it can anticipate and serve their needs and develop marketing strategies to increase business. In addition, it is important for guests to leave with a positive impression of the hotel—it will definitely affect how they talk about the hotel to others and may be the determining factor in whether they return to the property in the future.

Most property management systems use registration records to automatically construct a **guest history file** when a guest checks out. A guest history file is a collection of guest history records. Information in a guest history file allows the hotel to better understand its clientele and provides a solid base for strategic marketing. Guest histories, including details of the guests' spending at the hotel, are usually sent electronically to the company's central database management system for processing and storage.

The purpose of account settlement is to collect money due the hotel before guest departure. Depending on the guest's credit arrangements, the guest will pay cash; use a credit card, debit card, or smart card; or apply pre-established direct billing instructions. Account balances should be verified and errors corrected before the guest leaves the hotel. Problems may occur in guest account settlement when charges are not posted to the guest's account until *after* the guest checks out. These charges are called **late charges.** Even if payment is eventually collected, the hotel usually incurs additional costs through billing the guest. In addition, this can irritate guests, who may have to submit incomplete expense accounts to their employers. The task of settling accounts with outstanding balances for departed guests is generally transferred to a back office system to be handled by the accounting department, not the front office. However, the front office is responsible for providing complete and accurate billing information to assist the accounting department in its collection efforts.

Once the guest has checked out, the front office can analyze data related to the guest's stay. System-generated reports can be used to review operations, isolate problem areas, indicate where corrective action may be necessary, and highlight business trends. Daily system reports typically present information about cash and charge transactions and front office operating statistics. Operational analysis can help managers establish a standard of performance that can be used to evaluate the effectiveness of front office operations.

Front Office Systems

Before the 1970s, technology in the front office was almost nonexistent. Manual operations were the rule in lodging operations. The semi-automated operations through the early 1970s laid much of the groundwork for the development of automated operations in the 1980s. The implementation of comprehensive automated applications became prevalent in the 1990s and beyond. The first decade of the twenty-first century introduced analytical metrics, revenue management, online purchasing programs, and e-commerce solutions. Technology has become affordable, allowing lodging properties to manage many of their operations with automated applications that may rely on portable devices, wireless networks, and remote access, including select self-service applications.

Front Office Activities

Front office recordkeeping in an automated property management system (PMS) is mostly the result of programmed routines. Computer systems designed for use in the hospitality industry at first were not considered functionally viable or generally affordable. These initial systems tended to be expensive, making them attractive to only the largest hotel properties. As hardware, software, and netware became less expensive, more compact, and easier to operate, implementation became more commonplace. User-friendly applications that did not require sophisticated technical training evolved for various hotel functions and applications over the next several years. The development of versatile portable and wireless devices enabled system vendors to approach all classes of lodging properties. Systems are now cost-effective for hotels of all sizes. It is important to note that the addition of wireless mobile devices to the technology toolbox enabled applications in areas previously considered impractical.

Pre-Arrival Activities. The reservations software of a property management system usually interfaces with a central reservations system or other distribution network and may automatically quote rates and reserve rooms according to booking engine protocol. The reservations software may also automatically generate e-mail confirmations, produce requests for guest deposits, handle pre-registration activities, and establish the credit status of the traveler if a credit card, debit card, or smart card number is provided as part of the reservation record. Electronic folios can be used to track pre-registration transactions for guests with confirmed reservations. A reservations software package may also generate an expected arrivals list, occupancy and revenue forecast reports, and a variety of auxiliary reports.

Arrival Activities. Guest information collected during the reservation process is automatically transferred as a reservation record to the property management system's front office software. A front desk agent enters similar guest information for walk-in guests into the front office system. The agent may then present a computer-generated **registration card** to the guest for verification and signature. The installation of online payment authorization terminals enables front desk personnel to receive timely payment card approval. Registration data, stored electronically, can also be retrieved whenever necessary, thereby making a room rack unnecessary. Electronic guest folios are maintained and accessed through the system's application software.

Some properties offer self check-in/check-out terminals in the hotel's lobby area, onboard a shuttle van, or via mobile devices. In addition, the availability of automated teller machines (ATMs) and self check-in kiosks at airports and other off-premises locations has had a positive impact on guests willing to accept self-service technology in lodging establishments.

To use a self-service terminal, the guest inserts a credit card, debit card, frequent traveler card, or smart card into the machine, which reads the encoded card data and communicates with the property management system. The central system locates the guest's reservation and returns the information to the terminal. The guest may be asked to verify name, departure date, rate, and room type on the display. Some systems allow changes to this information, and some require that the guest be on property at the front desk if any changes are necessary. If the information is correct, the system assigns an available room within the lodging management system and may dispense a walking map to the room along with a downloadable guestroom door-lock code or guestroom key.

Some hotels may not employ self check-in/check-out terminals, as a means to keep personal contact between the hotel staff and the guest. Typically, self check-in terminals work especially well in large convention hotels where long check-in and check-out lines can undermine a guest's experience. These terminals are used to accelerate the check-in process and get guests to their rooms quicker. Other hotels, such as economy-priced hotels and some mid-range hotels that do not provide extensive personal service, often install and rely on self-service terminals. One additional advantage of these devices in economy and mid-range hotels is that they may reduce the size of the work shift at the front desk, since the equipment may be capable of processing check-ins and check-outs independently.

Some hotel companies allow guests to register via the Internet prior to arrival at the property. Guests access the hotel's website registration area and confirm their arrival information. When they arrive at the hotel, they simply stop by a convenient pre-registration desk, show identification, and pick up their room keys. The entire process takes only a few seconds once they arrive at the hotel. With the extension of wireless technologies, guests can also pre-register through a laptop computer, personal digital assistant (PDA), or smart phone.

Occupancy Activities. A hotel property management system typically includes work stations and related devices located throughout the hotel facility. These devices may include point-of-sale (POS) terminals, data workstations, smart identification tags, handheld units, pagers, and other formats. As guests charge purchases at revenue outlets, the charged amounts are electronically transferred to the property management system, and the appropriate guest account is automatically updated. Most automated devices are capable of supporting two-way (duplex) interfaces, so the status of each guest is verified before the system accepts the charge for posting. For example, if a guest checks out of the hotel and then attempts to purchase a gift shop item and charge it to his or her room account, the point-of-sale terminal notifies the gift shop clerk that the item cannot be charged to the guest's account because the account has already been settled and closed. Instantaneous postings, simultaneous guest account and departmental entries, and continuous trial balances free front office staff to spend time reviewing, rather than focusing on data entry and balancing guest accounts.

Departure Activities. An electronic or printed folio presented at check-out or e-mailed helps assure the guest that the statement of account is complete and accurate. Depending on the method of settlement, the system may automatically post the transactions to appropriate back office accounts. For a guest account that requires third-party billing, the system is capable of producing a bill to be sent to the sponsor or credit-granting agency. Once the guest's account is settled and the postings are considered complete, departed-guest information may be used to create an electronic record in the hotel's guest history file.

Off-premises outsourcing, application service providers (ASPs), and cloud computing networks enable hotels to implement automated applications without having to support a complete on-premises system. Such system solutions require the hotel to provide the servicing bureau with data for processing. A popular hospitality industry outsourced application has been payroll accounting. Employee time records are sent to the service bureau to convert into paychecks and payroll reports for management. However, service bureaus, which focus primarily on back office functions, are not always a feasible option for front office activities. On the other hand, cloud computing is capable of supporting aspects of both front office and back office operations.

Front Office Documents

The front office relies on various documents to monitor the guest's stay. This section discusses front office documents employed in the four stages of the traditional guest cycle. It is important to note that many of these reports may only be available initially in electronic format.

Pre-Arrival Documents

Since reservations initiate the guest cycle, capturing and maintaining reservation data is critical to effective front office operations. Regardless of the reservation's point of entry (in-house, the hotel's website, or the reservations office), reservations are formulated into an electronic **reservation file.** The guest may be sent a system-generated confirmation to indicate that a reservation has been made and that its specifications are accurate. The confirmation process permits errors to be corrected prior to guest arrival and verifies the guest's correct contact information for future communication. Digital confirmations have the advantages of lower costs to the hotel and a rapid response to guests.

Arrival Documents

The front office may use a front desk or concierge location for guest check-in. A registration record indicates the guests' personal data, including length of stay and method of settlement. Registration records may also provide guest information related to on-premises and in-room amenities and hotel policies. Additionally, registration records indicate the room rate and length of stay, allowing the guest to reconfirm this information. This reduces questions about the price of the room or intended length of stay at check-out.

Credit must be established, verified, or authorized during check-in as well. Most payment card companies require an online authorization of electronic data capture by a recording device to establish credit. A front desk agent will acknowledge online approval against the guest's method of payment for a pre-established amount. Should the balance exceed that amount during the stay, additional requests are made to the payment card company. Often, the front office system automatically requests the credit approval during check-in and, when the balance approaches or exceeds the approved level, the system may automatically request additional approvals from the payment card company.

Occupancy Documents

Once the guest is registered, the front office system creates an electronic guest folio to capture guest charges and credits. While folio information is comparable across front office recordkeeping systems, folio formats tend to vary. In nearly all electronic systems, information from guest registration data is used to create the folio. This is an example of data interchange within the flow of electronic records. The front office may retain a copy of the guest folio as a record of the guest's stay, and present a hard copy or electronic equivalent to the guest following check-out. Additional folio copies may be used for such purposes as assistance in direct billing after departure, for creating e-mail receipts, and to help reconcile departmental sales reports.

Electronic folios simplify transaction posting and handling. Once the information is captured, the system assigns a unique account number or carries forward the reservation number. In a property management system, an electronic folio is automatically created and available for immediate transaction posting. Electronic folios are stored internally and can be printed on demand.

A **voucher** is a support document detailing the facts of a transaction. A voucher does not replace the *source document* created at the point of purchase. Common types of vouchers include charge vouchers, allowance vouchers, transfer vouchers, and paid-out vouchers. During a system audit routine, vouchers help ensure that all transactions requiring account posting have been processed correctly. Automated properties require few paper vouchers, or, in some cases, no paper vouchers at all. This is because remote revenue centers are electronically connected (interfaced) with the front office system, thus reducing the need for support documentation.

Automated front office systems replace traditional filing techniques with desktop and mobile terminals, thereby eliminating the need for information racks and rack slips. These terminals can quickly access guest records and display comprehensive information. Interfacing technology enables other electronic equipment, such as point-of-sale terminals, electronic locks, call accounting devices, and energy management systems, to also be connected to the front office system.

Departure Documents

Guest folios are kept current throughout occupancy to ensure an accurate account balance for settlement at the time of departure. In addition to the guest folio, other documents may be required for account settlement. A payment card voucher, for example, may be necessary if the guest elects to settle the account with a payment card. In some hotels, a cash voucher is used to document a cash settlement. A transfer voucher may be necessary if the guest's account is direct-billed — that is, transferred from a guest receivable account in the front office to a non-guest receivable account in the back office. The property management system typically generates several records and reports that may be used to prove transactions and provide a basis for comprehensive front office auditing.

During the departure stage, the property management system may create a guest history file. As stated earlier, a guest history file stores information that can be used for marketing and sales efforts, and can be helpful in registering and serving the guest during a return visit. Most systems automatically create an electronic guest history file as part of the check-out process. A collection of guest history files forms a database of invaluable marketing information.

The Front Desk

Most front office functions are performed at the front desk. The front desk is where guests register, request information and services, relate complaints, settle accounts, and check out.

Most front desks are prominently located in the hotel lobby. A typical front desk surface is a counter approximately three-and-a-half feet high and two-and-a-half feet deep. Its length may vary according to the design of the desk area, the duties performed at the front desk, and the size of the hotel lobby. Signs may be placed on or above the desk to direct guests to the proper activity center for registration, cashier, check-out, information and mail handling, and other guest services. Front desk designs usually screen front office forms and equipment from guests or visitors standing at the desk, since much front office information is considered confidential and proprietary.

Functional Organization

The functional efficiency of a front desk configuration depends on the organization of the work stations located at the desk. The design and layout of the desk should provide each front desk employee with easy access to the equipment, forms, and supplies necessary for his or her assigned tasks. (Exhibit 5 presents a sample front desk design.) Ideally, the front desk layout is planned and its furniture and fixtures situated according to the functions performed at designated activity centers along the desk. However, as lines of responsibility overlap among front desk personnel, largely because of cross-training and automation, more front desks are being designed with position flexibility in mind.

Efficiency is an important concern in front office design. Whenever front office employees have to turn their backs to guests, leave guests unattended, or take too long to complete a process, front desk design could be improved. Studies that examine how front office personnel interact with guests and equipment often suggest changes in front desk design.

Design Alternatives

Various hotel companies have researched industry needs and redesigned front desk areas to make them more aesthetically appealing. For instance, there is general agreement that traditional mail, message, and other filing or compartment organizers visible to traffic in the lobby are unnecessary at the front desk, not to mention unwise from a security standpoint. Mail, messages, and other materials can be stored in drawers or slots located under or away from the front desk, thereby making the front desk area appear more streamlined.

Exhibit 5   Sample Layout of a Front Desk

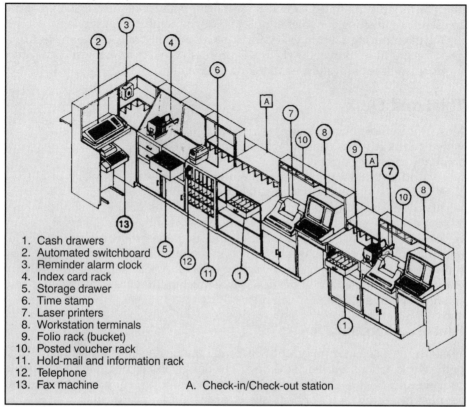

1. Cash drawers
2. Automated switchboard
3. Reminder alarm clock
4. Index card rack
5. Storage drawer
6. Time stamp
7. Laser printers
8. Workstation terminals
9. Folio rack (bucket)
10. Posted voucher rack
11. Hold-mail and information rack
12. Telephone
13. Fax machine   A. Check-in/Check-out station

Some hotels have circular or semicircular front desk structures. The circular desk encloses the front desk staff with its counter. In a semicircular arrangement, there is normally a straight wall at the back of the desk with a door leading to front office support services. Circular and semicircular desks allow greater service to more guests at the same time, and also tend to appear more modern and innovative than the traditional straight desk. This design, however, may present potential problems in the sense that guests can approach the desk from all angles, even though front office work stations and equipment are situated in specific spots. Extra care may be necessary to ensure the success of these and other innovative desk designs.

Some hotels have experimented with a lobby arrangement that includes no front desk at all. In a desk-less environment, registration and room assignment may be handled at a small table or personal desk in a low-traffic area of the lobby. A concierge, receptionist, or special guest service employee may serve as guest host. Although a guest host may perform many of the same functions as a front desk agent, the service is intended to be more personal and informal. Guests often enjoy a casual, seated registration instead of a long wait standing in line at a front desk counter.

Other hotels use self check-in terminals, with a small reception desk for those guests who are uncomfortable using technology or who may have questions. Also available are options for remote check-in.

Accessibility. The traditional standards for front desk design may not satisfy the physical needs of all hotel guests. Accessibility is an important consideration in the general design of a hotel, especially its front office area. The Americans with Disabilities Act stipulates that companies that serve the general public must make public areas and services readily accessible to the disabled. This means that public areas and accommodations in new and renovated lodging properties must be barrier-free, including front desk areas. According to the law, existing businesses will be required to make architectural and physical changes that are "readily achievable" given the company's size and financial resources. This may require changes in the size and setup of doorways, as well as the removal of architectural barriers such as curbs and steps. The law may also require that a portion of the front desk be of a more accessible height and design to accommodate people using wheelchairs or people with other special needs. When the front desk design cannot be changed, it is customary for front desk agents to go, when necessary, to the guest side of the desk to accommodate disabled travelers.

Point-of-Sale System. In some hotels, the front desk also serves as a place where guests can purchase items they may need while traveling. A front desk point-of-sale (POS) terminal is used to record cash transactions and maintain cash balances for front desk sales not associated with the guest cycle, such as the sale of newspapers, personal grooming items, sundries, or other items. In some limited-service properties, the hotel may offer a pantry of items that guests can purchase, such as sandwiches, canned food items, breakfast foods, toiletries, and snacks. Guests are expected to pay for these items at the front desk; the items may be paid for in full or posted to the guest's folio via the front desk POS terminal. Many specialized functions can be built into a POS system to facilitate close monitoring of front office transactions. The POS system is normally interfaced with the property management system to provide more complete control over financial transactions, folio postings, and other settlements.

POS systems possess the capabilities to produce transaction records, generate sales receipts, capture electronic settlement data, monitor inventory levels, and maintain item pricing. POS systems typically record the:

- Amount of the transaction
- Description of the transaction
- Affected departments
- Type of transaction
- Identity of the cashier
- Amount tendered
- Method of payment

A POS terminal may also feature a cash drawer divided into several money compartments, or may have removable drawers for individual cashier banks.

Support Devices. The front office may have numerous pieces of automated and manual support equipment. These devices can help simplify cumbersome procedures with logical information handling and adequate storage capacity for data and files. The following paragraphs describe just a few of the support devices found at a front desk.

An *electronic payment reader* captures the account type and number, expiration date, and select additional information assigned to the account. These devices may operate in a stand-alone or online mode connected to an automatic call-out transaction authorization network. In many cases, they are integrated with the property management system and can be used for several functions involving electronic data capture and settlement. Data that is magnetically encoded and stored on the magnetic stripe on the back of a plastic card or contained in a contactless signal exchange is transmitted to a clearinghouse or authorization service. On the basis of the transaction data and the cardholder's account status, the clearinghouse or authorization service either approves or disapproves the transaction. The technology integrates the reader and the front office system and may allow more information to be exchanged between the authorization service and the guest's electronic record. Guest loyalty programs can include a plastic membership card with a magnetic stripe that may also be read by the payment device. Membership information, including reward points, may be verified when guests check in by swiping or tapping the card.

In addition to credit and debit cards, guests may present gift cards or smart cards for partial or full account settlement. Gift cards represent a prepaid amount that can be applied against an outstanding folio balance. Smart cards differ from credit and debit cards in that they usually contain an integrated circuit on a silicon chip imbedded in them (instead of, or in addition to, a magnetic stripe) to store account information. A smart card is capable of storing much more information than a magnetic stripe card.

The front office area may also feature security monitors, such as closed-circuit television screens, allowing front office management or security personnel to monitor certain areas of the hotel from a central location.

Telecommunications

Hotels must be able to support a broad range of telephone traffic with adequate technology to ensure an efficient, effective telecommunications system. There are many types of calls a guest may place during a hotel stay:

- Local calls
- Direct-dial long-distance calls
- Pre-payment card calls
- Collect calls
- Third-party calls
- Person-to-person calls
- Billed-to-room calls

- International calls

- Toll-free calls

- 900 or premium-price calls

- Voice over Internet Protocol (VoIP) calls

While all of these calls can be completed without operator assistance, guests sometimes ask front office staff for assistance in placing calls. In addition, a single call often fits into more than one call category. For example, a direct-dial long-distance call could also be a pre-payment card call; a person-to-person call could also be a collect call; a local call could be to an Internet service provider; and an international call could be a person-to-person call. For many of these types of calls, the hotel may charge guests a surcharge for use of its telephone technology.

A hotel's telephone equipment may include a "call accounting" billing system. The system detects how the call is being placed (direct dial, calling card, etc.) and then calculates the amount the hotel needs to bill the guest once the call is finished. The charge is then posted to the guest's folio in the hotel property management system. Since a majority of guests carry a cellular phone, the volume of billable guest telephone traffic has been significantly reduced.

International calls typically not within the scope of a guest's cell phone plan can be direct-dialed or placed with operator assistance. To direct-dial an international call, the guest typically dials an international access code, a country code, a city code, and the telephone number. The hotel bills guests for direct-dialed international calls and may apply a fee in addition to the price of the call.

Toll-free calls can be direct-dialed from a guestroom as either local calls or long-distance calls. In either case, the guest receives access to an outside line and dials the toll-free access number (such as 800, 888, 877, etc.). The hotel may apply a surcharge or other fee for this service.

Calls made to businesses that charge callers a fee for the call (a fee separate from the one the telephone company charges for placing the call) may be 900 or premium-price calls. Problems can arise when these types of calls are made from guestrooms. Guests may be shocked and mistakenly blame the hotel upon receiving premium call charges. The businesses involved in premium-price telephone services charge widely varying rates. One business might charge $1.50 per minute; another might charge $3.50 for the first minute and $2.00 for each additional minute; a third business might charge a flat rate of $9.00 a call. Another problem that arises is that the hotel's telephone system may be able to track only the costs involved in placing the call and not the premium charged by the premium service company. A guest could settle a phone charge of $2.50 at check-out and the hotel could later receive a premium call bill of $40.50 for the same call. It is for these reasons that some hotels choose to block premium-price calls from guestrooms.

Calls placed and connected over Internet technology, as opposed to common carrier networks, tend to be less expensive. Use of the Internet for telecommunications is termed *Voice over Internet Protocol (VoIP)* and represents a viable alternative to traditional phone lines and switching equipment.

Telecommunications Equipment

To serve guests efficiently and price calls properly, hotels need the right mix of telephone equipment and lines. There are many types of telephone lines or *trunks*. Each type of line is designed to carry certain types of calls. There are lines dedicated to incoming calls, others dedicated to outbound calls, and two-way lines as well. Based on its level of guest service, each hotel must determine the types and number of lines it needs to install. Systems and equipment that hotels use for placing and pricing calls include the following:

- Telephone switchboards (also known as PBX or PABX systems)
- Call accounting system
- Guestroom phones
- Pagers and cell phones
- Related technology

Telephone Switchboards. Historically, an important piece of equipment controlling phone service at hotels was the switchboard or private branch exchange (PBX), now automated and often labeled the PABX (for "private automated branch exchange"). This equipment routes inbound calls to the hotel telephone operator's console. The hotel operator, in turn, connects these calls to particular extensions or station lines. These might be at the front desk or in guestrooms, administrative offices, hotel departments, or other areas. This arrangement allows the hotel to have a large number of telephones share a limited number of telephone lines. Outbound calls are usually placed without the hotel operator's help, although they often go through the same equipment. Some hotel PBX/PABX systems have advanced features enabling them to handle data as well as voice communications. For example, room attendants can update the status of guestrooms by dialing a code from guestroom phones.

Alternatively, some hotels have implemented voice over Internet protocol (VoIP) that conducts communications over the property's high-speed Internet connection without requiring any PBX/PABX equipment. The telephone traffic for VoIP calls is handled by automated network devices and routers.

Call Accounting System. A **call accounting system (CAS)** enables hotel-based technology to place, price, and post telephone calls to electronic guest folios without assistance from phone company personnel or front desk staff. A CAS is a set of software programs that initiates the routing, rating, and recording of calls emanating from guestroom and/or administrative office telephones. The CAS interfaces with a hotel's property management system to electronically post charges to guest folios or to print charge slips for the front desk staff to post appropriately. Some CASs have a least-cost-routing component that routes a dialed call to the type of line that can carry the call at the lowest cost to the hotel. Prior to folio posting, the CAS may add a surcharge or other property-imposed fee (PIF) to the telephone company's call pricing.

Guestroom Phones. Along with other telecommunications equipment, guestroom phones are increasing in sophistication and capabilities. For example, guests can connect a personal computer or other compatible portable device into a guestroom phone supporting an input jack or port for connectivity. Many hotels provide two-line guestroom phones, so one line can accommodate an electronic interchange while the guest talks on the other line. Other features found on some guestroom phones include: conference calling, caller ID, speed dialing, hold buttons, call-waiting, hands-free speakers, voice messaging, and a message-waiting alert. Some phones combine voice, data, e-mail, fax, and other technologies so guests can retrieve messages, order room service, receive text documents, and place wake-up call requests. In addition, some hotels place cordless phones in guestrooms. A cordless phone uses a radio frequency to connect to the telephone system. Although guests like the convenience of cordless, these phones are not as secure or reliable as wired telephones. Alternatively, a computerized device may be used for guest communication with a VoIP system.

Pagers and Cell Phones. Some hotels offer a pager or cell phone to guests at check-in. In the case of cell phones, the hotel bills the guest for the number of minutes of recorded use, as indicated by the phone's internal usage meter. Calls placed through cell phones may not go through the hotel's CAS and therefore are priced outside the system and may require manual posting to the appropriate guest folios. Some hotels have begun experimenting with internal cell phones that allow only hotel-issued cell phones to work exclusively on the hotel's premises. When used, internal cell phones are issued to guests in lieu of in-room phones.

Related Technology. Often, hotels install telephone systems with sophisticated features for reasons other than just cost effectiveness. Examples include automatic call dispensing systems, telephone/room status systems, high-speed Internet access, and call detection software.

In many cases, *automatic call dispensing* is limited to wake-up services. In a staff-operated system, the staff member receiving the wake-up-call request enters the room number and time for each wake-up call into the call-dispensing system. Some self-service systems allow guests to place their own wake-up requests. At the scheduled time, a telephone call is automatically placed to the guest's room. Once the guest answers the call, the system may activate a synthesized voice that gives a greeting along with the current time, temperature, and weather conditions. Another variation on automatic call dispensing allows hotel staff to call all rooms simultaneously in case of an emergency or to call all guests associated with a specific group to remind them of a meeting, event, or function.

Telephone/room status systems can assist with rooms management and prohibit the unauthorized use of telephones in vacant rooms. Housekeeping or room service employees can use guestroom telephones to enter data concerning room service charges (for example, what was consumed from an in-room bar), maintenance information, or current room status information. These features not only improve communication, they also contribute to lower payroll costs and help ensure a more efficient in-room monitoring and restocking system for guestrooms.

An increasingly popular guestroom service is *high-speed Internet access (HSIA)*. Hotels may charge guests for HSIA service on a per-transaction, fixed-fee, or daily-fee basis. HSIA data services are brought to the hotel by an Internet service provider (ISP). Often there is a revenue-sharing agreement between the hotel and the ISP. HSIA systems may be wired or wireless.

A hotel may also rely on *call detection software,* a component of the hotel's call accounting system, to sense when a placed call is answered. Call detection equipment can pinpoint the exact moment a telephone call is connected, thereby improving billing accuracy and leading to a reduction in call accounting discrepancies, since only the charges associated with answered calls will appear on a guest's folio.

Property Management Systems

There are many automated hotel property management systems available. However, they do not all operate identically. Some generalizations about property management systems may illustrate the nature of front office applications. A property management system consists of sets of automated software packages (referred to as modules) that can support a variety of activities in front office and back office areas. Four common front office software modules are designed to help front office staff perform functions related to:

- Reservation management

- Rooms management

- Guest accounting management

- General management

Exhibit 6 summarizes front office property management system applications.

Reservation Management Software

An in-house reservation management software module enables a hotel to rapidly process room requests and generate timely and accurate room availability, room revenue, and reservation forecasting reports. Most lodging chains participate in remote reservation networks known as global distribution systems (GDSs), Internet distribution systems (IDSs), and central reservation systems (CRSs). GDSs capture, process, and forward reservation information generated mostly by travel agents and airline companies. The largest and best-known worldwide GDSs are Sabre, Galileo International, Amadeus, and Worldspan. IDSs are intermediary websites that represent hotel companies and offer overnight accommodations on a commission or mark-up fee basis. IDSs capture guest reservation data and may be automatically connected to the hotel's reservation management system through a GDS or CRS. Examples of Internet distribution sites include travelocity.com, travelweb.com, priceline.com, hotels.com, and orbitz.com. CRSs are often operated by the hotel company and typically communicate reservations data, track rooms reserved, control reservations by room type and room rate, and monitor the number of reservations received. Most reservation management applications create reservation records for seamless connectivity to a property management system.

A property relying on an in-house reservation module may be able to receive data sent directly from any or all remote reservations channels (GDS, IDS, or CRS).

Exhibit 6 Front Office Property Management System Applications

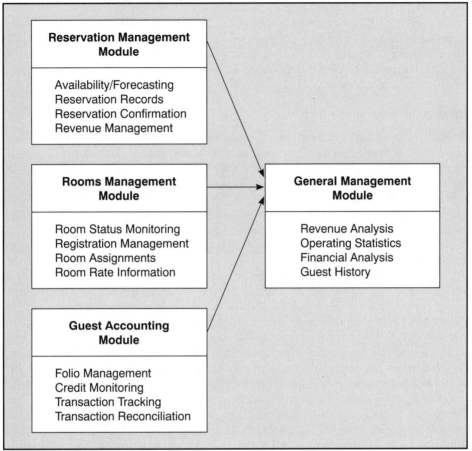

Automated in-house reservations records, files, and revenue forecasts are immediately updated as reservation data are confirmed. It is through electronic file updating that the system remains current and in control of reservations activities. Many systems allow real-time, two-way communication between remote reservations networks and property-level applications, thereby enabling instantaneous updates of inventory and guest information. With this approach, usually referred to as single image inventory, accurate guestroom availabilities and pricing are shared between systems through *seamless integration.*

In addition, previously received reservation data can be automatically reformatted into pre-registration applications, and a series of appropriate records and reports can be generated. Various reservation management reports summarize reservation data and guest account status information, as well as letters or e-mails of reservation confirmations sent to guests with processed reservations. Reservations management software also includes upgraded room rate control features, guest history referencing, and more detailed property information such as bed types, guestroom views, in-room amenities, convention space, public areas, recreational facilities, and other special features.

Reservations management software can also track deposit requests and keep a record of deposits received. This is especially important to resort hotels, which often require deposits to finalize reservation requests. Other hotels may also require deposits for special occasions, such as a special event weekend when a sold-out condition is likely.

Rooms Management Software

Rooms management software maintains current information on the status of overnight guestrooms, provides information on room rates, assists in room assignments, and helps front office personnel coordinate guest services. A rooms management module can also provide rapid access to room availability data during certain aspects of the reservation process. This information can be especially useful in short-term reservation confirmation and rooms revenue forecasting. Since rooms management software has replaced most traditional front office equipment, it is often a major area of consideration when a hotel is comparing one property management system over another.

Rooms management software can provide front office staff with a summary of each guestroom's status. For example, a front desk agent may enter a room number query at a front office terminal, and the current status of the guestroom will be displayed. Once the guestroom has been cleaned and readied for occupancy, the housekeeping staff can communicate the room's updated status through a device connected to the housekeeping software application, or, in some cases, through the guestroom telephone. With a property management system, changes in room status are instantaneously reflected in the front office system. In addition, when a guest requests a room, the front desk agent can enter the guest's preferences into the system to find a room that meets his or her needs. For example, an agent can request information on all vacant and clean rooms facing the golf course that have king-size beds. Some rooms management systems also feature maintenance and special-request dispatch capabilities. For example, a room with an air conditioning problem or needing extra towels can be registered and monitored through the property management system and a hotel engineer or housekeeper can subsequently be dispatched to fulfill the request.

Rooms management software also assists the reservations function. When rooms are temporarily taken out of inventory for maintenance or cleaning, the number of available rooms in the reservation office is automatically adjusted. This helps control future room inventory and ensure that all guests have rooms ready upon arrival.

Guest Accounting Management Software

Guest accounting management software increases the hotel's control over guest accounts and significantly modifies the front office audit routine. Guest accounts are maintained electronically, thereby eliminating the need for folio cards, folio trays, and account posting machines. The guest accounting module monitors predetermined guest credit limits and provides flexibility through multiple folio formats. At check-out, previously approved outstanding account balances may be automatically transferred to an appropriate back office accounts receivable file for subsequent billing and collection. Account management capabilities represent major benefits of a property management system. For example, a credit manager in a large convention hotel can automatically monitor the credit limits of all guests and receive a system-generated report for all accounts approaching or exceeding credit limits.

When the hotel's revenue outlets are connected to the front office system, remote point-of-sale terminals can seamlessly communicate guest charges to the property management system. These charges will be automatically posted to appropriate electronic guest folios. Automatic posting procedures are intended to improve accounting efficiency while reducing or eliminating late charges (charges posted to a guest account after the guest has checked out of the hotel).

General Management Software

General management software cannot operate independently of other front office software packages. General management applications tend to be report-generating packages that depend on data collected through reservations management, rooms management, and guest accounting management software modules. For example, general management software may be able to generate a report indicating the day's expected arrivals and the number of rooms remaining available for occupancy—a combination of reservation management and rooms management data. In addition to generating reports, the general management module serves as the internal link between front office and back office system interface applications.

Back Office Interfaces

A comprehensive property management system involves integrating the hotel's front office and back office areas. Although separate front office and back office software packages can operate independently of one another, integrated systems offer the hotel a full range of control over a variety of operational areas. Such areas include room sales, telephone call accounting, payroll, and account analysis. An integrated system cannot produce complete financial statements unless all the required data are stored in an accessible database. Many reports generated by the back office system depend on the accuracy of front office data collection. Most property management system vendors offer several back office application modules. Four popular back office applications are:

- *General ledger accounting software,* consisting primarily of accounts receivable and accounts payable application packages. Accounts receivable software monitors guest accounts and account billing and collection when integrated with the front office guest accounting module. Accounts payable software tracks hotel purchases and helps the hotel maintain sufficient cash flow to satisfy its debts.

- *Human resources software* may include payroll accounting, personnel recordkeeping, and labor scheduling. Payroll accounting includes time and attendance records, pay distribution, deductions, and withholdings. Personnel records include personal profiles, labor history, and job performance evaluations. Labor scheduling involves tracking employee skills and availability in relation to the hotel's staffing requirements.

- *Financial reporting software* enables the hotel to develop a chart of accounts to help in producing balance sheets, income statements, and transaction analysis reports.

- *Inventory control software* monitors stocking levels, purchase ordering, and stock rotation. Additional computations include inventory usage, variance, valuation, and extensions.

System Interfaces

A variety of property management system interface applications are available in an automated environment.

Non-Guest-Operated Interfaces. Common interfaces that are initiated and directed by hotel staff include the following:

- A *point-of-sale (POS) system* allows guest account transactions to be quickly transmitted from remote revenue centers to the property management system for automatic posting to electronic folios.

- A *call accounting system (CAS)* directs, prices, and tracks guestroom telephone use for pricing and automatic posting to electronic folios.

- An *electronic locking system (ELS)* typically interfaces with the rooms management module to provide enhanced guest security and service.

- An *energy management system (EMS)* can be applied to automatically control the temperature, humidity, and air movement in public spaces and guestrooms through a rooms management interface.

An EMS is an automated control system designed to manage the operation of mechanical equipment in a lodging property. An EMS interfaced to a property management system offers a number of opportunities for energy control. For example, assume that 50 percent occupancy is forecasted for tonight at a 300-room hotel. Minimizing the hotel's energy consumption on this night becomes a factor in determining which rooms to sell. One approach would be to assign guests only to the lower floors and significantly reduce the energy demands of rooms on the upper floors. By interfacing an EMS with a front office rooms management system, it is possible to automatically control room assignments and achieve desired energy-cost savings.

Guest-Operated Interfaces. Hotels can provide automated conveniences and services by installing a variety of guest-operated devices. In some properties, guests may inquire about in-house events and local activities through automated information kiosks in public areas, or through the television or a portable communication device in their guestrooms. Connecting a printer to an information terminal enables guests to print desired information.

Through connected devices, guests can review their folios and complete the check-out process from remote locations as well as the comfort and privacy of their guestrooms. In-room televisions or other communication devices interfaced with a guest accounting module enable guests to simultaneously access folio data and to approve and settle their accounts by selecting a pre-approved method of settlement. Guestroom telephones interfaced with the property management system may also be used for this purpose. In-room specialty devices linked to external information services allow guests to access e-mail, websites, transportation schedules, local restaurant and entertainment guides, weather reports, news and sports updates, shopping catalogs, and video games.

An *in-room entertainment system* can be interfaced with a front office module or can function as a stand-alone application. In-room entertainment systems allow guests to access various forms of entertainment through the guestroom television or other connected device. If there is a charge for the service, such as a pay-per-view movie, a video game, or Internet access, the charge can be automatically calculated and posted to the guest's electronic folio. To keep guests from inadvertently tuning to a pay channel, the television is usually preset to a non-pay channel or preview channel. Incorporating a preview channel can significantly reduce the number of guest disputes about the validity of applied pay TV or movie charges. In-room entertainment systems may require the guest to contact someone in the front office to request that a pay channel be activated. In addition, a preview channel provides the hotel with advertising opportunities. The preview channel can display information about the hotel's facilities and special amenities. The hotel can also sell advertising for local attractions, thereby creating a modest revenue source.

There are two types of *in-room vending systems. Non-automated honor bars* consist of beverage and snack items in both dry and cold storage areas within a guestroom. The bar's beginning inventory level is recorded, and hotel employees on a daily basis note changes in inventory. Appropriate charges for missing or consumed items are noted for posting to the guest's folio. Since honor bars are available at all times, this system often results in an unusually high volume of late charge postings. *Automated honor bars* or *in-room vending equipment* may contain fiber-optic sensors that record the removal of stored products from designated compartments. When a sensor is triggered, these devices assume a sale has transpired and transmit point-of-purchase information to a POS microprocessor that, in turn, communicates to the front office accounting module for electronic folio posting.

Other technology-based guest amenities may include an in-room device connected to online resources. This amenity is popular in hotels serving meeting, convention, and business travelers, and may link with other hotel systems that automatically calculate the cost of the application and forward the charge for folio posting.

Automated Guest Services. Outstanding guest services can provide a competitive advantage in attracting potential guests. For example, in-room entertainment companies are developing systems to provide local information through guestroom software browsers, satellite television and radios, hand-held mapping devices, and mobile devices. Guests can locate restaurants, museums, shops, and other points of interest through access to websites, virtual shopping malls, e-mail, and other online resources and services. In a similar way, hotels can promote their own services or other hotels in the chain. If a guest is interested in a particular hotel or restaurant, for example, the system can automatically connect to the business site, way-finding application, or reservation application.

High-speed Internet access (HSIA) service has evolved from an upgrade amenity to a "must-have" for most hotels. HSIA service, whether wired or wireless, is usually provided in guestrooms as well as in public areas and meeting facilities. At resort locations, wireless HSIA may also be available at pools and recreational facilities, as well as on the beach. Hotels may also offer Internet access through guestroom televisions, the hotel business center, and informational kiosks located throughout the property. While guest Internet access often is complimentary, some hotel brands charge for the service, based on market conditions.

Internet service has also become a major requirement for hotels with meeting facilities. Meeting room Internet service usually requires higher speeds and greater bandwidth, so there may be higher costs the hotel must recover.

Many hotels now provide business centers featuring airline check-in, fax service, photocopiers, conference telephones, and Internet access. There may be charges for use of hardware and software as well as network access arranged through the business center.

Sales Automation Systems

Property management systems and sales automation systems are usually integrated. Once viewed merely as a way to coordinate and manage group reservations and meeting-room space availability, sales automation software now is considered a strategic tool that maximizes revenue while tracking the monetary value of group business relationships.

For front office management, this can be vitally important. By entering group guestroom allocations into a sales automation application, a hotel salesperson can evaluate the number of remaining available rooms on a continuous basis. As with a front office reservation module, in a sales automation system group allocations decrease with each group room reservation commitment. The group allocation will increase when groups give room reservations back to the hotel, or management allocates more rooms to a particular group.

Maintaining accurate and consistent information about the status of group guestroom reservations in both the property management and sales automation systems is critical. The hotel reservations staff may actually have rooms available to sell but be unaware of them, since they may incorrectly appear allocated to a group in the sales automation system even though the group has yet to commit to those rooms. Conversely, group salespersons may oversell group allocations, thereby resulting in no rooms in its block remaining available. To avoid conflicts between these two systems, the information must be properly balanced. Most property management systems directly interface the sales automation function. Interfacing gives group sales managers a clear view of rooms inventory in the property management system, since both systems rely on a single data source. In addition, when group room reservations are returned to the hotel, the rooms will be made immediately available for sale.

Sales automation systems collect sufficient data to identify booking trends, and are capable of tracking group histories. Most group tracking systems store actual group guestroom usage (called **group pickup**), room rates, and non-room (food and beverage, facilities, amenities, etc.) rates. The next time the group books space at the hotel or at an affiliated property in the hotel chain, the system will be capable of providing the group's history and thereby be better able to allocate a group block. Some chains provide affiliate properties access to centralized group history files through a specialized database system. This allows a hotel on the West Coast, for example, to research a group that stayed earlier at an affiliate hotel on the East Coast. Group history files store information on group sales and revenues and the number of rooms blocked (allocated) and booked (reserved). In addition, banquet menus, meeting space usage, VIPs, billing history, meeting planner, group coordinator, and many other pieces of important information may also be available. Such information can be important to front office management. For example, knowing the check-in and check-out pattern of group members may prove helpful for front office staffing. Knowing the group's history regarding its number of no-shows, early departures, suites reserved, and rooms with rollaway beds reserved may also be helpful.

Summary

The functions, activities, and areas of the front office are geared toward supporting guest transactions and services. To many guests, the front office represents the hotel. It is the main source for coordinating nearly every guest service the hotel provides. The financial transactions a guest makes while staying at a hotel determine the guest cycle of business through the property. Transaction flows can be divided into four stages: pre-arrival, arrival, occupancy, and departure. Within each stage, important front office tasks related to guest services and guest accounting can be identified and analyzed. Front office staff needs to be aware of guest services and guest accounting activities throughout the guest stay.

The guest chooses a hotel during the pre-arrival stage of the guest cycle. The arrival stage of the guest cycle includes registration and rooming functions. During the occupancy stage, the front office provides the guest with services, information, and supplies. Other guest services and guest accounting aspects of the guest cycle are completed during the cycle's departure stage. Since activities and functions tend to overlap between stages, some properties have revised the traditional guest cycle into a sequence of pre-sale, point-of-sale, and post-sale events. This sequence improves coordination among hotel operating departments.

Most front office functions are performed at the front desk. The front desk, prominently located in the lobby, is traditionally where guests register, request information and services, relate complaints, settle accounts, and check out. The functional efficiency of a front desk depends on its design and layout. The desk configuration should provide front desk staff with easy access to equipment, forms, and supplies necessary for performing assigned tasks. A property management system comprises software modules capable of supporting a variety of activities in front office and back office areas. In addition, guest- and non-guest-operated interfaces can be connected to the hotel's property management system for greater effectiveness and efficiency.

🗝 Key Terms

call accounting system (CAS)—A device linked to the hotel telephone system that accurately accounts for guest telephone calls by identifying each phone number dialed from guestroom telephones and tracking charges.

group pickup—The number of guestrooms a group actually uses.

guest cycle—A division of the flow of business through a hotel that identifies the contacts and financial exchanges between guests and hotel employees.

guest folio—A paper or electronic form front desk staff uses to chart transactions on an account assigned to an individual person or guestroom.

guest history file—A collection of guest history records containing information about interactions between the hotel and former guests.

house limit—A guest credit limit established by the hotel.

late charge—A transaction requiring posting to a guest account that does not reach the front office system until after the guest has checked out.

property management system (PMS)—A computer software package that supports a variety of applications related to front office and back office activities.

registration card—A printed form for a registration record.

reservation record—An electronic document storing such guest data as date of arrival, type and number of rooms requested, deposit, and number of persons in the party.

reservation file—A collection of reservation records.

voucher—A document detailing a transaction to be posted to an electronic folio; used to communicate information from an unconnected point of sale to the front office system.

💬 Review Questions

1. What activities are involved in the four stages of the traditional guest cycle? Why have some properties replaced the traditional cycle with a three-stage sequence?

2. How does the departure stage of the guest cycle conclude both guest services and guest accounting activities? How can the front office use data about the guest stay?

3. How have front office recordkeeping systems evolved over the years?

4. What are some of the organizational concerns of front desk design? What criteria determine the appropriateness of a design?

5. What are some common telecommunications equipment items used in hotels? How do they work?

6. What are the four most common front office software modules? How do they streamline front office recordkeeping? How does a general management module depend on the other three modules?

7. How are newer technologies helping hotels offer more services?

Internet Sites

For more information, visit the following Internet sites. Remember that Internet addresses can change without notice. If the site is no longer there, you can use a search engine to look for additional sites.

Galaxy Hotel Systems
www.galaxyhotelsystems.com

MICROS
www.micros.com

Orbitz
www.orbitz.com

Pegasus Solutions
www.pegs.com

Priceline
www.priceline.com

Sabre Holdings
www.sabre-holdings.com

Travelocity
www.travelocity.com

Travelport
www.travelport.com

Case Studies

Making the Most of Moments of Truth

#1—Gordon Sumner's Food for Thought

Freelance writer Gordon Sumner stepped off the hotel elevator and glanced at his watch. It was 10:00 A.M. on a Thursday and he was grateful to have had the chance to sleep in late after his 11:30 P.M. arrival the night before. Now the only thing he needed to start the day off right was a hearty breakfast. He headed to the front desk for directions to the hotel restaurant.

"Good morning," the man behind the desk said. "How can I help you?"

"You have a restaurant here, don't you?"

"Yes, we do. In fact, it just received a Golden Palate award from our city magazine."

"Well, I don't know if I'd recognize award-winning food if I ate it, but I would like a good breakfast," Gordon said.

"Then we have just the place for you, sir."

Gordon got directions from the agent and within two minutes he was sitting at a table in a bright, well-decorated restaurant. Looking around, he noticed half-a-dozen other people lingering over breakfast and coffee at nearby tables. From what he could see, the food did look appetizing.

After several minutes passed without a visit from a server, Gordon finally noticed a server walking across the other side of the room. He caught her attention and asked to see a menu. Ten minutes later, he had to flag her down again. *Goodness*, he thought, *the food must be spectacular if this place can win awards despite such poor service.*

"Can I help you, sir?" she said as she approached his table.

"I'd like to order breakfast. Could I get a—"

"I'm sorry, sir, but we stopped serving breakfast at 9:45."

"Well, then, I guess an early lunch would be all right. I'm starving."

The waitress bit her lip. "Actually, we don't begin serving lunch until 11:15. That's about another hour from now."

It was frustrating to see people still enjoying their meals and to realize he wouldn't be able to join them. "All right," he said without enthusiasm, "could I get some coffee to go, then? Maybe I'll grab a newspaper from the gift shop and just—"

She was shaking her head. "I'm sorry, but the register is locked until lunch. We can't handle take-out orders."

"I see," he said, wondering why the man at the front desk hadn't bothered to explain any of this. "So tell me: where can a guy get something to eat around here?"

"You know, if I were you, I'd take the walkway over to the mall across the street. They have a pretty good food court."

Twenty minutes later, Gordon passed through the lobby on his way back from the mall and his fast-food meal.

The front desk agent called out to him, "And was your breakfast award-winning, sir?"

"No, I can't say that it was," Gordon replied icily as he walked by.

The agent looked stricken. "Oh! I'm sorry to hear that. I hope you'll give us the chance to serve you again."

"Not likely," Gordon said under his breath as he stepped into the elevator.

#2—Freddie Bulsara: Dancers, with Wolves

Reservations Manager Freddie Bulsara was looking forward to a glorious Sunday, thanks to his booking prowess. This weekend marked a double coup. On Saturday, the hotel had hosted 230 young ballet dancers and their adult chaperones who were in town for a Sunday morning dance competition. Today, they would check out, opening up a large block of rooms that would match—almost to the room— the needs of a 200-member contingent of conventioneers from the Royal Fraternal Order of Wolves.

Freddie marveled at the perfection of his plan. The dancers would check out by 9:00 A.M., before leaving for their competition; the Wolves were to begin arriving at exactly 1:00 P.M. *Groups like this are really going to put this property on the map,* Freddie told himself.

But something wasn't right. When Freddie stopped at the front desk to ask how things had gone with the dancers, LeighAnne Crenshaw looked up from her work and said, "I can't really say. I'll let you know once they leave."

Freddie felt his heart skip a beat. "It's 11:45, LeighAnne. What are you talking about?"

"When I came in this morning, I found a note here that says the dancers asked to be allowed a late check-out after their competition. I guess a lot of them wanted to be able to come back to their rooms and change their clothes before leaving. Their group leader had it all arranged."

"With *whom?*"

LeighAnne shrugged. "There's no name on the note, but it looks like Brian's handwriting. He would have been working the front desk when they all came in last night."

Brian. A new hire who hadn't been on the job for more than two months. *His misguided need to do anything a guest asks is going to ruin everything I've worked for,* Freddie thought. "Do you know when they'll actually be checking out, then?"

"Well, the competition started at 9:30, and they said it was about two hours long. With travel time, I'd guess they'll be coming back within the next thirty minutes, if that tells you anything."

It tells me we won't have time for housekeeping to finish with the rooms before the Wolves get here, Freddie thought. *We'll have to stall the conventioneers until their rooms are ready.*

"I take that back," LeighAnne said, nodding toward the front entrance. "That looks like their bus now."

"Thank goodness!" Freddie said. "The sooner they get back to their rooms, the sooner we can clear them out and get housekeeping started. It might be tight, but—"

Freddie stopped mid-sentence. His mouth dropped open as the bus doors sprang open and the passengers made their way across the sidewalk to the revolving doors. He expected a stream of little girls in pink tutus. What he saw was a huge pack of middle-aged men wearing wolf ears and shouting, laughing, and punching each other in the arm.

"Oh no," Freddie whispered. He glanced at the clock as the first members of the Royal Fraternal Order of Wolves crossed the lobby toward the front desk.

The man in front—a tall, barrel-chested individual—tugged off his wolf ears and stuck out his hand. "You must be Freddie!" he shouted with a grin. "Darrell Drucker. We spoke on the phone!"

Freddie tried to return the man's energetic handshake, but his heart wasn't in it. The Wolves were quickly filling up every available space in the lobby. "Hello, Mr. Drucker," he managed to say. "We weren't expecting you until one o'clock."

Mr. Drucker looked taken aback. "Why, it's one o'clock right smack on the dot!" Then surprise slowly spread across his face. "We musta forgot to turn our watches back when we crossed that time zone!" he said with a grin. "Well, Freddie, just point us to our rooms, and we'll get out of your hair."

"Actually, it's going to be—"

"Look at that!" one of the other Wolves shouted across the lobby. He was smiling and pointing at the entrance, where dozens of pre-teen girls in tutus and pink and white tights were pressing their way through the doors and into the packed lobby.

"They're ba-a-ack," LeighAnne said dryly, quoting a haunted-house movie from the 1980s.

Freddie just hoped there was a ghost of a chance he would be able to keep everyone happy until the situation was straightened out.

#3—Reg Dwight: A Night to Remember

It had been a quiet Monday night until front desk agent Reg Dwight picked up the telephone at 3 A.M. On the other end of the line was a representative from an international airline. "About half an hour ago, we received a bomb threat concerning a flight to London that already was fueled, filled with passengers, and preparing for take-off," the woman began. "For their own safety, we have had to deplane those passengers, and now we have 260 people who need rooms until we can clear the plane, scan the baggage, and arrange for alternate transportation. Can we send them your way for the duration?"

Although Reg had worked many nights alone at the front desk, this was the first time he had ever faced a situation like this. He took a deep breath. "How many rooms would be involved?"

"With all the families and couples, we would need only about 175 rooms. The airline will of course cover the lodging costs, as well as one meal for everyone at your restaurant."

Reg checked availability. The passengers would have to spread out over most of the hotel, but the rooms were there. He was just about to calculate the financial windfall of 175 rooms at a rack rate of $84 when the woman added, "At 'distressed passenger' rates, of course." *Oh,* Reg thought. *That's $35 per room.* Reg wasn't aware of any existing hotel policies for handling a situation like this. Although it definitely would not be a money-making proposition—it actually cost $40 to deliver a guestroom—Reg thought the value of providing a needed service would outweigh any financial drawbacks. He hoped his supervisor would think so, too.

He told the caller to send the passengers his way and he would take care of them. Reg then asked to be kept informed of the guests' new travel arrangements as soon as they were established. He figured the guests would arrive tired, anxious, and angry about having to get off a plane in the middle of the night and stay longer than expected. He hoped that, by being able to answer many of their questions, he could put them at ease.

"How soon will they arrive?" he asked.

"The buses should be leaving within fifteen minutes, so they will reach your hotel around four o'clock. Just one more thing. You may want to let passengers know that their carry-on and checked baggage will be sent over as soon as it is thoroughly scanned, but that may not be until six. We will send all the shoes over then too."

Did she say "shoes"?

"I'm sorry, I must go," she hurried on. "I will ring back as soon as we have any news to share. Thanks so much for working with us during this emergency."

As soon as she hung up, Reg dialed another call. He knew he was going to need much more help than was normally available at 4 A.M. He called his supervisor at home, waking her to find out who he should contact. In addition to saying that she would come to work herself, she recommended that he call in kitchen, dining room, housekeeping, and front desk staff. Since she had also faced a similar situation before, she explained about the shoes.

"Before passengers can deplane using the inflatable slides, they have to take their shoes off. They usually collect them later on the runway. But in situations like this, the airline will just dump them all in boxes and send them over—unsorted, unpaired—along with a jumble of unidentified carry-on bags and checked luggage. We can put all the baggage in the Heritage Room. The shoes can go in the Carlton Room if Lorenzo hasn't already set up the A-V equipment for the noon meeting that's scheduled there. Hopefully, the shoes will be out in time to allow A-V setup just before the group has to have it."

"I'll make sure that happens."

"Tell you what. I'll be there as soon as I can to help with checking everyone in and covering whatever else needs to be covered. I'll give this some thought myself, but I'd like you to have a list ready for me of all the things you can think of that might be affected by having 260 possibly upset and worried guests arriving—and what those guests might want or need. We're just lucky we had the rooms to give them."

Reg took a deep breath. "*Lucky* wasn't the first word that came to mind," he muttered.

Discussion Questions

1. What steps could the staff at Gordon Sumner's hotel have taken to improve their service?

2. What factors were out of Freddie Bulsara's control? How could he have prepared for problems?

3. What might Reg Dwight's list of affected areas and guest wants/needs include?

Case Number: 3323CA

The following industry experts helped generate and develop this case: Richard M. Brooks, CHA, Vice President, TWE Group; and S. Kenneth Hiller, CHA, General Manager, Holiday Inn, Beachwood, Ohio.

Family Reunions: Worth the Hassle?

Ten years ago, Mr. and Mrs. Johnson discovered the Boden Oceanside Resort and Lodge. Now they were checking in to the resort for the fourth time. But this time was special. They had planned a family reunion with their three children, their spouses, and five grandchildren—all of the grandchildren were under age six. Mr. and Mrs. Johnson were the first to arrive after the long drive from the city. Their check-in went smoothly and they made dinner reservations for thirteen people at 8 P.M. in the formal dining room.

What is the value of a customer? Ten years ago, who at the front desk could have predicted that the Johnsons would become frequent return guests and that this year they would have their small family reunion at the resort?

The week turned out to be a beautiful one for the Johnsons and their children's families. The front desk, on the other hand, was kept very busy by all of the requests. The staff wondered if they would survive the numerous families that had selected the resort for their reunions this summer. The many families were running the rooms division and restaurant staffs ragged. After the elder Johnsons checked in, the level of intensity seemed to take a quantum leap. The remaining Johnson family members arrived in separate vehicles, each having driven the six hours from the city where they had met the night before. The young children were full of energy and the parents were frazzled from being in the car for so long with the kids.

Two hours after check-in, the list of observations and special needs was growing. It included the following:

- Although it was in the high seventies, the night-time low was predicted to be in the mid-forties. One family from Florida requested a space heater because they were accustomed to sleeping in eighty-degree temperatures. The rooms in the lodge either have heat or no heat, with fans for moving the warm air rather than air conditioning. In the summer, the heat is turned off. However, even on cool nights, which most guests appreciate, the lodge stays warmer than the outside air. The space heater was placed in the room upon check-in.

- One of the Johnson children requested bumpers for the crib in her guestroom. Because the lodge had no bumpers ("bumpers" are padded pillows to keep children sleeping in cribs from hitting the side walls), the bell attendant took extra pillows to the room. They were placed in the crib with the child screaming all the while.

- By 8 P.M. it was obvious that the Johnson party would not be eating in the formal dining room. One of the couples came to the desk and canceled the reservation, stating that they would all eat on their own in the less formal lounge area.

- At 10 P.M., one of the families called down for room service. The kids had been too excited to sit in the lounge for their dinner and so didn't eat much. However, much to the family's disappointment, the lodge didn't have room service and didn't serve food after 9 P.M.

- One of the families walked through the lobby at least six times during their first three hours at the lodge. The mother was constantly saying "shhh" to the children while they ran around enjoying themselves.

- One of the families requested a room change to a smoking room. However, they would not accept a room on the ground floor. After a lengthy search, it was concluded that a room change would disrupt the expectations of many arriving guests over the next several days because the only available smoking room was on the ground floor of the lodge. The guests weren't moved after all.

At the front desk, Tabitha, the new front office manager, was shaking her head. This was only the first four hours of the Johnson family reunion at the lodge! What would the next four days be like? Was it worth it to attract families for reunions?

The Johnsons didn't even seem to want to be together. They had all requested rooms a good distance away from one another. How did the parents feel about this? What kind of psychological toll would this one family have on the staff of the lodge over the next four days?

But on the other hand, she considered, what would the revenue for the property be from this one family reunion? And what about future business? Could the staff continue to provide exceptional service to these guests even under the stressful circumstances?

Tabitha was out of the office for the next few days on a brief vacation. When she returned, she asked about the Johnson reunion. No one recalled any unusual occurrences. They remembered the name and a few members of the party. She called up the folio to see whether they had any unusual requests or had done many of the activities offered at the resort. What she found was a total bill of $8,900 with guest charges mainly for rooms and meals. She wondered how many other families would generate nearly $10,000 worth of business in just four days at the lodge. She closed the folio, taking note of the importance of frequent guests and their loyalty. When the next guests checked in for the first time, she couldn't help wondering whether they would someday be frequent guests.

Just a week later, she noticed that the lodge had sold six rooms for three nights to a family named Camper. When they checked in, it seemed like a small army had descended upon the resort. There were the grandmother and grandfather, their six grown children, and eighteen grandchildren, for a total guest count of twenty-six people. The average daily revenue for this small group was projected to be at least $3,000. Tabitha struck up a conversation with the grandfather, asking whether anyone from this party had stayed at the lodge in the past. He told her that no one had, but that they'd heard about the lodge from friends over the years.

As the front office manager, Tabitha thought about what she could be doing to be sure that more first-time guests would become frequent customers. What could they do, for example, to ensure that the twenty-six members of the Camper party would remember their visit and return again and again on their own or with the larger family group?

Discussion Questions

1. In order to make clear to your front office staff the value of an individual customer, how could you calculate the revenue a frequent customer may generate over a long period of time?

2. Family reunions are big business. As front office manager, how would you work with the sales department to ensure quality service for group business?

Case number: 608C17

This case also appears in Todd Comen, *Case Studies in Front Office Management* (Lansing, Mich.: American Hotel & Lodging Educational Institute, 2003).

Chapter 4 Outline

Competencies

1. Discuss the sales dimension of the reservations process, outline the different types of reservations, and describe reservation inquiries and their distribution channels. (pp. 139–152)

2. Describe the process of taking group reservations and discuss group reservation issues. (pp. 152–157)

3. Identify the tools managers use to track and control reservations availability, and discuss reservation records. (pp. 157–161)

4. Describe policies and procedures surrounding the confirmation, modification, and cancellation of different types of reservations. (pp. 161–164)

5. Explain the function of typical reservation reports, and summarize other reservation considerations. (pp. 164–174)

4

Reservations

FROM A GUEST'S POINT OF VIEW, the most important outcome of the reservations process is the hotel having a guestroom ready and waiting when the guest arrives. This guestroom should not be just *any* room, but *the* room that best meets the needs the guest expressed during the reservations process. At the same time, hotel managers have different objectives for the reservations process. They would like the reservations process to provide the highest occupancy and room revenue possible.

To achieve these outcomes, hospitality operations must have efficient reservations procedures in place. Finely tuned procedures allow reservations agents to perform many functions, including identifying what the guest requires and what rooms the hotel has available for the dates requested, recording and acting on reservation details, promoting hotel services, and ensuring accuracy. Reservations agents must be able to respond in a quick, accurate, and pleasant manner. The time an agent spends on researching rates and room package plans, creating records, filing, and other clerical tasks should be held to a minimum.

Processing reservations involves matching room requests with room availabilities and rates; recording, confirming, and maintaining reservations; and producing management reports. Reservation information is especially useful in other front office functions. For example, with the information gathered during the reservations process, front office personnel can use a property management system to finalize room assignments, initiate guest accounts, and track guests' special requests.

At the same time, achieving high occupancy and revenue takes considerable research, planning, and monitoring. In the past, the hotel reservations manager, the front office manager, the rooms division manager, and the general manager have been responsible for these duties. Since the duties associated with room sales have become more important and complex, many hotels have established the position of **revenue manager** to oversee them. A revenue manager is responsible for forecasting demand for each market segment the hotel seeks to attract—corporate transient, group, leisure transient, and others—as well as determining the guestroom rates that will provide sufficient room revenues and occupancies. The revenue manager must coordinate efforts with the reservations, front office, and sales departments to ensure a common base of operational information.

This chapter describes typical activities associated with the reservations process. These activities include:

- Formulating the reservation inquiry
- Determining room and rate availability

- Creating the reservation record
- Confirming the reservation record
- Maintaining the reservation record
- Producing reservation reports
- Researching, planning, and monitoring reservations

The nature of reservations is examined before these activities are addressed.

Reservations and Sales

Prior to automation, reservations agents focused primarily on basic room availability information; they did not have an effective way to identify available rooms by room type. When a guest requested a room, the reservations agent could confirm that a room was available. The agent, however, could not be sure that a particular type of room or that specific furnishings or features were available. Reservations agents would note special requests on the reservation record—such as a no-smoking room or a room with a scenic view or a certain type of bedding—but it was up to the front desk agent to fill such requests at the time of check-in. At the same time, the front desk agent was considered primarily responsible for maximizing hotel occupancy and room revenue. Front desk agents were often provided incentives to sell guests higher-priced rooms during check-in.

Automation of the reservations process provides accurate and current room and rate information. Since room features are normally categorized within the rooms management module, reservations agents can review room and rate information for a specific date. Requests for specific room types, location within the hotel, and special features can be immediately acknowledged and quickly confirmed as part of the reservations process. Many reservation systems automatically pre-assign specific rooms prior to the guest's arrival at the hotel. Pre-registration activities contribute to a more efficient check-in process for arriving guests.

Given the reservations department's increased role in the selling function, much of the responsibility associated with room revenue projections and profitability analyses has shifted to the reservations department. For this reason, many lodging companies currently view reservations as part of the sales department, even though the function has traditionally been part of the rooms division. Reservations agents are not merely order-takers; they are trained in sales techniques. Many hotel companies conduct extensive sales training programs with reservations agents, and use the position to identify staff members who would like to make sales their career. Many reservations offices have sales goals, including number of room nights, average room rate, and room revenue booked.

The ability of the reservations department to sell rooms, maximize revenue, enhance inventory control, and improve guest satisfaction is often cited as an important justification for investing in front office automation. With proper emphasis on sales and marketing techniques, properties can more accurately forecast and better react to business volumes. Gathering forecasted sales information and using it to determine pricing or room rate strategies is often referred to as *revenue management.*

As an increasing volume of reservations are completed online, without involvement of hotel personnel, there is greater reliance on designing intuitive websites that assist guests with self-reservations. When a web-based reservation application is connected to the hotel's property management system, reservation records can be seamlessly transmitted to the property level.

The Role of the Sales Department in Reservations

Since a great deal of the responsibility for achieving occupancy and revenue goals has shifted from the front desk to the reservations department, the sales department has taken a more important role in reservations. There are several reasons for this.

First, the sales department is a primary source of reservations for the hotel. Group sales managers or representatives create group reservations. These reservations are most commonly from corporations or trade associations holding important meetings. In addition, a sales representative may be assigned to attracting social, military, educational, religious, and fraternal groups, which together are usually referred to as the *SMERF market*. Although the actual guest reservations may go directly to the reservations office by telephone, central reservations office, group rooming list, group reservations mailer, or the hotel's website, the sales office typically originates the group sale. Therefore, management evaluates the sales department on how many group guestroom reservations it creates. Senior property managers frequently compare the number of rooms in a group's sales contract to the actual number of rooms the group reserves. In so doing, managers are able to verify that the sales department or the sales manager working with the group researched the group thoroughly before accepting the sales contract.

Second, the sales department is usually responsible for generating sales from other markets as well as the group market. The sales department may have a specialist assigned to corporations (to attract the business traveler market) and perhaps travel agencies as well (to pursue the travel agent market). In large or complex hotels, several managers may be assigned to these markets. The job of a sales agent is to familiarize local businesses and travel agencies with the features and benefits of the property. If the local company agrees to provide the hotel with a specific amount of business, it is often given discounted rates. Senior management must ensure that companies provided with discount plans are meeting their commitments.

Depending on the type of hotel, other sales managers may be assigned to work with online travel agencies (OTAs), Internet websites, and other reservation distribution channels. It is the responsibility of a specialized sales manager to familiarize distribution channels with the hotel's characteristics and its surrounding areas, in an effort to create a positive impression of the property and the travel destination. Distribution channels are regularly given current information regarding the property and the destination, and may also be offered special room rates and/or accommodation packages to help promote the property and attract guests.

Sales managers are often provided with financial or other incentives for meeting or exceeding their sales goals. In the past, goals were commonly established for room nights sold—that is, the total number of room nights the department and individual sales manager sold and the reservations office recorded. Unfortunately, this often led sales managers to significantly reduce room rates in order to close the sale. It is better for sales objectives and incentives (including promotions) to be related to the total revenue a sales manager generates, so that sales managers are not tempted to sell guestrooms at low rates just to meet room-nights-sold quotas.

The Reservation Sales Planning Process

The sales department can book business many months or years in advance. It is not uncommon to make group reservations five years in advance at large, group-oriented hotels. Some hotels have group contracts even further into the future, as the size of the group may limit the number of hotels that are able to accommodate the demand. Other hotels may have the majority of their group business booked no more than six months in advance. Either way, it is usually the sales department that initiates the reservation and revenue management processes, simply by focusing on committing rooms well into the future.

The reservations manager should be involved in every decision affecting the hotel's occupancy and revenue opportunities. In some cases, it is the reservations manager who monitors group and non-group business and informs the sales department of room availability. In other cases, the reservations manager may also be responsible for the hotel's revenue objectives. Every proposed group or corporate rate is evaluated, and the hotel's management team is notified when offering discounted rates jeopardizes revenue goals. Through this involvement, hotel managers can plan and control future business, rather than merely react to market conditions.

One example of planning and controlling group business is the mix of group and transient reservations a hotel accepts. This is generally decided in the annual budgeting process. The mix of business is very important, as it affects total room revenue. Since a hotel's sales department is generally focused on group sales, it is usually allocated a specific number of group rooms to sell. This is called a *group allocation*. The sales department is allowed to sell the rooms within the group allocation without additional approval. However, should sales managers desire to sell more rooms than have been set aside in the group allocation, they generally need the approval of the hotel's sales director or general manager. The reservations manager is usually the person who evaluates these requests and reports on their potential financial impact to room revenue forecasts.

Types of Reservations

The majority of hotel guests make reservations. Reservations may take many forms, but they can all be placed in one of two broad categories: guaranteed or non-guaranteed. It is important for hotel managers to know their state's law concerning guaranteed and non-guaranteed reservations. In some states, confirming a guaranteed reservation is considered a binding contract. If the hotel then fails to provide the room, legal penalties can be applied should the guest file a complaint with the proper state authority.

Guaranteed Reservations

A **guaranteed reservation** assures the guest that the hotel will hold a room until a specific time of the day following the guest's scheduled arrival date. This time may be check-out time of the following day or any other time the hotel chooses. The guest, in turn, guarantees to pay for the room, even if it is not used, unless the reservation is canceled according to the hotel's cancellation policies and procedures. Guaranteed reservations provide some protection for the hotel's revenues even in the case of a **no-show,** a situation in which a guest makes a reservation but does not register or cancel the reservation. Variations of guaranteed reservations are discussed in the following paragraphs.

Prepayment. A **prepayment guaranteed reservation** requires that a payment in full be received prior to the guest's day of arrival at the hotel. From the perspective of the front office, this is generally the most desirable form of guaranteed reservation. This type of guaranteed reservation is commonly used at resort hotels.

Payment Card. Major credit and debit card companies have developed systems to ensure that participating lodging properties receive payment for no-shows through **payment card guaranteed reservations.** Unless a credit or debit card guaranteed reservation is properly canceled before a stated **cancellation hour,** the lodging property will charge the guest's payment card account for one night's room rate plus tax; the card company will then bill the cardholder. Payment card guaranteed reservations are the most common form of guaranteed reservation. Resorts may charge a no-show guest for more than one room night, since the average length of stay at a resort is usually longer and it is more difficult for a resort to fill rooms that become available close to the day of arrival.

Advance Deposit. An **advance deposit guaranteed reservation** requires that the guest pay the hotel a specified amount of money prior to arrival. The amount of an advance deposit is typically large enough to cover one night's room rate and tax. (At resorts that traditionally have longer guest stays, advance deposits of several nights' room rate and tax are often required.) The pre-arrival amount will typically be larger if the reservation is for more than a one-night stay. If a guest holding an advance deposit guaranteed reservation fails to register or cancel, the hotel may retain the deposit and cancel the reservation for the remainder of the guest's stay. This type of guaranteed reservation is most common at destination resorts and convention center hotels. A variation on this type of deposit applies the deposit received to the last night of the stay. This is intended to ensure collection of room revenue should the guest depart earlier than scheduled.

Voucher or MCO. A type of travel agent guarantee is the travel agency voucher or miscellaneous charge order (MCO). The MCO is a voucher issued by the Airline Reporting Corporation (ARC) and is controlled by many of the same travel agency regulations that control airline tickets. Many resorts prefer MCOs if they must accept vouchers, because ARC guarantees payment if the travel agency defaults on the payment. With travel agency vouchers and MCOs, the guest has prepaid the amount of the deposit to the travel agent. The agent forwards a voucher or MCO to the hotel as proof of payment and a guarantee that the prepaid amount will be sent to the hotel when the voucher is returned to the travel agency for payment. Usually, with vouchers and MCOs, the travel agency deducts its commission before sending payment to the hotel.

Corporate. A **corporate guaranteed reservation** involves a corporation entering into an agreement with a hotel. A corporation may sign a contractual agreement with the hotel that states that the corporation will accept financial responsibility for any no-show business travelers the corporation sponsors. Such contracts are often popular in downtown or business center hotels catering to a large number of transient guests. The corporation, in turn, may receive a single comprehensive invoice from the hotel for several stays, thereby simplifying the billing process.

Non-Guaranteed Reservations

In the case of a **non-guaranteed reservation,** the hotel agrees to hold a room for the guest until a stated reservation cancellation hour (usually 4 P.M. or 6 P.M.) on the day of arrival. This type of reservation does not guarantee that the property will receive payment for no-shows. If the guest does not arrive by the cancellation hour, the hotel can release the room, meaning that it can add the room to the list of other rooms available for sale. If the guest arrives after the cancellation hour, the hotel will accommodate the guest only if a room is available.

It is common for hotels planning on full occupancy or nearing full occupancy to accept only guaranteed reservations. The goal behind this strategy is to maximize hotel revenue by reducing the number of potential no-shows. The efficiency and accuracy of a hotel's reservations process is especially critical in full or nearly full occupancy conditions.

Reservation Inquiries

A property receives reservation inquiries in a variety of ways. Regardless of the source, the reservations agent or website will collect information about the guest's stay through a process known as a *reservation inquiry.* The reservations agent or online process should collect such information as the guest's name, address, e-mail address, and telephone number; company or travel agency name (if applicable); date of arrival and date of departure; and the type and number of rooms requested. The reservations agent or online sequence should also try to establish the room rate, number of people in the party, method of payment or guarantee, and any special requests.

Distribution Channels

Hotel chains have come to realize that having multiple distribution channels for promoting their goods and services is critical to success. The more channels of distribution, the more opportunities guests will have to inquire about and book rooms. Reservation inquiries may come in through the property's reservations department (property direct), through a central reservations system, through a cluster reservations office, via a global distribution system (airline and travel agent network), via an intersell agency, or through Internet distribution systems

Exhibit 1   Sources of Reservations

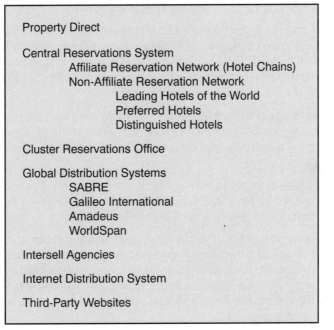

Property Direct

Central Reservations System
        Affiliate Reservation Network (Hotel Chains)
        Non-Affiliate Reservation Network
                Leading Hotels of the World
                Preferred Hotels
                Distinguished Hotels

Cluster Reservations Office

Global Distribution Systems
        SABRE
        Galileo International
        Amadeus
        WorldSpan

Intersell Agencies

Internet Distribution System

Third-Party Websites

(see Exhibit 1). Each of these distribution channels is discussed in the following sections.

Property Reservations Department. Hotels traditionally handled many of their reservation transactions directly. Depending on the volume of direct customer contact, a hotel may have a reservations department handle reservation inquiries rather than another department or online resource. A reservations department handles direct requests for accommodations, monitors any communication links with central reservations systems and intersell agencies, and maintains updated room availability information. Property-direct reservation requests can reach a hotel in several ways:

- *Telephone:* Prospective guests may telephone the hotel. For most hotels, this was one of the most common methods guests used to request a room reservation.

- *Mail:* Written requests for reservations are highly uncommon, except maybe for group, tour, and convention business. Generally, mail requests are sent directly to the reservations department.

- *Property website:* Hotel websites are among the most popular distribution channels today. A hotel's website handles reservation transactions through its automated links to the hotel's property management system.

- *Property-to-property:* Hotel chains typically encourage guests to plan their next hotel stay while in an affiliated property by offering direct communication between properties. This approach can significantly increase the overall number of reservations handled among affiliated properties.

- *Faxes and text messaging:* Faxes and text messaging account for a small portion of reservation transactions. Another text option involves communicating reservations through TDD equipment. This equipment is a specially designed teletype machine that allows people with hearing disabilities to communicate by telephone.

Reservations agent sales process. Most hotels have specific sales procedures for reservations agents to use when taking a reservation from a caller. Common components of the reservations agents' sales process include the following:

1. *Greet the caller.* A warm greeting always sets the proper tone for the conversation. A greeting such as, "Thank you for calling the Casa Vana Inn. This is Holly speaking. How can I help you today?" is always more favorably accepted than a curt greeting such as, "Reservations."

2. *Identify the caller's needs.* It is appropriate to ask the caller about arrival and departure dates, the number of guests, bed preference (double, king, etc.), group or corporate affiliation, and other information that helps define the caller's needs. For example, if a caller states that he or she is traveling with children, the reservations agent should attempt to identify the number of children and their ages.

3. *Provide an overview of the hotel's features and benefits, based on the caller's needs.* Reservations agents should listen closely to what the caller has said in Step 2. Based on that discussion, the agent should highlight the hotel features and benefits that align with the caller's needs. For example, mentioning a year-round swimming pool might be a feature welcomed by families, but they probably would not be interested in the hotel's business center. On the other hand, the business center may be an attractive feature to business travelers.

4. *Propose a room recommendation, and adjust it according to the caller's response.* This step comes after the image of the property has been established (Step 3) and reassures the caller that the reservations agent has truly been listening. If the caller says the recommended room is too expensive or doesn't meet his or her needs, the agent should revise the recommendation as necessary.

5. *Close the sale.* Ask for the reservation; don't wait for the caller to make a decision. Such questions as, "Mr. Bradley, would you like me to reserve that room for you now?" may be appropriate after Mr. Bradley's needs have been addressed.

6. *Gather the reservation information.* Record all the reservation information necessary, according to hotel procedures. This process typically involves repeating the guest's name, arrival date, departure date, room type and rate, and special requests to the caller to confirm the information. This is also the time to secure the reservation guarantee and provide a reservation confirmation number.

Exhibit 2   Sample Automated Reservation Form

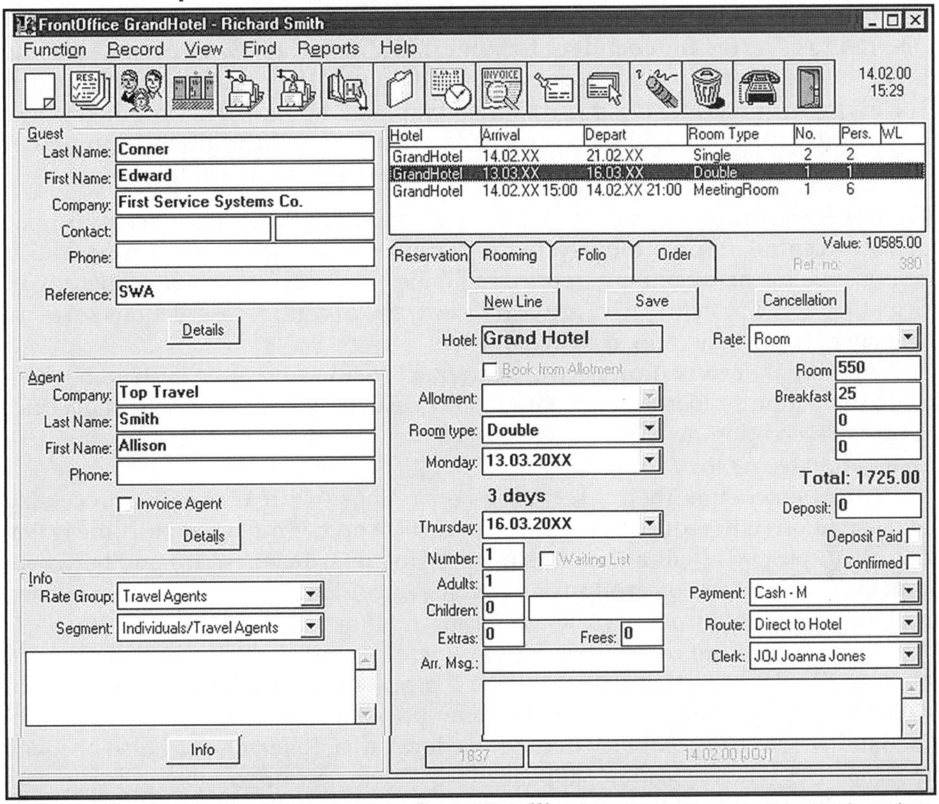

This electronic reservation record is from Hotellinx, a property management system offered by Hotellinx Systems Ltd., Turku, Finland. The company's Internet site (www.hotellinx.com) provides additional screen selections from its system.

7. *Thank the caller.* Closing a call as warmly as opening it leaves callers with a sense of confidence that they have selected the right hotel.

First and foremost, the reservations function is a sales process. One important quality of a successful reservations office is that the agents are trained to sell the hotel instead of being merely order-takers. They create a positive image of the property and instill a desire on the part of the caller to make a reservation. If the agents are excited about their work, their enthusiasm will carry over to callers. Conversely, if the reservations agent sounds unenthusiastic, the caller will not have a positive impression of the property and may decide to make a reservation elsewhere.

Most of the information gathered during the reservation inquiry will be used to create the **reservation record,** a process discussed later in the chapter. Exhibit 2 shows a sample reservation display screen used in an automated reservation system.

Reservations can be made for individuals, groups, tours, or conventions. A guest coming to the hotel as an individual and not part of a group is typically referred to as a **free independent traveler (FIT).** Reservations of persons coming to the hotel as part of a group may be handled differently from those of FIT guests. For example, reservations for group members may be recorded and filed under both the group's name and the guests' individual names. In addition, group reservations may receive special attention during pre-registration activities.

Central Reservations Systems. A majority of lodging properties belong to one or more **central reservations systems.** A central reservations system or CRS is responsible for maintaining a room availability inventory for each property participating in the system. There are two basic types of central reservations systems: affiliate networks and non-affiliate networks.

An **affiliate reservation network** is a hotel chain reservation system in which all participating properties are contractually related. Nearly every chain operates its own reservation network or outsources the central reservations function to a reservation technology supplier.

Chain hotels link their reservations operations to streamline the processing of reservations and reduce overall system costs. Another intended outcome is that one chain property will attract business for (or refer business to) another chain property. In the case of group reservations, information may be shared among affiliate properties through a sales office automation program.

Reservations are often passed from one chain property to another through an automated reservation network. If one property is fully booked, the reservations system handling the transaction may provide an online referral to accommodations at a chain property in the same local area. Referrals may also be made to properties whose locations appear more convenient or suitable to the guest's needs. Affiliate reservation networks that allow non-chain properties to participate in the reservation system are able to represent themselves to a broader market. Non-chain properties in an affiliate reservation system are referred to as **overflow facilities.** Reservation requests may be routed to overflow facilities only after all the available rooms in chain properties (within the targeted geographic area) have been booked. Overflow facilities typically pay a commission fee to the hotel or reservation network for these referrals.

A **non-affiliate reservation network** is a subscription system designed to connect independent or non-chain properties. Non-affiliate reservation networks enable independent hotel operators to enjoy many of the same CRS benefits as chain-affiliated operators. Like an affiliate reservation network, a non-affiliate network usually assumes responsibility for advertising its service and maintaining room availability data. Examples of non-affiliate reservation networks are The Leading Hotels of the World, Preferred Hotels & Resorts Worldwide, and Distinguished Hotels. In many cases, these non-affiliate networks accept only hotels of a certain quality or a limited number of hotels in any geographic area, to keep the value of their service high to participating members.

A central reservations office (CRO) typically deals directly with the public by means of a toll-free telephone number or online web address. Most large lodging chains support two or more reservation centers, with calls and contacts being directed to one of the centers. Reservation centers and websites operate twenty-four hours per day, most days of the year. At peak times, reservation centers will have a large number of agents and automated online servers available.

Central reservations offices typically exchange room availability information with member properties and communicate reservation transactions as they occur. This is normally accomplished through an online communications connection at the member hotel. In this way, reservations information is immediately transmitted between the central reservations entity and the hotel. Rapid-access reservation systems ensure that both the hotel and the central reservations system have accurate, up-to-date information on room availability and rates. Another approach is to have each hotel's property management system hold the master information for its room availability, rates, amenities, and so on; the central reservations system will then gain access when processing reservations. In either case, when a reservation is handled at a central reservations office, property-specific rate and availability data must be uploaded to the central reservation system, and completed reservation transactions processed by the central reservations office must be downloaded to the hotels' property management systems.

Central reservations systems normally provide participating properties with the communications equipment necessary for handling reservation transactions. Communication equipment may take the form of a desktop or notebook computer, an Internet website, an integrated network, a hand-held communication device, or a TDD (telecommunications device for the deaf). The central reservations system typically charges a fee to participating hotels for the services and support equipment it supplies. Hotels may pay a flat fee for the communication equipment and an additional fee for each reservation transaction processed through the system. Alternatively, some central reservations systems charge a flat percentage of room revenue to cover all CRO operational expenses. In turn, each property provides accurate and current room availability data to the central reservations office. Without such data, the central reservations office cannot effectively process reservation requests.

Affiliate and non-affiliate central reservations systems often provide a variety of services in addition to managing reservations processing and communications. A central reservations system may also serve as an inter-property communications network, an accounting transfer system, or a destination information center. For instance, a central reservations system may be used as an accounting transfer system when a chain hotel communicates operating data to company headquarters for processing. When a central reservations system communicates reports on local weather, special events, and seasonal room rates, it serves as a destination information center.

Cluster Reservations Office. Chains that have several properties in a geographic area may opt to establish a single reservation or "cluster" office or website. This satellite entity operates similarly to a hotel chain central reservations system, but serves one specific destination area instead of the entire company. Instead of a reservations agent at the hotel answering the telephone and processing reservation requests, all reservation transactions are channeled through the cluster reservation office or website. When a guest contacts one of the hotels directly for a reservation request, the hotel transfers the inquiry to the cluster entity. Similarly, the company's central reservations network is connected to the cluster network as well as the property itself.

There are several advantages to a cluster reservations office or website. First, there is usually a reduction in staffing; it takes fewer reservations agents or technology specialists to staff a central office than to staff separate reservations offices in every property. Since labor tends to be the highest expense at a hotel, any reduction in labor cost is generally welcome. Second, since reservations agents and websites are serving several hotels at the same time, cross-selling opportunities are created. For example, if Hotel A is full because of a convention, the cluster network can offer another company hotel nearby. This is a convenience for the guest and improves the occupancy of the alternative hotel. Finally, room rates and availability can be coordinated among properties, the brand's central reservations network, and the global distribution systems. This makes reservation processing even more efficient.

Cluster reservations offices and websites may operate centrally or remotely from hotel activities. This physical separation makes communication between the hotel reservation databases being served and the cluster network devices vitally important. Before clustering, general managers could easily review the work of their reservations agents by simply visiting the office within the hotel and observing them. With clustering, coordinating with remote offices and automated networks has its challenges. Perhaps the most important of these is accurate programming and facility descriptions, as there is less opportunity to become familiar with a hotel's rooms, convention services, and other amenities. It is essential, therefore, that the cluster office and website be current in regards to events, facilities, and services at all hotels.

Global Distribution Systems. Most central reservations systems, whether they are an affiliate or a non-affiliate network, connect with one of the **global distribution systems (GDSs).** Most airlines around the world are connected to one or more of these four GDSs: SABRE, Galileo International, Amadeus, and WorldSpan. Historically, GDSs have been owned by an airline or consortium of airlines, but that has changed, since airlines are no longer very involved in the lodging industry. GDSs provide worldwide distribution of hotel reservation information and provide a platform for selling hotel reservations worldwide. GDSs also support the distribution of airline tickets, automobile rentals, and other services required by travelers. By directly linking the reservation systems of hotels, airlines, car rental agencies, and travel agency companies on a global basis through the Internet or a private network, global distribution systems provide access to an extensive array of travel and tourism inventories around the world.

Selling hotel rooms is usually accomplished by connecting hotel companies' reservation systems with the GDSs. Most travel agents around the world have terminals connected to one or more of the many airline reservation systems to book airline travel. By having hotel accommodations and automobile rentals available in the automated system at the same time, most GDSs provide single-source access to most of a travel agent's selling requirements. In one transaction, a travel agent can sell an airline ticket, hotel room, and automobile rental.

Travel agents may be reluctant to book hotel rooms through GDSs, fearing that room availability and room rates are not current, and the confirmation process will not be efficient. Hotel companies have improved their service to guests and travel agents by linking their central reservations systems to GDSs, which allows travel agents to book reservations directly into hotel property management systems with immediate verification of room availability and rates. This linkage is called **seamless integration** or **seamless connectivity.**

Intersell Agencies. An intersell agency is a reservation system alternative to a GDS that contracts to handle reservations for more than one product line. Intersell agencies typically handle reservation services for airline companies, car rental companies, and lodging properties—a "one call does it all" type of approach. Although intersell agencies typically channel room reservation requests to a hotel central reservations system, they may also communicate directly with a destination hotel. The fact that a hotel participates in an intersell arrangement does not preclude its participation in other types of central reservations systems.

Internet Distribution Systems. Many hotel companies, airlines, and car rental firms offer online reservation services through an **Internet distribution system** or **IDS.** Examples of IDSs include Expedia, Hotels.com, Orbitz, Hotwire, Priceline, and Travelocity. IDSs enable travelers from many different market segments to use desktop and mobile devices to reserve hotel rooms, book flights, and select rental cars. Vacation travelers, business travelers, corporate travel offices, international visitors—all are able to use the World Wide Web to make travel and accommodation reservations. The variety of potential guests accessing reservation-capable websites to place reservations has prompted hospitality companies to develop user-friendly reservation search engine and booking procedures.

Large and small hotels alike have a presence on the Internet. Chains often have a website focusing first on the brand and its features, then on the individual properties within the chain. Most chain Internet sites allow visitors to book reservations. Independent hotels also support websites that, while they may not be as technically sophisticated as chain sites, provide similar information and allow visitors to complete a reservations process.

Some prospective hotel guests are concerned about the privacy and security of financial transactions over the Internet. However, hotel websites have adopted security procedures based on reliable encryption methods that protect against fraud. When users access online reservation systems, web browsers automatically engage a high-level security feature.

In addition to providing an effective reservations process and securing transactions, online systems are also capable of performing important marketing functions. Reservation features of many hotel websites enable users to participate in special events and rate promotions. Some enable users to access a multimedia presentation of the features and benefits of the hotel—complete with a "walk-through" of the property (a virtual tour of the various rooms and services offered). Others allow users to reserve golf tee-times, spa treatments, space on local tours, and other activities, as well as make dining room reservations.

Distribution Channel Revenues

Revenues derived by hotels (suppliers) and agents (sellers) forming distribution channels vary widely, depending on the channel or supplier/agent relationship. Central reservations offices typically charge affiliate properties either a fixed rate per night per room, regardless of reservation activity, or a transaction fee based on reservation activity, or both. The amount of revenue earned by the CRO depends on the financial arrangements contracted between the chain and its member properties. Global distribution systems and Internet distribution systems receive revenues from hotels through commissions, by levying transaction fees or transmission fees, and/or by selling hotel rooms that have been discounted.

To illustrate how revenues might be affected by various distribution channels, consider this sample transaction. Suppose a chain hotel is selling a guestroom for $100. If the sale came to the hotel directly, via its property reservations department, the hotel would receive $100. However, if a GDS agent sells the $100 room, the hotel receives less money. Why? Because there are multiple fees that reduce the net revenue to the hotel. The seller (a travel agency, for example) may earn a 10 percent commission ($10 in this case) and the GDS may charge a $3 transaction fee. In addition, the reservation transaction may be processed through the chain's CRS, which might charge $5 for its services. In this example, the hotel receives $82 for the sale, while paying out $18 in commissions and fees.

When hotels sell rooms via the various distribution channels discussed in this section, the objective is to offset associated commissions and other fees with an increase in occupancy and overall room revenue than would otherwise be realized.

Group Reservations

Group reservations can involve a variety of contacts: guests, meeting planners, convention and visitors bureaus, tour operators, and travel agents. Group reservations typically involve intermediary agents and require special handling. Usually, when a group selects a hotel, its representative deals with the hotel's sales or reservations department. If sufficient accommodations are available, an agreed-upon number of guestrooms, called a **block,** is set aside for the group's members. Group members may be given a special reservation identification code or reservation web address to use to reserve rooms within the group's assigned block. Reservations received from group members are applied against the rooms held in the group's block, thereby reducing the number of rooms available within the block. Rooms reserved for specific guests are referred to as **booked.** As group members reserve rooms, the room statuses change from *blocked* to *booked.* Normally, the hotel will establish progress dates to evaluate the degree of conversions from blocked to booked rooms. Unreserved rooms in the block may be released to the hotel's available room inventory at a predetermined date. This time frame is usually referred to as the group reservation **cut-off date.** Typically, the cut-off date is clearly stated in the contract the group's representative completes with the hotel. The hotel may honor reservation requests received after the cut-off date so long as rooms remain available.

Group Reservation Issues

Although group reservation procedures appear simple, a number of potential problems may develop. The following sections consider common group reservation participants and issues.

Creating a Group Block. Group business is often highly desired by hotels. Yet creating and controlling a group block has its pitfalls. When handling group blocks, the reservations manager should be aware of the following procedures:

- Group business demands that a contract be created specifying the exact number of rooms required and the quoted rates. The contract must also specify the main group arrival and departure dates, any special considerations such as suites or complimentary rooms, method of reservation, and the group and individual billing arrangements. Early arrival and late departure dates may also be included in the contract. The contract should also note the group cut-off date for room availability. This information should be applied to the front office system so that reservations can be automatically tracked.

- The reservations manager should verify the total number of rooms required for the group against what is available in the hotel. The sales department often has access to a front office terminal to verify general availability before booking the group. However, the group block should always be verified by the reservations manager to be sure the system inventory is accurate before confirming the room block to the group. If the group will take away rooms from transient (non-group) business, the reservations manager should notify the sales or general manager of the possible effect. This is called **non-group displacement.** Determining displacement is important, because the hotel may block rooms for group guests that it would normally sell to non-group guests, often at a higher rate. In addition, frequent guests of the hotel may have to be turned away and disappointed when a group takes these rooms. Transient guests may feel uncomfortable in a hotel dominated by group business, or will be forced to go elsewhere if they are not able to reserve rooms due to group blocks.

- Before blocking the rooms, the reservations manager should check the group's history with the hotel, if available. For example, if the group requests a fifty-room block and the record shows the group booked only forty rooms the year before, the reservations manager may wish to confer with the sales manager before finalizing the block. Reducing a block based on the group's history is called a **wash down** or a **wash.** If the group does not have a history at the hotel, it is sometimes possible to check with the hotel that last accommodated the group. By following these steps, the reservations manager helps control room inventories and ensures that as many rooms as possible are available for sale. It is important to note that the wash-down process must be handled very carefully. Contracts are legally binding and the hotel must provide the number of rooms specified in the contract. If a group leader finds out that a hotel does not have the number of available rooms specified in the contract, there can be significant legal consequences.

- As group reservations arrive, the reservations manager must monitor the room availability in the block. It is important for the reservations manager to notify the sales department when a block does not look like it will fill or if more rooms are needed in the block due to strong demand. The sales department can then contact the group and make adjustments to the room block. If more rooms are needed, there may be an impact on the group allocation and the hotel may have to choose between taking the additional group reservations or referring them to other hotels. If fewer rooms are needed than blocked, this can be an opportunity for the sales department to sell additional rooms.

- Group room sales programs are an important issue for the reservations manager to monitor. By definition, a *definite group* is a group that has signed a sales contract. All definite groups should be entered into the reservation system as soon as they have signed a contract, in order to maintain an accurate room inventory. A *tentative group* is a group that has had a contract sent to them, but has not signed or returned the contract to the hotel. Some hotels choose to enter tentative groups into their reservation system. In this way the hotels can keep track of what they believe they have sold of their group allocation. However, it is necessary to track tentative groups to be sure they are updated to definite status or removed from the reservation system. Holding tentative groups on the books for too long may prohibit the booking of a definite group and can cause confusion between the sales and reservation offices.

- The method of sending group reservations to the hotel is also important and often included in the sales contract. Attendees may be allowed to make reservations directly with the hotel and through the central reservations network or online. Direct registration activity may not always be desired. In other cases, the group sponsor may want to receive the reservation requests before they go to the hotel. Many corporate group reservations are provided to the hotel on a rooming list from the company; this may also apply to tour groups from travel agencies. Group leaders often prefer to closely control rooming and billing arrangements. Agents in the reservations office must be careful that they honor these arrangements and not accept reservations outside of the agreed-upon procedures.

Conventions and Conferences. Problems can occur during a convention or conference if a close working relationship is not established between the hotel's sales staff and the group's meeting planner. If good communication and a spirit of cooperation are established early on, many problems can be avoided. Suggestions for hotels dealing with convention groups include the following:

- Know the convention group's profile, including its cancellation, no-show, and last-minute reservation history.

- Review all relevant hotel reservation policies with the convention planner.

- Inform reservations agents that the convention has been scheduled, and go over the reservation process set up for the convention.

- Produce regularly scheduled reports to update the status of the convention block.

- Generate an up-to-date list of registrants at regular intervals.

- Correct errors found by the convention planner immediately.

- Confirm reservations from attendees as soon as they are received.

- Return rooms to the group's block when cancellations are received and inform the convention planner.

- Distribute a final rooming list to the convention planner and all hotel staff involved with the convention.

Convention and Visitors Bureaus. Large conventions sometimes require the use of rooms at more than one hotel to accommodate all the convention attendees. When conventions take rooms at many hotels in a city, they are often called city-wide conventions. Frequently, room requirements at several hotels are coordinated by a separate housing or convention bureau within the city. Special application software may be used to help monitor and coordinate this effort. Each hotel must determine the number and type of available rooms it is willing to set aside for convention use. The objective of the bureau is to accommodate all attendees by coordinating hotel availabilities with reservation requests. The convention and visitors bureau normally uses a communications network to notify participating hotels on a daily (or more frequent) basis. In return, each hotel informs the bureau of any requests or cancellations communicated directly to the hotel's reservation system. Through such an exchange of information, the bureau assists each hotel in effectively managing its convention block.

Tour Groups. Tour groups are groups of people who have had their accommodations, transportation, and related travel activities arranged for them by a professional tour operator. Hotels should be especially careful to research the reliability and past performance of tour operators and travel agents. Once acquainted with a tour operator's history, reservations managers may feel more secure when blocking and booking reservations for a tour group. Suggestions for dealing with tour group reservations include the following:

- Specify the number and types of rooms to be held in a group block, including rooms for drivers and guides.

- Clearly state a cut-off date, after which unused rooms in the block will be released for other hotel use. On or before the cut-off date, the tour operator should supply the hotel with a guarantee on the number of rooms the group will need (if the operator can't supply a final rooming list by this date).

- Specify a date by which the organizer will provide a final rooming list (if this date is different from the cut-off date).

- Monitor the amount of advance deposits required and their due date.

- Note on the reservation record any services and amenities the property will provide as part of the group package.

- Include on the reservation record the name and telephone number of the tour group's representative or agent.

- Note any special arrangements, such as early arrival, baggage handling, registration, and check-out procedures.

Attendee Management and Housing Systems Software. Attendee management and housing systems software is a supplemental reservation planning tool. Historically, group meeting planners and hotel reservation staffs had to coordinate group attendee reservation activities without the help of automated systems. Group reservations were once handled by telephone or via a printed reservation mailer. Group leaders would distribute mailers to potential attendees, who would complete the mailer and return it to the hotel. This was a time-consuming process that was often inaccurate, due to illegible guest handwriting or confusion over dates and rate plans or other issues. Hotels then had to report the reservations they received to group leaders, so they could keep track of group reservations on their end.

These problems were relieved when hotel companies allowed group reservations via their websites and call centers. Although a website can be helpful, the hotel staff must ensure that the site's group information is accurate. Group attendees using the website will receive the appropriate group rate for a guestroom allocated to the group only if the information is accessible at the time of the reservation.

Attendee management and housing systems software automates the group reservations and registration process. The software relies on the Internet to communicate with potential attendees. Attendee management applications focus only on meeting registration activities, while housing system applications are designed to handle guestroom reservations and meeting registration activities.

With an attendee management and housing registration system, the group leader creates a special website that provides information about the group event and reservation availability. The information is then linked to the group's main website, so people visiting the site can see the information. Some systems allow group leaders to load e-mail and postal addresses; the group leader can then send e-mail and printed messages via regular mail to prospective attendees. Attendees receiving the e-mail message can click on the Internet link contained in the message, then register for the meeting and reserve a room. Prospective attendees receiving the printed message are given the website address, so they can log on and make their reservations.

These systems capture guest information, including the guest's name, mailing address, e-mail address, payment card information, guestroom request, and much more. Guests can usually identify special needs; they may indicate that they plan to arrive early, for example, or request a no-smoking room. Group attendees can sign up for specific presentations, events, or recreational activities (they can reserve golf tee times or make spa reservations, for example).

Once the guest provides the information requested on the website, the information is sent to the group for processing. Simpler systems provide meeting planners with reports that are forwarded to the hosting hotel for manual processing. More sophisticated systems, like Passkey, actually interface with hotel reservation systems. When a reservation is made through a Passkey website to a "Passkey-enabled" hotel, the reservation is made, and confirmed to the guest, automatically. This eliminates the manual processing associated with transcribing printed reports into the hotel's reservation system. It also keeps the room inventories accurate between the group and the hotel. For large meetings, some systems combine the inventories of many hotels, thereby giving guests a choice of where to stay. This is especially important for meetings that use much of a city's guestroom inventory. Attendee management and housing system software can be very cost-effective because it simplifies the meeting registration and reservation processes. This is important to meeting planners and hotels alike, since it improves communications between them and reduces the amount of manual labor.

Reservation Availability

When a hotel or its website receives a reservation inquiry, it is important to compare the inquiry data with previously processed reservations. Processing a reservation request results in one of several responses. A hotel can:

- Accept the reservation as requested.

- Suggest alternative room types, dates, and/or rates.

- Suggest an alternative hotel.

In any **reservation system,** it is necessary to closely monitor the number of reservations in order to control **overbooking.** A hotel should use care when accepting reservations beyond its room capacity. Some states have laws concerning guests with guaranteed reservations who do not receive rooms when they arrive at a hotel. Reservation systems can be programmed to closely monitor overbooking.

Comparing historical reservation volumes against actual arrivals can produce an overbooking factor to serve as a booking guideline. Depending on the property's no-show reservation history, management may allow the reservations system to overbook. Overbooking is a strategy aimed at helping the hotel to achieve 100-percent occupancy by hedging against guests who do not arrive or cancel their reservations. Based on historical data and the experience of knowledgeable managers, reservation systems may be able to forecast cancellations, early check-outs, and no-shows with a high level of accuracy. Room reservation forecasts must be shared with the sales department and general manager, who may have additional information not entered in the reservation system, such as information about competitive pressures and other issues. By booking a hotel slightly beyond its available room capacity, the system attempts to ensure that as many rooms as possible are occupied.

Overbooking should be approached cautiously. If a reservation system is allowed to book too many rooms, guests with confirmed reservations may have to be turned away. This creates poor guest relations and discourages repeat business. To properly control overbooking, managers must monitor reservation system activity by controlling booking, blocking, and cancellation information.

Reservation Systems

An automated reservation management module in a property management system can keep close track of reservation activities. Such systems can tightly control room

Exhibit 3   Daily Arrival, Stayover, and Departure Report

ARRIVALS, STAYOVERS, DEPARTURES FOR KELLOGG CENTER
PAGE 001
01/19/XX   15:03

DATE	ARRIVE	STAYON	DEPART	GUESTS	SOLD	UNSOLD	REVENUE
01/19	19	83	4	135	102	43	5,185.00
01/20	34	57	45	131	91	54	4,604.00
01/21	37	55	36	130	92	53	4,495.50
01/22	15	6	86	29	21	124	1,116.00
01/23	12	14	7	36	26	127	1,252.00

Courtesy of Kellogg Hotel & Conference Center, Michigan State University, East Lansing, Michigan.

availability data and automatically generate many reservation-related reports. Exhibit 3, for example, shows a daily expected arrival, stayover, and departure report. It indicates that for January 19, nineteen arrivals, eighty-three stayovers, and four departures are expected. In addition, this report projects estimated room revenue based on reported reservation information. Automated systems can also generate reports summarizing reservations by room type, guest profile, and many other characteristics. The biggest advantage of an automated reservation system is the improved accuracy of room availability and rate information. As reservations agents input reservations and reservation modifications or cancellations into the system, the inventory of available rooms is immediately updated. In addition, front desk transactions involving no-shows, early departures, or walk-ins will immediately update the room availability. This is important, as it provides sales managers with the occupancy and room-rate information they need to help them achieve revenue objectives.

Exhibit 4 shows a guestroom control log from a hotel sales software package. For each day of the week, the screen shows the total number of rooms still available for sale, as well as the number of rooms allocated to definite and tentative group bookings and the number of rooms protected for front office sales to transient business. Room sales are coordinated in real time as salespeople, reservations agents, and the front office manager have instant access to the most current information.

Once all rooms in a specific category are sold, the reservation system can be programmed to refuse any further reservations in that category. When checking availability in a closed category, a reservations agent may receive a message such as the following displayed on the screen: *The category of rooms requested is not available.* Some reservation systems are programmed to automatically suggest alternative room types or rates, or even other nearby hotel properties. Systems can be programmed to itemize room availability for future periods and may display open, closed, and special event dates for an extended period of time. *Open dates* refer to available room days, while *closed dates* depict full-house forecasts. *Special*

Exhibit 4   Guestroom Control Log

Scheduler - Newmarket Hotel & Towers

File View Activity Reports Window Help

QuickBook...

| To Do List | Diary | GRC | Appointments |

Account tree (left panel):
- Account
  - Merck Pharmecutical, Inc
  - Ernst & Young
  - American Express Travel
  - Avery Labels
- Booking
  - American Medical Association
  - Brown and Smith Consulting
  - Avery Labels
  - Merck Pharmecutical, Inc
- Contact
  - Mr. Richard Durgan
  - Ms. Janet Evans
  - Mr. Rick Fennimore
  - Mr. Jake Thompson

Calendar: March 20XX

14 Bookings (2002)

				Tue 3/5	Wed 3/6	Thu 3/7	Fri 3/8	Sat 3/9	Sun 3/10	Mon 3/11
Total Available				175	190	30	170	190	330	390
Group Definite				175	155	170	40	40	0	0
Group Tentative				20	25	180	180	170	70	0
Trans Protected				130	130	120	110	100	100	110
MAR				110	120	110	90	90	90	110
Archer	D	BK	125	25	25					
Ernst & Young	D	BK	220	20						
Ambleside	D	BK	140	90	90	90				
Merck	D	BK	145	40	40	40				
Brown Co.	D	JRL	130				40	40	40	
AMA	T	LRH	125	20	25					
Exxon	T	CMK	225			180	180	170	70	
Avery Labels	P	BK	125	200	200					
Oceans, Inc	P	BK	120	90						
MPC Holdings	P	BK	45					45	45	
IBM	P		110							
Johnson & Co.	P	BK	123						45	45
Prudential	P	PH	230						100	100
Toyota	P	BK	120						100	

Source: Delphi for Windows/Newmarket International, Inc., Durham, New Hampshire. For more information, visit the company's Internet site at www.newmarketinc.com.

event dates can be programmed to alert reservations agents that a convention or large group is expected to occupy the hotel either before, during, or immediately following a caller's requested day of arrival. In addition, many reservation systems have a management override feature that enables overbooking. This override provision should be exercised with extreme care.

Reservation systems store reservation records electronically, thereby allowing the creation of waiting lists for high-demand periods. This feature contributes to the processing of group reservations and the implementation of revenue management strategies. The future time frame for tracking reservations is called the "reservation horizon"; most automated systems have horizons of two to five years.

Reservation Records

Reservation records identify guests and their occupancy needs before the guests' arrival. These records enable the hotel to personalize and/or customize guest service and schedule staff more accurately. Reservation records also contain a variety of data that the hotel can use to generate several important management reports.

Reservations agents or online hotel booking engines can create reservation records based on interactions with guests only after determining that a request for a reservation can be met. These electronic records initiate the guest cycle. To create a reservation record, the reservations system typically captures such guest data as:

- Guest's name (and group name, if applicable)
- Guest's home or billing address
- Guest's e-mail address
- Guest's telephone number, including area code
- Name, address, and telephone number of the guest's company, if appropriate
- Name of and pertinent information about the person making the reservation, if not the guest
- Number of people in the party, and perhaps the ages of any children
- Arrival date and time
- Number of nights required or expected departure date, depending on how the system is designed
- Reservation type (guaranteed, non-guaranteed)
- Special requirements (infant, disabled guest, or no-smoking accommodations, for example)
- Additional information as needed (method of transportation, late arrival, flight number, room preference, and so forth)

If a guest plans to arrive after the hotel's normal reservation cancellation hour, the guest should be informed of the property's policy for non-guaranteed reservations. Once the necessary information has been captured, the system may immediately assign a reservation confirmation number. Confirmation number assignment provides both the guest and the reservations department with a unique reference for the reservation record.

In the case of a guaranteed reservation, additional information is generally needed for the reservation record. Depending on the guest's method of guarantee, the following information may be required:

- *Payment card information:* This information consists of the payment card type, number, expiration date, security code number, and cardholder's name. Online reservation systems may be connected to a transaction processing service that allows for automatic verification of payment card information.

- *Prepayment or deposit information:* This information comes in the form of an agreement from the guest to submit a required deposit to the hotel before a specified date. A proposed advance deposit or prepayment guarantee should be closely monitored to ensure the correct amount is paid by the designated date; if it is not, the reservation may need to be canceled or reclassified as non-guaranteed. If the hotel's policy is to collect the deposit at the time of reservation, the guest should be notified. If a payment card is provided at the time the reservation is made, the transaction processing services will post the deposit to the hotel immediately.

- *Corporate or travel agency account information:* This information includes the name and address of the booking company, the name of the person making the reservation, and the client's corporate or travel agency direct billing account number (if previously assigned by the hotel). For efficiency, the hotel may preload an approved list of corporate and travel agency account numbers to expedite the verification process. Even if the corporation or travel agency does not require billing, a tracking account is usually set up in the reservation system to monitor the business the corporation or travel agency provides to the hotel. In this way the sales office will have the information necessary to negotiate or renegotiate contracts with such companies.

Reservations systems should disclose important aspects of guaranteeing a reservation. Guests must be aware that their accommodations will only be held until a specific time past their scheduled arrival time. Guests must also know that if they fail to cancel the reservation before a specified time, they may forfeit the deposit or the hotel may levy a charge against the guarantee.

Individual properties and chains may differ with respect to quoting and confirming room rates during the creation of a reservation record. Although published rates may be subject to change without notice, a rate quoted and confirmed during the reservations process must be honored. Reservation systems must be capable of modifying rates based on such factors as:

- Supplementary charges for extra services or amenities.
- Arrival or minimum stay requirements in effect for the dates requested (if any).
- Special promotions in effect for the dates requested (if any).
- Applicable currency exchange rates, which may alter final charges for international guests.
- Applicable room tax exemptions and percentages.
- Applicable service charges or gratuities.

Reservation Confirmation/Cancellation

A reservation confirmation means that the hotel acknowledged and verified a guest's room request and personal information. A written confirmation states the intent of both parties and confirms important points of agreement: names, dates, rate, type of accommodation, number of rooms, deposit required or received, and number of guests. *Confirmed reservations may be either guaranteed or non-guaranteed.*

Reservation systems normally generate a confirmation notice shortly after the reservation request is matched with availability. Information can be retrieved from the reservation record and automatically reformatted into a specially designed letter or e-mail format. While there are probably as many formats for confirmation letters and e-mails as there are hotels, all confirmation notices generally include:

- Name and address of guest
- Date and time of arrival

- Room type and rate
- Length of stay
- Number of persons in party
- Reservation classification (guaranteed or non-guaranteed)
- Reservation confirmation number
- Special requests, if any

Depending on the nature of the reservation, the confirmation notice may also include a request for a deposit or prepayment, or an update of the original reservation detailing reconfirmation, modification, or cancellation.

For guests requesting accommodations and services covered by the Americans with Disabilities Act, the confirmation notice is an important channel of communication. It assures these guests that their special needs are understood and the accommodations they need will be ready. Hotels often categorize guestrooms that are specially equipped for disabled guests in a separate inventory classification for improved control.

Confirmation/Cancellation Numbers

As part of the reservation confirmation process, systems may assign a reservation **confirmation number.** A confirmation number helps assure a guest that a reservation record exists. It can be especially useful to a hotel in referencing a specific reservation record requiring modification or cancellation. Similarly, reservation systems may issue a reservation **cancellation number** to guests properly canceling a reservation.

Issuing a reservation cancellation number protects both the guest and the hotel. In the event of any future misunderstanding, the assignment of a reservation cancellation number can prove that the hotel received the cancellation within policy guidelines. In the case of a canceled guaranteed reservation, a reservation cancellation number may relieve the guest of an obligation to pay any charges posted against the guarantee. Without a reservation cancellation number, a guest may have trouble disputing a no-show billing. Cancellation numbers are not normally assigned to guests who cancel their reservation after the hotel's stated cancellation hour. These reservations are considered canceled outside the available time frame. If the canceled reservation is non-guaranteed, the guest is not obligated to pay the hotel. Procedures for issuing cancellation numbers may be part of an established agreement between the hotel and a payment card company relative to no-show billing.

Each reservation system typically uses unique methods of generating confirmation and cancellation numbers. These numbers can include portions of the guest's scheduled arrival date, the reservations agent's initials, a property code, and other relevant information. For example, under one system, the cancellation number 36014MR563 represents these facts:

360   =   guest's scheduled date of arrival (from consecutively numbered days of the year)

14	=	property code number
MR	=	initials of the reservations agent issuing the cancellation number
563	=	consecutive numbering of all cancellation numbers issued in the current year

Calendar dates can be expressed in three digits when the days of the year are numbered consecutively from 001 through 365 (366 in a leap year). These are often referred to as *Julian dates*. For example, the number 360 in the example corresponds to December 26 in a non-leap year.

Confirmation and cancellation numbers should be stored in separate files for quick referencing. Cross-referencing reservation cancellation numbers by scheduled date of arrival can help facilitate other related functions. For example, the cancellation of a reservation will result in updated reservation reports that assist management in staffing and facility planning.

No matter how thorough the reservations process, there is no way to avoid an occasional reservation change or cancellation. This fact does not make the proper creation of a reservation record any less important. A system's capabilities for storing and retrieving reservation records and related files are vital to the reservations process. If a person contacts the hotel or hotel website to change a reservation, for example, the reservations agent or automated filing system must be able to quickly access the correct record, verify its contents, and process the modification. The system must also be able to promptly re-file the reservation record and update pertinent reservation reports.

Modifying Non-Guaranteed Reservations

Guests sometimes make non-guaranteed rather than guaranteed reservations when they expect to arrive at the property before the hotel's reservation cancellation hour. However, situations can arise that make it impossible for a guest to arrive on time. For example, delayed airline flights, road-construction bottlenecks, or weather conditions may hinder travel. When delays are apparent, experienced travelers often contact the hotel and notify the staff of the delay, or change their reservations from non-guaranteed to guaranteed in order to avoid being canceled at the hotel's reservation cancellation hour. Reservations systems capable of processing reservation changes must closely adhere to hotel policies. Typically, a system would:

1. Access the correct non-guaranteed reservation record.
2. Capture the guest's payment card type, number, and expiration date.
3. Assign the guest a new reservation confirmation number, if it is hotel policy.
4. Complete the change from non-guaranteed to guaranteed reservation status according to additional system procedures, if any.

Canceling a Reservation

A prospective guest does the hotel a service when he or she takes the time to cancel a reservation. A reservation cancellation informs the hotel that a previously reserved room is once again available, and helps the front office more effectively manage its rooms inventory. Hotels should make processing reservation cancellations easy and efficient. Reservation cancellations, like any guest service, require the reservations website or front office staff to be as guest-friendly and effective as possible.

Non-Guaranteed Reservations. To cancel a non-guaranteed reservation, the reservation system may require the guest's name and address, number of reserved rooms, scheduled arrival and departure dates, and reservation confirmation number, if available. This information will ensure that the correct reservation is accessed and canceled. After recording the cancellation, the system should assign a cancellation number.

Payment Card Guaranteed Reservations. Most payment card companies will support no-show billings only if the reservation system issues cancellation numbers for properly canceled reservations. Reservations systems may follow a cancellation procedure for payment card guaranteed reservations that involves the following steps:

1. Access the correct reservation record.

2. Assign a reservation cancellation number.

3. Add the cancellation number to the reservation cancellation file.

4. Verify updated room availability information (room returned to available inventory).

Advance Deposit Reservations. Policies related to the cancellation of advance deposit reservations vary greatly among hotel companies and reservation systems. The reservation system should follow procedures similar to those it uses for processing reservation cancellations. Deposits are normally returned to guests who properly cancel reservations. While reservation systems must always be precise when assigning and recording reservation cancellation numbers, it is especially important when an advance deposit is involved.

Reservation Reports

An effective reservation system helps maximize room sales by accurately monitoring room availabilities and forecasting rooms revenue. The number and type of management reports available through a reservation system are functions of the hotel's needs and the system's capability and contents. Popular reservations management reports include the following:

- *Reservation transactions report:* This report summarizes daily reservations activity in terms of reservation record creation, modification, and cancellation. Other possible reports include specialized summaries such as cancellation reports, blocked room reports, and no-show reports.

- *Commission agent report:* Agents with contractual agreements may be owed commissions for business booked at the property. This report tracks the amounts the hotel owes to each agent.

- *Regrets and denials report:* Regrets and denials are ways of classifying lost business. Regrets are recorded when guests choose not to make a reservation. There may be several reasons for this, including room rate, room type availability, location, and other factors. Denials are recorded when the hotel is unable to accept a reservation request. This is most often due to room availability or restrictions put on new reservations. In many hotels, each of these situations is recorded for review by management. If the hotel is getting too many regrets due to rate, management may need to adjust the rate to be more competitive. Denials help management decide such things as group allocations, or whether more rooms of a certain type need to be added to the property. Some companies call this report the "turnaway report" or "lost business report."

- *Revenue forecast report:* This report projects future revenue by multiplying predicted occupancies by applicable room rates. This information can be especially important for the hotel's long-range planning and cash management strategies.

Expected Arrival and Departure Lists

Expected arrival and departure lists may be generated according to a predetermined schedule or on demand to indicate the number and names of guests expected to arrive, depart, or stay over.

A list of expected arrivals may be displayed or printed in the reservations department or via any connected device. Front desk agents depend on having expected arrival information to facilitate an efficient guest registration process. Similarly, expected departure information can be used to anticipate and expedite guest account settlement and check-out. Expected departure lists also help front desk staff members identify guests who may be staying beyond their expected departure date but have not told the hotel (overstays). This can be very important, especially when the hotel expects a high percentage of occupancy and may have already pre-assigned the occupied room for an incoming guest.

Reservation systems can also perform preregistration functions and provide other services for special guests, such as VIPs or those staying in specially prepared rooms. Depending on the amount of information collected during the reservations process, a guest may need only to sign a pre-arrival form or submit his or her payment card for processing to complete the registration process. By securing comprehensive information during the reservations process, a more efficient guest registration process may be possible.

Processing Deposits

Advance deposits for reservations should be processed by employees who do not have direct access to reservation records. Reservations personnel should not handle advance deposit payments, as a separation of duties provides a higher level of security for the hotel. Someone independent of the reservations process—the hotel's general cashier, for example—may be a good candidate as an independent reviewer. This employee should endorse and record deposit payments immediately after receiving them and record the following information in a deposits-received system file: form of payment, identifying payment number, amount of payment, date received, guest name, arrival date, and reservation confirmation number. The file should then be accessible by the reservations department. Each reservation record should be updated with the status of its deposit information. A transaction report should verify that the recorded deposits balance with the total reservation deposits entered for the day.

Generally speaking, advance deposits received from guests should be processed with a high level of security. Hotels should discourage guests from sending cash payments through the mail. Checks are better, but payment card deposits are almost always preferred.

Reservations Histories

Front office managers can develop an understanding of the hotel's reservations pattern by analyzing reservation information. The hotel's sales and marketing division can apply reservations data and assorted system reports to identify trends, review products and services, and assess the impact of marketing strategies. Reservations histories include statistics on all aspects of the reservations process, including the number of guests, occupied rooms, reservations (by distribution channel), no-shows, walk-ins, overstays, and understays (people who checked out before a stated departure date). *Overstays* differ from *stayovers* in that a stayover is simply a guest who *continues to occupy* a room between his or her day of arrival and expected departure date. Knowing overstay and understay percentages can help management devise a plan for accommodating walk-ins or guests who request reservations at the last minute. Histories are also very helpful to track individual groups. Knowing the group booking pattern (arrivals prior to the start of the group block and departures after the end of the group block, for example) may be important for more accurately projecting future bookings. Tracking group guests who depart before their expected departure date is important because it may indicate to the hotel reservations manager that additional reservations can be taken on dates held by the group, since a certain number of attendees tend to leave before their departure date.

Other Reservation Considerations

The topics covered in this section are not part of the typical reservations process. Nonetheless, it is important for front desk and reservations personnel to understand the legal implications of a reservation and be familiar with waiting lists, promotional packages, potential problems in the reservations process, and the impact of e-commerce and online reservations.

Legal Implications

The reservation agreement between the hotel and the guest begins at the time of guest contact. This agreement may be oral or written. Confirming a reservation to a prospective guest in language that states that the guest will be accommodated on a particular date may constitute a contract binding the hotel to provide accommodations on that date. If the confirmation is in response to a reservation request from the prospective guest, it may bind both the hotel and the prospective guest to fulfill the reservation.

Waiting Lists

Occasionally, a reservation request must be denied because the hotel is fully booked on the date in question. However, with sufficient lead time, interested guests may be put on a waiting list for the proposed date. Hotels experiencing high-volume reservations may satisfy excess demand through this technique. A waiting list might be developed and used according to these guidelines:

- Advise the guest that no rooms are currently available for the requested date(s).

- Offer to take the guest's name, telephone number, and e-mail address.

- Agree to notify the prospective guest immediately if a room becomes available due to a cancellation or change.

- Help the guest find alternative dates or accommodations if no rooms become available.

Having a waiting list, when properly implemented and managed, is a good business practice that provides a service to guests that helps foster good will.

Promotional Packages

Many hotels and resorts offer special promotional packages to potential guests. These packages always include the guestroom, plus optional features such as meals, golf, tennis, sports lessons, limousine service, and sight-seeing or other activities in or near the property. Generally, hotels and resorts provide guests with some sort of discount for purchasing a promotional package. Guests often consider promotional packages a bargain and a convenience, since they don't have to arrange to separately purchase the items and activities offered in the package.

Reservations personnel and website content must be very informative about all the packages a property offers. Before buying a package, guests will usually interact with a reservations agent or visit the property's website to learn more about the package in detail, including features and all related prices. If a guest wishes to stay at a resort for four nights, and the resort offers only a three-night package, the reservations agent or the website must be capable of pricing and applying an extra night's stay. Packages can be very effective for hotels and resorts, especially when they are well designed and properly sold.

Potential Reservation Problems

Some steps of the reservations process are more susceptible to error than others. If reservations agents are aware of these trouble spots and can successfully deal with them, mistakes will be less likely. The following sections discuss some common reservation problems.

Errors in the Reservation Record. Unfortunately, there are many opportunities for a reservations agent or a guest at a website to make an error when creating a reservation record. For example:

- The record may be created with an incorrect arrival or departure date, a misspelled guest name, or first and last names mistakenly reversed (for example, *Troy Thomas* might be recorded as *Thomas Troy*).

- The name of the person making a reservation on behalf of the guest may be accidentally entered as the guest's name on the reservation record.

To avoid such problems, the reservations system or agent should verify the information entered on the reservation record by displaying or reciting the information back to the person creating the reservation record. In addition, displaying or quoting the hotel's cancellation policy is appropriate as part of this process, as it can help avoid later problems related to no-show billings or non-return of deposits. Such communication can be especially important to hotels catering to international travelers. An error that prevents access to a reservation record can be disastrous to a hotel-guest relationship.

Misunderstandings Due to Industry Jargon. Sometimes reservations agents or web-based systems use industry jargon that is not always widely understood. This can lead to problems. For example:

- A family with a *confirmed reservation* may arrive two hours after the cancellation hour only to find that the hotel has no rooms available; the family thought a confirmed reservation was the same as a *guaranteed reservation*.

- Two business travelers book a *double room,* anticipating two beds; they are displeased to learn their room has only *one double bed.*

- Parents wishing to have their children stay in a *connecting room* mistakenly request an *adjacent room.* At check-in, the parents find that the children's room is across the hall or next door with no direct connection.

To avoid such problems, reservations agents or web-based systems should make every effort to minimize industry jargon and explain what various terms mean at a particular property. After accepting a reservation, the terms and conditions of reserved accommodations should be provided in addition to the hotel's general reservations policies and procedures.

Miscommunication with Central Reservations Systems. There are some unique possibilities for miscommunication between guests and reservations agents or online central reservations systems. For example:

- A central reservations system serving several hotels in the same city may confuse the guest, causing the guest to make a reservation at the wrong hotel, such as a chain's airport property rather than its mid-city property.

- A system that handles hotels in similarly named cities may book the guest into a hotel in the wrong city or state (for example, Charleston, West Virginia, instead of Charleston, South Carolina; Pasadena, California, instead of Pasadena, Texas).

To avoid such problems, the hotel's reservations agents or website should furnish the guest with the full name and address of the property at which a reservation has been made. When a reservation system serves more than one hotel in the same city, a thorough description of the hotel's location is extremely helpful to guests. One feature of automated systems is a zip code check or a displayed map of the area. With this program, the reservations agent or guest enters the zip code of the hotel and the system identifies the city associated with the zip code, along with a map with directions to the property, thereby helping to minimize address errors.

Online Reservation System Failures. Unless a reliable communication linkage between the hotel and an online reservation application is maintained effectively, problems can occur. For example:

- The hotel may fail to update its online reservation system database with current room availabilities and rate changes.

- The online reservation system may be delinquent in communicating reservations it has booked to the property.

- Communications equipment, affecting either the online reservation system or the hotel, may become inoperable.

- The hotel may close reservations on a particular date with the online reservations system, but apply this change too late to be effective.

- The hotel may discover that it has rooms available on a certain date due to cancellations or early departures but fail to update the online reservation system in time to gain last-minute reservations.

- Global distribution systems and Internet distribution systems may present similar problems. Reservation systems without effective interfaces to GDSs and IDSs may have to constantly update room availability data through an off-line process. This can be time-consuming and error-prone.

To avoid such problems, hotel management must ensure accurate and timely communication between the hotel and the online reservation systems. This is typically a duty of the reservations manager. When closing reservations for a certain date, the hotel must check for any reservations an online reservation system may have confirmed but not yet communicated. Many companies have automated links between the hotel reservations system and central reservations network that eliminate the timing issues of opening and closing availability and changing rates (seamless integration). Faulty equipment at either end of the communication channel may impair the effectiveness of the reservations process. Attention must be paid to ensuring a sound working relationship between the online reservation system(s) and the hotel's reservation system.

In addition, it is appropriate to frequently double-check the global distribution systems and Internet distribution systems to be sure room availability and rates are correctly displayed. This can be done by reviewing the content of GDS and IDS online offerings on a regular basis.

E-Commerce

E-commerce is an important component in hotel reservations management. (The chapter introduced e-commerce earlier, but it is covered here in more detail because of its importance.) E-commerce extends the reach of hotels far beyond the traditional distribution channels of a hotel reservations office, call center, and global distribution system. Hotels have a presence in multiple distribution channels and direct access to the consumer through the Internet. Regardless of whether a hotel is part of a chain or is independent, it can participate in online commerce via the Internet. Linking with guests through the Internet is actually the easiest part of e-commerce. The more difficult part is knowing which sites provide the best distribution opportunities, which hotel features to present, and which room rates to display.

Initially, the Internet was recognized as an emerging force in hotel reservation distribution, and most hotel companies sought a web presence. At first, most hotels simply placed the content of their printed property brochures online. With first-generation websites, hotel guests desiring to make a reservation contacted the hotel's reservations office by phoning the number displayed on the website. The second generation of hotel website development offered guests the ability to book reservations online. Offering fully interactive reservation capabilities with multiple room types and rates and real-time confirmation quickly became the standard.

At first, many prospective guests checked the Internet to make a hotel selection, and then contacted the hotel directly to make their reservations. But, over time, "lookers" have become "bookers," as consumer confidence in online hotel reservation processing increased.

Hotel companies have expanded their website capabilities by adding specialized search engine capabilities, group sales, and advanced navigational features. Visitors to hotel websites typically can experience 360-degree panoramic tours of facilities, peruse restaurant and banquet menus, and many even receive hotel-generated web-cam streaming video. Searches can be conducted according to such parameters as city, number of guestrooms, types of guestrooms, brand of hotel, function room type, convention settings, nearby businesses, and local area points of interest. For example, potential guests can search for hotels with swimming pools, located near an airport, offering high-speed Internet access, and with twenty-four-hour room service. With some additional clicks, individual traveler and group reservations can be completed and confirmed. In the same transaction, guests may be able to reserve golf tee-times, spa treatments, dining room seating, and shuttle van arrangements.

E-commerce has become so important that a hotel may assign a manager to be responsible for overseeing online content and transactions (the revenue manager, for example). Some hotel companies assign corporate-level managers and implement elaborate technology to coordinate revenue management and e-commerce requirements company-wide.

Potential guests who search the Internet for overnight accommodations do so for convenience as well as price. Many websites offer air transportation and car rentals with hotel reservations through a comprehensive booking engine for the ease of bundled purchasing and potential pricing discounts.

The Internet provides many specialized travel-related sites for specific traveler profiles. For example, there are sites dedicated to:

- Brand-loyal travelers (for example, hilton.com, marriott.com, choicehotels. com, etc.)

- Meeting professionals (for example, mpoint.com, starcite.com, etc.)

- Bargain shoppers (priceline.com, site59.com, and so on)

- Cruise travelers (celebrity.com, cruise.com, cruisesonly.com, etc.)

- All-inclusive hotels (resortvacationstogo.com, for example)

- Interval-ownership vacations (rci.com, intervalworld.com, etc.)

There are many more travel-related websites, some general-purpose, others appealing to specific travel markets.

E-commerce is an effective and expanding distribution channel for potential guest reservations. However, e-commerce must be effectively managed on a daily basis, so management can be sure that hotel information and pricing are properly presented.

Single Image Inventory. In order for e-commerce to be effective, accurate and timely room rate and inventory data must be available to all hotel electronic distribution channels simultaneously. The best means to accomplish this is through single image inventory technology. Simply stated, *single image inventory* means that all reservation distribution channels draw from the same room availability, pricing, rate rules, services, and amenities information. Failure to have all online distributors working from the same data source can be chaotic and lead to unintentional overselling, availability shortages, and erratic levels of occupancy. When using single image inventory, all sellers base transactions against identical information.

E-Commerce Site Categories. E-commerce sites can be categorized as merchant-model or wholesaler sites, and as opaque or transparent sites. Each of these categories is examined in the following sections.

Merchant model. The merchant model, also called the *markup model*, is a hotel e-commerce strategy for an online intermediary, such as an IDS, negotiating room pricing with the hotel. The participating hotel is asked by the online seller (merchant) to provide rooms at a discount (for example, 20 to 30 percent) below the lowest published rate normally charged for the room type, or an alternate discounted rate (at the discretion of the hotel). This discounted rate is called the *net rate* and represents the amount paid to the hotel for each room sold at the agreed-upon discount by the merchant. In turn, the merchant or online seller takes on the responsibility for marketing the inventory allocated to it. The merchant will mark up the net rate to achieve the room rate charged to the guest. This is termed the gross rate.

For example, consider a standard room with a lowest published rate of $100. To determine the net rate, assume the merchant has negotiated a 25 percent discount with the hotel, thereby producing a net rate of $75. The merchant then determines the new selling price of the room (that is, the room's gross rate) by adding a set amount of dollar mark-up or by multiplying the net rate by a desired percentage. In the present example, using a 25 percent markup, this will generate a gross rate of $93.75 ($75 plus the 25 percent markup of $18.75). Therefore, the merchant earns a gross margin (gross rate minus net rate) of $18.75, the guest pays $6.25 less than the $100 rack rate, and the hotel earns $75.

Merchant-model sites tend to rank hotels based on their discounts; the more a hotel discounts its rooms, the more prominently the hotel is listed at a merchant website. Therefore, many hotel managers feel pressured to provide significant discounts to merchant-model websites, fearing that otherwise the hotel will not be promoted as well as its competition. Examples of merchant-model sites include Hotels.com (www.hotels.com), Lowestfare.com (www.lowestfare.com), Orbitz (www.orbitz.com), Lodging.com (www.lodging.com), and Travelocity (www. travelocity.com).

Wholesaler model. With the wholesaler model, the hotel tends to maintain greater control over its room price, as a commission is paid to the wholesaler based on a percentage of the hotel's net rate. Simply stated, the hotel sets the selling price and the wholesaler receives an agreed-upon sales commission (that is, percentage of the price). For example, consider a hotel company that offers a room with a rate of $100 to a wholesaler at a net rate of $80. In turn, the hotel agrees to allow the seller to add a 10 percent ($8) commission. In this example, the room will have a gross rate of $88 and the guest will pay $12 less than the hotel's $100 published rate. Some wholesalers, like Priceline and Hotwire, may negotiate a minimum margin (for example, $5 per room) to be added to the net rate rather than work on a percent commission.

Sellers using the wholesaler model tend to earn less than sellers using the merchant model. It is for this reason that online sellers tend to favor the merchant model; hotels, on the other hand, tend to favor the wholesaler model, because they maintain greater control over their rooms' final price to guests. Examples of wholesaler model sites include Expedia (www.expedia.com), Hotwire (www.hotwire.com), Priceline (www.priceline.com), Travelweb (www.travelweb.com), and Orbitz (www.orbitz.com). It is not uncommon for online reservation websites to work on both the merchant model and a wholesaler model platform.

Opaque sites. At an opaque website, a hotel room is marketed by a price and/or rating category. For example, a hotel may be described simply as a "three-star property" without any reference to brand or property specifics. At an opaque website, hotel rooms are treated as a commodity and are offered based on the action of the highest bidder. The services, amenities, and ambience of the property may not be considered in the hotel selection process. With opaque websites, the brand of the hotel and its features are hidden from the buyer until the transaction is completed. Only a quality rating and the room's general location are known to the buyer at the time of commitment to reserve, hence the use of the term *opaque*. Since neither the hotel's identity nor its brand is disclosed until after the sale is completed, defining whether the guest is a customer of the e-commerce site or the hotel can be challenging and confusing. Since both hotels and travel sites may offer loyalty club points or frequent shopper rewards, this can be important to determine.

Opaque sites often work on an auction basis. Potential guests may specify a rate they are willing to pay, and the site then works with available inventory within the guests' specified quality rating and/or price range. If it has no inventory to sell in the rating or price range specified, it may contact participating hotels to see if they will accept the guest's bid price. Since these rates may be significantly below the hotel's published or even usual discounted rates, profit margins are reduced. For this reason, many hotel companies do not offer loyalty club points or room upgrades for reservations made through opaque sites. Examples of opaque sites include Priceline (www.priceline.com) and Hotwire (www.hotwire.com). It is important to note that several opaque sites offer a transparency-site option as a special feature.

Transparent sites. As with opaque sites, rooms at transparent sites are classified or categorized based on room rate or star ranking. But, unlike opaque sites, transparent sites reveal the identity of hotels in the qualifying range before buyers make a purchase. Transparency allows the guest to select a preferred property among competing entities. Examples of transparent sites include Expedia (www. expedia.com), Hotels.com (www.hotels.com), lastminute.com (www.lastminute. com), and Travelocity.com (www.travelocity.com).

E-Commerce Trends. While most hotels rely on multiple e-commerce distribution channels simultaneously, the channels have become much more sophisticated in the hotel's overall selling strategy. For years, many hotels offered the same rooms on different channels at different rates, often underselling their own brand websites by offering special pricing to unbranded websites. This resulted in a significant erosion of the hotels' average room rates and therefore overall room revenue. Hotels have learned to exercise caution in selecting e-commerce sites, and have developed distinct strategies for each online partner. The majority of hotel branded sites offer a best rate guarantee, which assures the traveler that the lowest online rate appears on the hotel website; should a traveler find a lower rate for the same room on the same date, the hotel company will compensate the traveler (that is, refund the difference plus a premium). A guaranteed rate program normally applies to all distribution channels except opaque websites, since travelers do not learn the identity of the hotel property they are buying (until the transaction is completed), and therefore it is difficult to equate two quoted rates. An individual hotel that allows e-commerce sites to offer rates lower than the brand site may be penalized by its brand or chain.

As hotel e-commerce has evolved, its focus has shifted toward the processing of group room reservations and group meetings, embracing issues such as large room blocks, food and beverage catering menus, tradeshow space allocation, meeting room reservations, and audiovisual equipment scheduling. On some hotel websites, group leaders can use an online request for proposal (RFP) script to enter meeting dates, room and space requirements, and other meeting needs, to which the hotel can respond based on a database query. Catering considerations, the need to control meeting space, and the desire to maximize group revenues make an automated response beyond the capabilities of most hotel companies. The implementation of an automated group RFP response process, based upon sophisticated formulas that involve guestroom-to-meeting-space ratios and projected revenue ratios, has also helped coordinate group activities. Examples of online group search and RFP engines are PlanSoft (www.mpoint.com) and StarCite (www.starcite.com).

Another online booking trend involves the awarding of affinity or loyalty club points (generated by the online booking site) for hotel, auto, air, cruise, rail, and other travel services. In awarding points to guests, the online booking site becomes the featured product, not the destination hotel. Some hotel companies allow loyalty club members to redeem rewards in real time on an affiliated website as well. However, as hotels struggle to promote their unique identity online, such online booking agency practices may be considered confusing and harmful.

A popular online application is dynamic package pricing. Historically, online booking sites have offered only predetermined, rigidly defined (static) hotel packages—for example, "stay five nights and receive a sixth night at no charge, along with a discount on a rental car and airfare." As online booking engines evolve, websites are able to offer on-the-fly (dynamic) pricing of custom packages selected and assembled by the guest (for example, inclusive of accommodations, food service, recreational activities, holiday events, special occasions, etc.). E-commerce technology allows guests to build and bundle components to create a personalized package, generate a unique package price, and simultaneously make multiple reservations for the services placed in the custom package.

In addition, e-commerce capabilities can enable online booking sites to create virtual hotel brands by grouping a proprietary set of preferred hotel properties at a destination site (for example, Expedia's Bargain Hotels). This creates a more complex level of competition within the marketplace.

Summary

Effective hotel operations require an efficient reservations procedure. Reservation systems must be able to respond quickly, accurately, and pleasantly to requests for overnight accommodations. Reservations processing involves matching room requests with room availabilities; recording, confirming, and maintaining reservations; and producing management reports. Reservation information is especially useful in other front office functions.

The reservations office and hotel sales office must coordinate their activities and information regularly. The reservations manager participates in regular sales meetings and ensures that current reservation information is provided to the sales department. Successful reservations agents sell their hotel, creating positive images of the facilities and services. Hotels use specific sales processes to ensure that guests have the right information about the property, and the reservations agent collects all the guest information necessary to process a reservation. The reservation system should contain detailed and timely information covering room types and available rates. Given the capabilities of automation, much of the responsibility for room sales has shifted from the front office to the reservations department and associated websites. Requests for specific room types, locations, and special features can be acknowledged and confirmed as part of the reservations process.

The two major types of hotel reservations are guaranteed and nonguaranteed. Hotels can draw reservations from various market sources within the hospitality industry, including central reservations systems, intersell agencies, and property-direct reservations. There are two basic types of central reservations systems: affiliate networks and non-affiliate networks. In an affiliate network, all of the hotels participating in the network are contractually related (that is, part of a chain); in a non-affiliate network, participating properties are independent (non-chain). Global distribution systems connect central reservations systems with airline computer systems and terminals around the world. The term *intersell agency* describes a central reservations system that contracts to handle more than just hotel rooms. A property-direct system handles all requests for accommodations, monitors any communication links with central reservations systems and intersell agencies, and maintains updated room availability status reports for a single hotel.

Processing a reservation request can result in one of several responses: reservation acceptance; suggestion of alternative room types, dates, and/or rates; and suggestion of an alternative hotel property. In any reservation system, it is necessary to closely monitor the number of reservations accepted in order to avoid overbooking. A reliable reservation system can assist management in maintaining tight control over room availability data and can generate many reservation-related reports.

Reservation records identify guests and their occupancy needs prior to actual arrival. These records enable the hotel to personalize guest service and more accurately schedule staff. Reservation records are created based on interactions with potential guests. A reservation record initiates the hotel guest cycle. A reservation confirmation indicates the hotel's acknowledgment and verification of a guest's room request and personal information. A written confirmation states the intent of both parties and confirms important points of agreement, including the room type and rate for a specific date. Confirmed reservations may be guaranteed or non-guaranteed. As part of the reservation confirmation process, a reservation confirmation number may be assigned to each accepted reservation record. A confirmation number assures the guest that a reservation record exists. It can be especially useful to the hotel in retrieving a reservation record for updating, prior to guest registration. Similarly, hotels may issue a reservation cancellation number to guests properly canceling a reservation. Issuing a cancellation number to guests protects both the guest and hotel in the event of a no-show or a misunderstanding.

An effective reservation system helps maximize room sales by accurately monitoring room availabilities and forecasting rooms revenue. The number and type of management reports available through a reservation system are a function of the hotel's needs and the system's capability and contents. Typical reservations management reports include: reservation transactions report, commission agent report, regrets and denials report (or turnaway report), and a revenue forecast report.

Other reservation considerations include the legal ramifications of reservations, waiting lists, promotional packages, potential problems in the reservations process, and the impact of e-commerce on reservations.

🔑 Key Terms

advance deposit guaranteed reservation—A type of reservation guarantee that requires the guest to pay a specified amount of money to the hotel in advance of arrival.

affiliate reservation network—A hotel chain's reservation system in which all participating properties are contractually related.

block—An agreed-upon number of rooms set aside for members of a group planning to stay at a hotel.

book—To sell or reserve rooms ahead of time.

cancellation hour—The hour after which a property may release for sale all unclaimed non-guaranteed reservations, according to property policy.

cancellation number—A number issued to a guest who has properly canceled a reservation, proving that a cancellation request was received.

central reservations system—A network for communicating reservations in which each participating property is represented in an automated database and is required to provide room availability data to the central reservations center on a timely basis.

confirmation number—A code that provides a unique reference to a reservation record and assures the guest that the reservation record exists.

corporate guaranteed reservation—A type of reservation guarantee in which a corporation signs a contractual agreement with the hotel to accept financial responsibility for any no-show business travelers it sponsors.

cut-off date—The date agreed upon between a group and a hotel after which all unreserved rooms in the group's block will be given back to the general rooms inventory for sale.

free independent traveler (FIT)—A traveler who is not part of a group.

global distribution system (GDS)—A distribution channel for reservations that provides worldwide distribution of hotel reservation information and allows the selling of hotel reservations around the world; usually accomplished by connecting the hotel company reservation system with an airline reservation system.

guaranteed reservation—A reservation that assures the guest that a room will be held until a specific time of the day following the guest's scheduled arrival date. This time may be check-out time, the start of the hotel day, or any time the hotel chooses. The guest, in turn, guarantees to pay for the room, even if it is not used, unless the reservation is canceled according to the hotel's cancellation procedures.

Internet distribution system (IDS)—A direct-marketing distribution channel that provides property exposure and reservations management for independent hotels, chain hotels, and third-party intermediaries representing hotel companies.

non-affiliate reservation network—A central reservations system that connects independent (non-chain) lodging properties.

non-group displacement (or displacement)—The turning away of transient guests for lack of rooms due to the acceptance of group business.

non-guaranteed reservation—A reservation agreement in which the hotel holds a room for the guest until a stated reservation cancellation hour on the day of arrival; the property is not guaranteed payment in the case of a no-show.

no-show—A guest who made a room reservation but did not register or cancel.

overbooking—Accepting more reservations than there are available rooms.

overflow facility—A property selected to receive central system reservation requests after room availabilities in the system's participating properties within a geographic region have been exhausted.

payment card guaranteed reservation—A type of guarantee supported by payment card companies; these companies guarantee participating properties payment for reserved rooms that remain unoccupied.

prepayment guaranteed reservation—A type of reservation guarantee that requires a payment in full before the day of arrival.

revenue manager—The manager responsible for forecasting demand for each market segment the hotel seeks to attract—corporate transient, group, leisure transient, and others—as well as determining the guestroom rates that will provide sufficient room revenues and occupancies. Also typically manages e-commerce functions.

reservation record—A collection of data that identifies a guest and his or her anticipated occupancy needs before arrival at the property; enables the hotel to personalize guest service and accurately schedule staff.

reservation system—Software specifically designed to handle the creation, modification, confirmation, and/or cancellation of reservation records.

seamless connectivity/integration—The ability of travel agencies to book reservations directly into hotel reservation systems, as well as verify room availability and rates.

wash down (or wash)—Blocking fewer rooms than the number requested by a group, based on the group's history.

 Review Questions

1. What role does a reservations manager or supervisor play in the sales department? What role does the reservations manager or supervisor play in forecasting occupancy and revenue?

2. What are the major types of reservations? What are the responsibilities of the guest and the hotel in each case?

3. What information does a reservations agent need to create a reservation record?

4. How do non-affiliate reservation networks differ from affiliate reservation networks? How do central reservations systems differ from intersell agencies?

5. What methods can be used to guarantee a reservation? What is the difference between them?

6. What are common reservation control devices used by hotels? How is each used to monitor room availabilities?

7. What guest information is necessary for a reservations agent to guarantee a reservation?

8. What is the main purpose of a confirmation letter or telephone call?

9. How does proper cancellation of a reservation benefit the hotel? How can hotels make cancellations as easy as possible for guests?

10. What is the purpose of a cancellation number? How might a cancellation number be generated?

11. What management reports can be generated from reservations data? What are the uses of expected arrival lists and reservations histories?

12. How can reservation procedures for conferences, conventions, and tour groups be made more efficient? What precautions should a reservations manager take before creating a group block?

Internet Sites

For more information, visit the following Internet sites. Remember that Internet addresses can change without notice. If the site is no longer there, you can use a search engine to look for additional sites.

Internet Reservation Sites

BizTravelBrokers.com
www.biztravelbrokers.com

Business Travel Net
www.business-travel-net.com

Hotels and Travel on the Net
www.hotelstravel.com

HotelsOnline
www.hotelsonline.com

Priceline
www.priceline.com

Resorts Online
www.resortsonline.com

Travelocity
www.travelocity.com

Technology Sites

Agilysys Hospitality Solutions
www.agilysys.com/home/Hospitality/
Solutions/

Hospitality Financial & Technology
  Professionals
www.hftp.org/HITEC

Hotel Electronic Distribution Network
  Association
www.hedna.org

Hotellinx Systems Ltd.
www.hotellinx.com

MICROS Systems, Inc.
www.micros.com

Newmarket International, Inc.
www.newmarketinc.com

Passkey
www.passkey.com

StarCite, Inc.
www2.starcite.com

Case Studies

Sarah's Serious Reservations—Working with the CRO

Sarah Shepherd was visiting her hotel chain's Midwest central reservations office in Des Moines, Iowa, wondering why her general manager had wanted her to spend a day touring the facilities with other reservations managers. She had a lot of work to do back in Bloomington, and she didn't understand what good it could do her to see how a roomful of reservations agents took orders over the telephone. "Frankly, I don't know either," her GM had told her. "I just have the suspicion that we could make a lot better use of our central reservations system. We're currently booking 30 percent of our rooms with them. Maybe we could do better. I'd like you to find out if that's true and bring back some recommendations."

Right now, I'd recommend catching an early flight home, she thought as the tour leaders began dividing the large group into smaller teams. Recognizing Gabe Culberson, the reservations manager from her sister property in Bloomington, she went to join his team. "At least I'll have a friend to commiserate with," she said under her breath. Sarah and Gabe were joined by Gwen Hsu, a reservations manager from one of the chain's St. Louis properties.

The tour began "on the floor," where Sarah, Gabe, and Gwen watched as 200 reservations agents answered an unending stream of telephone calls. "This is really the nerve center for the operation," their guide was telling them, trying hard to be heard without interrupting any of the ongoing phone conversations. "Every potential guest who picks up the phone and dials our toll-free number ends up talking to someone in this room. Using the information you've provided that appears on these monitors, agents answer guest questions about rates, availability, amenities, local attractions—the whole works. To the best of their ability, that is."

"What do you mean by that?" Gwen asked.

"Well, we can only pass along the information that managers like you provide. If it isn't in our reservations system, we don't know about it."

Gabe leaned toward Sarah. "That's for sure. You wouldn't believe the difference it made when we posted information about the new children's museum downtown." Then he chuckled. "What am I saying—you've probably noticed the healthy bump in family business, too, right?"

"What do you mean?" Sarah started to ask, but their tour guide was moving on.

The guide stopped behind a reservations agent who was telling a caller about one of the chain's downtown Chicago properties. "This is Michelle," the guide said, "and she's one of our most enthusiastic sales agents. I just wanted you to hear how she works her magic over the phone."

"—that's right, Mr. Davis," Michelle was telling the caller. "Now, I have you booked for a room with two double beds and a rollaway bed for five days. Since you mentioned that you and your wife will be traveling with three small children, though, I would personally encourage you to consider the benefits you would gain by staying in a suite instead. You're right. It is a more expensive room, but it will give your family substantially more room to spread out in during a long stay in the city. Plus, with the suite reservation I can also offer you a special family package price that includes reduced admission to the Field Museum of Natural History, the Museum of Science and Industry, and Shedd Aquarium. That will give your family something fun to do while you're at your conference." Michelle paused, scanning her terminal. "Yes, a hotel shuttle offers transportation to those attractions. Great, I'll reserve a suite in your name and make sure you get the family package price. You'll be able to pick up your museum and aquarium tickets at the concierge desk in the hotel lobby. Oh, and you might tell your wife that the hotel is just one block off of the Magnificent Mile, one of the best shopping districts in the nation. Thank you for calling, Mr. Davis. I hope you and your family will have a great stay."

Wow! Sarah thought with surprise. *She sounds just like one of my own sales agents. In fact, she might even be better than they are!*

The group started moving on when Michelle answered another call. Suddenly Sarah heard Michelle say the name of her own property in Bloomington.

"Wait a second," she called to their guide. "I'd love to hear this."

Michelle was studying her screen. "I'm sorry, sir. I do know that there's a new children's museum in Bloomington, but I don't have any information here about it. Other attractions? There is an annual Frontier Fest, but that's the only attraction I have a record of."

"What?" Sarah said, a bit too loudly. *The Frontier Fest died out two years ago. Why wasn't Michelle-the-Wonder-Agent telling this caller about the Worlds of Water Fun Park that opened less than a mile away last year or the new mall and movie theaters? And why didn't she know anything about the children's museum?*

"It's five minutes from the airport and shuttle service is provided. One moment while I check. I'm sorry, I don't have any information about fees or whether that's a hotel shuttle or an airport shuttle. There may be a charge."

But there isn't, Sarah thought, her heart sinking. *It's our own courtesy van. Why don't you know that?*

"I'm showing a rate of $105 for that room. Would you like me to reserve that for you, then, Ms. McQueen?" This time, Michelle paused for what felt like minutes to Sarah. "I understand. Well, thank you very much for your call. I hope we'll be able to serve you in the future."

Dejected, Sarah turned to her friend Gabe. "She just lost that sale for me."

Gabe peered at Michelle's monitor for a minute. "Actually, Sarah, I think *you* just lost that sale for your hotel." He explained what he meant over coffee during a break in their tour.

"Tell me how you work with central reservations," he said.

"I'm not sure I know what you mean. We tell them how many rooms they can sell, and usually they sell them. It's simple: people call in and the agents take orders."

"But it's not that simple—at least, it shouldn't be. You heard Michelle's conversation with that guy staying in Chicago. She definitely was not 'taking an order.' She was *selling*. She could do that because the Chicago property provided her with every piece of information she'd need in the selling process. That's what I try to do at our property. Anything that I'd normally tell our in-house sales staff I post to the central res system. If the pool is out for repair, if we've changed our menu, if we've added amenities or know of area attractions, if we offer special corporate discounts—all of that information gets added to the database here so it comes up on their screens when a guest calls in."

Sarah was suddenly thoughtful. "So you're saying Michelle didn't know about the children's museum or the defunct Frontier Fest or the courtesy van or our new rate structure because I didn't post the information."

Gabe nodded. "I also noticed that there wasn't any information about that renovation you guys did about a year and a half ago."

"Just rub it in, Gabe," Sarah said, starting to smile. "I admit I had no idea they could be such effective salespeople."

Just then Gwen Hsu walked up. "Oh, they're effective, all right. *Too* effective, if you ask me. My problem is that central res keeps overbooking my property, so I get a seemingly constant stream of guests—with confirmations—that I don't have any room for."

"So you walk them," Gabe said.

"Well, I sure don't walk the folks who've reserved with us directly. They're our regulars. The central res guests are usually one-timers who have to be in town for a meeting; odds are, I'll never see them again."

"Gwen, how often do you update your allocation of rooms with central reservations?" Sarah wondered.

"What do you mean?"

"Gabe's been telling me that central reservations can only work with the information we give them. I just wondered how often you changed their allocation or posted new occupancy information."

"I guess it's usually first-thing-in-the-morning, last-thing-at-night. In the morning, I post the allocation for the day; at night, I check in to see where they stand in relation to the reservations we've developed in-house. That's usually when I get the bad news."

"That may be the problem," Gabe interjected. "I'm on our system probably twelve times a day, updating information and adjusting the allocation. And we don't have a pattern of overbooking."

Gwen frowned, saying that sounded like a lot of work. She would have to evaluate it to decide whether the benefits warranted the extra effort. She then left to ask their guide a specific question before the second half of their tour began.

"That was a good question, Sarah," Gabe said. "You know, by the time the next trip to central res rolls around, I bet your property will be just as involved in and enthusiastic about the system as mine is."

"Actually, Gabe, I was thinking that, next time around, it'll be *your* property's turn to play catch-up," Sarah said, flashing a smile.

Discussion Questions

1. What kinds of information does Sarah need from other departments at her hotel that will enable her to work better with the central reservations office?

2. As the reservations manager, what might Sarah do to improve the effectiveness of her property's work with central reservations?

Case Number: 3324CA

The following industry experts helped generate and develop this case: Richard M. Brooks, CHA, Vice President, TWE Group; and S. Kenneth Hiller, CHA, General Manager, Holiday Inn, Beechwood, Ohio.

Booking Online

Most of the arrivals had checked in to the Boden by 5:00 P.M. on this beautiful late spring day. They seemed to want to get in their first swim of the season and maybe even a stroll on the beach before going to dinner. The computer showed that three more arrivals were expected, a party of three and two couples. Since it was going to be such a nice weekend, many of the guests had arrived without prior reservations, but, given the fact that the season was just getting underway, the resort was able to accommodate all of them. However, the last three parties would nearly fill the resort and lodge for the weekend. Rooms still available included a honeymoon suite, two mini-suites, and three double-double standard rooms. The front office supervisor, Sasha, was pleased with the results.

While Sasha reviewed the departure print-out for Saturday, a handsome tall couple and their daughter stepped from their vehicle under the porte cochere. The valet attended well to their needs, and before long the bell attendant had unloaded their luggage. Sasha assumed that this was the party who had reserved room 314, a room with two double beds and an ocean view, for the weekend. Indeed it was. She welcomed the party to the Boden Oceanside Resort and Lodge. The guest, Mr. Pardonme, said hello and handed Sasha a reservation confirmation. It was immediately obvious that the reservation had been made online by Mr. Pardonme.

Sasha brought up the reservation file on the computer screen and scanned the guest file to determine if the Pardonme party had been assigned a room comparable to the one specified on the reservation confirmation. She knew that sometimes guests who booked online were sold rooms that were not always available when they arrived at the resort. Her concerns were confirmed when she saw that they had been assigned room 314 when they had actually purchased a mini-suite. The price they were paying, however, was for a standard room like the one they had been assigned. Sasha wondered if the Pardonme party would even notice.

She checked them in to room 314 without mentioning the difference, hoping that the two double beds, the nice view, and a reasonably spacious bathroom would satisfy the guests. As it was, there weren't many choices left for them anyway! Sasha decided that if they were dissatisfied she would show them the last mini-suite available, but also let them know that it was usually sold for $145 rather than the $85 bargain online price they were paying per night. Moments later the Pardonmes returned to ask about the suite they were promised. Sasha asked the bell attendant to show them a suite that was usually saved for handicapped guests.

The bell attendant and the Pardonme party went to the suite and, upon entering, Mr. Pardonme thought that the hotel must have gone mad. "Where is the second bed?" he asked, looking a little perplexed.

"It's here on the wall," said the bell attendant. "It's a Murphy bed." Mr. Pardonme looked around the room, looked at his confirmation letter that described the room he had reserved, and shook his head.

Back at the front desk, Mr. Pardonme was a little upset. He told Sasha that the room he had reserved over the Internet was the one that he expected to sleep in for the next three nights. He purposely had phoned the Boden prior to reserving online to be sure that he could get the room of his choice. Whoever had been on reservations that day had told him not to worry because there were plenty of the mini-suites available for the nights he was booking for. She told him the rate that would guarantee him the room was $145 per night if he booked directly with the Boden through the reservations department. She wasn't sure why the online rate was so much lower, but she couldn't lower her rate. So Mr. Pardonme decided to try booking online, and now the room he had selected was not the one he had been assigned. He told Sasha that he wasn't interested in the alternative she had given him because the Murphy bed didn't give him and his wife any more privacy than the double-double that they had first been assigned.

Sasha didn't have any other rooms available that met his specific needs. She told Mr. Pardonme that the best she could do was either of the two rooms that they had been shown. The Pardonme party finally settled for the mini-suite with the Murphy bed. The room would be more comfortable than the first one they had been shown. Sasha did a room move on the computer and gave them the proper keys. She hoped they would enjoy that room. How much time would they spend in it anyway, she thought to herself. And they are getting a great price on the room anyway, so why were they being so picky?

Discussion Questions

1. What were the expectations of the guests?

2. What other options might Sasha have considered in this case?

Case number: 608C02

This case also appears in Todd Comen, *Case Studies in Front Office Management* (Lansing, Mich.: American Hotel & Lodging Educational Institute, 2003).

Overbooked at the Boden Oceanside Resort and Lodge

It was 9:30 P.M. and a couple was at the front desk insisting that they placed a reservation for three nights at the lodge over two months ago. The front desk agent, Rob, was unable to find their reservation anywhere. Rob had been with the hotel for two years and he knew his way around the front office. He had seen this trick before and didn't have much patience for it. As was the routine, however, he checked the reservation system, called the toll-free reservation service and thumbed through the manager's files trying to uncover anything that would suggest that the guests had a reservation for this evening. The guests' names were neither in the history file nor anywhere in the central reservation system.

The hotel was oversold and Rob was in no mood to work with the guests. He had already walked three other parties, two families with reservations and one couple from off the road who didn't have reservations for the evening. He had been taught to walk first-time guests or walk-ins with no reservations. Rob was always advised to hold rooms at whatever cost for those frequent guests who stayed at the resort for at least a week each year. These guests were sacred and never to be sacrificed, even if they didn't show up on the night they were expected. He told the couple politely that there were no rooms available and suggested they try another resort of similar quality down the road. The couple was getting quite belligerent by then and insisted on speaking with a manager.

Matt, the manager on duty, had been busy since coming on duty late that afternoon due to a fully booked house. As he approached the desk, he wondered why Rob couldn't deal with the situation. Matt listened to all of the details and noted that the guests claimed to have had a reservation for a couple of months. He checked the time, noting that it was relatively late, and also checked to see how many arrivals were expected. There were reservations that hadn't been claimed yet and they were all held with a credit card. He wondered if any of the late arrivals had phoned the hotel earlier to cancel their reservation and the message hadn't been entered into the system for some reason.

After pondering for a moment he made up his mind to check the couple in to a double-double that wasn't in the new section of the resort. He figured that they might complain that it wasn't their first choice, but at least it was a room. The couple was pleased when he told them that they could have a room for the night, but that the hotel was overbooked for the next three nights due to a number of small family reunions and that he couldn't guarantee them a room for the following evening. Rob was puzzled by Matt's quick decision, but graciously and smoothly checked the guests into the room that Matt had assigned them.

The remainder of the evening was quiet, with a couple of late arrivals. Rob had time to think over the events of the evening and wondered if he should stay with the resort or if he should apply at the new Four Winds resort that was advertising for an opening team just down the road.

The next day Rob called his manager and gave his two weeks' notice.

Discussion Questions

1. Which guests would you walk to another hotel?

2. What would be a guest-friendly way to walk guests?

3. What are the costs of walking a guest?

Case number: 608C05

This case also appears in Todd Comen, *Case Studies in Front Office Management* (Lansing, Mich.: American Hotel & Lodging Educational Institute, 2003).

Chapter 5 Outline

The Registration Process
    Preregistration Activities
    Creating the Registration Record
    Assigning the Guestroom and Room
        Rate
    Establishing the Guest's Method of
        Payment
    Verifying the Guest's Identity
    Issuing the Room Key or Access Code
    Responding to Special Requests
Creative Registration Options
    Self-Registration
Selling the Guestroom
Denying Accommodations
    Walk-In Guests
    Guests with Non-Guaranteed
        Reservations
    Guests with Guaranteed Reservations
Summary

Competencies

1. List the seven steps of the registration process, explain the function of preregistration, and identify preregistration activities. (pp. 187–190)

2. Describe the function of registration records and registration cards, and identify factors that affect room and rate assignments during the registration process. (pp. 190–198)

3. Outline procedures for establishing the guest's method of payment at registration. (pp. 198–206)

4. Explain the importance of verifying the guest's identity, outline proper procedures for issuing guestroom keys or access codes to guests, and describe the front desk agent's role in addressing special requests from guests during registration. (pp. 206–208)

5. Discuss creative registration options, describe techniques used to upsell guests during registration, and explain how to handle situations in which guests cannot be accommodated by the hotel. (pp. 209–215)

5

Registration

ON-SITE REGISTRATION BEGINS when the front desk agent extends a sincere welcome to the arriving hotel guest. The front desk agent moves the guest into the registration process after determining the guest's **reservation status.** To a great degree, registration relies on the information recorded in the guest's reservation record. Front office personnel will find registration simpler and smoother when accurate and complete information has been captured during the reservations process.

This chapter examines the seven steps of the hotel registration process. The chapter also presents alternate registration options, discusses the front office sales role, and reviews potential strategies when guests cannot be accommodated.

The Registration Process

From a front desk agent's perspective, the registration process consists of seven steps:

1. Preregistration activities
2. Creating the registration record
3. Assigning the guestroom and room rate
4. Establishing the guest's method of payment
5. Verifying the guest's identity
6. Issuing the room key or access code
7. Responding to special requests

We will discuss each of these steps in the following sections.

Preregistration Activities

Preregistration activities (registration activities that occur before the guest arrives at the property) help accelerate the registration process. Guests can be preregistered using the information collected during the reservations process. Typically, preregistered guests need only verify information already entered onto a registration record and provide a valid signature in the appropriate place on a **registration form** or card.

Preregistration normally involves more than merely producing a registration document in advance of guest arrival. Room and rate assignment, creation of a guest folio, and other functions may also be part of the preregistration process.

However, some front office managers may be reluctant to assign a specific room to a guest in advance of check-in, since reservations are sometimes canceled or modified. Specific room assignments often become jumbled when last-minute changes in reservation status are made. In addition, assigning a large percentage of vacant rooms in advance of arrival may limit the number of rooms available to guests who are not preregistered. This imbalance can slow the registration process and create a negative impression of the hotel. Hotels will tend to develop pre-registration policies based on operational experience.

In some front office operations, preregistration services may be limited to specially designated or VIP guests or groups. However, most experienced front office managers prefer to preregister guests with reservation records because it shortens the check-in process and also helps them identify what rooms are available for those guests who do not have a reservation. Since data recorded during the reservations process serve as the basis for preregistration, front office systems will reformat data contained in a reservation record into a registration record. A sample system-generated preregistration card is shown in Exhibit 1. Although a hotel may have to void some pre-arrival room assignments due to last-minute changes, the registration time saved by guests who register without complications usually compensates for the inconvenience caused by the small percentage of cancellations or modifications.

Preregistration helps managers plan for the special requirements of guests as well as the hotel. For example, frequent guests may have a special room they enjoy at the hotel, and guests with disabilities may need rooms outfitted to their special needs. By preregistering these guests, the front desk agent can be sure to satisfy these guests or can notify the department responsible for satisfying the request. Consider the situation in which a room has been assigned to a family requesting an additional bed for an infant. The front desk can then notify the housekeeping department of the room assignment so that a crib can be delivered in advance of the family's arrival. In addition, preregistration helps managers when they anticipate the hotel will be at full occupancy over the next several days. In order to allocate guestrooms properly, it may be necessary to apply reservations management software that enables guest reservations of one or two nights to be preregistered into rooms that have been specially blocked beginning one or two nights in the future. In this way, rooms that are blocked will be available when the early arriving guests check in. In some hotels, this process may be closely monitored several days in advance to ensure that the required rooms remain available.

Preregistration lends itself to innovative registration options. For instance, a hotel courtesy van might pick up a guest arriving at the airport who has a hotel reservation. The driver of the van, equipped with a mobile device, could request the guest's signature on a pre-printed registration card, imprint the guest's payment card, and give the guest a pre-assigned room key—all before the guest arrives at the hotel.

Another variation on preregistration for air travelers involves actual services at the airport. Some luxury hotels have arrangements with nearby airports to provide guests with convenient check-in services. The guest may swipe or tap a major payment card at a remote kiosk interfaced to the hotel's property management system. This arrangement allows the front office to approve the guest's

Exhibit 1   Sample Computer-Generated Preregistration Card

Kellogg Hotel & Conference Center
at Michigan State University

Mike Kasavana
555 IT Lane
East Lansing, MI 48824
US

Arrival Date:	01-24-07	Confirmation #:	1067009
Departure Date:	01-25-07	Room Type:	SQN
No. of Nights:	1	Room:	703
Company:	Kasavana	Guests:	1 /0
Group:		Daily Rate:	$ 129.00
		Deposit:	$

Billing Info: Direct Bill All Charges to MSU Account

Please note that checkout time is 12:00 Noon.

If any of the above information is incorrect or incomplete, please use the section below.

Name: _____   Telephone: _____

Address: _____   City: _____

State/Prov: _____   Zip Code: _____   Country: _____

The Kellogg Hotel & Conference Center is not responsible for, items in the vehicle, loss of property, including money and jewels, unless placed in a safe deposit box at the Front Desk. I agree that I am personally liable if my indicated company or group does not honor any charges billed to me. Such charges will include the cost of repairs to the guest room due to the damage other than normal wear and tear, and expenses incurred due to the extraordinary security measures undertaken due to bad behavior by me or my guests.

DEBIT CARD AUTHORIZATION WILL IMMEDIATELY BE DEDUCTED FROM YOUR CHECKING ACCOUNT

Credit Card: _____   **Debit Card:** _____   **Direct Billing:** _____   **Cash/Check:** _____

VA___   MC___   AX___   DS___   DC___

Signature: _____

55 S. Harrison Road, East Lansing, MI 48824 * Ph: 571-432-4000 * www.kelloggcenter.com

Courtesy of Kellogg Hotel & Conference Center, Michigan State University, East Lansing, Michigan.

credit, prepare guest registration records, prepare room keys, and print any waiting messages. When the guest arrives at the hotel front desk, the guest will experience an abbreviated check-in process.

A more sophisticated approach to preregistration involves registering guests designated for VIP service in a hotel area other than the front desk—for example, at a concierge desk. Some hotels arrange for VIP guests to be pre-processed and escorted directly to their guestrooms, thereby avoiding possible delays encountered at the front desk.

A hotel may take care to preregister guests who are members of the hotel's frequent traveler program, are part of an arriving group, or are travelers from a preferred corporate account. Preregistration ensures that these guests receive appropriate accommodations based on their level of loyalty or business affiliation. Some hotels make special provisions for reservations from e-commerce websites, as these reservations may be sold on a **run of the house** basis, meaning that the guest will be assigned whatever room is available at check-in time. Generally, a run-of-the-house guest does not benefit from preregistration activities.

Some hotel companies have centralized guest history systems. Guest reservations can be researched and compared to guest history files through advanced automation techniques. A guest history file will reveal guest preferences exhibited in prior stays that can be acted on as part of the current guest preregistration activity. For example, Wyndham Hotels & Resorts has a guest-loyalty program called "Wyndham ByRequest." Members of Wyndham ByRequest can enter certain personal preferences to create a guest profile or guest history file. This file contains such items as the type of pillow the guest prefers, or whether he or she would like complimentary bottled water placed in the guestroom prior to arrival. Through the preregistration process, the front office can notify housekeeping or room service about guest profile/history requests and preferences.

Creating the Registration Record

After a guest arrives at the hotel, the front desk agent verifies a preregistration record or creates a **registration record** containing important guest information.

Registration records facilitate the registration process. The registration record requires a guest to enter or verify his or her name, address, telephone number, e-mail address, company affiliation (if appropriate), and other personal data. Exhibit 2 shows a sample registration record. As this sample indicates, some registration records may include a statement about the hotel's responsibility for storing guest valuables, as state law may require such a statement. The registration record usually contains a space for the guest's signature to indicate acceptance of the room rate and date of departure. In some states, a guest's signature is a legal prerequisite to establishing an innkeeper/guest relationship. In many states, however, this requirement has been replaced by other provisions, such as the intentional establishment of credit by the guest at the time of registration.

Although a state or local municipality may require a signed registration form, an electronic record establishes the basis for registration processing. Guests arriving without reservations (walk-ins) normally will experience a different registration routine. Front desk agents will need to collect guest data and subsequently input that data into a front office system to create a registration record. Required registration information should be collected from guest responses during check-in.

Registration records require guests to indicate an intended method of payment for the guestroom and other hotel goods and services. In addition, front desk agents should confirm the guest's planned departure date and pre-assigned room rate. These elements are critical to rooms and revenue management. Clarifying the

Exhibit 2   Sample Registration Record

ROOM	NAME		RATE	RESV. ID		

Courtesy of The Sheraton Inn, Lansing, Michigan.

room rate at registration minimizes confusion and adjustments to the guest's folio at check-out. Many registration records also contain some form of acknowledgment on the part of the guest that he or she is responsible for payment in case the payment card or direct billing arrangement is not accepted for settlement.

Exhibit 3 diagrams the flow of guest registration information to electronic files and to other areas and functions of the hotel. The guest's intended method of payment may determine his or her point-of-sale charge status. For example, a guest paying one night's room rate by cash at registration is likely to have a *no-post status* in the hotel's revenue centers. In other words, the guest will not be allowed to charge purchases to a room account, as the guest did not provide a deferred payment method during registration. A guest presenting a valid payment card during registration may be allowed point-of-sale charge privileges, as the deferred payment for such items will eventually be charged to his or her room account. The decision to allocate charge privileges to a guest usually depends on the establishment of an acceptable method of credit at check-in.

At check-out, the information in a guest's registration record may be used as the primary source for creating a guest history file. This file may then become part of the hotel company's database to be used in the future by the hotel's sales and marketing staff. The information in a guest history database can be analyzed to assist management in developing contact strategies, marketing lists, and detailed reports.

Exhibit 3   Flow of Guest Registration Information

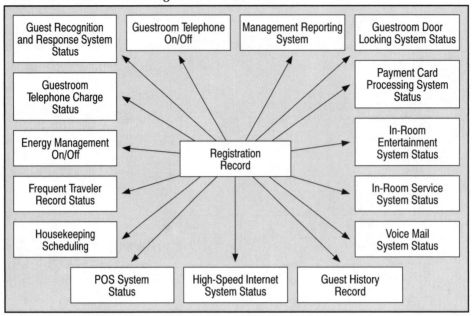

Assigning the Guestroom and Room Rate

Guestroom assignment is an important part of the registration process. Room assignment involves identifying and allocating an available room in a specific room category to a guest. When the guest request is ambiguous, or when a guestroom is unavailable in the guest's preferred category, a front desk agent may query the front office system to locate an acceptable available room.

On the basis of reservation information, specific rooms and rates may be pre-assigned (before the guest's arrival). Pre-assigning a specific room depends on the room's forecasted availability status and how appropriately the room meets the guest's needs. This requires the reservations system to interact with the rooms management module in the front office system. Guestroom assignments are finalized during the registration process.

Determining the guest's needs by room type alone is often insufficient. Hotels typically offer a variety of room rates for similar types of rooms. Room rates for rooms with identical bed configurations may vary based on room size, quality of furnishings, location, amenities, and other factors. Front desk agents must know the differences between the room types and be capable of querying the system to determine each room's rate category, current occupancy status, furnishings, location, and amenities to best satisfy guest requests. Future reservation commitments must also be considered during room assignment so that rooms are not assigned in conflict with near-future reservation needs.

The front desk agent's knowledge of the hotel and ability to use the system to determine room status and an appropriate room rate is critical to an effective registration process. The important topics of room status, room rates, room locations, and reservation blocks are addressed in the following sections.

Room Status. Effective room and rate assignment depends on accurate and timely guestroom status information. Room status information is usually discussed in terms of two timelines. In the long term (beyond the present night), a room's readiness is described by its reservation status. In the short term (tonight), a room's readiness is described by its housekeeping status, which refers to its availability for immediate assignment. Typical housekeeping status descriptions include:

- Occupied—the room has a registered guest or guests assigned to it.
- Vacant—the room is currently unoccupied.
- On-Change—the room is currently being cleaned for the next guest.
- Out-of-Order—the room has a condition that does not allow it to be rented.

An important aid to the registration of guests arriving early is the prompt relay of housekeeping information to the front desk. This is especially true during high-occupancy or full-occupancy (sold-out) periods. The more efficient the registration process, the more impressed an arriving guest is likely to be with the hotel's efficiency of operation. At most properties, the front desk agent is not authorized to assign a guestroom until the room has been cleaned, inspected, and released by the housekeeping department. Even though a guest arriving early may have to wait for a room, he or she will perceive the wait for a readied room as a better option than simply receiving a room key to a guestroom that has not been properly prepared.

Room status discrepancies can occur in front office systems for several reasons. First, there may be an actual variance, caused by incomplete or inaccurate recordkeeping. For example, a guest may settle his or her account for the nights the guestroom was originally reserved, but request to stay in the room for an additional night. While the front desk agent settles the account, the agent may accidentally indicate to the property management system that the guest has checked out, creating a room status discrepancy, since the front office will show the guest checked out, but the housekeeping department will indicate that someone continues to occupy the guestroom. (In this case, the guest is termed a **sleeper.**) Another room status discrepancy occurs when a guest leaves the hotel without settling his or her account; the front office still shows the room as occupied, but housekeeping lists the guestroom as vacant. (In this case, the guest is termed a **skipper.**) Room status discrepancies may also arise from delays in communicating housekeeping status updates from the housekeeping department to the front desk system.

In many properties, the property management system produces a daily front office report called the **occupancy report,** which lists rooms occupied for the current night and indicates those guests expected to check out the following day. The executive housekeeper typically receives a copy of this report on a daily basis and uses it to schedule housekeeping staff for the following day. A housekeeping staff scheduling report is created each morning, and the executive housekeeper uses it to assign staff members to specific floor sections. The rooms occupied by guests expected to check out are usually scheduled to be cleaned last, since many guests

Exhibit 4   Housekeeping Status Report

Housekeeper's Report

Date _____ , 20 _____

A.M.
P.M.

ROOM NUMBER	STATUS	ROOM NUMBER	STATUS	ROOM NUMBER	STATUS	ROOM NUMBER	STATUS
101		126		151		176	
102		127		152		177	
103		128		153		178	
104		129		154		179	
105		130		155		180	
106		131		156		181	
107		132		157		182	
108		133		158		183	
120						195	
121		146		171		196	
122		147		172		197	
123		148		173		198	
124		149		174		199	
125		150		175		200	

Remarks:

_____

_____

_____

_____

Housekeeper's Signature

Legend:

✓	-	Occupied
000	-	Out-of-Order
—	-	Vacant
B	-	Slept Out (Baggage Still in Room)
X	-	Occupied No Baggage
C.O.	-	Slept In but Checked Out Early A.M.
E.A.	-	Early Arrival

tend to occupy the guestroom until just prior to the hotel's departure time. Thus, if these rooms were assigned to be cleaned early, they might have to be cleaned again, should the guest use the room following its cleaning. Rooms of departed guests require more cleaning time than do rooms of guests who are staying over (making the room a stayover room). If a guest checks out before the stated departure date, the front desk must notify housekeeping that the room should no longer be classified as a stayover. A special housekeeping routine coordinated with the front desk is often needed for cleaning and inspecting early check-out rooms.

At the end of a work shift, the housekeeping department prepares a **housekeeping status report** (see Exhibit 4) based on a physical check of all guestrooms. This report indicates the current housekeeping status of each room. It should be compared with the front desk occupancy report, and any room status discrepancies should be brought to the attention of the front office manager. This process helps ensure that front desk agents work with accurate and timely room-availability information; this can be especially important when processing late check-ins.

Many front office systems define room status in more detail than just occupied or on-change. Typical status designations in front office systems include:

- V/O—vacant and on-change
- V/C—vacant and cleaned, but not yet inspected
- V/I—vacant and inspected
- O/C—occupied and cleaned

Room Rates. A **room rate** is the price a hotel charges for overnight accommodations. The cost structure of the hotel dictates the minimum rate for a room, and competition helps the hotel establish its maximum rate. The room rate range is the range of values between the minimum and maximum rates. A hotel will usually designate a standard rate for each room. This rate is typically called the **rack rate** because historically the standard rate was the one posted at the front desk in a device called a room rack. The rack rate is considered the retail rate for the room. In most cases, room rate discounts provided by the hotel are discounts to a room's rack rate.

In summary, the room rate is the actual price charged for a given room on a given night. The rack rate is the standard or non-discounted rate for a given room type (such as rooms with two double beds, rooms with one king-size bed, suites, and so forth). If a guest does not qualify for a discounted price, the guest is charged the rack rate. If the guest qualifies for a discount—for example, 10 percent off the rack rate as a result of membership in a qualifying group—the price charged for the room is 10 percent off the rack rate. Hence, when a guest is charged a non-discounted price, the rack rate is also the room rate, but when a discount is applied, the room rate is a percent of the rack rate.

Room rates are typically confirmed as part of the reservations process. Assigning rates for walk-in guests is usually the responsibility of the front desk agent, guided by the hotel's policies and sales guidelines. Front desk agents are often allowed to offer a room at a lower price than its rack rate. Normally, this occurs only with managerial approval. For example, hotel management may be expecting a low rate of occupancy. To attract as much business as possible to the hotel, walk-in guests may be offered a rate below the rack rate to entice them to register and stay at the hotel. Some hotels establish seasonal rate schedules in order to anticipate business fluctuations. The objective of room rate flexibility is to provide greater value during low-demand periods and to maximize room revenue during high-demand periods (a form of revenue management).

Other room rate schedules may reflect variations in the number of guests assigned to the room, service level, amenities, and room location. For example, room rates may include dining room meals. Under the **American Plan (AP),** room charges include the cost of the guestroom and may include three meals per day in the hotel's food service outlets. Under the **Modified American Plan (MAP),** the daily rate includes charges for the guestroom and two meals per day (typically breakfast and dinner). Sometimes, the phrase *full pension* is used in place of American Plan, and *semi-pension* in place of Modified American Plan. Some resorts use an **All Inclusive** rate that includes the cost of the guestroom plus meals, beverages, and hotel-supported activities. Under the **European Plan (EP)**, meals are priced separately from guestrooms. American resorts frequently use either the American Plan or the Modified American Plan. Most non-resort hotels in the United States set their rates according to the European Plan.

Room rates may also vary based on type of guest. If authorized, front desk agents should know how and when to apply a special room rate during the registration process. Special room rates may include:

- *Commercial* or *corporate rates* for companies that provide frequent business to the hotel.

- *Complimentary rates (no charge)* for business promotions to special guests and/or industry leaders, or for compensation to dissatisfied guests.

- *Group rates* for a pre-determined number of affiliated guests.

- *Family rates* for parents and children sharing the same guestroom.

- *Day rates* for less than an overnight stay (check-in and check-out on the same day).

- *Package-plan rates* for guestrooms sold in a bundled package that includes special events or activities.

- *Frequent traveler rates* for guests earning discounts through a loyalty or rewards program.

Eligibility for special rates is generally contingent on management policy and the guest's profile.

Room Locations. When assigning guestrooms, a front desk agent must be aware of the characteristics of each room type. In most hotels, guestrooms within specific room categories tend to be approximately the same size and offer similar furnishings and amenities. Some hotels, due to different construction techniques and materials, may have room types that vary significantly in size and configuration. Differences between guestrooms generally are attributable to their furnishings, amenities, and location. Front desk agents should be familiar with various guestroom configurations, as well as the hotel's floor plan, in order to satisfy guest rooming requests. Exhibit 5 provides an example of a simplified hotel floor plan. Note the connecting rooms and handicapper-accessible rooms depicted in the floor plan.

The front office system contains specific data about each room, such as its type, rate, floor, view, bedding, and other pertinent information. Front office systems can be programmed to provide other guestroom information, such as special room features and amenities, in an easy-to-reference format.

Individual guests or groups of guests may specify certain room locations in the hotel as part of a reservation request. Groups may be promised preferred rooms by the sales and marketing department or catering department. However, the department booking the rooms should be careful to check room availabilities with the reservations department before committing specific rooms or facilities

Exhibit 5 Simplified Hotel Floor Plan

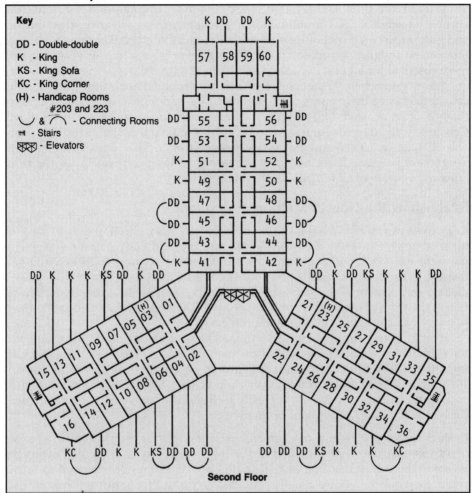

Courtesy of The Sheraton Inn, Lansing, Michigan.

to incoming guests or groups. Although the reservations department may block the desired rooms in advance, it is the responsibility of the front desk agents to assign guestrooms at registration to those group members not previously assigned a room from the preferred group block of rooms.

Reservation Blocks. A primary concern in the room assignment phase of registration concerns which rooms will be available in the near future, based on reservation blocks. Usually, a reservations agent or the front office supervisor blocks reserved rooms through an automated reservations file. If for any reason reserved rooms are incorrectly blocked or inadvertently overlooked, room assignment conflicts may result.

For instance, suppose a walk-in guest is assigned a room for a two-night stay. But if that room is booked for a guest arriving the next day—and the front desk agent is unaware of this commitment—rooming problems will arise when the second guest registers. Front office systems help reduce such booking errors because they can be designed to prohibit the front desk agent from selecting a pre-assigned room reserved for a guest expected to check in at a later date.

Many guests believe that once they occupy a room, there is little that the hotel can do to change their status. Any attempt to move a registered guest to another room is often resisted; bad feelings may arise even if the guest agrees to move. Conversely, the incoming guest, who was promised a particular room, will probably be inconvenienced and may be wary of the front desk's control over its room assignment process. These and related reasons make it imperative for the front office to be aware of all future guestroom commitments.

Establishing the Guest's Method of Payment

Regardless of whether the guest intends to pay by cash, check, payment card, or other acceptable method, the hotel should take precautionary measures to ensure payment for goods and services rendered. Effective account collection and settlement depends on the steps taken during registration to determine the guest's method of payment. The establishment of proper settlement or credit authorization at the time of registration will greatly reduce the potential for unauthorized payments and subsequent collection problems.

Just as hotels vary in size, structure, and organization, so do the guidelines for establishing a guest's method of payment. The registration process plays an important role in front office guest accounting, since front desk agents are responsible for gathering information at check-in related to the intended method of payment. Methods of payment typically include cash, personal checks, payment cards, direct billing, and special promotions.

Cash. Some guests prefer to pay guestroom charges during registration, in advance of occupancy, using cash. As stated earlier, guests who pay cash for their overnight accommodations at the time of registration are typically not extended in-house credit. Revenue outlets are usually provided access to **PIA (paid-in-advance)** lists of cash-paying guests who are thereby not authorized to have charge purchases posted to their guestroom accounts *(no-post status)*.

In most properties, PIA lists are created automatically by a front office system that interfaces guest electronic folio files to the hotel's revenue outlets. Such systems will not allow outlet employees to post charges at the point of purchase to guest accounts that are not authorized for in-house charges. Guests without in-house charge privileges must settle their purchases at the point of sale with an acceptable form of payment. At some hotels, during check-in, front desk agents may require a cash-paying guest to leave an imprint of a payment card in order to extend in-house charge privileges to a cash-paying guest.

Hotels consider cashier's checks, traveler's checks, and money orders equivalent to cash. A hotel that accepts such forms of legal tender should require proper guest identification and treat such transactions as cash payments. Front desk agents should compare the picture and signature on the guest's identification with the appearance and signature of the person presenting the check or money order. When there is doubt, the check or money order should be verified with the issuing bank or agency.

Personal Checks. Some lodging properties allow transactions to be paid by personal check, while others have a strict policy against accepting personal checks. Although a hotel has no obligation to accept personal checks, it cannot refuse to accept a personal check on the basis of sex, race, or other grounds that would warrant illegal discrimination. Individual properties must establish policies for accepting personal checks. Hotels should also consider adopting policies relative to payroll checks, personal checks written on out-of-state and foreign bank accounts, government checks, and second- and third-party checks.

Some hotels allow guests to cash personal checks as long as they have a payment card on file that provides a check-cashing guarantee and the amount of the check is within the payment card company's established credit limit. When this is the case, front desk agents should imprint the payment card onto the back side of the guest's personal check or the guest's registration card. Some hotels accept personal checks only during standard banking hours; this provision often allows the daytime shift of the front office to obtain bank verification of the check, if necessary. Some hotels allow guests to write personal checks equivalent to the total amount of the guestroom rate and taxes only. When this is the case, cash or payment card payment will be required for all other purchases beyond this amount.

Hotels that accept personal checks should require proper identification. The guest's driver's license or passport number, address, telephone number, and e-mail address should be recorded on the *back* of a personal check as part of the hotel endorsement. Bank stamps and clearing house imprints will also be recorded on the *back* of the check. In some hotels, the amounts and dates of cashed personal checks are recorded on the guest's registration card. This procedure helps ensure that guests do not exceed the property's pre-established check-cashing limits (if any). If front office cashiers are not authorized to accept personal checks, they must be aware of what procedures to follow when a guest attempts to cash a personal check at the front desk.

Properties can also protect themselves against potential losses incurred through acceptance of fraudulent or bogus personal checks by following these basic guidelines:

- Do not refund cash if the original transaction was settled by personal check. If possible, return the guest's original personal check and, when appropriate, require an alternate form of payment. Some properties do not write a refund check, even if a refund is warranted, until the guest's bank verifies that the personal check in question was valid and has been cleared for payment.

- Accept personal checks written only on the current day. Do not accept undated or post-dated personal checks—that is, checks carrying no date or a future date instead of the current date. Such checks are not acceptable.

- Require that personal checks written to settle an account be made payable to the hotel, not to "Cash." Or, to put it another way, if guests want to write a check to "Cash," the guests should be given money in exchange for the check, and not be allowed to use such a check to pay their hotel bills. Such a policy would undermine a non-paying guest's (skipper's) claim that a personal check made out to "Cash" was used to pay his or her hotel account when in fact it was used to gain spending money.

- Do not accept checks written on foreign banks unless the hotel's credit department has pre-approved acceptance of these types of checks.

Exhibit 6 shows some additional procedural steps for avoiding check fraud.

Second- and third-party checks. In general, hotels should not accept second- or third-party checks. A *second-party check* is one made out to the guest presenting the check. A *third-party check* is one made out to someone who has in turn signed the check over to the guest presenting it. When accepting such checks, hotels may experience collection problems, especially if the maker of the check has registered a "stop payment" order on the check. If the hotel accepts a second-party check, the front desk agent should require the guest to endorse the check at the front desk, in view of the front desk agent, even if the guest had previously endorsed the check. The front desk agent can then compare the guest's two signatures (previous and current endorsements) prior to accepting the check.

Check guarantee service. Some hotels use a check guarantee service to ensure that the checks guests present are valid. A check guarantee service relies on critical information appearing on the check, which the front desk agent can provide either by entering the information on a terminal keypad or by passing the check through a special magnetic ink reader. The check guarantee service, in turn, determines the check writer's credit history and either guarantees or denies payment support. If a supported check later is found to be invalid, the guarantee service is liable for the amount of the check, not the hotel.

Alternatively, some hotels use a system capable of providing immediate payment through electronic transfer, much like a debit card transaction. The equipment functions similarly to a payment card reader with an interconnected verification system. Valid checks have specially encoded bank identification and account numbers printed at the bottom front of the check. Check readers can capture and decipher the special numbering and use data transfer technology to contact the bank identified on the check and verify that the account has sufficient funds. Basically, the check is passed through the reader, which records the bank and account information and sends it forward through the system. If the information is valid, the funds are set aside and paid to the hotel through the same system. If the check is not valid, or the balance in the account is not sufficient to cover the amount of the check, the hotel is immediately notified and the check is declined.

Since check services typically charge a transaction fee, hotels use the services only for personal checks written to settle guest accounts. It is important to note that there are no service guarantees for checks drawn on foreign banks.

Payment Cards. There are two forms of payment (credit and debit) cards that can be used for payment of guest charges: contact cards that rely on a magnetic stripe being swiped for account access, and contactless cards that rely on wireless transmission for account exchange. Contact credit or debit cards are plastic cards with a magnetic stripe that are assigned a line of credit by the issuer of the card. When

Exhibit 6   Suggested Steps for Accepting Checks

Steps to Follow when Accepting Checks

1 Be cautious of new checking accounts

Of all the insufficient, "hot" checks, 90% are drawn on accounts less than a year old. The consecutive numbers in the upper right hand corner begin with 101 and you should be especially careful when taking low numbered checks. Because knowing the age of the account is so important, some banks now print a code of when the account was opened (for example, 0278 means February, 1978) on all checks.

2 Place all information on front of check

As described in Regulation CC, either write the information consecutively across the top of the front or use the cross method.

Driver's license number	Credit card number
Clerk's initials	Other ID or manager's approval

3 Examine driver's license carefully

After you have the license out of the customer's wallet and in your hand, quickly ask yourself the following questions: Is the person in the photo and in front of you the same person? Are the addresses on the check and license the same? When does the license expire? More than 60% of the forged checks last year were cashed with an expired driver's license. Also, the courts have ruled that licenses are legally worthless for identification as soon as they expire. Be sure you examine the driver's license carefully.

4 Other Negotiable Instrument Codes

On drafts issued by savings and loan institutions and mutual savings banks, magnetic bank routing numbers may start with the digit 2 or 3. Credit union drafts are honored by the bank on which they are drawn. International traveler's checks have routing numbers starting with 8000. U.S. Government checks contain the routing number 000000518.

5 Traveler's check identification

VISA—When held above eye level, a globe of the world will appear on the front left and a dove in the upper right.

MASTERCARD and THOMAS COOK—When held above eye level, on the right side of the check in a circle, a woman with short black hair will appear.

CITICORP—When held above eye level, a Greek god will appear on the right.

BANK OF AMERICA—No distinguishing watermarks.

AMERICAN EXPRESS—Turn check over. Moisten your finger tip and run it over the left denomination. If it smears it is good. Right side will not smear.

6 Be impressed with the check—not the person

Don't let a customer's appearance lull you into ignoring any of these steps. Frank Abagnale, the retired master forger, once cashed a $50 check written on a cocktail napkin, before a hidden camera for television, because the bank teller was more impressed by his appearance than by the item he presented. When you're in a hurry, or want to make an exception, think how you will defend your decision if the check is returned. Then, only the check will matter —not the circumstances in which you took it.

Developed by Frank W. Abagnale

Frank W. Abagnale & Associates/PO Box 701290, Tulsa, Oklahoma 74170/Telephone 918-492-6590

Courtesy of Frank W. Abagnale & Associates, Tulsa, Oklahoma.

a charge purchase is made against the card, it is applied to the cardholder's credit line. Statements are sent to cardholders every month. Some card accounts, called travel-and-entertainment (T&E) cards, are expected to be paid in full each month. American Express is an example of a T&E card. Cardholders of bank cards (Visa, MasterCard, and others) are typically provided an installment payment plan that applies a rate of interest on balances carried forward to the next payment cycle. Payment card purchases may be rejected by the issuing bank or agency if the account is over the pre-approved limit or if the purchase in question will take the account over the limit. Debit cards differ from credit cards in that a debit card is attached to a deposit account (that is, a savings or checking account). When a charge is incurred, it immediately reduces the balance in the debit cardholder's account; there is no credit extended. Debit card charges can be rejected if there are insufficient funds to cover the cost of the transaction, or if a charge will result in the account balance going below a predetermined minimum balance.

Careful authorization and verification of card payments are as important to front office cash flow as the precautions taken with any other method of payment. The front office usually compiles a set of steps for processing payment card trans-actions. In addition, payment card companies often require that front desk agents adhere to exact procedures in order to ensure transaction settlement. As shown in Exhibit 7, payment card companies also provide helpful tips for avoiding fraud and implementing sound processing procedures. Hotels should have an attorney review their payment card procedures to be sure the hotel adheres to state and federal laws, payment card industry (PCI) standards, and additional specifications contained in card company contracts. Local banks may also provide procedural guidelines. Front office management may also consider the following points when establishing a front desk policy for handling payment cards.

Expiration date and location validation. When a guest presents a payment card, the front desk agent handling the transaction should immediately check the card's expiration date. If the date shows that the card has expired, the front desk agent should bring this to the guest's attention and request an alternative method of payment. Since payment card companies are not required to honor transactions processed with an expired card, the acceptance of such a card places the hotel in an untenable position. If the hotel inadvertently accepts an expired or invalid card, it may not be able to collect payment for the guest's charged purchases. In addition, some banks issue cards that are good only in a specific country. The front desk agent must be especially careful when dealing with international trav-elers, as they may present payment cards that are clearly marked as being valid only in specific countries.

Online authorization. After checking a card's expiration date, the front desk agent should make sure the card is otherwise valid. Swiping or tapping a payment card will connect the card reader to an online clearinghouse service. Once a com-munication connection is established, the required card and transaction data are exchanged through an electronic-data-capture (EDC) process. On the basis of the captured data, the card verification service consults an account database and gen-erates either an **authorization code** or a **denial code** for the transaction.

Invalid card. Front desk staff members should follow established front office and card-payment-company procedures when a card appears to be invalid, such

Exhibit 7 Tips from Payment Card Companies

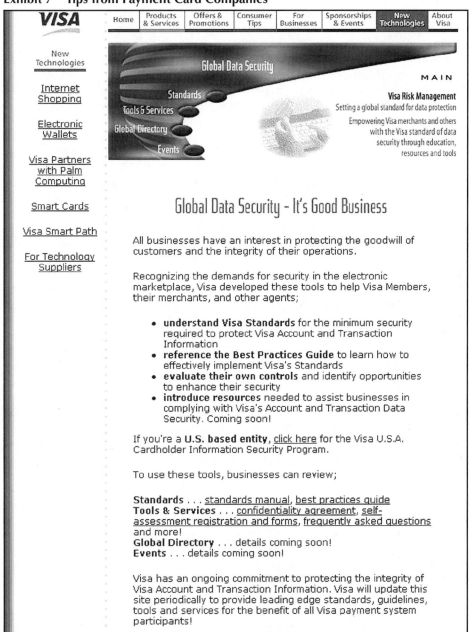

as when it has been tampered with, or the signature on the card does not match the signature on the hotel registration form. Normally, it is appropriate for staff members to politely request an alternate form of payment, without attracting attention or embarrassing the guest. If the guest has no other acceptable means of payment, front desk agents typically will refer the situation to the front office credit manager or hotel general manager for resolution.

If a guest presents a card that appears invalid, the front desk agent might be advised to contact hotel security. Although the federal government has made payment card fraud a criminal offense, lodging properties should exercise care in detaining guests they suspect of theft or fraud. Such detention, especially if unjustified or improperly instituted, might expose the hotel to a lawsuit based on false imprisonment and slander. The hotel's attorney should provide advice on the proper handling of invalid cards and on the hotel's vulnerability to related lawsuits.

Imprinting the voucher. Although rapid online verification and approval of payment cards has become the industry standard, some hotels may not have direct access to verification systems. In this case, front desk agents may need to imprint approved, valid cards onto approved payment card vouchers. Some hotels require front desk agents to circle the card's expiration date and initial the validation number on the imprinted voucher as proof that procedures have been followed. The imprinted card voucher can be attached to the guest's printed folio, or placed in a voucher file for safekeeping. Usually, the guest is not asked to sign the voucher until final account settlement at check-out.

Floor limits. Payment card companies may assign hotels a **floor limit.** A floor limit is the maximum amount in payment card charges the hotel can accept without requesting special authorization on behalf of a cardholder. If the amount a guest wants to charge to his or her card account exceeds the hotel's floor limit, the front office should contact the card company to request approval for the transaction.

In some cases, the penalty to the hotel for not obtaining authorization for charges exceeding the floor limit is forfeiture of the entire amount charged, not just the amount above the floor limit. An automated front office system that monitors guest account balances can identify guest accounts approaching the floor limit. Some lodging properties ask payment card companies to assign unusually high floor limits, given the hotel's room rates and other pricing structures. By receiving a higher floor limit, front desk agents will not have to inconvenience guests by frequently authorizing transactions or by having to secure alternate methods of payment.

Reserving credit. The front office may reserve a specified amount of pre-authorized credit in a guest's payment card account to ensure payment for goods and services. For instance, a guest who arrives and plans to stay for several nights likely will incur room charges in excess of the hotel's floor limit. To avoid a potential payment card authorization problem, the front office may want to reserve a credit line of *at least* an amount equal to the anticipated charges to be incurred on the guest's folio.

Management must be aware of the laws that pertain to reserving credit, as well as related card policies. Consider the case of a guest who decides to leave earlier than planned, and tries to make a subsequent purchase elsewhere, only to discover that his or her credit is tied up in a reserve created by the hotel. Laws related to reserving credit vary by state. In some states, the hotel would be obligated to notify the payment card company to release the unused portion of the reserved line of credit when the guest checks out. Also, some states stipulate that a hotel

Exhibit 8   Suggestions for Resolving Credit Problems

When a payment card issuer refuses to authorize a transaction:

- Discuss the matter with the guest in private.

- Use care when describing the guest's unauthorized transaction (for example, do not call the guest's payment card "bad" or "worthless").

- Offer the use of a telephone to help resolve the matter with a payment card company representative.

- Allow the guest a chance to provide alternate, acceptable means of payment.

When a guest's personal check cannot be accepted:

- Explain the hotel's check cashing policy.

- Remain friendly and cooperative.

- Discuss alternative methods of payment with the guest.

- If local banks are open, direct the guest to a nearby branch, or offer the use of a telephone.

can reserve an anticipated amount of credit only if it informs the guest beforehand, and obtains the guest's consent. Hotels should consult legal counsel before establishing a front office policy for reserving credit against payment card accounts.

When a guest arrives to check in, the front desk agent should request a method of payment before retrieving the guest's registration information. The agent may then swipe or tap a payment card using the card reader attached to the front office system. The card reader processes the captured data and attempts to identify the arriving guest by displaying the registration record to the agent or by providing a list of possible matches. Once the agent has identified the proper guest, the system automatically calculates the amount of credit to be reserved and contacts the card company without intervention by the front desk agent. By the time registration is completed, the hotel should have an approval or denial code received from the payment card company displayed in the guest's electronic record.

Denying a credit request. When a front desk agent discovers that a guest's credit has been denied by the issuing card company, extreme care should be exercised in notifying the guest of the problem. In discussing problematic credit issues, the front desk agent must be as diplomatic as possible. The agent's tone of voice should remain friendly and subdued, no matter how belligerent the guest may become. While hotel staff members have certain rights to review and evaluate credit information, the guest also has the right to know why the front office will not accept his or her personal check, payment card, or direct-billing arrangement. Exhibit 8 suggests some procedures for resolving credit problems. These suggestions should be modified to fit the problem, the guest, and the hotel's policies.

Direct Billing. Some hotels extend credit to guests by agreeing to bill the guest or the guest's company for charges. **Direct billing** (also called "bill to") arrangements are normally established through communication between the front office and the guest or the guest's sponsoring company, and in advance of the guest's arrival. A potential guest or a sponsoring company representative may be asked to complete the hotel's application for credit. The front office manager normally reviews and is responsible for approving a guest's credit application. A list of approved direct billing accounts is usually maintained at the front desk for reference during registration. At check-out, a guest with approved credit simply signs his or her guest folio after approving its contents, and a statement is direct-billed to the third party for collection. In a direct billing arrangement, the hotel itself, not a payment card company or other agency, assumes full responsibility for account collection.

Special Promotions. During registration, guests may present vouchers, coupons, gift certificates, gift cards, or special incentive awards received from businesses, airlines, or other authorized agencies. Front desk agents must be aware of hotel agreements to honor such items and must know how to properly credit the bearer. Front desk agents must use care when handling special program vouchers because such documents tend to differ in value, conditions, or terms. Since program vouchers represent a form of payment and may be the actual documents the front office uses to reconcile the guest's folio, careful handling is warranted. Since vouchers and coupons represent pre-paid revenue to the hotel, the front desk should maintain a set of samples of all currently acceptable vouchers, coupons, gift cards, and certificates. This collection should be discussed with front desk staff in front desk training sessions and should be readily available to agents in case questions arise.

Payment Issues for Groups. Front desk agents must be careful when registering group guests and establishing the method of payment for them, because group members arriving at the hotel to attend a meeting or convention often have individual billing arrangements pre-established. In some cases, the guest's room and tax charges are direct-billed to a group master folio or account, while other charges, called **incidental charges** (such as Internet, food, beverage, and dry cleaning charges), may be the guest's personal responsibility. In such a case, credit for incidental charges will need to be established for each member of the group. However, when the group agrees to pay for all of the charges made by its members, it may not be necessary to establish individual guest lines of credit. Groups often pay guestroom, tax, and incidental charges for VIP guests or invited speakers, so these individuals may be asked to simply sign a registration form to verify date of departure before being issued a room key or guestroom access code.

Verifying the Guest's Identity

Many hotels require front desk agents to obtain positive guest identification before completing the registration process for any arriving guest. It is very common for front desk agents to ask for photo identification in the form of a driver's license or passport to ensure positive identification of the guest's name, address, signature, and photograph. Since the terrorist attacks of September 11, 2001, verifying the identity of guests has become common practice at nearly all hotels. For domestic guests, a driver's license or other form of photo identification is usually sufficient. International guests normally will need to present a passport. In both cases, the type of identification and identification number on the document should be recorded in the guest record. As an additional security measure, if the guest does not speak the local language, this fact should also be noted in the guest's record, as it can assist in identifying guests requiring foreign language translation, and is helpful in emergency situations.

Issuing the Room Key or Access Code

The front desk agent completes the guest registration process by issuing a room key. In some hotels, a newly registered guest is simply handed a guestroom key and directed to the guestroom by the front desk agent. In other hotels, the guest may be given a map showing guestroom location as well as the location of other hotel facilities such as the dining rooms, cocktail lounges, swimming pool, fitness center, meeting rooms, and parking facilities. For the security of both the guest and the property, room keys must be carefully controlled. The theft, loss, or unauthorized duplication and use of guestroom keys threaten hotel security.

Hotels should have written procedures governing guestroom key control. These procedures should state who is authorized to issue guestroom keys, who receives such keys, and where and how guestroom keys are created and/or stored at the front desk.

For security reasons, the front desk agent should never announce the room number of the guest when presenting the guestroom key to the guest. The front desk agent can, however, draw the guest's attention to the room number by writing it down or pointing to the room on the hotel map. Front offices that use a special code on guestroom keys instead of room numbers should have their front desk agents write the room number for the guest or discreetly explain to the guest how to interpret the room code on the key. Many hotels provide guestroom keys in envelopes, which gives front desk agents a convenient place to write the room number for guests.

If the hotel provides bell service, the front desk agent should ask whether the guest would like assistance from a bell attendant. If so, the front desk agent should introduce the bell attendant to the guest, hand the bell attendant the guest's room key, and ask the attendant to show the guest to the room. On the way to the room, the bell attendant should familiarize the guest with hotel information by explaining the special features of the hotel and such things as the locations of emergency exits, emergency procedures, restaurant locations, retail outlets' hours of operation, locations of ice and vending machines, and other appropriate information. Once inside the guestroom, the bell attendant can explain the features of the room, show the guest how the thermostat and in-room amenities work, answer any questions, and hand the room key to the guest. If the guest is displeased with the room or if the room is not prepared as the guest expected, the bell attendant should listen attentively and bring the matter to the attention of the front desk agent for corrective action. For example, if a family arrives at a hotel expecting a rollaway bed for a child to already be in the guestroom and it isn't there, the agent or bell attendant should make arrangements to ensure the bed is brought to the room.

Responding to Special Requests

Part of the guest registration process involves acknowledging and acting on special guest requests. For example, a guest may have requested two connecting rooms during the reservations process. These rooms should be blocked in advance of check-in to ensure availability when the guest arrives. If it appears that the guest's reservation requests were not properly handled, the front desk agent should strive to satisfy the guest's requests during the registration process, if possible.

Other special requests may involve guestroom:

- Location
- View
- Bed type
- Smoking/no-smoking status
- Amenities
- Special furnishings for disabled guests
- High-speed Internet access
- Entertainment systems, such as on-demand video systems and video game systems

A guest may request a room close to or far from an elevator; one that over-looks the ocean, pool, or city; one that has a king-size bed; or one that has a refreshment center or entertainment area. In addition, guests may ask for special furnishings in the guestroom. A couple arriving with a young child may request a crib. If the room was not pre-set with a crib, the front desk agent should contact housekeeping to arrange for prompt delivery of a crib. Special requests are best handled during preregistration. Some guests may ask for other special items, such as bed boards or ironing boards. Disabled guests may require rooms with certain design features—grab bars in the bathroom, for example, or special lights attached to smoke and fire detection systems. The Americans with Disabilities Act requires most lodging establishments to have special accommodations for disabled guests. These rooms should be specially reserved whenever possible and not sold to anyone who is not disabled unless there are no other rooms available in the hotel.

Sometimes special requests are made by another person on behalf of the guest. For example, the general manager may want to welcome a frequent guest by placing a fruit basket in the guest's room. Travel agents may order champagne to be delivered to a client's guestroom. Relatives of a honeymooning couple may request that champagne and flowers be placed in the room before the couple arrives.

While many of the details surrounding special requests can be handled during preregistration, it is important for the front office to follow up on each request. Guests are quickly disappointed if, upon arrival at the guestroom, they find that the hotel did not honor their requests. Front desk agents should mention the guest's special requests at check-in to ensure that the hotel has provided what the guest requested. In this way, guests are satisfied that their requests have been met.

Creative Registration Options

The registration process described in this chapter is typical of most hotels. Some hotels, however, have experimented with different techniques to make registration more efficient and effective. Registration techniques tried, with varying degrees of success, include the following:

- *Eliminating the front desk.* Instead of a front desk agent behind a front desk, a host waits in a reception area with a list of expected arriving guests and their pre-assigned guestrooms. The host identifies guests, completes an abbreviated registration process, and sometimes escorts guests to their rooms. The guest's credit is established when the reservation is made through a special interface between the central reservation software and the payment card company. With everything else in place, all the host or front desk agent has to do is preregister the guest and assign a room key. When the guest arrives, a simple verification of the information on the registration form completes the process. Sometimes this service is tied to the hotel's frequent traveler program or handled by the concierge staff.

- *Registering group guests at a special location.* An area separate from the front desk may be screened off and used only for managing guest services and/or providing check-in or check-out services for arriving group members at peak times.

- *Creating a unique, separate registration area for VIP guests.* This approach is similar to the hotel host or greeter concept just mentioned, but is available only to VIPs.

- *Combining hotel registration and meeting registration in a separate area for arriving group members.* Separating group guests from other guests enables the front office to offer specialized services to the group.

- *Registering guests off-site,* such as in airports, convention centers, and shuttle vans, allows guests to check in prior to arrival at the front desk.

The challenge is to make the hotel registration process innovative while treating guests with expediency and care.

Some front office registration services include temporary luggage storage for guests who arrive during busy periods. In addition, front desk agents may offer complimentary food or beverages to guests who may be inconvenienced during registration. Such guests may be directed to the hotel's lounge or restaurant to enjoy a more relaxed and leisurely wait while their guestrooms are being readied for occupancy.

Self-Registration

A guest registration concept that is becoming popular is **self-registration.** Self-registration terminals may be located on or off hotel grounds or made available through a mobile device or property website. Limited-service lodging brands as well as full-service brands are providing unattended terminals for guests who prefer to use self-service technology. Regardless of which guest-operated device is used, self-registration can significantly reduce guest registration time.

To use a self-registration option, a guest generally must have made a reservation that led to the creation of a reservation record. At the time of self-registration, the guest may need to enter a reservation confirmation number or swipe or tap a valid payment or guest-loyalty-program card. The terminal can capture and exchange data with the hotel's property management system to link to the reservation record. A self check-in terminal may also prompt the guest to enter additional registration data. Most terminals connect to a rooms management system, thereby enabling automatic room and rate assignment. Some terminals print or display registration materials (identifying the assigned room number) and a map (showing the location of the room). Customized greetings or messages about special hotel events or promotions can be displayed on the self-service device. The terminal may automatically dispense a guestroom key as a result of interaction with an electronic guestroom lock system.

Selling the Guestroom

Front desk agents will not have the chance to use efficient or innovative registration techniques if the guest is not convinced of the value of occupying a hotel room. Part of the front desk agent's job is to create consumer acceptance of the hotel's products: guestrooms, amenities, facilities, and services. Front desk agents can take several approaches to selling guests on the value of staying at the hotel.

Front desk agents should practice sales techniques specific to their work. The registration process, for example, must move through certain stages to ensure quick and careful registration. Within such stages, front office staff members have the opportunity to make individual sales presentations. Properly trained front office staff members can improve room revenue by applying front office sales techniques, especially the technique of upselling.

Upselling refers to the efforts of reservations and front desk agents to offer guests the opportunity to reserve rooms in categories above standard rate accommodations. Hotels normally have several rate categories based on such factors as room decor, size, location, view, amenities, and furnishings. Sometimes the rack rate differences among guestrooms are substantial. Exhibit 9 lists some general suggestions for upselling guestrooms.

To upsell, front office and reservations staff must be trained to be more than simply order-takers; they must be trained to be salespeople. Staff members should upsell rooms in much the same way that a food server in a restaurant sells an extra item such as an appetizer, beverage, or dessert. Reservations and front office staff should learn effective techniques for suggesting room upgrade options to guests. Upgrading involves knowing how and when to ask for a sale in a non-pressuring way and how to direct the sales effort toward a successful conclusion.

Offering guestroom options to an inquiring guest is the key to the reservations and registration sales process, and it requires thoughtful planning and practice. Although the majority of upselling is conducted during the reservations process, front desk agents will have similar sales opportunities with walk-in guests. Some hotels, as a matter of policy, offer registering guests more than one room option (when more than one option is available) and leave it to the guests to decide. To create guest acceptance, the front desk agent must know how to describe the

Exhibit 9   Suggestions for Upselling Guestrooms

- Always greet each guest with a smile in your voice as well as on your face. Be pleasant and businesslike. Remember: you are selling yourself as much as you are selling the hotel and its services.

- Establish and maintain eye contact with the guest.

- Find out the guest's name immediately and use it at least three times during the conversation. Always use courteous titles such as "Mr." or "Ms." when addressing the guest. Do not call a guest by his or her first name.

- Attempt to identify the needs of the guest, since these needs may not have been identified during the reservations process. Match the guest's needs to the furnishings and/or amenities from among available rooms. For example, a guest staying at the hotel for three or four nights may appreciate and be more willing to pay for a larger or more isolated room than a guest staying only one night. Guests on a honeymoon or special vacation may be willing to pay for a room with a scenic view.

- Upsell rooms when possible. Offer an upgraded room by pointing out its features and benefits first, then mention its rate. If the guest has a reservation, describe the differences between the reserved and the upgraded room. Walk-in guests provide the best opportunity for upselling. If two different types of rooms are available, mention the features, benefits, and rates of both. Do not risk losing the sale by mentioning only the higher-priced room.

- Complete the registration process.

- Thank the guest and wish him or her a pleasant stay.

hotel's facilities and services in an attractive and positive manner. It is not uncommon for hotels to offer incentive programs for reservations and front desk staff who successfully upsell guestrooms.

A guest will likely provide several clues about what is an acceptable accommodation to him or her; some information may even be available on the guest's reservation record. Front desk agents should mention the physical features as well as the benefits and conveniences of the various types of available rooms. A guest may select a room immediately after it is described, or may wait until the front desk agent describes all the options. In some cases, the only guestrooms available may be those in the higher-priced categories. Successful reservations and front desk agents can briefly and efficiently explain to the guest the value in a higher-priced room. However, if a guest has reserved a lower-priced room and does not want to pay the higher rate, a room should then be provided at the reserved (quoted) rate.

The front desk agent normally directs the guest through the remainder of the registration process after the guest has selected a room. As the guest is completing the registration, the front desk agent may reinforce the guest's choice by recapping the room's location and special features. As the registration process draws to a close, the front desk agent should inform the guest about the hotel's revenue outlets, services, and facilities. Most guests appreciate this information.

Before the guest leaves the front desk, the front desk agent should thank him or her for choosing the hotel and express a personal interest in making the stay pleasant. Some hotels require front desk agents to place a phone call to the guest's room shortly after registration, to ensure that the guest's accommodations are satisfactory.

Denying Accommodations

In general, a hotel is obligated to accommodate guests if rooms are available. Discrimination is prohibited in places of public accommodation on the basis of race, sex, sexual orientation, religion, or national origin. Legitimate reasons for refusing to accommodate a guest may include a lack of available rooms, the potential guest's disorderly conduct, or the guest's inability or unwillingness to pay for accommodations or services. In addition, state law may stipulate other reasons for denying accommodations. A front desk agent should not be the person who determines whether someone will be roomed or not; this is the responsibility of front office management. Management is also responsible for telling guests why they are being turned away. Management, with the advice of legal counsel and the state hotel association, should instruct front office staff on policies and procedures concerning the acceptance or rejection of potential guests.

Sometimes a hotel may be short of available rooms and may not be able to accommodate guests. It is imperative that the hotel set policies and procedures for handling these situations. Seldom, if ever, should a hotel be unable to accommodate a guest who has a reservation, especially a guaranteed reservation. When this happens, most hotels will make other arrangements for the guest. In the case of a guaranteed reservation, some hotels will arrange for and may pay for the guest's room at another property. It is important to remember that hotel policy may dictate no obligation to guests who do not hold guaranteed reservations. Generally speaking, guests with reservations who arrive before the hotel's reservation cancellation hour should be accommodated.

Walk-In Guests

A **walk-in** guest who has been traveling for an extended time may be disappointed to find that a hotel is fully occupied. Hotels have no obligation to accommodate guests who arrive without a reservation when no guestrooms are available. If a walk-in guest cannot be accommodated, front desk agents can assist the guest by providing directions to nearby hotels. The front desk agent might also offer to contact another hotel on behalf of the displaced guest.

Most of the time, guests who cannot be accommodated at the hotel would prefer to stay at a similar property. Hotels should keep a list, with contact information, of comparable properties in the local area. Hotels can benefit through mutual guest referrals in this way. Guest referrals allow one hotel to compare how well it is doing on a given night with other area hotels. Competing properties may reciprocate by sending overflow business to neighboring properties when the opportunity arises. Most importantly, however, referrals should be viewed as part of the hotel's guest relations program. The extra care paid to turned-away guests helps create an industry-wide atmosphere of caring and concern for all guests.

The situation may be more difficult when a walk-in guest incorrectly believes that he or she has a reservation. The hotel might take the following steps to clarify the situation:

- If the guest presents a letter of confirmation, verify the date and the name of the hotel; the guest may have arrived on a different date or at the wrong property. Most confirmation letters have a confirmation number that can help the front desk agent locate the reservation record in the hotel's system.

- Ask whether another person might have made the reservation for the guest; the reservation may be at another property, or it may be misfiled under the name of the person making the reservation, not the guest's name.

- Double-check reservations records for another spelling of the guest's last name. For instance, "B," "P," and "T" may have been confused when the reservation was made during a telephone conversation or entered incorrectly in a text document. Also, check to see if the guest's first and last names were inadvertently reversed in the reservation record.

- If the reservation was made through a travel agency or corporate representative, give the guest an opportunity to contact the originating source for clarification.

- Verify no-show registration information from the previous day, just in case the guest was mistakenly classified as a "no-show" because of an incorrect date of arrival.

If there seems to be no alternative to **walking** (turning away) the guest, a manager, not a front desk agent, should explain the matter to the guest in a private area away from the front desk. Registering one guest in view of another who cannot be accommodated can be extremely awkward and embarrassing to both the guest and the front office staff member.

Guests with Non-Guaranteed Reservations

A number of circumstances can delay a guest's scheduled arrival time or date. Guests frequently do not have the chance to change a non-guaranteed reservation to a guaranteed reservation by the time they realize they will arrive past the hotel's reservation cancellation hour. As a result, the hotel may not hold the reserved room for the guest and may not have a room available at the time the guest arrives. If the hotel cannot provide a guestroom, front office management must be extremely tactful when informing the guest. Blame should not be placed on either party, since the lack of accommodations may not be the fault of the guest or the front office staff.

Guests with Guaranteed Reservations

If reservations are carefully handled and sound forecasting procedures are followed, the hotel should not have to deny accommodations to a guest who has a guaranteed reservation. It is a serious matter to turn away a guest with a guaranteed reservation: some states have laws prohibiting hotels from doing so, and, should a hotel not be able to accommodate such a guest, penalties may be imposed upon the hotel by the state, at the guest's request. Even though hotels should do all they can to avoid turning away guests who have guaranteed reservations, they should have a policy for front desk staff members to follow if the situation occurs.

The front office manager should take charge and make the necessary decisions when it appears that the property does not have accommodations for a guest who has a guaranteed reservation. The manager may do the following:

- Review all room status reports and expected arrivals lists to ensure full occupancy is expected.

- Conduct an accurate count of rooms occupied, using all relevant data.

- Compare information in the rooms availability file, the housekeeper's report, and guest folios, looking for discrepancies in occupancy status.

- Contact in-house **due-outs** (guests expected to check out today) who have not yet checked out to confirm their departure times. Housekeeping staff can also visit select guestrooms to verify occupancy status. A guest may have left the hotel without properly completing check-out, and therefore the guestroom can be made available for an arriving guest. A departing guest may have left the hotel expecting to be billed, or may have paid in advance, or may simply have forgotten to check out. An early discovery of a room departure allows that room to be made available.

- Verify guestrooms with a status of "out-of-order" to ensure that they are not qualified to be occupied. Perhaps an out-of-order room might be readied for sale, if the room problems are minor—no bedspread, for example, or missing window drapes. If a guest is willing to occupy an out-of-order room, its rate could be appropriately adjusted. These decisions must be made by front office management. An out-of-order room should never be offered if the room has serious deficiencies, like no running water or telephone service. In addition, an out-of-order room should never be offered unless it is inspected first, and the department placing the room on out-of-order status is notified that it will be occupied. The front office manager should check the out-of-order report daily to ensure that all rooms are made available as quickly as possible.

- Identify rooms that have been pre-blocked for one or two days in the future. A guest can be assigned to one of these rooms, if the guest will depart early enough to not affect the room block.

Front desk staff should be consistent when discussing the lack of accommodations with arriving guests. Helpful suggestions include the following:

- Guests should be encouraged to return to the hotel at the earliest date of availability. Upon their return, they may be placed on a VIP list, provided a complimentary room upgrade, or presented with a small amenity as compensation for the inconvenience of having been turned away on their last visit.

- Management should prepare a follow-up letter to be sent to guests who arrived with a reservation but could not be accommodated, apologizing for the inconvenience and encouraging the guests to consider returning to the hotel (with appropriate incentives).

- If a member of a convention block cannot be accommodated, the group's meeting planner should be notified. The planner may be able to solve the problem by arranging for some attendees to alter their current rooming status. In such cases, it is important for the front office staff to have a positive working relationship with the group coordinator or meeting planner. This notification may better enable the coordinator or planner to properly deal with the problem and subsequent membership complaints.

Summary

Through the reservations process, a guest provides nearly all the information needed to complete registration. The focus of front office operations shifts to the registration process once the arriving guest's reservation status is known. Front office personnel will find registration smoother and simpler when the information in a reservation record is accurate and complete. The registration process can be divided into seven steps: preregistration activities, creating the registration record, assigning the room and rate, establishing the method of payment, verifying the guest's identity, issuing the room key or access code, and filling special requests.

Preregistration activities occur before guest arrival and are intended to accelerate the registration process. Guests can be preregistered when reservations agents or hotel websites with registration capabilities gather the proper information. Typically, preregistered guests need only verify registration information and provide a valid signature to complete the registration process. In addition, room and rate assignment, creation of a guest folio, and other functions may be part of a hotel's preregistration activities.

The registration record is a collection of important guest information, and is created at the time of check-in. Registration cards, or their computer-generated equivalent, should prompt front desk agents to inquire about the guest's intentions regarding method of payment and planned date of departure. Front desk agents should always confirm the guest's departure date and pre-assigned room rate.

Room assignment involves identifying and allocating an available room in a specific room category. Based on reservation information, specific rooms and rates may be assigned before the guest arrives. Pre-assigning a specific room depends on the room's forecasted availability status and how appropriately the room meets the guest's needs. Room assignments are finalized during the registration process. Effective room and rate assignment depends on accurate and timely room status information (long-term *reservation status* and short-term *housekeeping status*).

Effective account settlement depends on the steps taken during registration to determine the guest's method of payment. Proper settlement or credit authorization at the time of registration will greatly reduce the potential for subsequent collection problems. Just as hotels vary in size, structure, and organization, so do their guidelines for establishing the guest's method of payment. The registration process may also play an important role in guest accounting, since it deals directly with method of payment.

Many hotels require positive guest identification to complete the registration process. This has long been common practice in Europe, and has become common in the United States since 9/11. Hotel managers want to be sure they know who is staying at their property. For domestic guests, a driver's license or other form of photo identification is usually sufficient. International guests should be asked for their passports.

By issuing a room key, the front desk agent completes the registration process. Hotels should have written policies governing guestroom key control. If the hotel provides bell service, the front desk agent should ask whether the guest would like assistance from a bell attendant and then communicate specific room information to the bell attendant.

Part of registration is making sure that any special requests made by guests are acknowledged and dealt with. While many of the details surrounding special requests can be addressed during preregistration, it is important to follow up on each request. Guests will be disappointed if they arrive at their room and find that the hotel did not honor a request. Front desk agents should mention special guest requests during registration to assure the guest that the hotel will meet the guest's wants and needs.

Some hotels are trying creative registration options in an effort to better accommodate guests. A relatively new concept in front office registration is self-registration. Self-registration terminals can be located off-site (in airports, for example) or in the hotel lobby. These terminals vary in design and may resemble automated bank teller machines.

Upselling at the front desk is a common practice used to enhance the value of the guest's lodging experience while increasing hotel revenues. Front desk agents should identify opportunities for offering better accommodations to guests and selling their value. For example, guests who travel regularly as part of their work may appreciate rooms with special business amenities at a small increase in the room rate they confirmed. Many hotels provide incentive programs for agents making the most of such selling opportunities.

Relocating (or walking) guests must be done with great care and concern. Most guests who believe the hotel has not acted in their best interest will become upset; some may cause a disturbance or vow never to return. Further, they may criticize the hotel to friends and co-workers, creating an even larger negative image of the hotel. Walking a guest should be done by a manager, not a front desk agent. Hotels should attempt to bring the guest back as soon as possible. Front office managers must take care to minimize the number of guests who must be relocated, and be aware of any laws pertaining to guests who have guaranteed reservations. Upscale hotels usually pay for the guest's transportation to and from the hotel to which the guest is relocated (in addition to paying for the guestroom), and advise their telecommunications department to redirect incoming telephone calls and faxes to the other location.

🔑 Key Terms

All Inclusive—A billing arrangement under which room charges include the guestroom, meals, beverages, and activities.

American Plan (AP)—A billing arrangement under which room charges include the guestroom and three meals; also called "full pension."

authorization code—A code generated by an online payment card verification service, indicating that the requested transaction has been approved.

denial code—A code generated by an online payment card verification service, indicating that the requested transaction has not been approved.

direct billing—A credit arrangement, normally established through correspondence between a guest or a company and the hotel, in which the hotel agrees to bill the guest or the company for charges incurred.

due-outs—Guests expected to check out on a given day who have not yet done so.

European Plan (EP)—A billing arrangement under which meals are priced separately from rooms.

floor limit—A limit assigned to hotels by payment card companies indicating the maximum amount in payment card charges the hotel is permitted to accept from a card member without special authorization.

housekeeping status report—A report prepared by the housekeeping department indicating the current housekeeping status of each room, based on a physical check.

incidental charges—Charges made to a guest account other than the charges and tax for the guestroom.

Modified American Plan (MAP)—A billing arrangement under which the daily rate includes charges for the guestroom and two meals, typically breakfast and dinner.

occupancy report—A report prepared each night by a front desk agent that lists the rooms occupied that night and indicates those guests expected to check out the following day.

PIA (paid-in-advance)—A guest who pays his or her room charges in cash during registration; PIA guests are often denied in-house credit.

rack rate—The standard rate established by a hotel for a particular category of rooms.

registration form—A document used to help formulate a registration record; in many states, the guest's signature on a registration form is required by law.

registration record—A collection of important guest information created by the front desk agent following the guest's arrival; includes the guest's name, address, telephone number, and company affiliation; method of payment; and date of departure.

reservation status—An indicator of a room's long-term availability for assignment.

room rate—The price a hotel charges for overnight accommodations.

room status discrepancies—A situation in which the housekeeping department's description of a room's status differs from the room status information that guides front desk employees in assigning rooms to guests.

run of the house—Room assignment based on room availability at the time of check-in.

self-registration—A computerized system that automatically registers a guest and dispenses a guestroom key, based on the guest's reservation and payment card information.

skipper—A guest who leaves without paying for the room.

sleeper—An unoccupied guestroom wrongly shown as occupied on the property management system.

upselling—A sales technique whereby a guest is offered a more expensive room than what he or she reserved or originally requested, and is then persuaded to rent the room based on the room's features and benefits, and his or her needs.

walk-in—A guest who arrives at a hotel without a reservation.

walking—Turning away a guest who has a reservation, due to a lack of rooms.

 Review Questions ───────────────────────────────

1. What are the seven steps of the registration process?

2. What are the advantages of preregistering guests? What might limit the front office's ability to preregister guests?

3. What information is usually requested on a guest registration card? How is this information useful to the front office?

4. Why is current room status information essential to an effective guest registration process?

5. What are the advantages of a computerized room status system?

6. What are some examples of special room rates?

7. What major methods of payment do guests use? What forms of tender are generally considered equivalent to cash?

8. What procedures do front desk agents use for accepting a payment card as a method of payment during registration?

9. What are some creative registration options?

10. What is upselling? When is it appropriate? What are some things a hotel can do to upsell a guest?

11. What actions should the front office consider when a guest cannot be accommodated?

Internet Sites

For more information, visit the following Internet sites. Remember that Internet addresses can change without notice. If the site is no longer there, you can use a search engine to look for additional sites.

American Express Company
www.americanexpress.com

MasterCard Worldwide
www.mastercard.com

Diners Club International
www.dinersclub.com

Visa Inc.
www.visa.com

Discover Card
www.discovercard.com

Wyndham Rewards
www.wyndhamrewards.com

Case Studies

Checking In to the Boden Oceanside Resort and Lodge

Checking in to the Boden Oceanside Resort and Lodge should have taken John five minutes, even though the check-in line was three deep. However, there was only one front desk agent in sight and the people checking in seemed to have all kinds of questions. To complicate matters, their room keys couldn't be encoded for some reason, and the agent was trying to take a phone call from a guest at the same time.

When John finally reached the desk, the agent didn't make eye contact. John's name was on the reservation list and all of the details of his stay were in order. John was given a handful of brochures but the clerk didn't really explain any of them specifically. There was a map of the town, a brochure describing local events, and a brochure featuring various restaurants in the area. The map of the property was so small that it was difficult to make out exactly where one was on the property.

The best part of check-in was the 20 percent discount coupon for the Saturday brunch.

As John picked up his luggage, he looked around for a bell attendant. He wasn't quite sure where his room was, but knew its general direction. The desk clerk had not looked up at him while explaining where the room was on the map. He hoped that there would be signage to direct him once he got outside the main lobby.

After settling into his room, John noticed a constant humming sound coming from behind the wall. It sounded somewhat like a fan. John hated any extra noise and called the front desk to find out what the noise was.

The desk agent who had checked John in was on break and the new one informed him that the noise was indeed a fan from the kitchen that ran from 8 A.M. until 11 P.M. and that the room wasn't usually sold unless the hotel was sold out. John asked to be moved, since he would be in the hotel for five days. The agent told him it would be no problem and that he should come back to the front desk to get another room key. She asked whether he needed assistance with his luggage and then asked if he could hold the line for a second.

John waited on the phone for what seemed three or four minutes when the agent finally got back to him. She apologized and he said he would like help with his luggage.

After waiting for about ten minutes, John finally left his luggage in the room and went back to the front desk. The agent who had helped him was taking a phone reservation, but her assistant asked if he could help. John mentioned his desire to change rooms. The assistant leaned down to talk to the agent on the phone but was ignored momentarily. He told John he didn't know which room she had arranged for him and that she would be off the phone in a moment.

Twenty minutes later John was checked into a new room with an ocean view. He decided to go out for a walk and stopped first at the front desk to see if his luggage could be delivered to his new room. "Oh no!" said the agent. "I forgot to let the bell attendant know about the move and now he has gone home."

John found his way to his old room, picked up his luggage and took it to his new room.

As he lay on his bed substituting a rest for a walk, John couldn't help seeing a few cobwebs in the upper corners of the room, cracking wallpaper, and some dust on the ceiling trim.

After his nap, John had to call down to the front desk because there was no toilet paper in the bathroom. He was transferred to housekeeping, where the executive housekeeper answered cordially. She apologized and told him that she was severely understaffed due to budget freezes but would send someone up right away.

As John went for a walk later that afternoon, he was nearly knocked over in the hallway by a load of laundry being carried by a very small woman. She said something he couldn't understand in broken Spanish and English and hurried along on her errand.

As it turns out, John had been hired to inspect the property by the owners of the Boden Oceanside Resort and Lodge. He began to jot down some notes that he would use in his report to the owners.

Discussion Questions

1. What suggestions do you have for the front desk manager?

2. How many departments did John interact with during the arrival stage?

3. Why would the owners hire John to check out the property?

Case number: 608C04

This case also appears in Todd Comen, *Case Studies in Front Office Management* (Lansing, Mich.: American Hotel & Lodging Educational Institute, 2003).

Everybody Sells: Turning Front Desk Agents into Salespeople

"Come in, come in!"

Ben, a slim, gray-haired figure in a dark three-piece suit, rose from his leather desk chair and waved Keith into one of the two chairs on the other side of the massive oak desk. Keith said thank you and glanced around the general manager's office as Ben settled into the chair next to his. Keith had been in the office a few times before, but he was still impressed by the floor-to-ceiling bookshelves behind the desk, the lithographs of old hotels that lined the walls, the awards and testimonial plaques that were sprinkled throughout the room.

"The reason I wanted to talk with you today," Ben began, "is to discuss what we can do to bring up our average daily rate. You've been at the hotel a couple of weeks now and I assume you've learned your way around a bit."

"Yes sir."

Ben's eyes twinkled. "I've told you before, just because my hair is gray and I've been in the hotel business a hundred years, there's no need to call me 'sir.' 'Ben' will do."

Keith smiled and just stopped himself from saying "Yes sir" again.

"I've received word that corporate wants us to raise our ADR ten percent by the end of the quarter, and the front desk has got to do its part." Ben leaned back in his chair and clasped his hands over his vest. He reminded Keith of a kindly, long-time family lawyer getting set to dispense some grandfatherly advice. "I don't want to be insulting, but, since this is your first job as a front office manager—in fact, you're not that long out of college, is that correct?"

"That's right, just a few years," Keith said. "Still 'wet behind the ears,' you might say."

"Well, if you'll indulge me, I'd like to relate a little history of the relationship between the reservations department and the front desk; I think it will help you appreciate how we got to where we are today, and put into perspective what I'll be asking you to do to help us get that extra ten percent."

"Okay." Keith settled back for a long story.

"My first hotel job was in the reservations office. Back then there were no computers. We did have phones, however, in case you were wondering." Keith smiled as Ben chuckled. "People would call in requesting a room, and we would roll an index card into a typewriter and type out a reservation. The caller didn't make special requests, such as 'a room with a desk, please,' or 'a king-size bed, please,' and we didn't ask for any of that information, because we weren't sure what type of room would be available—back then inventory control was all done at the front desk. The card was simply a request that a room be held for the caller on a certain day. The cards would all be gathered up at the end of the shift and taken to the front desk, where they would be filed by the day the reservation was for.

"When the guest arrived at the hotel, the front desk agent would pull the card ('Yes, Mr. Whosis, we have a room for you') and then the selling would begin, based on what types of rooms the agent knew were still available: 'Would you like a king-size bed?' 'We have several rooms with a nice view of the park—would you care for one of those?' and so on. In other words, the front desk agents were the hotel's salespeople, because they had control of the guestroom inventory. They knew which rooms were available and which were not.

"Well, along came computers, and suddenly sales moved from the front desk to the reservations department. Why? Because computers allowed the reservations department to keep track of guestroom inventory. Now when a caller phoned the hotel, the reservationist could look at a computer screen and tell exactly what rooms were still available on the day the caller wanted to stay at the hotel. So the reservationist, instead of merely reserving 'a' room—the old card system could do that much—could now reserve a *particular* room. The reservationist could ask the caller all of the questions the front desk agent used to ask: 'What size bed would you like?' 'Would you like a room with a view?' 'For five dollars more I can reserve a room near the pool; would you like that?' and so on. Therefore, once computerized reservations systems arrived and guestroom inventory control shifted from the front desk to the reservations department, the sales function and all of the sales training shifted from the front desk to the reservations department, too."

Ben spread his hands in a gesture of regret. "Consequently, salesmanship was not emphasized at the front desk anymore. In fact, many agents saw no need to sell, because most guests had already told the reservationist exactly what types of rooms they wanted. Many front desk agents thought they would be 'bothering' a guest if they suggested a room other than the one called for by the reservation already entered into the computer.

"But—and this is something I could never get your predecessor to understand, or at least to act on," Ben frowned, "front desk agents can still have a tremendous impact on a hotel's bottom line, through upselling. For example, if a guest walks in with his wife, and the front desk agent sees that he has reserved a standard room, the agent should say something like the following: 'Sir, we have a room available that you might enjoy more than the one you've reserved. The room I'm thinking of is a corner room with a great view. It also has a whirlpool tub that's great for relaxing, a sitting area, and a king-size bed—which would be an upgrade from the two double beds in your present room—all for only $15 more. Would you like me to reserve this room for you?'

"Or, if an agent sees a guest come in lugging three sample cases, he can assume that this is a businessperson who probably would like enough space in his room to spread out business papers or samples or what have you. The agent should say something like this: 'Gee, it looks like you're really loaded down, sir. I see that you've reserved a standard guestroom, but I have a bigger room with plenty of desk space for only $10 more.' What's wrong with that?"

Ben stopped talking and looked at Keith expectantly.

"Nothing?" Keith ventured.

"That's right, there's nothing wrong with that!" Ben said enthusiastically. "The agent made a suggestion that might make the guest's stay more pleasant and also increase revenues for the hotel. That's all there is to upselling. But so few agents are trained to do that anymore. Like I said, computers changed everything. In the old days, reservationists were 'order-takers' and the front desk agents were the salespeople; now the roles are completely reversed. And it shouldn't be that way. Front desk agents still have a sales role to play."

Ben chuckled again. "Thank you for letting me climb up on my soapbox. You're probably wondering, 'What does all this have to do with me?' Well, what I want you to do is turn your front desk agents into salespeople again. We've got to teach them how to sell and give them the tools to sell so they'll have the confidence to sell."

"I hope this doesn't sound naive," Keith said, "but, can upselling really make that much difference? I mean, $5 here, $10 there, and not every guest is going to agree to an upgrade." Keith paused. "I guess I'm not sure how much that's really going to add to the bottom line."

"That's the beauty of upselling," Ben replied. "Every extra dollar you bring in through upselling falls to the bottom line. We've already spent the money to get the guest to the hotel—through advertising, the reservationist taking the call, and so on. Now that he's here, anything extra we can entice him into spending is pure gravy."

Ben smiled. "Now, don't get the wrong idea. I don't want to sound manipulative, because upselling—done properly—is not the art of tricking a guest into buying something he doesn't want. A front desk agent should never pressure a guest. However, there's nothing wrong with pointing out to a guest that, for a few dollars more, his or her experience at the hotel might be enhanced. Usually, guests are unaware that there are rooms available that might better fit their needs. Maybe the reservationist didn't do a great job of selling, who knows? So agents aren't trying to 'gouge' guests when they upsell—they are merely offering a guest some options that the guest might not have thought about, options that might make the guest's experience at the hotel more enjoyable. That's the way you should present upselling to your agents."

"I'll be glad to try," Keith said, "but I'm not sure how to go about it."

"Well, the first thing I'd do is assess the current sales skills of the staff," Ben said. "Is anyone selling right now? You've only been here a couple of weeks and I know you're not fully acquainted with your personnel, so I'd spend some time observing the agents. This might also give you ideas on what types of upselling opportunities the agents are missing. If you discover a pattern, that will give you a plan of attack on good ways to raise the ADR.

"What I suspect you're going to find," Ben continued, "is that few, if any, agents are upselling right now. But don't be discouraged. There are lots of techniques we can use in-house to train them; we may even send them to some outside seminars, or bring a trainer here if we have to. Also, you'll probably want to set up an incentive program to encourage the agents to sell."

Ben stood up to signal an end to the meeting and placed a hand on Keith's shoulder. "Don't worry, I'm confident you can do it. And you're not alone. All we need from the front desk area is an additional five percent; reservations and the sales department have targets to meet, too, and—working together—we'll make our numbers and corporate will be happy. If you run into trouble, don't hesitate to come see me."

"Thank you, Ben."

During the next week, Keith observed the front desk agents as they checked in guests. As Ben predicted, they didn't make any effort to upsell. They were polite and professional, but invariably they sent the guests to whatever room they had previously reserved. Even with walk-in guests there was no salesmanship. The agents always offered the walk-ins one of the hotel's standard guestrooms—the lowest-priced rooms in the house—and almost every walk-in simply accepted it. Keith observed only one walk-in guest who asked if there were better rooms available. The agent said yes, the hotel had some deluxe rooms available, and there was even one club room still available. (The hotel had three basic types of rooms: "standard" guestrooms with either two double beds, two queen-size beds, or one king-size bed; "deluxe" guestrooms with the same bed combinations but with slightly more floor space and better appointments; and "club" rooms that were really mini-suites with king-size beds, sitting areas, and special amenities such as thicker towels, upgraded toiletries, turn-down service, and so on.) When the guest asked the agent to describe the differences in the rooms, Keith was surprised to hear the agent do a terrible job of outlining the different features and amenities that accompanied each type of room. Later, Keith checked with some of the other agents and was shocked to learn that many of them had never seen any of the hotel's guestrooms.

As the week wore on, Keith noticed a pattern that concerned him: most of the hotel's club rooms were given away as upgrades to the hotel's business guests. Those rooms were supposed to be real money-makers for the hotel, because the hotel sold them at a higher rate than the standard and deluxe guestrooms, but that was precisely the problem—the rooms were rarely sold. As part of its special corporate rates, the hotel promised business travelers free upgrades to club rooms "subject to availability." And club rooms were always available, because front desk agents weren't selling them! If Keith did nothing more than get his agents to sell more club rooms, that would have a dramatic impact on ADR, because the rooms would be sold rather than given to guests who were already enjoying a discounted corporate rate.

At the end of the week, Keith met with his front desk agents at the beginning of their shifts and explained the situation. "The overall goal of the hotel is to raise ADR by ten percent; our contribution is to increase our numbers by five percent. We can do that by upselling—to all of our guests, but especially to our walk-ins. According to my research, about 12 percent of our guests are walk-ins, and since these guests have no prior reservations, they're not committed to a particular room and should be easier to upsell. If we start out by offering walk-ins our club rooms, rather than our standard rooms, then offer a deluxe room as a compromise if they don't want a club room, I think we can almost make our numbers right there, not even counting upselling to guests who already have reservations.

"Let me give you an example of how a little bit of upselling can make a big difference," Keith continued. "We sold about 1,000 rooms to walk-ins last month. All but fourteen of those guests were booked in standard rooms at around $55 per night. If we sell club rooms, which sell for $40 more, to 200 of those walk-ins— that's just one upgraded guest out of five—that brings in an additional $8,800 for the month. Project that over twelve months, and we're bringing in over $100,000 more revenue per year for the hotel. Just moving 200 walk-ins from a standard to a deluxe room at $75 a night would bring in $4,400 more a month. And those dollars fall right to the bottom line.

"If we sell out the club rooms—and that should be our goal every night— they are no longer available as free giveaways to businesspeople, which saves us money and gives us upselling opportunities: 'I'm sorry, Ms. Businessperson, but our club rooms are full tonight. I can go ahead and book you into your standard room, or I can upgrade you to a deluxe guestroom with lots of space and a king-size bed for just $20 more.' Don't save the club rooms so you are sure to have some available to give away as upgrades. What you want to do is sell them out, so we don't have to give them away."

"Isn't that unfair to the business travelers?" asked one agent.

"Not really," Keith replied. "Our deals with business travelers state that we will upgrade them to club rooms if any are available—but we certainly aren't obligated to deliberately not sell club rooms to make sure they're available. That's not good business, and businesspeople don't expect us to do that. The hotel put a lot of money into those club rooms, and it's entitled to try to recoup that investment if it can.

"I know the idea of upselling is a new one for many of you," Keith said in conclusion, "but it isn't that difficult, and I'm not going to just shove you out there unprepared. You're going to get some training, and I'm also going to come up with an incentive plan so you can share in the rewards of bringing more revenue to the hotel.

"Upselling can be enjoyable if you approach it the right way, so get ready to have some fun! And here's a slogan I want you to remember from now on: 'Everybody Sells!'"

Discussion Questions

1. What are some ways Keith can train his front desk agents to be salespeople?

2. What types of incentive plans might Keith put in place to encourage his front desk agents to sell?

Case Number: 3325CA

The following industry experts helped generate and develop this case: Richard M. Brooks, CHA, Vice President, TWE Group; and S. Kenneth Hiller, CHA, General Manager, Holiday Inn, Beachwood, Ohio.

Risking the Upgrade!

Things were hopping in the front office this Friday afternoon. Guests had been checking in for the Glamder wedding, which would last two days and was taking up a block of twenty rooms. It was a major wedding for the resort, and the sales department was very pleased. It was still the shoulder season, so an event such as this was welcome at this time of year. With the wedding room block, the resort was nearly fully occupied.

At 7:30, two men arrived at the front desk to check in a little late for the rehearsal dinner. The front desk agent, Clarice, greeted them cordially and requested their names. One introduced himself as John Jones. Clarice identified the correct guest record for John Jones, scanned it briefly to determine if indeed he was with the wedding party, how many days he would be staying, and the number of people in the room. She noticed that there was only one person booked for the room and asked whether he was traveling alone. He explained that his buddy had decided to attend the wedding at the last minute so they drove down together from Oregon.

Clarice reviewed the guest record again, taking notice of the room assignment and the price quoted for the room. Mr. Jones had been assigned to a small, less expensive room in the south wing of the resort for the low rate of $120. This room had only one queen size bed and a pull-out sofa. She took a look at the men and wondered who would get the pull-out sofa, since both of them were well over six feet tall.

While pondering what to do next, she asked whether they had ever stayed at the resort before. Mr. Jones said that he and his wife and two children had stayed at the resort just eight months ago and loved it. They had planned to go to Europe, but world circumstances influenced them to stay closer to home. They had stayed in a lovely suite and really enjoyed their time at the resort. The friend, however, had never stayed there.

Clarice then asked whether they would be comfortable in a room with a queen bed and a pull-out sofa. Mr. Jones quipped that since he was paying for the room, he would take dibs on the queen bed. The other gentleman didn't complain, but was a little disappointed. Clarice thought for a moment and asked whether they would like an upgrade to a more comfortable room. She couldn't guarantee one, but would see what she could do if they gave her a few moments. She asked them if they would like to have a refreshing drink in the lounge while she checked on room availability.

Since the men were late already, they decided a few more minutes wouldn't matter and that they would have a drink. After ten minutes and another check-in, the men were back wondering if anything had been found. Clarice said that the only thing she could find was a junior suite with two queen beds. It was a very comfortable room and would be the envy of the other wedding guests. She said it was $100 more per night. As the wedding party would last two nights, the total additional cost would be $200. Mr. Jones was quick to respond to the suggestion by saying he would be pleased to split the difference with the resort, meaning that the additional charge would be $50 per night.

Clarice pondered the offer. She cringed, wondering what her supervisor would have to say about upgrading guests from the lowest-cost room to one of the nicest the resort had to offer for only $50 per night. Her superiors had always pushed for getting top dollar for the suites.

On the other hand, Clarice had noticed that the suites hadn't been selling to walk-in customers. At this time of night, the room might not sell anyway, she thought to herself. And what were the chances of the room selling the following night when it wasn't reserved in advance? Clarice wondered whether to take the additional $50 per night and risk upsetting the supervisor whom she knew didn't like selling below rack rate, or just leave the two guys in the less expensive room. She thought for a moment and then decided to go with the upgrade. The two gentlemen were thrilled when they passed the front desk later that evening on their way to the rehearsal dinner. They had called their wives and told them of the warm reception and that they would have to plan a visit to the resort in the near future.

The following day the assistant front office manager asked to have a word with Clarice about the upgrade decision she'd made the previous afternoon. They had a brief discussion while Clarice answered phones for the PBX operator who was taking a dinner break. As expected, the assistant front office manager wasn't very pleased with the upgrade decision. Even though Clarice tried to explain her reasoning for the upgrade, the manager couldn't see her point and asked her never to do it again.

Discussion Questions

1. Did Clarice use good business sense or was she just being nice?
2. Should the manager have been called to help with this decision?

Case number: 608C07

This case also appears in Todd Comen, *Case Studies in Front Office Management* (Lansing, Mich.: American Hotel & Lodging Educational Institute, 2003).

Chapter 6 Outline

Competencies

1. Describe front office procedures for communicating with guests, and describe communications between the front office and other hotel areas. (pp. 229–240)

2. Identify typical service requests that guests make at the front desk, and describe general approaches to handling guest complaints. (pp. 240–248)

6

Communications and Guest Services

COMMUNICATION IS VITAL to front office operations, because nearly everything that happens in a hotel affects the front office, and vice versa. All functions of the front office rely in part on clear communication. Front office staff must communicate effectively with one another, with personnel in other departments and divisions, and with guests. Effective communication is a prerequisite to an efficient front office. This chapter examines the importance of communication and several ongoing responsibilities of the front office.

Front Office Communications

Communication involves more than memorandums, face-to-face conversations, e-mail, and text messaging. Effective front office communication also involves the use of transaction files, information directories, internal and external networks, search engines, and mail and telephone procedures. The complexity of front office communication tends to be directly related to the number of guestrooms and the size and extent of the hotel's public areas and facilities. The larger the hotel and the more people involved, the more complex the communication network. Even in small hotels, establishing and maintaining communication links can be more complex than anticipated.

Guest Communications

Communication takes many forms in a hotel, but none is more important than how front office staff members communicate with guests. Guest communications must present a professional, positive image for the hotel, whether in person, over the telephone, online, or remotely. The proper greeting, attitude, and follow-up all set expectations and influence how guests perceive the hotel.

For example, when front office staff members answer the telephone, it is appropriate for them to provide an informative and warm greeting. Using an introduction such as: "Thank you for calling the Casa Vana Hotel. This is Emily speaking. How can I help you?" provides a warm welcome to the caller. By contrast, answering with "Casa Vana Hotel" may seem cold or abrupt and fail to create an impression of hospitality. The same principle applies to departmental calls within the hotel. A warm greeting, such as, "Thank you for calling the Casa Vana Hotel Reservations Office. This is Brad. How may I help you?" is much more professional than simply answering the call with a curt, "Reservations." An effective and informative, friendly greeting identifies who is speaking and offers assistance, all in a concise expression.

When front desk agents contact a guest, it is important for them to introduce themselves and give the reason for the contact. For example: "Good afternoon, Mr. Wilson. This is Greg at the front desk. I'm calling to follow up on the service request you made this morning to repair the room's air conditioning unit. Is it working to your satisfaction now?" With this approach, Mr. Wilson knows who is calling and why the call is being made. Also, it's less likely that he will consider the call an intrusion, since Greg made it clear that the call is in response to Mr. Wilson's prior request.

Face-to-face communication is just as important. Unlike telephone communication, where words and tone of voice alone determine how the message is received, face-to-face communication also includes body language and eye contact. Guests do not respond well when a front desk staff member doesn't make eye contact during a conversation. Guests checking in at the front desk may become irritated when the front desk agent looks only at a desktop screen and not at them, for example. Guests tend to respond well when employees convey a sense of interest, confidence, and honesty when they communicate. This is done through the use of proper language, a professional demeanor, and an attitude of hospitality.

Transaction File

Front desk agents may maintain an automated **transaction file** or non-automated **log book** so front office staff members have access to a record of important events and decisions that occurred during previous work shifts. A typical front office transaction file (sometimes referred to as a *concierge file*) is a chronological journal that lists unusual events, guest complaints or requests, and other relevant information. Front desk agents may make entries to the transaction file throughout a work shift. These notes should be clearly entered in a prescribed format or template, so they serve as effective reference material for staff members on the next front office shift.

Before beginning a shift, front desk supervisors and agents should review the transaction file, noting any current activities, situations that require follow-up, or potential problems. For example, a front desk agent on the morning shift may have noted that a guest phoned the front desk requesting engineering service for a plumbing problem. The agent should have entered the request as well as what action was taken to resolve the situation, if any. Notations become an important link in the communication network that informs employees on subsequent shifts of previous happenings. The front office transaction file should detail what happened, why, and when, as well as who recorded the entry (in case questions arise). After reviewing these notes, the front desk agent on duty can respond intelligently if the guest contacts the front desk for a status report.

When entries are made in the transaction file concerning guest requests, it is appropriate for the person who noted the request to personally follow through, if possible. For example, if a guest calls the front desk to request extra towels for the guestroom, the agent who took the call should check with the guest later in the

Exhibit 1   Rapid Response Software

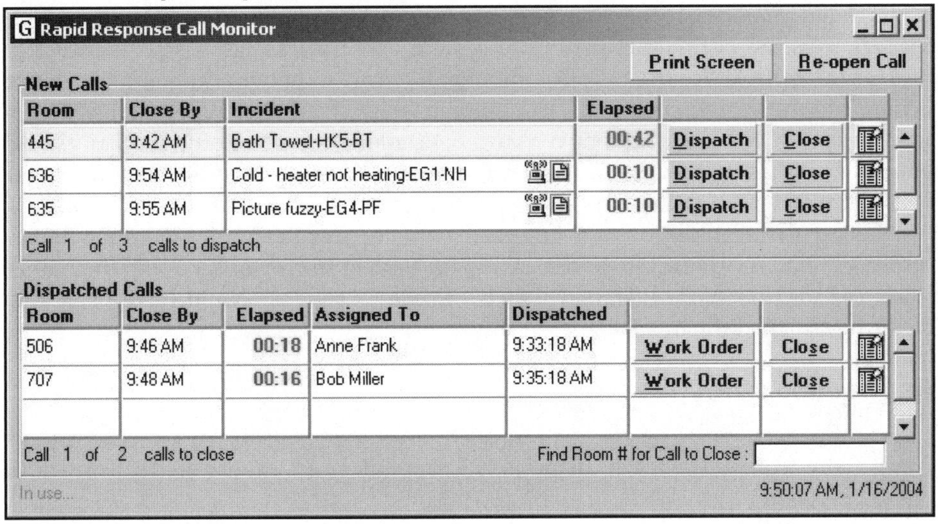

Source: GuestWare (Diversified Computer Corporation). For more information, see www.guestware.com/products/guestware-modules/rapid-response.

day to ensure that the towels were delivered by the housekeeping staff. If the agent who took the initial call was unable to place a follow-up call, an agent working the very next shift should do so. Sometimes it's not possible to respond to a guest's request until the following day. In that case, the guest should be told at the time the request is made (or some time shortly thereafter) when action will be taken. If no information is provided, the guest may feel uneasy and become irritated. Once a guest's request has been filled, an entry should be made in the transaction file showing that the follow-up call was made and how the guest responded to it. It is important to (1) record the final action taken concerning the guest request, or (2) communicate with other hotel departments if follow-up action on their part is required. This is the most efficient way to track and monitor the situation.

The front office transaction file is also important to hotel managers. It helps them understand the activity of the front desk staff and presents a documented record of historical issues. For example, if there are recurring problems with housekeeping or engineering functions, a way to analyze these challenges is through examining entries in the front office transaction file. Also, should there be guest complaints, compliments, or unusual activity, the transaction file explains what happened and how each situation was handled or resolved.

Hotel automation applications may include **rapid response software** for the recording, tracking, and completion of guest service requests (see Exhibit 1). Several software systems allow hotel employees to record guest service requests via workstations or mobile devices. Incoming requests are automatically distributed to the appropriate hotel department, which alerts staff to the need for corrective actions. For example, a guest may notice that a guestroom light bulb is burned out and needs to be replaced, and phones the front desk agent to report the problem.

The front desk agent enters the guest request into the guest services system. The department responsible for changing light bulbs, either housekeeping or engineering, receives the notification from the system and may assign a staff member to replace the bulb. Once the task is complete, the staff member enters the corrective action into the system. Front office managers as well as other hotel managers can use the system to track and report a variety of maintenance-related information to ensure that guest concerns are resolved quickly and completely, leading to higher levels of guest satisfaction.

Using the transaction file or guest services application is a much better approach than receiving a negative rating on a guest survey and having the hotel's guest satisfaction score decline because of something that could have been successfully handled during the guest's stay.

Information Directory

Front office staff must be able to respond in a knowledgeable way when guests contact the front desk for information. Common guest questions to front desk agents involve:

- Recommending local restaurants
- Contacting transportation companies, including taxi, limousine, and airport shuttle service companies
- Providing directions to a nearby business, office building, or landmark
- Providing directions to a shopping center, drugstore, or gas station
- Providing directions to a place of worship
- Providing directions to a bank or automated teller machine
- Providing directions to a theater, stadium, or ticket agency
- Providing directions to a university, library, museum, or other point of interest
- Providing directions to a federal building, capitol, district court, or city hall
- Providing information about hotel policies (for example, check-out time, or rules concerning pets)
- Providing information about the hotel's recreational facilities or those near the hotel

Often front desk agents need to access somewhat obscure information to answer guest questions. Some front offices accumulate such data in a bound guide or an electronic file called an **information directory.** The front office information directory may include simplified maps of the area; taxi and airline company telephone numbers; bank, theater, church, and store locations; information about local restaurants (including their menus); and special event schedules. Front desk agents should be familiar with the information directory's format and content as well as be able to use an online search engine and/or map software.

Some hotels have installed automated information terminals or kiosks in their lobbies and other public areas. Information kiosks are the electronic equivalent of the front office information directory and may involve online searches and map services. Self-service information kiosks are typically accessed by guests without front office staff assistance. Such ease of access allows front desk agents to attend to other guest needs.

Reader Board

Many hotels provide a schedule of daily events through information display screens or an in-room television system. A traditional industry term for the device used to display daily events is the **reader board.** Information on a reader board usually includes the names of groups staying at the hotel and their meeting room(s), agenda items, and meeting times. Digital reader boards may be placed near the front desk, in elevators, in the lobby, and in the meeting room section of the hotel; reader board information may be displayed on a guestroom television channel as well (this helps reduce the number of inquiries received by front desk agents). Digital monitors may be placed in convenient locations so that guests can review the list of daily events by scrolling or using a touchscreen index. Interfacing the electronic reader board system with the hotel's sales and catering system allows the information to be updated automatically by the sales and catering staffs as well as front desk staff.

Group Résumé Book/File

In convention hotels, it is common to have a **group résumé** book or electronic group history file available to front office staff. Each group staying in the hotel will generate a summary of its activities, billing instructions, key attendees, recreational arrangements, arrival and departure patterns, and other important information to be entered into the system. Some hotels prefer to store the group history by group name. Many hotels make the group file required reading for front desk and uniformed staff at the beginning of each work shift. Front desk staff members should become familiar with the history of all incoming groups to be sure they know what arrangements have been made in the past as well as the present. In addition, front desk staff should know where the group file is located so that any questions concerning the group can be answered quickly and correctly. Prior to a group checking in, it is common to have a pre-convention meeting, or "pre-con." The hotel catering or convention services manager responsible for the group usually leads the meeting. Group résumés are usually distributed and reviewed at these meetings. Group leaders attend these meetings along with key hotel department managers. Last-minute changes are discussed and any outstanding issues should be resolved prior to the group's arrival. The department managers are then expected to familiarize their staffs with the information contained in the file.

A frequent guest concern involves understanding group billing arrangements. Most property management systems have the ability to monitor and post group room and non-room charges and to allocate charges to predetermined accounts (if desired). For example, it is common for corporate meeting planners to require that the room and tax portion of every guest bill be forwarded to the group master account, while directing that incidental charges (for Internet access, dry cleaning service, alcoholic beverages, in-room refreshments, and entertainment) be paid by guests individually. Property management systems can be programmed to automatically split folio charges according to the specifications of the group's coordinator or leader. However, guests may not clearly understand these arrangements. By having a group file available, the front desk agent can quickly verify billing arrangements and direct the guest to the group leader for further billing clarification, if necessary.

The group file should be kept current and include background information on groups due to arrive within the next few days as well as groups that departed within the past week. By having information on groups arriving in the near future, the front office manager can verify the detailed arrangements for the group. For example, if a group expects an early arrival pattern, or is a group with a history in which many attendees request late departures following a meeting, these facts should be in the file so the front office manager can plan accordingly. Maintaining a file for departed groups helps the front office manager refer to group arrangements should departed guests have questions concerning billing or other matters.

Mail and Package Handling

Registered guests rely on the front office to relay delivered mail and packages quickly and efficiently. Front office managers normally develop policies for mail and package handling based on the policies and regulations supplied by the United States Postal Service.

In general, the front office is expected to time-stamp all guest mail when it arrives at the property. Doing so documents the date and time that the mail was received in case a question arises about when the mail arrived or how quickly the guest was notified of its arrival. When mail and packages arrive, front office records should be checked to verify that the guest is currently registered, is due to check in, or has checked out. Different mail handling procedures should be prescribed for each of these three circumstances.

Usually, mail for a registered guest is held at the front office in the appropriate slot in a mail and message rack or in an alphabetical rack according to the guest's last name. Due to security issues, mail and packages received are maintained out of public sight behind the front desk. This approach prevents other guests or hotel visitors from learning that a particular room is occupied because there is mail in the slot for that room. A front desk agent should promptly attempt to notify a guest when mail is received. Some properties notify guests by turning on an in-room message light on the guestroom telephone; others deliver a printed message to the guestroom or leave a voice mail message on the phone. If mail arrives for a guest who has not yet registered, a notation should be made on the guest's reservation record and the mail held until the guest arrives. Guest mail that is not picked up or has arrived for a guest who has already checked out should be time-stamped a second time and returned to its sender or sent to a forwarding address if the guest has provided the front office with one.

Guests may also receive registered letters, express mail packages, or other mail requiring a signature upon delivery. Some hotels permit front desk agents to sign for such mail. After doing so, the agent records the item's delivery in the front office mail signature book, and may have the guest sign for the mail at the

Exhibit 2   Sample Page from a Mail Signature Book

MAIL SIGNATURE BOOK

DATE	Room No.	Registry No.	NAME	WHERE FROM	SIGNATURE	Clerk	DATE	FORWARDED TO	ADDRESS	REMARKS

ORIGAMI INC

Courtesy of Origami, Inc.

time of pickup or delivery (a sample page from a mail signature book is shown in Exhibit 2). If the sender restricts who can receive the mail, the front office staff may be directed to follow other procedures. For example, if the sender stipulates guest signature *only*, a front desk agent cannot sign for the mail. Instead, the front desk agent may page the guest or provide a notice to the guest's room that a delivery attempt had been made.

Packages are usually treated in a similar fashion. If the package is too large to store at the front desk, it should be taken to a secure storage area. The package and its location should be recorded in the front office mail signature book.

Telecommunications Services

Historically, hotels provided in-room local and long-distance telephone service twenty-four hours a day. Regardless of whether front desk agents or hotel telephone operators answer incoming calls, all employees answering calls should be courteous and helpful. The telephone call may be the first point of contact with hotel staff, and the way that callers are treated will certainly affect the hotel's image. Front office management may restrict the type of information the front office staff may furnish to callers, due to guest privacy and security issues.

Telephone messages taken by front office staff should be time-stamped and relayed to the guestroom phone or maintained at the front desk for arriving guests. If guestroom telephones are equipped with a message indicator light, the front desk agent may switch on the in-room message light to alert the guest that a message is waiting for pickup. In some properties, messages can be entered directly into the front desk system for relay to a switchboard operator or front desk agent.

Building Telephone Skills

Regardless of whom you talk with over the telephone, it's essential that you make a positive impression. Answering the telephone is an opportunity for you to portray a professional image as well as a positive image for the property.

During any business telephone conversation, you should:

1. **Smile even though you are on the telephone.**
   When you smile, you automatically improve your vocal quality. You'll sound pleasant and interested.

2. **Sit or stand up straight.**
   By sitting or standing up straight, you'll be more alert and pay better attention to what is being said.

3. **Use a low voice pitch.**
   A lower voice pitch will make you sound more mature and authoritative.

4. **Match your speaking rate to the caller's.**
   Let the caller set the tempo of the conversation. For example, he or she may be in a hurry; in that case, you should provide information more quickly.

5. **Avoid extremes in volume.**
   If you speak too loudly, you may sound rude or pushy. If you speak too softly, you may sound timid or uncertain.

6. **Avoid expressions such as "uh-huh" and "yeah."**
   Such expressions make you sound dull, indifferent, and uninterested.

Front office staff often take phone messages for other employees or guests. Most front offices have a standard telephone message form. If you answer the phone, it's important that you listen carefully and take accurate written notes while speaking with the caller. When you take a telephone message, be sure to get the following information:

- Date
- Time of the call
- Name of the person being called
- Caller's full name
- Caller's department (if the call is internal)
- Caller's company (if appropriate)
- Caller's time zone (if out of state)
- Caller's telephone number (and area code, if needed)
- Message (do not abbreviate—provide a full message)

If the message is urgent, mark it as such. It is also a good practice to repeat the telephone number to the caller for accuracy. Some front offices recommend that the message also be repeated. Finally, sign your name and follow front office procedures for storing or delivering the message.

Any telephone conversation can be improved by following these simple guidelines. Remember to treat all callers, guests, and employees with courtesy and respect.

The telephone system may be programmed to automatically turn on the guest-room message light when it receives a voice mail message. When the guest returns to the room, the flashing light on the phone informs the guest that a message is waiting to be accessed. The guest can then access an automated message system or telephone the switchboard operator or front office message center. In some hotels, the guest may be able to display the received message on the guestroom television screen or other in-room device.

Many hotels have added guest voice mail systems. **Voice mailboxes** are devices that can record spoken messages for guests. A caller wishing to leave a voice mail message simply speaks into the phone when prompted and the message is recorded by the voice mailbox system. To retrieve the message, the guest typically presses a special telephone key or enters an access code that connects with the voice mailbox, then listens to the recorded message. A major advantage of voice mail is that the message is captured in the caller's voice. This is especially helpful with foreign callers who may not speak the local language clearly. Voice mail also offers improved confidentiality of messages and eliminates the need for front desk agents or hotel telephone operators to try to interpret unclear messages left with them by callers.

Another popular feature of voice mail systems is group broadcast. This feature allows guestrooms associated with a specific group to automatically receive the same special message simultaneously. For example, a group leader may send a voice mail to everyone in the group, informing all members that the time for a function has been rescheduled. All group attendees are automatically linked and notified.

Facsimiles. Facsimiles or faxes are usually treated like mail but with special care, as guests are often waiting for these documents. If the incoming fax has special delivery instructions, such as *deliver immediately to a specific meeting room*, the front desk agent should dispatch a bell attendant with the fax to the room right away. If no special instructions are provided, the hotel may store the fax in the mail rack and turn on the message light in the guestroom. Faxes are different from mail in that they are automatically time-stamped and do not come in an envelope. (The hotel may opt to deliver the fax in an envelope to the guest.) The fax document will contain the date and time of transmission. Faxes should always be treated as confidential; front desk staff members should never read a fax. It is their job simply to deliver the document.

Front desk agents should record when the guest was notified of a received fax and when the guest picked up the fax. A similar record is kept of outgoing faxes if the property offers public fax service. If a fax is undeliverable, the hotel should immediately notify the party sending the fax. Most hotels charge guests to send faxes, since there are telecommunication costs involved. Some hotels charge guests for received faxes as well. Whether or not there is a charge, front desk agents should process and deliver faxes quickly.

Wake-Up Services. Since a guest may miss an important appointment, a flight, or simply a head start on a vacation by oversleeping, front desk agents must pay special attention to wake-up call requests. Front office mechanical devices or a front office automated system can remind front desk agents to place wake-up calls, or the systems can be programmed to automatically place the calls and play a recorded wake-up message. Despite advances in technology, some hotels may prefer that front desk agents or telephone operators make wake-up calls to provide a more personal touch.

Typically, the clock in the telephone department used for wake-up purposes is called the **hotel clock.** It carries the official time of the hotel. Therefore, the clock should be checked regularly to ensure it is correct. Other clocks in the front office, such as front desk time stamps, should be synchronized with the hotel clock to be sure time accuracy is maintained.

Instead of calling the hotel operator or front desk agent to place a wake-up call request, guests often can simply dial a special telephone extension from the guestroom phone and follow the instructions provided by the system to request a wake-up time. This self-service feature gives the guest direct control of the process. Hotels can also combine a wake-up call with room service, thereby allowing the guest to confirm a breakfast meal request when receiving a wake-up call.

E-Mail and Data Services. Most hotel guests have business and personal e-mail accounts or company data files that they may need to access while traveling. A guest who has a laptop, notebook, or mobile device can use the guestroom's high-speed Internet access to connect to the web. Once connected, the guest can access web-based e-mail or download e-mail or other files via specialty software. Alternatively, guests may use a guestroom telephone line as a data port, but such access typically operates at a much lower transfer speed. Connecting to the Internet enables communication with corporate networks, virtual private networks, home office networks, public access networks, cellular networks, and other networks. If the hotel provides wireless high-speed Internet access, travelers may also be able to access the web from public areas (indoor and outdoor venues) as well as from meeting rooms and exhibit floors. Hotels may provide such services on a complimentary basis or charge a fee.

TDDs. A special hotel guest service involves telecommunications devices for the deaf (TDDs) for hearing- and/or speech-impaired travelers. A TDD is a specially designed piece of equipment for placing and conducting telephone calls. The Americans with Disabilities Act requires that hotels make available, upon request, a TDD for use by a guest who has an impairment. Similarly, the front desk should have a TDD device to handle in-house calls from hearing- or speech-impaired guests.

Call Broadcast. Many hotels have a call broadcast feature on their telephone equipment that allows the system to place calls to all occupied guestrooms. Some equipment can be selective, calling only certain subgroups of guests. For example, a group leader may want to leave a message for all in-house group members, reminding them that the awards reception has been changed from 6 P.M. to 6:30 P.M. More importantly, in case of an emergency, the call broadcast feature can operate like a reverse 911 system. The system enables emergency announcement calls to be placed simultaneously to all rooms identified as occupied. The emergency message can be sent and note if the telephone was answered by someone in the room. This feature is very important, especially if the hotel has to be evacuated, or if guests need to be instructed about safety procedures.

Interdepartmental Communications

Many services in a hotel require coordination between the front office staff and staff in other departments or divisions. The front office staff generally exchanges most of its information with personnel in the housekeeping, engineering, and maintenance departments.

Housekeeping

The housekeeping department staff and the front office staff must keep each other informed of changes in guestroom status to ensure that guests are roomed efficiently and without complication. The more familiar the front office staff is with housekeeping procedures, and vice versa, the smoother the relationship will be between the two departments. Housekeeping personnel must know the status of every room, along with any guest requests. In most cases, property management systems support workstations and mobile devices used by housekeeping staff to update arrival and departure information. It remains common for front desk agents to phone housekeeping staff members with requests, whether for extra towels for a guestroom or to tidy up the lobby.

The front office manager and housekeeping manager should meet frequently to review upcoming hotel activities. For example, if the hotel is expecting a large check-out and check-in on the same day, the front office manager and housekeeping manager should discuss what priorities should be set for arriving guests and stayovers. Special requests, like rooms for VIP guests, are very important, since the hotel does not want to inconvenience VIPs or make a bad impression on them.

Engineering and Maintenance

In many hotels, engineering and maintenance personnel begin each shift by examining the front office log book or specialty software for repair work orders. Front desk agents use the log book or application software to track maintenance problems reported by guests or staff, such as faulty heating or cooling, poor plumbing service, noisy equipment, or broken furniture. The front office log serves as an excellent reference for the hotel's engineering and maintenance staff.

Many hotels use a multiple-part work order form, or real-time data entry, to report maintenance problems. When the work is completed, the engineering and maintenance staff informs the department that filed the work request order. If a maintenance problem renders a room unsalable, housekeeping staff must be informed immediately when the problem is resolved so the room can be readied and placed back in the available rooms inventory. Immediate notification of changes in room status helps minimize lost room revenue. To enhance hotel operations, a hotel may employ engineering and maintenance staff around the clock.

Revenue Centers

Although hotels enjoy their greatest revenues through guestroom sales, additional services and activities may support or boost overall profitability. In addition to the rooms division, hotel revenue centers may include:

- Dining rooms, snack bars, and specialty restaurants
- Bars, lounges, and nightclubs
- Room service operations
- Business centers
- Dry cleaning/valet service
- Vending machines
- Gift shops, barbershops, and newsstands
- Banquet, meeting, and catering facilities
- Local and long-distance telephone service
- Health clubs, golf courses, and exercise rooms
- Car rentals, limousine services, and tours
- Casinos and gaming activities
- Pay-per-view television movies
- In-room entertainment (video games, web TV)
- Valet parking and parking garages

Guests frequently learn about these services and facilities through the hotel's website, printed directory, or advertising on the guestroom television. Front desk agents and uniformed staff members must also be familiar with these facilities and services so they can answer guest questions in a positive and knowledgeable manner. The transactions charged to room accounts by guests at hotel revenue centers must be communicated to the front desk in a timely manner to ensure prompt payment and avoid late charges.

Marketing and Public Relations

The front office staff should be among the first to know about events the hotel schedules for publicity. In many ways, the effectiveness of a hotel's marketing and public relations efforts depends on the participation and enthusiasm of front office staff. Guest receptions, special hotel promotions, health and fitness programs, family events, and even complimentary coffee in a hotel's lobby may provide settings for guests to socialize and can help promote repeat business for the hotel. Front office staff may contribute to hotel newsletters, guest history files, and customized registration and check-out processes that can greatly help personalize services for returning guests.

Guest Services

As the center of front office activity, the front desk is responsible for coordinating guest services. Typical guest services involve providing information and special equipment and supplies. Guest services may also include accommodating guests through special procedures. A guest's satisfaction with the hotel hinges in part on the front desk's ability to respond to special requests. A request that falls outside the front office's responsibility should be directly referred to the appropriate person or department.

A growing number of hotels employ a concierge or other designated staff member to handle guest requests. A concierge should embody the spirit of hospitality of the entire property. As more hotel functions have become automated, the concierge plays an important role in reinforcing the hotel's personal touch in guest services.

Several hotel companies have introduced centralized guest service centers. Guests have only to dial one telephone number (or press one button on their guest-room telephone) to place a request. Guest service requests may include requests for valet parking, room service, luggage assistance, dry cleaning service, conference information, local directions, and other requests. The staff of these service centers should be specially trained to handle all of the various guest requests that come in.

Equipment and Supplies

Guests may request special equipment and supplies while making a reservation, at the time of registration, or during occupancy. Reservations agents should have a reliable method for recording special requests to ensure that the requests are properly met. After registration, a guest who needs special equipment or supplies will almost always contact the front desk. The front desk agent, in turn, follows through by contacting the appropriate service center or hotel department. Equipment and supplies commonly requested by guests include:

- Rollaway beds and cribs

- Additional linens/pillows

- Irons and ironing boards

- Additional clothes hangers

- Audiovisual and office equipment

- High-speed Internet connectors (for example, cables or wireless adapters)

- Special equipment for visually impaired, hearing impaired, or physically challenged guests

Front desk agents should have alternative ways to meet guest requests when the department that normally provides the equipment or service is closed or inaccessible. The housekeeping department, for example, attends to many guest requests, but may not be staffed around the clock. In some hotels, front office staff may have access to housekeeping supplies during late-night hours. Alternately, the housekeeping department may stock a centrally located linen closet and issue a key to appropriate front office staff. Such arrangements enable the front office staff to satisfy guest requests for additional linens and pillows in a timely manner, even when the housekeeping department is closed.

Special Procedures

Guests may ask for special considerations when making a reservation or at any point during the hotel stay. Reservations agents should have a reliable method of recording special requests made during the reservations process and communicating such requests to appropriate front office staff. Front desk agents should also have a way to record any requests they receive or process. Completing some special guest requests might call for exceptions to standard front office procedures. For this reason, front desk agents should exercise caution and sound judgment when attempting to satisfy guest requests.

Procedural requests may require more time and effort to fill than equipment and supply requests. Typical procedural requests include:

- Split account folio balances

- Audit master account folios

- Provide wake-up calls

- Schedule transportation arrangements

- Place entertainment reservations

- Complete newspaper delivery

- Provide secretarial services, including language translation and photocopying services

- Secure bonded child-care services

A knowledgeable front desk agent usually can fill a special request involving authorized guest folio adjustments. **Split folios** are most often requested by business travelers. Essentially, these folios separate guest charges onto two or more separate folio accounts. One folio account may be set up to record room and tax charges; this part of the folio may be billed to the guest's company or to a group master account. A second folio account may be set up to track incidental charges such as Internet access and food and beverage purchases; this part of the folio will most likely be paid directly by the guest.

A convention group meeting in the hotel may request a **master folio.** Typically, only authorized charges incurred by the group are posted to the master folio and subsequently billed to the convention's sponsor. Each group member may be held responsible for other charges posted to his or her individual folio account. The purpose of a master folio is to collect authorized charges that are not appropriately posted elsewhere. The master account is one of the most important items on a group résumé and is usually discussed in detail during the hotel staff's pre- and post-convention analysis for the group.

A concierge may be assigned to handle other procedural requests. Hotels not employing a concierge may have front desk agents update and use the front office information directory as a resource for referrals and outside services requested by guests.

Some hotels operate a guest service center. Hotels can be confusing places for guests, and when guests have a question or special request, they may not know whom to call to resolve the issue. A designated guest service center makes it easier for guests to place requests and for the hotel to respond to them in a timely fashion. Some hotels instruct guests to call a single extension number, usually printed in bold numbers on the guestroom telephone. These calls are routed to the guest service center, where specially trained staff handle the incoming requests. Working a guest service center requires staff members to have knowledge about a wide variety of hotel products, services, and procedures. For example, when a guest calls to request a bell attendant to pick up luggage from the guestroom, the guest service agent must know to ask about the quantity of luggage to be retrieved, because this will help determine the kind of cart the bell attendant brings to the guestroom.

Guest Relations

Despite front office staff efficiency and attentiveness, guests will occasionally be disappointed or find fault with something or someone in the front office. The front office manager should anticipate guest complaints and devise strategies that help staff members effectively resolve problems.

The high visibility of the front office staff means that front desk agents are frequently the first to learn of guest complaints. Front desk agents should be especially attentive to guests with complaints and seek a timely and satisfactory resolution to the problem. Nothing annoys guests more than having their complaints ignored, discounted, or overlooked. While most front office staff members do not enjoy receiving complaints, they should understand that few guests enjoy complaining. Employees must realize that guests who do not have the opportunity to complain to front office staff often tell their friends, relatives, and business associates instead.

When guests find it easy to express their opinions, both the front desk staff and the guests benefit. The front office staff learns of potential or actual problems and has the opportunity to resolve them. For a guest, this can mean a more satisfying stay. When problems are quickly resolved, a guest often feels that the hotel cares about his or her needs. From the guest perspective, every complaint should be perceived by the front office staff as an opportunity to strengthen guest relations. On the other hand, guests who leave a hotel dissatisfied may never return. A popular axiom in the lodging business is that it takes $10 to attract a guest for the first time, but only $1 to keep the guest coming back. By handling guest relations positively, the investment is likely to be repaid many times.

Complaints

Guest complaints can be separated into four categories of problems: mechanical, attitudinal, service-related, and unusual.

Most guest complaints relate to hotel equipment malfunctions. *Mechanical complaints* usually concern problems with guestroom climate controls, lighting, electricity, furnishings, ice machines, vending machines, door keys, plumbing, television sets, elevators, and so on. Even an excellent preventive maintenance program cannot completely eliminate all potential equipment problems. Effective use of a front office file and maintenance work order system can help reduce the frequency of mechanical complaints. Sometimes a complaint may shift to a focus on the speed of the response. It is essential, therefore, that the appropriate staff member be dispatched as quickly as possible with the proper tools to correct the problem. Good tracking methods help ensure timely service and reliable recording of the situations.

Guests may make *attitudinal complaints* when they feel they have been poorly treated by hotel staff members. Guests who overhear staff conversations or who receive complaints from hotel staff members may also express attitudinal complaints. Guests should not be exposed to employees arguing, or become sounding boards for employee problems. Hotel managers and shift supervisors, not guests, should listen and attend to the complaints and problems of staff members. This can be especially critical to maintaining effective guest relations.

Guests may make *service-related complaints* when they experience a problem with hotel service. Service-related complaints can be wide-ranging and about such things as long lines, lack of assistance, untidy guestrooms, missed wake-up calls, ill-prepared food, or ignored requests for additional guestroom supplies. Front office staff members generally receive more service-related complaints when the hotel is operating at or near full occupancy.

Guests may also complain about the absence of a swimming pool, lack of public transportation, bad weather, and so on. Hotels generally have little or no control over the circumstances surrounding *unusual complaints*. Nonetheless, guests expect the front office staff to be sympathetic and patiently listen to such complaints. Front office managers should alert front desk agents that there will be times when guests will complain about things that the staff can do nothing about. Through such orientation, staff members will be better prepared to handle unusual complaints with appropriate guest-relations techniques and avoid challenging situations.

Identifying Complaints. All guest complaints deserve attention. An excited guest complaining loudly to front desk staff requires immediate attention. A guest making a more discreet comment deserves no less attention, although the need for action may be less immediate.

Guest relations stand to improve when the front office systematically identifies and resolves its most frequent guest complaints. By reviewing a properly kept front office transaction file, management can often identify and address recurring complaints and problems.

Another way to identify complaints involves the evaluation of guest comment cards, online surveys, or questionnaires. Exhibits 3, 4, and 5 demonstrate the level of detail and sophistication that can be expected of a thorough analysis of guest responses to well-designed comment media. Exhibit 3, "Guest Perception Detail," groups comment questions by specific hotel departments (in this exhibit, the bellman/valet department and the front desk department are shown). Within each department, the specific questions asked of guests are listed, with the individual responses tabulated. Current month, last month, and year-to-date favorability rating percentages are shown for purposes of comparison. Exhibit 4, "Guest Perception Graph," shows the overall favorability ratings of all hotel departments,

Exhibit 3   Guest Perception Detail

Quantitative Details:

1. Name of report and date of survey.
2. The specific department or area the report is detailing.
3. All questions are grouped by the specific departments/categories.
4. Response Option—Guests are given the choice of options from which to mark their opinion.
5. Response Percentages—This number represents the percentage of guest responses per response option.
6. Guest Response—The number of guests who responded to the specific question.
7. Comparison of the overall rating by question for the current month, last month and year-to-date.
8. Response Option Averages—The average of all respondents per response option.
9. Overall Favorability Average—Overall average for all questions compared to current month, last month and year-to-date for the entire department/category.

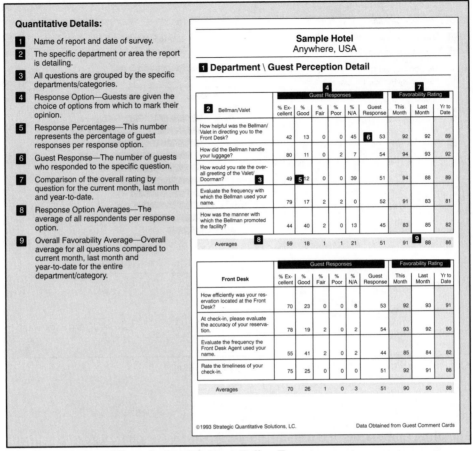

Sample Hotel
Anywhere, USA

1 Department \ Guest Perception Detail

2 Bellman/Valet	% Excellent	% Good	% Fair	% Poor	% N/A	Guest Response	This Month	Last Month	Yr to Date
How helpful was the Bellman/Valet in directing you to the Front Desk?	42	13	0	0	45	6 53	92	92	89
How did the Bellman handle your luggage?	80	11	0	2	7	54	94	93	92
How would you rate the overall greeting of the Valet/Doorman? 3	49	5 12	0	0	39	51	94	88	89
Evaluate the frequency with which the Bellman used your name.	79	17	2	2	0	52	91	83	81
How was the manner with which the Bellman promoted the facility?	44	40	2	0	13	45	83	85	82
Averages 8	59	18	1	1	21	51	91	9 88	86

Front Desk	% Excellent	% Good	% Fair	% Poor	% N/A	Guest Response	This Month	Last Month	Yr to Date
How efficiently was your reservation located at the Front Desk?	70	23	0	0	8	53	92	93	91
At check-in, please evaluate the accuracy of your reservation.	78	19	2	0	2	54	93	92	90
Evaluate the frequency the Front Desk Agent used your name.	55	41	2	0	2	44	85	84	82
Rate the timeliness of your check-in.	75	25	0	0	0	51	92	91	88
Averages	70	26	1	0	3	51	90	90	88

©1993 Strategic Quantitative Solutions, LC.   Data Obtained from Guest Comment Cards

Courtesy of Strategic Quantitative Solutions, Dallas, Texas.

in descending order for ease of comparison. The overall hotel average ("Overall Perceptions") is also shown on the graph. Departments falling below the overall average generally signal areas that need to be improved. Exhibit 5, "Favorability Trending Graphs," depicts the overall rating trend for all questions asked about specific departments. This exhibit shows the trend graphs for the bellman/valet, front desk, and housekeeping departments. Trend graphs not only help identify areas that need improvement, but help measure the success of current and future improvement efforts.

Identifying problems is one of the first steps in taking corrective action. By examining the number and type of complaints received, front office management may gain insight into common and less-common problems. Front office staff members may be better equipped to handle frequent complaints courteously and effectively, especially if they are aware the problem cannot be immediately corrected.

Exhibit 4   Guest Perception Graph

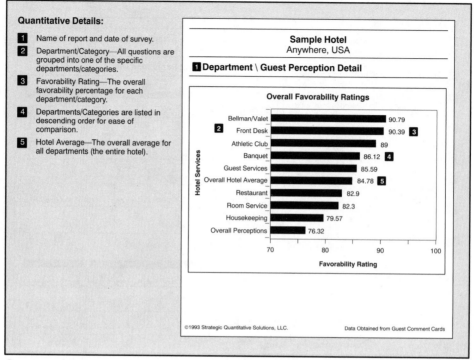

Courtesy of Strategic Quantitative Solutions, Dallas, Texas.

Handling Complaints. It is usually counterproductive to ignore a guest complaint. In many hotels, front desk agents are instructed to promptly refer complaints to supervisors or managers. Front office staff may receive complaints about the hotel's food and beverage operations, regardless of whether those operations are managed by the hotel. Unless the front office manager and the food and beverage manager establish procedures for cooperating and resolving complaints, guests may continue to be upset and the front office staff will continue to hear about the problem. The hotel manager and revenue center managers should maintain close communications and develop procedures designed to satisfactorily address guest complaints.

Front office management and staff should keep the following resolution guidelines in mind when handling guest complaints:

- Front office staff members should not go alone to a guestroom to investigate a problem or otherwise risk potential danger. When expressing a complaint, the guest may be quite angry and a one-on-one situation may be ill-advised.

- Front office staff members should not make promises that exceed their authority or ability to deliver.

Exhibit 5   Favorability Trending Graphs

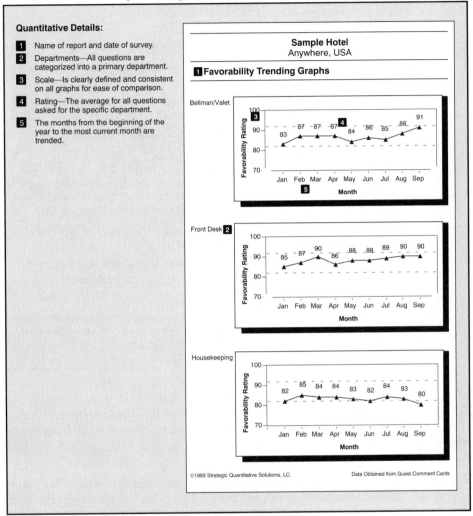

Courtesy of Strategic Quantitative Solutions, Dallas, Texas.

- If a problem is not likely to be resolved in a timely manner, front office staff should admit this to the guest. Honesty is always the best policy when dealing with guest complaints.

- Front desk agents should be advised that some guests are just prone to complain. The front office staff should develop an approach for dealing with chronic complainers.

Exhibit 6 lists guidelines for handling guest complaints in a professional manner. Learning to deal effectively with guest complaints requires experience. Front

Exhibit 6   Guidelines for Handling Complaints

1. Listen with concern and empathy.

2. Isolate the guest if possible, so that other guests won't overhear.

3. Stay calm. Avoid responding with hostility or defensiveness. Don't argue with the guest.

4. Be aware of the guest's self-esteem. Show a personal interest in the problem. Use the guest's name frequently. Take the complaint seriously.

5. Give the guest your undivided attention. Concentrate on the problem, not on placing blame. Do NOT insult the guest.

6. Take notes. Writing down the key facts saves time if someone else must get involved. Also, guests will tend to slow down when they are speaking faster than you can write. More important, the fact that a front office staff member is concerned enough to write down what they're saying is reassuring to guests.

7. Tell the guest what can be done. Offer choices. Don't promise the impossible, and don't exceed your authority.

8. Set an approximate time for completion of corrective actions. Be specific, but do not underestimate the amount of time it will take to resolve the problem.

9. Monitor the progress of the corrective action.

10. Follow up. Even if the complaint was resolved by someone else, contact the guest to ensure that the problem was resolved satisfactorily. Report the entire event, the actions taken, and the conclusion of the incident.

office staff should anticipate how to resolve some of the most typical complaints. Role-playing among front office staff can be an effective method for learning to deal with guest complaints. By anticipating complaints, planning and practicing responses, and receiving constructive feedback, front office staff will be better prepared to deal with actual guest complaints.

Follow-Up Procedures. Front office management may use the front office transaction file to initiate corrective action, verify that guest complaints have been resolved, and identify recurring problems. This comprehensive record helps management contact guests who expressed dissatisfaction with some aspect of their stay. If the guest has departed the hotel, a letter or e-mail from the front office manager expressing regret about the guest's unsatisfactory experience is usually sufficient to promote goodwill and demonstrate concern for the guest. It may be wise for the front office manager to telephone a departed guest to get a more complete description of the problem or incident that caused the dissatisfaction. Chain hotels may also receive guest complaints channeled through chain headquarters. Cumulative records of guest complaints about hotels in the chain may be compiled and reported to each manager. This method of feedback allows the chain's corporate headquarters to evaluate and measure each hotel's guest relations performance. Hotels with a consistent high volume of guest complaints may receive visits from chain managers to bring attention to the serious nature of these issues.

Summary

Effective communication is essential to an efficient front office. Front office employees must communicate effectively with one another, with personnel in other departments and divisions, and with guests. Professional communication with guests starts when the reservation is made and carries through the entire guest stay. Whether communicating by telephone or in person, all employees in guest contact positions should be properly trained in what to say and how to say it.

The complexity of front office communication tends to be directly related to the number of guestrooms and the size and extent of the hotel's public areas and facilities. The larger the hotel, the larger and more complex the communication network is likely to be. The front desk may maintain a front office transaction file or log book (typically, a journal that chronicles unusual events, guest complaints or requests, and other relevant information) so that front office staff can be aware of important events and decisions that occurred during previous work shifts. Rapid response software is an electronic version of a log book. A group résumé book is also helpful in handling group arrangements at the front desk.

In addition, front desk agents may need to access non-hotel information (for example, maps; bank, theater, church, and store locations; and special event schedules) to answer guest inquiries. Some front offices accumulate such data in a bound guide or an electronic file called a *front office information directory*. Daily hotel activity is communicated to guests and visitors through reader boards placed conveniently in various locations. The hotel maintains a hotel clock to synchronize the various departments and services it offers.

Registered guests rely on the front office to quickly deliver mail and messages. Front office staff should time-stamp all guest mail when it arrives. Doing so provides evidence of when the mail was received and helps ensure timely delivery. Guest mail that is not picked up or has arrived for a guest who has already checked out should be time-stamped a second time and returned to its sender.

Due to privacy and security issues, front office managers may restrict the information that front office staff members answering telephones may furnish to callers. Voice mail allows callers to record messages for guests.

Many services in a hotel require coordination between the front office and other hotel departments or divisions. The front office generally exchanges the most information with personnel in the housekeeping department and the engineering and maintenance department. For example, housekeeping and the front office must keep each other informed of changes in room status to ensure that guests are roomed efficiently and without complications. In many hotels, the engineering and maintenance staff begins each shift by examining the front office log book for repair work orders.

Front desk agents can influence the performance of the hotel's revenue centers through the use of marketing and public relations skills. Front desk agents should be familiar with all revenue centers so they can answer guest questions about them. The transactions charged by guests at hotel restaurants, gift shops, and other remote points of sale must be communicated to the front desk to ensure eventual payment.

As the center of front office activity, the front desk is responsible for coordinating guest services. Typical guest services involve providing information and special equipment and supplies. Guest services may also include accommodating guests through special procedures. A request that falls beyond the responsibility of the front office should be referred to the appropriate person or department.

Despite staff efficiency and attentiveness, guests will occasionally be disappointed or find fault with something or someone at the hotel. The front office should anticipate guest complaints and devise strategies that help staff effectively resolve the problem. Guest complaints can be divided into four categories of problems: mechanical, attitudinal, service-related, and unusual.

Key Terms

group résumé—A summary of all of a group's activities, billing instructions, key attendees, recreational arrangements, arrival and departure patterns, and other important information; usually stored in a binder at the front desk or in an electronic file.

hotel clock—The clock by the hotel switchboard that keeps the official hotel time.

information directory—A collection of information kept at the front desk for front desk agents to use in responding to guest requests and questions, including simplified maps of the area; taxi and airline company telephone numbers; bank, theater, church, and store locations; and special event schedules.

log book—A journal in which important front office events and decisions are recorded for reference during subsequent shifts. In many hotels, the log book has been replaced by a transaction file maintained by the property management system.

master folio—A folio used to chart transactions on an account assigned to more than one person or guestroom, usually reserved for group accounts; a master folio collects charges not appropriately posted elsewhere.

rapid response software—An electronic form of a maintenance log book system.

reader board—A posting or closed-circuit broadcast of daily events at a hotel.

split folio—A folio in which a guest's charges are separated into two or more folios.

transaction file—A chronological recording of important front office events and decisions for reference during subsequent front office work shifts.

voice mailbox—A device capable of storing, recording, and playing back messages for guests through the telephone system.

Review Questions

1. What front desk procedures help ensure the proper delivery of mail, packages, messages, and faxes to guests?

2. How are communications between the front office and the maintenance division handled? What are the functions of the front office log book and maintenance work orders?

3. What are three main types of requests guests make at the front desk?

4. What is the purpose of the group résumé book? What kind of information is contained on group résumés, and how does the front desk use such information?

5. What is the purpose of a front desk information directory? What sort of information might such a directory contain?

6. Why should the front office staff welcome guest complaints? How may a property benefit from analyzing the complaints it receives?

7. What are the four major types of guest complaints? Which is most common? What are some general approaches to handling guest complaints?

Internet Sites

For more information, visit the following Internet sites. Remember that Internet addresses can change without notice. If the site is no longer there, you can use a search engine to look for additional sites.

Lodging Publications—Online and Printed

Hospitality Net
www.hospitalitynet.org

Technology Sites

CSS Hotel Systems
www.csshotelsystems.com

First Resort Software
www.firstres.com

Hospitality Financial and Technology
  Professionals
www.hftp.org/Pages/Events/HITEC.
aspx

The Host Group
www.thehostgroup.com

Hotellinx Systems Ltd.
www.hotellinx.com

MICROS Systems, Inc.
www.micros.com

Newmarket International
www.newmarketinc.com

Guest and Employee Satisfaction

Market Metrix
www.marketmetrix.com

UniFocus
www.unifocus.com

Case Studies

Service Recovery at the Simpson Hotel

"Carrie, what are you doing? It's almost time to go."

"I'm looking for my new book, Mommy. Have you seen it?"

Abraham Nichols's voice echoed up the stairway. "Almost set up there?"

"We'll be a few more minutes, Abe," answered his wife, Angela.

"All right, but remember, we'll be getting in late as it is. I'll put the baby in the car."

Two weeks ago, Abe had been asked to attend a two-day conference in a town five hours from his home. He and Angela had decided to make it a weekend getaway for the family. When making reservations at the Simpson Hotel for the family, Abe informed the reservations agent of all their special requirements: their 11:00 P.M. Thursday-night arrival; a clean, no-smoking double-double with a crib in place for six-month-old Jason and food service available for their eight-year-old daughter; a pool and fitness center; and the group rate for Thursday and Friday nights.

Thursday night before they left, the Nicholses took a quick supper. Carrie didn't eat much, as her parents had expected; she always got excited about vacations. Then they were on their way.

When the Nicholses arrived, everyone was more than ready for bed—everyone except Carrie, who had found the snacks that her parents had packed inadequate. "I'm still hungry, Daddy. Do they have vending machines at this hotel?"

"Well, don't worry, honey. I talked to the people at the hotel ahead of time, and they said we could get food delivered to our room even at eleven at night. You're going to love it here; there's a big pool where you can swim all you want. And here we are," said Abe as they pulled in under the marquee.

Angela pulled the baby out of the car seat while Abe wrestled with the two large suitcases and the baby's bag and Carrie unloaded her day pack. "You'd think a place like this would have a bellperson," Abe grumbled to Angela.

"I know—and valet parking," she answered. "Go ahead and park, we'll bring the luggage inside." Angela grabbed Jason's bag with the hand with which she was holding him, took one suitcase in the other hand, and pushed the last suitcase with her foot.

Carrie yawned. "Can you get the other suitcase for me, honey?" her mother asked.

Once they were inside, the front office agent looked up from what he was doing and said, "Oh, I'm sorry, let me help you with those. There's usually a bellperson to help with luggage, but he was sick and there was no replacement for this shift. Welcome to the Simpson Hotel. Once we get your things over by the front desk, I'll get you checked in right away."

Abe returned a few minutes later and the family checked in. They noticed a vending machine on their way upstairs, but it had nothing that interested Carrie. When they got to their room, they found it clean and smelling fresh. It had two double beds, but no crib. Abe called the front desk right away. "The agent I talked to on the phone when I made the reservation said you'd have a crib for us," he told the front desk agent.

"Oh, I'm very sorry, sir. I'll chase one down for you right away," the agent responded.

"And could you bring us your room service menu?" Abe asked.

"You'll find that in the guest information directory in your room, sir. It's in the blue binder on the desk," the agent answered.

"Oh, okay, thank you," Abe replied.

Carrie went through the menu with her mother, but Carrie wasn't interested in anything on it. "It looks like all they have available right now are two kinds of salad and some cold deli sandwiches," she told her parents. Angela tried to console Carrie. Between the excitement and the hunger, it looked as if Carrie was going to have trouble getting to sleep. Eventually Angela ordered her a small bag of chips, but the room service order-taker told her that they were making an exception for her; usually chips were only available with the sandwiches.

The chips arrived at the same time as the crib. The crib was delivered by a breathless gentleman who had a five-minute explanation of why it had taken him so long. Abe politely thanked him and turned to put Jason down.

"The first session of the conference isn't until ten tomorrow morning, so let's try to sleep in," Abe told Angela.

"We can try, but we'll see what Jason does. He doesn't know we're on vacation," she answered.

The next morning the family was awakened at 8:30 A.M. by noise. Abe and Angela were both surprised that it was not Jason's crying, but a knock on the door. "Housekeeping," said a voice on the other side. Abe opened the door and blinked at the housekeeper. Jason started crying.

"Very sorry, sir, I didn't mean to wake you," said the housekeeper. "Didn't you see the—never mind, I'll come back later. Very sorry." *It's not my fault they don't use the Do Not Disturb signs,* thought the housekeeper to herself.

The Nicholses had breakfast, then Abe was off to the conference. Carrie was eager to get into the pool, but first Angela had to ask front desk agents where it was. "I'm very sorry, ma'am," the agent said, "Didn't anyone tell you? The pool is closed for repairs." Carrie groaned.

Angela tried to salvage the situation. "Will it be reopened soon? by Sunday?"

"I'm afraid not, ma'am," answered the agent.

"All right, then, there's a museum I read about in a magazine that's supposed to be close by—the Pinkerton Museum of Natural History?"

The front desk agent recognized the name but had no brochures handy. She drew Angela a map on the back of an envelope and gave her directions for how to walk to the museum. The agent couldn't remember all the street names, nor did she know the museum's hours or admission charges. In spite of this, Angela and the children headed out and had a good time that day at the museum. Carrie was so excited that she told the front desk agent all about it when they got back. Angela thanked the agent for her directions.

Abe finished up with the conference meetings late Friday afternoon. He realized that he could have put up a Do Not Disturb sign the night before, but he looked around the room and found none.

After Abe had unwound a bit, Angela left the children with him so she could go work out at the fitness center. She used the treadmill for a while, but when she went to use the rowing machine, she noticed that one of its handles was much looser than the other. She reported it to the front desk on her way back to the room. She also asked the front desk agent about family restaurants in the area. The agent pulled out a phone book and started scanning the yellow pages. "All I see for family restaurants is places across town," the agent told her, "but there's an upscale place just down the road...." Angela thanked him, and the family had their favorite pizza delivered for supper.

That night the Nicholses realized that their room was right over the lounge. They could hear the live music until about midnight, but that wasn't too bad, because the singer was singing songs they knew and liked. Saturday night was different; the driving beat seemed to make the whole room vibrate. Somehow the kids managed to fall asleep in spite of the noise; Abe and Angela were still trying to get to sleep at 2:00 A.M. They talked about when they wanted to leave the next day and decided to leave earlier than they had originally planned. After a night like this, they reasoned, they were not going to be in the mood for recreation. Abe began filling out a guest comment card.

The Nicholses learned at check-out the next morning that the hotel had incorrectly billed them the full rack rate for all three nights. "We'll generate a new bill in just a few moments, Mr. Nichols," the front desk agent told him.

Abe was dropping the comment card into the designated slot while he was waiting when Tom Girard, the hotel's general manager, introduced himself. "I'm just taking an informal guest survey today. How was your stay here?"

Abe gave him the whole story—good points and bad points. Tom listened carefully, taking notes on a pad. He thanked Abe for his feedback and apologized for the difficulties the family had. He offered the Nicholses a free lunch at the hotel's restaurant and told Abe that if the family was ever in the area again, they should call Tom's office and he would arrange for a free night's stay.

Three weeks later, the Nicholses received a very thoughtful follow-up letter from Tom Girard. It explained what he and his staff had done to correct the problems the Nicholses had experienced. But Abe reported to Angela that the credit card bill for the hotel stay was $14 higher than their folio had been when they checked out. A call to the Simpson Hotel revealed that the minibar charges were not posted until after the family had left.

Discussion Questions

1. What went right with the Nichols's stay? What went wrong? Was the overall impression they received of the hotel good or bad?

2. How did the general manager do at responding to Mr. Nichols's feedback?

3. How should the GM relay the Nichols's feedback to his department heads and staff? Should a property offer a 100-percent guest-satisfaction guarantee? If so, how should it be implemented?

4. How can the Simpson Hotel's staff develop a process for improving communication, quality control, and accountability—ultimately, for improving guest service?

Case Number: 3326CA

The following industry experts helped generate and develop this case: Richard N
Brooks, CHA, Vice President, TWE Group; and S. Kenneth Hiller, CHA, Genera
Manager, Holiday Inn, Beachwood, Ohio.

To Serve or Not to Serve

It was a typically warm summer afternoon and check-ins were brisk. This was one
of the first big weekends of the summer and the front office staff was still adjusting to the large number of arrivals. As another car pulled under the porte cochere,
Drew, a bell attendant, gave an audible sigh.

"I hope this one tips better than the other two I just had," he muttered
loudly enough that Chris, the front desk agent, and Philip, the manager on duty
(MOD), could hear. Drew was still leaning against the front desk taking a short
breather as the couple got out of their car, looked around, and then proceeded
to the front desk. After the front desk agent completed the check-in process,
she asked whether they would like assistance with their luggage. After a brief
pause, they said yes and—like many other guests—looked around for the bell
attendant.

Drew had moved from the front desk he had been leaning on to a part of the
lobby where he wasn't easily seen, hoping that the guests would turn down the
offer for assistance. He wasn't in the mood for another poor tipper even though a
gratuity of 15 percent was placed on every room charge. This meant that the guest
was paying for bell service whether they used it or not. Also, if they did request
assistance, they were not even obliged to pay an additional sum because the tip
was covered in the cost of the room.

Once the front desk agent knew that the guests required assistance, she radi-
oed Drew. As he heard the radio call, Drew proceeded to the back area where the
luggage carts are kept. Philip caught Drew's eye and suggested with a point of the
finger that the people who had just checked in were in need of assistance. Drew,
however, ignored this cue from the MOD.

A few minutes later, Philip noticed the guests taking their belongings from
their car and placing them on the walkway. He wondered what happened to Drew.
Philip found Drew in the service corridor talking with the other bell attendant,
Jim. "I thought you were going straight out to assist those guests," said Philip in a
rather disturbed and impatient tone of voice. "What are you two doing? Don't you
know guests are waiting to be helped?"

Drew backed up and told Philip in an angry voice that his shoulder was really
hurting and he went to get Jim so he could assist the guests. Jim had been eating
his dinner and wasn't very pleased to be asked to assist the guests when Drew was
the one on duty. Jim was even off the clock at the moment.

Philip said that he would do the job if the other two couldn't take the time for
it or were too tired. "Maybe you should go home if your shoulder is hurting too
much to assist guests," suggested the MOD.

"Hey," said Drew, "I've been working hard all day, it's hotter than blazes, and I'm going in to the doctor next week. I haven't been sitting on my you-know-what, you know!"

Finally, Jim took the luggage cart and proceeded to the entrance to assist the guests. By this time they were looking around inside the lobby for a bell attendant.

As Philip returned to assist the front desk agents during this busy check-in afternoon, he counted the number of times he practically had to drag Drew and some of the other bell attendants away from their place at the front desk counter to assist guests with their luggage. "Isn't this their job?" he asked himself. "What messages are they sending by just standing around watching our guests help themselves? Why include the 15 percent gratuity if we aren't helping every guest with his or her luggage?"

Philip pondered these questions for a long time. Now, with Drew being so difficult to direct, he thought about how to communicate his concerns with the front office manager.

Discussion Questions

1. What nonverbal message is Drew sending to the arriving guests?

2. When Jim interacts with the guests waiting for luggage assistance, what will be his greatest communications challenges?

3. How would you suggest Drew and the other bell attendants behave during this vital arrival stage of the guest cycle?

4. Was the MOD acting appropriately toward the bell attendants? How else could he have communicated with them that could have been more effective?

Case number: 608C06

This case also appears in Todd Comen, *Case Studies in Front Office Management* (Lansing, Mich.: American Hotel & Lodging Educational Institute, 2003).

Something Old, Something New: Meeting Tour Group Needs

The bus coach tour group from San Francisco arrived three hours late. Coach sales staff had long since gone home, having made last-minute rooming changes. The dining room had finally blocked 6:30 P.M. for an entire busload of forty customers. And the thermometer hovered just shy of eighty-five degrees.

Stacy looked tired as she disembarked from the coach. She was the tour escort, a job she had performed very well for many years. Three hours behind schedule on what should have been an eight-hour drive revealed the wear on her. The hotel staff greeted the arriving passengers while they remained seated on the coach, advising them of their dinner reservations, suggesting that washing up but not changing would be the most expedient for the resort as the dining room was booked through the evening. Room keys were distributed while the guests left the bus. Guests were informed that their luggage would be delivered to the guestrooms while they were at dinner.

The majority of the passengers were in their mid-sixties to late seventies, with a wide range of health, from good to really poor. Numerous passengers, the hotel staff was to discover, had respiratory problems. And one was on oxygen twenty-four hours a day.

As the guests entered the lobby, they were directed to their rooms by one of the front desk agents, who was stationed between the entrance and the elevators. It was a slow process, as many of the guests were stiff from the long bus ride. Some decided to go directly to the dining room, while others either took the stairs or waited for the elevator to the second, third, and fourth floors.

As the lobby cleared, it quieted down at the front desk while the guests refreshed themselves and got acquainted with their rooms. The front desk staff was feeling pretty good thus far, as no one had complained about his or her room assignment. The hotel was unusually full for this time of year because of some small functions, including a wedding party and an executive retreat. As there were only a few expected arrivals left, the desk staff knew that they had three additional rooms that could be sold to walk-in customers.

At 6:50, a distinguished looking elderly couple stopped abruptly at the front desk, obviously upset. The woman wore two large diamonds on her wedding ring and they were both well dressed, as if going to an upscale restaurant in the city. They introduced themselves as the Kavaliers and asked Trisha, the front desk agent, how to turn on the air conditioning, as the room was very warm. She politely informed them that there wasn't any air conditioning in their room and that the fan would circulate the air when the windows in the room were opened.

With a distraught look on his face, Mr. Kavalier said, "My wife has to have air conditioning or she can't breathe. If we had known this, we never would have come on this trip. The owner of the tour company assured us that there was air conditioning at this resort." This guest was now visibly angry and very upset. He informed Trisha that if he couldn't have an air-conditioned room, he and his wife would have to rent a car and drive home.

Trisha apologized and said that she understood their concern. She assured the guests that there had never been air conditioning in the guestrooms and that the only rooms with air conditioning were in the new addition that had only twenty-five rooms. She also explained that the resort was very full, but, if they would proceed to their dinner, she would see what could be done. The guests were reluctant to leave, but Philip, the manager on duty (MOD), assured the guests that Trisha would do what she could to meet their requirements. If a room could not be found for the next two nights, the guests would have the option to move to another resort that could meet their requirements.

The situation wasn't so bad yet, as there were a number of guests still to arrive and a few rooms still available. Trisha and Philip went to work to identify a solution for the Kavaliers. The front desk agent first checked to see if there were any air-conditioned rooms available for two consecutive nights. These rooms, however, were more than twice the cost per night of the rooms that the coach guests were assigned. They discussed whether it was a good idea to upgrade a coach guest to these fine rooms. What would the other coach guests demand if they knew that one of their party was assigned an executive room?

Soon after this first complaint about the lack of air conditioning, Stacy approached the front desk. She was in good spirits, but she said many in her party were uncomfortable with their room assignments. Several guests were placed in smoking rooms when they had specifically requested no-smoking. Her guests were having trouble breathing as they had minor respiratory problems. One of her party had actually requested a smoking room but had been placed in a no-smoking room. And others were saying they couldn't take the humidity and heat. The rooms were hot and they couldn't find the air conditioning.

On top of this deluge of new information, one of the coach guests in room 340 had just called the desk to say that her husband, who is on oxygen twenty-four hours a day, could not attach his portable oxygen unit to the bulk tank that was delivered to their room earlier in the day by an outside vendor. She wondered if the company was close by so that the proper equipment could be delivered. Her husband, she said, had about two hours' worth of oxygen left in his portable tank.

As Trisha relayed this information to Philip, he began to wonder just how this night was going to end up. Where should he and his staff focus now? Things were heating up as the weather turned more humid. He knew that not only were the guests uncomfortable, but that this heat and humidity caused the resort employees to become cranky and less patient. His main problem was to find a solution to the oxygen tank problem. This he assumed was a life-and-death situation. The guests with complaints about air conditioning may or may not be in a life-threatening situation. He would leave the rooming challenges to the front desk agents and focus on getting oxygen to the resort before two hours elapsed.

As he was considering his options, an elderly man emerged from the elevator pushing a wheelchair. He was breathing with the assistance of an oxygen tank. This was the man who had two hours of oxygen left, and he was heading for the dining room without his wife. She came down the stairs minutes later, berating him for walking down himself. He seemed fairly relaxed, and Philip wondered if he really needed the oxygen continuously or if he could live without it for a time.

Room-move requests from the coach tour group only were as follows:

Current room number	Possible room number change	Reason for change
245	103	No-smoking to smoking
434	243	No stairs involved (physical challenge to climb stairs)
103	345	Smoking to no-smoking
212	367	Must have air conditioning
322	464	Must have air conditioning
342	102	Escort willing to move to smoking room, but needs ozone treatment
102	343	Smoking to no-smoking

Finally, at 10 P.M., Trisha decided to move room 212 to 367, the last air-conditioned room available. She first went to discuss this room change with the guests to be sure this would work. While she was away from the desk, Philip met two of the last arriving guests for the evening, Mr. and Mrs. Vogel, who had driven more than 400 miles that day. The Vogels were very tired but happy to have arrived at the resort. Philip checked them into room 367. When the front desk agent returned after confirming the room move to 367, she was shocked to learn that the Vogels had just been checked in to that same room. Now what would she tell the guests she had just shown the room?

As the night wore on, small groups from the coach tour could be overheard in the lounge and public areas complaining about the resort accommodations. Even the bus driver was upset because his room was different from the room he had the last time he had driven a group to the resort.

Finally, at 11 P.M., most of the guests had gone off to their rooms. Oxygen had finally been delivered to the gentleman in room 340. He was hooked up for the night, but the oxygen firm had to return the next morning with a nozzle that would fit his canister. The MOD had spent a couple of hours on this project, finally calling the local rescue squad for an emergency oxygen tank while they awaited delivery of oxygen from the regular supplier. It turned out that the regular supplier was more than an hour away and couldn't guarantee delivery before the guest ran out.

The last of the coach tour guests passed the front desk on her way up to her room. She looked at Trisha and Philip and just shook her head. "Some people just can't be satisfied with being alive," she said. "I'm doing great and very happy to be here."

Trisha and Philip looked at each other and sighed, wondering why all of the coach guests couldn't be that easy.

Discussion Questions:

1. How should the work associated with the problems outlined in the case be delegated among the staff on duty? Who should do what?

2. Who is the most important guest in this group? What steps would you take in order to meet that person's needs?

3. If you were on the morning shift, what do you think your morning would be like following a night such as this described in the case?

4. Are room moves really necessary, or do they just result in more work for everyone?

Case number: 608C08

This case also appears in Todd Comen, *Case Studies in Front Office Management* (Lansing, Mich.: American Hotel & Lodging Educational Institute, 2003).

Chapter 7 Outline

Competencies

1. Explain important issues in developing and managing a security program. (pp. 261–273)

2. Describe the role that managers play in a property's security program. (pp. 274–275)

3. Explain the importance of setting up a security program, including security staffing and having a liaison with local law enforcement. (pp. 275–281)

4. Identify the elements of security training that are critical to an effective security program. (pp. 281–287)

5. List and describe the legal concepts and societal concerns related to security issues. (pp. 287–290)

7

Security and the Lodging Industry

This chapter has been adapted largely from material found in Chapter 1 of *Security and Loss Prevention Management*, Second Edition, by Raymond C. Ellis, Jr., and David M. Stipanuk

LODGING PROPERTY MANAGERS have many responsibilities, one of which is **security**. From the earliest days of the hospitality industry, one of the most important duties of an innkeeper has been to protect guests from harm while on the property. Although interpretations of protection may vary from state to state, every legal jurisdiction imposes some form of security obligation on hotels. Security regulations go beyond the innkeeper-guest relationship to include hotel employees and others on the property who are not guests. Therefore, providing security in a hotel is the broad task of protecting people—guests, employees, and others—and assets. Crimes involving the theft of assets usually result in greater immediate monetary losses to lodging properties than crimes against persons, but crimes against persons have a greater effect on public relations (and therefore occupancy) and may lead to high legal expenses and large punitive damage awards.

Lodging property security efforts may involve such areas of concern as guestroom security, key control, locks, access control, perimeter control, alarm systems, communication systems, lighting, closed-circuit television, safe deposit boxes, inventory control, credit and billing procedures, computer security, staffing, pre-employment screening, employee training, responsible service of alcoholic beverages, emergency procedures, safety procedures, recordkeeping, and more.

The industry's concern with security increased dramatically after the terrorist attacks of September 11, 2001. Hotels, because they are so open to the public, are potential targets for terrorist activities. For example, immediately after the tragic events of 9/11, hotels in New York and Washington, D.C., received dozens of bomb threats, including threats to use poisonous gas and other types of destructive devices. Additionally, two prominent hotels were among the targets of the terrorist attacks in Mumbai, India, in late 2008.

Of course, terrorism is not the only security concern hotels face. The crime rate against both people and assets continues to increase. In addition, the rapidly growing number of lawsuits filed against innkeepers—and even individual employees—for failure to provide adequate security has raised the industry's security awareness. Newspaper and television exposés make the public aware of many hotel security issues.

In most states, innkeepers have a legal duty to provide "reasonable care" to protect guests and guests' invitees. Innkeepers may be held responsible if employees injure guests. Innkeepers accused of negligence for not providing reasonable care for someone who was injured or victimized on their premises are losing millions of dollars every year in court judgments and out-of-court settlements.

Even if financial considerations were the only security concern (which they certainly are not), the urgent need for hotels to implement a security program if one is not already in place is obvious. It must be stated, however, that each lodging property is different and has different security needs. Therefore, the material included in this chapter should not be construed as recommending any industry standard. We can only explore general security concerns in the following pages.

Developing the Security Program

A lodging property's security program should stress the prevention of security problems. It is far more desirable to keep security incidents from occurring than to catch a criminal after a crime has been committed. Certain security actions and procedures may help to prevent or discourage incidents. Nonetheless, it must be recognized that *not all crime is preventable.*

Each property should continually review its security procedures and update them to meet changing security needs. The following list indicates general areas that might be part of a property's security program:

- Doors, locks, key control, and access control
- Guestroom security
- Control of persons on premises
- Perimeter and grounds control
- Protection of assets (money on hand, guests' assets, equipment, inventories)
- Emergency procedures
- Communications
- Security records
- Staff security procedures

We will discuss each of these security areas in the following sections.

Doors, Locks, Key Control, and Access Control

During a grand opening, a hotel traditionally throws out the keys to the front door. This symbolizes that everyone is welcome. Yet the symbolism doesn't preclude the need to provide access control to all parts of the building and grounds. When most people think of access control, they first think of guestroom access, but there are many other hotel areas that require security control, including offices, pool and fitness centers, meeting rooms, storerooms and lockers, and other areas. For example, locking hotel storerooms helps prevent hotel employees from unauthorized entry and from stealing hotel property, whether it is food, linen, or other supplies.

Locking fitness centers and pools helps prevent guests, visitors, and employees from using the facilities when they cannot be properly supervised.

Guestroom-access security is the most common security need, however. Electronic guestroom locks have replaced mechanical systems in most lodging properties. Electronic systems have great flexibility. Different key types can be issued to guests and hotel employees. Electronic systems can record every authorized entry and every unauthorized entry attempt. If a guest reports a robbery, the person responsible for hotel security can query the guestroom lock and identify the keys that were used in the last ten, twenty, or fifty entries. For guests, security is enhanced because new key codes are issued each time a guest checks in. Keys are issued during the check-in process, and usually will only work for a limited time period—for example, the issued key is good until noon on the scheduled date of departure. If the guest decides to extend the stay, the key must be recoded. Similarly, if the guest departs a day early, the key can be rendered invalid by checking in another guest to the room.

For employees, guestroom keys are coded by department, and may also have time limits on them. For example, a hotel maintenance employee may be given a temporary guestroom key to fix a problem in a guestroom. The key may be good for a specific time period, such as between 10 A.M. and 11 A.M. If more time is needed, the key must be recoded.

Guestroom door locks also may include chains or other backup locks on the inside of the door, so that guests can control access once they are in the room. Most guestroom locks have a deadbolt mechanism. This allows the guest to provide extra security by turning a lever that extends a thick piece of metal into the guestroom doorframe.

Guestroom locks are also found on connecting-room doors and balcony or patio doors. These locks are usually not electronic, so extra care must be taken to ensure that they provide guests with good security. Balcony and patio locks may include not only the lock on the door, but also an extra lock that is controlled from inside the room. When connecting rooms are not needed, it is important that the connecting door be closed and locked. Only hotel employees should have the keys to open those doors.

Most hotels have multiple key-security levels. The lowest level is the individual guestroom, office, storeroom, or meeting room. The next level is often called a "section master" key. Section master keys are generally used in housekeeping when a room attendant is assigned a specific group of rooms to clean or inspect; he or she can carry one section master key instead of carrying many separate guestroom keys. A floor master key is generally the next level up; it provides access to an entire floor. There can be several building master keys. One building master can cover the guestroom section of the building, including all storage closets in that part of the building. Another building master can cover all public areas, such as dining and meeting rooms. A grand master key gives access to all door locks in the building. An emergency key or "E-Key" is an emergency override key that allows access to all rooms, even if they have been locked from the inside.

All of a lodging property's keys, no matter what level they are, should have controls on them. Guestroom keys are recoded every time new guests check in or change their departure date. Other keys do not need to be changed as often, but still need to be controlled. For example, an E-Key should be issued only upon the permission of the hotel general manager or security manager. When an E-Key is issued, an entry should be made in the security log, stating who was issued the key, the time and date it was issued, who approved the issue, what lock it was issued for, and the reason for the key's issuance. E-Keys must have a time limit on them as well. Section master keys and floor master keys should be issued a day at a time, with the original keys being returned to a security checkpoint at the end of every shift. If a key is lost or stolen, it must be reported immediately and appropriate actions taken to invalidate that key.

Guestroom Security

We have been discussing guestroom key control, but guestroom security extends beyond the guestroom's door locks. Another security device found on guestroom doors is the peephole. Peepholes usually contain a fish-eye lens that allows guests to see to the left and right when looking out. Peepholes are usually placed conveniently in the door for guests of average height. In rooms that are specially equipped to comply with the Americans with Disabilities Act, a second peephole is provided for guests in wheelchairs. Hotel hallways should be brightly lit, to allow guests to see all areas of the hall.

Telephones are also an important part of guestroom security, as they allow guests to call for help when necessary. Clear instructions, such as "Dial 0 for Emergencies," should be on or near every guestroom telephone.

Control of Persons on Premises

Controlling people on the premises is one of the most difficult issues for hotel managers and security personnel. By their nature and history, hotels hold themselves open for public accommodation. Unfortunately, however, there are times and circumstances when not everyone is welcome. Hotels are private property, so people can be excluded if they have no specific reason for being on the premises. It is in these situations where training the hotel staff in security issues is so important. Training should include how to identify people who may not belong at the hotel, and what to do if such people are identified. For many hotels, surveillance systems assist in this effort, since employees cannot directly view every area of a hotel at all times. Surveillance systems use video cameras, motion detectors, and other security devices to monitor hotel areas. Cameras are usually connected to monitors in the security office, front desk, telephone department, or other areas where there is generally someone to watch them. Motion detectors and other forms of passive security can set off alarms. Some hotels have signs posted stating that they are private property. This public warning may be required to take advantage of local trespass laws.

Perimeter and Grounds Control

Perimeter and grounds control can take many forms. Surveillance systems are very useful in providing security monitoring of such outdoor areas as parking lots, pools, tennis courts, and other areas. Parking lots should be well-lit; guests and employees feel safer in well-lighted parking lots or structures. Parking facilities may also have gates to control traffic; sometimes these gates are staffed for extra protection. Fences are often needed, especially in high-risk areas. For example, most states require swimming pools to be fenced and gated if they are outside and not physically surrounded by the hotel structure. Fences may also be used to separate the hotel from its neighbors. The hotel's management should train valet parking attendants, landscape staff members, maintenance staff members, and others to watch for unauthorized people on the grounds.

Protection of Assets

The physical and intellectual assets of the hotel must be protected as well. Important devices for securing the assets of guests are hotel safe deposit boxes and, for those hotels that offer them, in-room safes. All states require hotels to provide some sort of safe deposit box facility for guests at no charge. Guests must be notified of the availability of these boxes, usually through notices in guestrooms. Some states also require that notices be posted in public areas, such as the front desk. The safe deposit boxes are usually at or near the front desk. Upscale and world-class hotels usually have a separate room for safe deposit boxes, where guests can have privacy while using the boxes. These rooms cannot be entered from the lobby without someone from the hotel opening the door. In other properties, the safe deposit boxes are at the front desk, and guests may have to open and close them in the lobby. Guests must sign a signature card every time they use the safe deposit box, and the hotel employee must verify the signature before allowing access to the safe. In addition, the safe deposit box keys must also be secured to prevent them from being lost or stolen. Hotels usually have only one key per safe deposit box. If the key is lost or stolen, the box lock must be removed and a new lock installed. If a hotel has more than one key per safe deposit box, a guest claiming a loss from the contents of the box may have legal grounds for claiming that hotel employees could open the box with the other key.

Guestroom safes are becoming more popular, as they offer convenience to guests. However, some states do not have clear rulings at this time as to whether in-room safes can take the place of guest safe deposit boxes. Some in-room safes have unique keys, some are digital and use codes entered by the guest, and some work with guest payment cards.

Another important security device is a robbery alarm at the front desk. Usually this is a silent alarm that sends a signal to the local police department. The activation device is generally placed out of sight, such as near an employee's foot where it can't be easily seen from the guest side of a counter. This device may work with the hotel's surveillance system, so that when it is activated, a camera records what is going on at the alarm location.

There may be more than one safe for hotel use. For example, a hotel can have a main safe, where cash and important records are secured. As computer software becomes more important, it is not uncommon to find the software stored in the hotel safe, or in another secure area, such as the computer room. There may also be a cashier drop safe. A cashier drop safe is a special safe that allows items to be dropped into it; the only way to remove the items is to open the safe with a combination. Drop safes are used to temporarily store the cash received in the day's transactions from the front desk and the various hotel revenue outlets. When a deposit is made into the safe, the amount, date, time, revenue outlet, and name of the person dropping the amount is entered in a log near the safe. Many hotels require someone other than the person responsible for the drop to witness the deposit and co-sign that a drop was actually made. The person opening the safe then compares the log to the actual envelopes found in the safe as the first step in ensuring that the contents are accurate. Both general hotel safes and drop safes are fire-rated to protect the contents from fire.

An important procedure used to protect the contents of a cashier bank is the bank audit. Bank audits may be done on a scheduled basis or without notice. Most hotels conduct audits without notice so that employees do not have time to make corrections to their banks. The purpose of the bank audit is to make sure that the contents of the bank are correct and money is not missing. This prevents hotel employees from making "loans" to themselves.

Hotels must also protect the assets of employees. Employee changing and locker rooms should be secure and safe. Many hotels provide locks for employees. When uniformed employees arrive for work, they each receive a uniform and a lock for the locker they store their personal valuables in. When they leave the hotel after their shift, the lock must accompany the uniform. Other hotels use a more flexible system, involving a lockable storage bag that holds employee clothing and other items. The bag is turned in to a secure storage area after it is filled, and it is claimed at the end of the employee's shift.

Most departments have secure storage areas for women's purses and other employee personal items that may be needed during the day. Good front desk designs allow for lockable drawers at the front desk or in a nearby area. Each employee gets a drawer to use during his or her shift.

Emergency Procedures

Sooner or later, every hotel will have some sort of emergency to deal with. Injuries, robberies, destruction of assets, fires, or other emergency situations will require extraordinary action on the part of the hotel staff. The hotel should have well-documented procedures for all emergencies that can be anticipated. These procedures should be included in the initial and ongoing employee training program. For example, many hotels invite the local fire department to the hotel to train employees on the proper use of fire extinguishers. Lifeguards must be properly trained on water safety and cardiopulmonary resuscitation (CPR). Front desk staff must know what to do during a robbery or when a guest calls asking for medical assistance. Hotel staff members working at hotels located in hurricane or flood-prone areas need to know what to do when these emergencies occur.

If a fire is reported, all employees should know how to respond. Some employees may be assigned to directing guests out of the building, while others may be assigned to directing the fire department to the fire's location.

One of the most important emergency procedures is to assist guests with disabilities during an emergency. Most hotel computer systems have special codes in them for identifying where guests with disabilities have been roomed. If a hotel is being evacuated, employees must go to these guestrooms to assist the disabled guests. For example, if the hotel has a fire, elevators will not work, and guests who use wheelchairs or are otherwise unable to move easily will need assistance to fire exits.

All states require guests to be notified in their guestrooms of emergency exits and procedures. Most full-service hotels have bell attendants provide a brief emergency orientation while escorting guests to their rooms. Evacuation routes are generally posted in guestrooms, often on the back of the main guestroom door.

Communications

Good communication forms the backbone of any successful security program. Providing mobile communication devices, such as radios and pagers, to key employees is one way to ensure good communication during emergency situations. Another good communication strategy is to post security information in high-traffic employee areas to help keep security awareness high at the hotel. Security should be a frequent topic of discussion in department meetings and other staff meetings. In addition, the hotel should regularly publish security information. For example, if a hotel is notified of a counterfeit ring in the area, employees should be given a description of how to identify the fake bills, and, if known, a description of the persons distributing them. This applies to drug or theft gangs as well. Employees should be given very specific instructions on what to do when they identify a possible security problem.

Guests in need of medical assistance often communicate their need to the front desk, so the hotel should have procedures in place for front desk agents to follow when helping these guests. Guests may be referred to doctors or hospitals; in real emergencies, the local emergency medical service (EMS) should be contacted. However, employees should be given clear instructions on when to call for EMS assistance.

Just as important, all hotel staff members should receive training on how to communicate to guests and other people during an emergency. For example, in the case of a building evacuation, staff members must show composure and confidence. If the staff seems panicked, the panic may spread to guests. Dealing with the public at large is just as important. When the news media becomes aware of a hotel emergency, reporters and others will attempt to contact the hotel for comment. Every employee should be aware of the hotel's policy concerning media contact and why compliance with the policy is so important.

Security Records

Any activity that has a security-related dimension to it should be recorded for future reference. For example, the issuing of an E-Key should be recorded in writing. The audit of a cashier bank requires more than one person counting the bank, and all employees involved should sign a security record as to the results of the audit. Reports about robberies, assaults, personal injuries to guests or employees, and property damage or theft; vehicle maintenance records; and preventive maintenance records all should be part of an ongoing security record program.

Security records are important for several reasons. First, they allow hotel management to track issues. For example, the hotel may identify an ongoing problem with a guestroom lock by recording every time a security officer is called to a room because the issued key doesn't work properly. Vehicle maintenance records allow the hotel to track maintenance issues, such as tire wear. Most municipalities mandate periodic testing of the fire alarm system and recording of the results.

Another important reason for security records is to protect the hotel from legal action. Hotels should use a standard form for all reported security violations (see Exhibit 1 for a sample incident/loss report). The form should have space for recording a clear description of the situation and what actions the hotel took when it was notified. These records are confidential and must remain in the hotel's custody unless the general manager directs otherwise.

Finally, security records may assist the hotel with insurance claims made by either the hotel's insurance carrier or a guest's. In either case, security records can present the hotel's view of what happened. This is especially helpful when hotel staff members are called upon to describe a security incident that occurred many months ago.

Staff Security Procedures

Investing in security technology and equipment is a good idea, but a properly trained hotel staff is still the best way to provide security in a hotel. Although every hotel differs, certain common security procedures should be standard practice. Some examples include:

- Never say a guest's room number out loud at the front desk. If someone asks what room a guest is in, he or she should be directed to a house telephone; the hotel operator can then connect the person to the appropriate room without mentioning the number. This also means not saying the room number when issuing a key to a newly arrived guest at the front desk. Room numbers and directions to guestrooms should be written down for guests or given to guests via pre-printed materials.

- Front desk agents should require identification from anyone who comes to the front desk and asks for a key. If photo identification is not available, the person asking for the key should provide some personal information that can be verified in the hotel computer system, such as his or her home address, telephone number, or company affiliation.

- Room attendants should not allow anyone in a guestroom without a key. People asking to have a guestroom door opened should be directed to the front desk; if the situation warrants it, hotel security should be called.

- Valet parking should use a numbered three-part form to control cars. The first part goes to the guest as a receipt. The second and third parts stay with the vehicle keys. When the guest claims the car, the second part stays with the valet office as an official record; the third part goes with the keys and should be matched to the guest's receipt before the car is released. Some hotels use a four-part form.

Exhibit 1   Incident/Loss Report

INCIDENT/LOSS REPORT

Time_____
Guest_____Room_____
Employee_____Dept._____
Other_____

(Please type or print)

Type of Incident/Loss (Fire, Theft, Disturbance, Etc.)

_____

Person Reporting Incident/Loss (Victim)

Name_____Phone #_____

Address_____

City/State/Zip_____

Place of Employment_____Phone #_____

Date & Time of Incident/Loss Date_____Time_____

Date & Time Hotel Notified   Date_____Time_____

Description of Incident (Who, What, Where, When, Why)_____

_____

_____

_____

_____

Stolen Vehicle_____|_____|_____|_____|_____|
    Year   Make   Model   Color   Serial#   License#

Witness to Incident_____Phone #_____

Value of Property_____

Were Police Notified?_____By_____

Police Officer's Name & Badge No._____Report #_____

Action Taken

General Manager Notified   ☐ Yes   ☐ No

Security Notified   ☐ Yes   ☐ No

_____ Notified   ☐ Yes   ☐ No

Person Taking Report_____

Position/Department_____

Home Phone #_____

- Hotels should provide standard guest safety information in their guestrooms. The American Hotel & Lodging Association has published a "Traveler Safety Tips" card that can be placed in guestrooms for guests (see Exhibit 2).

- Hotel guests should be asked for a room key or other proof of occupancy when they ask to charge purchases to their room.

- Employees should immediately report possible security issues. For example, burned-out light bulbs in guest corridors should be reported and replaced right away. Open emergency doors, unlocked gates, and other security issues should be addressed with the highest priority.

Security procedures are also important with regard to the acceptance of payment cards for payment and the protection of sensitive information that, in the wrong hands, could facilitate identify theft.[1]

Throughout the guest cycle, hotels frequently receive payment for various transactions via payment cards. Due to the sensitive information that is found in payment cards, hotels must be extremely careful in keeping card data secure. Some countries and states have laws regarding these issues that must be obeyed, but there is no single, consistent set of laws applicable to everyone. In an effort to address the security of card data, the payment card industry has imposed its own comprehensive set of requirements. All businesses that accept payment (credit and debit) cards, including hotels, are required to comply with the Payment Card Industry Data Security Standard (PCI DSS or simply PCI or DSS), which the major payment card companies created to reduce risk and prevent problems related to the misuse of cardholder data.

As set forth in the PCI DSS, all merchants accepting payment in the form of payment cards must adopt a series of security measures to protect sensitive customer credit and debit account information. Most merchants were given notice and a period of time to prepare their organizations and secure their systems. That grace period ended in the fall of 2007, at which point compliance enforcement began. Any merchant, regardless of size or type, that accepts credit and/or debit cards that is not currently compliant with this standard faces potentially strict financial penalties and runs the risk of losing the privilege to accept credit and debit cards.

The PCI DSS affects all merchants globally—regardless of size, industry, location, or type of business—that accept credit and/or debit cards, and covers the collection, storage, transmission, and use of customer and account information embedded in these cards. The PCI DSS is defined by six major categories and twelve key compliance requirements (see Exhibit 3). The extensive procedural details of the PCI DSS are beyond our scope here, and they involve not only the procedures used when accepting payment, but also the computer security protocols that must be in place when saving and transmitting information electronically. For a full explanation of the PCI DSS, see *The Payment Card Industry Compliance Process for Lodging Establishments*, an excellent resource published by the American Hotel & Lodging Educational Institute.[2]

There are also a number of privacy issues that need to be addressed where payment cards are concerned, such as payment card fraud, identity theft, and misuse of data. The Federal Trade Commission (FTC) estimates that as many as nine

Exhibit 2 Traveler Safety Tips Card

TRAVELER SAFETY TIPS

American Hotel & Motel Association

1. Don't answer the door in a hotel or motel room without verifying who it is. If a person claims to be an employee, call the front desk and ask if someone from their staff is supposed to have access to your room and for what purpose.

2. When returning to your hotel or motel late in the evening, use the main entrance of the hotel. Be observant and look around before entering parking lots.

3. Close the door securely whenever you are in your room and use all of the locking devices provided.

4. Don't needlessly display guest room keys in public or carelessly leave them on restaurant tables, at the swimming pool, or other places where they can be easily stolen.

5. Do not draw attention to yourself by displaying large amounts of cash or expensive jewelry.

6. Don't invite strangers to your room.

7. Place all valuables in the hotel or motel's safe deposit box.

8. Do not leave valuables in your vehicle.

9. Check to see that any sliding glass doors or windows and any connecting room doors are locked.

10. If you see any suspicious activity, please report your observations to the management.

We Support the National Citizens' Crime Prevention Campaign.

TAKE A BITE OUT OF CRIME®

♻ Printed on recycled paper

Copyright 1993 by
The American Hotel
& Motel Association
1201 New York Avenue, N.W.
Washington, D.C. 20005-3931

Source: American Hotel & Lodging Association, Washington, D.C.

Exhibit 3   A Synopsis of the PCI Data Security Standard

Twelve Steps to PCI Compliance*

Control Objectives	Compliance Requirements
Build and maintain a secure network	1. Install and maintain a firewall configuration to protect data
	2. Change vendor-supplied defaults for system passwords and other security parameters
Protect cardholder data	3. Protect stored data
	4. Encrypt transmission of cardholder magnetic-stripe data and sensitive information across public networks
Maintain a vulnerability management program	5. Use and regularly update antivirus software
	6. Develop and maintain secure systems and applications
Implement strong access control measures	7. Restrict access to data to a need-to-know basis
	8. Assign a unique ID to each person with computer access
	9. Restrict physical access to cardholder data
Regularly monitor and test networks	10. Track and monitor all access to network resources and cardholder data
	11. Regularly test security systems and processes
Maintain an information security policy	12. Maintain a policy that addresses information security

*The Payment Card Industry Data Security Standard (PCI DSS) includes numerous sub-requirements not listed here. To see these, visit http://www.pcisecuritystandards.org.

Source: IT Compliance Institute. (2007, June 22.) *Compliance Insight: Challenges and Opportunities of PCI*, p. 3.

million Americans have their identity stolen annually. Identities are stolen when a thief claims to be someone else, and uses the victim's Social Security number or payment card account, or conducts transactions without the victim's permission, thereby committing fraud and/or other criminal activity. Identity theft can take many forms, including renting an apartment, obtaining a payment card, signing a contract, or establishing a telephone account in someone else's name. Unfortunately, victims of identity theft often do not discover the theft until they learn about an unexplainable transaction, receive a doubtful credit report or invalid payment card account statement, or are contacted by a debt collection agency.

Popular techniques for capturing unauthorized guest information include, but are not limited to, the following:

- *Dumpster diving*—This term refers to the practice in which a thief rummages through hotel trash cans and/or dumpster contents in search of receipts, folios, bills, records, or other documents that may contain personal information about guests.

- *Skimming*—This term describes the activity by which a thief steals a credit card or debit card account number by using an illegal data-capture device while supposedly processing a legitimate transaction (such as a magnetic-stripe-swipe data capture).

- *Change of address*—Front office staff should be wary of anyone contacting the front desk or the accounting department in an attempt to change or divert guest billing statements or transaction records to an alternate address without confirming the authorization of such a change.

The hotel's privacy obligation relative to payment card fraud is to secure payment card numbers from theft. The most effective ways to secure card numbers include:

- To "mask" or not display complete card numbers on folios, POS receipts, confirmations, screen displays, and reports. Rather, show only a portion of the card number.

- Destroy obsolete transaction records that may contain card numbers, as required by the PCI DSS.

- Secure all databases containing card numbers (PMS, POS, CRS, booking engine) from unauthorized access either locally or online.

- Secure all back-up tapes from unauthorized removal.

- Use systems that encrypt payment card numbers if at all possible.

Identity theft frauds can take various forms, but usually involve a thief getting credit in some manner (payment card, bank loan, even a mortgage) using the victim's name and SSN and/or other payment card numbers. The hotel can help prevent identity theft by securing guest payment cards using the methods listed above.

Many of the perceived threats to payment card privacy revolve around the fear that someone could abuse private data to discriminate or otherwise act against a victim. While hotels should have clear policies in place regarding the protection of sensitive guest (or employee) information, hotels should be prepared to release data to legitimate investigators or others with warrants supported by a subpoena. A difficult gray area occurs when, for example, a police officer or detective requests information in a situation where there is no time to get a subpoena and delay could put someone at risk or permit time for a crime to be committed on hotel premises.

There are other very real threats to payment card privacy that the hotel is obligated to protect guests from. For example, folio detail should include only enough information to identify the transaction. Hotels must ensure that requests for copies of folios are legitimate and are in fact from the guest himself or herself, rather than, say, his or her spouse's divorce attorney. The process for confirming folio copy requests should be clear, documented, and adhered to.

The general rule of thumb must be, "It is no one else's business what the guest did in the hotel, so the hotel must protect that information from accidental or by-deception exposure." It is important that staff members understand their roles and responsibilities in safeguarding sensitive information.

Management's Role in Security

All managers at a property should be involved in developing security guidelines that address the hotel's unique security needs. Legal counsel should review these guidelines. Once approved, these guidelines should be communicated to all employees. If guidelines were prepared for each individual department, they can be provided on a department-by-department basis. There is a greater likelihood that employees will review the material if it addresses their specific areas without detailing the total security operations of the property. Employee turnover and changes in job assignments necessitate a regular review program to make sure all employees are aware of their security responsibilities.

Lodging properties should clearly define the security role of their managers, whether the size of the property requires a large security staff or the security function is assigned to one or several on-premises supervisory staff. The protection of guests, employees, and assets requires all managers (and, indeed, all employees) to be constantly alert to possible security breaches.

Areas of Vulnerability

A more mobile worldwide society, the criminal by-products of the drug culture, and a climbing crime rate have all created new security problems for hotels. Many decades ago, hotel security problems related primarily to room thefts—assaults or rapes were almost unheard of. In a famous lawsuit, a jury awarded 1960s entertainer Connie Francis $2.5 million after she was assaulted in a hotel. The case considerably raised the public's awareness of hotel safety issues. Hotels have gained an unfortunate visibility with regard to criminal incidents that can include assault, arson, and armed robbery. Crimes against guests, even if few in number, can generate adverse publicity, can seriously damage the reputation of the property, and may be extremely costly during subsequent litigation.

One problem in designing a security program to deal with serious crime is that the security effort must take into consideration the property's image. The lodging industry is, after all, a service industry. A hotel markets an image of hospitality as its main product. Security procedures that evoke impressions of martial law may be good for security, but they will probably be bad for the hotel's image of hospitality and therefore will be bad for business. Poorly thought-out security procedures may offend or inconvenience guests and drive them away altogether.

Another area of asset vulnerability results from the use of inadequate procedures for checking and giving credit. Such procedures may lead to losses by permitting the unauthorized or fraudulent use of payment cards, personal checks, and traveler's checks. This type of incident is less visible to the public than personal crime and is therefore less likely to greatly affect public relations efforts. Nonetheless, when establishing credit procedures to protect a property from incurring losses through bad debts, care must again be taken to avoid offending one's guests.

A high degree of vulnerability exists in the protection of the physical assets of a lodging establishment. Tableware, ashtrays, linens, and towels are taken from hotels so often that, in many hotels, these expenses are virtually ignored and are merely written off as a cost of doing business. However, because the theft of these items results in a monetary loss to the organization, management has a responsibility to take preventive action.

Unfortunately, another area of vulnerability for hotels is theft by employees. Studies by the U.S. Small Business Administration have indicated that business failures can often be directly related to employee theft, which may appear in numerous forms within lodging properties and, taken together, may combine to constitute a major security concern.

Security Requirements

The number of lodging properties and the variety of lodging concepts have proliferated in recent decades. Each new lodging concept or expansion of a successful format for serving the traveling public has added to both the variety of lodging properties and the variety of communities in which lodging properties are located. Such diversity is clearly one of the strengths of the lodging industry, but it also provides some of the industry's profoundest challenges. This is perhaps nowhere truer or more evident than in the area of hotel security. For example, some extended-stay lodging brands operate with minimal or no staff on duty at night, making security a greater issue for these types of properties.

No two hotels have identical security requirements; therefore, national security standards are not feasible for such a varied industry. The ever-growing diversity of lodging operations, locations, layout, staff, functions, and clientele makes it impossible for lodging managers to develop security requirements that could reasonably apply to all properties. Because each property is different, something that is a required security procedure for one property may not be of any value to another. Managers do not have an easy task when it comes to creating and implementing security programs that are uniquely suited to their properties.

Setting Up the Security Program

A lodging property's management must evaluate whether a special security presence is warranted by its property's security requirements. If it is, management must decide how that presence may best be integrated with the operation of the hotel. A management team's commitment to security is necessary to integrate security concerns into the day-to-day operation and administration of the property.

Setting up such an integrated security system is a process that involves many elements. These may include establishing working relationships with local and regional law enforcement and other agencies, choosing whether to use contract or in-house security personnel, and creating an appropriate and effective security training program for all personnel.

Relations with Local Governmental Agencies

A hotel is part of a larger community. Many hotel managers actively participate in civic organizations such as the Rotary Club, Kiwanis Club, and other organizations. Involvement can be beneficial for business, as many important relationships can develop through such affiliations.

Establishing good relationships with people from government agencies like police, fire, health, and emergency management agencies is also very important for hotel managers. This became very apparent in New York City after September 11, 2001. Manhattan Island, where the tragedy occurred, was intentionally cut off from the rest of the city. To get home, many people in Manhattan had to walk, sometimes for miles, because the subways, trains, and some bridges and auto-mobile tunnels were closed. Foot traffic across bridges was allowed, but nothing more. People turned to hotels for shelter and, in some cases, protection. Yet hotels were not part of New York City's master plan for emergencies. Hotel managers responded well to the emergency and accommodated many guests, whether they could pay or not, during the crisis. This example proves that civic emergency plans that consider hotels isolated from the rest of the community and region may be inadequate, and underscores the wisdom of hotel managers getting to know lead-ers of the various emergency-response agencies in their communities.

Hotel managers can gain insight into potential security and emergency planning issues by coordinating their security plans with local and regional law enforcement and other agencies. This goes well beyond just looking at crime rates and past experiences at the hotel and its surrounding community. Liaisons with police, fire, health, and emergency management agencies are essential to an effec-tive hotel security and emergency plan.

Each emergency agency requires special attention, because each is unique. For example, police specialize in solving and preventing crimes. Fire departments spe-cialize in fire prevention, protection, and extinguishing. Some health agencies focus on sanitation, while others respond to urgent emergency situations. Emergency management agencies, created to coordinate the activities of local and regional resource agencies, are important hotel contacts as well. On a national level, simi-lar responsibilities are under the control of the Federal Emergency Management Agency, better known as FEMA. Hotel managers should coordinate hotel involve-ment with these agencies and actively participate in their planning processes. For example, in 1993, Hurricane Iniki struck the island of Kauai in Hawaii. The resorts along the coast ended up in the direct path of the hurricane and were severely damaged. Resort managers involved in regional emergency planning efforts were able to ensure that their guests found safe shelter in designated locations outside the storm's path. Resort managers who did not participate in the emergency plan-ning process found themselves unable to assure their guests of a similar level of safety and protection.

Hotels that have a security or loss prevention department should make that department the hotel's official contact with local agencies. For hotels without such a department, this role is delegated to the general manager or front office manager. Therefore, understanding the role each emergency agency plays can be critical to the front office manager.

As part of a property's security program, hotel managers should cultivate cooperative relationships with local law enforcement and other agencies. Manag-ers should invite the appropriate law enforcement personnel to visit the hotel, so they can become familiar with it. Some hotels hire off-duty police officers as addi-tional security for special occasions. If possible, review hotel security procedures with the local law enforcement authorities. Be sure to request police guidance in crime prevention. A good relationship with local law enforcement agencies often encourages a more prompt response to security incidents at the hotel and will likely result in more frequent police patrols. A police presence at the hotel can also be a deterrent to certain crimes.

Most hotel managers think of the fire department when they think of emergencies. In many hotels, the fire department is the most visible government agency, because of frequent hotel inspections performed by the fire marshal. Working cooperatively with the fire department goes beyond identifying fire hazards, however. The fire department can train hotel managers and staff members in how to use fire extinguishers, help the hotel develop fire escape routes, and prescribe evacuation procedures. Improper handling of emergency fire equipment can be just as dangerous to hotel staff members, guests, and property as a raging fire. In many communities, fire departments are also responsible for the emergency medical teams (EMTs) that respond to emergency calls for medical assistance. An EMT may be willing to train hotel staff members in first aid and other emergency procedures.

Coordinating with health agencies helps ensure hotel access to medical services when needed. Establishing a relationship with a local hospital should be considered part of the hotel's emergency planning. Guests may request or require medical assistance, and being familiar with a local hospital helps make things easier when it's time to call the hospital for medical assistance or to notify it that someone is in transit who requires emergency treatment.

The need to coordinate with local and regional emergency management agencies is especially important for hotels in geographic areas that are subject to severe weather and other natural disasters. Since 9/11, however, coordinating with emergency management agencies has taken on added importance for hotels everywhere, since terrorists can strike anywhere. Hotel managers should be involved in the community's emergency notification planning, so that hotel guests and staff members can be notified of the need to evacuate. In certain cases, hospitals may not be large enough to handle emergency situations, so they may request that hotels serve as emergency medical treatment centers. Another reason to participate in local and regional emergency planning is to be sure hotels are included in emergency service plans. Such participation can help ensure that hotels will be listed as high-priority buildings for the maintenance or restoration of electric, telephone, transportation, medical, and other vital services during emergencies.

A Potential Communications Problem. Unfortunately, law enforcement, fire, medical, and emergency management agencies and private security personnel have not always cooperated well with each other. Police have sometimes viewed private security efforts as staffed with poorly trained older (or retired) personnel who are largely ineffective. In today's changing security scene, this stereotype often does an injustice to a lodging property's security personnel, as private security has become more professional and sophisticated. Better communication is the key to educating local agencies about the broad scope of a lodging property's security and emergency programs and about the growing professionalism of the industry's security personnel.

The most effective cooperation results when government agencies and hotels understand each other's needs. For example, the police should know enough about a property and its security program to be able to offer appropriate assistance in a given situation. They should be informed of any special events or visitors (for example, political or entertainment figures) that may create an unusual security risk at the property. On the other hand, the property's staff should have a basic understanding of police procedures so that they can be of greatest assistance to the police once they arrive. Representatives of the various government agencies will be able to explain the type of assistance they would find most helpful. This information should be included in a property's ongoing security training program.

Security Staffing

A hotel must choose whether to hire its own full-time security personnel, outsource the security function by contracting with a local security company, arrange for part-time protection with local off-duty police personnel, or use any combination of these or other options.

Because of a facility's size and organizational structure, it may be appropriate to assign security responsibility to a member of the management staff, such as a resident or assistant manager, a chief engineer, or the human resources director. Most large hotels have full-time security staffs, with one or more employees on each shift. Smaller properties may not be able to afford a full-time staff, so a combination of part-time security employees and properly trained full-time hotel employees may be an appropriate approach. If management decides the property needs a security department, it must determine whether the department should be a proprietary unit with in-house staff or a security program run through a reputable licensed contract security company. In some situations, it may be feasible to employ off-duty police to cover certain hours of operation, while certain members of the property's staff provide daytime coverage as one of their responsibilities.

If the security department or function is staffed by hotel employees, additional considerations include determining whether the staff will wear uniforms, whether certain or all members of the security staff will be armed, and whether there are work shifts on which security personnel need not be assigned. Unless mandated by a local or state jurisdiction, the senior security executives of the lodging industry are unanimously opposed to the use of firearms by security staff. The rare instance where an armed security officer could have been of value in a specific security incident is far outweighed by the insurance costs and the potential for accidental injury or death of innocent bystanders in a shoot-out.

All decisions concerning security staffing deserve careful thought and should be discussed with legal counsel. Each option has its adherents.

Contract Security. The proponents of contract security organizations argue that such organizations can provide sophisticated security services at considerable savings. In addition, they assert that a reputable contract security company will provide thoroughly screened, tested, and trained personnel. It may also provide consulting services, including in-depth surveys of hotel security requirements, electronic audio countermeasure sweeps (a debugging tactic), data processing security, and assistance in contingency planning for bomb threats and natural disasters. Finally, they contend that an in-house security staff may become too familiar and friendly with the other employees. If a guard catches a friend stealing, he or she might hesitate to report that friend. Some people believe that this situation may be less likely to occur if the hotel's security personnel are supplied by an outside agency.

In selecting a security company, make sure that extensive guard training, geared specifically to each facility, is provided. Review contract and insurance requirements (that is, named insured clauses and requirements for proof of insurance) with legal counsel. Check the previous lodging experience of the company's managers and line security employees, as well as specific training in dealing with guests, employees, and others. If your state or community requires that such agencies be certified, verify that the agency you choose meets this legal requirement. Be clear and specific regarding the services to be provided by the contract organization. Require the security firm's supervisory personnel to conduct frequent unannounced inspections, day and night, to ensure that its guards are in compliance with company regulations. Determine whether the security service can provide a sufficient number of personnel on short notice in the case of a large-scale emergency. Insist that security officers be required to file daily and unusual-incident reports. Determine the percentage of the security firm's hotel customers that it retains on an annual basis; rates of retention are an excellent indication of a company's service level.

If hotel managers give orders or instructions to contract security employees, a different relationship is established. The responsibility for the actions of the contract security employee becomes blurred, and there are instances in which the contract employee has been considered a workers' compensation case for the property rather than for the contract security company. Contract companies have held (and their viewpoint has prevailed in court) that the instructions from the hotel executive may have placed the contract employee in jeopardy and may have been contributory to the workers' compensation incident. In other instances, the contract employee has turned to his or her company for the workers' compensation relief, but has sued the lodging establishment under general comprehensive liability, which affords the opportunity for a much greater settlement than would be available through workers' compensation only.

A contract security organization will almost always be willing to perform an in-depth security survey for a property if the property has not already performed one for itself or had one performed by another agency. Remember, however, that a contract security organization is selling services. This fact may sometimes lead such an organization to overstate a property's security needs, which can pose an unfortunate problem for an innkeeper. Suppose a property implements some (perhaps even most) of a contract security organization's recommendations, yet despite such efforts, a security incident occurs on the premises. It is possible that a **plaintiff** might subpoena and use the security organization's written recommendations in court as evidence of the innkeeper's knowledge of alleged "inadequate security." Even if the recommendations overstated the needs, if the innkeeper failed to implement every suggestion, a jury may be more likely to judge the innkeeper negligent.

In-House Security. Proponents of proprietary or in-house security departments point out a number of advantages to this system. They emphasize the fact that the hotel has greater control over its own security officers or staff members. They also argue that training for in-house security staff members can be much more directly related to the lodging industry. They believe that the peculiarities and special needs of the industry are more effectively addressed by those within the industry than by those in a contractual relationship with the industry. In addition, they emphasize that the quality of personnel is under the direct control of the hotel in a proprietary system, rather than under the control of the contract security company, and that the director and staff of an in-house department are more effectively integrated with the other hotel departments and personnel. If the security staff is in-house, the security director can be a member of the property's executive committee, an action that would not be possible with a contract security agency. They point out that a greater sense of loyalty may be developed among in-house staff members, since career paths can be established that move security personnel into other roles in the organization. Finally, another important concern is the typically high turnover of contract security employees.

Off-Duty Police. Some properties use off-duty police officers for their security staff. There are certain benefits associated with this practice. Such officers have superior training in reacting to and dealing with crimes and other emergencies, they understand the law, they are used to dealing with people, they may be better able to identify known criminals, they are immediately recognized as authorities, and they often do in fact have more authority than ordinary citizens (as a deputized individual, they are not limited to a "citizen's arrest"). In addition, the hotel's relationship with the local police department may be enhanced.

However, there may be potential drawbacks as well. First, police officers may be oriented more toward apprehension functions than toward prevention. Second, some jurisdictions require off-duty officers to be armed, and this may not be desirable (if they are armed and injure someone, the property may be liable). In addition, off-duty officers may not be permitted to wear uniforms in some jurisdictions. Finally, an officer may be working at the hotel following a full-duty police shift and may be fatigued.

Other Security Staffing Considerations. Security concerns should be addressed during the selection and hiring of all employees. It is especially important, though, when hiring a member of the security department, given that this individual is responsible for the protection of the property. If legal counsel approves, the hotel could use an authorization statement and affidavit. Such a statement, signed by the job applicant, allows the property to more easily investigate the applicant's background. Bonding (insuring for protection from employee theft) through an insurance company permits more effective screening of applicants and is certainly warranted in the case of security staff members who, by virtue of their function, have access to most areas of the hotel. It is appropriate to have everyone employed as a driver to have a police background check to make sure they have a valid driver's license for the type of vehicle they are driving, and to see if they have any traffic violations on their driving records. This background check should be done before hiring and at least annually from that time on. This procedure applies not only to specialized employees, such as airport bus drivers, but also to other employees who may drive a hotel vehicle as part of their other assigned duties, such as a maintenance staff member.

Properties must also decide how they will schedule security staff on the property. During daytime operations, involving all employees as the "eyes and ears" of the property may make it possible to reduce the security staff to a few key persons able to respond to a security-related call from an employee. In setting schedules, special programs and activities that may affect the number of security staff needed during a particular work shift should be taken into consideration. In many properties, additional security staff members are assigned during the nighttime hours.

Security Training

Whether or not a hotel has a full-time security staff, no security staff can be everywhere at once. Therefore, every hotel employee must be trained to identify security issues and take appropriate action when they are discovered. Training can include company-provided security training programs, as well as visits by local police departments.

Everyone must understand the limits of an on-premises security officer's authority under the local codes and regulations of the jurisdiction. Factors to review in such training are: procedures to follow in a citizen's arrest, the arrest authority of a deputized security guard, and the legal limits placed upon an off-duty police officer.

In addition, since every employee of a lodging facility may act as an integral part of its security program, all employees should be given a thorough security orientation at the time they are hired and should be regularly exposed to an ongoing security education program throughout their term of employment. Such continuing security education programs can occur at department or other staff meetings. Management then can maintain and preserve records of attendance and minutes of such meetings for future reference.

Comprehensive training should include all aspects of the protection of guests, the general public, employees, and the assets of guests, employees, and the property. Depending on a particular facility's needs, training may be expanded to include the special concerns of emergency management and interconnections with the other departments in the hotel.

The key point is that the unique needs of each lodging property call for the development of individually designed security systems and individualized security training programs. Of course, this is not to say that no two lodging properties will ever have security systems with common elements. Though never identical, the security needs of various properties are sometimes similar. Common elements are likely to arise from the common potential problems that lodging properties face. However, each property also has security needs that are unique to it.

Insights that have an impact on security training may also be gained when security personnel keep abreast of the latest thinking and developments in the security field by reading the various security publications available. Because new security equipment is regularly being introduced, and approaches to security are constantly being refined, such periodicals can provide important supplemental

Exhibit 4 Selected Security and Law Enforcement Publications

Hospitality Law
747 Dresher Road
P.O. Box 980
Horsham, PA 19044-0980
(215) 784-0860

Hotel/Motel Security and Safety Management
Rusting Publications
402 Main Street
Port Washington, NY 11050
(516) 883-1440

The Police Chief
International Association of Chiefs of Police
515 N. Washington Street
Alexandria, VA 22314-2357
(703) 836-6767

Research in Brief
National Institute of Justice
Office of Justice Programs
810 7th Street, NW
Washington, DC 20531
(202) 307-2942

Security Letter
166 East 96th Street
New York, NY 10128
(212) 348-1553

Security Management
American Society for Industrial Security
1655 North Fort Meyer Drive
Arlington, VA 22209
(703) 522-5800

Security Technology & Design
Locksmith Publishing Corp.
850 Busse Highway
Park Ridge, IL 60068
(847) 692-5940

SecurityWorld
Cahners Publishing Company
Cahners Plaza
1350 East Touhy Avenue
Des Plaines, IL 60018
(847) 635-8800

information that may help management keep its particular security program up-to-date. Exhibit 4 lists several of these publications.

It is unfortunate when a hotel manager does not realize the importance of implementing a well-planned security training program. Having a well-documented and implemented security program, including a trained staff, can play a part in protecting a hotel against certain lawsuits; being able to prove that staff members were given security training can make a positive impression on a jury attempting to determine negligence or reasonable care. In numerous lodging cases, the presentation of an effective and well-organized security program has been persuasive to both the jury and the court.

Admittedly, it takes time and money to develop an effective security training program. Management must carefully examine its operation and premises to discover potential security problems. It then must decide how to best use its resources (systems, procedures, and personnel) to deal with the potential problems. Every aspect of management's plan that relies on the performance of personnel then must be explained through training to the affected personnel.

An important part of preparing a security training program is determining not only what should be taught, but also who should learn it. Trainers should focus their efforts on providing employees with the information the employees need to know to operate more effectively in their jobs.

Each property should write down its security standards and procedures in a security manual that can be used to help train employees. A carefully written manual helps ensure consistency in employee training and performance. Just as important, actually having to write the manual forces managers to think carefully and to organize their thoughts about security in a way that often does not happen if managers and trainers are allowed to rely merely on their memories and on oral instruction. The formats of security manuals can vary; regardless of the format used, the contents of a security manual should cover the broad range of the property's security concerns in *specific* terms.

In addition, with the input of many of the lodging industry's corporate security executives, the American Hotel & Lodging Educational Institute developed a very effective training program for security officers. Successful completion of *Lodging Security Officer Training* provides the individual with a "certificate of completion."[3]

Who Is Responsible? When a property uses an in-house security staff, it is obvious to all concerned that the property is responsible for the actions of its staff. The property cannot evade this responsibility merely by using off-duty officers or a contract security service, because these security officers are usually considered agents of the property. If the security officers are negligent, the property may be held liable. Such services do not relieve a property of its legal responsibility to provide reasonable care.

The use of off-duty police officers poses certain potential legal problems as well. If an off-duty officer uses his or her legal authority to arrest someone who then proves that the arrest was inappropriate, whose agent is the officer: the community's or the property's? In some cases, the officer is considered the property's agent. This means the property could be held liable for false arrest and false imprisonment. Similar liability could result if an armed officer unlawfully injures someone.

The Authority of a Security Officer. The presence of a uniformed security officer may connote to some people the image of a public law enforcement officer. In fact, some security officers—once outfitted with a uniform, badge, and, at times, weaponry—sometimes wrongly believe themselves to possess the authority of public law enforcement officers. This attitude must be changed if the police, the public, and the individual security officer are to understand and accept the role and authority of the private security officer in crime prevention. The right of a property owner to protect his or her property and the role of the security officer as his or her agent is a key principle behind the security officer's authority.

A hotel security officer, in the absence of any special commission, deputization, ordinance, or state statute, possesses no greater authority than any other private citizen. However, because the security officer can be involved in protective functions on a daily basis, he or she may be in a position to use certain powers more than most other private citizens. The exercise of these powers may involve nothing more than simply stopping undesired conduct, or it may involve making a citizen's arrest. In *all* actions that interfere with the rights of others, the security officer should endeavor to obtain consent and voluntary cooperation from the person being interfered with.

Guns and Security Officers

Although security officers in some industries carry firearms or other weapons, few in the lodging industry do so. Lodging directors of security say there are many reasons why lodging security officers should not be armed. Chief among these reasons:

- Weapons lead to more injuries among lodging security officers. If criminals see that the security officer is armed, they are more likely to use a weapon if they have one. Or security officers could injure themselves. For example, one security officer accidentally shot himself while practicing "fast draws" during his coffee break.

- Weapons could increase the property's liability or damages awarded if courts deem officers have used unreasonable force. One security officer apprehended an intruder, put a gun to his head, and marched him off toward the manager's office. Before they got to the office, however, the gun went off and killed the intruder.

- Lodging properties are often crowded places where passers-by could be easily caught in cross-fire. An accidental shooting of an innocent bystander could be a disaster for the bystander, the officer, and the property.

Source: *Lodging Security Officer Training* (Lansing, Mich.: American Hotel & Lodging Educational Institute, 1995).

Most security officers will, at some point in their careers, be faced with situations in which they must determine the appropriate legal action to be taken, such as calling the police, questioning a suspect, or making a citizen's arrest. To prevent improper acts that could result in a liability suit against the security officer and/or the employer, an officer must understand what constitutes a crime according to the appropriate criminal law so that he or she may be more specific in relaying information to and working with public law enforcement agencies.

Criminal statutes set limits on the behavior of lodging security officers. Activity beyond these limits may result in the filing of criminal charges for assault, battery, manslaughter, or other crimes. **Tort law,** which provides legal grounds for one person to remedy a wrong committed against him or her by another, also restricts the actions of the security officer. Tort law permits an injured party to bring a lawsuit for damages against the security officer, as well as the employing property, for such unreasonable conduct as false arrest, false imprisonment, malicious prosecution, defamation, slander, and other tortious acts. Individuals charged with responsibility for security should be familiar with applicable state and local laws regulating private security, particularly those relating to citizen's arrest.

Citizen's arrests. Most states, through state statutes, judicial pronouncements, or common law, permit arrests by private citizens under certain circumstances. There is considerable variation among states concerning the privileges conferred and restraints imposed in a citizen's arrest.

A **citizen's arrest** occurs when an individual is *lawfully* deprived of his or her freedom. Normally, the task of arresting criminal offenders is one for a sworn police officer. Even where the law permits a security officer to make a citizen's arrest, he or she should do so only if a sworn police officer cannot respond in time and good judgment requires prompt action on the part of the hotel. Non-security personnel should not attempt to make a citizen's arrest.

Each security officer must be familiar with the statutory arrest authority of private citizens in the state in which he or she is employed. In New York, for example, a private citizen may make an arrest for a felony only when the suspect has in fact committed it; merely having reasonable grounds for believing the suspect committed a felony is insufficient to make a citizen's arrest. In other states, the felony must be committed in the presence of the citizen making the arrest. Some states do not permit a citizen's arrest for the commission of a misdemeanor of any type, while in other states, such as New York, a citizen's arrest for a misdemeanor is permitted, provided the offense is in fact committed in the presence of the citizen making the arrest. In any event, hotels in all states should check with local counsel before instituting any procedures for detaining persons on their premises. Moreover, security officers cannot exercise lawful arrest power for any purpose other than to turn the individual arrested over to the proper authorities.

An arrest made without proper legal authority may constitute false arrest and false imprisonment, and could result in civil and criminal liability on the part of the security officer and civil liability on the part of the lodging property. Except for a felony or misdemeanor arrest when and where permitted under state law, or except as provided for in some areas by state statutes relating very specifically to shoplifting, no other involuntary detention or confinement should be attempted. Any person who voluntarily consents to being detained must clearly understand that he or she is free to leave at any time.

Even situations in which sworn police officers make an arrest in response to a hotel complaint may present the lodging property with a potential problem. If a guest or patron is arrested without justification at the instigation of the hotel, the property might be faced with a suit for malicious prosecution.

Search. When a security officer makes a legal citizen's arrest for a felony or misdemeanor, the right of self-defense may in some states justify a search for an offensive weapon under certain circumstances. Individual properties, however, should check with local counsel to determine what circumstances, if any, would justify a search by a private citizen incidental to a lawful arrest. If a person consents voluntarily to a search, the consent should be obtained by the security officer in writing if at all possible, and should be witnessed by at least one other individual.

Use of force. Generally speaking, a private citizen may use only such force as is reasonably necessary to effect a lawful arrest or to prevent the escape of a person from custody who has been lawfully arrested. If excessive or unreasonable force is used, the security officer may be subject to criminal action by the state, and both he or she and the lodging property may be subject to a civil action for damages by the person against whom force was used.

No employee should use any force calculated to cause death or serious bodily harm unless there is a threat to his or her personal safety or the personal safety of another person. Deadly force should never be used to protect property.

The Team Concept. An important goal of a security training program is to turn a property's entire staff into a security-conscious team. The team concept may benefit a hotel in protecting guests, employees, and the property itself. In the team approach, all department heads and supervisors regard security as an aspect of their jobs. While they usually are not directly involved in routine security assignments, they can be invaluable in maintaining the security of the property. Similarly, each employee has a responsibility to assist in a security capacity. It is essential, for example, that room attendants call the security office or the property's management when they notice a suspicious person in the guestroom area or back in the service areas of the property. Such alertness on the part of employees has been instrumental in many cases in the prevention of incidents and in the arrest of criminals. Whether the security role is incorporated in the activities of an assistant manager, a resident manager, or an owner-manager at the small property level, or in the role of a full-time director of security at a large property, the team concept is still valid. Employees in properties of any size can, for example, be instructed to:

- Be alert to and report any suspicious activities or persons anywhere on the property.

- Avoid confronting a suspicious individual. Instead, the employee should step into a secured area (guestroom, locked linen room, or other space containing a phone), lock the door, and call the office designated to receive such emergency calls.

- Report any drug paraphernalia or other suspicious items that may be exposed to public view when working within a guestroom. (Never search through a guest's luggage or property, however.) In one case, a jewel thief was arrested when a room attendant noticed an open case filled with jewelry. The thief stayed at one hotel while breaking into the other hotels in the community. In another case, a thief left a case of burglar tools open.

- Alert security when rooming guests with large but empty pieces of luggage.

- Check on the proper posting of innkeeper laws, as the posting of such laws may be required in the jurisdiction in which the hotel is located.

- Check to make sure that any information cards or tent cards provided for the guest's information on security are in their proper locations.

This list contains only a brief selection from the wide range of activities a security training program can prepare a staff to perform. Every property will be able to construct its own list to deal with its unique security concerns.

In 1993, the "Traveler Safety Campaign" was introduced by the American Hotel & Lodging Association to inform the traveling public of safety/security concerns and enlist them as members of the lodging security team. The initiative included the following participating members:

- American Automobile Association (AAA)

- American Association of Retired Persons (AARP)

- American Society of Travel Agents (ASTA)

- National Crime Prevention Council and its mascot, McGruff the Crime Dog

Millions of "Traveler Safety Tips" cards (see Exhibit 2) were distributed and displayed in guestrooms. Some hotel chains incorporated the ten suggestions on their guestroom key folders. A video was also made available for review by guests on the information channel in each guestroom. There have been instances where crimes have been prevented when guests have followed the campaign's recommendation of calling the front desk to report a suspicious person or incident.

Security and the Law

Every state has its own statutes and court rulings on innkeeper laws. These laws deal with the rights and responsibilities of innkeepers and can be fairly extensive. Although such laws almost invariably deal with the same general topics, they can differ from state to state. Lodging management and security personnel should read the innkeeper statutory laws of their state. The understanding gained from this information can contribute to the development of a more effective security program.

Also, in determining what elements might be included in a particular security program, it may be wise to review recent court and jury decisions that deal with hotel security matters. Many recent cases have addressed one or more of the following issues: locking systems, key control, security personnel on the premises, lighting, door viewports or peepholes, police liaison, foreseeability or prior notice, crime in the community, security efforts tailored to the needs of a specific property, and the involvement of employees as the hotel "eyes and ears" with regard to the security function. Expert witnesses for the plaintiff frequently stress these areas of concern in depositions.

The frequency of all types of lawsuits is increasing annually, and hotels, motels, inns, clubs, restaurants, and resorts are not immune from this trend. Management cannot afford to ignore the financial ramifications associated with costly settlements. The hospitality industry, with its special emphasis on people and personal services, represents an area where the possibility for litigation is very great.

Legal Definitions

Generally, in a suit alleging negligence, the plaintiff must show that the **defendant** innkeeper had a duty to use reasonable care to protect the plaintiff or victim from foreseeable acts; that the defendant failed to perform this duty; that this failure was the proximate cause of the incident; and that the plaintiff actually suffered loss or injury.

The central legal issue is that innkeepers owe a duty of care to all persons on their properties. Failure to meet this duty may result in security-related liability. In most states, the innkeepers' duty or standard of care is legally defined as taking reasonable care to protect against foreseeable acts. There is probably no concept that has affected the lodging industry more than the court interpretation of **reasonable care**. Unfortunately for the innkeeper, there is no concise and clear-cut determination of what a court or jury may consider reasonable care in any given case. Whether reasonable care is exercised depends on the facts and circumstances in each case.

Like reasonable care, **foreseeability** is an imprecise term. Courts and juries may consider certain consequences foreseeable at some properties and not at others. Factors that may help determine foreseeability at a given property include the prior incidence of that type or similar types of crime on the premises, the prior incidence of all types of crime on the premises, and (in an increasing number of cases) the crime rate of the surrounding community. The practical result of many court and jury decisions as they relate to foreseeability has been to expand the innkeeper's duty to include being aware of criminal activities both on- and off-premises. For example, if certain crimes are taking place in a community, a court or jury might decide that a reasonable innkeeper should foresee the possibility of a similar crime happening on-premises; if such a crime does indeed occur on-premises and the victim alleges negligence on the innkeeper's part in not taking reasonable steps to prevent such a crime, it may be difficult for the innkeeper to plead successfully that he or she did not know about the crimes in the community if they were generally known.

Simply failing in a duty does not in itself establish liability for negligence. The breach of a duty to exercise reasonable care must be shown to be the underlying **proximate cause** of an incident. Proximate cause, sometimes called **legal cause,** is usually defined as that primary moving predominating cause from which an injury follows as a natural, direct, and immediate consequence, and without which the injury would not have occurred. It is not sufficient that the defendant's conduct has been one of the causes of the plaintiff's injury. It must be the proximate cause, which is sometimes said to depend on whether the conduct has been so significant and important a cause that the defendant should be legally responsible. A proximate cause of an incident need not be its only cause.

Foreseeability is again a factor. **Negligence** involves a foreseeable risk, a threatened danger of injury, and an injury that is caused by conduct unreasonable in proportion to the foreseeable danger. For example, if someone carelessly leaves a can of gasoline near an open flame and the gas then explodes, causing injury, a jury might find that such an act created a foreseeable risk of harm and that the injury was caused by conduct unreasonable in proportion to the foreseeable risk.

Suits alleging negligence request that the defendant be required to pay **damages**. There are two types of damages: compensatory and punitive. **Compensatory damages** are awarded to compensate the plaintiff for pain and suffering, loss of income during a period of absence from work, medical and hospital expenses, and recuperative facility or home-service expenses. Compensatory damages may sometimes be covered, perhaps after the payment of a deductible, by an individual's or corporation's liability insurance policy. In recent years, there has been a trend within the courts for juries to assess punitive damages in addition to compensatory damages. **Punitive damages** are damages awarded against a person to punish him or her for outrageous conduct. The chief purpose of punitive damages is to inflict punishment as an example and a deterrent to similar conduct. Some courts have allowed insurance coverage for punitive damages under certain circumstances, while other courts have disallowed insurance coverage of punitive damages as a matter of public policy. The size of punitive damage awards can be substantial, sometimes totaling several million dollars.

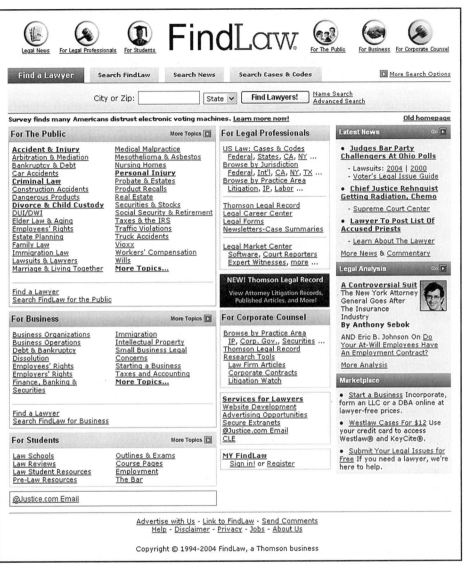

Nominated by the Webby Awards as one of the five best "Politics & Law" sites on the Internet, FindLaw (www.findlaw.com) offers a variety of free services designed to make legal and government information easy to find online.

The court in which a suit or case is first tried is often called the **trial court.** The suit is filed by the plaintiff against the defendant. At the commencement of a lawsuit, the defendant can ask for dismissal of the complaint. If the allegations in the plaintiff's complaint fail to establish a valid legal claim or the defendant has an absolute affirmative defense, the complaint should be dismissed. After each party has had an opportunity to discover the facts of the case, but before the case is tried, either the plaintiff or the defendant can ask for a **summary judgment.** A defendant can be granted summary judgment if, upon undisputed facts, the plaintiff fails to meet the factual and legal requirements to establish the case. A plaintiff can be granted summary judgment if, upon undisputed facts, the defendant's liability is absolute—that is, the plaintiff has a valid legal claim supported by the facts and no defense is possible. The jury will then deliberate only the amount of damages to be awarded.

After the close of proofs offered in evidence, either the plaintiff or defendant can ask for a **directed verdict.** The defendant can contend that it should be granted a directed verdict because the plaintiff failed to prove its cause of action. The plaintiff can request a directed verdict claiming that the defendant has been unable to establish a defense. Directed verdicts are rendered by judges, not juries.

If the case goes to the jury and the jury returns a decision, the losing party can ask for **judgment n.o.v. (notwithstanding the verdict)** and/or a new trial. In granting judgment n.o.v., the trial judge overrules all or part of the jury verdict. The judge can also grant a new trial.

Whichever party loses the suit can appeal the decision. The party appealing is the **appellant;** the party appealed against is the **appellee** or **respondent.**

Summary

From the earliest days of the hospitality industry, one of the most important duties of an innkeeper has been to protect guests from harm while on the property. Although interpretations of protection may vary from state to state, every legal jurisdiction imposes some form of security obligation on hotels. Of course, the industry's concern with security increased greatly after the terrorist attacks of September 11, 2001.

A hotel's security program should stress the prevention of security problems. It is far more desirable to keep security incidents from occurring than to catch a criminal after a crime has been committed. Certain actions and procedures may help to prevent or discourage incidents. Nonetheless, it must be recognized that not all crime is preventable.

There are many areas that require security control in a hotel, including offices, pool and fitness centers, meeting rooms, storerooms and lockers, and other areas. Guestroom-access security is the most common security need, however. Electronic guestroom locks have replaced mechanical systems in most lodging properties. Electronic systems have great flexibility; different key types can be issued to guests and hotel employees. Typically, these systems can record every authorized entry and every unauthorized entry attempt. Guestroom door locks may include chains or other backup locks on the inside of the door, so that guests can control access once they are in the room. Most guestroom locks have a deadbolt mechanism of some type.

By their nature and history, hotels hold themselves open for public accommodation. However, hotels are private property, and therefore people can be excluded if they have no specific reason for being on the premises. Staff training should include how to identify people who may not belong at the hotel. For many hotels, surveillance systems involving video cameras, motion detectors, and other security devices assist in this effort. Some hotels have signs posted stating that they are private property. This public warning may be required to take advantage of local trespass laws.

Perimeter and grounds control can take many forms. Surveillance systems are very useful in providing security monitoring of such outdoor areas as parking lots, pools, tennis courts, and other areas. Parking lots should be well-lit, and may also have gates to control traffic; sometimes these gates are staffed for extra protection. Fences are often needed to separate the hotel from its neighbors. The hotel management should train valet parking attendants, landscape staff, maintenance staff, and others to watch for unauthorized people on the grounds.

Important devices for securing guest assets are the hotel safe deposit boxes and, for those hotels that offer them, in-room safes. All states require hotels to provide some sort of safe deposit box facility for guests at no charge. Hotels must also protect the assets of employees. Employee changing and locker rooms should be secure and safe. Many hotels provide locks for employees. Most departments have secure storage areas for women's purses and other items that may be needed during the day. Good front desk designs allow for lockable drawers at the front desk or in a nearby area for use by employees.

When hotel guests use payment cards to settle purchases, a whole series of security issues arise because these cards contain sensitive information. Staff must be trained in proper procedures for safeguarding transaction information. In addition, the payment card industry imposes mandatory software and hardware protocols dealing with the storage and transmission of payment card data. Hotel staff must be especially sensitive to the fact that guest information, in the wrong hands, can help a criminal facilitate identity theft. For this reason, the hotel must safeguard files and business records.

Every hotel will have emergencies. They may be injuries, robberies, destruction of assets, fires, or other situations that require extraordinary action on the part of the hotel staff. The hotel should have well-documented procedures for all anticipated emergencies. One of the most important emergency procedures is to assist guests with disabilities during an emergency.

The hotel must have a plan in place for giving guests medical assistance when necessary. Guests can be referred to doctors or hospitals, or in real emergencies, the local emergency medical service (EMS) should be contacted. However, there should be clear instructions to employees on when to call for EMS assistance.

All lodging properties should keep good security records. Security records are important for several reasons. First, they allow hotel management to track security issues. Second, they help protect the hotel from legal action. Third, they may assist the hotel with insurance claims, either by the hotel's insurance carrier or a guest's. Security records can present the hotel's view of what happened. This is especially helpful when hotel staff members are called upon to describe a security incident that occurred many months ago.

Whether or not a hotel has a full-time security staff, no security staff can be everywhere at once. Therefore, every hotel employee needs to be trained to identify security issues and to know what to do when they are discovered. Training can include company-provided security training programs, as well as visits by local police departments. All employees should be given a thorough security orientation at the time they are hired and should be regularly exposed to an ongoing security education program throughout their term of employment. Comprehensive training should include all aspects of the protection of guests, the general public, employees, and the assets of guests, employees, and the property.

When a property uses an in-house security staff, it is obvious to all concerned that the property is responsible for the actions of its staff. The property cannot evade this responsibility merely by using off-duty officers or a contract security service, because these security officers are usually considered the hotel's agents. If the security officers are negligent, the property may be held liable. Hiring a security service does not relieve a property of its legal responsibility to provide reasonable care.

The use of off-duty police officers poses certain potential legal problems as well. If an off-duty officer uses his or her legal authority to arrest someone who then proves that the arrest was inappropriate, whose agent is the officer: the community's or the property's? In some cases, the officer is considered the property's agent. This means the property could be held liable for false arrest and false imprisonment. Similar liability could result if an armed officer unlawfully injures someone.

The presence of a uniformed security officer may connote to some people the image of a public law enforcement officer. However, a hotel security officer, in the absence of any special commission, deputization, ordinance, or state statute, possesses no greater authority than any other private citizen. However, because the security officer can be involved in protective functions on a daily basis, he or she may be in a position to use certain powers more than most other private citizens. The exercise of these powers may involve nothing more than simply stopping undesired conduct, or it may involve making a citizen's arrest. In *all* actions that interfere with the rights of others, the security officer should endeavor to obtain consent and voluntary cooperation from the person being interfered with. Criminal statutes set limits on the behavior of lodging security officers. Activity beyond these limits may result in criminal charges being filed against the officers for assault, battery, manslaughter, or other crimes.

Every state has its own statutes and court rulings on innkeeper laws. These laws deal with the rights and responsibilities of innkeepers and can be fairly extensive. Although such laws almost invariably deal with the same general topics, they can differ from state to state. Lodging management and security personnel should read the innkeeper statutory laws of their state. The understanding gained from this information can contribute to the development of a more effective security program.

Endnotes

1.   Much of the remainder of this section is drawn from Mark G. Haley and Daniel J. Connolly, *The Payment Card Industry Compliance Process for Lodging Establishments* (Lansing, Mich.: American Hotel & Lodging Educational Institute, 2008); and *Principles of Privacy: Defining and Implementing Sound Privacy Practices in Hospitality* (Lansing, Mich.: American Hotel & Lodging Educational Institute, 2005).

2.   For more information, contact the American Hotel & Lodging Educational Institute, 2113 N. High Street, Lansing, MI 48906, 800-349-0299 or 407-999-8100.

3. For more information on this program, contact the American Hotel & Lodging Educational Institute, 2113 N. High Street, Lansing, MI 48906, 800-349-0299 or 407-999-8100, or see *Lodging Security Officer Training Program* (Lansing, Mich.: American Hotel & Lodging Educational Institute, 1995).

🔑 Key Terms

appellant—The party appealing a previous court decision.

appellee—The party appealed against. Also known as the respondent.

citizen's arrest—Common law in most states, a citizen's arrest permits arrest by private citizens when an individual is *lawfully* deprived of his or her freedom. It should be done only if a sworn police officer cannot respond in time and good judgment requires prompt action.

compensatory damages—Damages awarded to compensate the plaintiff for pain and suffering, loss of income during a period of absence from work, medical and hospital expenses, and recuperative facility or home-service expenses.

damages—Monetary awards paid by the defendant to compensate the plaintiff, to punish the defendant, or both.

defendant—The side the suit is brought against.

directed verdict—An immediate decision rendered by a judge after the close of evidence, because either side failed to prove its cause.

foreseeability—The reasonable likelihood that a specific future incident could have been foreseen—and, therefore, prevented—based on knowledge of past similar incidents on the premises or in the surrounding community.

judgment n.o.v. (notwithstanding the verdict)—A judgment by a trial judge that overrules all or part of the jury verdict.

legal cause—The primary or predominating cause from which an injury follows as a natural, direct, and immediate consequence, and without which the injury would not have occurred. Also known as proximate cause.

negligence—Failure to exercise the care that a reasonably prudent person would exercise under like or similar circumstances.

plaintiff—The side that initiates and files the suit.

proximate cause—The primary or predominating cause from which an injury follows as a natural, direct, and immediate consequence, and without which the injury would not have occurred. Also known as legal cause.

punitive damages—Damages awarded against a person as punishment for outrageous conduct; punitive damages also act as a deterrent to similar conduct.

reasonable care—Actions that are ordinary or usual to protect against a foreseeable event—the central legal issue being that innkeepers owe a duty of care to all persons on their property. Failure to meet this duty may result in security-related liability.

respondent—The party appealed against. Also known as the appellee.

security—Protecting people and assets. Security efforts may involve such areas of concern as guestroom security, key control, locks, access and perimeter control, alarm and communication systems, lighting, closed-circuit television, safe deposit boxes, inventory control, credit and billing procedures, computer security, staffing, pre-employment screening, employee training, responsible service of alcoholic beverages, emergency and safety procedures, and recordkeeping.

summary judgment—A judgment granted (1) to the defendant when the plaintiff fails to meet the factual and legal requirements to establish its case, or (2) to the plaintiff when a valid legal claim exists supported by the facts with no possible defense.

tort law—Provides the basis for actions permitting one person to remedy a wrong committed against him or her by another. For example, it permits an injured party to bring a lawsuit for damages against a security officer and the employing property for such unreasonable conduct as false arrest, false imprisonment, malicious prosecution, defamation, and slander.

trial court—The court in which a suit or case is first tried.

 Review Questions

1. What are the general areas that should be considered for inclusion in a property's security program?

2. What are the main areas of vulnerability that create security problems for hotels?

3. Why is it important to cultivate a law enforcement liaison?

4. What are the various types of security staffing? What are the advantages and disadvantages of each?

5. Why is security training for the hotel staff so important? Why is good security recordkeeping so important?

6. Why is training critical to an effective security program? What specific elements should be incorporated into a training program? What are some of the myths about training?

7. Should security guards be armed? Why or why not?

8. What is the extent of a security officer's authority? What types of behavior can the officer legally engage in? What activities could result in civil and criminal liability?

9. What does the term *team concept* refer to in a security training program? What are some things that all employees can be instructed to do?

10. How can courts in different states come to different conclusions regarding similar issues?

Internet Sites

For more information, visit the following Internet sites. Remember that Internet addresses can change without notice. If the site is no longer there, you can use a search engine to look for additional sites.

American Hotel & Lodging
  Association (AH&LA)
www.ahla.com

American Hotel & Lodging
  Educational Institute
www.ahlei.org

American Society of Travel Agents
  (ASTA)
www.asta.org

CISA Security Products, Inc.
www.repla.com

FindLaw: Internet legal resources
www.findlaw.com

International Association of Chiefs of
  Police
www.theiacp.org

International Association of
  Professional Security Consultants
www.iapsc.org

International Foundation for
  Protection Officers
www.ifpo.com

National Crime Prevention Council
www.ncpc.org

National Fire Protection Association
  (NFPA)
www.nfpa.org

National Institute of Justice
www.ojp.usdoj.gov/nij

Case Studies

Steve's Royal Problem

Steve Tritsch was enjoying his first month as a full-fledged GM. He'd enjoyed his previous position at a large downtown property in Philadelphia. In fact, his GM there had been a valuable reference for his new job. But it was exciting to now be out on his own. Although the Royal Court was a smaller property, with 198 rooms, it was still a full-service hotel with numerous strengths: it was in a prime location just off the expressway, it was a well-known brand with a national reputation, and it seemed to have an excellent, well-trained staff. The only real problem was financial. Apparently, the previous GM had not been able to turn those strengths into a sufficient number of bookings. Steve's job was to keep expenses down, increase revenue as much as possible, and turn the Royal Court around. After thirty days on the job, he was well on his way to turning those goals into realities.

Then the letter from Lawhead, Alexander, and Fisk arrived. Apparently, a female guest had her purse snatched in the hotel's parking lot three months ago, on June 4. Now her attorneys were threatening to file suit unless the Royal Court made restitution. They requested payment of $25,000 as compensation for their client's loss of property, multiple injuries, and pain and suffering.

Steve took a deep breath. He knew what writing a check for $25,000 would do to his property's struggling bottom line: $25,000 represented an awful lot of room nights—especially when his insurance deductible was twice that amount. But he also wondered if the letter might be nothing more than an empty threat. He had to get the facts.

First, he checked the previous GM's files for any record of the incident. Although he did find one folder labeled "On-Premises Security," it contained only a form letter of dismissal that had apparently been sent to all of the hotel's security staff this past March, six months ago. He also paged through the previous GM's planner and found no notations regarding a June 4 incident. Increasingly frustrated, he dialed his executive housekeeper, a 15-year veteran who seemed to have an almost infallible memory. "Ginnie, do you remember anything about a purse snatching earlier this year?" Steve asked.

"You'll have to be more specific than that, Steve," she said. "There was one in late winter that happened in the corridor upstairs, and there was another one in June. That was out in the parking lot."

"So, it's true," Steve said. "A guest got injured during a purse snatching on our property."

"Well, there were injuries," Ginnie began, "but I seem to remember that she wasn't exactly a guest. I'd want to check on that."

"Thanks. I'll take care of it," ended Steve.

Steve picked up the letter and walked down to the front desk. Malia Etoise, another long-time staff member, was working this afternoon. "Hi, Malia. I need to find out if," he glanced down at the letter, "a Lauren Heidegger was a guest here on June third or fourth."

Malia entered the necessary information into her computer terminal. "Hmm," she began, "I'm not showing a Lauren Heidegger or any Heideggers for those dates. But for some reason that name's ringing a bell."

"She's claiming to have been the victim of a purse snatching on June 4," Steve prompted.

"Oh, I remember that," Malia said, nodding her head. "It was awful. She came running in here and her knees were bleeding and her dress was torn. Once all the other women heard about it, there was total chaos for a while."

"All the other women?" Steve asked.

"Mrs. Heidegger was here for a women's luncheon of some kind. I don't remember all the details. But once the word spread, women just streamed out of the Briar Room and filled the lobby wanting to know everything that happened, wanting us to call the police."

"Which you did, of course," Steve stated in a matter-of-fact tone.

Malia paused for a moment. "Yes, that time I'm sure we did call the police."

"That time? So, there were other incidents when you didn't call the police?" Steve asked.

Malia rolled her eyes and nodded. "Not my choice. But the way it was explained to me was that all police calls show up in the newspaper, and your predecessor didn't want that kind of publicity."

Steve returned to his office and fell into his chair, not certain what his next step should be. It certainly sounded as if the incident had occurred on Royal Court property and that there were witnesses to that fact. But Mrs. Heidegger wasn't a guest after all; maybe the property wasn't liable. Besides, the previous GM hadn't even felt the incident warranted a written record. At Steve's former job, the hotel was large enough to afford a full-time security staff and he hadn't paid much attention to their work. Now, it seemed the responsibility for security rested firmly on his shoulders, but he was stymied. "Maybe Carson has some advice for me," Steve thought, recalling how his former boss had gone out of his way to be a mentor for him. He picked up the phone.

"That's a tough spot," Carson agreed. "But I'm sure you'll handle it fine."

"Great," Steve said, sounding less than confident. "Where do I go from here?"

"I'll lay it out for you," Carson replied. "First, call the legal department at the corporate office. Let them know about the letter and that you're researching the matter. They may ask a lot of questions you can't answer yet, but you'll get the answers as you continue the investigation."

"To me the only real question is: do we settle or go to court?" Steve remarked curtly.

Carson calmly replied, "But you can't answer that until you know how strong your position is. You need to find out whether your operation has taken 'reasonable care.' There aren't any hard-and-fast rules about what that is—it can vary from community to community. You need to find out what reasonable care means for your location.

"First, contact the police department and get a computer print-out of all the calls made to your address. They can probably do it while you wait. Now, some incidents on that list may not really involve your hotel at all—maybe there was a car accident on the street and the driver came in to use the phone, that kind of thing. You'll need to go through the list and find out which incidents do apply.

"Next, I'd call up the local newspaper and ask them to search their morgue for all of the stories with the name of your hotel in it. Chances are, any problems that would generate a police call would also show up in the newspaper. There might even be some mentions in the paper that didn't involve the police. Give the newspaper's librarian a couple of days to get the information you need.

"While you're waiting, though, I'd recommend talking to some of the other GMs in your area. Ask them what types of crime problems they've had or are having. Some might not want to talk specifically about their own operation—you know, nobody wants to give the impression that their place isn't as safe as can be—but you should be able to get a good feel about what kind of neighborhood you're in.

"You've already started talking to your staff, and that's good. I'd suggest that you do more of that. Just walk around and ask your people what incidents they might remember, what their overall impression is of hotel security and crime in the area."

"Carson," Steve interrupted, "you and I both know that perceptions aren't always accurate. They're subjective."

"That's true," Carson replied. "But, accurate or not, do you want a dozen members of your staff on the witness stand telling a jury that they didn't feel safe at the Royal Court Hotel? I don't think so. Better to find out sooner than later."

"I understand," Steve sighed.

"One last thing," Carson added. "Drive around your neighborhood and try to see it through the eyes of a plaintiff's attorney who wants to prove negligence. Is yours the only property without a fence? Without security lighting? In other words, does it look as if you care about security?"

The next few days proved both valuable and anxiety-filled.

The police call sheet noted only the June purse snatching, not the late-winter incident that Ginnie remembered. But it also listed three car burglaries in the parking lot, one break-in during a wedding reception (in which the bride and groom's wedding gifts and honeymoon luggage were stolen), some vending machine vandalism, and two calls in response to guestroom parties that resulted in property damage. All during the last twelve months.

The first local GM Steve called began the conversation by thanking Steve's predecessor. "If he hadn't let those three security officers go," she said, "I'd still be reviewing résumés." She went on to explain that a rise in criminal activity throughout the area had led most of the other hotels to actually increase their security. As far as she knew, Royal Court was the only property to eliminate staff—and she had immediately added two of them to her payroll. Another property down the road had hired the third security officer. "I think a lot of us felt he was just shooting himself in the foot," she admitted. "Sure, he saved some money up front—and I know things have been tight for everybody—but...." She didn't have to finish the sentence. Steve was beginning to understand.

Other incidents surfaced once Steve began chatting with his staff. Some tires were slashed by vandals. Some fights erupted in the bar. Malia recalled that there had even been rumors that the Royal Court recently had a reputation as a favored place to buy drugs for dealers who wanted fast interstate access. That activity had diminished, though, when the Carriage Bridge Hotel across the street started offering doughnuts and coffee to the police working the night shift; the close proximity of a squad car was enough to scare the dealers away—at least at night. Unfortunately, that didn't completely convince the staff at the Royal Court. Some employees continued to ask not to work the night shift and others only entered and left the hotel in pairs.

The newspaper search only confirmed what Steve had already learned: the Royal Court had seen more than its share of security problems. Apparently, he'd just been lucky in not seeing any new incidents during his first thirty days on the job. He realized that luck was not good enough. Not only did he have to present the facts of his investigation to the corporate legal department along with his recommendation, he also had to implement an effective security program immediately.

With his notes in front of him, Steve picked up the telephone and placed a call to the corporate office.

Discussion Questions

1. What evidence can Steve share with the corporate legal department that would support a recommendation either to settle for $25,000 or to take the case to court?

2. What steps can Steve and his staff take to effectively reduce the number of security incidents at the Royal Court, while still working to keep expenses to a minimum?

Case Number: 3871CA

The following industry experts helped generate and develop this case: Wendell Couch, ARM, CHA, Director of Technical Services for the Risk Management Department of Bass Hotels & Resorts; and Raymond C. Ellis, Jr., CHE, CHTP, CLSD, Professor, Conrad N. Hilton College, University of Houston, Director, Loss Prevention Management Institute.

Doughnuts and Dilemmas

Phil Watson, the general manager of the Bluestone Hotel, was just settling down to some early morning paperwork when the buzzer on his intercom sounded. He pushed the speaker button: "Yes, Jean?"

"There's a Douglas Koneval on line two. He wants to know if you've still got 'Calamity Jane' in your 'bag.' He said you'd know what he's talking about."

Phil chuckled. "Put him through, put him through." Phil waited for the muffled click, and then said: "Doug!"

"Phil! You still trying to make putts with that beat-up old putter of yours!?"

"Hey, that putter was good enough to send you back to the clubhouse a broken and defeated man! How've you been? I haven't heard from you in a while."

"Actually, I've been pretty busy," Doug said. "You heard I'm at the Wellington now, right?"

The Wellington was an independent hotel upstate. "No, I didn't know that."

"Yes, I took the GM job a couple of months ago."

"Your first job as a general manager! That's great! How's it working out for you?"

"Well, that's why I'm calling. Things have been going pretty smoothly so far—there's a good staff here, and I've got ideas for improving some things, but something happened yesterday that got me thinking about security issues here at the hotel. It was nothing major—we had a loud guest get a little belligerent when we asked him to quiet down—but it hit me that I don't have a contact at the local police department yet and I really don't know how to go about making one. You've been at the Bluestone for a lot of years, and I know you have an excellent relationship with the police. I was hoping I could pick your brain a bit this morning and get some ideas on how I can establish a good relationship with the police here in my little community."

Phil laughed. "Well, I don't know that I've got anything spectacular to offer, but I can share some basics with you that just about any general manager would probably try."

"That's just what I need."

"Well," Phil began, "the first thing I'd do is arrange to have lunch with the police chief. I can't remember—does the Wellington have F&B?"

"Yes, we have a nice little restaurant on-site."

"Well, I'd invite him to the restaurant. Is the police chief a 'him' or a 'her,' by · the way?"

"It's a 'him,'" Doug replied. "Malcolm Ramsey is his name. I've never met him, but I've heard he's an okay guy to deal with."

"Invite Malcolm to the restaurant, have a nice lunch, and just introduce yourself and get to know him a little. If he has the time, ask him to walk around the property with you after lunch and point out any security concerns you should be aware of."

"Great idea! I could even have him write something up for me, a report that I could—"

"Whoa, stop right there!" Phil interjected. "You do not want anything in writing from Malcolm."

"I don't? Why not? He might come up with some great suggestions that would really make the property safe."

"Yes, he might, but he might also come up with suggestions that you could never afford to implement. If you have a written report lying around with some security advice in it that you didn't act on and something happens at the hotel—" Phil shrugged. "You could be in serious trouble if that report winds up in court."

"Good point. Okay, nothing in writing. What else should I do?"

"Well, let Malcolm know that you're interested in a good relationship with his department and that you're willing to do what you can to accommodate his officers. Let him know that officers out on patrol are welcome to stop by and use the hotel's restrooms, for example. If the officers are tired of writing out police reports with their clipboards balanced on their knees or on a steering wheel, they can come by and use a table in the employee breakroom. And they're welcome to just stop by for coffee and pastries."

"Doughnuts still work," Doug laughed.

"Yes, they do," Phil agreed. "And little courtesies can pay big dividends when something happens at your property. Three weeks ago we had a 'domestic situation' occur in one of our rooms. Our front desk got a call around midnight—'Hey, there's a racket going on next door, I can't sleep'—and Sylvia at the front desk says, 'Okay, I'll take care of it.' She calls the room—410, I think it was—and asks them to pipe down. She gets a response like: 'Oh, no problem. Sorry,' et cetera, et cetera. A few minutes later, the phone rings again—'Hey, they're still going at it in Room 410; now some woman's crying in there'—so Sylvia contacts the security guard and the manager on duty, Bret Russell. The two of them go up to the room and knock on the door. 'What's going on? Is everyone okay?' 'Yeah, yeah,' the man inside says, 'we're just arguing a little bit.' 'Open the door, please.' So the door opens and this guy is standing there in his underwear, the desk lamp's turned over, and a woman's standing on the other side of the bed in a nightshirt, a hand cupped over one eye. 'Ma'am, are you okay?' 'Yeah, I'm okay, we're just having a little disagreement, that's all. Everything's cool.' 'Are you sure?' 'Yeah, we're done.' 'We'll pay for the damages,' the guy says, so Bret says, 'All right, we'll leave, but take it easy in here, okay?' 'Sure thing, we're sorry,' the guy says. So Bret and the security guard leave the room and they don't even get all the way down the hall to the elevator before they hear the guy start yelling again and another lamp go over. 'That's it,' Bret says, 'we're calling the police.'

"And the officers were great. Two squad cars were at the hotel within five minutes, and ten minutes later the husband was in one of them, on his way to jail. The other officer stayed with the wife while she packed and went to the front desk to pay the bill, then he took her to a shelter for battered women. The whole thing was over in twenty minutes and they handled it beautifully. Real quiet. None of the other guests even knew the officers had been there."

"That's the kind of cooperation I'm looking for," Doug said. "What about hiring off-duty police officers for hotel security work? Is that a good idea?"

"Two words," Phil replied. "'No guns.'"

"'No guns'?"

"That's right. Off-duty officers can be good additions to your staff—if you tell them that you don't want guns on your property. It's a liability issue. Even though these officers are on the city's police force, when you hire them, they're working for you. If they accidentally shoot an innocent bystander, the hotel is on the hook, not the city."

"That's good to know," Doug said. "Should I just approach the officers individually with offers?"

"I'd ask the chief about it during your lunch with him. Just tell him what you're considering, and ask him what his policy is. Some police departments don't allow their officers to do freelance security work. At the other extreme, some departments have a sergeant in charge of evenly distributing that kind of work among the officers. Other departments let individual officers cut their own deals."

"You've given me a lot to think about," Doug said, in that tone of voice people get when they are winding down their phone call. "I really want to get started on the right foot with Malcolm. A good relationship with the police is really important."

Phil took his cue to sum up. "Well, the thing to do first is to set up a lunch with Malcolm and let him know that you want to do what it takes to have a positive working relationship with his department."

"Hey, thanks for the time, Phil. I gotta run, but I really appreciate your ideas. I'll let you know how things work out."

"Do that, Doug, and best of luck to you. I know you'll do well."

Phil no sooner hung up the telephone when the intercom buzzer sounded again. "Yes, Jean?"

"Lieutenant Foster is here to see you."

What a coincidence, Phil thought. "Send him in, please."

The office door opened and Jean showed in one of the lieutenants on the local police force. Phil came around from behind his desk and shook his hand warmly. "Hi, Glenn, nice to see you again. What brings you out our way?"

"Good morning, Phil." Glenn took a seat in one of the two chairs in front of Phil's desk. Phil, rather than sit behind his desk, sat in the other.

"I got a problem that maybe you can help me with," Glenn continued. "The FBI called me a few minutes ago, looking for—," Glenn paused to pull a notebook out of the inside pocket of his sport coat—"looking for a 'Ruben Drosha.' I guess this guy's really bad news. We need to know if he's at the hotel, what phone calls he's made, and his credit card number. They're trying to track where he's been. You know the drill."

Phil shifted in his seat uncomfortably. "Do you have subpoenas for any of that stuff, Glenn? Because if you don't, you know the only thing I can legally tell you is whether he's registered at the hotel."

Glenn snorted. "Get real, Phil, this is a Saturday. All the judges are up north getting their fishing boats out about now. Like I said, the FBI just called me. I was hoping we could keep this on an informal, friendly basis."

Phil shook his head. "Sorry, Glenn, but I just can't do it. I can tell you if he's here or not, and I can put a call through to his room if you want to talk to him, but that's as far as I can go without a court order."

"I'm sorry you feel that way." Glenn stood up, signaling an end to the discussion. Phil stood up, too. "The chief will be disappointed. He thought you'd be more cooperative," Glenn said quietly. "But I guess you gotta do what you gotta do. Let's go check reservations and see if Drosha's here. It's not much, but at least I won't go back to the FBI entirely empty-handed."

Discussion Questions

1. In addition to the things Phil mentioned to Doug, what other things can Doug do to promote a good relationship with his local police department?

2. The "domestic situation" that occurred at Phil's hotel could have turned out much worse. What are some of the things that could have gone wrong, had it been handled less effectively by hotel staff members?

3. Despite Phil's advice to Doug about establishing a good working relationship with the police, and despite Phil's wish to preserve his relationship with his own local police force, Phil turned down Lieutenant Foster's request for information about a man wanted by the FBI. Why did Phil refuse to give Foster all of the information he wanted?

Case Number: 3871CB

The following industry experts helped generate and develop this case: Wendell Couch, ARM, CHA, Director of Technical Services for the Risk Management Department of Bass Hotels & Resorts; and Raymond C. Ellis, Jr., CHE, CHTP, CLSD, Professor, Conrad N. Hilton College, University of Houston, Director, Loss Prevention Management Institute.

The Case of the Missing Jewels

It was 3:40 in the afternoon and I had been on property for less than an hour when I overheard a guest speaking rather loudly about something to do with the manager. It was a thick accent and coming from a woman who seemed to be rather upset. I couldn't tell if she was speaking English or not, but knew that the voice was one of an upset woman.

Within a minute, the front desk agent had come to my side to tell me that there was an Italian guest who spoke little English demanding to speak to the manager. She wasn't clear on what the problem was, but told me that the woman was very upset. Turning around I saw an elegantly dressed, elderly woman looking directly at me. I knew right away that she was with the wedding party that was up from Los Angeles. The bride had selected the resort many months ago, and today was the big day. Thus far, however, many of the wedding guests were not satisfied with their experience at the resort. It seemed that they would rather have been at a five-star hotel than an oceanside resort.

As I walked over to the guest, I made eye contact with her and smiled. I greeted her with my usual, "How can I be of service to you?" After a long while of trying to decipher her limited English combined with Italian, it became clear that her jewelry was missing. She claimed that jewelry valued at more than $2,000 had been stolen by our room attendants.

The guest was staying in the old south wing where the locks on the sliding glass doors are broken so it is not possible to lock the guestrooms completely. In addition, there are no safes in the rooms. However, the lodge does offer safe deposit boxes in the front office. We had never had a robbery before, but I never assume anything until I hear the whole story.

I patiently listened to the guest as she raised her voice accusing the room attendants and demanding that we pay her for her loss. I informed her that we would need to treat this as a theft and call the police so she could file a report. First, though, I asked her whether there could be any other reason the jewelry might be missing, because our room attendants are quite responsible and honest. She insisted that the jewelry had been stolen from the room, and she was ready to file the police report. She also continued to demand that we compensate her immediately.

I phoned the police.

The guest went back to her room still visibly upset.

I wondered if the lodge was responsible for the jewelry, since the registration card that the guest receives states that the property is not responsible for lost or stolen items.

The police arrived within a half hour. It took a while to complete the report, given the limited English of the guest. It was now time for the wedding to begin, so the guest departed, although still very disgruntled. She let all of us know that we didn't meet her high standards for service and luxury accommodations. I knew that she would be back as soon as the wedding was over to demand compensation for her jewels.

Later that afternoon, I retired to my office to consider my options. I wondered if this was really a security issue. I knew that the sliding glass doors could be secured if the bar was placed behind the door once it was closed. Security guards were always scheduled from 9 P.M. to 8 A.M., when the front office manager arrived. We had theft insurance, but it carried a high deductible. I wondered if the front desk agent who had checked in this guest had offered the use of the resort's safe deposit boxes.

Later that evening, as I was making my rounds, the father of the bride called me aside. He told me that the jewels had actually been worn by his daughter for the wedding but that her aunt hadn't remembered giving her permission the night before at the rehearsal dinner. I returned to my office and wondered whether I should let the police know that this was just another mistake.

Discussion Questions

1. How should the Manager on Duty (MOD) have approached the irate guest?

2. What steps would you have taken to gather the relevant information from the guest?

3. Would you have called the police?

4. Is the property following a good procedure for storing and protecting guest valuables?

Case number: 608C11

This case also appears in Todd Comen, *Case Studies in Front Office Management* (Lansing, Mich.: American Hotel & Lodging Educational Institute, 2003).

Chapter 8 Outline

Accounting Fundamentals
    Accounts
    Folios
    Vouchers
    Points of Sale
    Ledgers
Creation and Maintenance of Accounts
    Automated Recordkeeping Systems
    Charge Privileges
    Credit Monitoring
    Account Maintenance
Tracking Transactions
    Cash Payment
    Charge Purchase
    Account Correction
    Account Allowance
    Account Transfer
    Cash Advance
Internal Control
    Cash Banks
    Audit Controls
Settlement of Accounts
Summary

Competencies

1. Summarize front office accounting fundamentals, including issues surrounding accounts, folios, vouchers, points of sale, and ledgers. (pp. 307–313)

2. Describe the process of creating and maintaining front office accounts. (pp. 313–316)

3. Explain typical procedures for processing and tracking common front office accounting transactions. (pp. 316–321)

4. Describe internal control procedures for front office operations and explain typical settlement procedures. (pp. 321–327)

8

Front Office Accounting

WHILE FRONT OFFICE ACCOUNTING may seem intimidating at first, it is actually grounded in straightforward logic and requires only basic math skills. A front office accounting system monitors and charts the transactions of guests and businesses, agencies, and other non-guests using the hotel's services and facilities. The front office staff's ability to perform accounting tasks in an accurate and complete manner will directly affect the hotel's ability to collect revenue against **outstanding balances.**

This chapter examines the fundamentals of front office accounting, including creating and maintaining accounts, tracking transactions, adhering to internal control procedures, and settling accounts.

Accounting Fundamentals

An effective front office accounting system captures and records guest data during each stage of the guest cycle. During the pre-arrival stage, a front office accounting system captures data related to the type of reservation guarantee and tracks prepayments and advance deposits. When a guest arrives at the front desk, the front office accounting system documents the application of room rate and tax at registration. During occupancy, the system tracks authorized guest purchases at the hotel's revenue centers. Finally, the system helps ensure payment for outstanding goods and services at the time of check-out.

The financial transactions of non-guests may also be processed within the parameters of front office accounting. By allowing authorized non-guest transactions, a hotel can promote its services and facilities to local businesses, or track transactions related to conference business. The area of non-guest accounts may also include the accounts of former guests that were not properly settled at checkout. The responsibility for collecting non-guest account balances shifts from the front office to the back office accounting division.

In brief, a front office accounting system:

- Creates and maintains an accurate accounting record for each guest or non-guest account.

- Tracks financial transactions throughout the guest cycle.

- Ensures internal control over cash and non-cash transactions.

- Records settlement for all goods and services provided.

While there are generally accepted accounting principles for the lodging industry, front office accounting procedures are often uniquely tailored to each hotel operation. Accounting terminology and report formats often differ among hotels as well as between hotel chains. The following sections provide a brief review of some general concepts of front office accounting.

Accounts

An **account** is a form on which financial data are accumulated and summarized. An account may be imagined as a bin or container that stores the results of various business transactions. The increases and decreases in an account are calculated and the resulting monetary amount is the **account balance.** Any financial transaction that occurs in a hotel may affect several accounts. Front office accounts are recordkeeping devices to store information about guest and non-guest financial transactions.

In its simplest written form, an account resembles the letter T:

This form of recording is called a T-account. The growing use of front office automated systems has diminished the popularity of T-accounts. However, T-accounts remain a useful tool for teaching bookkeeping principles. For a front office account, *charges* are increases in the account balance and are entered on the left side of the T. *Payments* are decreases in the account balance and are entered on the right side of the T. The *account balance* is calculated by subtracting the T-account right-side total from the left-side total.

Front office accounting documents typically use a journal form. In a non-automated or semi-automated recordkeeping system, a journal form might contain the following information:

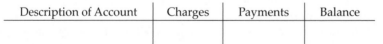

Similar to a T-account, increases in the account balance are entered under charges, while decreases in the account balance are entered under payments. In a fully automated system, charges and payments may be listed in a single column with the amounts of payments placed within parentheses or noted with minus signs to indicate their effect (a decrease) on the account balance.

In accounting terminology, the left side of an account is called the **debit** side (abbreviated **dr**) and the right side is called the **credit** side (abbreviated **cr**). Despite their prominence in other branches of hospitality accounting, debits and credits play a relatively small role in front office accounting. Debits and credits do not imply anything good or bad about an account. The value of debits and credits results from the use of double-entry bookkeeping, which is the basis for accounting in most modern businesses. In double-entry bookkeeping, every transaction creates entries that affect at least two accounts. The sum of the debit entries created by a transaction must equal the sum of the credit entries created by that same transaction. This fact forms the basis for an accounting process called the *night audit* or simply termed "the audit."

Guest Accounts. A **guest account** is a record of financial transactions that occur between a guest and the hotel. Guest accounts are created when guests guarantee their reservations or when they register at the front desk. During occupancy, the front office is responsible for and records all transactions affecting the balance of a guest account. The front office staff usually seeks payment for any outstanding guest account balance during the settlement stage of the guest cycle. Certain circumstances may require the guest to make a partial or full payment at other times during the guest cycle. For example, if the front office is to enforce the hotel's house limit, guests who exceed that limit may be asked to settle part or all of the outstanding balance. When there is a house limit, account settlement action is initiated when the account balance exceeds a predetermined limit, not at the time of check-out.

Non-Guest Accounts. A hotel may extend in-house charge privileges to local businesses or agencies as a way to promote sales. Management may also offer in-house charge privileges to groups sponsoring meetings at the hotel. In each of these cases, the front office staff will create a **non-guest account** to track deferred transactions. Non-guest accounts set up for local businesses and agencies are usually called *house accounts* or *city accounts*. Such accounts set up for groups are termed *master accounts*.

A non-guest account can also be created when a guest fails to settle his or her account at the time of departure. Whenever a guest's status changes from in-house to non-guest, the responsibility for account settlement shifts correspondingly from the front office to the back office accounting division. The hotel's accounting department normally bills non-guest accounts on a weekly or monthly basis, unlike guest accounts, which the front office staff compiles daily.

Folios

Front office transactions are typically charted on account statements called **folios.** A folio is a statement of all transactions (debits and credits) affecting the balance of a single account. When an account is created, it is assigned a folio with a starting balance of zero. All transactions that increase (debits) or decrease (credits) the balance of the account are recorded on the folio. At settlement, a guest folio should be returned to a zero balance by cash payment or by transfer to an approved payment card or direct billing account.

The process of recording transactions on a folio is called **posting.** A transaction is *posted* when it has been recorded on the proper folio in the proper location, and a new balance has been determined. When posting transactions, the front office staff may rely on handwritten folios (if it uses a non-automated system), machine-posted folios (with a semi-automated system), or automated folios (with the guest accounting module of the hotel's property management system). Regardless of the posting technique or system used, the basic accounting information recorded on a folio remains the same.

There are basically five types of folios used in front office accounting:

- **Guest folios:** accounts assigned to individual persons or guestrooms

- **Master folios:** accounts assigned to more than one person or guestroom; usually reserved for group accounts

- **Non-guest** or **semi-permanent folios:** accounts assigned to non-guest businesses or agencies with charge privileges at the hotel

- **Employee folios:** accounts assigned to employees with charge privileges

- Permanent folios: accounts assigned to firms or agencies with which the hotel has an ongoing relationship (e.g., credit and debit card companies)

Additional types of folios may be frequently created by front office management to accommodate special circumstances or requests. For example, a business guest may request that his or her charges and payments be split between two personal folios: one to record expenses to be paid by the sponsoring business, and one to record personal expenses to be paid by the guest. In this situation, two folios are created for one guest. If the room and tax portion are to be separated from other charges, the room and tax is posted to the *room folio.* This is sometimes called the *A folio.* Food, beverage, Internet, and other charges are posted to a second *incidental folio* or *B folio.*

Every folio should have a unique identifier (i.e., a serial number or code number). Folio identifiers are necessary for several reasons. First, they serve as labels that help ensure that all folios are accounted for during a front office audit. Second, folio identifiers may be used to index information in an automated system. Automated systems frequently create folio identifiers when a reservation record is created. The reservation record is assigned an identifier that is carried forward to the front office system as the folio identifier. Finally, folio identifiers help provide a chain of documentation.

Most hotels restrict the use of employee folios to those individuals who have been granted charge privileges for business reasons. For example, a sales manager may have charge privileges in the hotel's dining room to entertain clients.

Vouchers

A **voucher** details a transaction to be posted to a front office account. This document lists detailed transaction information gathered at the source of the transaction, such as the hotel dining room or gift shop. The voucher is then sent or electronically transferred to the front office staff or system for posting. For example, hotel revenue outlets use vouchers to notify the front office of guest charge purchases that require posting. Several types of vouchers are used in front office accounting, including cash vouchers, charge vouchers, transfer vouchers, allowance vouchers, and paid-out vouchers. Most automated front office systems require few paper vouchers, since revenue-outlet terminals interfaced with a front office system are capable of transmitting transaction information directly to electronic folios. As a result, the use of paper vouchers has been significantly reduced.

Points of Sale

The term *point of sale* describes the physical location at which goods or services are purchased. Any hotel department that collects revenues for its goods or services is considered a revenue center and, thus, a point of sale. Large hotels typically support many points of sale, including restaurants, lounges, room service, dry cleaning, valet service, parking garage, telephone service, fitness centers, athletic facilities, spas, and retail shops. The front office accounting system must ensure that all charge purchases at a point of sale are posted to the proper guest or non-guest account.

Some hotels offer guest-operated devices that function as self-service points of sale. Similar to an actual revenue outlet, these devices result in charges that must be posted to guest or non-guest folios. Three such devices are in-room movie systems, Internet-access devices, and in-room vending systems.

The volume of goods and services purchased at scattered points of sale within the hotel requires a complex internal accounting system to ensure proper posting and documentation of sales transactions. Exhibit 1 charts the flow of information that results when a guest charges a restaurant purchase to his or her guest account. An automated **point-of-sale (POS) system** typically enables remote terminals at the point of purchase to communicate directly with a front office system. Automated POS systems significantly reduce the amount of time required to post charge purchases to guest folios, minimize the number of times transactional data must be handled, and virtually eliminate after-departure (late) charges. Overall, automation helps front office staff create a well-documented, legible folio statement with a minimum number of errors.

No matter the location, points of sale must provide some basic information when posting a charge to the front office system. The information includes the source document or transaction number, the amount of the charge, name of the point-of-sale outlet, guestroom number, name of the guest, and a brief description of the charge. If the charge is supported by a source document, the signature of the guest and the identity of the employee capturing the transaction may also be required. When a POS charge is posted through a remote terminal, employee identification is captured by the system and attached to the folio posting, along with the time of the posting. Posting through an automated terminal may require a guest signature on a sales slip for audit purposes or in case there is a dispute regarding the transaction or amount. Some POS systems allow the swipe of a guestroom key as sufficient verification for posting a charge to a guest folio.

Ledgers

A **ledger** is a summary grouping of accounts. The front office ledger is a collection of front office account folios. The folios represented in the front office are a part of the front office **accounts receivable ledger.** An **account receivable** represents money owed to the hotel. Front office accounting commonly separates accounts receivable into two subsidiary groups: the **guest ledger** (for guest receivables) and the **city ledger** (for non-guest receivables).

Guest Ledger. The *guest ledger* refers to the set of guest accounts that corresponds to registered hotel guests and guests who have made advance deposits for upcoming

Exhibit 1   Restaurant Charge Posted to Guestroom Account

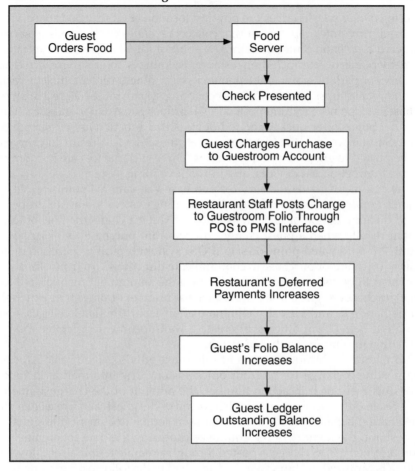

hotel stays. Guests who use a payment card (or make credit arrangements for billing to their accounts) are extended privileges to charge purchases to account folios during their stays. Guests may also make payments against their outstanding balance at any time during occupancy, thereby reducing deferred account balances. Guests' financial transactions are recorded onto guest ledger accounts to assist in tracking guest account balances. In some front office operations, the guest ledger may be called the *transient ledger, front office ledger,* or *rooms ledger.* When an advance deposit is received, it is posted to the guest ledger and appears as a credit balance. When the guest arrives, the amount of the credit balance is diminished throughout the stay by the charges posted to the account. In hotels that have a high volume of advance deposit activity (resorts, for example), the guest ledger may be divided into advance deposits and in-house guest ledgers. In hotels that have few advance deposits, posting the deposits to the guest ledger usually provides sufficient financial control. For non-automated and semi-automated hotels, the credit associated with an advance deposit may be posted to the guest's folio immediately. When the guest arrives, the deposit on the guest's folio is applied against charges to the account.

City Ledger. The city ledger, also called the *non-guest ledger,* is the collection of non-guest accounts. If a guest account is not settled in full by acceptable payment at check-out, the guest's folio balance is transferred from the guest ledger in the front office to the city ledger in the back office accounting division for collection. At the time of account transfer, the responsibility for account collection shifts from the front office to the accounting division (back office). The city ledger can contain credit and debit card payment accounts, direct billing accounts, and accounts of past guests due for collection by the hotel.

Creation and Maintenance of Accounts

The task of accurately and completely recording all transactions that affect guest ledger accounts is the responsibility of the front office staff. The front office may also be responsible for recording transactions affecting non-guest accounts. Usually, the back office accounting division is ultimately responsible for collection of non-guest ledger accounts.

Guest folios are created during the reservations process or at the time of registration. To prepare a folio for use, information from the guest's reservation or registration record may be automatically transferred to the folio. In an automated front office system, guest information is automatically transferred from an electronic reservation record or captured at registration and entered onto an electronic folio. Electronic folios are automatically cross-referenced with other property management system–based records within the front office system. Unlike manual or semi-automated systems, automated systems can track an unlimited number of postings in each account created. In some systems, a preliminary electronic folio is created automatically and simultaneously with the reservation record. This enables postings to guest accounts prior to registration. Such items as pre-payments and advance deposits can then be accurately monitored through electronic recordkeeping. An automated system can also be programmed to create the proper number of folios needed for pre-registration of arriving guests.

At check-in, reservations data are verified and combined with room rate information and the guest's assigned room number to finalize an in-house electronic folio. For a walk-in guest, equivalent information is captured during registration and entered into the front office system. Creating an electronic folio within a front office system can significantly reduce the possibility of transactional account entry errors. One of the major advantages of electronic data processing is that captured data need be handled only once. By handling data only once, an automated system can significantly reduce errors usually associated with repetitive data handling.

Automated Recordkeeping Systems

Point-of-sale transactions may be automatically posted to an electronic folio. In a printed copy of a folio, debits (charges) and credits (payments) may appear in a single column with payments distinguished by parentheses or a minus sign. Printed folio copies may also be produced in the traditional multiple-column

Exhibit 2   Sample Folio Data

Description	Charges	Credits	Balance
Previous Balance			$0.00
Restaurant	$14.25		$14.25
Guestroom	$60.00		$74.25
Long-Distance Telephone	$6.38		$80.63
Allowance		$18.38	$62.25
Cash Payment		$62.25	$0.00

account format. It is unnecessary to manually maintain an account's previous balance in a fully automated system, since automated systems maintain current balances for all folios. Exhibit 2 is an example of a guest folio used in an automated front office system.

Charge Privileges

To establish an in-house line of credit, a guest may be required to present an acceptable and valid payment card or a direct billing authorization at the time of registration. An automated front office system will allow credit to be established at the time a reservation record is created. This is usually done by obtaining the number and expiration date of the guest's payment card and electronically transmitting this information to the card company with a request for an amount guarantee. Once a line of credit has been approved, guests are authorized to make charge purchases at hotel points of sale. These transactions are communicated electronically from remote points of sale locations to the front office accounting module.

Guests who use cash to pay for accommodations at registration are typically not extended charge purchase privileges. These guests are typically called **paid-in-advance** or **PIA guests.** In an automated front office accounting system, PIA accounts are typically set to a *no-post* status. Since point-of-sale terminals throughout the hotel have immediate access to stored account information, a no-post status account is one that cannot accept charge purchase transactions. This means that revenue center cashiers will not be able to post charges for a guest with a no-post status account. In non-automated and semi-automated properties, a PIA list is manually distributed to all revenue centers.

Local businesses or residents may apply to the hotel and qualify to establish a house account or non-guest account. Charge purchases for house accounts, like those for guest accounts, move from the hotel's revenue centers to the front office accounting system for posting. Since point-of-sale transactions are posted to a folio for eventual collection, front office staff may be responsible for monitoring guest and non-guest accounts.

Credit Monitoring

The front office staff must monitor guest and non-guest accounts to ensure they remain within acceptable credit limits. Typically, a line of credit is set for guests who establish charge privileges during the reservations or registration process. Guests who present an acceptable payment card at registration may be extended a line of credit equal to the **floor limit** authorized by the issuing payment card company. This means the front office may not have to seek approval from the card company as long as the charges do not exceed the floor limit specified by the card company. Guest and non-guest accounts with other approved credit arrangements (bill to accounts) are subject to limitations established by the front office. These internal credit restrictions are called **house limits.**

Front office management may need to be notified when a front office account approaches its floor or house limit. Such accounts are called high-risk or **high-balance accounts.** The front office manager, or front office auditor, is primarily responsible for identifying accounts that are approaching or have reached or exceeded predetermined credit limits. The front office may deny additional charge privileges to guests with high-balance accounts until the situation is resolved. A front office manager may periodically review guest ledgers throughout the day to ensure that guests have not exceeded their approved credit limits. Automated front offices may generate a guest list on demand that highlights the names of guests whose accounts are near or over their approved credit limits. Front office management may ask the payment card company to authorize additional credit, or request the guest to make a partial payment to reduce the outstanding account balance.

In some hotels there may be a full-time credit manager to review high-balance accounts. The credit manager may also request additional authorization from credit card companies for guests near or over their floor limits. In addition, it is the credit manager's responsibility to obtain settlement from present and past guests who have not settled their accounts.

Account Maintenance

A folio is used to record transactions that affect a guest or non-guest account balance. Guest folios must be accurate, complete, and properly filed, since guests may inquire about their account balance or check out of the hotel with little or no advance notice. Transaction postings conform to a basic **front office accounting formula.** The accounting formula is:

$$\text{Previous Balance} + \text{Debits} - \text{Credits} = \text{Net Outstanding Balance}$$
$$\text{PB} + \text{DR} - \text{CR} = \text{NOB}$$

Recall that debits increase the balance of a guest or non-guest account, while credits decrease the account balance.

This formula can be applied to the folio data shown in Exhibit 2. The guest registered on July 27. The first debit—a charge purchase of $14.25—occurred that evening in the hotel's restaurant. Since the guest charged the purchase to a guestroom account, the first net outstanding balance on the account is $14.25:

$$\text{PB} + \text{DR} - \text{CR} = \text{NOB}$$
$$\$0.00 + \$14.25 - \$0.00 = \$14.25$$

Or, stated another way:

Previous Balance: $ 0.00
+ Debits: + 14.25
− Credits: − 0.00

= Net Outstanding Balance: $14.25

Later that evening, the front office accounting system automatically posted the guest's room and room tax charges ($160) to the account. This transaction, which appears on the second line of the folio, results in a new net outstanding balance:

PB	+	DR	−	CR	=	NOB
$14.25	+	$60.00	−	$0.00	=	$74.25

Next, the guest's long-distance telephone call was posted, resulting in a $6.38 debit posting. The front office later applied a miscellaneous credit (account allowance) of $18.38, and received a cash payment of $162.25 from the guest at checkout. When each of these transactions is applied, the front office posting formula yields a zero net outstanding balance for the account:

PB	+	DR	−	CR	=	NOB
$74.25	+	$6.38	−	$ 0.00	=	$80.63
$80.63	+	$0.00	−	$18.38	=	$62.25
$62.25	+	$0.00	−	$62.25	=	$ 0.00

At this point, the guest checks out of the hotel and the account is brought to a zero balance and properly closed.

Tracking Transactions

Charge purchase transactions must be correctly documented in order for the front office to properly maintain accounts. Front office staff may rely on electronic vouchers to provide a reliable set of support documentation for postings on a guest or non-guest folio. Even with POS systems communicating directly to the front office system, guests may still question charges when the folio is reviewed. A major concern of the front office accounting process involves the communication of transactional information from remote points of sale to the front office system. The front office audit is intended to verify transactional data to ensure that the front office collects accounts receivable balances for all goods and services provided by the hotel.

A transaction initiates activity within the front office accounting system. From an accounting perspective, nothing happens until a transaction occurs. For this reason, the front office accounting system can be described as a transactional accounting system. Proper posting procedures depend on the nature of the transaction and its monetary value. A transaction can be classified as:

- Cash payment
- Charge purchase (account receivable)

- Account correction

- Account allowance

- Account transfer

- Cash advance

Each type of transaction will have a different effect on the front office accounting system. Each may be communicated to the front office through the use of a different type of electronic voucher, thereby simplifying front office auditing procedures.

Cash Payment

Cash payments made at the front desk to reduce a guest's net outstanding balance are posted as credits to the guest or non-guest account, thereby decreasing the balance of the account. Since most guests establish credit by using a payment card at the time of check-in, the front office may use a **cash voucher** to document cash received. Only cash payment transactions that take place at the front desk will create entries that appear on a front office account folio. Front office account balances are also affected by cash payments made to settle an account or to prepay accommodations.

When cash is paid for goods or services at a location other than the front desk, no entry will appear on any guest or non-guest account folio. The "account" for a cash transaction is created, increased, settled, and closed at the point of sale, thereby eliminating the need for front office system documentation or posting. For example, a cash payment for a guest's lunch in the hotel's restaurant would not appear on the guest's folio, since it was settled at the point of sale. In addition, some hotels sell items such as newspapers at the front desk. When guests pay for these items with cash, there is no charge to post to any guest or non-guest account.

Personal checks are negotiable instruments and should be treated as cash by the front desk staff. However, personal checks require a high level of scrutiny before the staff can accept them as payment of an account or exchange them for cash. Most hotels have a very specific procedure for accepting checks from guests. It is customary for the name, address, and telephone number of the guest to be preprinted on the check. The bank name and branch identification, along with the check number, should also be preprinted. In addition, the bank account number and bank routing number must clearly appear at the bottom of the check. Cashiers should verify the signature on the check with another form of guest identification, preferably one with a photo. The check should then be endorsed by the front desk agent with a special bank deposit stamp, designating payment to the hotel only. Finally, the guest's proof of identification, such as the driver's license number, should also be recorded on the check. The hotel casher verifies the signature on the personal check against the guest's signature on a second signed document. This ensures that the signature on the check is valid.

An additional precaution should be taken with personal checks relating to the actual currency used. Cashiers should be sure the payment is in local currency, not foreign currency. If the instrument is issued in foreign currency, the front desk cashier may be required to calculate the currency conversion to local currency before payment is accepted. Hotels usually charge the guest a small fee for currency conversion.

Hotels often subscribe to a check guarantee service to ensure that the personal checks they receive from guests are authentic. When using a guarantee service, the account number, bank routing number, check number, and amount of the check need to be provided to the service. Once the check is accepted for payment, the service guarantees payment to the hotel. Guarantee services charge a fee to hotels, but in most cases hotels will absorb the fee as a cost of doing business.

Charge Purchase

Charge purchases represent deferred payment transactions. In a deferred payment transaction, the guest (buyer) receives goods and services from a hotel revenue center (seller), but does not pay for goods or services at the time they are provided. A charge purchase transaction (debit) increases the outstanding balance of a guest or non-guest folio account.

If the transaction occurs somewhere other than at the front desk, it must be communicated to the front desk system for proper folio posting. In non-automated and semi-automated properties, this communication is normally accomplished by means of a **charge voucher,** also referred to as an *account receivable voucher.* When the revenue center in which the charge originated uses a form to record the sale (for example, a guest check in the dining room), the form itself is usually considered a source document. To communicate the existence of this transaction, the support document (a voucher) is completed and sent to the front desk for posting. Many non-automated and semi-automated hotels use a multi-part food and beverage check. When the guest signs the charge to his or her guestroom, a copy of the signed guest check may be sent to the front desk for posting in place of a charge voucher.

Many hotels contain retail stores that the hotels do not own or operate. Instead, the hotels may lease the stores to non-affiliated merchants. Hotel management and the merchants may form a business arrangement that allows hotel guests to charge store purchases to their guestroom accounts. When this is the case, the hotel's management and non-affiliated merchants must agree on a secure and reliable procedure for accurately tracking and posting purchase transactions. Once guest charges are posted, the hotel's management becomes liable for settlement with merchants for all shop charges posted to guest and non-guest accounts. It therefore becomes incumbent on hotel management to meticulously monitor and record all legitimate deferred transactions. Hotel management must identify a proof-of-sale procedure and establish a resolution process in the event a transaction is disputed.

When guests charge purchases to a guestroom account, merchants must require the guest to present a room key and an additional form of identification. If the merchant's point-of-sale system is not linked to the front office system, the merchant will likely contact the front desk and request account verification before completing the sale. Once the front desk agent verifies the guest's status, the merchant may also ask the guest to sign the receipt or sales voucher. This is done to avoid guest disputes at a later time.

When the shop's point-of-sale system is electronically linked to the hotel front office system, the merchant can use the system to verify that a guest's name is associated with an authorized guestroom account (that is, that the guest is checked in with credit established). If the guest's account is not authorized to accept charge purchases (that is, the guest's account has a no-post status), the system will not accept the charge.

Hotels are often not liable for retail charges presented for posting after the guest has departed.

Account Correction

An account correction transaction resolves a posting error on a guest or non-guest folio. By definition, an account correction is made on the same day the error is discovered, *before* the close of business (that is, before the daily audit). An account correction can either increase or decrease a guest or non-guest account balance, depending on the nature of the error. For instance, an account would need to be adjusted if a front desk agent inadvertently posted an incorrect charge to a particular guestroom. A **correction voucher** is used to document an account correction transaction. Usually the front desk agent posting the correction signs the correction voucher, and presents it to the front office manager or supervisor on duty for review and approval.

Account Allowance

Account allowances involve two types of transactions. One type of account allowance is a decrease in a folio balance for such purposes as compensation for poor service or rebates for coupons and/or other discounts. Another type of account allowance corrects a posting error detected *after* the close of business (that is, after the daily audit). Such an error will be separately entered into the accounting records of the appropriate revenue centers, thereby also correcting their corresponding accounting records.

An account allowance is documented by the use of an **allowance voucher.** Allowance vouchers normally require management approval. Exhibit 3 contains sample account correction and account allowance vouchers that may be used in a semi-automated property. Just as when dealing with correction vouchers, the front office agent posting the allowance may have to secure the front office manager's or supervisor's approval to validate the allowance voucher.

Account Transfer

Account transfers involve two different guest or non-guest accounts and tend to have offsetting impacts on subsequent account balances. For example, when one guest offers to pay a charge posted to another guest's folio, the charge will need to be transferred from the first account to a second account. A **transfer voucher** supports the reduction in balance on the originating folio and the increase in balance on the destination folio.

Cash Advance

The difference between a cash advance and other types of transactions is that cash advances reflect cash flow out of the hotel's resources, either directly to, or on

Exhibit 3   Sample Account Correction and Account Allowance Vouchers

ROOM# DATE AMOUNT

221538

DO NOT WRITE IN ABOVE SPACE
DATE   SYMBOL   AMOUNT

DO NOT WRITE IN THIS SPACE

TOTALS EFFECTED

EXPLANATION

AMOUNT   CASHIER   APPROVED

NCR Systemedia Group
481250   **CORRECTION**

ROOM# DATE AMOUNT

311811

DO NOT WRITE IN ABOVE SPACE   DATE   19
NAME   ROOM OR
                                           ACCT. NO.
DATE   SYMBOL   AMOUNT

DO NOT WRITE IN THIS SPACE

EXPLANATION

NCR Systemedia
481205   **ALLOWANCE**   SIGNATURE

behalf of, a guest. Cash advance transactions are considered debit transactions, since they increase a guest folio's outstanding balance. Cash advances are supported by **cash advance vouchers.** Cash disbursed by the front office staff on behalf of a guest (and charged to the guest's account as a cash advance) is typically called a **paid-out.** In some front office operations, a paid-out voucher is used instead of a cash advance voucher.

In the past, front office staff often allowed guests to sign a paid-out slip and receive cash on account; this is no longer common practice. Many hotels refer guests requiring cash to bank automated teller machines (ATMs) located on, or near, the hotel property. A paid-out reduces the amount of cash held in the front office cash drawer. For example, a guest may order a floral delivery and request that the front desk agent accept the order should the guest not be reachable at time of delivery. Since the guest most likely will not leave money with the front desk agent for this purpose, payment on behalf of the guest by the front office staff member constitutes a cash advance on the guest's behalf. The front office staff member pays for the delivery from cash at the front desk on the presumption that the guest will reimburse the purchase amount. Front office policy should dictate how cash advances are handled. Paid-outs should require a manager's approval before the cash is actually dispensed.

Internal Control

Internal control within the front office system involves:

- Tracking transaction documentation
- Verifying account entries and balances
- Identifying vulnerabilities in the accounting system

Auditing is the process of verifying front office accounting records for accuracy and completeness. Each financial interaction is documented in terms of the nature and dollar amount of the transaction. For example, consider the transaction that occurs when a guest charges a meal to his or her individual guestroom folio. This transaction will likely be supported by a restaurant guest check, POS recording, and creation of a charge voucher (or electronic equivalent). A charge voucher originates in a revenue center and is transmitted to the front office system for posting. In a semi-automated front office, a front desk agent retrieves the guest's folio, posts the charge purchase transaction, re-files the guest folio, and files the charge voucher. Later that day, a front office audit ensures that all vouchers sent to the front office have been properly posted to the correct account. In this example, the audit should match the front office total of charges transferred from the revenue center to the total of charges posted. Discrepancies in accounting procedures are easy to resolve when complete documentation is readily available to substantiate account entries.

Cash Banks

An important set of front office accounting control procedures involves the use of front office cashier banks. A **cash bank** is an amount of cash assigned to a cashier to handle the various transactions that occur during a work shift. The hotel may issue cash banks with a specific amount of money to each cashier. That amount is to be used for making change when guests settle their accounts, for processing paid-outs, and for providing other cash-related services during the cashier's shift. The **bank limit** is the starting amount the bank should have in it when it is issued at the beginning of the shift. Control procedures typically require that cashiers sign for their bank at the beginning of their work shift and that only the person who signed for the bank has access to it during the shift. At the end of a work shift, the front office cashier is solely responsible for depositing all cash, checks, and other negotiable instruments received during the work shift into the hotel safe (or other designated location). The amount being deposited is itemized on the front of an office cash envelope holding the deposit. After the deposit has been made, the bank should be restored to its original bank limit.

In hotels that do not assign individual banks, cashiers usually pass the banks to the next shift. In these cases, the cashier that has used the bank is required to verify the balance of the bank at the end of the shift, depositing any amounts over the bank limit in the hotel's safe. The cashier receiving the bank should also verify that the bank has the proper starting amount in it, since the responsibility for the bank will shift to him or her. At the end of the shift, the cashier typically separates out the amount of the initial bank, and then enters the amount of remaining cash, checks, and other negotiable items (such as paid-out vouchers) into a specially designed cash voucher or front office cash envelope. The cashier normally itemizes and records the contents of the front office cash envelope on the outside of the envelope before dropping it into the front office vault. From an internal control perspective, at least one other employee should witness this cash banking procedure, and both employees should sign a log attesting that the drop was performed correctly, noting the time of the drop.

Monetary differences between the money placed in the front office cash envelope and the cashier's net cash receipts should be noted on the envelope as overages, shortages, or due backs. **Net cash receipts** are the amount of cash, checks, and other negotiable items in the cashier's drawer, minus the amount of the initial cash bank, plus any paid-outs.

For example, assume the front office cashier began the work shift with a $175 cash bank. During the shift, the cashier made paid-outs totaling $49. At the end of the work shift, the amount of cash, checks, and other negotiable items in the cash drawer totals $952.

To determine the amount of net cash receipts, the front office cashier would first add together the value of the cash, checks, and other negotiable items in the cash drawer ($952). The cashier would next subtract the value of the initial cash bank ($175). By adding the amount of paid-outs ($49), the front office cashier will arrive at a net cash receipt position ($826):

$$\$952 - \$175 + \$49 = \$826$$

An **overage** occurs when, after the initial bank is removed, the total of the cash, checks, gift certificates, and paid-outs in the cash drawer is greater than the net cash receipts. An overage can occur when a front desk agent receives a cash payment from a guest for more than the amount of the folio balance and returns less cash to the guest than required. For example, the guest may have a gift certificate or gift card value that represents a prepayment to the hotel. The hotel cashier treats this coupon or card value as cash. A **shortage** occurs when the total of the contents of the drawer is less than the net cash receipts. A shortage can occur when a front desk agent receives a cash payment from a guest for more than the amount of the folio balance and returns more cash than appropriate. Neither an overage nor a shortage is typically considered acceptable by front office management when evaluating the job performance of a front office cashier. Overages and shortages are determined by comparing the cash totals of the cashier's postings against the actual cash, checks, and negotiables in the cashier's bank. Effective recordkeeping systems, whether they be non-automated, semi-automated, or fully automated, will provide proper cash posting documentation. Since cashiers deal with cash and related assets, it is essential to have proper procedures to ensure financial integrity.

A **due back** occurs when a cashier pays out more than he or she receives; in other words, there is not enough cash in the drawer to restore the initial bank. Due backs are not unusual in front office operations. A special kind of due back may occur when a cashier accepts many large-denomination currency bills during a work shift. This situation can make it difficult to restore the initial bank. Since checks and large bills are not very useful for processing cash transactions, they are usually deposited with other receipts. Consequently, the front office deposit may be greater than the cashier's net cash receipts, with the excess *due back* to the front office cashier's bank. Front office due backs are normally replaced with smaller denomination currency before the cashier's next work shift, thereby restoring the cash bank to its full and correct amount. Due backs do not reflect positively or negatively on the cashier's job performance, and may occur regardless of whether net cash receipts are in or out of balance.

Audit Controls

A number of front office audit controls help ensure that front office staff members properly handle cash, guest accounts, and non-guest accounts. Publicly held lodging companies are required to have both their front and back office accounting records audited yearly by an independent certified public accountant. In addition, companies with multiple lodging properties often employ internal auditors at a headquarters site who make unannounced visits to individual properties for the purpose of reviewing accounting procedures and records. A report is subsequently prepared for management and ownership review. Exhibit 4 presents one firm's internal control inspection checklist. The checklist includes items related to standard front office procedures designed to protect the integrity of front office operations.

Settlement of Accounts

The collection of payment for outstanding account balances is called account settlement. Account settlement involves bringing an account balance to zero as a result of proper payments. An account can be brought to a zero balance as a result of a payment (cash or payment card) in full or a transfer to an approved direct billing account. All guest accounts should be brought to a zero balance at the time of check-out. Transfers to approved deferred payment plans move outstanding folio balances from the guest ledger to the city or non-guest ledger.

Although guest account settlement normally occurs at check-out, guests may make payments against outstanding folio balances at any time prior to check-out. Non-guest folio balances may be initially billed on the day the transaction occurred. Settlement may be due in fifteen to thirty days, depending on accounting department policy. For example, consider the case of a guest who makes a

Exhibit 4   Sample Internal Control Inspection Checklist

(A)   GUEST ACCOUNTS

  1.   Accounts Receivable per audit:

   a. _____ Sleepers $ _____
   b. _____ After departure charges   _____
   c. _____ Prepaid accts. with charges   _____
   d. _____ Disputed accounts   _____
   e. _____ Delinquent accounts (over 60 days)   _____
   f. _____ Skips   _____
   g. _____ Tour vouchers   _____
   h. _____ Employee accounts   _____
   i. _____ Intercompany accounts   _____
   j. _____   _____
   k. _____   _____
   l. _____   _____
                                                       SUBTOTAL $ _____
   m. Other direct billing accounts   _____
                                          TOTAL DIRECT BILLING $ _____
   n. Total guest accounts
                                     TOTAL ACCOUNTS RECEIVABLE $ _____
   o. Less advance deposits   _____
                                    BALANCE ACCOUNTS RECEIVABLE $ _____
   p. Variance
       _____ Direct billing accounts
       _____ Accounts confirmed by letter $ _____
       Reset control number per report   _____
       Reset control number per machine   _____

		Sat.	Unsat.
2.	Direct billing accounts signed by guest.	_____	_____
3.	Follow-up on accounts receivable in accordance with company policy.	_____	_____
4.	Only authorized individuals permitted to sign direct billing accounts.	_____	_____
5.	Direct billing accounts have copies of all correspondence and supporting charges pertaining thereto.	_____	_____
6.	Direct billing checks deposited promptly.	_____	_____
7.	Monthly listing of accounts receivable prepared properly.	_____	_____
8.	Direct billing payments, posting, billing, separated and supervised.	_____	_____
9.	Corporate credit authorization on file for direct billings.	_____	_____

(B)   ADVANCE DEPOSITS

1.	Folios are complete (date of arrival shown on folios, etc.).	_____	_____
2.	Advance deposit folios are secured.	_____	_____
3.	Revenues or refunds processed promptly on stale dated credit balance accounts.	_____	_____
4.	Advance deposit checks deposited promptly.	_____	_____

Exhibit 4 *(continued)*

			Sat.	Unsat.
(C)		**CREDIT CARD PROCEDURES**		
	1.	Credit card imprinters are dated correctly.		
	2.	An examination of all completed credit card vouchers shows:		
		a. Approval where required.	___	___
		b. All cards current (not expired).	___	___
		c. All imprints are legible.	___	___
		d. Clerk's initials and folio number.	___	___
	3.	Credit card transmittals completed correctly (totals correct, non-national credit card charges itemized, adding machine tape included).	___	___
(D)		**CHECKS**		
	1.	Clerk's initials, folio number, endorsement and payee portion completed properly.	___	___
	2.	Deposit daily.	___	___
	3.	Correct check cashing policies in force.	___	___
	4.	Check register maintained correctly.	___	___
(E)		**FRONT OFFICE**		
	1.	Reset control number controlled properly.	___	___
	2.	Revenues balanced to D card: (check 3 days)		
		a. Room	___	___
		b. Restaurant	___	___
		c. Long Distance	___	___
		d. Laundry	___	___
		e. Miscellaneous	___	___
	3.	Paid-outs and allowances are completed and approved by management.	___	___
	4.	Corrections controlled and balanced.	___	___
	5.	Copies of all vouchers kept on property.	___	___
	6.	Long-distance calls taxed properly.	___	___
	7.	Long-distance service charges only as permitted by law.	___	___
	8.	Room tax charged correctly.	___	___
(F)		**GUEST FOLIOS AND REGISTRATION CARDS**		
	1.	Registration cards and folios filled out completely.	___	___
	2.	Folios and registration cards are time stamped in and out.	___	___
	3.	Continuation folios marked to and from.	___	___
	4.	Alphabetical and numerical filing current and in good order.	___	___
	5.	Numerical sequence of unused folios in order.	___	___
	6.	Void folios handled correctly.	___	___
(G)		**SECURITY AND SAFETY**		
	1.	Drop facilities constructed properly.	___	___
	2.	Deposit witness log used properly.	___	___
	3.	House banks stored properly when not in use.	___	___
	4.	Night Auditor's clearance key secured.	___	___
	5.	Safe deposit boxes:		
		a. Log maintained correctly.	___	___
		b. Keys available for unused boxes.	___	___

(continued)

Exhibit 4 *(continued)*

			Sat.	Unsat.
6.	Vehicle drivers properly licensed.		_____	_____
7.	Cash drawers locked when not in use.			
8.	Hotel safe:			
	a. Safe combinations last changed: _____		._____	_____
	b. No terminated employees have safe combinations.		_____	_____
9.	Proper security over keys when not in use.		_____	_____
10.	Adequate security over storerooms.		_____	_____
11.	TV log up to date.		_____	_____
12.	Adequate linen inventory control.		_____	_____

(H)   FOLIO ACCOUNTABILITY

1. Unused folios (unopened boxes only):
   Total on hand _____ from number _____ to number _____
   Where are unused folios stored: _____
   How long will supply last: _____
   Per attached check sheets, the following folios were not accounted for: _____
   Total folios checked: _____   Period covered from _____ to _____
   Total number of folios missing: _____

COMMENTS: _____
_____
_____
_____
_____
_____

I acknowledge receipt of this inspection and concur that the ratings given my property are factual and accurate (list any exceptions above).

_____   _____
Manager   Date

Same Manager present at last audit?
Yes _____   No _____

I hereby certify that on the above date I performed an audit of the above property.

_____
Field Auditor, Audit Services Division

guaranteed reservation but does not arrive to check in at the hotel. This is called a *no-show* guest. The account cannot be settled at check-out, since the guest never registered. Instead, the front office cashier sends a statement to the payment card processor for the amount of the guarantee, hoping to settle the account balance in a timely manner. Once the billing is transmitted, the account is often transferred to the back office accounts receivable department for collection.

When a guest account is paid, the folio is updated to indicate account settlement and closure. Sometimes a guest settles an account but a charge is posted in the system after the account has been closed. This situation is called a **late charge.** Guests may dispute or refuse to pay a late charge, often resulting in an account adjustment in the front office accounting system. An example of a typical late charge is a transaction arising from the guest's in-room refreshment center that is posted to the front office accounting system after the guest has departed the hotel.

Summary

A front office accounting system monitors and charts the transactions of guests and businesses, agencies, and other non-guests using the hotel's services and facilities. The front office's ability to perform accounting tasks in an accurate and complete manner will directly affect the hotel's ability to collect outstanding balances.

A front office accounting system is uniquely tailored to each hotel operation. Accounting system terminology and report formats often differ from hotel to hotel. In general, an account is a form on which financial data are accumulated and summarized. The increases and decreases in an account are calculated and the resulting monetary amount is the account balance. All of the financial transactions that occur in a hotel affect accounts. Front office accounts are recordkeeping devices used to store information about guest and non-guest financial transactions. For a front office account, charges are increases in the account balance and are entered on the left side of the "T" (when using a simple written T-account). Payments are decreases in the account balance and are entered on the right side of the "T." Front office accounting documents typically use a journal form.

A guest account is a record of financial transactions between a guest and the hotel. Guest accounts are created when guests guarantee their reservations or when they register at the front desk. A hotel may also extend in-house charge privileges to local businesses or agencies as a means of promotion, or to groups sponsoring meetings at the hotel. The front office creates non-guest accounts (also called *house accounts* or *city accounts*) to track these transactions.

Front office transactions are typically charted on account statements called *folios.* A folio is a statement of all transactions (debits and credits) affecting the balance of a single account. All transactions that increase (debit) or decrease (credit) the balance of the account are recorded on the folio. At settlement, a guest folio should be returned to a zero balance by cash payment or by transfer to an approved credit/debit card or direct billing account. The process of recording transactions on a folio is called *posting.* A transaction is posted when it has been recorded on the proper folio in the proper location, and a new balance has been determined.

There are basically four types of folios used in the front office: guest folios, master folios, non-guest or semi-permanent folios, and employee folios. Additional types of folios are frequently created by front office management to accommodate special circumstances or requests.

A voucher details a transaction to be posted to a front office account. This document lists detailed transaction information gathered at the source of the transaction. The voucher is then sent to the front office. Auditing is the process of verifying front office accounting records for accuracy and completeness.

The term *point of sale* describes the location at which goods or services are purchased. Any hotel department that collects revenues for its goods or services is considered a revenue center and, thus, a point of sale. An automated point-of-sale (POS) system may allow remote terminals at the points of sale to communicate directly with a front office system. Automated POS systems may significantly reduce the amount of time required to post charge purchases to guest folios, the number of times each piece of data must be handled, and the number of posting errors and after-departure (late) charges.

A ledger is a grouping of accounts. The front office ledger is a collection of front office account folios. The folios used in the front office form part of the front office accounts receivable ledger. An account receivable represents money owed to the hotel. Front office accounting commonly separates accounts receivable into two subsidiary groups: the guest ledger (for guest receivables) and the city ledger (for non-guest receivables). The guest ledger is the set of guest accounts that correspond to registered hotel guests. Guests who make appropriate credit arrangements at registration may be extended privileges to charge purchases to their individual account folios. The city ledger, also called the *non-guest ledger*, is the collection of non-guest accounts. If a guest account is not settled in full at checkout, the guest's folio balance is transferred from the guest ledger in the front office to the city ledger in the accounting division for collection. Shops in the hotel may have arrangements to allow guests to charge purchases to their rooms. In these cases, the hotel posts the charges to the guests' accounts, collects the amount due from the guests, and pays the shopkeepers the money due them.

Front office policy may require the completion of a cash voucher as support documentation for cash transactions affecting front office accounts.

In large hotels, establishing and monitoring the credit of guests is often the responsibility of a credit manager. In small hotels, these tasks may be part of the front desk manager's duties. The credit manager assists guests in establishing credit and reviews the guest and non-guest ledgers to ensure that accounts do not exceed established credit limits.

🔑 Key Terms

account—A form on which financial data are accumulated and summarized.

account balance—A summary of an account in terms of its resulting monetary amount; specifically, the difference between the total debits and total credits to an account.

account receivable—An amount owed to the hotel.

accounts receivable ledger—A grouping of accounts receivable, including the guest ledger and the city ledger.

allowance voucher—A voucher used to support an account allowance.

bank limit—The amount of cash contained in a cashier bank when it is issued at the beginning of a work shift.

cash advance voucher—A voucher used to support cash flow out of the hotel, either directly to, or on behalf of, a guest.

cash bank—An amount of money given to a cashier at the start of a work shift so that he or she can handle the various transactions that occur. The cashier is responsible for this cash bank and for all cash, checks, and other negotiable items received during the work shift.

cash voucher—A voucher used to support a cash payment transaction at the front desk.

charge voucher—A voucher used to support a charge purchase transaction that takes place somewhere other than the front desk; also referred to as an account receivable voucher.

city ledger—The collection of all non-guest accounts, including house accounts and unsettled departed-guest accounts.

correction voucher—A voucher used to support the correction of a posting error that is rectified before the close of business on the day the error was made.

credit (cr)—An entry on the right side of an account.

debit (dr)—An entry on the left side of an account.

due back—A situation that occurs when a cashier pays out more than he or she receives; the difference is due back to the cashier's cash bank. In the front office, due backs usually occur when a cashier accepts so many checks and large bills during a shift that he or she cannot restore the initial bank at the end of the shift without using the checks or large bills.

employee folio—A folio used to chart transactions on an account assigned to an employee with charge purchase privileges at the hotel.

floor limit—A limit assigned to hotels by payment card companies indicating the maximum amount in payment card charges the hotel is permitted to accept from a card member without special authorization.

folio—A statement of all transactions affecting the balance of a single account.

front office accounting formula—The formula used in posting transactions to front office accounts: Previous Balance + Debits – Credits = Net Outstanding Balance.

guest account—A record of the financial transactions that occur between a guest and the hotel.

guest folio—A form (paper or electronic) used to chart transactions on an account assigned to an individual person or guestroom.

guest ledger—The set of accounts for all guests currently registered at the hotel; also called the *front office ledger, transient ledger,* or *rooms ledger.*

high-balance account—An account that has reached or exceeded a predetermined credit limit; typically identified by the night auditor; also called a *high risk account.*

house limit—A credit limit established by the hotel.

late charge—A charge posted to a guest account after the guest has settled the account and departed the hotel.

ledger—A grouping of accounts.

master folio—A folio used to chart transactions on an account assigned to more than one person or guestroom. Master folios are usually reserved for group accounts; they collect charges not appropriately posted elsewhere.

net cash receipts—The amount of cash and checks in the cashier's drawer, minus the amount of the initial cash bank.

non-guest account—An account created to track the financial transactions of (1) a local business or agency with charge privileges at the hotel, (2) a group sponsoring a meeting at the hotel, or (3) a former guest with an outstanding account balance.

non-guest/semi-permanent folio—A folio used to chart transactions on an account assigned to (1) a local business or agency with charge privileges at the hotel, (2) a group sponsoring a meeting at the hotel, or (3) a former guest with an outstanding account balance.

outstanding balance—The amount the guest owes the hotel—or the amount the hotel owes the guest, in the event of a credit balance at settlement.

overage—An imbalance that occurs when the total of cash and checks in a cash register drawer is greater than the initial bank plus net cash receipts.

paid-in-advance (PIA) guest—A guest who pays his or her room charges in cash during registration; PIA guests are often denied in-house credit.

paid-out—Cash disbursed by the hotel on behalf of a guest and charged to the guest's account as a cash advance.

point-of-sale (POS) system—An automated network that allows electronic cash registers at the hotel's points of sale to communicate directly with a front office system.

posting—The process of recording transactions on a guest folio.

shortage—An imbalance that occurs when the total of cash and checks in a cash register drawer is less than the initial bank plus net cash receipts.

transfer voucher—A voucher used to support a reduction in balance on one folio and an equal increase in balance on another; used for transfers between guest accounts and for transfers from guest accounts to non-guest accounts when they are settled by the use of payment cards.

voucher—A document detailing a transaction to be posted to a front office account; used to communicate information from a point of sale to the front office.

 Review Questions —————————————————————————————

1. What are the specific functions of a front office accounting system? What tasks are performed during each stage of the guest cycle?

2. What is the purpose of an account? How are transactions recorded in an account? How are guest accounts and non-guest accounts different?

3. What are the four types of folios in common use in front office accounting? How is a folio related to an account?

4. What is a point of sale? How can fully automated point-of-sale systems and guest-operated devices streamline the flow of accounting information to the front office?

5. What information is necessary to create a folio? How does the process differ in non-automated, semi-automated, and fully automated front office record-keeping systems?

6. What is the basic front office accounting formula? How is it used in posting transactions?

7. How does accounting for a cash payment differ from accounting for a cash advance at the front desk?

8. What is a cash bank? What are good cash bank control procedures?

9. What are overages, shortages, and due backs? How might these conditions reflect on a front office cashier's job performance?

10. What is the difference between an account correction and an account allowance? Why is it important to differentiate between the two?

Internet Sites

For more information, visit the following Internet sites. Remember that Internet addresses can change without notice. If the site is no longer there, you can use a search engine to look for additional sites.

CSS Hotel Systems
www.csshotelsystems.com

Innfinity Software Systems
www.innfinity.com

Execu/Tech Hospitality Solutions
www.execu-tech.com

Prologic First
www.prologicfirst.com

Hotellinx Systems Ltd.
www.hotellinx.com

Case Study

Front Office Accounting at the Magic Crest Hotel

One of the major problems with front office accounting at the Magic Crest Hotel is monitoring guest and non-guest accounts. Management has always extended local businesses and government officials charge privileges, the idea being that, with the convenience of deferred payments, local patrons would be more likely to dine and/or host clients at the hotel. This program has proved to be highly successful. The volume of purchases charged to such non-guest accounts now approximates the level of sales incurred by registered guests. Unsure if this is a good or bad situation, Mr. Aerial, the front office manager, requests the front office accounting staff to study the problem and to report its findings at next week's front office meeting.

At the weekly front office meeting, the hotel's accountant, Ms. Letsche, reports that there are at least three problems related to the hotel's non-guest charge purchasing policies: its impact on the daily hotel audit, the billing procedures to collect payment, and the number of applications for additional non-guest accounts.

When asked to be more specific, she begins with a review of the daily hotel audit. She states that since the front office receives charge vouchers from the hotel's revenue centers, it is the front desk agent's responsibility to separate guest from non-guest accounts. Since registered guest charges are posted by room number, one would think it easy to sort those charges from the others. Unfortunately, both the hotel's room numbers and the non-guest account numbers are three digits, thereby making the sorting more time-consuming. Mr. Aerial asks if it is really necessary to separate the charges. Ms. Letsche explains that it is, since the hotel must maintain accurate guest folio balances. She further states that the non-guest vouchers are accumulated and posted on Saturday afternoons, when the hotel's business is less hectic.

The billing procedures to collect non-guest account balances are tricky, Ms. Letsche said. Since the hotel bills non-guest accounts on the last day of each month, some charges occurring in a particular month may not be posted in time to appear on that month's bill. In addition, non-guest accounts usually are not paid in a timely fashion. In fact, 47 percent of last month's non-guest account balances remain unpaid and tomorrow is the date of the next billing cycle. Mr. Aerial explains that the local customers are important to the hotel and suggests that maybe Ms. Letsche is over-sensitive to the billing problems.

Lastly, Ms. Letsche relates the fact that there are at least ten new applications for non-guest accounts. She has instructed her staff not to authorize any new accounts without her written approval. She further states that she is reluctant to authorize any additional non-guest accounts, and looks to Mr. Aerial for advice. Convinced of the positive aspects of such business, Mr. Aerial directs her to approve the requests and to assign account numbers effective the first day of next month. Ms. Letsche so instructs her staff.

Discussion Questions

1. What ideas would you suggest to facilitate a more effective processing of guest and non-guest charge vouchers? How might the daily audit be aided by such changes? Is the accumulated-postings routine for non-guest accounts an effective plan?

2. What could be done to improve the hotel's billing of non-guest accounts? What could be done to improve collection of outstanding balances?

3. What are the advantages and disadvantages to having a high volume of non-guest accounts? What about the cost of carrying and collecting outstanding balances? How might the hotel's cash flow be affected by such transactions?

Case Number: 3327CA

The following industry experts helped generate and develop this case: Richard M. Brooks, CHA, Vice President, TWE Group; and S. Kenneth Hiller, CHA, General Manager, Holiday Inn, Beachwood, Ohio.

Chapter 9 Outline

The Check-Out and Settlement Process
Departure Procedures
    Methods of Settlement
    Late Check-Out
Check-Out Options
    Express Check-Out
    Self Check-Out
Unpaid Account Balances
Account Collection
    Account Aging
Front Office Records
    Guest History File
    Marketing Follow-Through
    Data Privacy
Summary

Competencies

1. Identify functions and procedures related to the check-out and settlement process, including departure procedures involving methods of settlement and late check-outs. (pp. 335–341)

2. Describe express check-out and self check-out procedures. (pp. 341–343)

3. Explain how hotels handle unpaid account balances and summarize account collection procedures. (pp. 343–348)

4. Describe how managers use guest history files, outline how the front office staff can support the hotel's marketing program through the check-out process, and summarize front office data privacy concerns. (pp. 349–354)

Check-Out and Account Settlement

Check-out and settlement are part of the final stage of the guest cycle. The services and activities of the departure stage are performed primarily by a member of the front office staff. Before the age of automation in hotels, the workload of the front desk staff in medium and large hotels was sufficiently busy that registration (check-in) and front office cashiering (check-out) were separately staffed functions. A guest would be checked in by a front desk agent and checked out by a front desk cashier. Cross-training of staff members was rare. Only in small hotels did the same person perform both jobs. With front office automation, most front desk agents can perform both check-in and check-out procedures. This adds variety to front desk work and permits more flexible staffing schedules and better service to guests. Personnel from the front office accounting staff may be involved as well. Before departing the hotel, guests will generally stop at the front desk to review their folio, settle any outstanding account balance, receive a receipt of the account statement, and return their room key. However, self check-out has become quite common, allowing guests to check out via an in-room television set or remote terminal, thereby bypassing the front desk entirely. Following self check-out, a final statement of the guest account can be picked up at the front desk, mailed, or e-mailed to the guest.

Two of the most stressful times for hotel guests occur during check-in and check-out. Guests may forget the previous courtesy and hospitality exhibited by the hotel staff if check-out and account settlement are not professional, accurate, friendly, and efficient. This chapter covers the final phase of the guest cycle by examining the various activities involved in guest check-out and account settlement.

The Check-Out and Settlement Process

Front office staff performs at least three important functions during the check-out and account settlement process:

- Resolution of outstanding guest account balances
- Updating of room status information
- Creation of a guest history record

Guest account settlement depends on an effective front office accounting system that maintains accurate procedures related to guest folios, verifies and authorizes a method of account settlement, and helps resolve discrepancies in account balances. Generally, the front office staff finds it most effective to settle a guest's account while the guest is still on the hotel premises. A guest can settle an account by paying cash, charging the balance to a payment card, deferring payment to an approved direct billing entity, applying a gift card, or using a combination of payment methods.

Front office policy usually requires guests to specify an anticipated method of eventual account settlement at the time they check in. This procedure enables front office staff to verify or confirm the status of the guest's payment card or direct billing information in advance of check-out and guest account settlement. Pre-settlement verification activities accelerate check-out time and significantly improve the front office staff's ability to efficiently settle outstanding account balances. Despite the fact that a guest may later change his or her mind and settle using another form of payment, pre-settlement verification activities help ensure that the hotel will receive payment for the accommodations and services it provides during the guest's stay.

Effective front office operations depend on accurate room status information. When a guest checks out and settles his or her account, the front desk agent performs several important tasks. First, the agent updates the guestroom's status from *occupied* to *on-change* in the room status file. *On-change* is a housekeeping term that means that the guest has checked out and the guestroom that previously had been occupied needs to be cleaned and readied for the next guest. When the room status is changed, the front office system may automatically notify housekeeping department staff that the guest has departed. Some front office systems will also remind housekeeping of any extra equipment to be removed from the guestroom, such as a crib or rollaway bed.

In the past, the front desk staff communicated information to the housekeeping department by telephone or through an electronic room status board or a telewriter. Today, this information is more commonly relayed automatically by the front office system to housekeeping department staff when the front desk agent completes the check-out process. Once housekeeping staff receives the information, a housekeeper may be dispatched to clean and prepare the room for inspection and resale. To maximize room sales, the front office system must maintain current occupancy and housekeeping status for all rooms and must be capable of exchanging room status information with the housekeeping department quickly and accurately.

Check-out and settlement also involves the creation of a *guest history record* that will become part of the front office system's *guest history file.* Since a hotel often can gain a valuable competitive advantage in the hospitality marketplace through the proper analysis of guest history data, guest history files form a powerful database for strategic marketing.

Departure Procedures

Guest check-out and account settlement can be an efficient process when the front office staff is well-prepared and organized. The departure stage of the guest cycle involves several procedures designed to simplify check-out and account settlement. These procedures include:

- Inquiring about additional charges not appearing on the guest folio.

- Posting outstanding charges awaiting posting.

- Verifying account information.

- Presenting the guest folio.

- Verifying the method of payment.

- Processing the account payment.

- Checking for undelivered mail, messages, and documents such as faxes.

- Securing the room key.

- Updating the room's status.

- Inquiring about the guest's experience at the hotel.

- Requesting the guest to complete a guest satisfaction survey.

- Updating the guest history file.

The procedures used vary among front office operations, depending on the hotel's level of service and degree of automation. The amount of personal contact between guests and front desk staff may also vary, since most front office operations include express and self check-out services.

The check-out procedure affords the front office staff yet another opportunity to make a positive impression on guests. A guest approaching the front desk should be greeted promptly and courteously. The front desk agent should check for any messages or mail awaiting guest pickup. The front desk agent should also verify that the guest has cleared any safe deposit box or in-room safe used during the stay, and make sure the guest has returned the guestroom key. In many systems, the guest's electronic folio can be flagged to notify the front desk agent if the guest has any outstanding messages, mail, or items in a safe deposit box. This simplifies front office recordkeeping and also minimizes the chance of overlooking these matters during check-out.

To ensure that the guest's folio is accurate and complete, the front desk agent should process any outstanding charges awaiting posting. In addition, the front desk agent should ask the guest if he or she incurred any recent charges and update the necessary postings to the guest's folio. Guests expect their final folio to be accurate and ready when they are ready to check out. No matter what degree of automation at a hotel, the guest may leave with a poor impression of the property if the guestroom folio is not complete and accurate at check-out time.

Traditionally, at check-out the guest is given a final copy of the guest folio for review and settlement. During this time, the front desk agent should confirm how the guest intends to settle the account, regardless of which method of settlement the guest specified during registration. This request is necessary, because front office policy may require the guest to establish credit at check-in, regardless of how the guest eventually plans to settle the account. A guest may establish credit by presenting a payment card at check-in, and then decide to settle his or her account balance by cash, credit card, debit card, gift card, or personal check. VIP guests or special guests of a group or corporate account should not be asked for settlement if their account is marked as a direct billing account.

After determining the guest's preferred method of payment, the front desk agent should then bring the guest's account balance to zero by applying the payment method. This is typically called **zeroing out** the account. A guest's account balance must be settled in full or transferred to an acceptable alternative account for a guest account to be considered zeroed out. As long as full payment is assured, the account should be considered as brought to a zero balance. For example, if the guest pays cash, the account is brought to a zero balance immediately. If the guest settles using a payment card, the hotel will get an approval from the payment card company for the amount due. Approval of a transaction by the payment card company guarantees payment to the hotel for the amount approved, so the account can also be brought to zero. Hotels may be paid amounts due from payment card companies within a day or two of the settlement transaction, but upon receiving a payment guarantee, the hotel assumes that payment in full will follow, and closes the folio. If the account is to be paid through direct billing, the account is brought to a zero balance through transferring the amount due to a non-guest ledger entry in the back office accounts receivable system.

Methods of Settlement

A guest account can be brought to a zero balance in several ways. Methods of settlement include cash or debit card, credit card, direct billing, or a combined settlement method.

Cash or Debit Card. A cash payment in full at check-out is the most direct way to bring a guest account balance to zero. When processing a cash payment in full, the front desk agent should mark the folio as paid. As mentioned previously, front office policy may sometimes require the guest to present a credit or debit card at check-in to establish charge privileges at hotel revenue centers. A guest may have had a credit card accepted and verified at registration, even though he or she intended eventually to settle the guest account using cash. The front desk agent should destroy the guest's credit card voucher created at registration when the guest pays the account in full with cash (or some other alternate form of payment). When the guest registers and the front desk agent establishes credit by obtaining a credit card authorization, in effect the credit card processing company commits to reserving projected funds for potential payment to the hotel. This practice reduces the amount of funds available to the credit card holder for other purchases. If the guest settles his or her account with another form of payment, it is essential that the funds being held for the hotel by the card company be released at check-out. Otherwise, the credit card processing company may reserve the funds for up to thirty days. This can be a burden to guests, and will result in complaints and dissatisfaction after the guest has departed the hotel.

Debit card settlements are considered to be similar to cash payments, because funds are drawn directly from the guest's personal checking or savings account when the card is processed. Banks issuing debit cards will not process a withdrawal transaction against the card unless there are sufficient funds in the account at the time of transaction settlement. Even though the guest's folio is brought to a zero balance at check-out, the amount due the hotel may be transferred from the guest ledger to the city ledger until final payment is received.

Guests desiring to settle their account in foreign currency should first convert their money to the local currency (that is, the currency that the hotel normally accepts). Account settlement is customarily handled in local currency only. Hotels may charge guests a fee to convert their foreign currency to the local currency, since the hotel's bank will charge a currency-conversion fee to the hotel at the time that funds are deposited. The front office cashier may have currency conversion rates readily available, based on online financial information.

Cash payments are the most likely to be involved in fraud by front desk agents. It is important that the hotel have procedures in place to record the processing of cash transactions. Some hotels require that a front office supervisor approve all cash settlements. This is to verify that the cash paid by the guest is actually put into the front desk agent's cash bank. In addition, front desk agents should be trained on how to identify counterfeit currency, especially $20 bills and higher denomination bills, as these are among the most common counterfeited.

Credit Card. Even though credit card settlement brings a guest account to zero, the amount of the charge must be tracked until payment is actually received from the credit card company. Therefore, credit card settlement creates a transfer credit on the guest's folio and moves the account balance from the guest ledger to a credit card account in the city (or non-guest) ledger. After the front desk agent processes the transaction, the guest may be asked to sign a copy of the folio, acknowledging and agreeing to the credit card balance. The guest's signature on the folio completes this transaction. When an international guest presents a credit card for payment, the credit card company will apply payment in local currency. In these cases, hotels do not have to be concerned with currency exchange fees, since these fees are charged to the cardholder.

Direct Billing. Like credit card settlement, direct billing transfers a guest's account balance from the guest ledger to the city ledger. Unlike credit card settlement, responsibility for billing and collecting a direct billing lies with the hotel rather than an outside agency. Direct billings are not normally an acceptable method of settlement unless the billing has been prearranged and approved by the hotel's back office credit department before or during guest registration. To complete a direct billing settlement, the front desk agent has the guest sign the folio to verify that its contents are correct and that the guest will accept responsibility for payment, should the direct billing agent refuse payment. A copy of the final guest folio is sent to the direct billing agency for payment.

Combined Settlement Methods. A guest may elect to use more than one settlement method to bring the guest folio balance to zero. For example, the guest may make a partial cash payment and charge the remainder of the account balance to a credit card. Front desk agents must accurately record the combined settlement methods and exercise care that required paperwork is properly completed. Properly completed paperwork helps facilitate an effective front office audit.

Once the guest has settled the folio balance, the front desk agent should provide the guest with a copy of the final folio. Check-out and account settlement are among the last opportunities the front office staff has to convey the spirit of hospitality. The front desk agent should ask the guest if everything at the property met the guest's expectations, especially the guestroom, facilities, and service areas.

Check-out and account settlement is an excellent time for the front desk agent to demonstrate the staff's concern relative to the quality of the guest's hotel experience. The front office may provide guests with comment cards at check-out or via e-mail following the guest's stay, hoping to receive an evaluation of the hotel's effectiveness. The front desk agent should always thank guests for staying at the hotel and wish guests safe travels. The front desk agent should also encourage guests to consider returning to the property during a return trip to the area.

Sometimes guests may settle their account before check-out time and not actually depart the hotel premises. For example, a guest may complete check-out at 8 A.M. but may participate in a business meeting at the hotel until noon. Such a guest will not be able to post additional charges to his or her guestroom account, since the account was closed at check-out. This can be an inconvenience or embarrassment for some guests. For this reason, front desk agents should verify that guests are actually leaving the hotel upon completion of check-out, and, if they are not, let them know that they will not be able to post additional charges to their account.

Late Check-Out

Guests do not always check out by the hotel's posted check-out time. To minimize **late check-outs,** the front office staff should post check-out time notices in conspicuous places, such as on the back of all guestroom doors and in a prominent location at the front desk. A reminder of the check-out time can also be included in any pre-departure materials distributed to guests expected to depart on the current day. Late check-outs can be a problem for some hotels and resorts. Guests may wish to stay throughout the day on the last day of their stay and use hotel facilities, including the guestroom, pool, spa, and other areas. It is important for front office staff to properly communicate and tactfully enforce the check-out time in order to provide the housekeeping staff sufficient time to prepare the room for arriving guests.

Hotel management may authorize the front desk staff to charge **late check-out fees.** A guest will probably be surprised to find such a fee on the folio, especially if he or she is not familiar with the hotel's check-out policy. Whenever a guest inquires about a late check-out, the front desk agent should inform the guest of the hotel's policy regarding late check-out times and charges.

Some guests may resent being charged an additional expense and may try to negotiate to avoid payment. Front desk agents should approach such situations calmly, offering a well-reasoned explanation for late check-out policies. A front office manager may need to be summoned to discuss and resolve the matter with the guest.

Front office staff should not be apologetic about a late check-out fee. The hotel's check-out time is carefully determined, not arbitrarily set. It is not intended to inconvenience guests. Management establishes a check-out time that allows the housekeeping department sufficient time to prepare rooms for newly arriving guests. Guestrooms should be cleaned and readied for arriving guests before the housekeeping staff completes its work shift. Late check-outs granted by a front desk agent can lead to additional expense for the hotel, especially in the housekeeping department, where room attendants may have to work beyond their regular shifts to finish cleaning all of their assigned rooms. In addition, the inconvenience and potential dissatisfaction of arriving guests should also be taken into consideration. For these reasons, it is often justifiable for hotels to apply a late check-out fee.

Check-Out Options

Changes in technology and guest needs have prompted front office managers to develop alternatives to standard check-out and account settlement procedures. These options combine advances in technology with special guest services to expedite departure activities.

Express Check-Out

At many hotels, guests encounter long lines at the front desk when trying to check out during a prime check-out period. To ease front desk volume, some front office staffs initiate check-out activities in advance of the guest actually being ready to depart. A common pre-departure activity involves producing and distributing guest folios to those guests expected to check out. Front office staff, housekeeping staff, or even hotel security staff may quietly slip printed folios under the guest-room doors of expected check-outs before 6 A.M. (These folios should be placed so that they can't be read or accessed from outside the room.)

Normally, the front office will distribute an **express check-out** form with each pre-departure folio. Express check-out forms may include a note requesting guests to notify the front desk if departure plans change. Otherwise, the front office will assume the guest is leaving by the hotel's posted check-out time. This procedure usually reminds and encourages guests to use the express check-out service.

A sample express check-out form is shown in Exhibit 1. By completing such a form, the guest authorizes the front office to transfer his or her outstanding folio balance to the payment card that was presented during registration. (If no payment card information was captured or if no credit was established at registration, the front office staff may not offer express check-out service.) After completing the form, the guest deposits the express check-out form at the front desk container designated for express check-out when departing. After the guest has left the hotel (it may be hours afterward), the front office staff completes the guest's check-out by transferring the outstanding guest folio balance to a previously authorized method of settlement. Any additional charges the guest incurs before leaving the hotel (telephone call charges, for example) will be added to his or her folio balance before the front desk agent brings the account to a zero balance via account transfer. Due to the possible occurrence of late charges, the amount due on the guest's copy of the express check-out folio may not equal the amount actually applied to the guest's payment card account. This possibility should be clearly stated on the express check-out form to minimize guest confusion. When after-departure charges are added to the account, a copy of the updated folio should be mailed or

Exhibit 1 Sample Express Check-Out Form

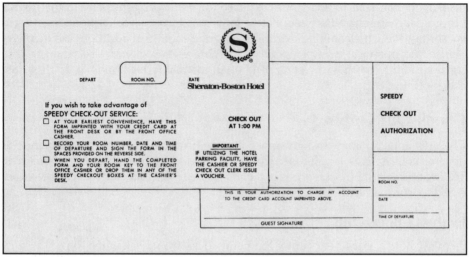

Courtesy of The Sheraton-Boston Hotel, Boston, Massachusetts.

e-mailed to the guest so that he or she has an accurate record of the stay. In this way, the guest is not surprised when his or her payment card bill arrives with a different amount.

Express check-out must not be offered to guests who paid in advance using cash, because it is unlikely the amount due the hotel will equal the amount prepaid by the guests, and, since front office records to not contain credit information on cash-paying guests, the hotel can't bill them for any additional money owed. As soon as an express check-out form is received by the front office staff, a front desk agent should change the room's status in the front office system so the housekeeping department receives the information in a timely manner and the room can be scheduled for cleaning.

Self Check-Out

In some hotels, guests can complete check-out procedures by accessing **self check-out terminals** in the hotel's lobby or meeting areas, or by using a mobile device or in-room device. Self check-out devices can interact with the front office system to reduce check-out time and minimize front desk traffic. Self check-out terminals vary in design. Some resemble automatic bank teller machines, while others possess touchscreen video and audio capability. Self-service devices may be located in areas of the hotel away from the front desk, such as in a convention registration area or the hotel parking garage.

To use a self check-out terminal, the guest accesses the proper folio and reviews its contents. Guests may be required to swipe or tap a payment card to initiate the process. Settlement can be automatically assigned to an acceptable payment card account.

Check-out is complete when the guest's account balance is transferred to a payment card account and an itemized account statement is prepared for the guest. A self check-out system should then automatically communicate updated room status information to the front office system. The front office system, in turn, relays room status information to the housekeeping department while simultaneously initiating the creation of a guest history record.

In-room folio review and check-out often relies on an in-room television set with a remote control device. The guest can simply confirm a previously approved method of settlement for the account, because the in-room television system is connected to the front office system. The front office system directs the self check-out process. Guests can pick up a copy of their printed folio at the front desk after completing self check-out, or request that one be e-mailed to them. In-room self check-out technology, like other self check-out procedures, automatically updates room status and creates a guest history record. Another advantage of in-room folio review is that guests can look at their folios at any time during their stays.

Laptop computers, mobile devices, and personal digital assistants (PDAs) can replace the guestroom television set as a self check-out device. Some hotel companies and front office system suppliers also feature self check-out capabilities through web access. Guests are able to access their account through a secure Internet link. Access enables online folio review and payment approval. The final billing may be sent to the guest via e-mail or instant messenger service.

Unpaid Account Balances

No matter how carefully front office staff monitors a guest's stay, there is always the possibility that the guest will leave without settling his or her account. Some guests honestly forget to check out; others depart the hotel with no intention of settling their account (these guests are commonly referred to as **skippers**). Sometimes front office staff discovers late charges for guests who have checked out and departed the hotel. Regardless of the reason, after-departure charges or outstanding guest account balances represent **unpaid account balances.**

Late charges are a major concern in guest account settlement. A **late charge** is a transaction requiring posting to a guest account that does not reach the front office system for posting until after the guest has checked out and closed his or her account. Restaurant, telephone, and room service charges are examples of potential late charges. Since the guest should have paid for these purchases before leaving, the hotel may have problems collecting after-departure charges.

Even if late charges are eventually paid, the hotel incurs the additional costs involved in after-departure billing. Sometimes the extra expenses for labor, postage, stationery, and special statements may cost more than the amount of the late charge. Many hotel managers will not bill a departed guest who owes for late charges unless the charges are above a certain set amount (for example, anywhere from $8 to $15). If the late charge is less than this set amount, management is likely to write off the amount and zero the balance through accounting. Few hotels can afford to finance a large volume of late charges, however. That's why reducing the possibility of late charges is important to cost containment.

A front office automated system that interfaces with revenue center outlets is often the most effective means of reducing or eliminating late charges. For example, a restaurant point-of-sale system with an interface to the front office system can instantly verify room account status, verify credit authorization, and post charges to the guest's folio, all before the guest leaves the restaurant. Similarly, a call accounting system interface to the front office system can help eliminate telephone call late charges. Guests who make telephone calls from their guestrooms and then go directly to the front desk to check out are likely to find all of their telephone call charges, even their last-minute calls, listed on their folios.

At hotels with front office systems that are not interfaced to point-of-sale or other systems, front desk agents can follow several guidelines to help reduce the occurrence of late charges. Front desk staff can:

- Post transactional vouchers as soon as the vouchers are received for posting. This procedure will help minimize the volume of unposted charges prior to and during the check-out period.

- Survey front office vouchers and folio racks for unposted charges before checking a guest out. For example, in-room movie systems may possess transactional information not yet transmitted to the front office system for posting.

- Ask departing guests whether they have incurred any charge purchases that are not listed on their final folios.

While most guests will respond honestly to a direct question, many guests may not feel obligated to volunteer information about charges not posted to the folio. These guests will simply pay the outstanding balance on the folio and ignore unposted charges. Some guests may be unaware that they are responsible for paying unposted charges.

Front office management at hotels without interfaced point-of-sale and other systems may establish a process to ensure that revenue outlet charges are delivered quickly to the front desk staff for posting. This is especially important during peak morning check-out periods. In an effort to minimize late charges, front desk staff may employ runners to collect revenue outlet vouchers, or may telephone other hotel departments to gather charge purchase information.

Guests who present a payment card at check-in may assume that all charges will automatically be transferred to their payment card account for billing. Depending on the hotel's contractual agreement with a payment card company, the hotel may simply write "signature on file" on the signature line of the payment card voucher to receive payment for the guest's outstanding balance. *Signature on file* means the guest has signed the hotel's registration form or its equivalent at check-in and, by doing so, has agreed to pay the final folio balance in full. It is important to note that a payment card company may allow after-departure charges to be added to a guest's signed payment card voucher. Front desk agents must be sure that the payment card company will accept additional charges before posting charges to a signed voucher. When after-departure charges are posted to a folio and added to a payment card voucher, the front desk staff should send a copy of the updated folio to the guest so that the guest will understand why additional charges appeared on the folio.

Account Collection

Late charges that are billed to departed guests should not be classified as uncollectible until the front office staff or accounting department personnel have exhausted all billing and collection procedures. A properly completed registration form should contain the guest's signature and home and business addresses, e-mail address, and telephone numbers. Procedures for billing late charges to a guest who settled an account using cash may differ from procedures used to bill late charges to a guest who settled an account with a payment card. Guests who paid with a payment card will be billed according to the policies and procedures of the payment card company governing late charge collection. Unpaid folio balances of guests who paid with cash may be transferred from the control of the front office to the hotel's accounting division in the back office for collection.

Typical city ledger accounts include:

- *Payment card billings* to authorized payment card companies
- *Direct billings* to approved corporate, travel, and other agencies
- *Travel agency accounts* for authorized tours and groups
- *Bad check accounts* resulting from departed-guest personal checks that were returned unpaid
- *Skipper accounts* for guests who left the hotel without settling their folios
- *Disputed bills* for guests who refused to settle their accounts (in part or in full) because of a discrepancy in posting
- *Guaranteed reservation accounts* for billing and tracking no-show guests
- *Late charges accounts* for guests who checked out before some charges were posted to their guestroom accounts
- *House accounts* for non-guest business and promotional activities

To be effective, front office management and the accounting department leadership must jointly establish a procedure for billing departed guests who have overdue accounts. Accounts receivable billing includes determining:

- When outstanding account balances are payable
- The number of days between account billings
- How to contact a departed guest whose account is overdue

The sooner the collection process is started, the more likely the hotel will receive payment on unpaid account balances. Timing is often the key to success in preparing departed-guest accounts for collection. Each hotel needs to develop its own collection schedule. Collection schedules can range from aggressive (short-cycle) to lenient (long-cycle), depending on the hotel's financial needs, guest profile, history of collection patterns, and so on. In some hotels, it is usually the front office credit manager who is responsible for collections. In other hotels, it may be the front desk manager or an accounts receivable clerk who is assigned the responsibility. Exhibit 2 shows a bill scheduling chart that may be used to monitor

Exhibit 2   Bill Scheduling Chart

Schedule	Method	Timing
1st billing	_____ Statement with back-up invoice	Mailed no later than _____ hours after the guest's account is transferred to the city ledger.
2nd billing	_____ Statement _____ Telephone call _____ Letter	_____ Days later
3rd billing	_____ Statement _____ Telephone call _____ Letter	_____ Days later
4th billing	_____ Statement _____ Telephone call _____ Letter	_____ Days later
5th billing	_____ Statement _____ Telephone call _____ Letter	_____ Days later
and so on.		

the methods and timing cycles for payment collections. Sometimes guests dispute charges because they do not remember making them. This is especially true of late charges.

In all collection cases, it is important for hotel staff to be polite but firm in any encounter involving a delinquent payment account. However, collection activities that violate a consumer's rights may prove to be more costly than the original debt. The Federal Fair Debt Collection Practices Act and the Fair Credit Billing Act clearly state the responsibilities and rights of parties involved in collection activities.

Regardless of the collection procedures followed, problems in accounts receivable billing may develop. Hotel management should have a documented procedure for collecting overdue accounts and may appoint a credit committee to examine overdue accounts.

Just as individual guest accounts must be monitored closely, so must the master folio accounts established for groups. Credit arrangements for groups should be established well before their arrival. Sometimes an advance deposit or prepayment will be required to ensure at least a partial payment. Front office staff may prepare a preliminary master folio account statement prior to the group's departure and review it with the group leader to expedite the final payment process. It is common for front office management to require individual guests to establish personal credit during registration, as the group master folio may be authorized to handle only certain expenses, such as room, tax, and arranged meals.

Master folio accounts can be complex in design for some meetings and conventions. For this reason, billing arrangements are usually clearly specified in the group function contract and reviewed and confirmed with the group leader before the group's arrival. Should there be changes, the front office manager and other affected hotel department heads must be notified. It is customary for the front office manager to meet daily with the group leader or designated representative to review group transactions. The objective of this daily meeting is to review all charges with the group leader and obtain his or her approval of the charges applied to the group folio for that day (or the previous day). This procedure allows the front office manager time to resolve any billing disputes before the group departs the hotel. In addition to informing the group leader of billing balances, this daily tally-authorization meeting helps expedite the payment collection process. Depending on hotel policy, the responsibility for obtaining charge authorization may be assigned to the front office manager, the credit manager, the catering manager, or the conference service manager. Of particular interest are banquet charges, since food-service charges are usually assessed on a per-guest basis. Guest and meeting room charges to be posted to the master account should also be regularly reviewed to ensure that the group is being properly charged. At some resort properties, unique or unusual charges may be commonly posted to the master folio account. For example, there may be a golf or tennis tournament for which all associated charges are posted to the group's master folio account. Special events can add complexity to the billing process. When the final master account statement is presented to the accounting department, all previously authorized invoices, vouchers, and related documentation should be attached to verify that the group leader has reviewed and approved the charges.

From an accounting perspective, some hotels attribute erroneous postings back to the department that originally accepted the uncollectible charge. For instance, the front office may be assessed the amount of an uncollectible transaction if charges were wrongly billed. The hotel's credit committee, credit manager, or general manager should analyze the originating department's procedures and recommend corrective action. Collection problems may indicate the need for employee retraining or closer supervision.

Account Aging

Payment card billings are normally paid according to the hotel's contractual agreements with the payment card companies. The hotel accounting department might receive payment immediately after billing or might have to wait several days or more. Factors that affect this include the volume of payment card transactions, frequency of payment voucher submission, and transaction fees levied by the payment card company. Most city ledger accounts are usually settled within thirty days of billing. Some city ledger accounts, however, may experience a collection period longer than thirty days. The hotel should establish methods for monitoring past due accounts based on the date the charges were incurred. This practice of scheduled billings is normally referred to as **account aging.**

Exhibit 3   Aged Accounts Receivable Report

Name	Balance	Current	Outstanding			
			30–60	**60–90**	**90–120**	**120+**
Elizabeth Penny	$125					$125
Mimi Hendricks	$235			$235		
M/M Phil Damon	$486	$100	$386			
Harrison Taylor	$999			$999		
TOTALS	$1,845	$100	$386	$1,234		$125

AGED ACCOUNTS RECEIVABLE — As of _____, 20 _____

Account aging analysis tends to differ among hotels, depending on the variety of credit terms in effect. At some properties, the hotel accounting division typically monitors account aging. At other properties, the front office auditor may assume this responsibility. An account age analysis sheet identifies accounts receivable of thirty, sixty, ninety, or more days old. Exhibit 3 shows a simplified aged accounts receivable report. Accounts that are less than thirty days old are considered **current.** Accounts that are older than thirty days are considered **overdue.** In some cases, accounts that are older than ninety days are considered **delinquent.** The front office staff and accounting department staff should maintain a list of outstanding accounts. Guests with an overdue account balance may be denied credit privileges until the account is paid or at least classified as current.

Overdue accounts represent an expense to the hotel. Hotel management cannot use the revenue attributed to overdue accounts because the revenue has not yet been collected. In addition, the older an account gets, the more difficult it becomes to collect. For this reason, many accounting departments maintain a report indicating the average age of accounts receivable. Hotel owners and senior managers use this report to ensure that collections are being handled properly.

Front Office Records

At the time of check-out, guest folios are stored electronically and can be accessed by guest name, folio number, guest history record number, or arrival/departure date. Front office staff can use electronic records to document original billings and establish guest history records following check-out.

Guest History File

Front office management can better understand hotel clientele and determine guest trends through **guest history files.** An automated guest history file is a collection of personal and financial data about guests who have stayed at the hotel (or at another property in the chain, in the case of chain hotels). An individual **guest history record** within the file normally contains personal and transactional information relevant to the guest's previous stay. (Guest history records are confidential and proprietary; front office managers are obligated to protect guests from invasions of privacy.)

Creating the guest history record is one of the last steps in the check-out and account settlement process. Many front office system operations construct a simple guest history file from a collection of expired guest registration information and guest folios. The front office system may automatically re-format guest information into a guest history database. Some front office systems can apply a pre-formatted template to automatically generate an electronic guest history record. See Exhibit 4 for a sample guest history record.

A hotel loyalty program may provide a special form or online script requesting such information as name of spouse and children, birthday, guestroom preference, bedding and pillow preference, and favorite foods. Having such personal information on file helps the hotel staff provide better, more comprehensive guest service during subsequent visits. Several hotel chains allow members of their frequent guest programs to provide this information through a dedicated preferred-guest website.

The hotel's sales and marketing staff can use guest history information as a database for mailing lists or to identify guest characteristics important for strategic marketing. This information may help hotel staff develop advertisements or link websites in a way that appeals to the types of clientele the hotel is attempting to attract. Guest history records may also reveal the need for new, supplementary, or enhanced guest services.

An automated guest history system is based on specialty software that allows the application of guest history data for marketing and related efforts, and for measuring the effectiveness of past promotional efforts. For instance, a guest history database may enable the hotel staff to determine the geographic distribution of guests' home and business addresses. Hotel advertisements may be placed more effectively based on this type of data. Some hotel chains centralize their guest history database, so that all affiliated hotels in the brand can access guests' preference information. Guests are often surprised to discover that a stay at one chain hotel has alerted another property in the chain to provide some extra, personalized courtesy. This approach tends to create strong loyalty to the brand, as well as across multiple brands of the same company.

Exhibit 4   Guest History Record

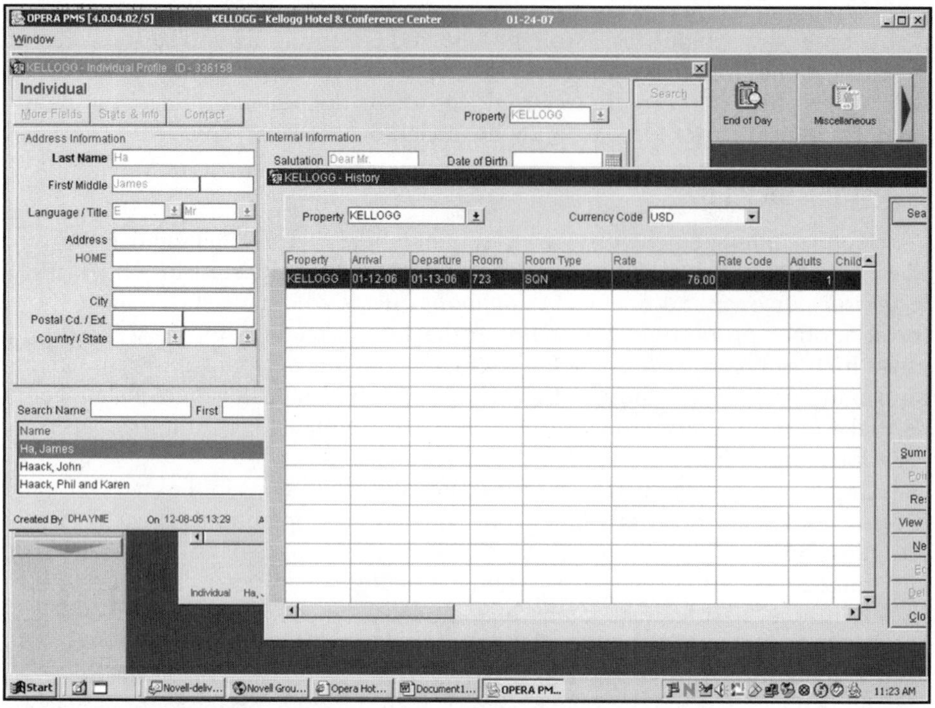

Courtesy: Kellogg Hotel & Conference Center, Michigan State University, East Lansing, Michigan.

Exhibit 5 diagrams the automated guest history system at The Ritz-Carlton Hotel Company. This system enables Ritz-Carlton staff members to use online guest preference information to provide uniquely personal levels of service to returning guests.

Many hotels keep detailed group and corporate account history files, to maintain positive relations with the group's leadership and help with group reservations. For example, a group may request 100 guestrooms for three nights for a corporate meeting scheduled for June, but fill only seventy rooms of those blocked for the group. The number of group rooms actually booked compared to the number originally blocked is called the *pick-up rate*. The hotel's sales and marketing system will track the group's pick-up rate so that the next time the group holds a meeting at the property, the sales staff can work with the meeting planner to block a more appropriate number of guestrooms. Hotel sales representatives commonly require that the group fill a minimum number of blocked guestrooms by a certain date, or an attrition charge will be applied to the group's master account. The attrition charge is intended to help compensate the hotel for blocking rooms that might otherwise have been saleable had they not been held out of availability only to be unoccupied. The attrition charge represents an extra expense to the group, so, if the hotel's sales representative can help the group to more accurately determine its rooming needs, the group may avoid such a charge.

Exhibit 5   The Ritz-Carlton Repeat Guest History Program

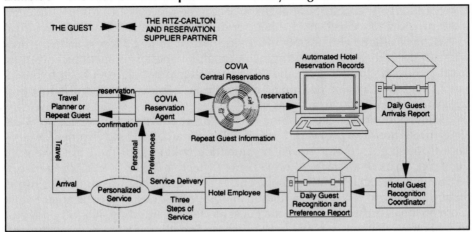

Source: *Application Summary: The Ritz-Carlton Hotel Company.*

Group leaders and meeting coordinators often negotiate with hotel sales staff for special discounted group or corporate rates. These discounted rates are usually based on the number of guestrooms the group or company is willing to guarantee to occupy over a specific time period (usually one year). By maintaining a detailed history of a group or company's guestroom usage, as well as its spending in hotel revenue centers, the hotel sales staff can be more fully informed and therefore more flexible when negotiating rates.

Marketing Follow-Through

Just as a hotel's marketing department may rely in part on guest history files to develop new marketing strategies for individual guests, so too may the department depend on a front office agent's performance and follow-through at checkout. Many hotel companies have implemented frequent guest or frequent traveler affinity programs to encourage brand loyalty. Frequent guest programs are often important components of enhanced guest-relations-management programs. Such programs generally award credits to guests (accrued after departure) for room nights occupied or dollars spent across a brand of properties. Before completing the check-out process, it is appropriate for the front desk agent to verify the guest's club membership status or to offer a membership opportunity to a guest who is not already a member.

For example, if the hotel's marketing department creates a program to reward frequent guests with a free overnight stay following a specified number of room night visits, the front office staff will be responsible for ensuring that a guest's number of room nights is properly posted within the system. Hence, the frequent guest's record becomes associated with the folio and subsequent guest history file. Front desk agents may have to validate and record coupons or adapt to some other form of recordkeeping system if the guest history file is not interfaced to the system controlling the frequent guest affinity program.

Hotel companies usually centralize the database of a frequent-guest program to more effectively enable the application of accrued rewards. In addition, frequent-guest programs are excellent channels for direct communication with brand-loyal guests. Since affinity club members provide both a mailing address and an e-mail address, the club is able to notify members about special promotions, including vacation, dinner, theater, golf, and other recreational packages. A hotel frequent-guest program may also be co-marketed with airline, car rental, cruise line, and independent marketing firm programs.

Many hotels place guest comment cards or feedback stations at various locations throughout the property. Some hotels offer an electronic channel for feedback through guestroom televisions, hotel lobby kiosks, or the hotel's website. However, no method has been proven more effective than a front desk agent collecting guest feedback during check-out. If the experience was not good, this is an opportunity to correct the situation and have the guest leave the hotel with a more positive impression. Once the guest has left the building, it is very difficult to deal effectively with a negative experience. Sometimes a simple apology is all that is necessary, while at other times an adjustment to the guest's folio balance may be appropriate. If the situation is serious, it should be noted in the front desk transaction file and the front office manager should meet with the guest, time permitting. If the guest doesn't have time to discuss the issue in detail, the manager should contact the guest later to identify the issue and take appropriate action.

If a guest needs a guestroom reservation for the next stop on his or her trip, the front office staff may be helpful in making the reservation at a hotel specified by the guest. A front desk agent can also make a reservation for a guest's return trip to the hotel. Front desk agents should keep in mind that check-out is the last opportunity to offer personalized services. Offering to make reservations for guests in transit or to make reservations for a future trip back to the hotel often leads to repeat business regardless of whether the guest makes a reservation at that time or not. Guests tend to remember the friendliness, convenience, and special services that help distinguish one lodging property from another.

Data Privacy

Front office managers and staff members become the guardians of proprietary data by virtue of the fact that the front office system contains records of guest preferences, transactions, account settlement methods, and behaviors. There is an implied expectation of privacy as a basic component of the guest-hotel or employee-employer relationship. Historically, data privacy has been codified in both statutory and case law, since innkeepers are privy to innumerable details of guest interactivity with various facets of the property. Hoteliers must meet the expectations of guests and employees regarding data privacy. If a hotel company is not vigilant about proper data collection and protection, potential security threats will likely arise. The threat of undesirable publicity, litigation, or fraud serves as a driver for industry adoption of sound privacy practices. Articulating and executing strong privacy policies typically strengthens and reinforces guest and employee relations.

PCI Compliance. The payment card industry (PCI) has developed a set of comprehensive data security standards (DSS) that must be adhered to by all retail merchants accepting payment cards, which of course includes hotel operators. PCI DSS requirements were developed in response to the increasing number of identity thefts and related payment card fraud cases resulting from improper cardholder data-handling procedures by businesses. The security policies contained in PCI DSS regulations are intended to thwart transaction data thieves (hackers) seeking to steal a guest's financial identity in order to make unauthorized purchases or create counterfeit payment card accounts.

PCI standards are designed to help businesses protect customer information through strict data security measures. PCI standards establish procedures aimed at minimizing or eliminating the potential risk of mishandling cardholder data by enhancing the recording and transmission of transactional data. All business operations accepting payment cards must adopt processes to protect sensitive customer payment information. It is important for hotel managers to realize that PCI compliance is not only mandatory, it increases guest confidence in front office data-handling procedures.

Interestingly, 80 percent of all data-handling compromises occurred at businesses that process less than one million payment card transactions per year. The American Hotel & Lodging Association has noted that the hospitality industry has been responsible for more than half of all payment card fraud committed in the United States in the past several years. Clearly, there is a need for hospitality businesses to adopt PCI processes to protect sensitive guest payment account information.

Hotel properties can meet PCI requirements through implementation of payment application software, in both property management systems and point-of-sale systems, that have been reviewed, validated, and certified as meeting DSS requirements. If a merchant is deemed non-compliant with PCI DSS principles and a data breach occurs, the penalties applied by the PCI Council can be significant and harmful to the reputation of the merchant. Sample penalties include reimbursement for the expense of a forensic investigation, heavy financial fines for data breaches, increased transaction processing fees, and even the possible loss of the ability to accept electronic payment transactions.

To be certified as PCI compliant, hotel operators must pass a security review and be periodically recertified. The following compliance considerations are central to a PCI DSS program, as specified by the PCI Security Standards Council:

1. Install and maintain a firewall configuration to protect cardholder data.

2. Do not use vendor-supplied defaults for system passwords and other security parameters.

3. Protect stored cardholder data through creative encryption or parsing.

4. Encrypt transmission of cardholder data across open, public networks.

5. Use and regularly update anti-virus software.

6. Develop and maintain secure systems and applications.

7. Restrict access to cardholder data on a need-to-know basis.

8. Assign a unique ID to each person with computer access.

9. Restrict physical access to cardholder data.

10. Track and monitor all access to network resources and cardholder data.

11. Regularly test security systems and processes.

12. Maintain a policy that addresses information security.

PCI compliance is the responsibility of hotel management, not the hotel's software vendor. Front office managers can use the following questions to perform a quick evaluation of their department's basic PCI conformity:

- Are front office system users automatically logged off the system following a 10–15 minute period of inactivity?

- Is retained cardholder data (folios, transaction receipts, and department reports) disguised so that no more than 4–6 digits of a cardholder's account data are viewable?

- Is cardholder data encrypted or masked in all system databases?

Summary

Check-out and account settlement are among the final transactions the guest has with the front office. Before departing the hotel, the guest will generally stop at the front desk to review his or her folio, pay any outstanding account balance, receive a copy of the account statement, close his or her safe deposit box, and return the room key. During check-out and account settlement, the front office accomplishes several important functions, including reconciling the guest account balance, updating the room status information, and initiating a guest history file. Through the use of pre-settlement verification activities, the front office can reduce the guest's check-out time and improve the front office's ability to collect outstanding account balances.

Effective front office operations also involve the resale of rooms once a guest has checked out. This entails prompt communication of room status information with the housekeeping department.

In addition to collecting any unpaid balances and updating room status information, the front desk agent may check for guest mail, messages, and faxes; post outstanding charges; verify account information; inquire about additional recent charges; present a final guest folio; verify the method of payment; process account settlement; secure the room key; and create a guest history file. A guest account can be brought to a zero balance in several ways. Methods of settlement include cash or debit card payment, credit card or direct billing transfer, or a combined settlement method.

To minimize late check-outs, the front office should post check-out time notices in conspicuous places. A reminder of the check-out time can also be included in any pre-departure materials distributed to guests expected to depart on the current day.

Changes in technology have prompted the front office to develop alternatives to standard check-out and settlement procedures. These check-out options help to minimize the time required for completing departure activities. Express check-out is a popular pre-departure activity that involves producing and distributing guest folios to guests expected to check out in the morning. Typically, guest folios are quietly slipped under the guestroom doors before 6 A.M. This enables guests in a hurry to depart without having to stop at the front desk. Another check-out option involves self check-out. In some properties, guests can check themselves out by accessing self check-out terminals in the lobby or by using an in-room system. Self check-out terminals and in-room systems are interfaced with an automated front office system and are intended to reduce check-out time and front office traffic.

No matter how carefully the front office monitors the guest's stay, it is always possible that a guest will leave without settling his or her account. Some guests may honestly forget to check out, while others intentionally avoid paying their bill. The front office may also discover late charges after a guest has legitimately checked out. Regardless of the reason, after-departure (late) charges represent unpaid account balances. Guest accounts not settled at check-out by payment in full, regardless of the credit established or prepayments made during registration, are transferred from the guest ledger to the city (non-guest) ledger for collection. At the time of transfer, responsibility for account settlement is transferred from the control of the front office to the hotel's general accounting division. Hotels monitor accounts in the city ledger carefully to ensure prompt payment. Accounts are aged according to the date of the last billing. Hotels work hard to minimize accounts that are older than thirty days.

Master accounts are set up for some meetings and conventions held at hotels. The designated manager should review group transactions with the group leader daily to obtain his or her written authorization for the transactions. The daily meeting allows for the resolution of any billing disputes before the group departs, and also apprises the group leader of billing totals.

Many hotel companies have implemented frequent guest or frequent traveler clubs. Such clubs award guests with credits for room nights occupied or dollars spent at the property or brand of properties. The hotel marketing department may rely on front office agents to verify the guest's membership status or offer membership opportunities in the frequent travel program to those guests who are not already members.

Hospitality managers and employees are guardians of guest proprietary data because the hotel's property management system stores information regarding guest preferences, transactions, and behaviors. Hotels must vigilantly collect and protect private guest and employee data, and take steps to make sure that they comply with payment card industry regulations concerning payment card transactions.

Key Terms

account aging—A method for tracking past-due accounts according to the date the charges originated.

current account—A city ledger account that is within the current billing period.

delinquent account—A city ledger account that has not been settled within a reasonable collection period, usually ninety days.

express check-out—A pre-departure activity that involves the production and early morning distribution of guest folios for guests expected to check out that morning.

guest history file—A collection of guest history records, constructed from expired registration cards or created through sophisticated automated systems that automatically direct information about departing guests into a guest history database.

guest history record—A record of personal and financial information about hotel guests relevant to marketing and sales that can help the hotel serve guests on return visits.

late charge—A transaction requiring posting to a guest account that does not reach the front desk for posting until after the guest has checked out and closed his or her account.

late check-out—A room status term indicating that the guest is being allowed to check out later than the hotel's standard check-out time.

late check-out fee—A charge imposed by some hotels on guests who do not check out by the established check-out time.

overdue account—A city ledger account that is unpaid beyond the current billing period, usually between thirty and ninety days.

self check-out terminal—An automated system, usually located in the hotel lobby, that allows the guest to review his or her folio and settle the account using the payment card authorized at check-in.

skipper—A guest who has left a hotel and has intentionally not settled his or her account.

unpaid account balance—Charges remaining in a guest account after the guest has left the hotel.

zeroing out—Settling a folio account balance in full as the guest checks out.

Review Questions

1. What are three important functions of the check-out and account settlement process? Why are these functions essential to the hotel's accounting, house-keeping, and marketing functions?

2. What is the definition of *zeroing out*? What happens to a guest account that is not settled at check-out?

3. What are four methods of guest account settlement at check-out? How are they different from each other? What effect does each have on the guest ledger and city ledger?

4. What are the differences between a debit card settlement and a credit card settlement?

5. What difficulties arise from late check-outs? How might these problems be reduced by the use of late check-out fees?

6. How does a typical express check-out procedure work? How does a typical self check-out terminal work? What are the advantages and disadvantages of each?

7. What are late charges? What steps can the front office take to reduce late charges?

8. What types of guest information are useful in collecting payment for late charges and unpaid account balances?

9. What are some elements of an effective billing and collection process? How can tracking uncollectible accounts to the departments responsible improve internal control?

10. What is account aging? Why is it important? Who might be responsible for account aging analysis?

11. What are the uses of guest histories? How can the front office construct a guest history file?

Internet Sites

For more information, visit the following Internet sites. Remember that Internet addresses can change without notice. If the site is no longer there, you can use a search engine to look for additional sites.

American Express Company
www.americanexpress.com

Asian Information Management
 Systems Ltd.
www.aimshk.com

Diners Club International Ltd.
www.dinersclub.com

Discover Card
www.discovercard.com

Fair Credit Billing Act (PDF)
www.ftc.gov/os/statutes/fcb/fcb.pdf

Fair Debt Collection Practices Act
www.ftc.gov/bcp/edu/pubs/consumer/
credit/cre18.shtm

InnQuest Software
www.innquest.com

MasterCard Worldwide
www.mastercard.com

On Command Corporation
www.spectravision.com

Visa
www.visa.com

Case Studies

Accounts Receivable at the Montrose Hotel

For about two months, Kathy Cole, the general manager of the Montrose Hotel, has been noticing a problem with the accounts receivable ledger. It has grown more than it should have, even though occupancy has been improving recently. The total ledger has grown by over 50 percent, with most of the growth being aged at over thirty days. Kathy cannot let this condition continue for very long, so she is addressing it with Glenna Danks, the hotel controller. Glenna tells Kathy that they are having trouble collecting on accounts sent to them from the front office.

The front office manager, Russ Fleming, has been on the job for about three months. Russ came to the Montrose Hotel from another of the chain's properties, where he was the assistant front office manager. The hotel Russ came from has a front office computer system, but the Montrose Hotel will not have one until next year. Kathy asks Russ to work with Glenna to find an answer to the issues. Upon researching the problems, Russ and Glenna find the following:

- Registration cards are not being filled in by guests with correct, billable, or readable addresses. Guests are sometimes leaving the space open.

- Payment card vouchers are difficult to read.

- Many payment card vouchers have after-departure charges on them.

- Groups are paying their master accounts more slowly than usual.

- Guest comment cards show many complaints about inaccurate bills and the time it takes to check out of the hotel.

Kathy, Glenna, and Russ must act quickly to bring the accounts receivable ledger back to its usual small amount.

Discussion Questions

1. Which departments must be involved in the actual problem resolution?

2. Write an action plan describing what each department must do to resolve the problem. Be sure to include employee training, any departmental procedure updates that are necessary, and specific accountabilities for ensuring the work is done properly.

3. Since the front office computer system is not scheduled to be installed for some time, what can hotel managers do now, with what they currently have to work with, to resolve the guest comment card complaints?

Case Number: 3328CA

The following industry experts helped generate and develop this case: Richard M. Brooks, CHA, Vice President, TWE Group; and Michael L. Kasavana, NAMA Professor in Hospitality Business, *The* School of Hospitality Business, Michigan State University, East Lansing, Michigan.

Owning the Problem!

"You own the problem," Matt, the valet, heard from his supervisor. Matt took a deep breath, recovering from the shock of learning that he would have to solve this one for the departing guest.

It was Matt's first day on valet after two weeks of intensive training. The training had begun with the two-day orientation program during which the vision and mission of the company were explained, guest service values were presented, and general policy and procedures were discussed. Following the orientation were five days of practical training in the functions of the front office, including all uniformed services such as bell attendant, valet, concierge, and front desk. Matt had thought that this was overkill. He often thought to himself that if they would just let him do the job, he would have the opportunity to gain the skills. But no, this resort and lodge demanded that everyone, including the groundskeeper and housekeeping staff, go through the full orientation and training program. So, after five days, Matt hoped he was prepared for this one.

Mr. Nauman had been a frequent guest at the Boden Resort and Lodge for many years. His wife and daughter usually accompanied him, but on this occasion he was on business and had decided to take a side trip to the lodge for a little relaxation. He was now on his way back to the city for an important business meeting, but Matt couldn't find his rental car. Mr. Nauman was a patient but efficient man. He was accustomed to the highest level of service; his typical business hotel was a Ritz-Carlton. Matt knew that Mr. Nauman was an important guest. Matt was responsible for solving this problem no matter what it took. Fortunately for Matt, the resort would back him up—even if it meant spending a lot of money or time to solve the problem. The Boden's philosophy was to satisfy every guest need.

Matt thought for a moment. He had brought around the Lincoln Town Car that he thought was Mr. Nauman's. However, Mr. Nauman had said that his wallet and briefcase had been left in the car and they were nowhere to be seen. Mr. Nauman was certain that this was not his rental car. Matt wondered if someone else who had checked out earlier may have also rented a Lincoln Town Car and perhaps the valet had switched the cars. What a nightmare that would be! He checked with valet services and, sure enough, a Mr. Bowman had checked out earlier that morning driving a Lincoln Town Car of the same color. Mr. Bowman had left for the airport many miles away and would be difficult to reach. Matt wondered if Mr. Bowman would realize that he had the wrong car once he looked around. Matt concluded that Mr. Bowman would have to turn in the rental car upon arrival at the airport.

In the meantime, Mr. Nauman was waiting for an answer. He was an action-oriented person and Matt knew he didn't have much time to make some decisions before Mr. Nauman would get antsy. He had to think fast, and he knew from his orientation and training that he had to focus on the guest. Matt thought about Mr. Nauman's business meeting and the need to get there immediately. He also knew that he would have to somehow retrieve Mr. Nauman's valuables from the other car.

It occurred to Matt that he would have to take a car to the airport rental agency fifty miles away, and he would have to find Mr. Nauman a car so that he could get to his meetings that were in the opposite direction. Mr. Nauman was planning to return for another night, so Matt could bring him his valuables plus his rental car. Matt thought about lending Mr. Nauman his car, but dismissed the idea quickly, as his car wasn't in the best of condition. He decided that he'd ask the Boden's general manager whether Mr. Nauman could borrow the company sedan for the day while Matt drove the other rental to trade in at the airport. A novel idea, thought the general manager, and perhaps the only real solution to this messy problem.

Five minutes later, Mr. Nauman, while still pretty angry, was on his way to his business meetings and Matt was on the phone to the rental agency at the airport. They would be on the lookout for Mr. Bowman, who was scheduled to arrive within the half hour. Matt jumped into the Lincoln Town Car and raced off toward the airport. He wondered whether this was the right approach and whether his supervisor would back him on this solution. The general manager already demonstrated support, so he was pretty sure that his direct supervisor would go along with it. But who would cover for him while he was away? This was a busy checkout time, and all valets were needed to meet the demand of the guests. As he pulled onto the freeway, he wondered whether this was the only time that this problem had ever happened.

Discussion Questions

1. Is Matt prepared for this level of responsibility after five days of training?
2. How can Matt's supervisor show his support for this action to solve the problem?
3. What else could Matt do to solve this problem?

Case number: 608C18

This case also appears in Todd Comen, *Case Studies in Front Office Management* (Lansing, Mich.: American Hotel & Lodging Educational Institute, 2003).

Chapter 10 Outline

Competencies

1. Describe the role of the housekeeping department in communicating room status. (pp. 363–365)

2. Explain the relationship between the housekeeping and maintenance departments and identify typical cleaning responsibilities of the housekeeping department. (pp. 366–372)

3. Explain how executive housekeepers use such tools as area inventory lists, frequency schedules, performance standards, and productivity standards to plan the work of the housekeeping department. (pp. 372–376)

4. Discuss equipment and supply inventory issues, and distinguish between recycled and non-recycled inventories. (pp. 376–377)

5. Summarize the issues involved in a dilemma many hotels face: whether to cut back or eliminate housekeeping supervisors. (pp. 377–380)

10

The Role of Housekeeping in Hospitality Operations

This chapter has been excerpted from material in Chapters 1 and 2
of *Managing Housekeeping Operations*, Second Edition, by
Margaret M. Kappa, Aleta Nitschke, and Patricia B. Schappert.

BECAUSE OF ITS IMPORTANCE to the efficient operation of the front office, in this chapter we will take a detailed look at the housekeeping department. The housekeeping department has frequent communication with the front office department, specifically with the front desk staff. Normally, front desk agents cannot assign guestrooms until the rooms have been cleaned, inspected, and released by the housekeeping department. In most properties, the housekeeping department is part of the rooms division along with the front office department, and the executive housekeeper works closely with the front office manager. In this chapter, we will look at the importance of communication between the front office and housekeeping departments, how housekeeping interacts with maintenance, the role of planning in the housekeeping department, and the changing involvement of housekeeping supervisors.

Communicating Room Status

Each night, a front desk agent or the property management system produces an **occupancy report.** The occupancy report lists rooms occupied that night and indicates guests who are expected to check out the following day. The executive housekeeper consults this list early the next morning and schedules occupied rooms for cleaning. As guests check out of the hotel, the front desk notifies housekeeping, either through the hotel's front office system, via telephone, or through some other room status update process. Housekeeping ensures that checked-out rooms are given top priority so that they can be cleaned and readied for arriving guests.

The executive housekeeper also uses the ten-day and three-day forecast reports prepared by the front office system. Forecast reports indicate how many rooms are projected to be occupied each day; this helps the executive housekeeper effectively prepare staff schedules to ensure that enough room attendants will be scheduled for each day's workload.

At the end of each work shift, the housekeeping department staff prepares a **housekeeping status report** (see Exhibit 1) based on a physical check of each room in the property. This report indicates the current housekeeping status of each room. It is compared to the front desk occupancy report, and any discrepancies are

Exhibit 1   Sample Housekeeping Status Report

| Housekeeper's Report | | | | | | A.M. | |
| Date _____ , 20 _____ | | | | | | P.M. | |

ROOM NUMBER	STATUS	ROOM NUMBER	STATUS	ROOM NUMBER	STATUS	ROOM NUMBER	STATUS
101		126		151		176	
102		127		152		177	
103		128		153		178	
104		129		154		179	
105		130		155		180	
106		131		156		181	
107		132		157		182	
108		133		158		183	
120		145		170		195	
121		146		171		196	
122		147		172		197	
123		148		173		198	
124		149		174		199	
125		150		175		200	

Remarks:

_____

_____

_____

Legend:
- ✓ - Occupied
- 000 - Out-of-Order
- —— - Vacant
- B - Slept Out (Baggage Still in Room)
- X - Occupied, No Baggage
- C.O. - Slept In but Checked Out Early A.M.
- E.A. - Early Arrival

_____
Housekeeper's Signature

brought to the attention of the front office manager. A **room status discrepancy** is the difference between the housekeeping department's description of a room's status and the room status information the front desk staff uses to assign guestrooms. Room status discrepancies can seriously affect a property's ability to accommodate guests and maximize rooms revenue.

Promptly notifying the front desk staff of the housekeeping status of rooms can be a tremendous asset in registering guests who arrive early, especially during high-occupancy or sold-out periods. Keeping room status information up to date requires close coordination and cooperation between the front desk and housekeeping department staffs.

In an automated room-status system, housekeeping staff and the front desk staff have instantaneous access to room status information. When a guest checks out, a front desk agent enters the departure into a front office terminal. Housekeeping is then automatically alerted that the room has been vacated and needs cleaning through a remote terminal located in the housekeeping department. Next, housekeeping attendants clean the room and notify the housekeeping supervisor when the room is ready for inspection. Once the room is inspected, the inspector enters this information into the room-status system. This housekeeping status update is then communicated to the front office system which, in turn, categorizes the room as clean, vacant, and available for sale.

While room occupancy status within an automated system is almost always current, reporting of each room's housekeeping status may lag behind. For example, the housekeeping supervisor may inspect several rooms in sequence but not update the room-status files until the end of a long inspection round. In a large hotel, contacting the housekeeping department after each room is inspected is generally inefficient, since answering a phone call or responding to a page leads to frequent interruptions. A delay in status reporting may also occur when a list of clean, inspected rooms is furnished to a staff member in the housekeeping department who does not immediately enter the data into the system.

The problems in promptly reporting each room's housekeeping status to the front office system can be reduced when the system is directly connected to the guestroom telephone system. With such a network, supervisors can inspect rooms, determine their readiness for sale, and then enter a code on the room telephone to change the room's status in the front office system. No one needs to answer the phone, since the computer automatically receives the relay, and there is minimal chance for error. Within seconds, the room's updated status can be displayed on the screen at the front office. This procedure can significantly reduce not only the number of guests forced to wait for room assignment but also the length of registration.

Teamwork between housekeeping and front office staffs is essential to daily hotel operations. The more familiar housekeeping and front office personnel are with each other's procedures, the smoother the relationship between the two departments.

Advanced housekeeping and front desk communication systems rely on wireless connectivity via a hand-held terminal carried by each housekeeper. The terminal may be a personal digital assistant (PDA) or similar device that resembles the mobile devices people carry with them to record appointments, telephone numbers, and personal notes. However, a housekeeping PDA is programmed for housekeeping purposes and uses the wireless connectivity for two-way communications between the housekeepers and other housekeeping department staff. With a PDA, a housekeeper's work schedule can be pre-loaded into his or her terminal before the beginning of the work shift. As the housekeeper's work is completed, the housekeeper records the information in the terminal and transmits it to the front office system so that the system's room status data is updated. If the housekeeping manager has an urgent request for a particular guestroom to be readied, the manager can use the terminal to communicate this information to the housekeeper working in that area. In addition, if a housekeeper needs additional supplies or identifies a maintenance problem, he or she can use the PDA to communicate such needs to the housekeeping or maintenance department. PDAs can also be used to dispatch housekeeping staff members in response to special guest requests—for more towels or for a crib, for example. The responding housekeeper can use the PDA to report when the request has been filled. In a large hotel with multiple buildings or a very large housekeeping department, the cost of PDA devices can be justified based on improved service to guests.

Housekeeping and Maintenance

In most non-lodging commercial buildings, housekeeping and maintenance personnel generally report to the same department manager. This makes sense, because these functional areas have similar goals and methods and operate most efficiently when they enjoy a close working relationship. In most midsize and large lodging operations, however, housekeeping personnel tend to report to the rooms division manager, while engineering and maintenance staff often constitute a separate division. Differing lines of accountability can become a barrier between these important support centers in a hotel.

It is unfortunate that support centers often seem to have an almost adversarial relationship. For example, housekeeping personnel sometimes resent having to clean up after various types of maintenance, while engineering personnel may be upset if the misuse of chemicals and equipment by housekeeping personnel results in additional work. To ensure the smooth operation of both departments, housekeeping and engineering managers need to devote attention to improving the working relationship between their departments. Teamwork is the key to successful hotel operations. Although the general manager is ultimately responsible for fostering a teamwork philosophy, each department and every employee can help.

Communicating Maintenance Work

Room attendants are the most logical and first line of offense in preparing the guestroom for an arriving guest. The housekeeping staff cleans the guestrooms and also is counted on to recognize guestroom deficiencies or malfunctions that can lead to guest dissatisfaction.

For instance, what happens if a room attendant does not recognize that a light bulb is burned out? Probably the guest will try to turn on the lamp, notice the burned-out bulb, become disgruntled, and call the front desk for assistance. Such an inconvenience is a strike against the hotel's image. The hotel can avoid this type of guest dissatisfaction by setting up a proactive system whereby housekeeping employees recognize deficiencies or malfunctions, report them, and ensure repair before guests occupy the guestroom. The following items are essential to a positive guest experience and can provide a starting point for training room attendants to understand their first-line responsibilities:

- *Sleep set:* Guests are uncomfortable when mattresses sag. A room attendant can tell when a mattress is sagging by inspecting it when the sheets are stripped away. Guest comfort can best be maintained by rotating mattresses periodically and replacing them when necessary. Most mattresses built for hotels have a convenient label identifying a rotation schedule, although housekeeping managers often create their own schedule. Whichever schedule is used, the goal is to make sure that every mattress is properly rotated in accordance with the manufacturer's recommendations.

- *Heating/air conditioning:* If a guestroom's temperature makes a room attendant feel uncomfortable while he or she is cleaning the room, chances are that guests who stay in that room will also be uncomfortable. For this reason, housekeepers should be trained to recognize and report problems or potential problems with heating or air conditioning systems.

- *TV, radio, telephone:* Room attendants should test the radio and TV while cleaning the guestroom. When wiping off the telephone, they should make sure the phone is working properly.

- *Bedspreads:* One of the first things guests notice in a guestroom is the condition of the bedspread. Since a positive first impression is so important, room attendants should promptly report and replace worn bedspreads.

- *Lighting:* If the room attendant thinks the room seems dark, a guest may feel the same way. Housekeepers should check each lamp's placement and each bulb's wattage, and check whether the switch/fixture works.

- *Door:* Door hardware must work properly; if it doesn't, the guest will be irritated. In addition, faulty door hardware is a serious security issue. If a room attendant has difficulty entering the room to clean it, he or she should recognize and report this situation, and make sure the door is repaired before calling the room "vacant and ready."

- *Toilet:* If it takes more than one flush to get everything down the drain, or if the water continuously runs, the room attendant needs to report it to the maintenance staff immediately.

- *Vanity and tub:* Sparkling porcelain can make the guest feel the room is extra clean, especially if the faucets are shiny. Room attendants must be alert to stains, drips, or corroded hardware.

- *Towels:* "Soft" is the word most people use to describe how they want their towels. A soft towel that is clean and free of stains will feel new. If the linen is something less than soft and clean, it should be considered for replacement.

- *Bathroom walls and door:* Wall coverings become dated quickly. When coverings begin to peel or look worn, this should be reported. Privacy is important to many guests; room attendants should ensure that the bathroom door is working properly and report any problems to the maintenance staff.

- *Water temperature:* For safety's sake, room attendants need to evaluate the temperature of faucet water. How warm is it as it flows from the tap? How long does it take to get hot? Unusual extremes of cold or hot water should be recognized and reported.

- *Ventilation:* If a mirror fogs up while the bathroom is being cleaned, a similar fogging problem will probably frustrate the guest. The room attendant should check the bathroom fan and be sure it is clean and working properly.

Types of Maintenance

The housekeeping department is involved in many hotel maintenance activities and alerts the engineering department when serious maintenance problems are discovered. There are three kinds of maintenance activities: routine maintenance, preventive maintenance, and scheduled maintenance.

Routine maintenance activities are those that relate to the general upkeep of the property, occur on a regular (daily or weekly) basis, and require relatively minimal training or skills. These are maintenance activities that occur outside of a formal work order system and for which no specific maintenance records (time or materials) are kept. Examples include sweeping carpets, washing floors, cleaning readily accessible windows, cutting grass, cleaning guestrooms, shoveling snow, and replacing burned-out lightbulbs. The housekeeping department performs many of these routine maintenance activities. Proper care of many surfaces and materials by housekeeping personnel is the first step in the overall maintenance program for the property's furniture and fixtures.

Preventive maintenance consists of three parts: inspection, minor corrections, and work order initiation. For many areas within the hotel, housekeeping personnel perform inspections in the normal course of their duties. For example, room attendants and inspectors may regularly check guestrooms for leaking faucets, cracked caulking around bathroom fixtures, and other items that may call for action by engineering staff. Attending to leaking faucets and improper caulking around sinks and tubs can control maintenance costs by preventing greater problems, such as ceiling or wall damage in the bath below. Such maintenance protects the physical plant investment and contributes to guest satisfaction.

Communication between the housekeeping and engineering departments should be efficient so that most minor repairs can be handled while the room attendant is cleaning the guestroom. In some properties, a full-time maintenance employee may be assigned to inspect guestrooms and perform the necessary repairs, adjustments, or replacements.

Preventive maintenance sometimes identifies problems and needs beyond the scope of a minor correction. These problems are brought to the attention of engineering through the work order system and the building engineer then schedules the necessary work. This type of work is often referred to as **scheduled maintenance.**

Scheduled maintenance activities are initiated at the property based on a formal work order or similar document. Work orders are a key element in the communication between housekeeping and engineering. A sample work order is shown in Exhibit 2. In many properties, work orders are numbered, three-part forms. Each part of the form is color-coded for its recipient.

When a member of the housekeeping department fills out a work order form, one copy is sent to the executive housekeeper and two copies to engineering. The chief engineer gets one of these copies and gives the other to the tradesperson assigned to the repair. The individual completing the task indicates the number of hours required to complete the work, any parts or supplies required, and other relevant information. When the job is completed, a copy of the tradesperson's completed work order is sent to the executive housekeeper. If this copy is not returned to the executive housekeeper within an appropriate amount of time, housekeeping issues another work order, which signals engineering to provide a status report on the requested repair.

Engineering personnel generally keep data files and history records on all equipment. Equipment data files contain basic information about each piece of equipment. This information can include technical data, manufacturers'

Exhibit 2   Sample Maintenance Work Order

Maintenance/In-House Work Order
(Maintenance use)
Kellogg Center Maintenance Request Form

Kellogg Hotel & Conference Center
at Michigan State University

Date_____

Location/Room Number_____

Contact Person_____

Requested Service/Nature of Problem _____

_____

_____

_____

_____

_____

_____

_____

_____

Additional Comments _____

_____

_____

_____

_____

Work Performed _____

_____

_____

Person Completing Work_____

Date Performed _____

Maintenance Supervisor Signature _____

K7659

Courtesy of Kellogg Hotel & Conference Center, Michigan State University, East Lansing, Michigan.

Exhibit 3 Sample Equipment History Record

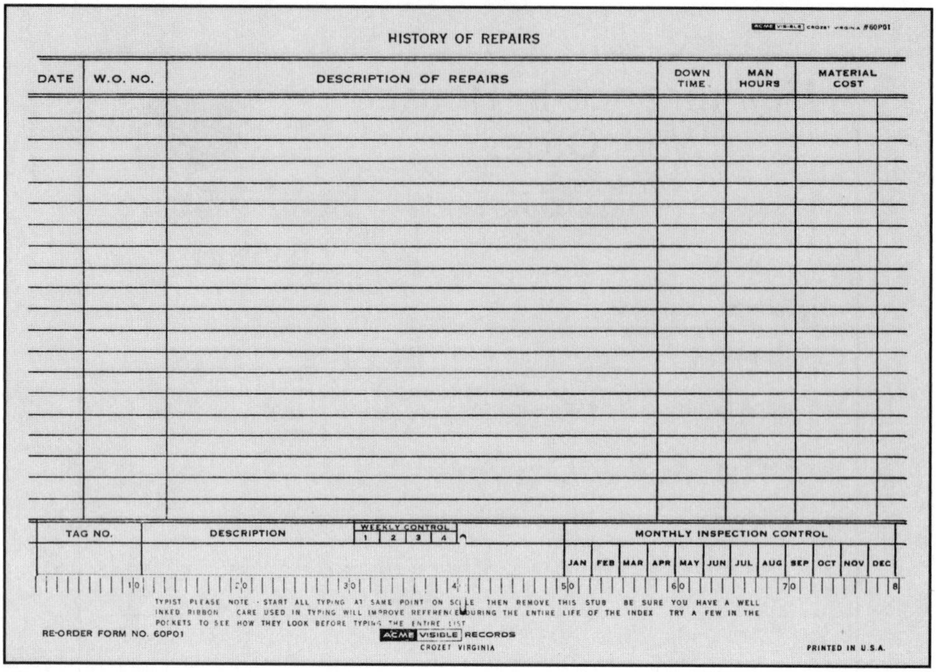
HISTORY OF REPAIRS

DATE	W.O. NO.	DESCRIPTION OF REPAIRS	DOWN TIME	MAN HOURS	MATERIAL COST

TAG NO.	DESCRIPTION	WEEKLY CONTROL 1 2 3 4	MONTHLY INSPECTION CONTROL
			JAN FEB MAR APR MAY JUN JUL AUG SEP OCT NOV DEC

TYPIST PLEASE NOTE - START ALL TYPING AT SAME POINT ON SCALE THEN REMOVE THIS STUB BE SURE YOU HAVE A WELL INKED RIBBON CARE USED IN TYPING WILL IMPROVE REFERENCE DURING THE ENTIRE LIFE OF THE INDEX TRY A FEW IN THE POCKETS TO SEE HOW THEY LOOK BEFORE TYPING THE ENTIRE LIST

RE-ORDER FORM NO. 60P01

ACME VISIBLE RECORDS CROZET VIRGINIA

PRINTED IN U.S.A.

Courtesy of Acme Visible Records.

information, the item's cost, special instructions, warranty information, and references to other information as well (such as the storage location of manuals and drawings). Equipment history records (see Exhibit 3) are logs of the inspection and maintenance work performed on a given piece of equipment. History records may be on separate cards or may be incorporated into the equipment data files. The purpose of historical records is to provide documentation of the maintenance activities performed on a given piece of equipment. Many properties have automated these recordkeeping functions, thereby making it easier for the executive housekeeper to retrieve pertinent information when determining the need to request new equipment. Historical records also help the chief engineer determine how many and how often spare parts should be ordered.

Identifying Housekeeping's Responsibilities

Regardless of the size and structure of a housekeeping department, it is typically the responsibility of the hotel's general manager to identify which areas housekeeping will be responsible for cleaning. Most housekeeping departments are responsible for cleaning the following areas:

- Guestrooms
- Corridors

- Public areas, such as the lobby and public restrooms
- Pool and patio areas
- Management offices
- Storage areas
- Linen and sewing rooms
- Laundry room
- Back-of-the-house areas, such as employee locker rooms

Housekeeping departments of hotels offering mid-range and world-class service are generally responsible for additional areas, such as:

- Meeting rooms
- Dining rooms
- Banquet rooms
- Convention exhibit halls
- Hotel-operated shops
- Game rooms
- Exercise rooms

Housekeeping's cleaning responsibilities in the food and beverage areas vary from property to property. In most hotels, housekeeping has very limited responsibilities in relation to cleaning food preparation, production, and storage areas. The special cleaning and sanitation tasks required for maintaining these areas are usually carried out by kitchen staff under the supervision of the chief steward. In some properties, the dining room staff cleans service areas after breakfast and lunch periods; housekeeping's night cleaning crew does the in-depth cleaning after dinner service or early in the morning before the dining room opens for business. The executive housekeeper and the dining room managers must work closely together to ensure that quality standards are maintained in the guest service and server station areas.

The same cooperation is necessary between housekeeping and banquet or convention services. The banquet or convention staff generally sets up banquet and meeting rooms and is responsible for some cleaning after the rooms are used. The final in-depth cleaning is left to the housekeeping crew. This means that the final responsibility for the cleanliness and overall appearance of these areas falls squarely on the shoulders of the housekeeping staff.

As stated, the general manager typically designates which areas housekeeping will be responsible for cleaning. However, if areas of responsibility cross department lines, the managers of those departments must get together and settle among themselves any disputes about cleaning responsibilities. The agreement among the managers is then reported to the general manager for his or her approval. A good housekeeping manager can effectively solve problems with other managers, thereby relieving the general manager of day-to-day operational problems.

It is a good idea for the executive housekeeper to obtain a floor plan of the hotel and color in those areas for which housekeeping is responsible. Different colors can designate those areas for which other department managers are responsible. To ensure that all areas of the property have been covered—and to avoid future misunderstandings about responsibilities—copies of this color-coded floor plan should be distributed to the general manager and to all department managers. This way, everyone can see at a glance who is responsible for cleaning each area in the hotel. The color-coded floor plan also presents a clear and impressive picture of the housekeeping department's role in cleaning and maintaining the hotel.

Once housekeeping's areas of responsibility are identified, planning focuses on analyzing the work required for cleaning and maintaining each area.

Planning the Work of the Housekeeping Department

Planning is probably the executive housekeeper's most important management function. Without competent planning, every day may present one crisis after another. Constant crises lower morale, decrease productivity, and increase expenses within the department. Also, without the direction and focus that planning provides, the executive housekeeper can easily become sidetracked by tasks that are unimportant or unrelated to accomplishing the hotel's objectives.

Since the housekeeping department is responsible for cleaning and maintaining so many different areas of the hotel, planning the work of the department can seem like an enormous task. Without a systematic, step-by-step approach to planning, the executive housekeeper can easily become overwhelmed and frustrated by the hundreds of important details. These details must be addressed to ensure that the work is not only done, but done correctly, efficiently, on time, and with the least cost to the department.

Area Inventory Lists

Planning the work of the housekeeping department begins with creating inventory lists of all items within each area that will need housekeeping's attention. Preparing **area inventory lists** is the first planning activity, because the lists ensure that the rest of the planning activities address every item for which housekeeping is held accountable. Inventory lists are bound to be long and extremely detailed. Since most properties offer several different types of guestrooms, separate inventory lists may be necessary for each room type.

When preparing a guestroom area inventory list, it is a good idea to follow the sequence in which room attendants will clean items and in which supervisors will inspect items. This enables the executive housekeeper to use the inventory lists as the basis for developing cleaning procedures, training plans, and inspection checklists. For example, items within a guestroom may appear on an inventory list as they are placed from right to left and from top to bottom around the room. Other systematic techniques may be used, but the point is that *some* system should be followed—and this system should be the same one used by room attendants and inspectors in the daily course of their duties.

Exhibit 4 Sample Frequency Schedule

PUBLIC AREA #2—LIGHT FIXTURES			
LOCATION	TYPE	NO.	FREQ.
Entrance #1	Sconce	2	1/W
Lobby	Chandelier	3	1/M
Entrance #2	Crown Sconce	2	1/M
Behind Fountain	Sconce	3	1/W
Catwalk	Pole Light	32	1/M
Lower Level	Pole Light	16	1/M
Fountain Area	Pole Light	5	1/M
Restaurant Courtyard	Pole Light	10	1/M
Restaurant Courtyard	Wall Light	5	1/M
Restaurant Patio	Half-Pole Light	16	1/W
Restaurant Entrance	White Globe Pole Light	6	1/W
Crystal Gazebo	White Globe Pole Light	8	1/W
2nd Stairs to Catwalk	White Globe Pole Light	2	1/W
Fountain	White Globe Pole Light	4	1/W
Lounge Patio	Wall Light	4	1/W
Restaurant Entrance	Chandelier	1	1/W

Frequency Schedules

Tasks on an area's **frequency schedule** (see Exhibit 4) that are made part of house-keeping's deep cleaning program should be transferred to a calendar plan and scheduled as special cleaning projects. The calendar plan guides the executive housekeeper in scheduling the appropriate staff to perform the necessary work. The executive housekeeper must take into account a number of factors when scheduling **deep cleaning** of guestrooms or other special projects. For example, whenever possible, days marked for guestroom deep cleaning should coincide with low occupancy periods. Also, the deep cleaning program must be flexible in relation to the activities of other departments. For example, if the maintenance department schedules extensive repair work for several guestrooms, the executive housekeeper should make every effort to coordinate a deep cleaning of these rooms with maintenance's timetable. Careful planning will produce good results for the hotel with the least possible inconvenience to guests or to other departments.

Performance Standards

The executive housekeeper can begin to develop **performance standards** by answering the question, What must be done in order to clean or maintain the major items within this area? Standards are required quality levels of performance. Per-formance standards state not only *what* must be done, they also describe in detail *how* the job must be done.

One of the primary objectives of planning the work of the housekeeping department is to ensure that all employees carry out their cleaning tasks in a consistent manner. The keys to consistency are the performance standards that the executive housekeeper develops, communicates, and manages. Although these standards vary from one housekeeping department to another, executive housekeepers can ensure consistency of cleaning by demanding 100 percent conformity to the standards established for their departments. When performance standards are not properly developed, effectively communicated, and consistently managed, housekeeping department productivity suffers, because employees will not perform their tasks according to the necessary standards.

The most important aspect of developing standards is gaining consensus on how cleaning and other tasks are to be carried out. Consensus can be achieved by having individuals who actually perform the tasks contribute to the standards that the department eventually adopts.

Performance standards are communicated through ongoing training programs. Many properties have developed performance standards and have included them between the covers of impressive housekeeping procedure manuals. However, all too often, these manuals simply gather dust on shelves in the offices of executive housekeepers. Well-written standards are useless unless they are applied. The only way to implement standards in the workplace is through effective training programs.

After communicating performance standards through ongoing training activities, the executive housekeeper must manage those standards. Managing standards means ensuring conformity to standards by inspection. Experienced housekeepers know the truth of the adage, "You can't expect what you don't inspect." Daily inspections and periodic performance evaluations should be followed up with specific on-the-job coaching and retraining. This ensures that all employees consistently perform their tasks in the most efficient and effective manner. The executive housekeeper should review the department's performance standards at least once a year and make appropriate revisions as new work methods are implemented.

Productivity Standards

While performance standards establish the expected quality of the work to be done, **productivity standards** (see Exhibit 5) determine the acceptable quantity of work to be done by department employees. An executive housekeeper begins to establish productivity standards by answering the question, "How long should it take for a housekeeping employee to perform an assigned task according to the department's performance standard?" Productivity standards must be determined to properly staff the department within the limitations established by the hotel's operating budget.

Since performance standards vary in relation to the unique needs and requirements of each hotel, it is impossible to identify productivity standards that would apply across the board to every housekeeping department. Since the duties of room attendants vary widely among economy, mid-market, and luxury hotels, the productivity standards for room attendants will also vary.

Exhibit 5 Sample Productivity Standard Worksheet

Step 1

Determine how long it should take to clean one guestroom according to the department's performance standards.

Approximately 27 minutes*

Step 2

Determine the total shift time in minutes.

8½ hours ✕ 60 minutes = 510 minutes

Step 3

Determine the time available for guestroom cleaning.

Total Shift Time .... 510 minutes

Less:

    Beginning-of-Shift Duties .... 20 minutes

    Morning Break .... 15 minutes

    Lunch .... 30 minutes

    Afternoon Break .... 15 minutes

    End-of-Shift Duties .... 20 minutes

Time Available for Guestroom Cleaning   410 minutes

Step 4

Determine the productivity standard by dividing the result of Step 3 by the result of Step 1.

$$\frac{410 \text{ minutes}}{27 \text{ minutes}} = 15.2 \text{ guestrooms per 8-hour shift}$$

*Since performance standards vary from property to property, this figure is used for illustrative purposes only. It is not a suggested time figure for cleaning guestrooms.

When determining realistic productivity standards, an executive housekeeper does not have to carry around a measuring tape, stopwatch, and clipboard and conduct time-and-motion studies on all the tasks necessary to clean and maintain each item on an area's inventory list. The labor of the executive housekeeper and other management staff is also a precious department resource. However, housekeeping managers must know how long it should take a housekeeping employee to perform the major tasks identified on the cleaning frequency schedules—such as guestroom cleaning. Once this information is known, the executive housekeeper can develop productivity standards.

Quality and quantity can be like two sides of a coin. On one side, if the quality expectations (performance standards) are set too high, the quantity of work that can be done accordingly may be unacceptably low. This forces the executive housekeeper to add more and more staff to ensure that all the work gets done. However, sooner or later (and probably sooner than expected), the general manager will cut the high labor expense of the housekeeping department. This action would force the executive housekeeper to reduce the staff size and realign quality and quantity by redefining performance standards in light of more realistic productivity standards.

On the other side, if performance standards are set too low, the quantity of work that can be done accordingly will be unexpectedly high. At first, the general manager may be delighted. However, as complaints from guests and staff increase and the property begins to look dingy because of neglect, the general manager may, once again, step in with a solution. This time, the general manager may choose to replace the executive housekeeper with someone who will establish higher performance standards and monitor department expenses more closely.

Actual productivity standards should be finalized after the hotel has been operating for a while. To determine the property's productivity standard for room cleaning, the housekeeping manager must take guestroom size, furnishings, bedding arrangement, bathroom design, and room configuration into consideration. If a housekeeper has to move from floor to floor or building to building, this travel time must be considered, since travel time takes away from cleaning time. In addition, the number of rooms in a suite must be considered. For example, a three-room suite with an elaborate living room, wet bar, and patio may be counted as four rooms to clean, given its complexity. As a result, housekeepers who clean suites may be assigned fewer rooms to clean.

The challenge is to effectively balance performance standards and productivity standards. Quality and quantity each can serve to check and balance the other. A concern for productivity need not necessarily lower performance standards—it can sharpen and refine current work methods and procedures. If room attendants constantly return to the housekeeping area for cleaning and guestroom supplies, something is wrong with the way they set up and stock their carts. Wasted motion is wasted time, and wasted time depletes the most important and most expensive resource of the housekeeping department: labor. The executive housekeeper must be constantly on the alert for new, more efficient work methods.

Remember, an executive housekeeper will rarely have all the resources necessary to do everything he or she may want to accomplish. Therefore, labor must be carefully allocated to achieve acceptable performance standards and realistic productivity standards.

Equipment and Supply Inventory Levels

After planning what must be done and how the tasks should be performed, the executive housekeeper must ensure that employees have the necessary equipment and supplies to get their jobs done. The executive housekeeper plans appropriate inventory levels by answering the following question: What amounts of equipment and supplies are necessary for the housekeeping staff to meet the performance and productivity standards of the department? The answer to this question ensures smooth daily housekeeping activities and forms the basis for planning an effective purchasing system. A purchasing system must consistently maintain the necessary amounts of items in housekeeping inventories.

Essentially, the executive housekeeper is responsible for two types of inventories: items that are recycled during the course of hotel operations, and non-recyclable items. Non-recyclable items are consumed or used up during routine activities of the housekeeping department. Due to limited storage facilities and management's desire not to tie up cash in overstocked inventories, the executive housekeeper must establish reasonable inventory levels for both recyclable and non-recyclable items.

Recycled Inventories. Recycled inventories include linens, most equipment items, and some guest supplies. Recycled equipment includes room attendant carts, vacuum cleaners, carpet shampooers, floor buffers, and many other items. Recycled guest supplies include such items as irons, ironing boards, cribs, and refrigerators, which guests may need during the course of their stay. Housekeeping is responsible for storing and maintaining these items as well as issuing them as guests request them.

The number of recycled items that must be on hand to ensure smooth operations is expressed as a **par number.** Par refers to the number of items that must be on hand to support daily, routine housekeeping operations. For example, one par of linens is the total number of items required to outfit all the hotel guestrooms once; two par of linens is the total number of items required to outfit all the hotel guestrooms twice; and so on.

Non-Recycled Inventories. Non-recycled inventories include cleaning supplies, guestroom supplies (such as bath soap), and guest amenities (which may range from toothbrushes and shampoos and conditioners to scented bath powders and colognes). Since non-recyclable items are used up in the course of operations, inventory levels are closely tied to the property's purchase ordering system. A purchase ordering system for non-recyclable inventory items establishes a par number that is based on two figures—a minimum quantity and a maximum quantity.

The **minimum quantity** is the fewest number of purchase units that should be in stock at any time. Purchase units are counted in terms of normal-size shipping containers, such as cases, drums, and so on. The inventory level should never fall below the minimum quantity. When the inventory level of a non-recyclable item reaches the minimum quantity, additional supplies must be ordered.

The actual number of additional supplies that must be ordered is determined by the **maximum quantity**. The maximum quantity is the greatest number of purchase units that should be in stock at any time. This maximum quantity must be consistent with available storage space and must not be so high that large amounts of the hotel's cash resources are tied up in an overstocked inventory. The shelf life of an item also affects the maximum quantity of purchase units that can be stored.

Supervisor Dilemma

The state of the economy has prompted a trend to eliminate middle managers. In the lodging industry, this trend has brought the position of housekeeping supervisor into question. General managers seem to be searching for more profit and, perhaps, a way to empower hourly employees. Is it possible to operate a clean and profitable hotel without housekeeping supervisors to inspect rooms?

Although the housekeeping supervisor position may have begun as a management extension of the executive housekeeper for larger properties, the job has centered on inspecting rooms in the past twenty years or so. Is it, then, an essential role? Does the hotel get its money's worth from this position?

Key issues hotels must consider are:

- Did the hotel hire the right people to be supervisors?

- Do the hotel's systems support the responsibilities of the supervisor?

- Is the hotel's mission enhanced as a direct result of the position?

- How would the "no supervisors" idea be introduced and then implemented?

- Would the number of room inspections be reduced or totally eliminated?

- Who would conduct room inspections if any are required?

- Who would conduct training?

- What changes would be made to job descriptions?

- How would quality standards be maintained or improved?

- What system would be used to ensure accurate room status updates?

The Rooms Chronicle surveyed some readers about housekeeping supervisors. Some managers eliminated supervisors, only to be disappointed by a gradual decline in the condition of guestrooms. Others, after making the change, saw guest comments and employee morale improve. One of the surveyed hotels reinstated inspections in 100 percent of the rooms after six months, while another did so after one year. Some have been successful at keeping 50 to 75 percent of their room attendants working independently.

How Is the Program Initiated? Most hotels based their decisions to eliminate supervisors on a desire to save payroll, although many were motivated by the total quality management philosophy of empowerment. At one hotel they eliminated supervisors because they wanted to speed up reporting of clean rooms to the front desk.

The hotels that successfully eliminated housekeeping supervisors gave advance, careful thought to all of the ramifications of this decision and involved the employees in planning. Some approached room attendants with the question, How does it make you feel to have someone check everything you do? When some frustration was expressed, they began to explore alternative ways to operate, incorporating room attendants' ideas for working independently.

Are Any Rooms Inspected? One of the properties surveyed operates without any room inspections. Management credits the work ethic of their room attendants for the attendants' ability to take full responsibility for the condition of their areas. Most hotels, however, inspect from one to five rooms per room attendant per week. As a rooms executive of a luxury hotel in the Midwest expressed it, "We conduct random verifications of our housekeepers' work. It should be like testing a pool for the level of chlorine—only a small sample is needed to know the condition of the entire pool."

Who Inspects if There Are No Supervisors? Most properties use housekeeping management to conduct random inspections, depending on the size of the hotel. Large hotels retain one or more supervisors for this purpose. The general manager of a resort hotel in Florida involves the entire hotel staff. "The use of supervisors does not have to be an all-or-nothing decision," says a general manager of a Midwestern resort. "We use supervisors only in the summer to work with our seasonal employees. During the rest of the year, our room attendants work independently. We've used this system for over a year and our comment card scores are still high, at 94 percent."

Are Job Descriptions Changed? If a hotel eliminates housekeeping supervisors, its room attendant job description is usually changed to make room attendants responsible for the cleanliness, readiness, and status updates for the rooms they clean. The room attendant must check equipment in the room to ensure that a guest will not find something in disrepair. Some hotels add responsibility for the hallway area around the guestroom and specify who will do the running if a bedspread or some other item needs to be replaced. The houseperson or porter job description usually is changed to complement the new structure.

How Do Pay Rates Change? Pay rates of room attendants are sometimes changed if supervisors are eliminated, with the majority of properties either setting rates according to quality of work or paying bonuses for exceeding quality standards. One hotel pays a $35 bonus biweekly if inspection scores are 90 percent or higher and if at least 1.9 rooms are cleaned per hour. The general manager of one all-suite hotel has a program in which room attendants earn the right to work without supervisors by achieving high scores on quality, attendance, and uniform care and are then paid 25 cents more per hour. At other hotels, pay rates are not increased.

Who Does the Training? Since most hotels use supervisors to train new housekeeping hires, who does the training if housekeeping supervisor positions are eliminated? Housekeeping managers could train, but, in these days of high turnover, the training function is often a full-time job. One option is to designate one or more room attendants as on-the-job trainers. In other hotels, at least one supervisor is retained who concentrates on training and retraining. "If I hire the right people and conduct ongoing training, my staff will be able to meet our standards," said one rooms executive.

What About Room Status? The morning check of vacant rooms is usually incorporated into the room attendant's job description by assigning him or her an area of responsibility rather than a list of dirty rooms. All rooms, hallways, vending areas, and elevator lobbies within this area are assigned. The room attendant will be the last person to see the rooms or area before the guest arrives or returns, so special care must be taken to ensure that the front desk always has the correct room status, whether occupied or vacant, clean or dirty.

Many property management systems are interfaced so a code can be entered on the guestroom phone or a mobile device to update a room's status. In other hotels, the room attendant must call either housekeeping or the front desk to change a room's status. When the front desk questions the status, someone is sent to double-check the room.

If a hotel eliminates its housekeeping supervisors, it should expect to spend more time checking room status discrepancies. Room attendants might clean a room, thinking it is a stayover, but while they are in another room, the first room's guest could check out. If the hotel has not adequately planned for this aspect, payroll saved on supervisors could easily be lost by poor room inventory management.

Tips for Success. A well-thought-out plan will provide for the cleanliness, maintenance, and status of every room. Since supervisors usually help prepare VIP rooms, do touch-ups on late check-outs, help with hurry-ups, assist with inventories, translate for room attendants who don't speak English, and clean rooms when there is a shortage of room attendants, all of these responsibilities must be reassigned elsewhere by hotels that wish to eliminate housekeeping supervisors.

If a hotel wishes to cut back or eliminate its housekeeping supervisory staff, it should involve its room attendants in the design of the new program, to help them have ownership of it. The new plan must be a win-win situation for the hotel and its room attendants, because employees are sensitive to management's efforts to save payroll at their expense. The program should be fine-tuned before implementation, because changes to pay rates or incentive plans after the fact serve as disincentives.

If the no- or fewer-supervisors concept is planned to suit the property's needs and implemented carefully, housekeeping employees and the hotel should make a successful transition.

Summary

The housekeeping department has frequent communication with the front office department, specifically with the front desk area. Normally, front desk agents cannot assign guestrooms until the rooms have been cleaned, inspected, and released by the housekeeping department. In most properties, the housekeeping department is part of the rooms division and the executive housekeeper works closely with the front office manager.

Each night, a front desk agent or the property management system produces an occupancy report, which lists rooms occupied that night and indicates guests who are expected to check out the following day. The executive housekeeper consults this list early the next morning and schedules occupied rooms for cleaning. The executive housekeeper also uses the ten-day and three-day forecast reports prepared by the front office system when creating staff schedules.

At the end of each work shift, the housekeeping staff prepares a housekeeping status report based on a physical check of each guestroom. This report is compared to the front desk occupancy report. A room status discrepancy is a situation in which the housekeeping department's description of a room's status differs from the room status information available at the front desk. Keeping room status information accurate and up to date requires close coordination and cooperation between the front desk and housekeeping departments.

In an automated room-status system, housekeeping staff and the front desk staff have instantaneous access to room status information. When a guest checks out, a front desk agent enters the departure into a front office terminal. Housekeeping is then automatically alerted that the room has been vacated and needs cleaning. Next, housekeeping attendants clean the room and notify the housekeeping supervisor when the room is ready for inspection. Once the room is inspected, the inspector enters this information into the room status system. This housekeeping status update is then communicated to the front office system. Advanced housekeeping and front desk communication systems rely on wireless connectivity via a hand-held terminal or some other mobile device carried by each housekeeper.

The housekeeping staff not only cleans guestrooms, it is also counted on to recognize guestroom maintenance needs that can lead to guest dissatisfaction. There are three kinds of maintenance activities: routine maintenance, preventive maintenance, and scheduled maintenance. Routine maintenance activities are those that relate to the general upkeep of the property, occur on a regular basis, and do not require a formal work order. Preventive maintenance consists of three parts: inspection, minor corrections, and work order initiation. Preventive maintenance sometimes identifies problems and needs beyond the scope of a minor correction. These problems are brought to the attention of engineering through the work order system. This type of work is often referred to as scheduled maintenance. Work orders are a key element in the communication between housekeeping and engineering.

Most housekeeping departments are responsible for cleaning the following areas: guestrooms; corridors; public areas, such as the lobby and public restrooms; pool and patio areas; management offices; storage areas; linen and sewing rooms; laundry room; and back-of-the-house areas, such as employee locker rooms. Housekeeping departments of hotels offering mid-range and world-class service are generally responsible for additional areas, such as meeting rooms, dining rooms, banquet rooms, convention exhibit halls, hotel-operated shops, game rooms, and exercise rooms. Housekeeping's cleaning responsibilities in the food and beverage areas vary from property to property. In most hotels, housekeeping has very limited responsibilities in relation to cleaning food preparation, production, and storage areas.

Planning the work of the housekeeping department begins with creating inventory lists of all items within each hotel area that require housekeeping's attention. Inventory lists ensure that the rest of the planning activities address every item for which housekeeping will be held accountable. When preparing a guestroom area inventory list, it is a good idea to follow the sequence in which room attendants will clean items and in which supervisors will inspect items. This enables the executive housekeeper to use the guestroom area inventory list as the basis for developing cleaning procedures, training plans, and inspection checklists.

The executive housekeeper can begin to develop performance standards by answering the question, What must be done in order to clean or maintain the major items within this area? Standards are required quality levels of performance. Performance standards state not only *what* must be done, they also describe in detail *how* the job must be done. While performance standards establish the expected quality of the work to be done, productivity standards determine the acceptable quantity of work to be done by department employees. An executive housekeeper begins to establish productivity standards by answering the question, How long should it take for a housekeeping employee to perform an assigned task according to the department's performance standard? To determine the property's productivity standard for guestroom cleaning, the housekeeping manager must consider room size, furnishings, bedding arrangement, bathroom design, and room configuration. If a housekeeper has to move from floor to floor or building to building, this travel time must be considered. In addition, the number of rooms in a suite must be considered. The challenge is to effectively balance performance standards and productivity standards.

After planning what must be done and how the tasks are to be performed, the executive housekeeper must ensure that employees have the necessary equipment and supplies to get their jobs done. Essentially, the executive housekeeper is responsible for two types of inventories: (1) recycled items, and (2) non-recyclable items. Recycled inventories include linens, most equipment items, and some guest supplies. Recycled equipment includes room attendant carts, vacuum cleaners, carpet shampooers, floor buffers, and many other items. Recycled guest supplies include such items as irons, ironing boards, cribs, and refrigerators, which guests may need during the course of their stay. Housekeeping is responsible for storing and maintaining these items as well as issuing them as guests request them. Non-recycled inventories include cleaning supplies, guestroom supplies (such as bath soap), and guest amenities (which may range from toothbrushes and shampoos and conditioners to scented bath powders and colognes).

The state of the economy has prompted a trend to eliminate middle managers, including housekeeping supervisors. Some hotel managers have eliminated these supervisors, only to be disappointed by a gradual decline in the condition of guestrooms; others have seen guest comments and employee morale improve after eliminating supervisors. Because hotels differ so widely, each hotel must decide this question based on its own needs and the expectations of its guests.

🔑 Key Terms

area inventory list—A list of all items within a particular area that need cleaning by or the attention of housekeeping personnel.

deep cleaning—Intensive or specialized cleaning undertaken in guestrooms or public areas. Often conducted according to a special schedule or on a special-project basis.

frequency schedule—A schedule that indicates how often each item on an area inventory list must be cleaned or maintained.

housekeeping status report—A report the housekeeping department prepares that indicates the current housekeeping status of each room, based on a physical check.

maximum quantity—The greatest number of purchase units that should be in stock at any given time.

minimum quantity—The fewest number of purchase units that should be in stock at any given time.

occupancy report—A report prepared each night by a front desk agent or the property management system that lists rooms occupied that night and indicates guests who are expected to check out the following day.

par number—A multiple of the standard quantity of a particular inventory item that must be on hand to support daily, routine housekeeping operations.

performance standards—A required level of performance that establishes the quality of work that must be done.

preventive maintenance—A systematic approach to maintenance in which situations are identified and corrected on a regular basis to control costs and keep larger problems from occurring.

productivity standards—An acceptable amount of work that must be done within a specific time frame according to an established performance standard.

room status discrepancy—A situation in which the housekeeping department's description of a room's status differs from the room status information at the front desk.

routine maintenance—Activities related to the general upkeep of the property that occur on a regular (daily or weekly) basis and require relatively minimal training or skills to perform.

scheduled maintenance—Activities related to the upkeep of the property that are initiated through a formal work order or similar document.

 # Review Questions

1. Why are two-way communications necessary between the front desk and housekeeping?

2. What are the systems the front desk and housekeeping use to track current room status?

3. What are the three kinds of maintenance activities?

4. What is the ideal relationship between housekeeping and maintenance? What is the actual situation in some properties?

5. What areas are most housekeeping departments responsible for cleaning in a hotel?

6. What additional areas may housekeeping be responsible for cleaning, depending on the property's service level?

7. What is the purpose of an area inventory list? What is an ideal way to sequence such a list?

8. What is a frequency schedule? How is it used in conjunction with a property's deep cleaning program?

9. What is the difference between a performance standard and a productivity standard?

Internet Sites

For more information, visit the following Internet sites. Remember that Internet addresses can change without notice. If the site is no longer there, you can use a search engine to look for additional sites.

Resort Data Processing, Inc.
www.resortdata.com

The Rooms Chronicle...online
www.roomschronicle.com

Case Studies

VIP Gets Lost in the Service Shuffle, or How the ABC Hotel Dropped the Ball

Monday
10:00 A.M.

The eight o'clock Monday-morning sales meeting had been more tedious than most, Ms. Sarah Salesperson thought as she made her way back to her office. She poured herself a cup of coffee before sitting at her computer to compose a memo. The director of sales had hammered away at one of her pet themes that morning: "The secret to sales is, 'Don't drop the ball!'" I suppose she's right, Sarah mused as she began to type; dropping the ball is certainly easy enough to do at a 600-room hotel. In light of the morning meeting, she thought it might be wise to send a note about Mr. Bigbucks to Ray Smith, the front office manager. Mr. Bigbucks was a director at XYZ Corporation, an international firm that could mean $500,000 or more in room bookings in the next two years—if Mr. Bigbucks could be persuaded to place some of his group meetings and other business with the hotel. He was due to arrive at 1:30 P.M. today, and Sarah wanted everything to be perfect for him.

> Dear Ray:
>
> Just wanted to remind you that Mr. Bigbucks of the XYZ Corporation is arriving at 1:30 P.M. today for an overnight stay. *Please* make sure he gets the full VIP treatment. I've chatted with him on the phone a few times, and will meet with him in person next month about the possibility of booking some business with the hotel, but I won't be able to connect with him this visit—I'm flying to Dallas this morning.
>
> Don't worry—I remembered to fill out the VIP forms this time and everybody should have them by now!
>
> Sincerely,
> *Sarah*

10:30 A.M.

To make doubly sure Ray understood the importance of Mr. Bigbucks, Sarah walked down to the front office to deliver her memo in person, but Ray was not at his desk. Oh well, he'll probably be back in a minute, she thought. She left the memo on Ray's chair so he would notice it first thing.

11:10 A.M.

Ray finally escaped for a few minutes from a meeting the general manager called that morning, and went straight to his desk to check for messages. He read Sarah's memo and decided to drop it off at the front desk on his way back to the meeting.

11:20 A.M.

At the front desk, Evert was trying to stay calm and friendly despite the crowd milling in the lobby. He had been a front desk agent for only three weeks and still got nervous when tour buses pulled up outside the hotel. That morning two groups, the American Society of Poets and the Plate Glass Producers, were checking in; this afternoon the American Pharmaceutical Association would arrive for a four-day regional meeting. Evert didn't even notice Ray until Ray tapped him on the shoulder. "Make sure housekeeping knows about this," Ray said, and placed Sarah's memo beside Evert's computer keyboard. Evert half-turned and nodded while continuing to check in a guest.

11:45 A.M.

Evert took advantage of a lull to read what Ray had dropped off. He quickly picked up a walkie-talkie and called Gail, the executive housekeeper. "Hi Gail, it's Evert at the front desk. We've got a VIP, Mr. Bigbucks, arriving at 1:30 this afternoon. I'm changing room 816 from 'clean and ready' to 'out of order' until you can give it the VIP treatment, okay? Thanks."

11:50 A.M.

Why am I always at the other end of the hotel when I get a call like this? Gail thought as she hurried to the employee lunchroom. And why is it always when my staff is eating lunch or taking a break? She asked Mary and Teresa, two of her best room attendants, to interrupt their lunches and follow her to room 816. As the three of them were walking to the linen closet to get fresh bedspreads and blankets, she called Roger, the head of maintenance and engineering, and asked him to send someone to 816. Then she called George in the kitchen. "George, this is Gail. Are the amenities for 816 ready?" George said he was just finishing up and someone would drop them off soon.

1:20 P.M.

Gail stood in the doorway and cast a critical eye over room 816 one last time. The quiet and order she surveyed were in sharp contrast to the noise and bustle of the last hour and a half. A small army had descended on the suite and performed all the tasks needed to transform a guestroom from merely "excellent" to "perfect." As Mr. Thompson, the hotel general manager, had said to Gail on more than one occasion, "It's your job to put the 'wow factor' in every VIP room. When they open that guestroom door for the first time, that's what I want them to think: 'Wow!'"

Gail reviewed her informal "wow" checklist in her mind. The clean bed linen, blankets, and bedspread were upgraded to freshly ironed sheets, new blankets, and a new bedspread. Mary edged the carpet with a whisk broom to get every speck of dust, the furniture was pulled out and the carpet vacuumed underneath, and the chair and chair cushions were vacuumed. Then the carpet was spot-cleaned. All the drawers in the bedroom and bathroom were wiped out to make sure no dust or hair was hiding. As the drapes were taken down and replaced with freshly cleaned ones, Chris Jones arrived from maintenance and checked over all the room's mechanicals. While he was checking the bathroom, he noticed a small rust stain on the toilet seat. Teresa could not scrub it off, so Chris went off to find a new toilet seat to replace the old one. Nothing in the room made of wood escaped the polishing cloths. At around 1:00 P.M., Jessie arrived from the restaurant with the hotel's platinum amenities package: a miniature wicker chair about two feet high containing cheese, crackers, a bottle of wine, fruit, nuts, and bread sticks interlaced with packets of hard candy made by the hotel chef. Personalized matchbooks embossed with Mr. Bigbucks' initials, a vase of fresh-cut flowers, and a gilt-edged note signed by Mr. Thompson himself completed the amenities. The installation of the sparkling new toilet seat was completed just ten minutes before.

Gail gazed down at the undisturbed herringbone pattern in the carpeting, left by the vacuum Teresa ran as the last touch, and couldn't think of a thing she had missed. "Room 816's ready," she called in to the front desk, and went off to see if she could sneak in a few bites of lunch.

4:35 P.M.

Mr. Bigbucks arrived at the hotel looking a bit rumpled from the long plane trip and the taxi ride shared with four other people. The hotel lobby was crowded with pharmacists and late-arriving poets checking in at the conventions desk. He walked up to an unoccupied spot along the regular front desk area and waited until a front desk agent could break away from the group check-ins.

"Good afternoon, welcome to the ABC Hotel, my name is Joan. How can I help you?"

"Hi, my name is Bigbucks. I have a reservation for tonight."

"Let me check that for you." The computer keys ticked quickly. "Yes, you'll be staying for one night. Do you need help with your luggage?"

"No, I have just one small bag."

Joan finished the check-in process, smiling and remembering to make frequent eye contact, and gave Mr. Bigbucks the key packet to room 616.

4:40 P.M.

When Mr. Bigbucks opened the door to 616, he was mildly disappointed to find nothing waiting for him in the room. The room was spotless and fresh, but at most hotels he found flowers, chocolates, maybe a note to welcome him. Here…nothing. Maybe it's because I'm only staying one night, he thought, although he didn't know why that would make a difference. His flight had been delayed, so he had arrived at the hotel much later than he'd planned and had just enough time to unpack and take a quick shower before heading out to dinner at the home of XYZ's president.

5:15 P.M.

Dr. Lucky, a dentist from Omaha, walked up to the front desk with a suitcase in each hand. He was in town for a three-day meeting at the city's convention center near the hotel. "I'd like a suite please," he said.

Dr. Lucky put his bags down while the front desk agent scanned the computer terminal. "We have a suite on the eighth floor available." A bell attendant started to place Dr. Lucky's bags on a luggage cart but Dr. Lucky stopped him. He liked to save money on his business trips whenever he could. He collected his room key, rode the elevator to the eighth floor, and followed the arrows to 816. He set his suitcases down and fumbled briefly with the electronic door lock before swinging the door open. He bent to pick up his bags. When he caught sight of the suite, he straightened up slowly, the bags forgotten. "Wow!" he sighed reverently.

5:35 P.M.

After hesitating a moment over stepping on the perfectly groomed carpeting, Dr. Lucky walked into the suite. He paused a moment to take it all in—the shining surfaces, the hint of fragrance from the flowers, the wicker basket (was that a tiny chair?)—before bringing in his suitcases, shutting the door, and opening up the wine. He usually didn't stay at hotels as nice as the ABC Hotel, but he had decided to splurge a bit on this trip. I've got to do this more often, he thought, I had no idea ordinary guests were treated so well at these posh hotels. He was munching happily on the cheese and crackers and looking curiously at the candies—he'd never seen any quite like them before—when he noticed a note on the dresser:

Dear Mr. Bigbucks:

We hope you enjoy your stay with the ABC Hotel. If there is anything we can do to make your experience with us more pleasant, please let us know.

Jim Thompson, General Manager

Dr. Lucky stopped in mid-chew. Oh, no, he thought, I've already eaten half the stuff in the basket. Will I have to pay extra for this?

5:40 P.M.

Mr. Bigbucks got in the elevator and pushed the button for the hotel lobby. At the third floor, the elevator stopped and the hotel's director of sales got in. The director and Mr. Bigbucks rode in silence to the lobby, where they both got off and headed in opposite directions.

6:00 P.M.

Dr. Lucky changed into more casual clothes and decided to spend the evening finding the convention center and exploring the city around the hotel. It was an easy decision to wait until tomorrow morning to call the front desk and straighten out the mix-up.

Tuesday
8:00 A.M.

Dr. Lucky went down to the hotel restaurant for breakfast. Since he planned to go back to his room before leaving for the convention center, he decided he would call the front desk later to discuss the wine-and-flowers mix-up. At the restaurant, he ran into a dentist he knew. They ate breakfast together and shared a cab ride directly to the convention center. Dr. Lucky promised himself he would stop at the front desk and get things straightened out when he got back.

8:30 A.M.

Mr. Bigbucks picked up his bag and pulled the door to room 616 closed behind him. He hadn't slept well. He was hoping the all-day meeting at corporate headquarters would end early so he could change his seven o'clock flight back home to something earlier. At the front desk, the agent was exceptionally friendly and efficient. On the way out to his cab Mr. Bigbucks passed Ray Smith. Ray was in a hurry; he had another meeting with the general manager about improving guest service.

Discussion Questions

1. What did the ABC Hotel do wrong?

2. How could the hotel have recovered with Mr. Bigbucks had it discovered its mistake while he was still at the hotel? How can the hotel recover with Mr. Bigbucks now?

3. What procedures should the hotel put in place to avoid such a mix-up in the future?

The following industry experts helped generate and develop this case: Gail Edwards, Director of Housekeeping, Regal Riverfront Hotel, St. Louis, Missouri; Mary Friedman, Director of Housekeeping, Radisson South, Bloomington, Minnesota; and Aleta Nitschke, Founder and Web Publisher of *The Rooms Chronicle*, Stratham, New Hampshire.

Tension in the Housekeeping Department

It was going to be a busy day at the Boden Oceanside Resort and Lodge. Today was Friday and 160 guests were checking out this morning. More than 200 rooms would be checked into by the end of the day for what was going to be a beautiful weekend. Maria, the front office manager, reviewed the arrival list and wondered if her counterpart in housekeeping would have the staff to ensure that all the rooms needed would be available by 3:00 P.M.

Staffing was still an issue for nearly all departments at the resort. Some of the larger resort operations in the state had trouble fully staffing for the busy seasons. The challenge for the front office manager and the director of housekeeping was to find qualified employees in a time of low unemployment for the local area. The executive housekeeper, Fran, was pleased because she had just hired a new room attendant, Adele. Fran had been in housekeeping for more than twenty years, and had been the executive housekeeper of the Boden for ten years.

Her problem this morning centered on a seasoned veteran, Mona, who had been with the hotel more than seven years. She had never moved up from room attendant, however, because her co-workers found her difficult to work with. The next step in her career would have been to move to supervisor, but that entailed inspecting rooms and giving direction. While she was not a team player, she did a great job on her own. Recently she had hurt her back for the third time and the doctor had ordered her not to do jobs that required repetitive motions. This restriction meant that she needed to work with another room attendant to get the job done.

Yesterday, Mona was teamed with Adele. The executive housekeeper thought that Mona could teach Adele the ropes, since the department trainer was off for a week. It seemed that the day went well for the two room attendants, so she assigned the two to work together again this morning. Since the resort was expecting a busy check-in, Fran had given the two the maximum number of rooms to clean for the day. Fran hoped that the two could work well as a team so that they could get their work done in a timely way.

At 10:00 A.M., Fran received a call from Maria. There were problems between two of Fran's room attendants. A guest had called in to the front desk exclaiming that two room attendants were screaming at each other in one of the rooms they were cleaning. Fran went immediately to the south wing of the resort. There she found Mona and Adele still arguing about a tip that had been left in room 309.

The guests had checked out by 8:30 A.M. after a four-night stay and left a $15 tip for the room attendants. Mona had pocketed the ten dollar bill and given the five to Adele. Although Adele had been on the job only a day, she knew that tips were to be split among the room attendants who had cleaned the room during the guest stay. In this case, not only was Adele entitled to two days of tips, but someone else would be expecting a portion of the tip as well.

Fran was furious because guests shouldn't be subjected to the sour energy of disgruntled room attendants. She quieted Adele and Mona down and asked them firmly to report to her office. She would be there in ten minutes after attending to the guest who had called the front office. Fran called the front office manager on the radio to ask if she would accompany her to the guest's room to be sure that the guest knew that her complaint was appreciated. Fran had never felt really comfortable interacting with guests. She still thought of housekeeping as being back of the house, and didn't expect her room attendants or supervisors to go out of their way to interact with resort guests.

Back in her office, Fran met with the two room attendants to work out the problem. Mona thought that, since she was the trainer, she was entitled to the majority of the tip. She believed that since Adele was only just learning, she should be prepared to assist wherever necessary. Adele said that Mona had made her clean all the bathrooms and that Mona wasn't even helping scrub the floor or toilet. Fran was very firm in her discussion with the two and told them that guests could be upset very easily when room attendants argued in public. "If there is a problem," she said, "come see me!"

"The mood was so tense you could cut it with a knife," said Fran later to her general manager, who stopped in to see how things were going. "I had to do something!"

Fran sent Adele and Mona home for the day to cool down. The following day, Mona was teamed with another room attendant, as was Adele. Fran figured that Mona was the problem and Adele just needed to work with someone with a different attitude.

Maria, the front office manager, caught up with Fran the next afternoon in the employee dining area and asked how things were going. Fran said that things seemed quiet, but she wasn't sure how the new room attendant would work out.

Discussion Questions

1. What are the advantages and disadvantages of the training that Adele received?

2. How could Fran have prevented some of the tension between the two room attendants?

Case number: 608C12

This case also appears in Todd Comen, *Case Studies in Front Office Management* (Lansing, Mich.: American Hotel & Lodging Educational Institute, 2003).

Filling the Shoes of a Veteran Executive Housekeeper

Mike wasn't a newcomer to housekeeping. He was most recently the assistant housekeeping manager at a hotel in Naples, Florida. Now he was walking into the shoes of a veteran of the housekeeping department at the Boden Oceanside Resort and Lodge. Mike had been hired to replace Fran, who had just retired after many years with the Boden. He was finding that Fran had run her operation almost flawlessly out of her head, rather than from written rules and guidelines.

Mike had met with numerous surprises during his first weeks at the Boden. Recently, housekeeping had been receiving low ratings from guests on the comment cards. The front office had been directing numerous guest complaints to the housekeeping department—mostly concerning towel shortages, stained sheets, and the need for new soap and shampoos. Mike understood that sometimes front desk agents misinterpreted complaints, but Mike knew better than to confront the front office manager about the possibility of her staff exaggerating the circumstances. He had learned long ago to take complaints as an opportunity for improvement.

This morning, shortly after Mike had arrived, the room attendants came to him to let him know that they were out of bathroom cleaning fluid. He wondered how this could be, as just last week he had requested an inventory of all housekeeping supplies and linens on hand. He had done so after noticing that linens were running low. In particular, frayed hand towels were being placed in bathrooms because good-quality ones were in short supply.

He assumed that, after the inventory, the assistant housekeeping manager would have ordered whatever was in low supply. Mike knew that the department had been understaffed for some time due to cost-cutting measures the hotel owners and general manager had instituted. He also knew that money hadn't been budgeted for new linens, even though the busy season would soon be upon them and the supply was inadequate for higher occupancy levels.

Now, as he entered the storage closet for the first time since his quick orientation tour (he always relied on his assistant to deal with inventory and stocking), Mike realized that he should have explored the purchasing process sooner.

Mike's strategy for moving into his new position was to let people continue to work at their jobs as before, observing and getting to know his staff, the guests, and the other department managers. He had enough on his plate just getting to know the culture of Boden's management, what was expected of him, and how the other managers worked to achieve the overall mission of the resort.

The storage room he now peered into was typical of many he had seen and worked in. Supplies were stocked by category, although there were no labels on the shelves. Linens were neatly folded and everything seemed to be in full view. It looked like most supplies were well stocked, so Mike wondered why the bathroom cleaner was out this morning. Mike looked around for an inventory sheet or anything that would tell him where the cleaner should have been stocked.

Just then Kit, his assistant manager, came down the corridor. Seeing Mike, she asked whether he needed anything. Mike told her that the front office manager was receiving complaints from guests about ragged hand towels and bath towels. Today, however, room attendants had informed him that they were out of bathroom cleaner. Kit was surprised that the cleaner was all gone because she always ordered a case every other week. Maybe someone stole some, she said.

Mike asked her what her ordering procedures were. Kit told him that she looks through the storeroom on a weekly basis and places an order every other week for cleaning supplies. She's been doing it for so long that she usually knows exactly what to order. She also told Mike that they don't run out of things very often, although they sometimes got down to the last unit. In those circumstances, she would run to the discount store to pick up some supplies if the order wasn't coming in for a few days.

After sending Kit out to the discount store for a case of bathroom cleaner, Mike sat down to figure out how to improve upon the system for purchasing housekeeping supplies. He also had to determine how he would ensure that guests would have acceptable linens for the upcoming season. He knew he couldn't order an entire new supply of linens and towels, so he had to develop a system to help him integrate new linens and towels into the system over a period of months.

Before putting pen to paper, Mike called the director of purchasing for the Boden to set up a meeting to discuss his needs.

Discussion Questions

1. What policies and procedures for inventory and purchasing would you put in place if you were Mike?
2. How does Mike's problem affect guest satisfaction?
3. What strategy should Mike use to convince the general manager to allocate more resources to the housekeeping department to meet his linen needs?

Case number: 608C13

This case also appears in Todd Comen, *Case Studies in Front Office Management* (Lansing, Mich.: American Hotel & Lodging Educational Institute, 2003).

Chapter 11 Outline

Functions of the Front Office Audit
    The Front Office Auditor
    Establishing an End of Day
    Cross-Referencing
    Account Integrity
    Guest Credit Monitoring
    Audit Posting Formula
    Daily and Supplemental Transcripts
    Front Office Automation
The Front Office Audit Process
    Complete Outstanding Postings
    Reconcile Room Status Discrepancies
    Verify Room Rates
    Balance All Departmental Accounts
    Verify No-Show Reservations
    Post Room Rates and Taxes
    Prepare Reports
    Prepare Cash Receipts for Deposit
    Perform System Back-Up Routine
    Distribute Reports
System Update
Centralized Front Office Audits
Summary

Competencies

1. Identify the functions of the front office audit. (pp. 393–398)

2. Identify the steps in the front office audit process. (pp. 398–407)

3. Explain the function of a system update and describe centralized front office audits. (pp. 407–409)

11

The Front Office Audit

SINCE HOTELS OPERATE twenty-four hours a day, seven days a week, front office management must regularly monitor the accuracy and completeness of guest and non-guest accounting records. A front office audit procedure is intended to fulfill this requirement.

The front office audit is a daily comparison of guest account transactions recorded in the front office system or at the front desk against revenue center transactions. This routine helps guarantee the accuracy, reliability, and thoroughness of front office accounting. The front office audit also may include active non-guest accounts. A successful audit will result in balanced guest and non-guest accounts, accurate account statements, appropriate account credit monitoring, and timely reports to management. An effective front office audit also increases the likelihood of correct guest and non-guest account settlement.

The **front office audit,** sometimes referred to as the **night audit,** is generally performed during the late evening hours. Before the implementation of automated front office systems, the most convenient time to perform the audit was during the late evening and early morning hours, when front office auditors could work with minimal interruption. Most, if not all, hotel revenue outlets are closed during late hours, thereby allowing the night audit to include all revenue department transactions for the day. Also, most hotels have an *accounting day* or *hotel day* that defines the daily business period of the hotel. The front office audit closes the transactions of one hotel day and, when completed, initializes the financial records for the next day.

With an automated front office system, the audit may be called a **system update,** since system files are electronically updated continuously as part of a transactional audit routine. Most of the manual work once performed by a front office auditor is now performed automatically. For example, a front office system can automatically post room charges and initiate an audit routine at a scheduled time or on demand. There is no reason that the front office audit routine must occur at night, other than to maintain reporting formats by hotel day. Much of the front office audit involves creating and distributing system reports, which can be done at any time.

Functions of the Front Office Audit

The main purpose of the front office audit is to verify the accuracy and completeness of guest and non-guest accounts against revenue center transaction reports. Specifically, the front office audit is concerned with the following functions:

- Verifying posted entries to guest and non-guest accounts
- Balancing all front office accounts
- Resolving room status and rate discrepancies
- Reviewing guest credit transactions against established limits
- Generating operational and managerial reports

It is important to understand that the front office audit is concerned only with front office activities. The audit of food, beverage, in-room refreshment centers, banquets, and other revenue outlets is usually the responsibility of the hotel accounting department and may occur the day after the revenue center outlet closes. Hotel management may require extensive auditing of food, beverage, and other revenue-producing departments. In some small hotels, the front office auditor may perform several parts of a complete audit in addition to the front office audit, since there may be fewer revenue outlets in the hotel.

The Front Office Auditor

Performing the front office audit requires attention to accounting detail, procedural controls, and guest credit restrictions. The **front office auditor** should also be familiar with the nature of transactions affecting the front office accounting system. The front office auditor typically tracks room revenues, occupancy percentages, and other standard hotel operating statistics. In addition, the auditor may use the front office system to prepare a daily summary of cash, check, credit card, debit card, gift card, and other activities that occurred at the front desk. These data collectively reflect the front office's financial performance for the day. The front office auditor summarizes and reports the results of operations to front office management. The hotel's accounting division (which is primarily responsible for back office auditing) may also rely on front office audit data in preparing additional statistical analyses.

Establishing an End of Day

The front office auditor compiles, balances, and reviews the transactions posted to guest ledger accounts throughout the day. Each hotel must decide what time will be considered the end of its accounting (or hotel) day. An **end of day** is simply an arbitrary stopping point for the business day. The front office manager must establish an end of day so that the audit can be considered complete through a specific, consistent point in time. Usually, the closing time of hotel revenue outlets determines the property's end of day. For hotels with twenty-four-hour room service, restaurants, or stores, the official end of day is the time when a majority of outlets close or no longer have frequent transaction activity. For casino hotels, for example, that tend to have revenue outlets constantly open, the end of day is determined by management as the best time to close the books, generally about 4 A.M., or later.

Typically, the business day ends when the front office audit begins, which may be after the hotel's night shift staff begins work. For example, if a front office audit begins at 1:30 A.M., the hotel's business day would end at 1:30 A.M. The period from

1:30 A.M. until the audit is completed is referred to as audit work time. Normally, transactions requiring front office accounting attention that are received during audit work time are not shown as posted until the end-of-day audit is completed. Transactions incurred during audit work time are considered part of the next business day.

Cross-Referencing

Hotel departments may generate paperwork to document transactions. For each revenue center transaction, the originating revenue center classifies and records the transaction type (cash, charge, or paid-out) and its monetary value. Front office personnel may review automated postings to ensure that the appropriate guest or non-guest folio has been properly accessed. In addition, revenue centers not interfaced to the front office system may need to use a voucher or alternate form of documentation to communicate transactional information to the front office staff for posting.

A front office accounting system depends on system interfaces and transactional documentation to establish accurate records and maintain effective operational controls. Transactional documentation (either electronic or paper-based) identifies the nature and amount of a transaction, and is the basis for data entry into a front office accounting system. This documentation may consist of charge vouchers, adjustment vouchers, and other support documents.

For internal control purposes, an accounting system should provide independent supporting documentation to verify each transaction. In a non-automated operation, supporting documents produced in different departments (for example, a coffee shop guest check and a front office guest folio) provide cross-reference information. Although the front office auditor receives information on room revenues from the front office system, the auditor should also check room rate postings on guest folios against the housekeeping department's report of occupied rooms and the front desk registration file. This is commonly called a **bucket check,** deriving its name historically from the old registration-card front desk storage file, which was frequently called "the bucket." This procedure helps ensure that accurate room rates have been posted for all occupied rooms and helps reduce the occupancy errors caused when front desk agents do not properly complete check-in or check-out procedures. Similarly, it is possible that some food and beverage postings to guest and non-guest accounts were documented through charge vouchers or guest checks sent from the revenue outlet to the front desk. In such circumstances, the auditor can use the outlet's register entries or sales journal as a cross-reference to prove front office postings.

The front office auditor relies on transactional documentation to prove that proper front office accounting procedures have been followed. The auditor's review of daily postings reconciles front office accounts with revenue center and departmental records.

Account Integrity

Sound internal control techniques help ensure the accuracy, completeness, and integrity of front office accounting procedures. Internal control techniques include cash control and the separation of duties. Duties are separated to ensure that no single individual is wholly responsible for accounting for all phases of a transaction.

Proper internal control techniques require different front office staff members to post, verify, and collect sales transactions at the front desk. If a front desk agent were allowed to sell a guestroom, post the charge, verify the posting, and collect cash for the room, no other staff member would be able to detect mistakes or possible embezzlement. Instead, duties should be split among employees: a front desk agent may perform the posting; a front office auditor, the verification; and a front office cashier, the settlement. In many properties, the front office auditor is the only person empowered to initiate the automatic posting of room rates and room tax charges to an electronic guest folio.

The front office auditor helps ensure that the front office receives payment for goods and services rendered. The front office auditor establishes guest and non-guest account integrity by cross-referencing account postings with departmental source documentation. The audit process is complete when the totals for guest, non-guest, and departmental accounts are **in balance** (that is, proven correct). As long as the audit process presents an **out-of-balance** position, the audit is considered incomplete. In essence, an out-of-balance position exists when the charges (debits) and credits posted to guest and non-guest accounts throughout the day do not match the charges (debits) and credits posted to the departmental revenue sources. An out-of-balance condition may require a thorough review of all account transactions, statements, vouchers, support documents, and departmental source documentation. With non-automated and semi-automated hotels, there may be several different forms of records to be reviewed, totaled, and combined as part of the balancing process. With a fully automated system, out-of-balance positions are rare.

Guest Credit Monitoring

Software responsible for monitoring the credit limits of guest and non-guest accounts helps maintain the integrity of the front office accounting system. Establishing lines of credit or credit limits depends on many factors, such as payment card company floor limits, the hotel's house limit, and the guest's status or reputation as a potential credit risk. The front office auditor should be familiar with these limits and how they relate to each guest and non-guest account. At the close of each business day, the front office auditor should identify guest and non-guest accounts that have reached or exceeded assigned credit limits (front office software can flag these accounts automatically). These accounts are typically called *high-balance accounts*. A report listing high balance accounts, or a **high-balance report,** should be prepared for appropriate front office management action.

Audit Posting Formula

Regardless of when the front office audit is conducted, the basic account posting formula (algorithm) applies, which is:

$$\text{Previous Balance} + \text{Debits} - \text{Credits} = \text{Net Outstanding Balance}$$
$$\text{PB} + \text{DR} - \text{CR} = \text{NOB}$$

The following example clarifies the use of this formula and its role in the front office audit. Assume a guest account has a previous balance of $280, departmental charges (debits) of $60, and payments received (credits) of $12.80. During the audit routine, the system posts the outstanding departmental charge transactions, such as the room and tax charges, and posts credits (cash payments, checks, and payment card payments) to yield a net outstanding balance of $327.20. This figure serves as the previous balance for the next transaction. Using the posting formula, these transactions are:

$$\text{PB} \quad + \quad \text{DR} \quad - \quad \text{CR} \quad = \quad \text{NOB}$$
$$\$280 \quad + \quad \$60 \quad - \quad \$12.80 \quad = \quad \$327.20$$

Daily and Supplemental Transcripts

A **daily transcript** is a detailed report of guest accounts that summarizes and updates those guest accounts that had transactional activity on that particular day. A **supplemental transcript** may track the day's transactional activity for non-guest accounts. Together, the daily transcript and supplemental transcript detail all transactions occurring on a single hotel day. Since guests can check out of the hotel at any time, the daily transcript must be processed with care.

Data appearing on a system-produced daily transcript is typically detailed by revenue center, transaction type, and transaction total. The daily transcript and the supplemental transcript form the basis for a consolidated report of front office accounting transactions from which revenue center totals can be checked. The total of charged purchases reported by the hotel's restaurant, for example, should equal the total amount of restaurant charge purchases posted to guest and non-guest accounts. The equality of these totals is an important concern in the front office audit process.

Daily and supplemental transcripts are simply electronic spreadsheets designed to eliminate posting discrepancies. Daily and supplemental transcripts can facilitate the front office audit routine by identifying out-of-balance figures in advance of a detailed review. An out-of-balance condition among non-guest accounts, for example, will help the front office auditor detect and correct errors without having to review all transactions occurring on that day.

Front Office Automation

Front office modules of a property management system (referred to as the front office system) can be interfaced with point-of-sale equipment, call accounting systems, in-room entertainment devices, and other revenue sources for timely, accurate, and automatic postings to electronic guest and non-guest account folios. Several audit functions can be performed continuously throughout the guest cycle. Automated systems enable the front office auditor to spend more time auditing transactions and analyzing front office activities and less time performing the postings and bookkeeping entries necessary with non-automated systems. Monitoring account balances and verifying account postings require a simplified procedure that compares guest ledger and non-guest ledger audit data with the front office daily report for balancing. When these documents are out of balance, there is usually an internal computational problem or an unusual data-processing error. For example, suppose the interface between the restaurant's point-of-sale system and the front office accounting system has been inoperative for a short time during the day. The point-of-sale system may show the total number and amount of the day's transfers to the front office system, but the front office system may have different totals due to the system interface failure. The front office auditor must reconcile the differences and post the adjusting entries to the appropriate guest accounts and ledgers to bring the two systems into balance.

An automated front office system may retain previous balance information for guest and non-guest accounts, along with appropriate transactional details, in an electronic database. Whereas previous balance entries were necessary in manual and semi-automated systems, automated front office systems calculate current balances quickly and do not need a previous balance entry as a starting point for transactional posting. During the audit, front office staff members may be guided through a series of procedures requiring them to provide information in response to system-generated directives or commands relative to the front office audit routine.

The front office system performs numerous mathematical verifications to ensure postings are correct. For example, a range check will recognize postings of unusual size, such as a $15 charge being posted as $1,500. Since most front office accounting systems are capable of tracking each posting by time, shift, employee, folio number, and revenue center, the system is capable of maintaining a detailed audit trail of transactional activity.

Front office systems can organize, compile, and print records faster than can be done manually. In an audit routine, a system can process a large quantity of data, perform numerous computations, and generate accurate account totals. A front office system update is often used to perform many of the automated functions necessary for monitoring the guest cycle. System updates are run daily to establish an audited end of day and allow for report production, file reorganization, and system maintenance.

Front office systems also offer rapid access to information, thereby enabling front office management to more knowledgeably plan, organize, and direct operations. Reports detailing revenue data, occupancy statistics, advance deposits, arrivals, no-shows, room status, and other operational information can be generated on request, or as part of the regular system update routine. Exhibit 1 presents a sample revenue center report.

The Front Office Audit Process

The front office audit focuses on two areas: (1) the discovery and correction of front office accounting errors, and (2) the creation of accounting and management reports. From an accounting point of view, a front office audit ensures the integrity of front office accounts through a cross-referencing process. Guest and non-guest accounts are compared with data entries and source documents from revenue centers to prove individual transaction entries and account totals. Discrepancies found during a front office audit must be corrected so that the front office accounting system is in balance. From a management perspective, the front

Exhibit 1 Sample Revenue Center Report

Trial Balance

Daily Transactions

Balance Brought Forward		16,413.67
Revenue		
1000	Room Revenue	9,556.20
1055	ADJ - Room Revenue - Tax Exempt	- 9.43
2009	SR Breakfast for Packages	20.00
2010	State Room Breakfast	629.45
2030	State Room Lunch	783.81
2040	State Room Dinner	2,920.02
2050	State Room Liquor	181.25
2060	State Room Beer	44.75
2070	State Room Wine	661.75
2110	KC Lounge Breakfast	36.25
2120	KC Lounge Lunch	17.00
2130	KC Lounge Dinner	436.20
2140	KC Lounge Liquor	251.50
2150	KC Lounge Beer	211.00
2160	KC Lounge Wine	246.00
2210	Room Service Breakfast	61.20
2230	Room Service Dinner	142.95
2250	Room Service Beer	3.75
2260	Room Service Wine	8.75
2310	Banquet Breakfast	625.00
2320	Banquet Lunch	4,035.75
2340	Banquet Break	2,440.00
2350	Banquet Reception	6,058.75
2380	Banquet Wine	245.00
2390	Banquet Room Rental	1,650.00
2400	Banquet Audio Visual	820.00
2410	Banquet Other	153.25
3010	Long Distance	16.75
3015	ADJ - Long Distance	- 8.15
3020	In Room Movies\ Games	51.96
3035	ADJ - Movies\Internet	- 11.99
4000	Parking	190.50
4010	Parking Special Events	4,000.00
4020	Parking Group	590.00
4060	Copies	6.37
4200	Gift Shop	574.46
6000	Stateroom Gratuity	972.08
6001	KC Lounge Gratuity	137.44
6002	Room Service Gratuity	68.73
6010	Banquet Service Charge	2,534.65
6020	Room Service -Service Charge	32.00
Revenue Total		41,384.95
Non Revenue		
7000	Room Sales Tax	326.11
7020	County Fee	408.41
7039	F&B Sales Tax for Packages	1.20
7041	Stateroom Food Sales Tax	207.60

Courtesy of Kellogg Hotel & Conference Center, Michigan State University, East Lansing, Michigan.

office audit provides important operating information, such as average daily rate (ADR), revenue per available room (RevPAR), occupancy percentage, number of package plans and other marketing programs, and the number of group rooms and complimentary (no-charge) rooms occupied.

Front office accounting systems perform a continuous system audit routine and provide summary reports at predetermined times as well as on demand. The degree of scrutiny required during the front office audit process depends on the frequency of errors and the volume of transactions to be reviewed. While the first of these factors relates to the quality of data entry work, the second correlates with the size and complexity of the hotel. Complex hotel operations typically require closer account scrutiny due to the potential high volume of transactions posted.

The following steps are common to the sequence of a front office audit:

1. Complete outstanding postings.
2. Reconcile room status discrepancies.
3. Verify room rates.
4. Balance all departmental accounts.
5. Verify no-show reservations.
6. Post room rates and taxes.
7. Prepare reports.
8. Prepare cash receipts for deposit.
9. Perform system back-up routine.
10. Distribute reports.

In an automated system update, several of these steps may be condensed or combined. The following sections present front office audit procedures from an operational perspective.

Complete Outstanding Postings

One of the primary functions of the front office audit is to ensure that all transactions affecting guest and non-guest accounts have been posted to appropriate folios. It is important that the system accurately post and account for all transactions as they occur. Posting errors are problematic and can lead to discrepancies and delays at check-out. This can prove time-consuming, since the debated charges will have to be researched for explanation.

While effective front office practice dictates that transactions be posted to the proper accounts as they occur, the front office auditor must confirm that all transactions have been posted before starting the audit routine. This may mean waiting until all food and beverage outlets, including banquet facilities, are closed. Incomplete postings will result in errors in account balancing and complicate summary reporting.

In addition to completing the posting function, the front office auditor will need to verify that all vouchers for revenue center transactions are posted. If the hotel does not have an interfaced automated telephone call accounting system, outstanding telephone charges may require manual posting. If the hotel supports point-of-sale or call accounting system interfaces to the front office accounting system, the previously posted totals should be verified to ensure that all outlet charges have been posted. This can be done by generating printed posting reports from the interfaced systems and comparing them with the totals reported by the front office accounting system. If the figures are identical, the systems are in balance. If they are not the same, the front office auditor should compare transactions between the two systems to identify the transactions that have been omitted or improperly posted.

Reconcile Room Status Discrepancies

Room status discrepancies must be resolved in a timely manner, since imbalances can lead to lost business and cause confusion in the front office. Errors in room status can lead to lost and uncollectible room revenues and omissions in account postings. The front office system must maintain current and accurate room status information to effectively determine the number and types of rooms that remain available for sale. For example, if a guest checks out but the front desk agent fails to properly complete the check-out procedure, the guest's room may appear elsewhere in the system as occupied when it is really vacant. This error in procedure could prevent the room from being sold until the error is discovered and corrected.

To minimize errors, housekeeping departments typically require staff to record the perceived status of guestrooms as they are serviced. While a preliminary reconciliation of the housekeeping and front office guestroom status is usually done on the shift before the front office audit, the auditor must review front office and housekeeping reports to reconcile and finalize the occupancy status of all guestrooms for a given night. If the housekeeping report indicates that a room is vacant, but front office staff considers it occupied, the auditor should search for an active guestroom folio and registration record. If the folio exists and has a current outstanding balance, there are several possibilities:

- A guest may have departed but forgotten to check out.

- A guest may be a skipper who left with no intention of checking out.

- A front desk agent or cashier may not have properly closed the folio at check-out.

- A guest may have used self-check-out but the system interface failed.

After verifying that the guest has left the hotel, the front office auditor should process the check-out and set the folio aside for front office management review and follow-up. If the folio has been settled, the front office room status system should be corrected to show that the guestroom is vacant. The front office auditor should verify the guest folio against the housekeeping reports and room status reports to ensure that all three are consistent and in balance. The check-out process, which is typically a rooms management function, automatically monitors and updates the room's status. Few, if any, room status discrepancies should occur in an automated front office system.

Verify Room Rates

Verifying room rates is usually done at the same time as reconciling room status, since both are part of the bucket check and are more efficiently completed simultaneously. The front office auditor will need to review a system-generated room report. This report provides a means for analyzing room revenues, since it indicates the room rack rate (price) for each room and the actual rate for which the room was rented. If a room's rack rate and actual rate do not match, the front office auditor should consider several factors:

- If the room is occupied by a member of a group or by a corporate-rate customer, is the discounted rate correct?

- If the room is occupied by a guest with a special package rate or promotional discount offered through the hotel's reservation distribution channels, is the discounted rate correct?

- If there is only one guest in a room and the actual rate is approximately half the rack rate, is the guest part of a shared reservation? If so, did the second guest register? Was the second guest properly charged?

- If the room is complimentary, is there appropriate supporting back-up for the rate (for example, a complimentary room authorization form)?

Guestroom rate verification is usually performed by comparing the registration to the front office system record. The registration record provides a snapshot of the guest's information, including room rate, at the time of check-in. Any changes made to the guestroom rate would happen during or after check-in, resulting in changes from the original record. The proper use of guestroom revenue and room count information is the foundation of room revenue analysis. The front office auditor may be required to produce this report for review by front office management, since it provides a method for measuring room revenue potential against actual room revenue. The actual room revenue posted is compared with the rack rate of the rooms occupied for the night. This comparison may be shown as a percentage or as a dollar amount.

Balance All Departmental Accounts

The front office audit process can become quite complicated when errors are discovered. It is generally considered more efficient to balance all departmental accounts first and then determine individual posting errors within an out-of-balance department.

The front office auditor typically balances all revenue center departments using source documents that originated in the revenue center. The front office auditor seeks to balance all front office accounts against departmental transaction information. Vouchers received electronically or manually at the front desk are totaled and compared with revenue center summaries. Source documents often help resolve discrepancies in an efficient manner.

When the front office accounting system is out of balance, the correctness and thoroughness of account postings must be investigated. A detailed department audit (by shift or by cashier) may be conducted and individual postings reviewed until the front office accounting error is detected and corrected.

The process used to balance revenue center departments is often called the **trial balance.** A trial balance is a test of the front office accounts to confirm proper balancing before the final audit is complete. The front office system will normally generate a trial balance before initiating final audit reports. The trial balance usually uncovers corrections or adjustments that need to be made during the audit process. The front office auditor may prefer to perform the trial balance before the system posts the day's guestroom and room tax charges. Doing so can simplify the final audit procedure. If the trial balance was correct and the final balance is wrong, the auditor can deduce that the error must relate to the guestroom and room tax posting.

It is important to note that a mathematical balance in guest and non-guest accounts against departmental totals does not necessarily mean that the proper accounts were selected for posting. Posting the correct amount to an incorrect account would still present an in-balance total. This type of error usually goes unnoticed until a guest has a problem with the validity of an entry on his or her statement.

Exhibit 2 presents a sample sequence of front office audit procedures useful in departmental balancing.

Verify No-Show Reservations

The front office auditor may also be responsible for clearing the reservation file or filing and posting charges to no-show accounts. When initiating a front office system posting of no-show charges, the front office auditor must be careful to verify that the reservation was guaranteed and the guest failed to register with the hotel. Sometimes duplicate reservations may be made for a guest or the guest's name may be misspelled and another record accidentally created by the front office staff or system. If these are not identified by front office staff, the guest may actually arrive but appear to be a no-show under the second reservation.

No-show billings must be handled with extreme care. A front desk agent who does not record cancellations properly may cause guests to be billed incorrectly. Incorrect billing may lead the payment card company guaranteeing the reservation to reevaluate its legal agreement and relationship with the hotel. Incorrect billing may also cause the hotel to lose the guest's future business and (if applicable) the business of the travel agency or intermediary that guaranteed the reservation. Front office staff must adhere to established no-show procedures when handling reservation cancellations or modifications.

Post Room Rates and Taxes

The automatic posting of guestroom rates and room taxes to guest folios typically occurs at the end of day. Once guestroom rates and taxes are posted, a rate and tax report may be generated for front office management review. The ability to electronically post room rates and room taxes is one of the most frequently cited advantages of an automated front office system. Once the front office initiates guestroom rate postings, the system auto-posts rates and taxes to the appropriate

Exhibit 2   Departmental Balancing Sequence

1. Sort vouchers by originating departments.

2. Consider each department's vouchers.

    a. Separate the correction vouchers according to the departments they are to be applied against.

    b. Total the corrections for each department.

3. After verifying each of the corrections with the departments affected, total the correction vouchers. The corrections total must coincide with the correction figures on the front office shift report.

4. Consider the vouchers again.

    a. Total the rest of the outstanding vouchers.

    b. Check individual transaction values on the bottom of the voucher against the figure appearing on the department detail report.

5. The vouchers should agree with the corrected figures of the departments. If the totals do not agree with either figure, the error should be resolved before proceeding.

    a. Verify that the date on the voucher is the current day's date.

    b. Check off each individual posting against its support document (voucher) until the error is found. This can be tedious if there are several errors. However, if the front office uses validating printers, a thorough check of the support document validations will help pinpoint errors.

    c. Post any additional corrections or adjustments.

6. In an automated system, revised individual shift reports can be generated after corrections and adjustments have been made. In any operations mode, backup data should be packaged for accounting office review.

electronic folio. System postings are highly reliable, since automatic charge postings are not prone to pickup, tax calculation, or posting errors. An auto-posting feature may be especially helpful to hotels located in municipalities subject to occupancy taxes in addition to a sales tax. Some hotels pre-set their front office systems to post daily recurring charges, such as valet parking or mandatory gratuities. Auto-posting charges saves front office audit time and improves accuracy.

Prepare Reports

The front office auditor typically prepares reports that indicate the status of front office activities and operations. Among those prepared for management review are the final department detail and summary reports, the daily operations report, the high balance report, and other reports specific to the property.

Final department detail and summary reports are produced and may be filed along with source documents for accounting division review. These reports help prove that transactions were properly posted and accounted for on a comprehensive basis.

The daily operations report summarizes the day's business and provides insight into revenues, receivables, operating statistics, and cash transactions related to the front office. This report is typically considered the most important outcome of the front office audit. The high balance report identifies guests whose charges are approaching an account credit limit designated by the hotel (the house limit).

In addition to regularly scheduled reports, the front office system may be programmed to produce a variety of management reports on demand. For example, the high balance report may be produced at any time during the day as a continuing check on guest transactions and account balances. Another important report is the daily summary report, also called the flash report. The daily summary report provides a dashboard or snapshot of important operating statistics on a daily, weekly, or monthly basis. Hotel managers typically find this summary report very informative and review its contents at the start of a work shift. The daily summary report may also indicate an occupancy and rate forecast for the following business day, alerting management to any changes that may have happened overnight.

In addition, an automated front office system can produce an assortment of specialty reports. For example, a group sales report can be produced for each registered group in the hotel, showing the number of rooms occupied by each group, the number of guests for each group, and the revenue generated by each group. This system-generated report can help the hotel sales department track group histories. The same type of report may be generated for guests on package plans or special promotion or advertising discounts. Other reports may list guests who stay frequently, are VIPs, or are celebrating a special occasion. This type of information may be automatically tracked, sorted, and reported by the front office system.

Prepare Cash Receipts for Deposit

The front office auditor frequently prepares a cash deposit voucher as part of the audit process. If front office cash receipts have not yet been deposited in a bank, the front office auditor compares the postings of cash payments and paid-outs (net cash receipts) with actual cash on hand. A copy of the front office cashier shift report may be included in the cash deposit envelope to support any overage, shortage, or due back balances. Since account and departmental balancing often involves cash transactions, accurate cash depositing may depend on an effective audit process.

The hotel may require the front desk cashier to deposit cash at the end of each shift without knowing the value of cash receipts the system has recorded. This is called a *blind drop,* since the cashier is not aware of the total that should be deposited according to the system. Blind drops are used when management is concerned that employees may not be reporting all cash received. When a blind drop is used, the front office auditor compares system totals per cashier with the cashier drop document. Variances are reported to the hotel general manager, front office manager, or controller.

Perform System Back-Up Routine

Since an automated system eliminates the need for a room rack, reservation cards, and a variety of other traditional front office forms and devices, front office accounting depends on the continuous functioning of the system. A system back-up in the

Exhibit 3   Guest Ledger Report

Lodgistix Resort & Conference Center (90003)

Preliminary Audit Report—July 12—Guest Ledger Balances

Status	Open Balance	Room/ Tax	Incdntl	Food	Beverage	Payment	Close Balance
Canceled-Keep	.00	.00	.00	.00	.00	220.00–	220.00–
Canceled-Return	.00	.00	.00	.00	.00	165.00–	165.00–
No Show	480.00–	.00	.00	.00	.00	.00	480.00–
Checked-out	312.31+	104.55+	.00	.00	.00	104.55–	312.31+
Registered	5485.36+	2441.23+	58.36+	311.31+	21.62+	1440.00–	6877.88+
House Accounts	.00	.00	8.40+	.00	.00	.00	8.40+
Group Master Accounts	.00	.00	15.00+	14.00+	21.00+	.00	50.00+
Total Guest Ledger	5317.67+	2545.78+	81.76+	325.31+	42.62+	1929.55–	6383.59+

Courtesy of Sulcus, Phoenix, Arizona.

front office audit routine is unique to an automated front office system. Back-up reports must be executed and various media duplicated in a timely manner so that front office operations can continue to run smoothly.

Normally, at least two guest lists are printed for back-up and emergency use: one for the front desk staff and one for the telephone switchboard operator. Additional guest lists may be printed for departments that may not have direct access to the front office system, such as the security department. A **room status report** enables front desk agents to identify vacant and ready rooms should the front office system become inoperable. A guest ledger report can be generated, such as the one shown in Exhibit 3. This report contains the opening and closing account balances for all registered guests. A front office activity report can also be generated; such a report contains expected arrival, stayover, and departure information for several days (a sample activity report is shown in Exhibit 4). In some front office systems, the next day's registration forms are pre-printed as part of the front office activity report. Due to requirements of the Americans with Disabilities Act, the front office staff must also keep track of guests with disabilities. One reason for this is to ensure that all disabled guests are accounted for in case of an emergency. This report is usually distributed to the managers of the various departments needing this information.

System-generated front office information should also be copied (backed up) onto a DVD optical disk or other media, depending on the system configuration. A system back-up should be conducted after each audit and stored in a safe place (maybe off the premises). Many front office systems have two types of system back-up: a daily back-up (a copy of front office files) and system back-up (eliminating account and transaction details no longer of value). For example, expired guest folio accounts that are at least three days old may be deleted from active storage files and be archived. If an account must be researched in the future, it can be located through an archived storage file search.

Exhibit 4   Activity Report

```
LODGISTIX RESORT & CONFERENCE CENTER (90003)                    PAGE   1
                                                                JUL12
Arrival/Stayover/Departure Activity Report                      13:14:23

              ---Arrivals--- ---Stayovers-- --Departures-- Rem
Date   Avl  Sold    Gtd  6/4  Shr   Gtd  6/4  Shr   Gtd  6/4  Shr  Blk Adlts Kids

JUL12   24    49 Trn  28    5    0    12    0    1    14    0    0        71   16
            67.1% Grp   2    0    0     0    0    0     0    0    0   3    2    0

JUL13   36    37 Trn   1    0    0    31    5    1     8    0    0        61   14
            50.6% Grp   0    0    0     0    0    0     2    0    0   0    0    0

JUL14   48    25 Trn   1    0    0    19    5    0    13    0    1        41    8
            34.2% Grp   0    0    0     0    0    0     0    0    0   0    0    0

JUL15   59    14 Trn   3    0    0    11    0    0     9    5    0        21    4
            19.1% Grp   0    0    0     0    0    0     0    0    0   0    0    0

JUL16   68     5 Trn   1    0    0     4    0    0    10    0    0         7    2
             6.8% Grp   0    0    0     0    0    0     0    0    0   0    0    0

JUL17   68     5 Trn   1    1    0     3    0    0     2    0    0         9    2
             6.8% Grp   0    0    0     0    0    0     0    0    0   0    0    0

JUL18   71     2 Trn   1    0    0     1    0    0     3    1    0         3    0
             2.7% Grp   0    0    0     0    0    0     0    0    0   0    0    0


              Total  Transient  Group  Rem Blk
Room Nights     511
  Available     374
       Sold     137       132       2       3
Occupancy %   26.8%     96.3%    1.4%    2.1%

End of report
```

Courtesy of Sulcus, Phoenix, Arizona.

Distribute Reports

Due to the sensitive and confidential nature of front office information, the front office auditor must promptly deliver appropriate reports to authorized individuals. The distribution of front office audit reports is the final step in the front office audit routine, and is important to efficient front office operations. Front office managers can make more informed decisions if front office audit reports are completed accurately and delivered on a timely basis.

System Update

A system update in a front office accounting system accomplishes many of the functions in the audit routine. System updates are performed daily to enable system file reorganization, system maintenance, and report production, and to provide an end-of-day closure.

Since front office systems audit transactional postings as they occur (in real time), there may be little or no need for the front office auditor to perform account postings. The front office system may be connected by remote communications to revenue centers for automatic postings. The front office system may support point-of-sale interfaces, call accounting technology, in-room entertainment, in-room vending, and the like. Interface capabilities enable the system to control and monitor charges made at revenue outlets throughout the hotel. Hotel management policies typically dictate the extent of system interface applications. The front office auditor should routinely review interface procedures to ensure the proper handling of automatically posted transactions from revenue outlets.

In the case of guaranteed reservation no-shows, for example, postings may be programmed to flow automatically to a billing file. If a transaction needs to be independently posted, the guest's electronic folio can be accessed for posting. Once complete, the folio will be automatically returned to electronic storage.

Room status discrepancies are somewhat unusual in an automated front office environment. Connecting registration and check-out with room status functions decreases the potential for such discrepancies. Housekeepers typically report the current occupancy status of a room through the room's telephone or a mobile device before leaving the room. This automatically updates the room's status in the front office system; if appropriate, a **room variance report** can be programmed to automatically flag discrepancies. Even in the case of a skipper, the system may help identify the problem quickly enough so that the housekeeping staff can ready the room for resale with minimal loss of room revenue.

In some front office systems, the balancing of front office and department accounts is continuously monitored in real time. As a charge purchase is entered at a remote point-of-sale terminal, for example, the charge may be instantaneously posted to an electronic guest folio and an electronic departmental control folio simultaneously. A **control folio** is an online internal accounting file that supports account postings originating from a revenue center. To balance departments, the front office system tests all non-control folio entries against individual control folio transactions. An imbalance is just as likely to identify a problem in automatic posting techniques as a shortcoming in front office accounting procedures. Detailed departmental reports can be generated and checked against account postings to prove account entries.

Front office systems can be programmed to produce a variety of reports of various lengths and content. Since a system update involves file reorganization as well as accounting detail, system output has a high degree of reliability. Reservation confirmations, revenue center summaries, expected arrival and departure lists, folios for departing guests, a daily report of operations, and billing statements for non-guest accounts may be produced as a result of an automated update.

Front office systems may also generate several other files as a safeguard against system failure. Activity reports, guest lists, room status reports, account statements, and the like may be duplicated and stored on auxiliary media as a hedge against system failure.

Centralized Front Office Audits

Front office automation significantly simplifies the front office audit process and allows multiple audit tests to be performed simultaneously. Centralization of multiple audits reduces staffing requirements for the participating properties and provides a basis for consolidated reporting. Centralized front office audits usually work best in limited-service hotels where there are few revenue outlets and operating departments are closed before the start of the audit process. At the central location, the auditor can obtain all the information necessary to complete the audit routine over secure data lines between participating hotels. The front office auditor is able to post corrective entries, back up the system, and produce reports for distribution to each hotel. The bucket check must be performed by the evening shift staff in participating hotels, since the originating documentation will not be available to the front office auditor in the central location. For chain hotels, being able to produce an aggregate or consolidated report for a group of hotels is beneficial. A hotel manager responsible for multiple properties gains access to diverse data and can directly generate reports without having to wait for individual front office managers to submit reports.

Summary

Hotels operate twenty-four hours a day, seven days a week, and the front office must regularly review and verify the accuracy and completeness of its accounting records. A front office audit process is intended to fulfill this need. The audit attempts to balance daily guest and non-guest account transactions against revenue center transactions. A successful audit will result in balanced accounts, accurate account statements, appropriate account credit monitoring, timely reports to management, and increased probability of account settlement. Traditionally, the front office audit has been called the *night audit*, since it is generally performed in the late night and early morning hours. The audit is also referred to as a *system update*, since electronic files are updated and backed up as part of the audit routine.

The chief purpose of the front office audit is to verify the accuracy and completeness of guest and non-guest accounts against departmental transaction reports and to provide reports for management. The front office auditor must be familiar with the nature and amount of transactions and must pay close attention to accounting detail, procedural controls, and guest credit restrictions. The front office auditor is usually responsible for tracking room revenues, occupancy percentages, and other standard operating statistics. In addition, the auditor will prepare a daily summary of cash, check, and payment card activities. This information is summarized to help managers evaluate the front office's financial performance on a particular day. For the audit to be consistent, the front office must establish an *end of day*, which is simply the end of the business day. Finally, the front office auditor may need to provide a variety of specialty reports to various departments in the hotel.

A front office accounting system depends on transactional documentation to establish accurate records and maintain effective operational controls. For internal control purposes, an accounting system must provide independent supporting documentation to verify each transaction. The front office auditor should check room rate postings on electronic folios against the housekeeping department's report of occupied rooms. This process helps ensure that rates have been posted for all occupied rooms and reduces the occupancy errors caused by front desk agents who do not properly complete check-in and check-out procedures.

Regardless of when the front office audit is conducted, the basic posting formula applies. The audit routine is somewhat simplified through the development of a daily transcript, which contains summary information on guest accounts. In some front office operations, a supplemental transcript may be used to monitor the transactional activity for non-guest accounts. Together, the daily transcript and supplemental transcript detail all transactions occurring on a single day.

Front office auditors typically follow a series of ten steps when conducting a front office audit: complete outstanding postings, reconcile room status discrepancies, verify room rates, balance all departmental accounts, verify no-show reservations, post room rates and taxes, prepare reports, prepare cash receipts for deposit, perform system back-up routine, and distribute reports.

Key Terms

bucket check—The night auditor's check of room rate postings on guest folios against the housekeeping department's report of occupied rooms and the registration cards in the file. This procedure helps ensure that rates have been posted for all occupied rooms and helps reduce the occupancy errors caused when front desk agents do not properly complete check-in and check-out procedures.

control folio—An automated front office system internal accounting file that supports account postings by department during a system update routine.

daily transcript—A detailed report of all guest accounts that indicates each charge transaction affecting a guest account for the day, used as a worksheet to detect possible posting errors.

end of day—An arbitrary stopping point for the business day.

front office auditor—An employee who checks the accuracy of front office accounting records and compiles a daily summary of hotel financial data as part of the front office audit; in many hotels, this is actually an employee of the accounting division.

high-balance report—A report that identifies guests who are approaching an account credit limit; typically prepared by the front office auditor.

in balance—A term describing the state of accounts when the totals of debit amounts and credit amounts are equal.

night audit (front office audit)—A daily comparison of guest accounts (and active non-guest accounts) with revenue center transaction information.

out-of-balance—A term used to describe the state of accounts when the totals of debit amounts and credit amounts do not equal.

room status report—A report that allows front desk agents to identify vacant and ready rooms, typically prepared as part of the front office audit.

room variance report—A report listing any discrepancies between front desk and housekeeping room statuses.

supplemental transcript—A detailed report of all non-guest accounts that indicates each charge transaction that affected a non-guest account that day, used as a worksheet to detect posting errors.

system update—A fully automated audit routine that accomplishes many of the same functions as a non-computerized front office audit; daily system updates enable file reorganization, system maintenance, and report production, and provide an end-of-day time frame.

trial balance—The process of balancing front office accounts with transaction information by department before the final balance is determined and the hotel day is closed.

Review Questions

1. What are the two basic purposes of the front office audit? Why is it generally performed at night? What is the definition of the term *end of day?*

2. What are the functions of the front office audit process? How does each contribute to the efficiency of the front office accounting system?

3. How do the concepts of cross-referencing and account integrity govern the front office audit process? What are the usual source documents for guest account transactions?

4. What information does a daily transcript provide? What related purpose does a supplemental transcript have?

5. How does the front office auditor reconcile room status discrepancies? Why is it important that these reconciliations occur as early as possible?

6. Why does the front office auditor verify room rates and no-shows before posting room rates and taxes? Why is it important that these postings occur as late as possible?

7. What accounting, management, and marketing reports are typically generated during the front office audit process?

8. What is the purpose of a system back-up for an automated front office system?

Internet Sites

For more information, visit the following Internet sites. Remember that Internet addresses can change without notice. If the site is no longer there, you can use a search engine to look for additional sites.

Technology Sites

CSS Hotel Systems
www.csshotelsystems.com

Execu/Tech Hospitality Solutions
www.execu-tech.com

First Resort Software
www.firstres.com

Galaxy Hotel Systems
www.galaxyhotelsystems.com

The Host Group
www.thehostgroup.com

MICROS
www.micros.com

Newmarket International
www.newmarketinc.com

Resort Data Processing, Inc.
www.resortdata.com

Case Study

Promoting the Front Office Auditor at The Macasa DeVille Resort

The Macasa DeVille is a majestic hotel located in the heart of rodeo country. The hotel until recently had been part of a national reservation system, but it canceled its participation and became independent. The Macasa DeVille has 110 guest suites, a formal dining room, two lounges, a health spa, and a horse riding stable. The Macasa DeVille is famous for its backpacking explorations and its fishing expeditions in nearby Lake Gregory. An outstanding view of the valley affords Macasa DeVille guests an excellent location for corporate seminars, executive management meetings, and training seminars.

The Macasa DeVille operates year-round at an average occupancy of 90 percent. Recently the general manager, Mr. Dailey, and the front office manager, Mr. Nagy, disagreed over two important issues. One dealt with discounted room rates, the other with the contents of the daily report of operations that Mr. Nagy's department produced for Mr. Dailey's review. Until Mr. Bradley, the front office auditor, brought these two matters to Mr. Dailey's attention, Mr. Dailey was unaware of the fluctuation in assigned room rates and the level of detail the daily report lacked.

Mr. Nagy felt that room rates should be flexible and vary according to the guest's ethnic background and politeness during registration. Each front desk agent was instructed to consult with Mr. Nagy before assigning a room rate during the registration process, regardless of the rate quoted at the time of reservation. In addition, Mr. Nagy believed Mr. Dailey should only be given occupancy statistics and average room rate information on a daily basis. Mr. Dailey did not like this approach and requested that Mr. Nagy resign. When the front office manager refused, Mr. Dailey fired him.

Mr. Dailey, who had not had to recruit or hire a front office manager, was faced with a challenge. He decided that, in his search for Mr. Nagy's replacement, he was going to seek someone with front office auditing experience. He believed that the information that existed within the confines of the front office audit would serve well in creating the daily report. Further, he believed he could instill a different room rate philosophy into the new front office manager without much trouble.

Mr. Dailey understood the urgency to recruit a new front office manager. He invited Mr. Bradley to apply and hired him two days after Mr. Nagy's departure. Many members of the front office staff were upset, believing that Mr. Bradley had blindsided Mr. Nagy in hopes of getting his job. Mr. Bradley had to work especially hard to prove to the staff that a former front office auditor could manage the department and put to better use much of the front office information.

Discussion Questions

1. Was Mr. Bradley correct in discussing the arbitrary variations in room rates and the shortcomings of the hotel's daily report with Mr. Dailey?

2. What information do you think the front office auditor most likely relied on to determine the room rate discrepancies? What key information may have been omitted from the daily report of operations?

3. Should a front office manager have front office audit experience? What are the advantages and disadvantages of such experience to the front office manager?

4. Develop a daily report format for the Macasa DeVille showing all the information Mr. Dailey should receive.

5. Briefly discuss the front office auditor's role in providing both daily financial information and overall information about the hotel's performance. What makes this information so important to management?

Case Number: 3329CA

The following industry experts helped generate and develop this case: Richard M. Brooks, CHA, Vice President, TWE Group; and Michael L. Kasavana, NAMA Professor in Hospitality Business, *The* School of Hospitality Business, Michigan State University, East Lansing, Michigan.

Night Audit Problem

This problem is a practical learning experience and a comprehensive review. It takes you step-by-step through an actual front office problem. The appendix at the end of the book contains the forms necessary for completing the problem. Read the instructions and work through the problem, filling in the forms based on the transactions stated below.

Instructions

1. Post the transactions to the guests' folios as they occur.

2. Create a folio for anyone who checks in. Use the following chart to establish the room rates by type of room and number of persons.

Room Type	1-Person Rate	2-Person Rate
Inner hall	$24	$30
Woods	$32	$38
Lake view	$34	$40
Pool	$40	$48
Deluxe	$48	$56
Suite	$60	$70

Extra per person: $6

3. After all transactions have been posted for the day, post the room rate and room sales tax (using four percent as the tax rate) for those guests who are still in the house.

4. Balance the folios.

5. Complete the transcript.

   a. Beginning with the rooms that have checked out:
      - List the room numbers sequentially.
      - Transfer the room statistics from the folio.
      - Bring the balance forward.
      - Enter the various charges and credits.
      - Carry the balance forward for each guest folio.

   b. Next, copy the same information for the rooms that are still occupied. List those rooms in numerical sequence.

   c. Total all significant columns of the transcript on the House Total line.

   d. Copy the City Ledger Control balance forward, the various charges and credits, and forward the balance.

   e. Enter the same information for the Advance Payments Control account.

   f. Total the significant columns of the House Total, the City Ledger, and the Advance Payments Control account.

   g. Balance and check the transcript.

Background

As of April 1, all the rooms on the hotel's first floor are occupied by individuals associated with the "Sunshine" group. The room charge and room sales tax are being picked up by the group; all other charges will be paid by the individuals. Five other rooms are occupied by guests not associated with the "Sunshine" group. The room rates and balances brought forward as of the morning of April 1 are:

Room No.	Name	Room Rate	Balance
101	Sunshine (Master)	$1,330	$(600.00)
245	Brown, Mr. & Mrs. Edwin	48	208.04
302	Jackson, Larry	70	72.80
324	Greenwood, Nelson	24	49.92
440	Foster, Mr. & Mrs. Jack	56	58.24
522	Straight, Mr. & Mrs. Tom	56	97.34

None of the "Incidentals" folios associated with the group guests have a balance. Also, the City Ledger Control Folio has a balance of $50,000 and the Advance Payments control (Deposits) has a credit balance of $2,930.

NOTE: Laundry, although done by an external business, should be treated as a departmental charge.

Transactions

1. Mr. Richard Russell checks in. He desires a "woods" room and is assigned room 206.

2. Mr. Charles McGraw and family (total of four persons) check in. They have a reservation with a deposit of $52. They desire a "lake view" room and are assigned room 409.

3. Mr. Jackson, room 302, checks out, charging his balance to his American Express card.

4. Mr. & Mrs. Carl Anderson arrive without reservations and are assigned to room 455, a suite. Mr. Anderson pays $100 when checking in.

5. Mr. Greenwood, room 324, makes two long-distance calls: one to Houston, Texas, for $7.28 and one to Atlanta, Georgia, for $6.24.

6. The room attendant reports that all luggage has been removed from room 522 and that Mr. & Mrs. Straight have disappeared.

7. Mr. & Mrs. Foster, room 440, check out. Mr. Foster charges his bill to the Allied Builders Co., a city ledger account.

8. Flash Cleaners laundry delivers for the Browns. The front desk agent posts the charge of $12 to the Browns' folio.

9. Flash Cleaners also delivers laundry for Mr. Davis, room 100, and Mr. Cotton. Mr. Davis is with the "Sunshine" group; the clerk posts the charge of $9 to his account. Mr. Cotton left his laundry when he departed on March 27 and is expected to return April 3; the charge is $6.

10. The credit manager informs Mr. Brown, room 245, that he has exceeded his credit limit of $200. Mr. Brown pays the cashier $350. He also complains about a lunch he had on March 29 for which he had paid in cash. The manager agrees to give him an allowance of $2.80.

11. Mr. & Mrs. Harry Goodman and their son check in. They are assigned to room 331, a "lake view" room. After checking in, they have lunch in the restaurant and charge the check of $15.60 to their room.

12. Mr. Bob Moose checks into room 401, a suite. After checking in, he spends the afternoon at the bar and charges his bill of $18.72 to his room.

13. Mr. Goodman complains to the restaurant manager about the lunch he had with his family. The manager agrees to make an allowance for the entire amount of the check.

14. Mr. & Mrs. Anderson have lunch in their room (455). They charge the amount of the meal, $8.32, to their room and add a tip of $1.50. The room service waiter collects the tip from the front office cashier.

15. A restaurant check arrives at the front desk for Mr. Foster; the charge is $4.76.

16. Mr. Greenwood, room 324, checks out. He disputes a long-distance charge of $6.24 and the charge is allowed (that is, removed or credited as an allowance). He pays the balance of his bill in full.

17. Mr. Russell, room 206, makes three long-distance calls to Chicago. The charges are $17.25, $14.25, and $6.98.

18. Two charge vouchers from the banquet department arrive at the front office for a dinner party held by the Westside Hospital, a city ledger account. The charges are $250 for food and $120 for beverages.

19. The cashier receives checks for $60 from Mr. Addison and $70 from Mr. Blue as deposits on reservations for April 9.

20. Mr. & Mrs. Brown wine and dine together. Mr. Brown charges the dinner check of $43.68 and the bar check of $15.60 to his room bill.

21. Charges for the "Sunshine" master folio, room 101, are as follows:

Food banquet:	$152.64
Cocktail banquet:	61.68
Cash advance:	43.50
Allowance for rooms:	30.36

22. City Ledger cash received was $1,140.

When you have completed the exercise, using either hand computation, machine posting, or a hotel computer, you will have experienced a night audit in miniature. A particular hotel may have slightly different procedures for handling many of the transactions, but this application illustrates a typical night audit for a small hotel.

Night Audit Problem ©1984. This problem was designed and written by George Conrade, CHA, CHE, Assistant Professor, Hotel, Restaurant & Institutional Management, University of Delaware.

Chapter 12 Outline

Competencies

1. Describe the management process in terms of the functions front office managers perform to achieve organizational objectives. (pp. 419–422)

2. Identify room rate categories and explain how managers establish room rates. (pp. 422–433)

3. Discuss issues involved with forecasting room availability and apply the ratios and formulas managers use. (pp. 433–444)

4. Explain how front office managers forecast rooms revenue and estimate expenses when budgeting for operations. (pp. 444–448)

5. Describe how managers use various reports and ratios to evaluate front office operations. (pp. 448–463)

6. Explain what front office managers can do to plan for disasters. (pp. 463–464)

12

Planning and Evaluating Operations

Most front office managers will readily admit that they rarely have all the resources necessary to accurately monitor the guest cycle. Resources available to managers include staff members, budgeted funds, work shifts, materials, and equipment. All are in limited supply. An important part of a front office manager's job involves planning how to apply limited resources to attain the department's objectives. An equally important function is evaluating the success of front office activities in meeting the department's objectives.

Management Functions

The process of front office management can be divided into specific management activities. Exhibit 1 illustrates how management functions fit into the overall front office management process. Although specific front office management tasks vary among hotels, fundamental management functions remain similar in scope.

Planning

Planning is probably the most important management function in any business, yet managers may fail to provide the attention it requires, and may overlook it entirely. Without competent planning, front office work would be chaotic. Without the direction and focus planning provides, the front office manager may become overly involved with tasks that are unrelated to or inconsistent with accomplishing the department's goals. A front office manager's first step in planning should involve determining the department's goals.

Managers should identify both near-term goals and long-term goals, and develop a plan for achieving them. An example of a near-term goal might be to increase next month's occupancy from 82 to 85 percent. A long-term goal might be to improve guest satisfaction scores well beyond the current level. The front office manager should use these general goals as a guide to planning more specific, measurable objectives. Planning also includes determining the strategies and tactics the department will use to attain the objectives.

An important component of planning is communication, which is essential for success. An effective front office manager will communicate the plans under development with supervisors to ensure that departmental activities are consistent with overall hotel planning. At the same time, it is a good idea to share tentative or preliminary plans with department members likely to be affected by the plan and

419

Exhibit 1   Overview of the Management Process

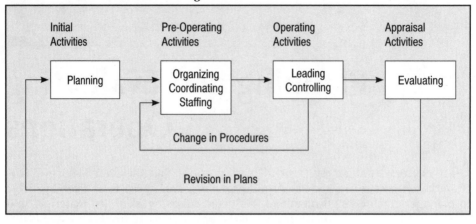

seek their input and feedback. Communication is most effective in written form so that ideas are documented and clearly illustrated for reviewers.

There are several benefits to communication and idea-sharing. First, department staff members can contribute to the planning process and thereby gain ownership of the plan (or portions of the plan). Staff members who are included in the planning process typically are more willing to accept and support the overall plan. Second, staff members involved in the planning process have the opportunity to provide constructive comments before the department manager finalizes the plan. If staff members have concerns about the plan, the department manager is able to address these issues during the planning phase. Third, once the plan is finalized, everyone involved will have a more comprehensive understanding of the goal or objective. If several different competing perspectives emerge during the planning process, compromises may be required. Staff members tend to develop a better understanding of the compromises that are made when they are part of the planning process.

Organizing

Using the planned goals as a guide, a front office manager organizes the department by dividing the work among front office staff. The manager should distribute work so that everyone participates and the work can be completed in a timely manner. Organizing includes determining the order in which tasks should be performed and establishing completion deadlines for each group and subgroup of tasks.

Coordinating

Coordinating involves bringing together and using available resources to attain planned goals. A front office manager must be able to coordinate the efforts of many individuals to ensure that work is performed efficiently, effectively, and on time. Coordinating front office procedures may involve engaging with other departments, such as sales, housekeeping, food and beverage, and accounting.

Many front office goals depend on other departments for achievement. For example, the goal of improving guest satisfaction scores may partially depend on the housekeeping staff's promptly notifying the front desk staff when a clean and vacant room has been readied for the next arriving guest. The front office manager's ability to coordinate with various department managers is closely related to his or her other management skills, such as planning and organizing.

Staffing

Staffing involves recruiting applicants and selecting those best qualified to fill available positions. To properly recruit employees, it is essential to develop job descriptions that thoroughly describe the position and that clearly identify the skills and qualities applicants must possess to satisfactorily fill it. The front office manager will work with the human resources department to develop job descriptions for front office positions. At most hotels, the human resources department is usually involved in the first level of qualifying and interviewing job applicants. Human resources staff members are also relied upon to resolve issues that may arise regarding whether a job description properly represents the position. The staffing process also involves scheduling employees. Most front office managers develop staffing guidelines based on formulas for calculating the number of employees required to meet guest and operational needs under specific conditions.

Leading

Leading is a complicated management skill that is exercised in a wide variety of situations, and is closely related to other management skills such as organizing, coordinating, and staffing. For a front office manager, leadership involves overseeing, motivating, training, disciplining, and setting an example for the front office staff. For example, to direct the work of others, a front office manager must first analyze the work to be done, organize the tasks in a logical order, and consider the environment in which staff will perform the tasks. In addition, if the department is behind in getting the work done, the front office manager steps in and assists until the workload is under control again.

A front office manager's leadership impact often extends beyond the front office. With so much of the hotel's business activity flowing through the front desk, other department heads count on the front office manager to provide direction. Senior managers at a hotel often depend on the front office manager's strong leadership skills to ensure that assignments are completed successfully.

One of the best ways to lead a department is by example. It is often necessary for department managers to participate in the department's day-to-day operations to demonstrate job knowledge and skills mastery. For instance, working at the front desk may involve greeting guests, checking guests in and out, pre-blocking rooms, working with housekeeping staff, charting room status, and more. When a manager leads effectively, this behavior demonstrates what is expected of all department employees. A manager must be available to department employees and will earn their respect as the unit leader if he or she leads by example. This often means working varying shifts to be available to all front desk staff, not just to the workers on one particular shift.

Controlling

Every front office department has a system of internal controls to protect the hotel's assets. For example, one form of internal control is requiring a witness's signature when a cashier makes a cash deposit at the end of the shift. Internal control systems work only when managers believe in the systems' importance and follow established procedures. The control process ensures that the actual results of business operations closely match planned results. The front office manager also exercises a control function when keeping front office operations on course in attaining planned goals.

Evaluating

Proper methods of evaluation determine the extent to which planned goals are, in fact, attained. The task of evaluating is frequently overlooked in many front office operations, or is performed haphazardly. Evaluating also involves reviewing and, when necessary, revising or helping to revise front office goals.

This chapter focuses on elements of two front office management functions: planning and evaluating front office operations. It begins by examining three important front office planning functions:

- Establishing room rates

- Forecasting room availability

- Budgeting for operations

It concludes by examining various methods a front office manager may use to evaluate the effectiveness of front office operations.

Establishing Room Rates

A front office revenue management system will almost always have more than one room rate category for each guestroom. Room rate categories generally correspond to types of rooms (suites, two beds, one bed, etc.) that are comparable in square footage and furnishings. Differences are based on criteria such as room size, location within the hotel, view, furnishings, and amenities.

The **rack rate** is the price for an overnight accommodation, as determined by front office management, for a particular room or room type. The rack rate is posted on the room rate schedule to inform front desk agents of the standard selling price of each guestroom in the hotel. Unless the guest qualifies for an authorized room rate discount, the rack rate will apply. The term *rack rate* predates front office automation and references the process by which an employee would identify the retail room rate from a manual filing system located at the front desk, called a *room rack,* hence the name *rack rate.* With front office automation, an electronic file replaces the rack. Electronically stored room rate data is accessed by front office staff members, as well as reservation agents, at the time of reservation or registration. Often, operational policies mandate that rack rates be reported to local and state authorities, and posted in public areas or inside the guestroom. Rack rates must be kept current and accurately reflect the appropriate accommodation charge for each room and room rate category.

Room rates are normally assigned by room type category. For example, a standard room with two double beds and no special amenities may be assigned the hotel's lowest rack rate. Larger rooms, with different sleeping accommodations and amenities, will be assigned a higher rack rate. Concierge floor rooms with more amenities and perhaps better outdoor views will likely be assigned an even higher rack rate. Suites usually command the highest rack rate because of size, number of beds, quality of furnishings, and other amenities.

When a resort property includes a meal plan in its room pricing (for example, Bed and Breakfast, Modified American, or Full American Plan), the rack rate is usually based on the room characteristics as well as the number of people expected to occupy the room. In this case, a resort's pricing for a single room rate may be greater than the value of the property's double occupancy rate divided by two, since the hotel incurs certain fixed costs no matter how many guests occupy the room.

Front office employees are expected to sell rooms at the rack rate unless a guest qualifies for a discounted room rate. Although rack rates are important, more often than not, guests may ask for and qualify for discount rates. For example, special rates are often quoted to groups and certain guests for promotional purposes, especially during low occupancy periods. Special room rate categories include:

- *Corporate or commercial rate:* the rate offered to companies that provide frequent business for an individual hotel or hotel chain.

- *Group rate:* the rate offered to group, meeting, and convention attendees staying at the hotel.

- *Promotional rate:* the rate offered to individuals who may belong to an affinity group such as the American Automobile Association or American Association of Retired Persons, to promote their patronage. The rate may also be extended during special low occupancy periods to other guests to promote occupancy.

- *Incentive rate:* the rate offered to guests in affiliated organizations such as travel agencies and airlines because of potential referral business. The rate may also be offered to promote future business; it is often extended to group leaders, meeting planners, tour operators, and other decision-makers capable of providing the hotel with additional room sales.

- *Family rate:* a rate reserved for families with children.

- *Package plan rate:* a rate that includes a guestroom in combination with other events, activities, or services, such as meals, golf, tennis, or parking.

- *Internet rate:* a special discounted rate that many hotel companies offer through an Internet website. A web rate is usually classified as the "best available rate" and is available to guests making an online reservation. Many hotel companies guarantee that the best available rate is at their own website and often offer a bonus plan for guests who find lower rates elsewhere. During projected lower occupancy business cycles, web rates tend to be discounted rates. Since a hotel company incurs less expense selling a guestroom through a private website, its rates will naturally be lower. Comparatively, global distribution systems, travel agency sites, corporate call centers, and other distribution channels may offer higher room rates.

- *Distressed-inventory rate:* a special room rate offered when a hotel projects or experiences low occupancy. This rate usually represents a significant discount off the rack rate and is implemented to help build occupancy. The idea behind distressed-inventory rates is that the discount will be sufficient to attract consumers who seek lower rates. Distressed-inventory rates are usually found on Internet websites that offer hotel rooms based on targeted price and not on a specific hotel property; in fact, online shoppers may need to commit to the room rate even before learning the identity of the hotel property or brand. Most hotels restrict the use of distressed-inventory rates to only those times when extremely low occupancy is predicted.

- *Complimentary rate:* a room rate provided to special guests, important industry leaders as a sales incentive, and those guests who have experienced a problem at the hotel to the point where management wishes to give them a complimentary rate as compensation. The term *complimentary rate* usually means that the guest will not be charged for the guestroom during the stay. However, the guest may still be charged for incidental items such as food and beverages, Internet access, etc.

The front office manager must be sure that the sale of rooms at special rates is rigidly controlled. Special rates represent discounts from the rack rate and therefore may adversely affect the average room rate and room revenue. The front office manager should examine the circumstances under which special rates are granted to ensure that front office staff members are adhering to prescribed policies. All policies should be clearly explained to front office staff, who should obtain proper approval when applying a special room rate. For example, a complimentary room (provided at no charge) does not increase room revenue, but it may or may not decrease the average room rate, depending on the front office accounting system. Most hotels require the general manager or another senior member of the management team to approve complimentary rates before guests arrive.

Establishing rack rates for room types, and determining discount categories and special rates, are some of the major duties of the hotel's revenue manager. The revenue manager recommends rack rates to senior hotel management after analyzing forecasted occupancy and business conditions in the marketplace. Rack rates are usually determined on a yearly basis (subject to frequent revision review) and are a major decision factor in the annual hotel budgeting process. Determining discounted rates is more tactical and is a decision the revenue manager, or possibly a revenue committee, must make. When determining rack rates or discounted rates, management should consider such factors as operating expenses, guest demand, market conditions, inflationary factors, and related business issues.

Room rates often serve as a market positioning statement, since they directly reflect service expectations to the hotel's target market. Room rate positioning can be critical to a hotel's success. For example, a property offering economy facilities and limited guest services will most likely not succeed if its rates are positioned in the mid-price or upscale levels.

The following sections examine three popular approaches to pricing rooms: the **market condition approach,** the **rule-of-thumb approach,** and the **Hubbart Formula.**

Market Condition Approach

The market condition approach reflects a relatively commonsense strategy. Managers identify comparable hotels in their geographic market and research their room rates. These comparable properties compose what is often referred to as the **competitive set,** which is usually made up of six to ten properties in a market area. The competition can be based on location, property ratings, property type, brand identification, or other factors. Not every lodging property in a particular location is a direct competitor. Guests who look for moderately priced lodging will generally limit their research to properties in that price range.

The thought behind this approach is that the hotel can charge only what the market will accept, and this is usually dictated by the competition. This information is available through various public domain sources. Hotels may also periodically make *blind calls* to competing hotels. Staff members making blind calls do not identify their hotel; they simply ask for availability and rates on specific dates at nearby hotels. (Note that, with caller ID, "blind" calls may not truly be blind unless the hotel takes steps to hide its identity within the caller ID system.)

A competitive analysis usually focuses on these questions:

- How do our hotel's room rates compare to those of our competition?

- Are our rates much lower or higher than those of the competition? How are our rates affecting our revenue and market share?

- What is our current occupancy percentage? What is the occupancy percentage of the competitive set? Will our total revenue improve if we increase (or decrease) our rates?

- Have any industry trends emerged during the past six months?

Most of the answers to these questions cannot be determined through simple phone calls to hotels or reviews of competitors' websites. Three well-known commercially available reports from neutral sources that provide this information are the TIMS, Phaser, and RateVIEW reports. Future occupancy and rate trends can be determined by studying the quoted rates and availability for the competitive set. The TIMS Report lists one month's rate information for a property and five local competitors. The rates are broken down daily and include information on sold-out nights, low rate, low rate variance from the subscribing property, low corporate rate, low corporate rate variance, special rates availability, high-low comparisons, and an index of room types and rates for the period. Exhibit 2 shows a sample TIMS report. A Phaser Report is a comparative analysis of room rates, including information from internal distribution channels (such as central reservations offices) and external distribution channels (such as global distribution systems) for a property and its competitive set. RateVIEW is a series of reports providing details on how a property compares with its competitive set for future dates, looking at many distribution channels.

Exhibit 2 Sample TIMS Report

TIMS Competitive Rate Analysis Report for the *Sample* TIMS Report		
TIMS Code: Sample	Reporting Period: Nov 10,'00 thru Dec 7,'00	Data Captured: Nov 8,'00

High - Low Rate Comparison

		Fri 11/10	Sat 11/11	Sun 11/12	Mon 11/13	Tue 11/14	Wed 11/15	Thu 11/16	Fri 11/17	Sat 11/18	Sun 11/19	Mon 11/20	Tue 11/21	Wed 11/22	Thu 11/23	Fri 11/24	Sat 11/25	Sun 11/26	Mon 11/27	Tue 11/28	Wed 11/29	Thu 11/30	Fri 12/01	Sat 12/02	Sun 12/03	Mon 12/04	Tue 12/05	Wed 12/06	Thu 12/07
SHERATON	High Rate	209	209	209	209	209	MLS	209	209	209	209	209	209	209	209	209	209	209	209	209	209	209	209	209	209	209	MLS	209	209
	Low Rate	135	135	125	169	169	MLS	155	89	125	89	125	125	125	79	79	79	89	129	129	129	89	89	89	89	129	MLS	129	89
	Variance	74	74	84	40	40		54	120	84	120	84	84	84	130	130	130	120	80	80	80	120	120	120	120	80		80	120
EMBASSY SUITES	High Rate	129	129	169	169	XXX	169	169	169	XXX	169	169	169	99	99	129	129	149	149	149	149	149	129	129	149	149	149	149	XXX
	Low Rate	89	89	89	169	XXX	169	169	169	XXX	169	169	169	99	99	89	89	89	149	149	149	149	89	89	89	149	149	149	XXX
	Variance	40	40	80	0		0	0	0		0	0	0	0	0	40	40	60	0	0	0	0	40	40	60	0	0	0	
HILTON	High Rate	104	104	184	184	194	XXX	184	164	214	184	184	184	184	184	104	164	184	184	184	184	184	164	224	184	194	194	194	194
	Low Rate	69	69	69	139	139	XXX	139	79	189	59	69	69	59	59	59	59	59	139	139	139	139	89	184	139	139	139	139	139
	Variance	35	35	115	45	55		45	85	25	125	115	115	125	125	45	105	125	45	45	45	45	75	40	45	55	55	55	55
MARRIOTT	High Rate	172	172	172	XXX	XXX	172	172	172	172	172	172	172	172	172	172	172	172	172	172	172	172	172	172	172	172	172	172	172
	Low Rate	84	84	159	XXX	XXX	172	169	84	159	159	159	159	69	69	69	69	159	159	129	129	84	84	129	129	129	129	129	129
	Variance	88	88	13			0	3	88	13	13	13	13	103	103	103	103	13	13	43	43	88	88	43	43	43	43	43	43
RADISSON	High Rate	139	139	139	139	139	139	139	XXX	XXX	XXX	XXX	139	139	139	139	139	139	139	139	139	139	139	139	139	139	139	139	139
	Low Rate	89	89	89	99	99	99	99	XXX	XXX	XXX	XXX	99	99	99	89	89	89	99	99	99	99	89	89	89	99	99	99	99
	Variance	50	50	50	40	40	40	40					40	40	40	50	50	50	40	40	40	40	50	50	50	40	40	40	40
WESTIN	High Rate	XXX	XXX	255	255	255	XXX	XXX	255	255	255	255	255	255	255	255	255	255	255	255	255	255	255	255	255	255	255	255	255
	Low Rate	XXX	XXX	169	189	179	XXX	XXX	119	159	129	169	169	119	79	79	79	79	169	169	169	169	85	85	179	179	230	179	179
	Variance			86	66	76			136	96	126	86	86	136	176	176	176	176	86	86	86	86	170	170	76	76	25	76	76

Another, more reliable way to determine historical market conditions is to subscribe to industry reports that provide this information from neutral sources. The best-known historical report is the Smith Travel Accommodations Research (STAR) Report. The STAR Report provides historical information on occupancy, average room rate, RevPAR, and market share. Exhibit 3 shows a portion of a sample STAR trend report, and Exhibit 4 shows a portion of a sample STAR summary report. By tracking this information over a period of months and years, the rates and occupancy of the competitive set can be well established.

There are many problems with this approach, although it remains popular. First, if a hotel is new, construction costs will most likely be higher than those of the competition. Therefore, a new hotel is not likely to have an identical cost structure or be as profitable as the competition initially. Second, this approach does not take the value of the hotel into consideration. Since the property is new, and perhaps offers newer amenities, the value of the property to guests can be greater. The market condition approach is really a marketing approach that allows the local market to determine the rate. It may not take into account what a strong sales effort may accomplish. It can, in effect, allow the competition to determine the rates, and this could significantly affect the profitability of a hotel's operation. Third, a drastic and uncharacteristic downturn of business (such as the Great Recession in the late 2000s) has the potential to render many historical views of rates less useful.

In the United States, hotel managers must not base their rates on the rates of other hotels through direct discussions with competitors. Such discussions would be considered violations of U.S. antitrust laws. This is one reason some hotels use a

Exhibit 3   Sample STAR Trend Report

Sample - STAR Trend Report

		Occupancy						Average Room Rate								REVF
Year Month	Prop	% CHG	Comp Set	% CHG	OCC Index	% CHG	Prop	% CHG	Comp Set	% CHG	ADR Index	% CHG	Prop	% CHG	Comp Set
20X1 May	62.4	2.0	60.2	8.5	103.7	11.5	90.89	18.3	104.40	4.6	87.1	14.4	56.74	16.6	62.87
20X1 June	72.5	20.4	68.2	8.3	106.3	11.2	94.69	3.3	105.97	4.4	89.4	1.0	68.67	24.4	72.24
20X1 July	71.7	5.4	64.9	3.6	110.5	9.4	93.82	.3	96.50	7.2	97.2	7.0	67.27	5.1	62.67
20X1 August	65.8	1.5	60.3	2.6	109.1	4.2	92.34	.8	94.52	3.7	97.7	2.8	60.80	2.4	56.99
20X1 September	68.2	4.4	64.9	5.7	105.1	10.7	110.07	1.6	116.46	5.6	94.5	6.8	75.07	2.8	75.57
20X1 October	83.3	4.9	80.7	6.0	103.2	1.1	128.09	22.3	131.06	20.6	97.7	1.5	106.69	28.4	105.71
20X1 November	67.6	3.0	64.6	2.4	104.6	.7	116.17	7.6	116.95	9.1	99.3	1.4	78.52	4.3	75.58
20X1 December	44.6	2.0	43.1	6.1	103.5	4.4	95.48	9.8	96.04	6.7	99.4	2.9	42.59	7.7	41.35
20X2 January	70.7	3.5	68.5	2.0	103.2	1.6	114.20	9.8	112.13	7.3	101.8	2.2	80.71	5.9	76.83
20X2 February	84.1	14.1	83.1	10.9	101.2	2.8	129.90	21.0	134.90	25.2	96.3	3.4	109.22	38.1	112.09
20X2 March	81.1	4.7	74.9	3.1	108.3	1.6	118.20	5.6	126.53	13.7	93.4	7.1	95.90	.7	94.75
20X2 April	67.7	1.6	65.1	.5	104.0	2.1	106.50	7.2	117.00	.8	91.0	7.9	72.11	8.7	76.12
20X2 May	69.5	11.4	64.3	6.8	108.1	4.2	106.07	16.7	118.23	13.2	89.7	3.0	73.68	29.9	76.06
20X2 June	73.6	1.5	59.8	12.3	123.1	15.8	111.34	17.6	112.26	5.9	99.2	11.0	81.93	19.3	67.19

Exhibit 4   Sample STAR Summary Report

Sample Inns & Suites Executive Summary Report - July

	Operating Performance Sample Inns & Suites						Room Revenue	Rooms Avail	Rooms Sold				Oper
July Monthly	Occupancy Percent			Average Room Rate						Occupancy Percent			A
Segment	1996	1995	% CHG	1996	1995	% CHG	% CHG	% CHG	% CHG	1996	1995	% CHG	199
United States	81.8	83.3	1.8	69.53	63.90	8.8	16.0	8.5	6.6	73.9	74.3	.5	70
Region													
New England	82.7	84.3	1.9	69.79	67.86	2.8	14.3	13.3	11.1	75.1	74.3	1.1	83
Middle Atlantic	84.4	85.0	.7	69.23	64.82	6.8	7.3	1.2	.4	75.7	74.3	1.9	87
South Atlantic	82.1	84.3	2.6	69.17	58.88	17.5	25.9	10.1	7.2	73.1	73.2	.1	70
East North Central	85.1	85.2	.1	62.39	58.80	6.1	9.3	3.1	3.0	73.4	75.1	2.3	67
East South Central	84.8	87.3	2.9	60.76	55.20	10.1	16.4	8.9	5.7	74.4	75.2	1.1	57
West North Central	83.4	83.9	.6	64.84	61.85	4.8	3.9	.4	.9	73.5	76.2	3.5	57
West South Central	75.0	81.7	8.2	64.79	61.80	4.8	34.0	39.1	27.8	69.9	71.3	2.0	59
Mountain	81.5	81.2	.4	76.19	71.37	6.8	14.6	6.9	7.3	75.0	76.1	1.4	61
Pacific	79.6	79.5	.1	79.35	74.44	6.6	13.0	5.9	6.0	75.9	75.1	1.1	80
Price													
Luxury	81.0	80.5	.6	97.65	84.71	15.3	21.2	4.4	5.1	75.2	74.9	.4	117
Upscale	81.7	83.3	1.9	80.09	74.67	7.3	14.5	8.8	6.8	76.0	76.8	1.0	87

blind-call approach to rate assessment among their competitive set. As previously mentioned, in a blind-call survey, staff at the researching property phone competitors pretending to be potential guests. During the calls, staff members inquire about room rates for select future dates. Rates may also be available from many public sources, such as the Internet, global distribution systems, published rate brochures, directories from the American Automobile Association, and many others.

Rule-of-Thumb Approach

The rule-of-thumb approach establishes the minimum average room rate at $1 for each $1,000 of construction and furnishings cost per room (and assumes the hotel maintains a 70 percent average occupancy). For example, assume that for a given hotel the average construction and furnishings cost for its guestrooms is $80,000 per room. Using the $1 per $1,000 approach results in an average minimum room rate of $80 per room for that hotel. Singles, doubles, suites, and other room types would be priced differently, but the minimum average room rate would be $80.

The emphasis placed on the hotel's construction and furnishings cost limits the applicability of using this approach, as it fails to consider the effects of inflation over time. For example, a well-maintained hotel costing $100,000 per room today may have been constructed at $20,000 per room forty years ago. The $1 per $1,000 approach would suggest an average selling price of $20 per room; however, a much higher rate would appear to be appropriate. The suggested rate of $20 per room does not take into account inflation and increased costs of labor, furnishings, and supplies. In these cases, management might consider the current replacement cost of the hotel, rather than its original construction and furnishings cost, as a basis for the rule-of-thumb application. Another way of accounting for inflation would be to index current costs against original costs. For example, if a hotel was built five years ago and inflation has increased at an annual rate of 3 percent, the $1 per $1,000 five years ago would require $1.16 per $1,000 now.

The rule-of-thumb approach to pricing rooms also fails to consider the contribution of other facilities and services toward the hotel's desired profitability. In most hotels, guests pay extra for goods and services such as food, beverages, Internet access, and dry cleaning. If these services contribute to profitability, hotel management may have less pressure to charge higher room rates.

The rule-of-thumb approach should also consider the hotel's occupancy level. As pointed out, the rule-of-thumb approach assumes 70 percent occupancy when determining the appropriate average room rate. However, if a lower occupancy percentage is expected, the hotel will have to capture a higher average rate to generate the same amount of room revenue. Hotels tend to have a very high level of fixed expenses (especially depreciation and mortgage expenses). For instance, a mortgage payment does not fluctuate and remains the same every month, regardless of the hotel's percentage of occupancy. The front office manager must understand the relationship between room rate and room occupancy on room revenue to ensure that revenue goals and financial obligations are met.

Hubbart Formula Approach

Another approach to average room rate determination is the Hubbart Formula. To determine the minimum average room rate, this approach considers operating costs, desired profits, and expected number of rooms to be sold. In other words, this approach starts with desired profitability, adds income taxes, then adds fixed charges and management fees, followed by overhead expenses and direct operating expenses. The Hubbart Formula is considered a *bottom-up* approach to pricing rooms because its initial item—net income (profit)—comes from the bottom line of a standard income statement. The second item needed for this formula—income taxes—is the second item from the bottom of the income statement, and so on. The Hubbart Formula approach involves the following eight steps:

1. Calculate the hotel's desired profit by multiplying the desired rate of return (ROI) by the owners' investment.

2. Calculate pretax profits by dividing desired profit (Step 1) by 1 minus the hotel's tax rate.

3. Calculate fixed charges and management fees. This calculation includes estimating depreciation, interest expense, property taxes, insurance, amortization, building mortgage, land, rent, and management fees.

4. Calculate undistributed operating expenses. This calculation includes estimating expenses for the following categories: administrative and general, information technology, human resources, transportation, marketing, property operation and maintenance, and energy costs.

5. Estimate non-room operated department income or loss—that is, food and beverage department income or loss, telecommunications department income or loss, and so forth.

6. Calculate the required rooms department income. The sum of pretax profits (Step 2), fixed charges and management fees (Step 3), undistributed operating expenses (Step 4), and other operated department losses less other operated department income (Step 5) equals the required rooms department income. The Hubbart Formula, in essence, places the overall financial burden of the hotel on the rooms department.

7. Determine the rooms department revenue. The required rooms department income (Step 6), plus rooms department direct expenses of payroll and related expenses, plus other direct operating expenses, equals the required rooms department revenue.

8. Calculate the average room rate by dividing rooms department revenue (Step 7) by the expected number of rooms to be sold.

Illustration of the Hubbart Formula. The Casa Vana Inn, a 200-room property, is projected to cost $9,900,000 inclusive of land, building, equipment, and furniture. An additional $100,000 is needed for working capital, bringing the total cost of construction and opening expenses to $10,000,000. The hotel is financed with a loan of $7,500,000 at 12 percent annual interest and cash of $2,500,000 provided by the owners. The owners desire a 15 percent annual return on their investment. A 75 percent occupancy is estimated; thus, 54,750 rooms are projected to be sold during the calendar year (200 × .75 × 365). The hotel's income tax rate is 40 percent, and additional expenses are estimated as follows:

Property tax expenses	$250,000
Insurance expenses	50,000
Depreciation expenses	300,000

Administrative and general expenses	300,000
Data processing expenses	120,000
Human resources expenses	80,000
Transportation expenses	40,000
Marketing expenses	200,000
Property operation and maintenance expenses	200,000
Energy and related expenses	300,000

Non-room revenue center income (loss) is estimated as follows :

Food and beverage department	$150,000
Telecommunications department	(50,000)
Rentals and other departments	100,000

The rooms department estimates direct operating expenses to be $10 per occupied room.

Exhibit 5 contains the calculations used in the Hubbart Formula and reveals a minimum average room rate of $67.81.

Exhibit 6 contains the formula for calculating room rates for single rooms (x) and double rooms ($x + y$), where the price differential between single and double room rates is represented by the variable y. Assume that the Casa Vana Inn has a double occupancy rate of 40 percent (that is, two out of every five rooms sold are sold at the double rate) and a room rate differential of $10. Applying the formula from Exhibit 6, single and double rates would be calculated as follows:

$$\frac{\text{Doubles Sold}}{\text{Daily}} = \frac{\text{Doubles Occupancy}}{\text{Rate}} \times \frac{\text{Numbers of}}{\text{Rooms}} \times \frac{\text{Occupancy}}{\text{Percentage}}$$

$$= .4(200)(.75)$$

$$= \underline{\underline{60}}$$

$$\frac{\text{Singles Sold}}{\text{Daily}} = \text{Rooms Sold Daily} - \text{Doubles Sold Daily}$$

$$= (200 \times .75) - 60$$

$$= \underline{\underline{90}}$$

Using the minimum average rate of $67.81 calculated in Exhibit 5, the required single and double rates can be determined as follows:

$$\text{Singles Sold } (x) + \left[\begin{array}{c} \text{Doubles Sold} \times \\ (x + \text{Rate Differential}) \end{array} \right] = \frac{\text{Average}}{\text{Room Rate}} \times \frac{\text{Daily Number}}{\text{of Rooms Sold}}$$

$$90x + 60(x + \$10) = (\$67.81)(150)$$
$$90x + 60x + \$600 = \$10,171.50$$
$$150x = \$9,571.50$$
$$x = \frac{\$9,571.50}{150}$$
$$x = \$63.81$$
$$\text{Single Rate} = \underline{\underline{\$63.81}}$$

$$\text{Double Rate} = \$63.81 + \$10.00$$
$$= \underline{\underline{\$73.81}}$$

Exhibit 5   Calculating Average Room Rate: Hubbart Formula

Item	Calculation	Amount
Desired net income	Owners' Investment ROI $2,500,000 \times .15 = \$375,000$	
	Pretax income $= \dfrac{\text{net income}}{1 - t}$	
	Pretax income $= \dfrac{\$375,000}{1 - .4}$	
	Pretax income $=$	$625,000
Plus: Interest expense	Principal $\times$ interest rate $=$ interest expense $7,500,000 \times .12 =$	+ 900,000
Income needed before interest expense and taxes		1,525,000
Plus: Estimated depreciation, property taxes, and insurance		+ 600,000
Income before fixed charges		2,125,000
Plus: Undistributed operating expense		1,240,000
Required operated departments income		$3,365,000
Departmental results excluding rooms		
Less: Food and beverage department income		(150,000)
Rentals and other department income		(100,000)
Plus: Telephone department loss		50,000
Rooms department income		3,165,000
Plus: Rooms department direct expense	$54,750 \times \$10 = \$547,500$	547,500
Rooms revenue		3,712,500
Number of rooms sold		÷ 54,750
Required average room rate		$ 67.81

Exhibit 6   Determining Single and Double Room Rates from an Average Room Rate

Singles sold (x) + Doubles Sold (x + y) = (Average Rate) (Rooms Sold)

where: x   =   Price of singles

y   =   Price differential between singles and doubles

x + y   =   Price of doubles

Alternatively, the double rate could be set as a percentage of the single rate. When this is the case, the formula is slightly altered:

$$\text{Singles Sold } (x) + \left[\frac{\text{Doubles Sold } (x) \times}{(1 + \text{Percentage Differential})}\right] = \frac{\text{Average}}{\text{Room Rate}} \times \frac{\text{Daily Number}}{\text{of Rooms Sold}}$$

The percentage differential is simply the percentage difference of the double rate over the single rate. To understand this approach, consider the Casa Vana Inn again. Assume a 40 percent double occupancy and a price differential of 15 percent:

$$\text{Singles Sold } (x) + \left[\frac{\text{Doubles Sold } (x) \times}{(1 + \text{Percentage Differential})}\right] = \frac{\text{Average}}{\text{Room Rate}} \times \frac{\text{Daily Number}}{\text{of Rooms Sold}}$$

$$
\begin{aligned}
90x + 60(x)(1.15) &= (\$67.81)(150) \\
90x + 69x &= \$10,171.50 \\
159x &= \$10,171.50 \\
x &= \frac{\$10,171.50}{159} \\
x &= \$63.97 \\
\text{Single Rate} &= \$63.97 \\
\text{Double Rate} &= \$63.97(1.15) \\
&= \$73.57
\end{aligned}
$$

The Hubbart Formula is most useful in setting *target* minimum average room rates as opposed to *actual* average room rates. It is important to note that the Hubbart Formula generates an average room rate as a target price at the hotel's point of profitability. It relies on management's accurate estimates of total rooms occupied and the single/double occupancy mix to determine target rates. If these estimates are incorrect, the targets will be incorrect.

Suppose a hotel company is planning to build a new property. Using the Hubbart Formula, management computes an average target room rate of $75. Knowing the current average rate for competing hotels in the area is only $50, management must consider whether the proposed hotel, projected to open in two years, has too high a targeted room rate.

To evaluate its potential, management assumes the competitor's average price will increase at 5 percent per year over the next two years, to $55.13 (that is, $50 × 1.05 × 1.05). Since the proposed hotel would be new construction, management reasons that a price premium may be acceptable in the marketplace. A projected average room rate difference of nearly $20, however, appears to be too large. A more reasonable initial average room rate might be $65; after three years of successive five percent price increases, the new hotel's daily average room rate would increase to just over $75, as follows:

	Annual increase at 5%	Selling Price
Initial room rate (new hotel)		$65.00
At the end of year 1	$3.25	$68.25
At the end of year 2	$3.41	$71.66
At the end of year 3	$3.58	$75.24

Considering this situation, hotel developers will have to finance the additional deficit in the first year ($75 for the targeted average rate versus $65 expected average rate when the hotel opens). In order to operate effectively, the hotel will need to devise some method of financing the projected room revenue shortfall. Unfortunately, hotels do not typically generate profits during the first few years of operation. When this is the case, operating deficits should be included in the hotel's financing plan.

Planned Rate Changes

Room rack rates are likely to change during a calendar year, depending on market factors such as location, seasonality, or major events in the area. Knowing this, hotels may publish a rack rate range instead of a specific room rack rate. For example, resorts may have several different rack rates for the same room types during a year, reflecting peak (high demand), shoulder, and off-peak (low demand) seasons. Room rack rates will tend to vary widely between these seasonal periods. Major events also can have a big impact on rates. For example, consider a planned rate change when a geographic area hosts the NFL Super Bowl. Hotels in the area may plan special (higher) room rates, given the expected high demand associated with upcoming Super Bowl events.

Forecasting Room Availability

The most important short-term planning that front office managers engage in is **forecasting** the number of rooms available for future reservations. *Room availability forecasts* are used to help manage the reservations process and guide front office staff in effective rooms management. Forecasting may be especially important on nights when a full house (100 percent occupancy) is likely.

A room availability forecast can also be used as an *occupancy forecast*. Since there is a fixed number of rooms available on any given night, forecasting the number of rooms available for sale and the number of rooms expected to be occupied can be useful in computing an expected occupancy percentage. The forecasted availability and occupancy numbers are very important to daily front office operations. Occupancy forecasts may be an important consideration for making room rate pricing decisions. This information can also influence when rooms can be placed on out-of-order status for maintenance or repair work. Without an accurate forecast, rooms may go unsold or be sold at less-than-optimal rates. Room occupancy forecasts can be useful to the front office manager attempting to schedule an optimal number of employees for an expected volume of business. These forecasts may be helpful to other hotel department managers as well. For example, the housekeeping department manager needs to know how many rooms the front office expects to be occupied to properly schedule room attendants. Restaurant managers must know the occupancy forecast to better schedule service staff, while the chef can use this information to determine how much food to purchase for the restaurant.

Obviously, a forecast is only as reliable as the information on which it is based. Since forecasts can serve as a guide in determining operating costs, every effort should be made to ensure forecasting accuracy.

Forecasting is a difficult skill to develop. The skill is acquired through experience, effective recordkeeping, and accurate counting methods. Experienced front office managers have found that several types of information can be helpful in room availability forecasting:

- A thorough knowledge of the hotel and surrounding attractions
- Market profiles of the targeted guests
- Occupancy data for the past several months and for the same calendar period of the previous year
- Reservation trends and a history of reservation lead times (how far in advance reservations are made)
- A listing of special events scheduled in the surrounding geographic area
- Business and historical profiles of specific groups booked for future dates
- The number of non-guaranteed and guaranteed reservations and an estimate of the number of reservations expected to be no-shows
- The cut-off date for group room reservation blocks being held for forecasted dates
- Estimated room availability of competing hotels for the forecast dates (which might be calculated based on information revealed through blind calls or website activity)
- The impact of citywide events or conferences on forecasted dates
- Plans for remodeling or renovating the hotel property that would change the number of available rooms
- Construction or renovation plans of competing hotels in the local area

Forecasting Data

The process of forecasting room availability generally relies on historical occupancy data as well as future reserved rooms already committed. Historical data is used to take part of the guesswork out of forecasting. To facilitate projections, the following daily occupancy data should be collected:

- Number of expected room arrivals: based on existing reservations and historical trends for projected reservations and cancellations prior to the arrival date.
- Number of expected room walk-ins: based on historical records of transient guests.
- Number of expected room stayovers (rooms occupied on the prior night that will continue to be occupied for the night in question): based on existing reservations.
- Number of expected reservation room no-shows: based on historical records.
- Number of expected room understays (check-outs occurring before expected departure date): based on historical data.
- Number of expected room check-outs: based on existing departure dates.

Exhibit 7   Occupancy History of the Holly Hotel

Occupancy History
First Week of March

Day	Date	Guests	Room Arrivals	Room Walk-Ins	Room Reservations	Room No-Shows
Mon	3/1	118	70	13	63	6
Tues	3/2	145	55	15	48	8
Wed	3/3	176	68	16	56	4
Thurs	3/4	117	53	22	48	17
Fri	3/5	75	35	8	35	8
Sat	3/6	86	28	6	26	4
Sun	3/7	49	17	10	12	5
Totals		766	326	90	288	52

Occupied Rooms	Overstay Rooms	Understay Rooms	Room Check-Outs
90	6	0	30
115	10	3	30
120	12	6	63
95	3	18	78
50	7	0	80
58	6	3	20
30	3	3	45
558	47	33	346

- Number of expected room overstays (check-outs occurring after the originally reserved departure date): based on historical records.

Hotels with a projected high double occupancy percentage may be as concerned with guest counts as room counts. For example, an all-inclusive resort with a large amount of business from vacationing couples may want to forecast the number of guests as well as room count activity. Convention hotels often have the same concerns.

Management often discovers that much of the data used in forecasting is contained in reports, documents, and other data sources at the property. Daily reports, for example, will likely be invaluable in forecasting work. Specialty reports can be summarized and stored in a way that is easily accessible to online applications.

Overall, these data are important to room availability forecasting, since they are used in calculating various daily operating ratios to help determine the number of available rooms for sale. Ratios are a mathematical expression of a relationship between two numbers that is determined by dividing one by the other. Most statistical ratios that apply to front office operations are expressed as percentages. The ratios examined in the following sections are percentage of no-shows, walk-ins, overstays, and understays. Occupancy history data shown in Exhibit 7 for a fictitious property (the Holly Hotel) are used to illustrate the calculation of each front office ratio. Managers should look for consistency in ratio values. Consistency may be finding identifiable patterns among ratio outcomes. Without consistency, forecasting ratios and projecting operating performance may be complex and more difficult.

Percentage of No-Shows. The percentage of no-shows indicates the proportion of reserved rooms in which the expected guests did not arrive to occupy (and did not cancel) on the expected arrival date. This ratio helps the front office manager decide when (and if) to sell already committed rooms to walk-in guests.

The percentage of no-shows is calculated by dividing the number of room no-shows for a specific period of time (day, week, month, or year) by the total number of room reservations for the same period. Using figures from Exhibit 7, the percentage of no-shows for the Holly Hotel during the first week of March can be calculated as follows:

$$\text{Percentage of No-Shows} = \frac{\text{Number of Room No-Shows}}{\text{Number of Room Reservations}}$$

$$= \frac{52}{288}$$

$$= \quad .1806 \text{ or } \underline{\underline{18.06\%}} \text{ of Reserved Rooms}$$

Some properties track no-show statistics in relation to guaranteed and non-guaranteed reservations. Non-guaranteed reservations typically have a higher no-show percentage than guaranteed reservations, since the potential guest with a non-guaranteed reservation has no obligation to pay for the accommodations despite not arriving and registering at the property. Properly incorporating no-show allowances into room availability forecasts also depends on the hotel's mix of business; for example, corporate groups generally have a much lower no-show percentage than do other types of groups or individual guests. A hotel that works with a large corporate meetings market will most likely have a low no-show percentage. Conversely, a hotel with very little corporate group business, such as a hotel located in a suburban area alongside an interstate highway, is likely to have a much higher percentage of no-show reservations, since most guests desire flexibility in their travel plans. Hotels and resorts strive to control no-shows through a number of policies and procedures, such as requiring an advanced deposit and/or contacting the guest before arrival to confirm that travel and room arrangements remain as planned.

Percentage of Walk-Ins. The percentage of walk-ins is calculated by dividing the number of rooms occupied by walk-ins by the total number of room arrivals for the same period. Using figures from Exhibit 7, the percentage of walk-ins for the Holly Hotel during the first week of March can be calculated as follows:

$$\text{Percentage of Walk-Ins} = \frac{\text{Number of Room Walk-Ins}}{\text{Total Number of Room Arrivals}}$$

$$= \frac{90}{326}$$

$$= \quad .2761 \text{ or } \underline{\underline{27.61\%}} \text{ of Room Arrivals}$$

Walk-in guests occupy available rooms that are not held for guests with reservations. Hotels may be able to sell rooms to walk-in guests at a higher room rate, since these guests usually have less opportunity to consider alternate properties. Front desk agents are sometimes asked to escort a walk-in guest to a guestroom under consideration. This tends to be a more effective method to sell rooms than online virtual tours or using descriptive adjectives when selling to people over the telephone. Walk-in guestroom sales help improve both occupancy and room revenues. However, from a planning perspective, it is generally preferred to have committed reservations in advance than to count on walk-in traffic.

Note that other ratios can dramatically affect the walk-in ratio. For example, if a hotel has ten no-shows beyond forecast, it may accept more walk-ins than usual to make up for the lost business. When this information is tracked for historical purposes, it is essential that the other ratios also be tracked to understand the interactivity between them. There will be a better opportunity for walk-ins (and possibly a higher room rate) if competing hotels are experiencing high demand.

Percentage of Overstays. Overstays represent rooms occupied by guests who stay beyond their originally scheduled departure dates. Overstay guests may have arrived with reservations or as walk-in guests. Overstays should not be confused with **stayovers.** Stayover rooms are rooms occupied by guests who arrived to occupy a room before the day in question and whose *scheduled* departure date isn't until after the day in question.

Using historical data, the percentage of overstays is calculated by dividing the actual number of overstay rooms by the total number of *expected* room check-outs for the same day or period. The number of expected room check-outs is the number of rooms shown by the front office system as due for departure. Stated another way, the number of expected room check-outs can be calculated from historical data as the number of actual departures minus understays plus overstays. Note that in this case, the term *understays* refers to guests checking out prior to the day in question, *not* to those guests who were *originally scheduled* to depart on that day but chose to check out a day early. For purposes of room availability forecasting, a guest is considered an understay if he or she checks out of the hotel before the stated date of departure.

Overstays and understays can be determined for periods beyond one day by summing the actual overstay and understay counts calculated separately for each day within the longer period. Using figures from Exhibit 7, the percentage of overstays for the Holly Hotel during the first week of March can be calculated as follows:

$$\text{Percentage of Overstays} \quad = \quad \frac{\text{Number of Overstay Rooms}}{\text{Number of Expected Check-Outs}}$$

$$= \quad \frac{47}{346 - 33 + 47}$$

$$= \quad .1306 \text{ or } \underline{\underline{13.06\%}} \text{ of Expected Check-Outs}$$

To help regulate room overstays, front office agents are trained to verify an arriving guest's departure date at the time of check-in. Such verification can be critical, especially when the hotel is at or near full occupancy and there are no provisions for overstay guests. Overstays may also prove problematic when specific rooms have been blocked for arriving guests. This is especially important for a specific room that may have special importance to an incoming guest.

Percentage of Understays. Understays represent rooms occupied by guests who check out before their originally scheduled departure dates. Understay guests may have arrived at the hotel with reservations or as walk-ins.

The percentage of understays is calculated by dividing the number of understay rooms by the total number of expected room check-outs for the same day or period. Using a similar approach to that just described for determining the percentage of overstays, the understays are counted as understays only on the day of their early check-out, and understay counts should be determined separately and summed for each day in a multi-day period. Using figures from Exhibit 7, the percentage of understays for the Holly Hotel during the first week of March can be calculated as follows:

$$\text{Percentage of Understays} = \frac{\text{Number of Understay Rooms}}{\text{Number of Expected Check-Outs}}$$

$$= \frac{33}{346 - 33 + 47}$$

$$= .0917 \text{ or } \underline{\underline{9.17\%}} \text{ of Expected Check-Outs}$$

Guests leaving before their stated departure date create empty rooms that typically are difficult to fill. Thus, understay rooms potentially represent lost room revenue. Overstays, on the other hand, are guests staying beyond their planned departure date and may represent a potential increase in room revenue. When a hotel is not operating at full occupancy, overstay guests often result in additional, unexpected room revenue. In an attempt to regulate understay and overstay rooms, front office staff should:

- Confirm or reconfirm each guest's departure date at registration. Some guests may already know of a change in plans that will affect their reservation, or a mistake may have been made in the original processing of the reservation. The sooner erroneous data are corrected, the greater the chance for improved room availability planning.

- Present an alternate guestroom suggestion to an overstay guest, explaining that an arriving guest holds a reservation for his or her assigned room.

- Review group history. Many groups hold large closing events on the last day of their meetings, and group members may even make reservations to attend. However, changes in plans or other priorities may require some guests to leave the hotel before the event. Front office managers may be better able to plan for these early departures, based on the group's departure history.

- Contact potential overstay guests about their scheduled departure date to confirm their intention to check out. Room occupancy data should be examined each day; rooms with guests expected to check out should be flagged. Guests who have not departed by the hotel's posted check-out time should be contacted and asked about their departure intentions. This procedure permits a revised count of overstays and allows sufficient time to modify previous room availability planning, if necessary.

Forecast Formula

Once relevant occupancy statistics have been gathered, the number of rooms available on any given date can be determined by the following formula:

	Total Number of Guestrooms
−	Number of Out-of-Order Rooms
−	Number of Room Stayovers
−	Number of Room Reservations
+	Number of Room Reservations × Percentage of No-Shows
+	Number of Room Understays
−	Number of Room Overstays
	Number of Rooms Available for Sale

Note that this formula does not include expected walk-in guests. Walk-in guests are not included in the formula since the number of walk-ins to be accommodated is determined by the number of rooms that remain available for sale. If a hotel is full due to existing reservations, stayovers, and other factors, it cannot accept walk-ins.

As an example, consider the Holly House, a 120-room property, where on April 1 there are three out-of-order rooms and fifty-five stayovers. On that day, there are forty-two guests with reservations scheduled to arrive. Since the percentage of no-shows has been recently calculated at 18.06 percent, the front office manager calculates that as many as eight guests with reservations may not arrive (42 × .1806 = 7.59, rounded to 8). Based on historical data, six understays and fifteen overstays are also expected. The number of rooms projected to be available for sale on April 1 can be determined as follows:

	Total Number of Guestrooms	120
−	Number of Out-of-Order Rooms	− 3
−	Number of Room Stayovers	− 55
−	Number of Room Reservations	− 42
+	Number of Room Reservations × No-Show Percentage	+ 8
+	Number of Room Understays	+ 6
−	Number of Room Overstays	− 15
	Number of Rooms Available for Sale	19

Therefore, the Holly House is considered to have nineteen rooms available for sale on April 1. Once this figure is determined, front office management can decide whether to accept more reservations and can determine a reasonable level of staffing. Front office planning decisions must remain flexible; they are subject to change as the front office learns of reservation cancellations and modifications. Note also that room availability forecasts are based on assumptions whose validity may vary on any given day.

Sample Forecast Forms

Front office managers may prepare several different room availability forecasts, depending on their needs and the needs of other managers in the hotel. For example, occupancy forecasts are typically developed on a monthly basis and reviewed by food and beverage and rooms division managers to forecast revenues, project expenses, and develop labor schedules. A ten-day forecast may be used to update labor scheduling and cost projections and may later be supplemented by a more current and accurate three-day forecast. Together, these forecasts help many hotel departments maintain appropriate staffing levels for expected business volumes and thereby help contain costs.

Ten-Day Forecast. At most lodging properties, the ten-day forecast is developed jointly by the front office manager and the reservations manager, possibly in conjunction with a room availability forecast committee. Many properties develop a ten-day forecast as an extension of the yearly forecast. A ten-day forecast usually consists of:

- Daily forecasted occupancy figures, including room arrivals, room departures, rooms occupied, and number of guests.

- The number of group commitments, with a listing of each group's name, arrival and departure dates, number of rooms reserved, number of guests, and perhaps quoted room rates.

- A comparison of the previous period's forecasted and actual room counts and occupancy percentages.

A special ten-day forecast may also be prepared for food and beverage, banquet, and catering operations. This forecast usually includes the expected number of guests, which is often referred to as the **house count.** Sometimes the house count is divided into group and non-group categories so that the hotel's dining room managers can better understand the nature of the business and their staffing needs.

To help various hotel departments plan their staffing and payroll levels for the upcoming period, the ten-day forecast should be completed and distributed to all department offices in advance of the coming period. This forecast can be especially helpful to the housekeeping department. A ten-day forecast form, as shown in Exhibit 8, is typically developed from data collected through several front office sources. (The occupancy multiplier mentioned in section 10 of the exhibit is discussed later in the chapter.) An equivalent report can be automatically generated by the hotel's property management system.

Exhibit 8   Sample Ten-Day Forecast Form

<table>
<tr><td colspan="12" align="center">**Ten-Day Occupancy Forecast**</td></tr>
<tr><td colspan="12">Location: _____   #: _____   Week Ending: _____</td></tr>
<tr><td colspan="12">Date Prepared: _____   Prepared By: _____</td></tr>
<tr><td colspan="12">To be submitted to all department heads at least one week before the first day listed on forecast.</td></tr>
<tr><td>1.   Date and Day (start week and end week the same as the payroll schedule)</td><td>Fri.</td><td>Sat.</td><td>Sun.</td><td>Mon.</td><td>Tues.</td><td>Wed.</td><td>Thur.</td><td>Fri.</td><td>Sat.</td><td>Sun.</td></tr>
<tr><td>2.   Estimated Departures</td><td></td><td></td><td></td><td></td><td></td><td></td><td></td><td></td><td></td><td></td></tr>
<tr><td>3.   Reservation Arrivals—Group (taken from log book)</td><td></td><td></td><td></td><td></td><td></td><td></td><td></td><td></td><td></td><td></td></tr>
<tr><td>4.   Reservation Arrivals—Individual (taken from log book)</td><td></td><td></td><td></td><td></td><td></td><td></td><td></td><td></td><td></td><td></td></tr>
<tr><td>5.   Future Reservations (estimated reservations received after forecast is completed)</td><td></td><td></td><td></td><td></td><td></td><td></td><td></td><td></td><td></td><td></td></tr>
<tr><td>6.   Expected Walk-Ins (% of walk-ins based on reservations received and actual occupancy for past two weeks)</td><td></td><td></td><td></td><td></td><td></td><td></td><td></td><td></td><td></td><td></td></tr>
<tr><td>7.   Total Arrivals</td><td></td><td></td><td></td><td></td><td></td><td></td><td></td><td></td><td></td><td></td></tr>
<tr><td>8.   Stayovers</td><td></td><td></td><td></td><td></td><td></td><td></td><td></td><td></td><td></td><td></td></tr>
<tr><td>9.   TOTAL FORECASTED ROOMS</td><td></td><td></td><td></td><td></td><td></td><td></td><td></td><td></td><td></td><td></td></tr>
<tr><td>10.   Occupancy Multiplier (based on number of guests per occupied room for average of the same day for last three weeks)</td><td></td><td></td><td></td><td></td><td></td><td></td><td></td><td></td><td></td><td></td></tr>
<tr><td>11.   FORECASTED NUMBER OF GUESTS</td><td></td><td></td><td></td><td></td><td></td><td></td><td></td><td></td><td></td><td></td></tr>
<tr><td>12.   Actual Rooms Occupied (taken from daily report for actual date to be completed by front office supervisor)</td><td></td><td></td><td></td><td></td><td></td><td></td><td></td><td></td><td></td><td></td></tr>
<tr><td>13.   Forecasted Variance (difference between forecast and rooms occupied on daily report)</td><td></td><td></td><td></td><td></td><td></td><td></td><td></td><td></td><td></td><td></td></tr>
<tr><td colspan="12">14.   Explanation (to be completed by front office supervisor and submitted to general manager; attach additional memo if necessary)</td></tr>
<tr><td colspan="12">APPROVED: _____   DATE: _____
        General Manager's Signature</td></tr>
</table>

First, the current number of occupied rooms is reviewed. The estimated numbers of overstays and expected departures are noted. Next, relevant reservation information is evaluated for each room (and guest) by date of arrival, length of stay, and date of departure. These counts are then reconciled with reservation control data. Then, the actual counts are adjusted to reflect the projected percentage

Exhibit 9   Refining a Forecast

A yearly forecast provides an excellent starting point for developing shorter-term, more accurate forecasts. Managers can better assess business by reviewing current reservations and booking pace. The closer the forecast is, the more accurate it will be.

Here is a checklist for revising forecasts:

- List all group bookings and transient reservations on the books.
- Examine arrivals, departures, and group information for the given period.
- Determine if demand for this particular period of time is high or low.
- Chart the peaks and valleys on a graph to better identify high/low demand.
- Have sales agents call competing properties for rates and consider adjusting your rates.
- Make decisions to maximize revenue during each time period.

of no-shows, anticipated understays, and expected walk-ins. These projections are based on the hotel's recent history, the seasonality of business, and the known history of specific groups scheduled to arrive. Finally, conventions and other groups are listed on the forecast to alert various department managers to possible periods of heavy, or light, check-ins and check-outs. The number of rooms assigned each day to each group may also be noted on the report.

Most automated systems provide a summary of recorded data in a report format for the front office manager to use. This is a key feature in revenue management systems that are programmed to forecast business. These revenue management systems possess special trend analysis and regression analysis applications. Starting with the revenue management system's forecast, the front office manager applies knowledge and skill to ultimately determine the accuracy of the forecast. Exhibit 9 presents a checklist that some revenue managers use when revising room availability forecasts.

Three-Day Forecast. A three-day forecast is an updated report that reflects a more current estimate of room availability. It details significant changes or events not highlighted on the ten-day forecast. The three-day forecast is intended to guide management in fine-tuning labor schedules and adjusting room availability information. Exhibit 10 shows a sample three-day forecast form. In some hotels, a daily revenue meeting is held to focus on occupancy and rate changes for the next several days. The results of this meeting are often reflected in the three-day forecast.

Room Count Considerations. Control books, charts, software applications, projections, ratios, and formulas can be essential in short- and long-range room availability planning. Each day, front office management performs several physical counts of rooms occupied, vacant, reserved, and expected to check out, to complete the occupancy statistics for that day. An automated system may reduce the need for most final counts, since the system can be programmed to continually update room availability information.

Exhibit 10   Sample Three-Day Forecast Form

Three-Day Forecast

Date of Forecast: _____   Forecast Completed By: _____

Total Rooms in Hotel: _____

		Tonight	Tomorrow	3rd Night
Day				
Date				
Previous Night Occupied Rooms[1]				
− Expected Departures				
− Early Departures				
+ Unexpected Stayovers				
+ Unoccupied Rooms[2]				
= Rooms Available For Sale				
+ Expected Arrivals				
+ Walk-ins & Same Day Reservations				
− No-Shows				
= Occupied Rooms				
= Occupancy %				
= Expected House Count[3]				

[1] Previous night occupied rooms is determined from either the actual number of rooms occupied last night or the forecasted number of rooms from the previous night.

[2] Unoccupied rooms equals the total number of rooms in the hotel less the number of rooms occupied.

[3] Expected house count equals the forecasted occupied rooms times the multiple occupancy percentage for the day (found on the computer report).

Distribution: General Manager, Front Desk, Housekeeping, All Food and Beverage, Accounting, Sales, Banquets, Security

It is important for front desk agents to know *exactly* how many rooms are available, especially if the hotel is expected to operate at nearly 100 percent occupancy. Once procedures for gathering room count information are established, planning procedures can be extended to longer periods of time to form a more reliable basis for revenue, expense, and labor forecasting. The checklist in Exhibit 11 may be applicable to non-automated and semi-automated operations alike.

Exhibit 11   Sample Daily Checklist for Accurate Room Counts

- Make counts of the rack and reservations. On tight days, a count should be made at 7:00 A.M., noon, 3:00 P.M., and 6:00 P.M. On normal days, a 7:00 A.M. and 6:00 P.M. count will suffice.
- Check room rack against the folio bucket to catch sleepers and skippers.
- Check housekeeping reports against the room rack to catch sleepers and skippers.
- Check for rooms that are due out, but still have balances on their folios, especially where payment cards are the indicated source of payment.
- Check reservations for any duplications.
- Call the reservations system to make sure all cancellations were transmitted.
- Check the switchboard, telephone rack, and/or alphabetical room rack to make sure that the guest is not already registered.
- Call the local airport for a report on canceled flights.
- Check the weather reports for cities from which a number of guests are expected.
- Check reservations against convention blocks to catch duplications.
- Check with other hotels for duplicate reservations if a housing or convention bureau indicated the reservation was a second choice.
- Check arrival dates on all reservation forms to be sure none were misfiled.
- Check the rooms cancellation list.
- If a reservation was made through the reservations manager, sales manager, or someone in the executive office and the property is close to full, call that staff person. Often, such guests are personal friends and are willing to help out by staying somewhere else.
- Close to the property's cut-off time, consider placing a person-to-person phone call to any guest with a nonguaranteed reservation who hasn't arrived. If the person accepts the call, confirm whether or not he or she will arrive yet that night.
- After the property's cut-off time, if it becomes necessary, pull any reservations that were not guaranteed or prepaid.
- If any rooms are out-of-order or not presently in use, check to see if they can be made up. Let housekeeping know when a tight day is expected, so that all possible rooms are made up.
- Before leaving work, convey in writing all pertinent information to the oncoming staff. Good communication is essential.

Budgeting for Operations

The most important long-term planning function that front office managers perform is budgeting for front office operations. The hotel's annual operations budget is a profit plan that addresses all revenue sources and expense items. Annual

Exhibit 12 Rooms Revenue Summary for the Emily Hotel

Year	Rooms Revenue	Increase in Dollars	Percentage Increase Over Prior Year
20X1	$1,000,000	—	—
20X2	1,100,000	$100,000	10%
20X3	1,210,000	110,000	10%
20X4	1,331,000	121,000	10%

budgets are commonly divided into monthly plans that, in turn, are divided into weekly (and sometimes daily) plans. These budget plans become standards against which management can evaluate the actual results of operations. In most hotels, room revenues are greater than food, beverage, banquet, or any other revenues. In addition, rooms division profits are usually greater than those of any other division. Therefore, an accurate rooms division budget is vital to creating the hotel's overall budget.

The budget planning process requires the closely coordinated efforts of all management personnel. While the front office manager is responsible for rooms revenue forecasts, the accounting division staff will be relied on to supply department managers with statistical information essential to the budget preparation process. The accounting division staff may also be responsible for coordinating the budget plans of individual department managers into a comprehensive property-wide operations budget for top management's review. The general manager and controller typically review departmental budget plans and may prepare a comprehensive hotel budget report for approval by the hotel's owners. If the budget is not satisfactory, elements requiring change may be returned to the appropriate division managers for review and revision.

The front office manager's primary responsibilities in budget planning are forecasting rooms revenue and estimating related expenses. Rooms revenue is forecasted with input from the reservations manager, while expenses are estimated with input from all department managers in the rooms division.

Forecasting Rooms Revenue

Historical financial information often serves as the foundation on which front office managers build rooms revenue forecasts. One method of rooms revenue forecasting involves an analysis of rooms revenue from past periods. Dollar and percentage differences are noted and the amount of rooms revenue for the budget year is predicted.

For example, Exhibit 12 shows yearly increases in net rooms revenue for the Emily Hotel. For the years 20X1 to 20X4, the amount of rooms revenue increased from $1,000,000 to $1,331,000, reflecting a 10 percent yearly increase. If future conditions appear to be similar to those of the past, the rooms revenue for 20X5 would be budgeted at $1,464,100—a 10 percent increase over the 20X4 amount.

Another approach to forecasting rooms revenue bases the revenue projection on past room sales and average daily room rates. Exhibit 13 presents rooms revenue statistics for the 120-room Bradley Hotel from 20X1 to 20X4. An analysis of

Exhibit 13   Rooms Revenue Statistics for the Bradley Hotel

Year	Rooms Sold	Average Daily Rate	Net Rooms Revenue	Occupancy Percentage
20X1	30,660	$50	$1,533,000	70%
20X2	31,974	52	1,662,648	73%
20X3	32,412	54	1,750,248	74%
20X4	32,850	57	1,872,450	75%

these statistics shows that occupancy percentage increased three percentage points from 20X1 to 20X2, one percentage point from 20X2 to 20X3, and one percentage point from 20X3 to 20X4. Average daily room rates increased by $2, $2, and $3 respectively over the same periods. If future conditions are assumed to be similar to those of the past, a rooms revenue forecast for 20X5 may be based on a one percent increase in occupancy percentage (to 76 percent) and a $3 increase in the average daily room rate (to $60). Given these projections, the following formula can be used to forecast rooms revenue for the year 20X5 for the Bradley Hotel:

$$\begin{aligned} \text{Forecasted Rooms Revenue} &= \text{Rooms Available} \times \text{Occupancy Percentage} \times \text{Average Daily Rate} \\ &= 43,800 \times .76 \times \$60 \\ &= \underline{\$1,997,280} \end{aligned}$$

The number of rooms available is calculated by multiplying the 120 rooms of the Bradley Hotel by the 365 days of the year. This calculation assumes that all rooms will be available for sale each day of the year. This will probably not be the case, but it is a reasonable starting point for projection. Note also that at some point occupancy will not be able to grow any further, and may actually decline. For example, new competitors may enter the market, taking occupancy away from the hotel. Management needs to anticipate this shift and adjust its forecasts to take into account the increased competition. The same logic applies to projecting rate growth. Hotel management may decide to hold or even reduce rates to maintain or improve occupancy when new competitors enter the market.

This simplified approach to forecasting rooms revenue is intended to illustrate the use of trend data in forecasting. A more detailed approach would consider the variety of different rates corresponding to room types, guest profiles, days of the week, and seasonality of business. These are just a few of the factors that may affect rooms revenue forecasting.

Estimating Expenses

Most expenses for front office operations are *variable expenses* in that they vary in direct proportion to rooms revenue. Historical data can be used to calculate an approximate percentage of rooms revenue that each expense item may represent. These percentage figures can then be applied to the total amount of forecasted rooms revenue, resulting in dollar estimates for each expense category for the budget year.

Exhibit 14   Expense Categories as Percentages of Rooms Revenue for the Bradley Hotel

Year	Payroll and Related Expenses	Laundry, Linen, and Guest Supplies	Commissions and Reservation Expenses	Other Expenses
20X1	16.5%	2.6%	2.3%	4.2%
20X2	16.9%	2.8%	2.5%	4.5%
20X3	17.2%	3.0%	2.6%	4.5%
20X4	17.4%	3.1%	2.7%	4.6%

Typical rooms division expenses are payroll and related expenses; guestroom laundry (terry and linen); guest supplies (bath amenities, toilet tissue); hotel merchandising (in-room guest directory and promotional brochures); travel agent commissions and direct reservation expenses; and other expenses. When these costs are totaled and divided by the number of occupied rooms, the cost per occupied room is determined. The cost per occupied room is often expressed in dollars and as a percentage. Exhibit 14 presents expense category statistics of the Bradley Hotel from 20X1 to 20X4, expressed as percentages of each year's rooms revenue. Based on this historical information and management's current objectives for the budget year 20X5, the percentage of rooms revenue for each expense category may be projected as follows: payroll and related expenses, 17.6 percent; laundry, linen and terry, and guest supplies, 3.2 percent; commissions and reservation expenses, 2.8 percent; and other expenses, 4.7 percent.

Using these percentage figures and the expected rooms revenue calculated previously, the Bradley Hotel's rooms division expenses for the budgeted year are estimated as follows:

- Payroll and related expenses
       $1,997,280 × .176 = $351,521.28
- Laundry, linen, terry, and guest supplies
       $1,997,280 × .032 = $ 63,912.96
- Commissions and reservation expenses
       $1,997,280 × .028 = $ 55,923.84
- Other expenses
       $1,997,280 × .047 = $ 93,872.16

In this example, management should question why costs continue to rise as a percentage of revenue. If costs continue to rise (as a percentage, not in real dollars), profitability likely will be affected. Therefore, one of the outcomes of the budget process will be to identify where costs are increasing as a percentage of revenue. Then, management can analyze why these costs are increasing disproportionately with revenue and develop a plan to address the issue.

Since most front office expenses vary proportionately with rooms revenue (and therefore occupancy), another method of estimating these expenses is to estimate variable costs per room sold and then multiply these costs by the number of rooms expected to be sold.

Refining Budget Plans

Departmental budget plans are commonly supported by detailed information gathered in the budget preparation process and recorded on worksheets and summary files. These documents should be saved to provide an explanation of the reasoning behind the decisions made while preparing departmental budget plans. Such records may help resolve issues that arise during the budget review. These support documents may also provide valuable assistance in the preparation of future budget plans.

If no historical data are available for budget planning, other sources of information can be used to develop a budget. For example, corporate headquarters can often supply comparable budget information to its chain-affiliated properties. Also, national accounting and consulting firms can usually provide supplemental data for the budget development process.

Many hotels refine expected results of operations and revise operations budgets as they progress through the budget year. Reforecasting is normally suggested when actual operating results start to vary significantly from the operations budget. Such variance may indicate that conditions have changed since the budget was first prepared. While operating budgets are seldom changed once the hotel's management and owners approve them, reforecasting provides a more realistic picture of current operating conditions.

Evaluating Front Office Operations

Evaluating the results of front office operations is an important management function. Without thoroughly evaluating the results of operations, managers will not know whether the front office is attaining planned goals. Successful front office managers evaluate the results of department activities on a daily, monthly, quarterly, and yearly basis. The following sections examine important tools that front office managers can use to evaluate the success of front office operations. These tools include:

- Daily report of operations
- Occupancy ratios
- Rooms revenue analysis
- Income statement
- Rooms schedule
- Rooms division budget reports
- Operating ratios
- Ratio standards

Daily Report of Operations

The **daily report of operations,** also known as the *manager's report,* the *daily report,* and the *daily revenue report,* summarizes the hotel's financial activities during a twenty-four-hour period. The daily report of operations provides a means of reconciling cash, bank accounts, revenue, and accounts receivable. The report also serves as a posting reference for various accounting journals and provides important data that must be input to link front and back office automated functions. Daily reports of operations are often uniquely structured to meet the needs of individual hotel properties.

Exhibit 15 presents a sample daily report of operations for a hotel with food and beverage service. Rooms statistics and occupancy ratios form an entire section of a typical daily report of operations. Enriched by comments and observations from the accounting staff, statistics shown on the daily report of operations may take on more significance. For example, statistics about the number of guests using the hotel's valet parking services take on added meaning when remarks indicate that valet sales are down while occupancy is up. The front office manager may presume that the front office staff is not properly promoting available guest valet parking services.

The information provided by the daily report of operations is not restricted to the front office manager or hotel general manager. Copies of the daily report of operations are generally distributed to all department and division managers in the hotel.

Occupancy Ratios

Occupancy ratios measure the effectiveness of the front office and reservations sales staffs in selling the hotel's primary product: guestrooms. The following rooms statistics must be gathered to calculate basic occupancy ratios:

- Number of rooms available for sale
- Number of rooms sold
- Number of guests
- Number of guests per room
- Net rooms revenue

Generally, these data are presented on the daily report of operations. Occupancy ratios that can be computed from these data include occupancy percentage, multiple (or double) occupancy ratio, average daily rate, revenue per available room (RevPAR), revenue per available customer (RevPAC), and average rate per guest. Computed occupancy percentage and average daily rate may also appear on a hotel's daily report of operations. These ratios typically are extensive and are usually calculated on a daily, weekly, monthly, and yearly basis.

The front office system typically generates occupied rooms data and calculates occupancy ratios for the front office manager, who analyzes the information to identify trends, patterns, or problems. (The front office system may be programmed to do much of this analysis.) When analyzing the information, there should be consideration of how a particular condition may produce varying effects on occupancy. For example, as multiple occupancy increases, the average daily room rate may also increase. This is because when a room is sold to more than one guest, the room rate may be greater than when the room is sold as a single. However, since the room rate for two guests sharing a room is usually not twice the rate for one person, the average room rate *per guest* decreases.

Exhibit 15   Sample Daily Report of Operations

DAILY REVENUE REPORT

Day _____ Of _____   Day _____ Date _____ Year: _____

Hotel _____   Completed By: _____

OCCUPANCY SUMMARY	ACTUAL TODAY	%	MONTH TO-DATE	%
SGL Rooms Occupied				
DBL Rooms Occupied				
COMP Rooms Occupied				
TOTAL Rooms Occupied				
O O O Rooms				
Vacant				
TOTAL Available Rooms		100%		100%
House Use				
TOTAL Hotel Rooms				
AVG House Rate (Inc. Comps & Perms)	$		$	
AVG Trans Rate (Excl. Comp & Perms)	$		$	
TOTAL # GUESTS				
Relocated				
Room Sales Efficiency				
TOTAL ROOMS OCCUPIED				
Forecast Frecast				
Budget				

REVENUE SUMMARY	TODAY	MTD	BUDGET MONTH END
Net Rooms			
Food			
Beverage			
Banquet Other			
Long Distance			
Local			
Laundry / Valet			
Garage			
Gift Shop			
Health Club			
Pro Shop (Merchandise)			
Golf Fees			
Tennis Fees			
TOTAL HOTEL			

ROOMS REVENUE ANALYSIS

Type	TODAY				MONTH-TO-DATE			
	# Rooms	%	Ave. Rate	Revenue	# Rooms	%	Ave. Rate	Revenue
Rack								
Corporate								
Guaranteed Corporate								
Preferred								
Weekend Rate								
Packages								
Government / Military								
Other								
Total Non Group								
Group								
Total Transient								
Permanents								
Complimentary								
Total		100%				100%		
Club Floor								
Frequent Guest								
RSVP								
Breakations								

COMPLIMENTARY ROOMS

Guest Name	Room No.	Company	Check In Date	Check Out Date	Authorized By

REORDER FROM STANDARD REGISTER FORMS SELECTOR R0750   PRINTED BY THE STANDARD REGISTER COMPANY U.S.A.

Exhibit 15 *(continued)*

FOOD & BEVERAGE ANALYSIS		TODAY			MONTH-TO-DATE		
Outlet		Revenue	# Covers	Ave. Check	Revenue	# Covers	Ave. Check
Room Service	Food						
	Food						
	Food						
	Food						
	Food						
	Food						
	Food						
Banquet	Food						
	Total Food						
Room Service	Bev.						
	Bev.						
	Bev.						
	Bev.						
	Bev.						
	Bev.						
	Bev.						
	Bev.						
Banquet	Bev.						
	Total Bev.						
Total Food & Bev.							
Room Rental							
Customer Sev. Inc.							
Miscellaneous							
Total Food & Bev. Dept.							

GROUP ANALYSIS					MARKET SEGMENTS	MONTH-TO-DATE		
Group	# Rooms	# Guests	Avg. Rate	Revenue	Group	# Rooms	Avg. Rate	Revenue
					National Assoc.			
					Reg & State Assoc.			
					Corporate			
					Incentive			
					SMERFE			
					Tour & Travel			
					Frequent Guest			
					Total Group			

ARRIVALS	YESTER-DAY	TODAY	ACTUAL MTD
6 PM Resv.			
Guaranteed Resv.			
Walk-ins			
Same Day Cancellations			
6 PM No Show			
Guaranteed No Show			
Relocated			
Total Actual Arrivals			

TOTAL

OUT OF ORDER ROOMS

Room No.	Reason	Number of Nights O.O.O.

DEPARTURES	YESTER-DAY	TODAY	ACTUAL MTD
Expected			
Unexpected			
Stayovers			
Total Actual Departures			

Anticipated Occupancy Tonight _____ %

The following sections examine how daily occupancy ratios are calculated for the Gregory Hotel. Rooms division data needed for the calculations are as follows:

- The Gregory Hotel has 120 rooms and a rack rate of $98. (For simplicity's sake, assume that this rack rate is applicable to both single and double room occupancies.)

- Eighty-three rooms were sold at varying rates.

- Eighty-five rooms were occupied by guests. (Rooms sold does not equal rooms occupied by guests because, on this particular day, single guests occupied two rooms at a complimentary room rate, thereby generating no rooms revenue. Note that the handling of complimentary rooms may differ among hotel properties.)

- Ten rooms were occupied by two guests; therefore, a total of 95 guests were in occupancy.

- $6,960 in rooms revenue was generated.

- $7,363.75 in total revenue was generated, including rooms, food, beverage, telecommunications, and other.

Occupancy Percentage. The most commonly used operating ratio in the front office is occupancy percentage. **Occupancy percentage** relates the number of rooms either sold or occupied to the number of rooms available during a specific period of time. It is important to note that some hotels use the number of rooms *sold* to calculate this percentage, while other hotels use the number of rooms *occupied* to calculate the statistic. Including complimentary rooms in the calculation can change certain operating statistics, such as average room rate. Using rooms sold, rooms occupied, or both is valid, depending upon the property's needs and history. This discussion will use rooms occupied to illustrate the occupancy percentage calculation.

Sometimes out-of-order rooms may be included in the number of rooms available. At properties that evaluate management performance partly on the basis of occupancy percentage, including out-of-order rooms in the number of rooms available provides the manager with incentive to get those rooms fixed and recycled more quickly. Including all rooms also provides a consistent base on which to measure occupancy. Conversely, not including out-of-order rooms may allow managers to artificially increase the calculated occupancy percentage simply by improperly classifying unsold rooms as out-of-order. Some properties do not include out-of-order rooms because the rooms are not available for sale. Also, to the extent that the occupancy percentage is used to evaluate the performance of front office staff having no control over out-of-order rooms, including those rooms may unfairly penalize the front office staff. Regardless of the approach chosen, it should be used consistently.

The occupancy percentage for the Gregory Hotel is calculated as follows:

$$\text{Occupancy Percentage} = \frac{\text{Number of Rooms Occupied}}{\text{Number of Rooms Available}}$$

$$= \frac{85}{120}$$

$$= \ .708 \text{ or } \underline{70.8\%}$$

Multiple Occupancy Ratio. The **multiple occupancy ratio** (frequently called the double occupancy ratio, although this phrasing may not always be accurate) is used to forecast food and beverage revenue, indicate clean linen requirements, and analyze average daily room rates. Multiple occupancy can be calculated by determining a **multiple occupancy percentage** or by determining the average number of guests per room sold or occupied (also called the *occupancy multiplier* or the *multiple occupancy factor*).

The multiple occupancy percentage for the Gregory Hotel is calculated as follows:

$$\text{Multiple Occupancy Percentage} \ = \ \frac{\text{Number of Rooms Occupied by More Than One Guest}}{\text{Number of Rooms Occupied}}$$

$$= \frac{10}{85}$$

$$= \ .118 \text{ or } \underline{11.8\%}$$

The average number of guests per room sold for the Gregory Hotel is calculated as follows:

$$\text{Average Guests per Room Sold} \ = \ \frac{\text{Number of Guests}}{\text{Number of Rooms Sold}}$$

$$= \frac{95}{83}$$

$$= \ \underline{1.14}$$

Average Daily Rate. Most front office managers calculate an **average daily rate** (ADR) even though room rates within a property vary significantly from single rooms to suites, from individual guests to groups and conventions, from weekdays to weekends, and from high- to low-demand periods.

The average daily rate for the Gregory Hotel is calculated as follows:

$$\text{Average Daily Rate} \ = \ \frac{\text{Total Room Revenue}}{\text{Number of Rooms Sold}}$$

$$= \frac{\$6,960}{83}$$

$$= \ \underline{\$83.86}$$

Some hotels include complimentary rooms in the denominator to show the true effect of complimentary rooms on the average daily rate. This statistic may also be referred to as the *average house rate*.

Revenue per Available Room (RevPAR). Revenue per available room or **RevPAR** is one of the most important hotel statistics, because it provides a statistical benchmark for comparison with similar hotels. RevPAR divides the total room revenue of the hotel by the number of available rooms.

The RevPAR for the Gregory Hotel is calculated as follows:

$$\text{RevPAR} = \frac{\text{Total Room Revenue}}{\text{Number of Available Rooms}}$$

$$= \frac{\$6,960}{120}$$

$$= \underline{\underline{\$58}}$$

Revenue per Available Customer (RevPAC). Revenue per available customer or **RevPAC,** while not as popular a statistic as RevPAR, can be an important industry statistic. RevPAC divides the total revenue generation of the hotel by the number of guests staying overnight, thereby showing the average revenue generated by each guest. For hotels with high volumes of multiple occupancy, this figure is especially important, since it provides an average room rate spending figure per guest. In most hotels, the higher the multiple occupancy, the greater the total revenue.

The RevPAC for the Gregory Hotel is calculated as follows:

$$\text{RevPAC} = \frac{\text{Total Revenue}}{\text{Number of Guests}}$$

$$= \frac{\$7,363.75}{95}$$

$$= \underline{\underline{\$77.51}}$$

Average Rate per Guest. Resort hotels, in particular, are often interested in knowing the **average rate per guest** (ARG). This rate is computed inclusive of every guest in the hotel. Some hotel companies include children in the number of guests.

The average rate per guest for the Gregory Hotel is calculated as follows:

$$\text{Average Rate per Guest} = \frac{\text{Total Room Revenue}}{\text{Number of Guests}}$$

$$= \frac{\$6,960}{95}$$

$$= \underline{\underline{\$73.26}}$$

Rooms Revenue Analysis

Front office staff members are expected to sell rooms at the rack rate unless a guest qualifies for an authorized discounted room rate. A **room rate variance report** lists those rooms that have been sold at other than their rack rates. With this report, front office management can review the use of various special rates to determine whether staff has followed all appropriate front office policies and procedures. Automated front office systems can be programmed to routinely generate a room rate variance report.

One way for front office managers to evaluate the sales effectiveness of the front office staff is to generate a **yield statistic,** which is actual rooms revenue as a percentage of potential rooms revenue.

Yield Statistic. Potential rooms revenue is the amount of rooms revenue that can be generated if all the rooms in the hotel are sold at rack rate on a given day, week, month, or year. The ratio of actual to potential rooms revenue is known as the achievement factor in a yield statistic. The potential revenue for the Gregory Hotel is $11,760 (all 120 rooms sold at the rack rate of $98). Given actual rooms revenue of $6,960, the yield statistic for the Gregory Hotel can be calculated as follows:

$$\text{Yield Statistic} = \frac{\text{Actual Rooms Revenue}}{\text{Potential Rooms Revenue}}$$

$$= \frac{\$6,960}{\$11,760}$$

$$= .5918 \text{ or } \underline{59.18\%}$$

This result reveals that, for the day in question, actual rooms revenue was 59.18 percent of the amount that could have been generated if all 120 rooms had been sold at the full rack rate of $98. This achievement statistic reveals that a significant amount of room rate discounting occurred.

Income Statement

The hotel's **income statement** or statement of income provides important financial information about the results of hotel operations for a given period of time. The period may be one month or longer, but should not exceed one business year. Since a statement of income reveals the amount of net income for a given period, it is one of the most important financial statements management uses to evaluate the overall success of operations. Although front office managers may not directly rely on the hotel's statement of income, it is an important financial indicator of operational success and profitability. The hotel income statement relies in part on detailed front office information that is supplied through the rooms schedule. The rooms schedule is discussed in the next section.

The hotel's statement of income is often called a consolidated income statement because it presents a composite picture of all the hotel's financial operations. Rooms division information appears on the first line, under the category of operated departments. The amount of income generated by the rooms division is determined by subtracting payroll and related expenses and other expenses from the amount of net revenue produced by the rooms division over the period covered by the income statement. Payroll expenses charged to the rooms division may include those associated with the front office manager, front desk agents, reservations agents, housekeepers, and uniformed service staff. Since the rooms division

Exhibit 16   Sample Consolidated Statement of Income

Eatonwood Hotel
Summary Statement of Income
For the year ended 12/31/20XX

	SCHEDULE	NET REVENUE	COST OF SALES	PAYROLL & RELATED EXPENSES	OTHER EXPENSES	INCOME (LOSS)
OPERATED DEPARTMENTS						
ROOMS	1	$ 6,070,356		$ 1,068,383	$ 473,487	$ 4,528,486
FOOD	2	2,017,928	$ 733,057	617,705	168,794	498,372
BEVERAGE	3	778,971	162,258	205,897	78,783	332,033
TELECOMMUNICATIONS	4	213,744	167,298	31,421	17,309	-2,284
RENTALS AND OTHER INCOME	5	188,092				188,092
TOTAL OPERATED DEPARTMENTS		9,269,091	1,062,613	1,923,406	738,373	5,544,699
UNDISTRIBUTED OPERATING EXPENSES						
ADMINISTRATIVE AND GENERAL	6			227,635	331,546	559,181
MARKETING	7			116,001	422,295	538,296
PROPERTY OPERATION AND MAINTENANCE	8			204,569	163,880	368,449
UTILITY COSTS	9				546,331	546,331
TOTAL UNDISTRIBUTED OPERATING EXPENSES				548,205	1,464,052	2,012,257
TOTALS		$ 9,269,091	$ 1,062,613	$ 2,471,611	$2,202,425	
INCOME AFTER UNDISTRIBUTED OPERATING EXPENSES						3,532,442
RENT, PROPERTY TAXES, AND INSURANCE						641,029
INCOME BEFORE INTEREST, DEPRECIATION AND AMORTIZATION, AND INCOME TAXES						2,891,413
INTEREST EXPENSE						461,347
INCOME BEFORE DEPRECIATION AMORTIZATION, AND INCOME TAXES						2,430,066
DEPRECIATION AND AMORTIZATION						552,401
GAIN ON SALE OF PROPERTY						1,574
INCOME BEFORE INCOME TAXES						1,879,239
INCOME TAXES						469,810
NET INCOME						$ 1,409,429

is not a merchandising facility, there is no cost of sales to subtract from the net revenue amount.

Revenue generated by the rooms division is usually the largest single amount produced by revenue centers within a hotel. Based on the figures in Exhibit 16, the amount of income earned by the Eatonwood Hotel's rooms division during the year was $4,528,486—or 81.7 percent of the total operated department income of $5,544,699.

Rooms Schedule

The hotel's income statement primarily contains summary information. The separate departmental income statements prepared by each revenue center provide

Exhibit 17   Sample Rooms Division Income Statement

Rooms—Schedule #1
Eatonwood Hotel
For the year ended 12/31/20XX

	Current Period
Revenue	$6,124,991
Allowances	54,635
Net Revenue	6,070,356
Expenses	
Salaries and Wages	855,919
Employee Benefits	212,464
Total Payroll and Related Expenses	1,068,383
Other Expenses	
Internet/Satellite Television	20,100
Commissions	66,775
Complimentary Guest Services	2,420
Contract Services	30,874
Guest Relocation	1,241
Guest Transportation	48,565
Laundry and Dry Cleaning	42,495
Linen	12,140
Operating Supplies	122,600
Reservations	40,908
Telecommunications	12,442
Training	7,122
Uniforms	60,705
Other	5,100
Total Other Expenses	473,487
Total Expenses	1,541,870
Departmental Income (Loss)	$4,528,486

more detail. Departmental income statements are called "schedules" and are referenced on the hotel's statement of income.

Exhibit 16 references the rooms schedule as *1*. The rooms schedule appears in Exhibit 17. The figures shown in Exhibit 17 for the rooms division revenue, payroll and related expenses, other expenses, and departmental income are the same amounts that appear for the rooms division under the category of operated departments in Exhibit 16.

The hotel accounting division, not the front office accounting staff, generally prepares the rooms schedule. The figures are derived from several sources, as follows:

Rooms Division Entry	Source Documents
Salaries and wages	Time cards, payroll records
Employee benefits	Payroll records
Commissions	Travel agency billings
Contract cleaning	Supplier invoices
Guest transportation	Invoices
Laundry and dry cleaning	Housekeeping and outside laundry/valet charges for employee uniforms
Linen	Supplier invoices
Operating supplies	Supplier invoices
Reservation expenses (if any)	Reservation system invoices
Other operating expenses	Supplier invoices (such as from equipment rentals, etc.)

(Reservation expenses are fees the hotel pays for central reservation services and reservations made through global distribution and Internet distribution systems.)

By carefully reviewing the rooms schedule, the front office manager may be able to develop action plans to improve the division's financial condition and services. For example, the income statement may indicate that the hotel's telecommunications revenue is down, due to the application of a long-distance surcharge. This analysis reveals that guests are choosing to make fewer telephone calls using the hotel's telecommunications system, because the cost per call was increased by the surcharge. Therefore, even though the revenue *per call* may have increased, overall telecommunications revenues have decreased.

Housekeeping provides another example. If the housekeeping department manager increases the number of rooms a room attendant is assigned to clean per day from fourteen to fifteen, the department will likely need to schedule fewer attendants. This can produce savings in wages, benefits, and possibly cleaning supplies. However, front office managers should be aware that taking measures to reduce costs may result in reduced guest services.

Rooms Division Budget Reports

Generally, the hotel's accounting division also prepares monthly budget reports that compare actual revenue and expense figures with budgeted amounts. These reports can provide timely information for evaluating front office operations. Front office performance is often judged according to how favorably the rooms division's monthly income and expense figures compare with budgeted amounts.

A typical budget report format should include both monthly variances and year-to-date variances for all budget items. Front office managers are more likely to focus on the monthly variances, since year-to-date variances merely represent the accumulation of monthly variances. Exhibit 18 presents a rooms division budget report for the Gregory Hotel for the month of January. This budget report does not yet contain year-to-date figures, since January is the first month of the business year for this particular hotel.

It is important to note that Exhibit 18 presents both dollar and percentage variances. The dollar variances indicate the difference between actual results and

Exhibit 18 Sample Monthly Rooms Division Budget Report

Gregory Hotel
Budget Report—Rooms Division
For January 20XX

	Actual	Budget	Variances $	Variances %
Revenue				
Room Sales	$156,240	$145,080	$11,160	7.69%
Allowances	437	300	(137)	(45.67)
Net Revenue	155,803	144,780	11,023	7.61
Expenses				
Salaries and Wages	20,826	18,821	(2,005)	(10.65)
Employee Benefits	4,015	5,791	1,776	30.67
Total Payroll and Related Expenses	24,841	24,612	(229)	(0.93)
Other Expenses				
Commissions	437	752	315	41.89
Contract Cleaning	921	873	(48)	(5.50)
Guest Transportation	1,750	1,200	(550)	(45.83)
Laundry and Dry Cleaning	1,218	975	(243)	(24.92)
Linen	1,906	1,875	(31)	(1.65)
Operating Supplies	1,937	1,348	(589)	(43.69)
Reservation Expenses	1,734	2,012	278	13.82
Uniforms	374	292	(82)	(28.08)
Other Operating Expenses	515	672	157	23.36
Total Other Expenses	10,792	9,999	(793)	(7.93)
Total Expenses	35,633	34,611	(1,022)	(2.95)
Departmental Income	$120,170	$110,169	$10,001	9.08%

budgeted amounts. Dollar variances are generally considered either favorable or unfavorable as follows:

	Favorable Variance	Unfavorable Variance
Revenue	Actual exceeds budget	Budget exceeds actual
Expenses	Budget exceeds actual	Actual exceeds budget

For example, the actual amount of salaries and wages for rooms division personnel in the month of January was $20,826, while the budgeted amount for salaries and wages was $18,821, resulting in an unfavorable variance of $2,005. This dollar variance is bracketed to indicate that it is unfavorable. However, if the revenue variance is highly favorable, an unfavorable variance in expenses (such as in payroll) is not necessarily negative. The comparative variance may merely indicate the greater expense associated with serving more guests than were anticipated when the budget was created. One way to verify whether a variance is really unfavorable or favorable is to divide the actual rooms occupied for the period into the actual cost and the budgeted cost. If the actual cost is at or below the budgeted cost per room, the variance is actually positive, even though there was more expense.

Percentage variances are determined by dividing the dollar variance by the budgeted amount. For example, the 7.61 percent variance for net revenue shown in Exhibit 18 is the result of dividing the dollar variance figure of $11,023 by the budgeted net revenue amount of $144,780.

The budget report shows both dollar and percentage variances because either dollar variances alone or percentage variances alone may not indicate the significance of the variances reported. For example, dollar variances fail to indicate the magnitude of change from the budgeted base. The monthly budget report for the front office of a large hotel may show that actual net revenue varied from the budgeted amount by $1,000. This may seem to be a significant variance, but if the $1,000 variance is based on a budgeted amount of $500,000, it represents a percentage difference of only 0.2 percent. Most front office managers would not consider this a significant variance. However, if the budget amount for the period was $10,000, a $1,000 variance would represent a percentage variance of 10 percent, a percentage variance most front office managers would consider significant.

Percentage variances alone can also be deceiving. For example, assume that the budgeted amount for an expense item is $10, and the actual expense was $12. The dollar variance of $2 represents a percentage variance of 20 percent. While this percentage difference appears significant, it probably would not be worth a front office manager's time to investigate a $2 variance.

The fact that actual results of front office operations differ from budgeted amounts on a budget report shouldn't be surprising. Any budgeting process, no matter how sophisticated, is unlikely to be perfect. Front office managers should not analyze every variance. Only significant variances require management analysis and action. The hotel general manager and controller can provide criteria by which the front office manager can determine which variances are significant.

Operating Ratios

Operating ratios assist managers in evaluating the success of front office operations. Exhibit 19 suggests more than twenty ratios that may be useful to managers in evaluating the success of front office operations.

Payroll and related expenses tends to be the largest single expense item for the rooms division as well as the entire hotel. For control purposes, labor costs are analyzed on a departmental basis. Dividing the payroll and related expenses of the rooms division by the division's net room revenue yields one of the most frequently analyzed areas of front office operations—labor cost.

Operating ratios should be compared against proper standards—budgeted percentages, for example. Any significant differences between actual and budgeted

Exhibit 19   Useful Rooms Division Operating Ratios

	Net Revenue	Payroll and Related Expenses	Other Expenses	Departmental Income
% of total hotel revenue	X			
% of departmental revenue		X	X	X
% of departmental total expenses		X	X	
% of total hotel payroll and related expenses		X		
% change from prior period	X	X	X	X
% change from budget	X	X	X	X
per available room	X	X	X	X
per occupied room	X	X	X	X

labor cost percentages must be carefully investigated, since payroll and related expenses represent the largest single expense category.

One method for analyzing payroll and related expenses involves a form similar to the one shown in Exhibit 20. Actual figures for the current and previous periods, as well as budgeted amounts, are itemized for comparative analysis. Any significant differences should be highlighted and explained in the remarks section. By conducting a payroll and related expenses analysis, the front office manager demonstrates to general management that he or she attends to the most important controllable expense in the rooms division. Careful attention to staffing as the number of rooms sold fluctuates can guarantee that the percentage of payroll and related expenses to total revenue remains relatively constant from month to month.

Ratio Standards

Operating ratios are meaningful only when compared against useful criteria such as:

- Planned ratio goals
- Corresponding historical ratios
- Industry averages

Ratios are best compared against planned ratio goals. For example, a front office manager may more effectively control labor and related expenses by projecting a goal for the current month's labor cost percentage that is slightly lower than the previous month's. The expectation of a lower labor cost percentage may reflect

Exhibit 20   Sample Payroll Analysis Form

Front Office Payroll Analysis

Hotel: _____   Period Ending: _____

JOB CATEGORY	Amount Last Year	Amount This Year	Amount Budgeted
Front Office	_____	_____	_____
PBX	_____	_____	_____
Head Housekeeper	_____	_____	_____
Asst. Housekeeper, Housekeeping Staff	_____	_____	_____
Housepersons & Porters	_____	_____	_____
Linen Staff	_____	_____	_____
Laundry Staff	_____	_____	_____
Reservations Staff	_____	_____	_____
Maintenance, Gardener, & Asst. Maintenance	_____	_____	_____
Security, Life Guard, & Uniform Service Staff	_____	_____	_____

	(Last Year)	(This Year)
Payroll and Related Expenses	_____	_____
Net Revenue	_____	_____
Labor Cost Percentage	_____	_____

STATISTICS

Rooms Rented	_____	_____
Rooms Cleaned	_____	_____
Housekeepers Hours Paid	_____	_____
Number of Rooms Per Housekeeper	_____	_____
Cost Per Room (Housekeepers)	_____	_____

REMARKS:

_____

_____

the front office manager's efforts to improve scheduling procedures and other factors related to the cost of labor. By comparing the actual labor cost percentage with the planned goal, the manager can measure the success of his or her efforts to control labor costs.

Industry averages may also provide a useful standard against which to compare operating ratios. These industry averages can be found in publications prepared by the national accounting firms and trade associations serving the hospitality industry.

Experienced front office managers realize that operating ratios are only indicators; they do not solve problems or necessarily reveal the source of a problem. At best, when ratios vary significantly from planned goals, previous results, or industry averages, they indicate that problems *may* exist. Considerably more analysis and investigation are usually necessary to determine appropriate corrective actions.

Planning for Disasters

Disaster planning is an area that front office managers, and even some senior hotel managers, often overlook. While this is not a day-to-day operating issue, it is important that front office managers have a disaster action and recovery plan in place and make sure that the front office staff is familiar with it.

There are various types of disasters to consider, ranging from power failures and automated systems failures to criminal activities, severe weather, floods, fires, and terrorism. While it is unrealistic to think that every conceivable disaster can be anticipated, many can, and plans should be in place to deal with them. If the hotel has a security department, its director should be involved in the design, documentation, implementation, and ongoing revision of front office disaster plans. If the hotel has no security department, various other sources from which to draw expertise include the American Hotel & Lodging Association (AH&LA) and the American Hotel & Lodging Educational Institute.

Given today's level of hotel automation, disaster plans must state which supplemental or corrective actions front office personnel need to take if essential technology applications fail. Training front office staff in what to do if the property management system, telecommunications system, electronic locking system, and other important automated systems fail is of critical importance. While most system outages are often relatively short-term and minor in scope, they definitely undermine the hotel's ability to serve its guests.

Unfortunately, one of the most common issues a hotel business experiences is criminal activity, whether it is at the front desk, in a revenue outlet, in a guestroom, or elsewhere. Front office managers should prepare for possible criminal activity affecting the front office by creating procedures for dealing effectively and safely with it. Front office staff should know whom to contact if they become aware of or witness criminal activity, and what additional procedures to follow. For example, hotel staff should know that it is unwise to touch or move anything in a guestroom if an incident has occurred that requires police investigation.

Severe weather, floods, and other natural disasters often require special planning to deal with them successfully. Hotel management's plans for coping with natural disasters should be coordinated with local and regional disaster planning agencies. In addition, these plans should consider the possible loss of utilities or the isolation of the property. For example, a snowstorm may prevent employees from reporting for a work shift or may prevent employees from departing the property at the end of a work shift.

A fire, terrorism attack, or other disaster may require a complete hotel evacuation and shutdown of operations. Front office staff must know how to conduct themselves, remembering at all times that they are representatives of the hotel.

They must know what documentation to remove from the property, what to secure by locks, and what to do with hotel assets like cash and cashier banks. Some front office staff members may be called upon to assist with evacuating guests, which might include directing them to various safe locations away from the property, as spelled out in the front office disaster plan.

Foreseeable disasters require planning and training so the front office department and the hotel as a whole can successfully deal with them should they occur. Management should periodically review and update disaster plans; plans should not be drawn up and then placed on a shelf to gather dust. Training, which can range from a simple fire drill to more elaborate instruction involving a simulated robbery or bomb threat, should not be a one-time event; it must be ongoing to be effective, with refresher sessions regularly scheduled.

Summary

Resources available to front office managers include staff members, budgeted funds, work shifts, materials, and equipment, each of which is in limited supply. The front office manager's job involves planning and evaluating the use of such limited resources in meeting the organization's objectives. The process of management can be divided into specific management functions: planning, organizing, coordinating, staffing, leading, controlling, and evaluating. Although specific front office management tasks vary from hotel to hotel, fundamental management functions are similar in scope.

Planning is probably the most important management function. Without competent planning, productivity may be extremely low. Without the direction and focus planning provides, the front office manager may become overly involved with tasks that are unrelated to or inconsistent with accomplishing the hotel's objectives. Communication is an important component of planning. An effective manager communicates department planning activities to managers he or she reports to, as well as to staff members likely to be affected. Using the planned goals as a guide, a front office manager performs an organizing function when dividing the work fairly among front office staff. Organizing includes determining the order in which tasks are to be performed and when each group of tasks should be completed.

The management function of coordinating involves using resources to attain planned goals. A front office manager must be able to coordinate the efforts of many individuals who are all doing different sets of tasks at the same time. The management function of staffing involves recruiting and selecting applicants and scheduling employees. Staffing guidelines are usually based on formulas for calculating the number of employees required to meet guest and operational needs under specified conditions.

Leading is a complicated management skill that is exercised in a variety of situations and is related to other management skills. For a front office manager, leading involves overseeing, motivating, training, and disciplining employees and making decisions. One of the best ways to lead a department is by example. Every hotel has a system of internal controls for protecting the assets of the business. The control process ensures that the actual results of operations closely match planned results. The management function of evaluating determines the extent to which planned goals are attained. Evaluating also involves reviewing and revising front office goals.

Three important front office planning functions are establishing room rates, forecasting room availability, and budgeting for operations. Hotels will normally have several different room rates. The rack rate is listed on the room rate schedule to inform front desk agents of the standard selling price of each guestroom in the hotel. Front office employees are expected to sell rooms at the rack rate unless a guest qualifies for an authorized room rate discount. Establishing rack rates for room types and determining discount categories and special rates are some of a revenue manager's major duties. When determining rack rates or discounted rates, management should consider such factors as operating expenses, guest demand, market conditions, inflationary factors, and related business issues.

Setting room rates through the market condition approach is the simplest and most commonly used. In this approach, the hotel's rates are set to be competitive with similar hotels in the market. The rule-of-thumb approach to setting room rates sets the rate at $1 for each $1,000 of construction and furnishings cost per room, assuming a 70 percent occupancy. The Hubbart Formula for determining the average price per room considers costs, desired profits, and expected number of rooms sold. The front office manager must understand the effects of rate and occupancy on room revenue to ensure that the hotel meets its revenue goals.

The most important short-term planning statistic is forecasting the number of rooms available for sale on any future date. Room availability forecasts are used to help manage the reservations process, guide room sales efforts, and plan staffing requirements. The process of forecasting room availability generally relies on historical occupancy data. Such statistics as the percentage of no-shows, walk-ins, overstays, and understays can be critical factors in effective forecasting.

The most important long-term planning function that front office managers perform is budgeting. The annual operations budget is a profit plan that addresses revenue sources and expense items. It is divided into monthly plans which, in turn, are divided into weekly (and sometimes daily) plans. Budget plans become standards against which management can evaluate operational results. The front office manager's primary responsibilities in budget planning are forecasting rooms revenue and estimating related expenses. The process requires the front office manager and accounting division personnel to coordinate their efforts.

Evaluating the results of front office operations is an important management function. Tools used in this function include the daily report of operations, occupancy ratios, rooms revenue analysis, the hotel income statement, the rooms schedule, rooms division budget reports, operating ratios, and ratio standards.

Operations planning must also include disaster planning. Disasters can include weather and other natural disasters, fires, criminal activities, terrorist acts, and automated systems failures. Front office management must create disaster action and recovery plans, often coordinating them with other hotel departments, as well as local and regional disaster planning agencies. Plans should be thoroughly documented, and front office staff members must be trained. This may involve simulation activities like fire drills or mock hotel evacuations.

Key Terms

average daily rate—An occupancy ratio derived by dividing net rooms revenue by the number of rooms sold.

average rate per guest—An occupancy ratio derived by dividing net rooms revenue by the number of guests.

competitive set—The group of hotels in a market that provides the most important competition for a hotel.

daily report of operations—A report that summarizes the hotel's financial activities during a twenty-four-hour period and provides insight into revenues, receivables, operating statistics, and cash transactions related to the front office; also known as the manager's report, daily report, and daily revenue report.

forecasting—The process of predicting events and trends in business; typical forecasting for the rooms division includes room availability and occupancy.

house count—The forecasted or expected number of guests for a particular period, sometimes broken down into group and non-group business.

Hubbart Formula—A bottom-up approach to pricing rooms; in determining the average price per room, this approach considers costs, desired profits, and expected rooms sold.

income statement—A financial statement that provides important information about the results of hotel operations for a given period of time.

market condition approach—An approach to pricing that bases prices on what comparable hotels in the hotel's competitive set are charging for a similar product.

multiple occupancy percentage—The number of rooms occupied by more than one guest divided by the number of rooms occupied by guests.

multiple occupancy ratio—A measurement used to forecast food and beverage revenue, indicate clean linen requirements, and analyze daily revenue rate; derived from the multiple occupancy percentage or by determining the average number of guests per rooms sold; also called the double occupancy ratio.

occupancy percentage—An occupancy ratio that relates the number of rooms sold to rooms available for sale during a specific period of time.

occupancy ratios—A measurement of the hotel's success in selling rooms; typical occupancy ratios include occupancy percentage, multiple occupancy ratio, average daily rate, revenue per available room, revenue per available customer, and average rate per guest.

operating ratios—A group of ratios that assist in the analysis of hospitality operations.

overstay—A guest who stays after his or her stated departure date.

rack rate—The standard rate the property establishes for a particular category of guestrooms.

revenue per available customer (RevPAC)—A revenue management measurement that focuses on revenue per actual guest.

revenue per available room (RevPAR)—A revenue management measurement that focuses on revenue per available room.

room rate variance report—A report listing rooms that have not been sold at rack rates.

rule-of-thumb approach—A cost approach to pricing rooms in which the room rate is set at $1 for each $1,000 of construction and furnishings cost per room, assuming an occupancy of 70 percent.

stayover—A room status term indicating that the guest is not checking out today and will remain at least one more night; a guest who continues to occupy a room from the time of arrival to the stated date of departure.

understay—A guest who checks out before his or her stated departure date.

yield statistic—The ratio of actual rooms revenue to potential rooms revenue.

Review Questions

1. How do the seven functions of management fit into the overall management process? How do these functions apply to the front office manager's position?

2. What kinds of special room rates might a hotel offer? What are the three common methods of establishing room rates?

3. What information do front office managers require to develop room availability forecasts? Why are these forecasts important? How reliable are such forecasts?

4. What steps can front office employees take to control understays and unwanted overstays?

5. What are the differences between RevPAR and RevPAC? How can the front office manager use each ratio?

6. How do ten-day and three-day forecasts help ensure efficiency in front office operations? What is the relationship between these forecasts? What departments in the hotel rely on these forecasts, other than the front office?

7. What are the front office manager's primary responsibilities in budget planning? How are they performed?

8. What occupancy ratios are commonly calculated by the front office? What is the significance of occupancy ratios?

9. What methods can a front office manager use to evaluate how effectively the front office is selling rooms?

10. How can front office managers use budget reports to analyze operations? Why is reporting both dollar and percentage variances valuable?

11. What are some useful standards against which front office managers should compare operating ratios? What is the significance of a variance from standards?

12. What can a front office manager do to prepare his or her staff to deal with disasters?

Internet Sites

For more information, visit the following Internet sites. Remember that Internet addresses can change without notice. If the site is no longer there, you can use a search engine to look for additional sites.

American Hotel & Lodging
  Association
www.ahla.com

American Hotel & Lodging
  Educational Institute
www.ahlei.org

Smith Travel Research
www.str.com

TIMS Reports.com
http://TIMSreports.com

TravelCLICK
www.travelclick.net

Chapter Appendix

Manual Operations Plans

The following plans and procedures are suggested as an outline for use whenever a disaster or something else causes the property management system to go down for a significant amount of time. (Illustration 1 outlines some immediate actions that can be taken.) The objective is to establish clear control and coordination responsibilities. Each property should prepare its own version based on its own operational needs and should prepare similar documents for all other critical systems (POS, sales and catering, etc.). All of these plans should be reviewed periodically to ensure that they stay current.

The key to running a hotel manually is good, organized communication between management and all operationally focused departments within the hotel, especially the front desk, reservations, and housekeeping. Most employees will never have worked in a manual environment and will be used to relying exclusively on the front office computer system. Consequently, all instructions to employees should be clear and precise, and the plans should be practiced regularly. Maintaining guest service is of utmost importance during this period.

Management/Staff Roles

The following roles are suggested for the key management and operations staff. The task assignments should be customized to the nature of each hotel's operations. For example, while many properties may not have a systems manager, they should have one person who has responsibility for coordinating all support activity on the automated systems. It is most important that the responsibility for performing each task be clearly understood by all.

General Manager/Hotel Manager

- Authorizes notification of all management personnel.
- Receives status reports from systems personnel.
- Makes/approves operational decisions regarding system downtime.

Systems Manager

- Determines magnitude of problem; estimates system downtime. Determines status of all correction activities in progress.
- Notifies response team on severity of problem and recommends degree of contingency to implement.
- Ensures that all necessary functions and personnel are prepared to begin manual operations, if necessary, and notifies appropriate service/vendor personnel.
- Keeps management updated regarding contingency status.
- Supervises repair, restoration, and replacement of data, components, systems, or entire computer room as needed.

Illustration 1 Downtime Quick Response Checklist

Quick Response Checklist

1. Alert managers.

2. If the system is down because of a power failure, *turn off all equipment immediately*. Failure to do so could result in further hardware damage. If the critical items are on uninterruptible power supplies (UPSs) with automated shutdown routines, monitor these to ensure that they are in fact closing down correctly.

3. Distribute the most recent downtime reports and destroy prior lists.

4. Designate a rack clerk, responsible for maintaining the room inventory and status, to begin to record all check-ins, check-outs, etc.

5. Designate a posting clerk, responsible for writing all charges on the guest folios.

6. Alert retail outlets that the system is inoperable and that they must close checks to the manual key. All room charges must be taken to the front desk for manual posting.

7. Alert the audit staff members no later than four hours before their shifts that the system is down and that they should report early to begin a manual audit.

8. Alert the central reservation help desk of the situation and estimated downtime, and arrange an alternative for continued delivery of reservations and feedback of hotel availability status.

9. The rooms division manager should write a letter to all in-house guests and arrivals notifying them of the situation.

10. Issue battery-operated radios to all key personnel, including the PBX operator.

- Prepares report for hotel management that details problems, causes, and solutions; plan performance; and suggestions for modifications as necessary.

Reception Manager

- Coordinates front office activity with the systems manager and reservations manager.

- Supervises the front office activity during downtime.

- Monitors controls and audit trails during downtime.

- Supervises in-house runners.

- Supplies food and beverage outlets with current guest list, no-post list, and cash guest list.

- Documents observed or perceived problems in plan operation for review and/or revision.

- Coordinates reconstruction of data, once system is restored.

Front Desk Supervisor

- Monitors and controls registration functions.

- Maintains room status control sheet.

- Maintains walk-in list.

- Communicates status changes to housekeeping.

- Maintains status change log.

- Supervises bucket clerk.

- Supervises re-entry of check-ins, check-outs, and moves once the system is restored.

Reception Agents

- Controls filing of guest charges and maintenance of current balances. Supervises generation of source documents, vouchers/receipts, etc.

- Assists cashiers in balancing shift.

- Assists with posting of charges/payments once the system is restored.

Reservation Manager

- Distributes thirty-day and one-year room availability reports to all reservation agents.

- Supervises manual booking of reservations.

- Maintains manual reservations file.

- Maintains a manual room availability control chart.

- Supervises re-entry of reservations once the system is restored.

PBX Operator

- Notifies computer staff when the system is down.

- Maintains and updates telephone reference list with assistance of front office.

All Outlet Managers

- Coordinates food and beverage contingency plan with systems manager.

- Supervises execution of contingency plan in all food and beverage outlets.

- Supervises manual operation of outlets, including ordering, service, payment, and posting of all checks.

- Supervises entering of all information once system is restored.

- Assists in balancing process during downtime.

Cashiers

- Responsible for three-part check and check control sheet distribution to outlet cashiers.

- Monitors the manual tip control sheet and disbursement of charge tips.

Assistant Controller

- Coordinates accounting department activity with the systems manager.
- Supervises execution of the contingency plan in the accounting office.
- Supervises data reconstruction after the system is restored.

Accounts Receivable Manager

- Works with the front desk supervisor and bucket clerk on maintaining the manual guest ledger.
- Maintains manual banquet billings.
- Coordinates advance deposit refunds with accounts payable during extended downtime.
- Maintains manual payment card account balances.
- Monitors advance deposit activity.
- Supervises restoration of data.

Housekeeping

- Supervises manual room status controls.
- Establishes initial room status sheet (P.M.) housekeeping report.
- Supervises vacant room inspection.
- Supervises distribution of updated room status lists to front desk.
- Supervises manual assignment of room attendants.
- Maintains room status change log.

Night Reception Manager

- Performs regular audit functions when and where necessary.
- Helps generate manual reports during extended downtime.
- Supervises the night clerks during downtime.
- Assists in the restoration of data.
- Performs update and distribution of reports.
- Balances hotel accounts at the end of the day.

Manual Front Desk Overview

Illustration 2 lists items and staff required to manually operate the front desk. Make sure that the room rack report (see Illustration 3) and any other standard forms are already filled out with the room numbers and other data that do not change. Prepare "crash kits" stocked with all necessary office supplies (pens, cards, pads, tape, etc.) and keep them in an area that is convenient to the front desk.

Illustration 2   Items and Staff Needed for Manual Front Desk Operations

Forms:	Manual Room Rack
	Cash Guest Report
	House Count Sheet
	Registration Cards (handwritten or pre-printed)
	Guest Folios (handwritten or pre-printed)
	Reservations Forms (handwritten or pre-printed)
	Most recent downtime reports from system
Miscellaneous:	Index cards and alphabetical file
	Calculator with tape (battery operated)
	Pencils with erasers
	Payment card imprinters
Personnel:	Posting Clerk: Responsible for posting all charges to guest folios
	Rack Clerk: Responsible for maintaining room inventory and current status
	Runners: Responsible for communications between departments, ensuring that departments are passing information correctly and that everyone is following the manual operating procedures

Returning to Automated Operations

When the system is fully operational again, it won't know that anything has happened since it went down, and it must be brought up-to-date through the manual entering of all transactions that occurred in the interim. This requires an organized effort on the part of all members of management to keep all users posting on the correct day. If all night audit work is organized into batches, all staff can concentrate on one day's activity at a time. A night audit must be run for each day that the system was down in order to bring the system up to the current date. Manual downtime procedures must be maintained until the system is running and its data has been verified as fully up-to-date. General steps in bringing the system up-to-date are:

1. Process the first day's work. Process all activity that was not posted on the day that the system went down, including check-ins, check-outs, all transactions, and room status changes.

2. Some systems (PBX, call accounting, mini bars, pay movies, etc.) that use an interface to post charges to guest folios may hold charges in a buffer. If these systems were operating during the time that the property management system was not, charges may post automatically when the interface is restored. This could result in charges being posted to the wrong accounts, double posting of charges, phones or mini bars being turned off or on inappropriately, and so on. Each of these systems should have a backup printer to report charges (including date, time, and room number) it was unable to send to the property management system. This is the information needed to post charges manually to the correct guests' folios, but the reports do not imply that charges are not still being held in a buffer. Check with the vendor for each of these systems to

Illustration 3   Sample Manual Room Rack Report

Manual Room Rack

Floor Number _____   Section Number _____

Room #: _____	Room Type: _____
Status: _____	Guest Name: _____
Room Features: _____	Check-Out: _____

Room #: _____	Room Type: _____
Status: _____	Guest Name: _____
Room Features: _____	Check-Out: _____

Room #: _____	Room Type: _____
Status: _____	Guest Name: _____
Room Features: _____	Check-Out: _____

Room #: _____	Room Type: _____
Status: _____	Guest Name: _____
Room Features: _____	Check-Out: _____

Room #: _____	Room Type: _____
Status: _____	Guest Name: _____
Room Features: _____	Check-Out: _____

Room #: _____	Room Type: _____
Status: _____	Guest Name: _____
Room Features: _____	Check-Out: _____

Room #: _____	Room Type: _____
Status: _____	Guest Name: _____
Room Features: _____	Check-Out: _____

Room #: _____	Room Type: _____
Status: _____	Guest Name: _____
Room Features: _____	Check-Out: _____

Room #: _____	Room Type: _____
Status: _____	Guest Name: _____
Room Features: _____	Check-Out: _____

Room #: _____	Room Type: _____
Status: _____	Guest Name: _____
Room Features: _____	Check-Out: _____

discuss how their systems work and how best to handle a situation where the property management system, the interface, or even the system in question is down. Add this information to the disaster action and recovery plan.

3. Perform a full rooms and financial audit for that day.

4. Run a night audit process on the computer system.

5. Once the above procedures are complete and the system is on the next day, process the remaining days' transactions in the same manner. Perform night audit and run a close-of-day for each day until the current day and time are reached.

Chapter 13 Outline

The Concept of Revenue Management
    Hotel Industry Applications
Measuring Revenue
    Formula 1: Potential Average Single
        Rate
    Formula 2: Potential Average Double
        Rate
    Formula 3: Multiple Occupancy
        Percentage
    Formula 4: Rate Spread
    Formula 5: Potential Average Rate
    Formula 6: Room Rate Achievement
        Factor
    Formula 7: Yield Statistic
    Formula 8: RevPAR
    Formula 9: Identical Yields
    Formula 10: Equivalent Occupancy
    Formula 11: Required Non-Room
        Revenue per Guest
    RevPAG and GOPPAR
Elements of Revenue Management
    Group Room Sales
    Transient Room Sales
    Other Revenue Opportunities
    Local and Area-Wide Activities
    Special Events
    Fair Market Share Forecasting
The Revenue Manager
Using Revenue Management
    The Revenue Meeting
    Potential High- and Low-Demand
        Tactics
    Implementing Revenue Strategies
Revenue Management Software
Summary

Competencies

1. Explain the concept of revenue management, and discuss how managers can maximize revenue by using forecast information in capacity management, discount allocation, and duration control. (pp. 477–482)

2. Discuss common formulas managers use to measure and manage revenue. (pp. 483–496)

3. Explain how revenue management decisions are affected by group room sales, transient room sales, other revenue opportunities, local and area-wide activities, special events, and fair market share forecasting. (pp. 496–506)

4. Discuss the revenue manager's role and position, summarize typical revenue meetings, outline potential tactics to use in periods of high and low demand, discuss revenue management tactics, and explain how revenue management software helps hotel managers. (pp. 506–519)

Revenue Management

Historically, a hotel's daily performance has been evaluated on either occupancy percentage or average daily rate (ADR). Unfortunately, such one-dimensional analyses fail to capture the relationship between these two factors. For example, hotel managers may decrease room rates, or ADR, in an effort to increase occupancy. This strategy, while helping to improve the occupancy percentage, may fail to offset the rooms revenue lost due to lower room rates. Unless occupancy increases can overcome the drop in rate, profits may actually decline. Similarly, increases in room rates, or ADR, may be accompanied by a decline in occupancy percentage. This means that some revenue will be lost because rooms that might have been sold at lower rates will remain unsold. Some hotel companies prefer to build occupancy percentage using low room rates to attract business, while others prefer to set a target average room rate and are willing to sacrifice occupancy to achieve it.

Revenue management presents a more precise measure of performance because it combines occupancy percentage and ADR into a single statistic: the *yield statistic*. Simply stated, revenue management is a technique used to maximize revenues. Revenue management, sometimes called yield management, takes into account as many of the factors influencing business trends as possible. It is also an evaluative tool that allows the front office manager to use potential revenue as the standard against which actual revenue can be compared.

There are various approaches to revenue management. Often, each approach is modeled to meet the needs of an individual hotel. This chapter presents many of the common elements and basic assumptions used in revenue management analysis. Although revenue management analysis can be performed manually, this approach is cumbersome, time-consuming, and prone to error. With the use of specialty application software, revenue management calculations can be automatically performed very quickly and accurately.

The Concept of Revenue Management

The concept of revenue management originated in the airline industry. Most travelers know that passengers on the same flight often pay different fares. Super-saver discounts, fourteen-day advance-purchase plans, non-refundable fares, and so forth have become the norm for airline pricing. What is not as widely known is the potential application of revenue management to other service industries. Revenue management has proven successful in the lodging, car rental, cruise line, railroad,

477

and touring industries—basically, in situations where reservations are taken for a perishable commodity. The key to successful implementation appears to be an ability to monitor demand and to develop reliable forecasts.

When hotels first started using revenue management, they focused strictly on guestroom rates and the basic economic principles of supply and demand. If demand for room nights was projected to be low—that is, if the forecast was for low occupancy, the revenue management strategy would dictate keeping room rates low in an attempt to attract as much business as possible. The idea was to convert every room availability inquiry into a reservation, even at a low rate. As demand increased for the targeted time frame, the hotel would increase its room rates. Hotels tended to align rate strategies with market segmentations by offering select discounts to featured groups, such as American Automobile Association members and AARP members. In addition, hotels did some specialized forecasting. For example, the number of current reservations for a future date may be low, but, if a city-wide convention was coming to town at that time, a hotel manager might believe the hotel would actually have higher occupancy and would fine-tune room rates and project occupancy accordingly. As hotel managers became more comfortable with the concept and application of revenue management strategies, they realized there were more effective ways to adjust rates while maximizing occupancy. Hotel companies conducted extensive analyses of guests who stayed at their hotels as well as those who preferred to stay elsewhere. Managers realized that room rates could accurately be adjusted based upon the demand of specific market segments, such as the following:

- Business travelers booking less than seven days prior to arrival

- Leisure travelers booking three to six months in advance of arrival

- Members of the hotel's frequent guest program

- Travelers making reservations over the Internet

- Travelers making reservations at the hotel's website

- Travelers requiring car rentals, airline reservations, and other components of a complete travel package

Hotel managers focused on making the best of each selling opportunity. The key to successful revenue management is to sell the right product (guestrooms, banquets, ancillary services) to the right customer (business, leisure, convention, or government guest) on the right day (weekday, weekend), for the right price (rack rate, corporate rate, group rate, government rate, or discount rate).

Many hotels use revenue management techniques to evaluate the total revenue potential of a guest or group. This includes all of the potential guest revenue beyond the guestroom rental, such as revenue from the sale of food and beverages, telephone service, Internet access, spa services, fitness center services, business center services, and other hotel goods and services. However, this discussion will focus on guestroom revenue, since this is the most important revenue stream for most hotels and therefore should receive the most attention from hotel management.

Revenue management, in one form or another, is pervasive across the lodging industry. Major hotel companies have developed unique revenue management systems that provide data for balancing room rates and occupancy levels at the property level. Some hotel managers do not support decisions based on revenue management analysis, evaluation, and strategy. These managers believe revenue management is too quantitative in nature, or fail to see the potential benefits derived from the work necessary for revenue management.

Revenue management is based on supply and demand. Prices tend to rise when demand exceeds supply; conversely, prices tend to fall when supply exceeds demand. Proper pricing adjustments, which take existing demand into account and can even influence it, appear to be the key to increased profitability. To increase revenue, the hotel industry is attempting to develop new forecasting techniques that will enable it to respond to changes in supply and demand with optimal room rates. The hotel industry's focus is shifting from high-*volume* bookings to high-*profit* bookings. By increasing bookings on low-demand days and by selling rooms at higher room rates on high-demand days, the industry can improve its profitability. In general, room rates should be higher (in order to maximize rate) when demand exceeds supply, and lower (in order to increase occupancy) when supply exceeds demand.

Revenue management is about making predictions and decisions—predictions about how much and what type of business to expect, and the subsequent decisions a manager makes to get the most revenue from that business.

Hotel Industry Applications

All hotel companies have a common problem: they have a fixed inventory of perishable products that cannot be stored if unsold by a specific time. The *real* commodity that hotels sell is time in a given space. If a room goes unsold on a given night, there is no way to recover the time lost and therefore the revenue lost. Thus, these products are typically sold for varying prices that depend on the timing of the transaction and the proposed date of delivery.

To make predictions, called **forecasts,** managers need information. They have to understand the property and the competitive market in which the property operates. They also need to consider future events—or variables—that might affect business.

Forecasts help determine whether room rates should be raised or lowered, and whether a reservation request should be accepted or rejected to maximize revenue. Front office managers have successfully applied such demand-forecasting strategies to room reservation systems; management information systems; room and package pricing; rooms and revenue management; seasonal rate determination; pre-theater dinner specials; and special, group, tour operator, and travel agent rates.

Front office managers have identified several benefits of revenue management, including:

- Improved forecasting
- Improved seasonal pricing and inventory decisions

- Identification of new market segments
- Identification of market segment demands
- Enhanced coordination between the front office and sales divisions
- Determination of discounting activity
- Improved development of short-term and long-term business plans
- Establishment of a value-based rate structure
- Increased business and profits
- Savings in labor costs and other operating expenses
- Initiation of consistent guest-contact scripting (that is, planned responses to guest inquiries or requests regarding reservations)

Selecting revenue management strategies and tactics is really about picking and choosing the reservations that most closely match the guest mix that hotel management desires. Most hotel managers seek a mix of two or more guest segments. (Some common guest segments are group guests, business travelers, leisure guests, government travelers, or contract guests.) Having a guest mix ensures that the hotel's business will not be significantly affected if business from one of the guest segments goes into decline. For example, business travel significantly decreased in the United States and overseas after the terrorist attacks of September 11, 2001. Some hotels managed to maintain acceptable profitability because they had a diversified guest base; hotels that relied primarily on business guests had much more difficulty maintaining profitability. The goal is to identify high-yield guest segments—the ones with guests who will pay the most and stay the longest—so the highest possible profits can be realized. This is accomplished by controlling room rates and availability through rate and stay restrictions.

Different demand situations call for different tactics. The challenge is to view each day as a separate situation and implement tactics best suited to the property and its guests, market, and demand conditions. This is done through capacity management, discount allocation, and duration control.

Capacity Management. Capacity management involves various methods of controlling and limiting room supply. For example, hotels will typically accept a statistically supported number of reservations in excess of the actual number of rooms available in an attempt to offset the potential impact of early check-outs, cancellations, and no-shows. Capacity management (also called selective overbooking) balances the risk of overselling guestrooms against the potential loss of revenue arising from room spoilage (rooms going unoccupied after the hotel stops taking reservations for a given date).

Other forms of capacity management include determining how many walk-ins to accept on the day of arrival, given projected cancellations, no-shows, and early departures. Capacity management strategies usually vary by room type. That is, it might be economically advantageous to overbook more rooms in lower-priced categories, because upgrading to higher-priced rooms is an acceptable solution to an oversell problem. The amount of such overbooking depends, of course, on the level of demand for the higher-priced rooms. In sophisticated computerized revenue management systems, capacity management may also be influenced by the availability of rooms at neighboring hotels or other competing properties.

The risks in overbooking should be clearly understood. It is generally better to have some rooms vacant at the end of the hotel day than to walk guests to other hotels. Walking guests leads to guest dissatisfaction. Guests will change hotels or brands if overbooking relocates them too often. In addition, hotel management must be aware of how local laws interpret overbooking.

Between late 2001 and late 2003, one of the most critical issues U.S. hotel managers faced was **group attrition**. The traditional process of handling group reservations normally occurs in two phases. The first phase involves blocking a set of rooms that the group expects its attendees to occupy. The second phase occurs as attendees actually register for the event and book the blocked rooms.

The number of rooms a group requires for a specific number of nights is one of the factors the hotel may consider when determining whether to accept the group's business. Once the hotel accepts the group's reservation, it hopes the group can sell all of its blocked rooms. When a group fails to book its committed number of room nights, the resulting shortfall is termed *attrition*. Before late 2001, group attrition did not pose a serious problem for a majority of lodging properties, since hotels could compensate for it through sales efforts in a variety of other market segments (such as by accepting short-term reservations for business travelers). In fact, some hotels actually allowed for a small percentage of group attrition and accounted for it in comprehensive capacity management strategies. Since 2001, three factors have contributed to elevating the importance of group attrition: group history, online shopping, and business sourcing.

- *Group history:* Meeting planners who contract for a large number of guestrooms tend to base their projections on the group's attendance history. If the group is notorious for missing its targeted room nights, hotel management will make adjustments to the expected business at the front end rather than wait until late in the reservation cycle.

- *Online shopping:* Group attendees have Internet access and can make their own reservations online, often shopping for a lower room rate than the rate negotiated for the group at the host hotel(s). Alternately, attendees may opt to stay at a nearby property instead of at the host hotel if they discover a lower room rate.

- *Business sourcing:* The volume of occupancy generated by non-group segments, such as business and leisure travelers, has significantly decreased, thereby placing a heavier emphasis on successfully marketing to group and convention business.

Hotel managers and meeting planners have worked together to minimize group attrition problems. Meeting planners now use various techniques to ensure that their groups meet their room-night pickup commitments. For example, many groups restrict attendance at meetings to those who stay in approved hotels. Furthermore, some city-wide groups will not provide transportation to attendees who do not stay in the host hotels. And sometimes group registration fees are significantly higher for attendees who do not stay in the host hotels. For their part, hotel managers are doing a better job of managing their hotels' discount rates, to ensure that in-house groups receive the lowest published rate. In addition, some hotels do not offer loyalty-program rewards to guests who pay significantly discounted rates.

Discount Allocation. Discount allocation involves restricting the time period and product mix (rooms) available at reduced or discounted rates. For each discounted room type, reservations are requested at various available rates, each set below rack rate. The theory is that the sale of a perishable item (the guestroom) at a reduced room rate is often better than no sale at all. The primary objective of discount allocation is to protect enough remaining rooms at a higher rate to satisfy the projected demand for rooms at that rate, while at the same time filling rooms that would otherwise have remained unsold. This process is repeated for each rate level from rack rate on down as demand indicates. Implementing such a scheme requires a reliable mechanism for demand forecasting.

A second objective of limiting discounts by room type is to encourage upselling. In upselling, a reservation agent or front desk agent attempts to place a guest in a higher-rated room. This technique requires a reliable estimate of price elasticity and/or the probability of upgrading. (*Elasticity* refers to the relationship between price and demand. If a small increase in price produces a dramatic drop in demand, the market is said to be price *elastic*. If a small increase in price produces little or no effect on demand, the market is said to be price *inelastic*.)

Duration Control. Duration control places time constraints on accepting reservations to protect sufficient space for multi-day requests (representing higher levels of revenue). This means that, under revenue management, a reservation for a one-night stay may be rejected, even though space is available for that night.

For example, if Wednesday is close to selling out but adjacent nights are not, a hotel may want to optimize its revenue potential for the last few remaining rooms on Wednesday by requiring multi-day stays, even at a discounted rate, rather than accepting reservations for Wednesday only. Similarly, if the hotel is projected to be close to capacity Tuesday, Wednesday, and Thursday, accepting a one-night stay during any of those days may be detrimental to the hotel's overall room revenue, since it may block occupancy on the other days. Hotels facing such situations may require that guests wishing to reserve rooms during projected full-occupancy periods make reservations for more than one night. Duration control is a common technique that resorts use during peak periods like Christmas, New Year's, Easter, and the Fourth of July.

These strategies may be combined. For example, duration control may be combined with discount allocation. A three-night stay may be available for discount, while a one-night stay may require the rack rate. It must be cautioned, though, that using these strategies must not be apparent to the guest. A guest might not understand why he or she must stay three nights to get a discounted rate if he or she wants to stay only one night. Proper use of revenue management relies on selling; it never divulges the revenue management strategy being used.

Measuring Revenue

Revenue management is designed to measure revenue achievement. One of the principal computations involved in revenue management is the hotel's **yield statistic,** the ratio of actual room revenue to potential room revenue. Actual room revenue is the revenue generated by the number of rooms sold. Potential room revenue is the amount of money that would be received if all rooms were sold at their rack rates (or, as described below, at the hotel's *potential average rate*).

Potential revenue can be determined in more than one way. First, some resorts calculate their potential revenue as the amount the resort would earn if all rooms were sold at the double occupancy rate. Resorts generally have a high percentage of double occupancy. Commercial hotels often calculate their potential revenue by taking into account the percentage mix of rooms normally sold at both single and double occupancy. The second method results in a lower total potential revenue figure, since single rooms are assumed to sell at less than double rooms. In fact, while it is unlikely that a hotel will attain a potential that is based on 100 percent double occupancy (first method), a hotel using the second method may actually be able to exceed its "potential" if demand for double rooms exceeds sales mix projections.

The hotel's yield statistic will vary with the method it uses; therefore, once the hotel has chosen a preferred method, it should use that method consistently. The second method (using both single and double occupancy) is illustrated in the formulas that follow. For hotels using the first method (based on 100 percent double occupancy), formulas 1, 3, 4, and 5 are not applicable; for such hotels, the potential average double rate (formula 2) will be the same as the potential average rate (formula 5).

The mathematical computations required for revenue management are relatively simple, even though a series of formulas are usually involved. This section is intended to introduce the basic formulations of revenue management calculations.

For the following discussion, assume that the Casa Vana Inn has 300 guestrooms, has an ADR of $80 per room, and is currently operating at a 70 percent average occupancy. The hotel offers 100 one-bed and 200 two-bed guestrooms. Management has established single and double rack rates for each room type. Any one-bed room sold as a single is priced at $90; as a double, it sells for $110. Any two-bed room sold as a single is priced at $100; as a double, it sells for $120.

Formula 1: Potential Average Single Rate

If the Casa Vana Inn had not varied its single rate by room type (for example, if all singles were $90), the potential average single rate would equal its rack rate. When the single rate differs by room type, as in this case, the potential average single rate is computed as a weighted average. It is computed by multiplying the number of rooms in each room type category by its single room rack rate and dividing the sum total by the number of potential single rooms in the hotel. For the Casa Vana Inn, the potential average single rate is computed as follows:

Room Type	Number of Rooms	Single Rack Rate	Revenue at 100% Occupancy Singles
1 bed	100	$ 90	$ 9,000
2 beds	200	100	20,000
	300		$29,000

$$\text{Potential Average Single Rate} = \frac{\text{Single Room Revenues at Rack Rate}}{\text{Number of Rooms Sold as Singles}}$$

$$= \frac{\$29,000}{300}$$

$$= \$96.67$$

Formula 2: Potential Average Double Rate

If the hotel had not varied its double rate by room type, the potential average double rate would equal its rack rate. When the double rate differs by room type, as in this case, the potential average double rate is computed as a weighted average. It is calculated by multiplying the number of rooms in each room type category by its respective double-room rack rate and dividing the sum total by the number of potential double rooms in the hotel. For the Casa Vana Inn, this computation is as follows:

Room Type	Number of Rooms	Double Rack Rate	Revenue at 100% Occupancy Doubles
1 bed	100	$110	$11,000
2 beds	200	120	24,000
	300		$35,000

$$\text{Potential Average Double Rate} = \frac{\text{Double Room Revenues at Rack Rate}}{\text{Number of Rooms Sold as Doubles}}$$

$$= \frac{\$35,000}{300}$$

$$= \$116.67$$

Note: For lodging properties basing potential revenue on 100 percent double occupancy, this step is all that is necessary to determine potential average rate (see formula 5).

Formula 3: Multiple Occupancy Percentage

An important element in determining a hotel's yield statistic is the proportion of the hotel's rooms that are occupied by more than one person—that is, the multiple occupancy percentage. This information is important because it indicates sales mix and helps balance room rates with future occupancy demand. In the case of the Casa Vana Inn, if 105 of the 210 rooms sold (at 70-percent occupancy) are normally occupied by more than one person, the multiple occupancy percentage is computed as follows:

$$\text{Multiple Occupancy Percentage} = \frac{105}{210}$$

$$= 0.5 \text{ or } \underline{\underline{50\%}}$$

Formula 4: Rate Spread

In addition to multiple occupancy percentage, another intermediate computation is important to yield statistics. The determination of a room **rate spread** among various room types can be essential to the use of yield decisions in targeting a hotel's specific market. The mathematical difference between the hotel's potential average single rate (formula 1) and potential average double rate (formula 2) is known as the rate spread. For the Casa Vana Inn, the rate spread is computed as follows:

$$\text{Rate Spread} = \text{Potential Average Double Rate} - \text{Potential Average Single Rate}$$

$$= \$116.67 - \$96.67$$

$$= \$ \underline{\underline{20.00}}$$

Formula 5: Potential Average Rate

A very important element in revenue management formulation is the **potential average rate.** A hotel's potential average rate is a collective statistic that effectively combines the potential average rate, multiple occupancy percentage, and rate spread. The potential average rate is determined in two steps. The first step involves multiplying the rate spread by the hotel's multiple occupancy percentage. The result is added to the hotel's potential average single rate to produce a potential average rate based on demand (sales mix) and room rate information. For the Casa Vana Inn, the potential average rate is computed as follows:

$$\text{Potential Average Rate} = \left(\text{Multiple Occupancy Percentage} \times \text{Rate Spread} \right) + \text{Potential Average Single Rate}$$

$$= (0.5 \times \$20) + \$96.67$$

$$= \underline{\underline{\$106.67}}$$

Formula 6: Room Rate Achievement Factor

The percentage of the rack rate that the hotel actually receives is expressed by the hotel's **achievement factor (AF),** also called the **rate potential percentage.** When revenue management software is not used, the achievement factor is generally calculated by dividing the actual average rate the hotel is currently collecting by the potential average rate.[1] The actual average rate equals total rooms revenue divided by either rooms sold or rooms occupied (depending on hotel policy). For the Casa Vana Inn, the room rate achievement factor is computed as follows:

$$\text{Achievement Factor} = \frac{\text{Actual Average Rate}}{\text{Potential Average Rate}}$$

$$= \frac{\$80.00}{\$106.67}$$

$$= 0.750 \text{ or } \underline{\underline{75.0\%}}$$

The achievement factor is also equal to 100 percent minus the discount percentage. By calculating its achievement factor, management discovers how much its actual room rates varied from established rack rates. In this case, the discount is 25 percent.

As shown below, the achievement factor can be used in one method of determining the yield statistic. It is not *necessary* to calculate the achievement factor, because the yield statistic can be determined without it. Nonetheless, the achievement factor is an important statistic in its own right because it allows management to monitor and therefore better control the hotel's use of discounting. For this reason, many hotels calculate the achievement factor as part of their revenue management efforts.

Formula 7: Yield Statistic

An important element in revenue management is the yield statistic. The yield statistic calculation incorporates several of the previous formulas into a critical index. There are various ways to express and calculate the yield statistic, all of which are equivalent:

1. $\text{Yield} = \dfrac{\text{Actual Rooms Revenue}}{\text{Potential Rooms Revenue}}$

2. $\text{Yield} = \dfrac{\text{Room Nights Sold}}{\text{Rooms Nights Available}} \times \dfrac{\text{Actual Average Room Rate}}{\text{Potential Average Rate}}$

3. $\text{Yield} = \text{Occupancy Percentage} \times \text{Achievement Factor}$

The first equation is used for a hotel that offers all its rooms at a single rack rate, regardless of occupancy. When (as is far more common) a hotel uses more than one rack rate for different room types and/or occupancies, potential rooms revenue equals total room nights available times the potential average rate.

The self-explanatory second equation is not demonstrated here. The third equation is illustrated below. For the Casa Vana Inn, the calculation is as follows: .

$$\text{Yield} = \text{Occupancy Percentage} \times \text{Achievement Factor}$$

$$= 0.7 \times 0.75$$

$$= 0.525 \text{ or } \underline{\underline{52.5\%}}$$

Consider another example. Assume that the Cybex Hotel has 150 rooms and a rack rate of $70. On average, the hotel sells 120 rooms per night at an average room rate of $60. What is the yield for this property?

$$\text{Occupancy Percentage} = 120 \div 150 = 0.8 \text{ or } 80\%$$

$$\text{Rate Achievement Factor} = 60 \div 70 = 0.857 \text{ or } 85.7\%$$

$$\text{Yield} = 0.8 \times 0.857 = 0.686 \text{ or } \underline{\underline{68.6\%}}$$

When using this approach to determine the yield statistic, note that complimentary rooms must be treated in the achievement factor the same way that they are treated in the occupancy percentage. That is, if complimentary rooms are included in the occupancy percentage, the actual average room rate used to determine the achievement factor must equal room revenues divided by rooms *occupied*, not rooms *sold*. If complimentary rooms are ignored in the occupancy percentage, they should be ignored in calculating the actual average room rate as well.

Formula 8: RevPAR

Instead of computing yield as a percentage, some lodging operations prefer an alternate statistic that focuses on revenue per available room **(RevPAR)**. RevPAR can be calculated using either of the following equations:

$$\text{RevPAR} = \frac{\text{Actual Room Revenue}}{\text{Number of Available Rooms}}$$

$$\text{RevPAR} = \text{Occupancy Percentage} \times \text{ADR}$$

For example, suppose the 300-room Casa Vana Inn sells 180 rooms for a total of $11,520. What is this hotel's revenue per available room?

$$\text{RevPAR} = \frac{\text{Actual Room Revenue}}{\text{Number of Available Rooms}}$$

$$= \$11,520 \div 300 = \underline{\underline{\$38.40}}$$

or

$$\text{RevPAR} = \text{Occupancy Percentage} \times \text{ADR}$$

$$= 60\% \times \$64 = \underline{\underline{\$38.40}}$$

where occupancy percentage $= 180 \div 300 = 0.6$ or 60%
and ADR $= \$11,520 \div 180 = \$64$

Formula 9: Identical Yields

Calculations of different combinations of occupancy and actual average room rate may result in identical room revenue and yield statistics. Suppose the Casa Vana Inn is currently operating at 70-percent occupancy with an average rate of $80, but is considering strategies designed to raise its average rate to $100. What occupancy percentage must it achieve to match the yield it currently achieves? The formula for determining identical yield occupancy percentage is as follows:

$$\frac{\text{Identical Yield}}{\text{Occupancy Percentage}} = \frac{\text{Current Occupancy}}{\text{Percentage}} \times \frac{\text{Current Average Rate}}{\text{Proposed Average Rate}}$$

$$= 70\% \times \frac{\$80}{\$100}$$

$$= 0.560 \text{ or } \underline{\underline{56.0\%}}$$

Identical yields do not generally represent identical operating situations, however. Consider the following three levels of room sales for which the Casa Vana Inn derives identical yield statistics:

Case	Number of Rooms Sold	Occupancy Percentage	Average Room Rate	Room Revenue	Yield
1	190	63.3%	$88.42	$16,800	52.5%
2	200	66.7%	$84.00	$16,800	52.5%
3	210	70.0%	$80.00	$16,800	52.5%

Are these three yield cases identical? Even though all three cases produce identical levels of room revenue and yield statistics, there are some significant differences to note.

Case 1, which represents the smallest number of rooms sold, will most likely have the lowest associated operating costs. Case 1 also generates the highest average room rate, and may appear to be the most profitable of the three cases. Case 3 represents the largest number of rooms sold and hence most likely the highest associated operating costs. This case also presents the lowest average room rate. These facts may be somewhat misleading, however. Often, the more rooms that are sold, the more likely the hotel is to collect greater non-room revenue. In other words, a higher occupancy percentage may result in greater total (room and non-room) revenue. Case 2 represents a middle position in terms of both number of rooms sold and average room rate. Some hoteliers may favor this case, since an intermediate position is achieved regarding associated operating costs and total revenues collected.

Clearly, identical yields should not be assumed to reveal equivalent operating positions. When identical yields are computed, judging which scenario is best often requires property-specific criteria and management evaluation.

Formula 10: Equivalent Occupancy

Management can use the **equivalent occupancy** formula when it wants to know what other combinations of room rate and occupancy percentage provide equivalent *net* revenue.

The equivalent occupancy formula is very similar to the identical yield occupancy formula, but takes marginal costs into account by incorporating gross profit or contribution margin. The **cost per occupied room** (also called the **marginal cost**) of providing a room is the cost the hotel incurs by selling that room (for example, housekeeping expenses such as cleaning supplies); this cost would not be incurred if the room were not sold (as opposed to **fixed costs,** which are incurred whether the room is sold or not). The **contribution margin** is that portion of the room rate that is left over after the marginal cost of providing the room has been subtracted out.[2]

To find the equivalent occupancy, use either of the following formulas (which are equivalent versions of the same equation):

$$\text{Equivalent Occupancy} = \text{Current Occupancy Percentage} \times \frac{\text{Rack Rate} - \text{Marginal Cost}}{\text{Rack Rate} \times \left(1 - \frac{\text{Discount}}{\text{Percentage}}\right) - \text{Marginal Cost}}$$

$$\text{Equivalent Occupancy} = \text{Current Occupancy Percentage} \times \frac{\text{Current Contribution Margin}}{\text{New Contribution Margin}}$$

Recall the example discussed under identical yield statistics. Now assume that the Casa Vana Inn is currently operating at 70-percent occupancy with an average rate of $80, and is considering strategies designed to raise its average rate to $100. Further assume that the marginal cost of providing a room is $12. What occupancy percentage must the Casa Vana Inn achieve to match the *net room revenue* it currently receives?

$$\text{Equivalent Occupancy} = \text{Current Occupancy Percentage} \times \frac{\text{Current Contribution Margin}}{\text{New Contribution Margin}}$$

$$= 70\% \times \frac{\$80 - \$12}{\$100 - \$12}$$

$$= 0.541 \text{ or } \underline{\underline{54.1\%}}$$

Recall from the discussion of identical yields that the Casa Vana Inn needs a 56-percent occupancy to produce an identical *yield statistic*—that is, equivalent gross revenue. However, the Casa Vana Inn does not need to match its gross revenue to achieve the same net revenue, since, by selling fewer rooms (at the higher price), it incurs fewer associated operating costs.

Although rack rates are raised relatively infrequently, discounting is a common practice in the lodging industry. What is the equivalent occupancy to 70 percent with an $80 average room rate if the average room rate is discounted by 20 percent (to $64)?

$$\text{Equivalent Occupancy} = 70\% \times \frac{\$80 - \$12}{\$64 - \$12}$$

$$= 0.915 \text{ or } \underline{\underline{91.5\%}}$$

A **discount grid** can help management to evaluate room rate discounting strategies. For example, if the average room rate of a hotel is $100 and its marginal cost (cost per occupied room) is $11, the grid in Exhibit 1 lists the occupancy percentages necessary to achieve equivalent net revenue, given different room rate discount levels. To prepare a discount grid, first calculate the marginal cost

Exhibit 1   Sample Discount Grid

Rack Rate		$100.00						
Marginal Cost		$11.00						
Current Occupancy		Equivalent Occupancy Percent Required to Maintain Profitability if Rates Are Discounted by:						
	5%	10%	15%	20%	25%	30%	35%
100%	106.0%	112.7%	120.3%	129.0%	139.1%	150.8%	164.8%
95%	100.7%	107.0%	114.3%	122.5%	132.1%	143.3%	156.6%
90%	95.4%	101.4%	108.2%	116.1%	125.2%	135.8%	148.3%
85%	90.1%	95.8%	102.2%	109.6%	118.2%	128.2%	140.1%
80%	84.8%	90.1%	96.2%	103.2%	111.3%	120.7%	131.9%
75%	79.5%	84.5%	90.2%	96.7%	104.3%	113.1%	123.6%
70%	74.2%	78.9%	84.2%	90.3%	97.3%	105.6%	115.4%
65%	68.9%	73.2%	78.2%	83.8%	90.4%	98.1%	107.1%
60%	63.6%	67.6%	72.2%	77.4%	83.4%	90.5%	98.9%
55%	58.3%	62.0%	66.1%	70.9%	76.5%	83.0%	90.6%
50%	53.0%	56.3%	60.1%	64.5%	69.5%	75.4%	82.4%
45%	47.7%	50.7%	54.1%	58.0%	62.6%	67.9%	74.2%
40%	42.4%	45.1%	48.1%	51.6%	55.6%	60.3%	65.9%
35%	37.1%	39.4%	42.1%	45.1%	48.7%	52.8%	57.7%
30%	31.8%	33.8%	36.1%	38.7%	41.7%	45.3%	49.4%
25%	26.5%	28.2%	30.1%	32.2%	34.8%	37.7%	41.2%

of providing a guestroom. Next, integrate this information into the equivalent occupancy formula and perform the calculations to fill in the grid. Completing a discount grid manually is quite time-consuming; spreadsheet programs greatly simplify the process.

Applying the yield and equivalent occupancy formulas to the same data will help illustrate their differences. Suppose once again that the Casa Vana Inn is currently operating at 70-percent occupancy with an average rate of $80 and a marginal cost of $12. Would the Inn be better off with an average rate of $100 and a 50-percent occupancy? What about $100 and 55-percent occupancy? Exhibit 2 presents these data and applies the yield statistic and equivalent occupancy formulas. Note that 50-percent occupancy falls below both the 56 percent necessary for identical yield and the 54.1 percent needed to produce equivalent net room revenue. Therefore, according to either approach, the Casa Vana Inn is worse off operating at a 50-percent occupancy and a $100 average room rate.

The second situation, however, finds the two approaches in conflict and illustrates the superiority of the equivalent occupancy formula. At 55-percent occupancy, the Casa Vana Inn falls short of the 56 percent needed to produce an identical yield statistic. When the yield statistic formula is used, the Inn appears to be worse off. However, the 55-percent occupancy level is higher than the 54.1

Exhibit 2   Application of Yield and Equivalent Occupancy Formulas

	Number of Rooms Sold	Occupancy Percentage	Average Room Rate	Gross Room Revenue	Total Contribution Margin*	Yield
Current	210	70.0%	$ 80	$16,800	$14,280	52.5%
Identical	168	56.0%	100	16,800	14,784	52.5%
Equivalent	162**	54.1%	100	16,200	14,280	50.6%
New	150	50.0%	100	15,000	13,200	46.9%
New	165	55.0%	100	16,500	14,520	51.6%

*Based on a marginal cost of $12. Since fixed costs are the same for all situations, the differences between total contribution margins will exactly equal the differences between net room revenues.

**Rounded down from 162.3. Based on this amount, net revenues would be $14,282.

percent required to produce equivalent net room revenue. With the equivalent occupancy formula, the Inn would be better off. A close look at the total contribution margin column—which shows that contribution (and therefore net room revenue) would rise—reveals that the equivalent occupancy formula provides more accurate and useful information.

Of course, the net gain in room revenue would have to be weighed against the potential loss of non-room revenue caused by a lower level of occupancy.

Formula 11: Required Non-Room Revenue per Guest

While equivalent occupancy accounts for marginal costs, unlike the yield statistic, both fail to account for changes in net non-room revenue due to changes in occupancy. A manager wanting some clear indication of whether a change in room rate will render more than an offsetting change in net non-room revenue may find an answer using **breakeven analysis.** This approach involves calculating or estimating a number of elements:

- The net change in room revenue due to room rate changes

- The amount of net non-room revenue needed to offset any reduction in net room revenue (when room rates are discounted) or the amount of net room revenue needed to offset any reduction in net non-room revenue (when room rates are increased)

- The average amount each guest spends in non-room revenue centers

- The change in occupancy likely to result from room rate changes

For example, a group may be negotiating for a lower room rate with a hotel. In order to make an appropriate group profit, the hotel may require some sort of additional food and beverage revenue, like a continental breakfast or group dinner. In other cases, the hotel may be unwilling to negotiate room rate but may add value to the group by hosting a complimentary cocktail reception or reducing parking fees. The same strategies apply to leisure guests coming to the hotel on a package plan. The package is priced competitively to attract guests, but the internal distribution of revenue should be designed to maximize profits.

The breakeven calculation is based on the **weighted average contribution margin ratio** (CMR_w) for all non-room revenue. While a detailed discussion of this topic is beyond the scope of this chapter, a simple formula for determining the CMR_w for all non-room revenue centers is as follows:[3]

$$CMR_w = \frac{\text{Total Non-Room Revenue} - \text{Total Non-Room Revenue Center Variable Costs}}{\text{Total Non-Room Revenue}}$$

Knowing the CMR_w and the average amount that guests spend in non-room revenue, and having estimated the probable change in occupancy (number of guests), the front office manager can then determine whether the net change caused by higher or lower room rates is likely to be more than offset by the net change in non-room revenue.

For example, suppose hotel management is considering room rate discounting in an attempt to increase occupancy and therefore net revenue. The formula used to determine the required non-room revenue per guest follows:

$$\text{Required Non-Room Revenue per Guest} = \frac{\text{Required Increase in Net Non-Room Revenue}}{\text{Number of Additional Guests}} \div CMR_w$$

The front office manager can compare the result of this equation with the actual average non-room spending per guest. If this number is higher than the actual average non-room spending per guest, the hotel is likely to lose net revenue by discounting its room rates; that is, the additional guests brought in through discounting will not spend enough to offset the net loss in room revenue. If the amount needed per additional guest is lower than the actual average amount spent, the hotel is likely to increase its net revenue through discounting.

As another example, assume that the 400-room Bradley Inn has a $144.75 potential average room rate (generating potential room revenue of $57,900) and a $12 marginal cost per room. The Inn currently operates at 60-percent occupancy (240 rooms sold per night) and an average room rate of $137.50. Management believes that it can raise occupancy to 75 percent (300 rooms sold per night) by lowering its average room rate to $110. It also believes it can raise occupancy to 90 percent (360 rooms sold per night) by lowering the average room rate to $91.67. Should management attempt either of these strategies?

It is important to note that since room revenue ($33,000) is the same for all three situations, looking simply at a yield statistic (57 percent) does not offer a solution. Equivalent occupancy calculations offer more useful information. A reduction in average room rate to $110 would require an equivalent occupancy of 76.8 percent (60 percent × $125.50 ÷ $98.00). A reduction to $91.67 would require an equivalent occupancy of 94.5 percent (60 percent × $125.50 ÷ $79.67). Based on management's forecasts of 75 percent and 90 percent occupancies, both average room rate reductions would result in a decrease in net room revenue.

Still, the average room rate reductions may be justifiable on the basis of increased *total* revenue. The first step in determining whether this is the case is calculating the total contribution margin (or, if fixed cost data are available, the net room revenue) of the three options:

Level of Occupancy		Number of Rooms		Room Contribution Margin		Total Revenue Contribution
60%	×	400	×	($137.50 − $12.00)	=	$30,120
75%	×	400	×	($110.00 − $12.00)	=	$29,400
90%	×	400	×	($91.67 − $12.00)	=	$28,681

An average room rate reduction to $110 brings in an additional 60 guests but results in a net room revenue loss of $720. A reduction in average room rate to $91.67 brings in an additional 120 guests but lowers net room revenue by $1,439. In either situation, to offset the loss, the Bradley Inn needs to earn an average net non-room revenue of $12 for each additional guest ($720 ÷ 60 extra guests; $1,439 ÷ 120 extra guests). If the non-room CMR_w is found to be 0.25, the required non-room spending for each additional guest is:

$$\text{Required Non-Room Spending} = \$12 \div 0.25 = \underline{\underline{\$48}}$$

In other words, if the Bradley Inn's guests typically spend an average of more than $48 per day in the Inn's non-room revenue centers, the Inn is likely to increase its total net revenue by offering either room rate discount.

Non-room revenue considerations can become critical factors in a revenue management analysis. Some hotels require that groups receiving discounted room rates contract for hotel food and beverage services to render the total revenue package attractive.

This discussion has thus far approached the breakeven analysis of required non-room revenue by examining a room rate *reduction* that decreases net room revenue and increases occupancy. Breakeven analysis can also be used to examine the net effects of a room rate *increase.* Consider the following situations.

When room rates are increased, occupancy percentage generally falls (unless demand is very inelastic). An increase in price may reduce room sales so much that net room revenue actually falls, despite the higher ADR. Because occupancy has declined, it is likely that non-room revenue will also decline. In this situation, it is clear that the price increase would hurt the hotel's financial position.

However, a room rate increase may in fact lead to higher net room revenue despite the decrease in occupancy it causes. Although higher net room revenue appears to be an outcome that management would desire, such a rate increase should not be implemented without careful analysis because, even if net room revenue goes up, *total* net revenue may still drop. This can occur when the occupancy decline reduces net non-room revenue by an amount greater than the net room revenue increase.

For example, assume that the 400-room Cybex Hotel is considering increasing its room rate from $80 to $90. Current occupancy is 80 percent. Forecasted occupancy after the price increase is estimated to be 75 percent. The marginal cost of selling a guestroom is $14. The average daily non-room spending per guest is

$75 and the weighted average contribution margin ratio for all non-room revenue centers is 0.30. Should management implement the rate increase? First, calculate the effect on net room revenue contribution:

Occupancy		Rooms		Room Contribution Margin		Total Contribution
80%	×	400	×	($80 − $14)	=	$21,120
75%	×	400	×	($90 − $14)	=	$22,800

Net room revenue would increase by $1,680 if the room rate were increased. The profit percentage per occupied room would increase from 82.5 percent ($66 ÷ $80) to 84.4 percent ($76 ÷ $90).

Next, calculate the effect on non-room net revenue:

Net Non-Room Revenue

At 80% occupancy: 320 guests × $75 × 0.30 = $7,200
At 75% occupancy: 300 guests × $75 × 0.30 = $6,750

Net non-room revenue would decrease by $450 if the room rate were increased.

Finally, subtract the net non-room revenue loss from the net room revenue gain. In this example, total daily net revenue would increase by $1,230 ($1,680 − $450) if the room rate is increased by $10. Given this net gain, management should implement the increase.

Now suppose that the front office manager had forecasted occupancy to be 71 percent after the rate increase rather than 75 percent. This change would lead to a different conclusion, as the following calculations demonstrate:

Occupancy		Rooms		Room Contribution Margin		Total Contribution
80%	×	400	×	($80 − $14)	=	$21,120
71%	×	400	×	($90 − $14)	=	$21,584

Net room revenue would increase by $464 if the room rate were increased. However, net non-room revenue would decrease by $810 if the room rate were increased:

Net Non-Room Revenue

At 80% occupancy: 320 guests × $75 × 0.30 = $7,200
At 71% occupancy: 284 guests × $75 × 0.30 = $6,390

In this revised example, total daily net revenue would decrease by $346 ($810 − $464). Given such circumstances, management should not implement the room rate increase.

RevPAG and GOPPAR

RevPAR is an established component of a revenue management analysis. Two additional measurements of hotel revenue and profitability have emerged as important considerations: RevPAG (revenue per available guest) and GOPPAR (gross operating profit per available room).

RevPAG is similar to RevPAR in that it measures total revenue; however, instead of reporting on a per-available-room basis, it uses the number of guests as a critical variable. The purpose of RevPAG is to determine the average revenue earned for each guest staying at a hotel. The RevPAG formula is:

$$\text{RevPAG} \quad = \quad \frac{\text{Total Revenue}}{\text{Number of Guests}}$$

RevPAG is most useful in hotels with multiple revenue outlets, such as restaurants, lounges, recreational activities, spa, and retail shops. It is a statistic that highlights the overall revenue derived per guest and is a more comprehensive measure than a per-room figure. Managers can also use RevPAG to identify areas in which the hotel is not capturing expected revenue. For example, a hotel may have a RevPAG of $110 per day, meaning that the average total revenue contributed by each guest (room revenue, food and beverage revenue, spa revenue, in-room entertainment revenue, etc.) is $110. However, if this average starts to decline, it indicates that the hotel is not earning as much revenue per guest as it did previously. Such a condition will lead hotel management to develop appropriate strategies and tactics to reverse the decline.

GOPPAR is a more sophisticated measurement than RevPAG, since it deals with gross operating profit. GOPPAR has the advantage of incorporating departmental expenses, not just revenue, resulting in a measure of gross operating profit, which is a number that represents the mathematical difference between departmental revenues and departmental expenses. By dividing the gross operating profit by the number of rooms available for sale, management can obtain a measure of profitability for the property. The purpose of GOPPAR is to quantify the hotel's profitability per available room. Industry analysts can also use GOPPAR to determine a hotel's financial value. Value can be especially important should the hotel's owner become interested in re-financing or selling the property. The GOPPAR formula is:

$$\text{GOPPAR} \quad = \quad \frac{\text{Departmental Revenues} - \text{Departmental Expenses}}{\text{Number of Available Rooms}}$$

Hotel management may do an adequate job generating revenue, but a less than satisfactory job controlling costs. If the hotel does not properly control expenses, all of its effort to maximize revenue will not produce an expected level of profitability. For example, a hotel may have a higher occupancy than expected, leading to a greater amount of revenue than initially projected. However, to accommodate the extra business, management may have scheduled more employees, leading to increased paid wages and possible overtime, and/or may have purchased more inventory (foods and beverages, etc.), thereby reducing eventual profitability of the unanticipated business increase.

While RevPAG and GOPPAR each have advantages, they also have potential shortcomings. For example, RevPAG may not be an effective measure for properties with limited revenue opportunities, such as budget or economy-service hotels. RevPAG may also produce somewhat distorted results for hotels with frequent short guest stays. In addition, since RevPAG is dependent upon the number of guests, it is difficult to use when making comparisons with other hotels, especially when double-occupancy percentages can vary significantly between similar properties.

GOPPAR has two major drawbacks. First, it is difficult to recognize as an industry-wide metric, since hotel profitability information tends to be proprietary and confidential. Whereas hotels are willing to provide average daily rate and occupancy statistics to neutral sources (such as Smith Travel Research), hotels consider operating profit data differently: usually only top-level managers and property owners are privy to profitability information. Second, GOPPAR is not timely; it may take up to one month after the close of business to calculate GOPPAR for an accounting period. Hotel management may prefer a metric that produces timelier results.

Elements of Revenue Management

The fact that flexible room rates affect both the number of guests and associated revenue transactions helps demonstrate the potential complexities of revenue management. Focusing attention only on room revenue potential may not present management with a comprehensive overview.

Revenue management becomes even more complex when room rate discounting is granted on a selective rather than general basis, and when it involves selling rooms for which there may be competing buyers. Hotels frequently offer discounts to certain categories of guests (for example, senior citizens and government employees). Hotels must also decide whether to accept or refuse group business at a discounted room rate. This section discusses various situations that can arise when hotels base their booking decisions on revenue management.

The following elements must be included in the development of a successful revenue management strategy:

- Group room sales
- Transient room sales
- Other revenue opportunities
- Local and area-wide activities
- Special events

One of the most important issues to understand about revenue management is that the practice changes from property to property. It may also change from season to season within a property, due to sources of business, competition, and other issues. However, there are certain elements important to developing basic revenue management skills.

Group Room Sales

In many hotels, groups form the nucleus of room revenue. It is common for hotels to receive reservations for group sales from three months to two years in advance of arrival. Some international business hotels and popular resorts commonly book groups more than two years in advance. Therefore, understanding group booking trends and requirements can be critical to the success of revenue management.

Sales and catering managers are in constant contact with new and existing clients. When a request comes in, the sales or catering manager must carefully research and document what the client is requesting. Then, the information is presented to the hotel's revenue meeting for consideration. Questions to be asked before a decision is made include:

- Does the group request fit into the hotel's strategy for the period? For example, the group requires 100 rooms, but that number will exceed the group allocation for the period.

- Are there other groups who are interested in the same period?

- What meeting space will the group require? Is it proportionate to the contracted number of guestrooms?

- What impact will this group have on booking additional group business for the same dates?

- What is the group willing to pay in room rate?

- Do the food and beverage functions include catered events or will the group use the hotel's restaurants?

- What revenue can the hotel plan to earn for rooms, food and beverage, and other sources?

To understand the potential impact of group sales on overall room revenue, the hotel should collect as much group profile information as possible, including:

- Group booking data
- Group booking pace
- Anticipated group business
- Group booking lead time
- Displacement of transient business

Group Booking Data. Management should determine whether the group blocks already recorded in the reservation file should be modified because of anticipated cancellations, historical overestimation of the number of rooms needed, or greater demand than originally anticipated by the group leader. If the group has a previous business profile, management can often adjust expectations by reviewing the group's booking history. Groups tend to block 5 to 10 percent more rooms than they are likely to need, in optimistic anticipation of the number of attendees. The hotel's deletion of unnecessary group rooms from a group block is called the **wash factor.** Management must be careful in estimating how many rooms should be "washed" from the block. If a group block is reduced by too many rooms, the hotel may find itself overbooked and unable to accommodate all of the members of the group.

Group Booking Pace. The rate at which group business is being booked is called the **group booking pace.** ("Booking" in this context refers to the initial agreement between the group and the hotel, not to the specific assignment of individual rooms in the block to group members.[4]) For example, suppose that in April of a given year, a hotel has 300 rooms in group blocks it is holding for scheduled functions in October of the same year. If the hotel had only 250 group rooms booked for October at the same time the year before, the booking pace would be 20 percent ahead of the previous year's pace. Once a hotel has accumulated several years of group booking data, it can often identify a historical trend that reveals a normal booking pace for each month of the year. Although this forecasting process appears simple, it can become very complicated due to unanticipated fluctuations, such as a one-time, city-wide convention. These variations should be noted so that they can be recognized in future booking pace forecasting. Management should strive to maintain a straightforward method for tracking group booking pace. Booking pace can be an invaluable forecasting variable.

Anticipated Group Business. Most national, regional, and state associations, as well as some corporations, have policies governing the locations of annual meetings. For example, a group may rotate its meeting location among three cities, returning to each every three years. Although a contract may not yet be signed, hotel management may be confident that the group will return according to the cycle. Of course, a group may not always return to the same hotel in the area. However, even when it goes to other hotels, the group may displace other group and non-group business that will need to find alternate accommodations in the area. The hotel analyzing these data can then forecast the "pressure" in the market and adjust its selling strategies accordingly. In addition, tentative bookings that await final contract negotiations should be included in the revenue management analysis.

Group Booking Lead Time. Booking lead time measures how far in advance of a stay bookings are made. Corporate group bookings tend to be smaller than association meetings and are often made within a year of the planned event. Larger association meetings may book two to five years in advance to ensure the availability of the required guestrooms and meeting space. Management should determine its hotel's lead time for group bookings so that booking trends can be charted. Booking trends can be combined with booking pace information to illustrate the rate at which the hotel is booking group business compared with historical trends (see Exhibit 3). This information can be very important when determining whether to accept an additional group and at what room rate to book the new group. If the current booking pace is lower than expected or lags behind the historical trend, it may be necessary to offer a lower room rate to stimulate increased occupancy. On the other hand, if demand is strong and the group booking pace is ahead of anticipated or historical trends, it may not be appropriate to discount room rates. Catering sales must also be taken into consideration when looking at booking lead times. For example, weddings are often planned a year or more in advance. If the catering department receives a request for the hotel ballroom a year in advance, management must decide to accept the catering request and potentially block group business, or hold out for the possibility that eventually a group will take guestrooms as well as the ballroom on the date in question. The group booking may never come, and, if the hotel turns down the catering business, the guestrooms and ballroom will be empty.

Displacement of Transient Business. Management should consult its demand forecast when determining whether or not to accept additional group business. **Displacement** occurs when a hotel accepts group business at the expense of transient guests. Since transient guests often pay higher room rates than group members and may be more likely to use hotel dining rooms, this situation warrants

Exhibit 3   Lead Time/Booking Pace for Sample Hotel

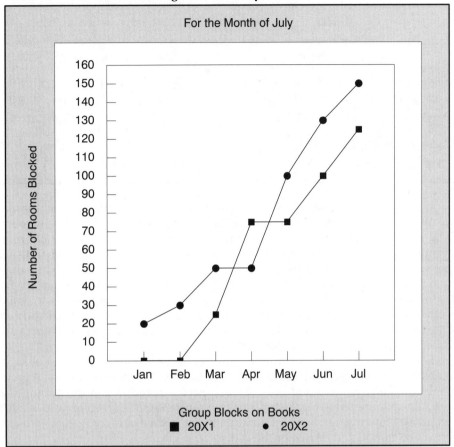

close scrutiny. Transient rooms are guestrooms sold to guests who are not affili-ated with a group registered with the hotel. A non-group guest may also be called a free independent traveler, or FIT.

Assume that the 400-room Halbrook Lodge has a potential average rate of $100, an actual average transient rate of $80, an actual average group rate of $60, and a marginal cost of $15 per occupied room. Consider the impact of a proposed group block of sixty rooms during an upcoming four-day period:

	Tuesday	Wednesday	Thursday	Friday
Rooms Available	400	400	400	400
Definite Groups Booked	140	140	150	150
Expected Transient Demand	200	180	220	210
Available Rooms	60	80	30	40
Proposed Group Block	60	60	60	60
Transient Displacement	0	0	30	20

Exhibit 4   Revenue and Yield Calculations

	Tuesday		Wednesday		Thursday		Friday	
	Without Group	With Group	Without Group	With Group	Without Group	With Group	Without Group	With Group
Gross revenue	$24,400	$28,000	$22,800	$26,400	$26,600	$27,800	$25,800	$27,800
Contribution*	19,300	22,000	18,000	20,700	21,050	21,800	20,400	21,800
Yield**	61.0%	70.0%	57.0%	66.0%	66.5%	69.5%	64.5%	69.5%

*Based on a marginal cost of $15.

**Potential revenue $=$ $100 potential average rate $\times$ 400 rooms $=$ $40,000.

If the proposed group block is accepted, no displacement occurs on Tuesday and Wednesday; the hotel clearly benefits on these days because it sells rooms it did not expect to sell (earning an additional $3,600 gross and $2,700 net room revenue each day). On Thursday and Friday, however, thirty and twenty transient guests, respectively, would be displaced. Still, as shown in Exhibit 4, Thursday's room revenue will rise by $1,200 gross and $750 net if the group is accepted. Friday's room revenue will rise by $2,000 gross and $1,400 net if the group is accepted. In other words, accepting the group business will increase the hotel's yield on each of the four days. Since it also raises the hotel's occupancy, this group's business will probably increase non-room revenue as well.

Several factors help determine whether a group reservation should be accepted. As just illustrated, the hotel should first look at revenue factors. A group should probably be accepted only if the expected revenue gain (including that from non-room revenue centers) offsets the transient guest revenue loss. In addition, management must consider what happens to the transient guests who cannot be accommodated. Whether these displaced guests are frequent or first-time guests, they may decide not to return to a hotel that has turned them away. The transient revenue lost may not be confined simply to the nights in question, especially when frequent guests choose not to return. Of course, turning away potential group business may also reduce future business.

Another situation in which the transient revenue lost may not be confined simply to the nights in question occurs when a non-group guest wishing to come in on Tuesday for three nights will be turned away if the group is taken. Even though the group is displacing actual non-group rooms on Thursday because of lack of inventory, it is affecting Tuesday and Wednesday as well.

Deciding whether to accept a group that forces transient displacement is an issue that deserves careful consideration. Management must consider the long-term impact on future business.

Keeping track of a group's history can help re-allocate group rooms to transient when those rooms may not be needed. As mentioned earlier, most groups overestimate the number of rooms they need by about 5 to 10 percent. That percentage is called the wash factor. By knowing each group's wash factor, a manager can safely release the excess rooms from the block. If a group's block is reduced by too many rooms, the property may find itself oversold and unable to accommodate all of the guests. If the group doesn't have a history with the property, a manager might contact other hotels where the group has previously stayed to try to determine its wash factor.

Dynamic Packaging. One of the most creative aspects of revenue management is the customization of a travel package according to a specific guest's needs. This practice is termed **dynamic packaging.** Although hotel sales representatives have offered packages to travelers for years, through travel agents, the Internet, and direct selling, these efforts have simply involved the bundling of existing services into a single package. Such deals were considered static packaging, since no personalization or customization was involved, and the deals often failed to meet the traveler's specific needs. Static packages might include a basic guestroom, parking fee, and dinner certificate for the hotel's dining room. A golf package might include one or two rounds of golf. Static packages often came with many associated restrictions, such as limited length of stay and limited day of arrival. Perhaps most important, static packages allowed no substitutions. For example, all guests would receive a dining certificate even when they did not want to dine at the hotel restaurant, since the certificate was part of the bundled services offered for a package rate. Hence, the guests would have had to pay for something they did not intend to use.

Dynamic packaging addresses the issue of preferred contents. Guests can use an Internet booking engine such as a hotel brand website, property website, select airline website, or a third-party travel website to create a custom (dynamic) package. The custom package can include only those services and amenities the guest desires. Dynamic packaging has been shown to increase the perceived value of a hotel package and to be more satisfying for the traveler. Dynamic packages may include airline tickets, hotel guestrooms, car rental agreements, recreational activities, sporting events, dining certificates, spa offerings, entertainment tickets, and other hospitality-related components. Hotels participating in online dynamic packaging offer hotel rooms at specific rates for a series of dates to Internet website representatives. Hotels usually find dynamic packaging especially effective during anticipated periods of low occupancy. By offering special deals then, hotels have a better chance of promoting business, since a customized travel package will have components designed to simplify the booking process. Hotels typically control the number of guestrooms available for dynamic packaging, so that, as occupancy increases, the hotels can either increase the available room rates or withdraw rooms from remaining available inventory previously committed to the packaging program.

Dynamic packaging also offers the opportunity for upselling. For example, a hotel may offer a standard guestroom as part of a basic package. Upselling the guest to a deluxe guestroom may be one of the alternate components available to the traveler. Upselling can effectively produce additional revenue for the hotel without its incurring significant additional expense.

Transient Room Sales

As mentioned earlier, transient rooms are those rooms sold to non-group travelers. Transient business is usually booked closer to the date of arrival than group business. A commercial hotel may book a majority of its group business three to six months before arrival, but transient business only one to three weeks before arrival. At a resort hotel, group bookings may be established one to two years in advance, while transient business may be booked three months in advance. As with group business, management must monitor the booking pace and lead time of transient business to understand how current reservations compare with historical and anticipated rates. This leads to the more complex subject of transient room rate discounting.

In a previous example, room rates were set by bed type and number in inventory. However, in today's market there may be many other reasons to price rooms differently. To maximize room revenue, front office managers may decide to classify rooms by location, desirability, or size, and charge a premium for better rooms. For example, rooms that are smaller, near noisy corridors, or unrenovated, or that offer less desirable views are likely to be offered at lower rates. Therefore, these rooms may be classified as standard and be assigned a lower room rate. More desirable rooms may be classified as deluxe and be assigned higher room rates.

To build business, hotels may offer deluxe rooms at standard rates to attract guests. This is especially true in times of low demand. Then, as demand improves to a predetermined threshold, any remaining deluxe rooms can be offered at or near full rack rate. Under this strategy, management attempts to maximize room revenue, not just average room rate or occupancy percentage. The reasoning is that lower demand creates a more competitive situation for the hotel. Discounting may reduce the amount of business lost because of rate resistance and allows the hotel to sell rooms that might otherwise remain vacant. An astute manager must know when to eliminate room rate discounts. If room rates are increased too soon, occupancy may be lost. If room rates are increased too late, some rooms may be sold for less than they could have been sold for. When discounting a deluxe room to a standard rate, the reservation or front desk agent should tell the guest that he or she is being upgraded. This will add perceived value to the guest's stay. It also reduces the confusion on the part of the guest the next time he or she comes to the hotel and is quoted a higher rate.

Managers must also consider the ethics of revenue management when choosing strategies. If a guestroom is classified as standard, there is usually a very good reason for it. Therefore, it would appear unethical to sell the room at a rate higher than its rack rate just because someone may be willing to pay the higher rate. Even though demand may provide the opportunity for a higher rate, charging the rate just because the market will accept it for the period is not always a good business practice. Some hotels have done this and received criticism from the market for doing it. This is one reason many states require that room rates be posted in each room.

Another issue to consider in transient room sales is the discounting offered to certain sources of business. Discounts can be offered to corporate and government travelers, as well as senior citizens, military and airline personnel, travel agents, and others. Quite often, these discounts apply to a substantial portion of a hotel's business. Some hotel companies are following the lead of airlines by offering discounts to guests booking through the Internet. Their justification for these discounts is that there are lower costs associated with Internet reservations.

These savings are being passed along to the consumer. However, this practice is still maturing and it will take time for the traveling public and hotel management to understand the impact of this type of discounting. For example, several hotel brands offer a best-rate guarantee at their own website, thus reducing the impact of discount sites that book guestrooms at significant reductions. At least one hotel company has taken this issue very seriously. It has notified its franchisees that offering discount rates below the company's rate guidelines may jeopardize their franchise arrangement with the company.

Controlling discounts is crucial to producing an optimal yield. For example, if a hotel has very few rooms reserved over a holiday period, it may open all discounts to callers just to attract business. As demand builds over the period, the discounts may be selectively closed. When the front office manager believes that rooms can be sold at a higher rate without an offsetting loss in occupancy, the discount should be closed. Some discounts cannot be closed off. Whenever possible, contracts for discounts should provide for flexibility when business conditions warrant.

Other Revenue Opportunities

Revenue management decisions for hotels that offer additional revenue outlets (non-room revenues) involve more than what to charge as an appropriate room rate. A hotel that offers meeting and banquet space, recreational facilities, spas, and other revenue centers gives guests many more opportunities to consider and gives management more revenue opportunities to evaluate. Negotiations with meeting and wedding planners focus on the total package of meeting space, banquet service, audiovisual equipment rentals, and the like, not solely on guestroom rates. A revenue management analysis must consider all revenue opportunities affecting potential profitability to determine the economic value of the total business to the hotel. Only after such analysis can management calculate a meaningful room rate.

While banquet functions generate food and beverage revenues, they might also affect guestroom revenues. For example, if a banquet with no associated guestrooms is scheduled to occupy the hotel's grand ballroom on New Year's Eve, another group wishing to use fifty guestrooms *and* the grand ballroom may have to be turned away. In most instances, the group requiring both catering and guestroom space will produce more profit for the hotel; therefore, the hotel must view the group in light of its potential contribution to hotel operations. Cooperation and communication between hotel departments is important to effectively execute a revenue management program.

When considering what rates to charge people attending a meeting at the hotel, management should consider all revenue opportunities, as well as the profitability each of those opportunities would provide. For example, guestrooms may contribute a 75 percent departmental profit margin; banquet meals, a 30 percent profit margin; meeting room rental, a 90 percent profit margin; and audiovisual rentals, a 60 percent profit margin. To determine the price to charge attendees needing a guestroom, meeting space, banquet service, and audiovisual rentals, managers should determine the potential revenue (or profit margin) for each affected department. Managers can easily accomplish this with spreadsheet software or a revenue management software application. Once the potential revenue resulting from the business has been calculated, it should be compared to the hotel's budget for the time period. If the meeting's revenue (or profit margin) exceeds the budget amount, a favorable decision is appropriate, and managers should develop a written agreement with the meeting planners.

Meeting planners may request concessions from hotel management in consideration of the meeting. A concession is some sort of improved value for the meeting. Concessions include items that would lower the expense of the meeting from the planner's perspective. Concessions made in negotiations may include the cost of meeting space and/or reductions in all aspects of the meeting. Suppose a meeting planner requests a VIP suite for the meeting's leader at no cost to the leader or group; this concession reduces the cost of the meeting from the planner's perspective but ignores the reduction in revenues for the hotel. Other concession items may involve reduced guestroom rates, as well as discounts on meeting room rental, food and beverage pricing, and audiovisual rental. The meeting planner may also request that complimentary items, such as daily decorative flowers or a wine and cheese tray, be placed in the VIP suite.

Concessions represent a loss in revenue or an increase in expense to the hotel, thereby reducing the overall value of the meeting. All such low- or no-cost items must be individually negotiated before the hotel determines a fair value for the meeting.

Many hotels will not accept banquet-only business during a projected high-demand period until the group's banquet-only booking date draws near. However, if the hotel's room sales history indicates low occupancy demand for a date such as New Year's Eve, the hotel might allow the sales department to book the banquet-only business well in advance.

Local and Area-Wide Activities

Local and area-wide activities can have dramatic effects on a hotel's revenue management strategies. Even when a hotel is not in the immediate vicinity of a convention, transient guests and smaller groups displaced by the convention may be referred to the hotel (as an overflow facility). When this occurs, the front office manager should be aware of the convention and the demand for guestrooms it has created. (Most local convention and visitors bureaus regularly publish information about large groups who book in the area.) If the demand is substantial, transient and group rates may need to be adjusted.

Convention business may render a trend analysis of group and transient activity invalid. If the booking pace of either group or transient rooms sales is significantly altered, the front office manager should immediately investigate. An increase in demand could indicate a convention in the area or a large booking at another property. A decrease in demand could indicate a major group cancellation at a competing property, which is now reducing its regular pricing to fill its guestrooms.

Ethics and good business practice should play an integral part in a yield strategy or tactic. It is appropriate and legal for competitors to occasionally meet and discuss general business trends. However, it is *not* legal to discuss room rates or the establishment (fixing) of room rates. There may also be additional sources of information that identify what is affecting business in the area. For example, most visitor and convention bureaus publish a list of meetings in their areas. Under no circumstances should employees of two different hotels discuss rate structuring or any other hotel operating issue, since such activity might be considered a violation of anti-trust laws in the United States.

Special Events

Quite often, special events such as holiday celebrations, concerts, festivals, and sporting events are held in or near a hotel. The hotel may be able to take advantage of such demand-enhancing activities by restricting room rate discounts or requiring a minimum length of stay. This is a common practice—for example, during the Christmas holidays at many Southern resorts. Guests wishing to stay over Christmas may be required to guarantee a four- or five-night minimum stay. Similarly, room discounts were eliminated during the 1996 Summer Olympic Games in Atlanta, Georgia, due to high demand and limited availability. Minimum stays were also required. These are all sound revenue management tactics, but they must be managed carefully so the hotel does not alienate frequent travelers.

Fair Market Share Forecasting

One of the other important elements of revenue management is understanding how well the hotel is doing in relation to the competition. This is known as the **fair market share**. It is important to know whether the rates being quoted are competitive and whether the hotel is actually getting its fair share of the available business in a market.

A primary tool for this analysis is the Smith Travel Accommodations Report, or STAR report. The STAR report is historical, so the information it provides tells hotel management how well their revenue management strategies and tactics worked in the past. By reviewing the past, however, management can make key decisions on how the hotel should be positioned in the future. The key statistic in the STAR report is the RevPAR Index. This statistic tells hotel management whether the property received its fair share of the business for the period reported compared to its competition or competitive set. For example, if a property had a 100 percent RevPAR Index, it would have received its fair share of business for the market. Keep in mind that RevPAR takes both occupancy and average daily rate into consideration. If a hotel received a score of 105 percent, it would have actually achieved more than its fair market share for the period. A score of 90 percent, on the other hand, would indicate that the hotel's competitive set did better for the period. It is important to note that, since RevPAR takes both occupancy and rate into consideration, a hotel may have a lower rate of occupancy than its competition but still have a higher RevPAR Index, because it maintained a higher average daily rate.

This information should be analyzed whenever the STAR report arrives, but also used for forecasting the next several months and the same period next year. For example, most hotels have peak and off-peak seasons. Management usually finds it convenient to classify each month into a business season. The STAR report can be used to position rates for a coming month, or develop next year's budget, by season. It may show opportunities for rate improvement or provide an indication of necessary rate repositioning. For example, management may look at the STAR report for the last two years and identify that their RevPAR Index for June has been over 105 percent. That could be an indication that they can continue to command higher rates during the month because of high demand. However, the STAR report should not be the only source of information on which to base decisions. For example, if another 300-room hotel is expected to open before June of next year, it may be more difficult holding or increasing rates because there will be more competition in the market.

While the STAR report is very valuable, it relies on hotels themselves to convey important statistics to the report producer. Since the data collection necessary to generate a comprehensive report is time-consuming, the STAR report tends to be somewhat historical in nature. For this reason, it may not accurately reflect the success of a hotel's revenue strategies in the short term. Hotels may experience a one- to two-month delay in performance due to variable market factors. Many industry observers consider the STAR report a solid basis for trend analysis, since it normally aggregates three months or more for each reporting period. Longer-term reports tend to provide a better indication of revenue management successes. Other trade resources are available to managers formulating revenue management strategies and tactics. For example, TravelCLICK produces a series of reports, including Hotelligence, Internet Hotelligence, and RateVIEW/Phaser. These reports are based on information collected from a diverse set of sources, including global distribution systems and Internet booking engines, and are considered forward-looking, since they are built on actual reservation transaction data.

The Revenue Manager

The duties of the revenue manager make this position among the most important to the hotel's financial success. A revenue manager can often mean the difference between a struggling hotel and a profitable hotel. Although much of this chapter's discussion of revenue management has concentrated on guestroom revenues, most large hotels include non-room revenue opportunities in the analysis. For example, when considering what rates to apply to a group, the revenue manager typically considers the total revenue projection for the group (rooms, food and beverage, audiovisual rentals, and other ancillary revenue) in a final rate quotation. The revenue manager must have an overview of the entire hotel's revenue structure and the guests who make up the majority of the business.

When a hotel wishes to hire a revenue manager, it is best to start with a job description. Job descriptions vary among different types of hotels. For example, a limited-service downtown hotel would likely prepare a job description that is different from a similarly sized property located in a suburban area near an interstate highway.

A successful hotel revenue manager typically possesses many of the following skills:

- *Operational skills:* A revenue manager must have had experience in one or more revenue-generating hotel departments. He or she must understand sources of revenues and associated cost structures for each operating department, and must be aware of the interdependencies among departments to meet hotel goals.

- *Analytical skills:* A revenue manager must understand historical, current, and future revenue data. He or she must be able to evaluate hotel booking trends and to project occupancy demands when determining pricing strategies that ensure a balance between room rates and levels of occupancy.

- *Strategic skills:* The revenue manager must understand what is going on in the market and how market forces are likely to affect the hotel. The revenue manager must then apply those assessments to take advantage of favorable market conditions.

- *Organizing skills:* A revenue manager must maintain detailed records of current operations in order to develop a database of information for future application.

- *Communications skills:* A revenue manager must be able to explain revenue processes and decisions with respect to short-term and long-term business projections.

- *Good listening skills:* The revenue manager must be able to listen to revenue management team members, hotel department heads, and other staff. He or she needs to appreciate issues that others raise and suggestions they make.

- *Team-building skills:* A revenue manager must work to build consensus among the revenue management team and hotel department heads and staff. Effective revenue management strategies and tactics depend on the revenue manager's ability to build and maintain trust and confidence in working relationships.

- *Training skills:* Successful revenue management requires ongoing training of all those involved in the process. The revenue manager must be able to train staff at all levels of the organization, including the general manager, the front office manager, sales managers, the food and beverage manager, the reservations manager, the banquet manager, and others actively involved in the program.

In addition, the successful hotel revenue manager has the following personal qualities:

- *Patience:* He or she must make many revenue management decisions three, six, and twelve months or more before the dates they actually affect. A revenue manager must be patient and not change strategies too quickly in reaction to unforeseen changes in hotel or market conditions. The successful revenue manager will also be patient with staff members as they learn how revenue management works and the roles they play in successfully implementing revenue management programs.

- *Creativity:* A revenue manager always looks for new data sources and ways to implement revenue management techniques.

- *Cooperativeness:* The revenue manager must be insightful and able to solicit information from department heads and other staff. The department managers who work most closely with the revenue manager are more likely to understand and support strategies and tactics they help create and implement.

- *Flexibility:* A revenue manager must be willing to change strategies and tactics as demand changes.

Using Revenue Management

The Revenue Meeting

Revenue management is an ongoing process. Whether the property is experiencing high demand or low demand, revenue management has a role and is part of the hotel's overall approach to business. Many hotels find it very useful to have a regular revenue meeting to share important business information and make appropriate revenue management decisions.

A common mistake is to consider revenue management a short-term process. Some managers try to make decisions within a few weeks of the arrival date. In fact, this is the opposite of what should be done. Successful revenue management looks months or years into the future, tracking business trends and guest demand. This is especially true of group-oriented hotels that have the majority of their rooms in their group allocation. These hotels usually book groups well into the future, so their revenue management decisions have impact well into the future as well. While changing rates within a few weeks of arrival in these hotels may improve ADR or RevPAR, the real impact is made when the group is booked and the rates are confirmed.

Because a property's staff members are essential to the success of revenue management efforts, they will want to meet as part of a revenue management team. This team usually includes representatives from key areas of the property. The general manager, all the sales managers and catering managers, and the reservations manager generally attend the revenue meeting as part of the revenue management team. If the hotel has a dedicated revenue manager, that person is also a regular attendee. Other managers may be invited to attend as needed. For example, the hotel controller may attend periodically to report on month-end results or special issues that the revenue meeting should address. The front office manager and food and beverage manager or catering manager may also be invited, as some decisions may need their involvement. Exhibit 5 lists ways that the revenue management team can encourage the entire staff to be involved in revenue management.

The team acts as satellite agents for implementing a revenue management plan. They can help a property determine whether past forecasts were accurate and may alert the revenue manager to significant patterns in group or transient behavior. The team can develop action plans for interdepartmental communication. With accurate forecasts in hand, all departments can prepare for the days ahead:

- Knowing how many guests are in-house can help food and beverage prepare

- Rate changes and adaptations in selling strategy affect the sales department

Exhibit 5   Getting the Staff Involved in Revenue Management

Here are some ideas for getting your staff involved in revenue management:

- Create a sense of competition. Show staff members the various forms and reports, such as TIMS or STAR. Let them know how your competition is doing and encourage them to exceed your biggest competitors.

- Post measurable, specific goals such as budgets or occupancy data. Staff members need to know exactly what is expected of them, so make sure the goals are challenging yet attainable.

- Show staff members how much they each affect the bottom line. Staff members who understand their role in the organization and the impact they have are more likely to support your efforts.

- Provide incentives or recognition for goal attainment. Seek and provide feedback on good work and follow up when goals aren't met. Coach staff members to correct problems.

- Train your staff. Simply telling them what you want them to do isn't enough. Take the time to show them *exactly* what you expect from them. Follow up continuously to make sure standards are being met.

- Occupancy percentages will affect housekeeping and uniformed services

The revenue management team may meet daily, weekly, and monthly. Daily meetings typically last only fifteen or so minutes. During the daily meeting, the team:

- Reviews the three-day forecast and makes sure that previously agreed-upon strategies and tactics are still in place. These strategies and tactics are then communicated to the staffs at the reservations office, central reservations office, and front desk.

- Reviews the previous day's (or weekend's) occupancy, room revenue, ADR, and yield statistic. These numbers are customarily available through night audit reporting. If there are variances from the forecast, they should be briefly discussed so that everyone understands what the differences are.

- Reviews the booking pace for near-term business (usually within three months). The revenue meeting attendees need to know whether the hotel is where it should be in the number of rooms and rooms revenue. The booking pace is compared to the day-to-day increase of business the hotel has planned. If the hotel is below the pace, there is a problem and action steps must be taken to build business. If the pace is above the plan, the hotel may have additional revenue opportunities to consider. Most commercial hotels do not have a lot of transient business on the books months in advance. In these properties, the booking pace is really concerned with group business. However, resorts may have strong transient demand months in advance. For instance, ski resorts and warm-weather resorts may track the booking pace of Christmas season packages sold to transient guests. The group booking pace may be checked weekly or less frequently for business further into the future.

- Reviews old business. In some cases, more research is necessary before a revenue decision can be made. For instance, group history may not be immediately available, the reservation pick-up of a city-wide convention may need to be checked, and a group's flexibility on meeting dates or its exact meeting room requirements may need to be checked before decisions can be made.

- Presents new business. There are two elements to new business: transient and group business. Transient business changes daily, especially within a week of arrival. This is true of all hotels. Because of this, the reservations manager must monitor transient demand closely and should present important changes during the revenue meeting. For instance, a hotel may expect to have 75-percent occupancy one week into the future, and transient demand has already driven occupancy above that forecast. The revenue meeting attendees need to know that, so they can review rates and other strategies. This should not be a reactive process. Plans should be set *in advance* for each day management believes an opportunity may arise to change rates. For example, suppose management believes that when a hotel reaches 90-percent occupancy, it should sell only rack rates. If a hotel is at 88-percent occupancy five days out, the reservations manager and front office manager should receive clear instructions at the revenue meeting about what to do when occupancy reaches 90 percent. The rate change should not have to wait for the revenue meeting the next day. At the same time, if last-minute cancellations take occupancy below 90 percent, the reservations manager should be able to offer selected discounts without having to wait for the next meeting.

- Discusses any last-minute adjustments that need to be made.

- Determines what information must be circulated as part of the interdepartmental communication plan.

- Reviews the 30–60 day outlook and communicates any updates in those forecasts.

- Reviews current channel distribution strategies.

  At weekly meetings, the team might meet for an hour to:

- Review forecasts for 30, 60, 90, and 120 days out.

- Discuss strategies for upcoming critical periods.

At monthly meetings, members of the revenue management team discuss issues that affect the big picture. They might look specifically at slow months and determine what efforts might boost sales, such as additional marketing, appeals to locals, or special sales force deployment. They would also review the ongoing annual forecast. Some teams also use monthly meetings to provide any necessary training on revenue management skills.

All elements of revenue management should be viewed together when making a decision. While the process is potentially complex, a failure to include relevant factors may render revenue management efforts less than completely successful.

Yield statistics should be tracked daily. Tracking yield statistics for an extended period of time can help managers recognize trends. However, to use revenue management properly, management must track yield statistics for *future* days. Future period calculations must be done every business day, depending on how far in advance the hotel books its business. If a hotel is currently at 50-percent yield for a day three weeks away, there may be plenty of time to put strategies in place to increase the projected level of yield. Discounts may be opened to raise occupancy, or closed to raise average rate. If achieving full potential room revenue is not possible (and it usually is not), the front office manager must decide on the best combination of rate and occupancy.

Each sales contract for group business should be reviewed individually. Contracts should be compared with historical trends as well as with budgets. Sales managers are expected to make a group rate recommendation for each group proposal they bring to the meeting. This rate recommendation needs to be compared to the budget and perhaps forecast. If it meets or exceeds the hotel's objectives for the period, there is usually little discussion. However, if the proposed rates fall below expectations, there must be a good reason. A hotel usually has a group sales target or budgeted figure for each month. Each group should be examined to see if it will contribute to meeting the overall profit budget. For example, one group may have a guestroom rate that falls below the budgeted room rate, but its food and beverage functions will bring its total profitability in line with the budget. If current transient demand is strong and the group will produce only minimal revenue, the hotel might consider not booking it. If demand is weak, the hotel may decide to accept the group simply to create revenue by selling rooms that would not otherwise be sold. Using group booking pace analyses will help management determine whether the hotel is on track to reach its target.

Another factor is the actual group booking pattern already on the books. For example, a hotel may have two days between groups that are not busy. Management may solicit a lower-revenue-generating group to fill the gap. The opposite may also occur. A group may desire space during a period when the hotel is close to filling its group rooms goal. Adding the group may move group sales above the hotel's goal. While this appears to be favorable, it may displace higher-rated transient business. If the group wants the hotel, it may need to be quoted a higher-than-normal group rate to help make up for the revenue lost through the displacement of transient guests.

The same type of analysis is required for transient business. For example, due to the discounts the hotel offers, corporate and government business may be assigned the standard category of rooms. As these standard rooms fill, the hotel may have only deluxe rooms left to sell. If demand is not strong, management may decide to sell the deluxe rooms at the standard rack rate to remain competitive. It is best to look at a combination of group and transient business before making firm occupancy and rate decisions.

Since the objective of revenue management is to maximize revenue, tracking business by revenue source helps determine when to allow discounted room rates. As various sources of business are identified, each should be analyzed to understand its impact on total revenue. Quite often, front office managers will authorize discounted room rates for groups if the groups have the potential to generate repeat customers.

Potential High- and Low-Demand Tactics

Hotels need to determine revenue management strategies for both high- and low-demand periods. During times of high demand, the normal technique is to increase room revenue by maximizing average room rate. Transient and group business market segments may each require a unique, specific strategy.

The following are some transient business tactics used during high-demand periods:

- Try to determine the right mix of market segments in order to sell out at the highest possible room rates. This strategy is highly dependent upon accurate sales mix forecasting.

- Monitor new business bookings, and use these changed conditions to reassign room inventory. Certain inventory may be assigned to specific market segments. For example, standard rooms may be assigned to travelers who have reservations with deep rate discounts. As occupancy begins to climb, consider closing out low room rates and charging rack rates only for the remaining inventory of standard rooms. Management should be prepared to re-open lower room rates should demand begin to slack off. Management must closely monitor demand and be flexible in adjusting room rates. It is important to note here that rooms can always be sold for less than their posted rack rate. However, it is unethical to sell them for more than their posted rack rate.

- Consider establishing a minimum number of nights per stay. For example, a resort that always fills to capacity during a national holiday weekend may consider requiring a three-day minimum stay in order to better control occupancy fluctuation.

A number of group business tactics may be appropriate during high-demand periods. When deciding between two or more competing groups, for example, management should select the group that produces the highest total revenue. Management must rely on its experience with groups to develop sound revenue management policies.

Given the focus on total revenue, it may be wise to sell blocks of guestrooms to groups that also book meeting space, food and beverage service, and hospitality suites. A group that books ancillary space and services is likely to spend more time and money in the hotel. This tactic usually requires restricting the access of local patrons to function, meeting, and public spaces; if local patrons book these spaces, potentially more-profitable groups needing such space may be forced to go elsewhere. Another tactic is to offer price-sensitive groups dates when the hotel's occupancy is expected to be low. Most group contracts are written today so that group dates cannot be changed without the group leader's agreement. Exhibit 6 offers some additional high-demand tactics that a hotel can use, while Exhibit 7 lists tactics for excess-demand periods.

The underlying strategy for transient and group business during low-demand periods is to increase revenue by maximizing occupancy. Front office managers may find the following business tactics helpful:

Exhibit 6   High-Demand Tactics

1. **Close or restrict discounts.**
   Analyze discounts and restrict them as necessary to maximize the average rate. You may offer discounts for those who book longer stays, or restrict bookings to shorter stays.

2. **Apply minimum length of stay restrictions carefully.**
   A minimum length of stay restriction can help a property increase room nights. For groups, study the groups' patterns and decide how many days they are likely to add to their stay.

3. **Reduce group room allocations.**
   Communicate with group leaders on a regular basis. Make sure the group actually needs the number of rooms identified in its contract. If not, make adjustments.

4. **Reduce or eliminate 6 P.M. holds.**
   Reduce or eliminate the number of unpaid rooms that are being held until 6 P.M. When demand is high, you will need rooms to be available for sale.

5. **Tighten guarantee and cancellation policies.**
   Tightening guarantee and cancellation policies helps to ensure payment for room nights. Charge payment cards for the first night's stay on the day the reservation is made.

6. **Raise rates to be consistent with competitors.**
   Charge rates consistent with the competition, but limit rate increases to those rates published in the central reservations system and listed in brochures for the period.

7. **Consider a rate raise for packages.**
   If you're already offering a package discount, consider raising the rate for that package.

8. **Apply full price to suites and executive rooms.**
   In a high-demand situation, charge full price for suites and executive rooms.

9. **Select close to arrival dates.**
   By allowing reservations to be taken for a certain date as long as the guest arrives before that date, a property is able to control the volume of check-ins. It is important to track and monitor denials that occur due to this restriction.

10. **Evaluate the benefits of sell-throughs.**
    With a sell-through, the required stay can begin before the date the strategy is applied. This is often used when one day has a peak in occupancy and management does not want the peak to adversely affect reservations on either side of the peak day.

11. **Apply deposits and guarantees to the last night of stay.**
    For longer lengths of stay, make sure the deposits and guarantees apply to the last night of the stay, minimizing early departures.

- Carefully design a flexible rating system that permits sales agents to offer lower rates in certain situations. Such rates should be determined early in the planning process in anticipation of low-demand periods.

- Ensure that all Internet distribution channels have current rates and availability dates. In some cases, it may be beneficial to improve the listing in Internet

Exhibit 7   Excess Demand Tactics

Apply high-demand tactics.

In an excess demand situation, where demand may exceed availability, it is important to consider all restrictions normally employed during a high-demand situation.

Understand the cause of excess demand.

Find out exactly what is causing excess demand. Ask questions such as:

- Is it a one-day or multi-day event?
- What type of event is it? What is the guest make-up?
- What other properties are likely to sell out due to the event?
- Is the demand local or for a larger area?
- Are the potential guests likely to accept a minimum length of stay requirement or other stay restrictions?

Answers to these questions will help determine the best strategy to apply.

Examples:

- If you find out that the demand is due to a two-day event, you may consider a two-night stay requirement to weed out other transients who will stay only one night.
- If you find out that the guests are likely to cancel depending upon the specific circumstances of the event, you can require a 48- or 72-hour cancellation notice. *(For instance, your guests may be participating in a sporting tournament where certain teams may or may not advance to subsequent rounds. They may choose to return home once their participation in the event has ended.)* A more positive approach would be to make rooms available to the fans of the teams who advance to the next round.
- If the event is located close to your property, you may be able to close off discounts for this period.

---

distribution channels by paying for an improved search engine ranking or buying a banner advertisement.

- Strive to accurately project expected market mix. The precision of this projection will influence the eventual yield statistic.

- Closely monitor group bookings and trends in transient business. Do not close off lower rate categories and market segments arbitrarily.

- As low occupancy periods become inevitable, open lower rate categories, solicit price-sensitive groups, and promote corporate, government, and other special discounts. Consider developing new room rate packages and soliciting business from the local community (for example, weekend getaways for the local transient market).

- Consider maintaining high room rates for walk-in guests. Since these guests have not contacted the hotel prior to arrival, they typically present an opportunity to increase the average rate through top-down upselling techniques.

- A non-financial tactic involves upgrading guests to nicer accommodations than they are entitled to by virtue of their room rate. This technique may lead to increased guest satisfaction and enhanced guest loyalty. The implementation of this policy is strictly a management decision and has some risks. For example, the guest may expect the same upgrade on future stays. This may not be possible and the reservations or front desk staff should take extra care to explain that this is a special, one-time upgrade because the hotel appreciates the guest's business.

The preceding list of suggested tactics is not exhaustive, but it is representative of industry strategies. Some additional low-demand tactics are listed in Exhibit 8.

Implementing Revenue Strategies

Once all of this revenue management information has been organized and analyzed, the front office manager must determine what rates the hotel will use on any given day. Certain strategies and tactics come with warnings. Applying restrictions too rigidly can actually discourage business. Managers must constantly keep in mind that the ultimate goal is to meet guests' needs. Any tactic that fails to do so will not produce the desired effect. Too much revenue management can be just as ineffective as no revenue management at all. That being the case, there are four tactics that must be applied cautiously:

1. Hurdle rate
2. Minimum length of stay
3. Close to arrival
4. Sell-through

Hurdle Rate. Rack rates are always left open, whether demand is high or low. Then, the front office manager must set the lowest rate for a given date based upon anticipated demand. Rates that fall below this minimum will not be offered. This is sometimes called the **hurdle rate.** Any room rate that can be sold at a rate above the hurdle rate is acceptable for that date. Any rate below the hurdle rate should not be offered. Some automated revenue management systems will not even display rates below the hurdle rate, thus preventing their use. Hurdle rates can fluctuate from day to day, depending upon the hotel's desired yield and market conditions. The hurdle rate usually reflects the front office manager's pricing strategy to maximize revenue.

Sometimes incentives are offered to front desk and reservations agents for selling rooms above the hurdle rate. For example, if the hurdle rate for a given day is $80 and a reservations agent sells a room for $90, he or she might receive ten promotion points. At the end of the month, all promotion points are totaled. For every 100 points, the reservations agent might receive a monetary reward. Incentives of this kind must be applied carefully, however. Reservations and front desk agents may elect not to offer lower rates that provide fewer incentive points, even though they are above the hurdle rate. While they are building incentive points, they may actually be turning away business.

Incentives may also be provided for longer guest stays. For example, a guest staying three nights may qualify for a lower rate than a guest staying for one night.

Exhibit 8   Low-Demand Tactics

1. **Sell value and benefits.**
   Rather than just quoting rates, make sure guests know you have the right product for them and the best value. Sell the various values and benefits of staying at your property versus others that guests may be considering.

2. **Offer packages.**
   To increase room nights, one tactic is to combine accommodations with a number of desirable products and services into a single package with one price. Mention any additions, renovations, or new amenities. Non-room revenue can be included, for example: free movies, discounted attraction tickets, and shopping coupons.

3. **Keep discount categories open.**
   Discounts are typically directed toward particular markets or are instituted during a particular time or season. During low-demand time it is important to accept discounts to encourage room nights.

4. **Encourage upgrades.**
   Move guests to a better accommodation or class of service to enhance their experience and encourage them to come back to the property again and again.

5. **Offer stay-sensitive price incentives.**
   A stay-sensitive price incentive provides a discount for guests who stay longer. For example, a guest staying three nights might get an additional $5-per-night discount, while a guest staying one night might not.

6. **Remove stay restrictions.**
   Remove any stay restrictions so guests are not limited as to when they can arrive or depart. Guests who can only stay one night will be encouraged to stay as well as the guest who is staying for a week. This will help to maximize occupancy. It is extremely important to communicate this to staff as well as to the central reservations system staff.

7. **Involve your staff.**
   Create an incentive contest to increase occupancy and room nights. Make sure to involve all members of your staff as well as central reservations staff.

8. **Establish relationships with competitors.**
   Having a cordial relationship with competitors can help with referrals and can help to carry out cross-marketing efforts.

9. **Lower rates.**
   There is great value in keeping guests at the property as long as you are at least covering the cost of occupancy. You may want to lower your rate as low as possible. Identify the hurdle rate, which is the lowest rate acceptable at that given moment.

This is a **stay-sensitive hurdle rate.** Reservations agents may receive incentives for booking a three-night stay, even if it is at a lower rate, because the total revenue generated from the reservation will be greater than the revenue of a one- or two-night stay.

Communicating hurdle rates can be done in various ways. Some hotels post the rate strategies in the reservations office and at the front desk where the agent can see them but the guest cannot. Some computer systems, as just stated, automatically display acceptable rates only. Whatever the communication method, it is essential that reservation information be kept current. Revenue strategies can change several times a day, and all front desk and reservations agents must know when a change occurs.

Minimum Length of Stay. A **minimum length of stay** strategy requires that a reservation must be made for at least a specified number of nights before it will be accepted. Examples of this were presented earlier in the chapter. The advantage of this strategy is that it allows the hotel to develop a relatively even occupancy pattern. It is common for resorts to use this approach during peak occupancy periods. Hotels may also use it during special events or high occupancy periods.

The use of minimum length of stay requirements is intended to keep an occupancy peak on one day from reducing occupancy on the days before and after the peak. This strategy should be applied with great care. With a strict minimum stay requirement, profitable guests who don't want to stay for the required time may choose to take their business elsewhere. This strategy should be applied only when it will encourage additional business rather than frustrate guests. To ensure that the strategy is working, managers can check denials and regrets on a daily basis.

Minimum lengths of stay can be applied with discount rates. For example, guests may have to pay rack rates for shorter stays, but be offered discounts for minimum lengths of stay.

Close to Arrival. A **close to arrival** strategy allows reservations to be taken for a certain date as long as the guest arrives before that date. For example, if the front office is expecting a 300-room check-in on a given date, the front office manager may decide that more than 300 rooms checking in may be too much of a strain on the front desk and its related departments. Therefore, guests arriving before that date and staying through the date will be accepted; however, additional arrivals on the peak arrival date will not be accepted. As with a minimum length of stay strategy, the reservations office should track the number of reservation requests denied due to this restriction.

Sell-Through. The **sell-through** strategy works like a minimum length of stay requirement except that the required stay can begin before the date the strategy is applied. For example, if a three-night sell-through is applied on Wednesday, the sell-through applies to arrivals on Monday, Tuesday, and Wednesday. Arrivals on each of those days must stay for three nights in order to be accepted.

A sell-through strategy is especially effective when one day has a peak in occupancy and management does not want the peak to adversely affect reservations on either side of the peak day. Hotels use a sell-through strategy as a technique to overbook the peak day. By properly forecasting no-shows, early departures, and reservation cancellations, management may be able to manage the peak day so that the overbooking is reduced and all guests with reservations are accommodated. Without such a strategy, the days before and after the peak may have reduced occupancy because the peak may block extended stays.

Room availability strategies can be used together with room rate strategies. For example, a three-night minimum length of stay can be used in conjunction with a hurdle rate of $90. If the guest desires only a two-night stay, the rack rate of $110 may be quoted to the guest or the reservation may not be accepted.

Revenue Management Software

Although the individual tasks of revenue management can be performed manually, the most efficient way to handle data and generate yield statistics is through revenue management software. This software can integrate room demand and room price statistics to simulate high-revenue–producing product scenarios.

Revenue management software does not make decisions for managers. It merely provides information and support for managerial decisions. Since revenue management is often quite complex, front office staff will not have the time to process the voluminous data manually. Fortunately, a computer can store, retrieve, and manipulate large amounts of data on a broad range of factors influencing room revenue. Over time, revenue management software can help management create models that show the probable results of decisions. Decision models are based on historical data, forecasts, and booked business.

Industries that have applied computer-based revenue management have observed the following results:

- *Continuous monitoring:* a computerized revenue management system can track and analyze business conditions twenty-four hours a day, seven days a week.

- *Consistency:* software can be programmed to respond to specific changes in the marketplace with specific corporate or local management rules resident in the software.

- *Information availability:* revenue management software can provide improved management information that, in turn, may help managers make better decisions more quickly.

- *Performance tracking:* a computer-based system can analyze sales and revenue transactions occurring within a business period to determine how well revenue management goals are being achieved.

Revenue management software can also generate an assortment of special reports:

- *Market segment report:* provides information regarding guest mix. This information is important for effective forecasting by market segment.

- *Calendar/booking graph:* presents room-night demands and volume of reservations on a daily basis.

- *Future arrival dates status report:* furnishes demand data for each day of the week. This report provides a variety of forecasting information that enables the discovery of occupancy trends by comparative analysis of weekdays. It can be designed to cover several future periods.

- *Single arrival date history report:* indicates the hotel's booking patterns (trends in reservations). This report relates to the booking graph by documenting how a specific day was constructed on the graph.

- *Weekly recap report:* indicates the sell rates for rooms, and the number of rooms authorized and sold in marketing programs with special and/or discounted rates.

- *Room statistics tracking sheet:* tracks no-shows, guaranteed no-shows, walk-ins, and turn-aways. This information can be instrumental in accurate forecasting.

Since management is interested in revenue enhancement, computer-based revenue management has become a popular hospitality industry software application.

Summary

Revenue management offers a more precise measure of room revenue and occupancy performance than other historical benchmarks. Revenue management is effective because it combines occupancy percentage and ADR into a single statistic. Revenue management focuses on maximizing room revenues while taking into account factors influencing business trends. It is an evaluative tool that allows front office management to use potential revenue as the standard against which actual revenue is compared.

Revenue management has proven successful in business environments in which reservations are taken for a perishable commodity. The key to successful revenue management appears to be reliable forecasting, since revenue management is based on conditions of supply and demand.

The key to successful revenue management is to sell the right product to the right customer on the right day for the right price. Major hotel companies have developed unique revenue management systems that provide data for balancing room rates and occupancy levels at the property level.

Between late 2001 and late 2003, one of the most critical issues U.S. hotel managers faced was group attrition. Since 2001, three factors have contributed to elevating the importance of group attrition: group history, online shopping, and business sourcing.

Because revenue management uses a set of demand-forecasting techniques to determine effective prices for a forecasted volume of business, it can be highly successful when applied to the rooms reservation process. Revenue management seeks to maximize revenue by controlling forecast information in three ways: capacity management, discount allocation, and duration control.

Capacity management involves a number of methods of controlling and limiting room supply. Capacity management may be influenced by the availability of rooms at neighboring hotels or competing properties. Group attrition affects capacity management by reducing the number of rooms actually occupied, even though the group committed to renting more rooms. Discounting involves restricting the time period and product mix (rooms) available at reduced prices. The primary objective of discount allocation is to protect enough remaining rooms at a higher rate to satisfy the projected demand for rooms at that rate, while at the same time filling rooms that would otherwise have remained unsold. Duration control places time constraints on accepting reservations in order to protect sufficient space for multi-day requests (representing higher levels of revenue).

The principal computation involved in revenue management is the yield statistic, which is the ratio of actual revenue to potential revenue. Actual revenue is the revenue generated by the number of rooms sold. Potential revenue is the amount of money the hotel would receive if all rooms were sold at full rack rate or potential average rate. The potential average rate is a collective statistic that combines the hotel's potential average single and double rates, multiple occupancy percentage, and rate spread into a single figure. The achievement factor is figured by dividing the hotel's actual average room rate by the potential average rate. Alternatively, some lodging operations prefer the statistic that focuses on revenue per available room (RevPAR).

The purpose of RevPAG is to measure the average revenue captured for each hotel guest. It is most useful in hotels that offer multiple revenue outlets. It can also help managers identify areas in which the hotel is not earning expected revenue. GOPPAR incorporates departmental expenses as well as revenue, resulting in a measure of gross operating profit.

Calculations of different combinations of occupancy and actual average room rate may result in identical room revenue and yields. Management must be careful not to assume that identical yields represent identical operating situations with respect to the number of rooms and number of guests in occupancy.

Dynamic packaging allows for the customization of a travel package to meet a specific guest's needs. It increases the perceived value of a hotel package and tends to be more satisfying for the traveler than static packaging. Hotels find dynamic packaging especially effective during periods of low occupancy.

A revenue management analysis must consider all revenue opportunities affecting potential profitability to determine the economic value of the total business to the hotel. Only after such analysis can management calculate a meaningful room rate.

The revenue manager's duties are among the most important to a hotel's financial success. A revenue manager can often mean the difference between a struggling hotel and a profitable one.

The revenue meeting is the forum that managers in most hotels use to make their important revenue management decisions. The revenue meeting is held as frequently as necessary. Both group and transient business issues are discussed and revenue strategies are implemented.

Revenue management becomes even more complex when discounting is granted on a selective rather than general basis, and when it involves selling rooms for which there may be competing buyers. Hotels frequently offer discounts to guests falling into certain categories (for example, senior citizens and government employees). Hotels must also decide whether to accept or refuse group business at a discounted rate. Understanding the impact of group business on the hotel's operating performance may be an important factor in how revenue management should be applied.

Since the objective of revenue management is to maximize revenue, tracking business by revenue source will also help determine when to allow discounted business. Some hotels may decide to allow specific types of discounted business, such as corporate business, because these markets are responsible for many repeat guests. As the various sources of business are determined, each should be analyzed to understand its impact on total revenue. Quite often, managers will take discounted business if it generates frequent customers, since the long-term impact is very positive.

Implementing yield strategies involves setting hurdle rates for rooms. The hurdle rate is the lowest rate that can be offered at a given time. The hurdle rate is sometimes stay-sensitive, meaning lower rates are available to guests who stay a minimum length of time. Sometimes incentives are used to encourage front desk and reservations agents to sell rooms at rates above the hurdle rate. Since hurdle rates change frequently, efficient communication of rates and changes is critical.

Revenue management often focuses on maximizing yield by controlling rates. Other strategies that focus on length of stay and arrival dates are also effective. These other strategies can be effectively combined with rate control to improve yield.

Endnotes

1. This method does not produce an achievement factor that is as precise as that which can be calculated by revenue management software. This is because the potential average rate is a weighted average of the rack rates of all rooms in the hotel. It is more accurate to use the weighted average of the rack rates of only the rooms that were actually sold (or occupied). Since the sales mix of rooms sold typically changes from day to day, so does the weighted average of those rooms' rack rates. Because it is impractical and cumbersome to manually calculate a weighted average of rack rates for rooms actually sold every day, the potential average rate of *all* rooms is generally used instead. The element of error this introduces may not be significant. Nonetheless, revenue management software is able to calculate the achievement factor more precisely because it can easily and automatically calculate the daily weighted average of the rack rates of rooms sold (or occupied).

2. In theory, and as used in our examples throughout the rest of the chapter, marginal costs are assumed to be constant at a given amount per room. In practice, this is not always the case. For example, certain labor costs may move incrementally; that is, as occupancy goes up, at some point management will have to add another front desk agent to help provide guest service. Also, room attendants are usually paid by the shift, not by the room; if a room attendant cleans twelve rooms one day and fifteen the next, the marginal cost per room will vary slightly. In addition, some properties are able to shut down wings not in use. If adding a guest means opening up an entire wing, the marginal cost of adding that guest will clearly be much higher than the marginal cost of simply adding a single room. For a more detailed discussion of these issues, see Raymond S. Schmidgall, *Hospitality Industry Managerial Accounting*, 7th ed. (Lansing, Mich.: American Hotel & Lodging Educational Institute, 2011), Chapter 6.

3. For a more detailed discussion of breakeven analysis and contribution margin ratios, see Schmidgall, Chapter 7.

4. Group business usually involves the hotel's sales division. The sales division typically *books* the group. It then turns the booking over to the reservations manager, who *blocks* the group. As individual group members contact the hotel, they are *booked* and the size of the block is reduced accordingly.

Key Terms

achievement factor—The percentage of the rack rate that a hotel actually receives; in hotels not using revenue management software, this factor is generally approximated by dividing the actual average room rate by the potential average rate.

booking lead time—A measurement of how far in advance bookings are made.

breakeven analysis—An analysis of the relationships among costs, revenue, and sales volume, allowing one to determine the revenue required to cover all costs; also called cost-volume-profit analysis.

close to arrival—A yield management availability strategy that allows reservations to be taken for a certain date as long as the guest arrives before that date; for example, a hotel may accept a reservation for a Wednesday night if the guest's actual stay begins on Tuesday night.

contribution margin—Sales less cost of sales for either an entire operating department or for a given product; represents the amount of sales revenue that is contributed toward fixed costs and/or profits.

cost per occupied room—The variable or added cost of selling a product that is incurred only if the room is sold; also called marginal cost.

discount grid—A chart indicating the occupancy percentage necessary to achieve equivalent net revenue, given different discount levels.

displacement—The turning away of transient guests for lack of rooms due to the acceptance of group business; also called non-group displacement.

dynamic packaging—The customization of a travel package according to a specific guest's needs. Hotels find dynamic packaging especially effective during expected periods of low occupancy.

equivalent occupancy—Given a contemplated or actual change in the average room rate, equivalent occupancy is the occupancy percentage required to produce the same net revenue as was produced by the old price and occupancy percentage.

fair market share—A comparison of a hotel's ADR and occupancy percentage, or RevPAR, against its competition to determine whether it is getting its share of business in the market.

fixed costs—Costs that remain constant in the short run even though sales volume varies.

forecast—A projection of estimated business volume.

GOPPAR—A revenue measurement that focuses on gross operating profit per available room.

group attrition—Under-consumption of, or failure to achieve, a committed number of group room nights.

group booking pace—The rate at which group business is being booked.

hurdle rate—In the context of revenue management, the lowest acceptable room rate for a given date.

marginal costs—The variable or added costs of selling a product, incurred only if the room is sold; also called cost per occupied room.

minimum length of stay—A revenue management availability strategy requiring that a reservation must be for at least a specified number of nights in order to be accepted.

potential average rate—A collective statistic that effectively combines the potential average single and double rates, multiple occupancy percentage, and rate spread to produce the average rate that would be achieved if all rooms were sold at their full rack rates.

rate potential percentage—The percentage of the rack rate that a hotel actually receives, computed by dividing the actual average room rate by the potential average rate; also called the achievement factor.

rate spread—The mathematical difference between the hotel's potential average single rate and potential average double rate.

revenue management—A technique based on supply and demand used to maximize revenues by lowering prices to increase sales during periods of low demand and raising prices during periods of high demand to increase revenue.

RevPAG—A revenue measurement that focuses on revenue earned per available guest.

RevPAR—A revenue measurement that focuses on revenue per available room.

sell-through—A revenue management availability strategy that works like a minimum length of stay requirement, except that the length of the required stay can begin before the date the strategy is applied.

stay-sensitive hurdle rate—In the context of revenue management, a hurdle rate (or minimum acceptable room rate) that varies with the length of the guest reservation.

wash factor—The deletion of unnecessary group rooms from a group block.

weighted average contribution margin ratio—In a multiple product situation, an average contribution margin for all operated departments that is weighted to reflect the relative contribution of each department to the establishment's ability to pay fixed costs and generate profits.

yield statistic—The ratio of actual rooms revenue to potential rooms revenue.

? Review Questions

1. What is the goal of revenue management?

2. Why is communication between the various revenue centers important to the successful implementation of revenue management?

3. What are the importance and limitations of using historical data when planning revenue management strategies?

4. What might be the impact of closing discount rates when business is down?

5. What role does booking pace play in revenue management?

6. What is a wash factor? How does it affect revenue management?

7. Why is transient displacement analysis so important in determining whether to accept a group reservation?

8. What is the difference between marginal cost and fixed cost?

9. What does the equivalent occupancy equation consider that the identical yield equation does not? Why is the difference significant? What important question does neither equation address?

10. Should a group reservation be accepted or rejected solely on the basis of its effect on room revenue? Why or why not?

11. What are several tactics that may be appropriate to take when room demand is low? When room demand is high?

12. What is the hurdle rate? How is it used in revenue management? What availability strategies are used as part of revenue management?

Internet Sites

For more information, visit the following Internet sites. Remember that Internet addresses can change without notice. If the site is no longer there, you can use a search engine to look for additional sites.

Smith Travel Research
www.strglobal.com

TravelCLICK
www.travelclick.net

TIMS Reports
www.timsreports.com

Case Study

Reviving Revenue Management

The Hearthstone Suites Hotel is an all-suite property with 250 rooms. A new property, the Fairmont Hotel, opened near Hearthstone Suites three months ago. Several months before the opening of the Fairmont, Laurie, the general manager at the Hearthstone Suites, pushed all her front office and reservations staff to sell as many rooms as possible. As she put it, "Whatever it takes, to stay competitive." The director of sales, Pat, supported the plan from day one, but Jodie, the front office manager, had misgivings from the start. Jodie was concerned that the revenue management program managers implemented a year and a half earlier would be totally useless because of the push for occupancy.

The most recent profit and loss statement indicates that Jodie's fears were realized. Though the occupancy is at budget year-to-date, the average daily rate (ADR) is down by $6. Also, the mix of commercial business is lower than planned—40 percent of guest mix instead of 50 percent. Also, the SMERF segment is higher than it should be—15 percent of guest mix instead of 5 percent. SMERF is a catch-all term for group business at substantially low rates—Social, Military, Educational, Religious, and Fraternal groups.

Jodie, Pat, and Laurie are in a meeting to discuss these latest figures. Laurie, the general manager, opens the meeting by saying, "Well, we've weathered the storm caused by the opening of the Fairmont. We managed to hold on to our occupancy level. But it looks like we have some regrouping to do. I trust you've each received the profit and loss statement I sent you. I'm concerned about the fact that we've lost so much of our share of the commercial business. And our ADR is much too low."

"I agree," says Jodie, "but I was just following orders when I had my staff focus on selling rooms. Our good occupancy rate has come at the cost of both revenue management and revenue. It will take quite a while to regain our former position."

"We all sat down and agreed months before the Fairmont opened that we should do our best to keep our occupancy numbers, and that's what we've done," says Pat. "You and your staff have worked hard and are to be commended, Jodie."

"Hear, hear," says Laurie, "and now we have some time to re-evaluate our position and start targeting that corporate segment again."

"I just hope it's not too late to win it back from Fairmont," sighs Jodie.

Later that day, Jodie gathers her front desk and reservations team to brief them about re-implementing the revenue management program. "I know you've all been putting a lot of extra effort into filling rooms over the past several months. I'm proud of you; the whole management team is. We've met our occupancy goals. The down side is that our guest mix is off. We've lost some of our commercial segment and gained too much of the SMERF segment. And our ADR is down a full $6. It's time we reviewed the revenue management program we use."

"The revenue what?" blurts Jack, a fairly new front desk agent. "You never told us about that."

"Now hold on a minute," counters Jodie, "some of you are so new that you haven't been fully trained in this program, but I know I've talked about it to some extent with all of you."

"Sure, you told me a little about it," offers Tracey, a reservationist. "I never have been comfortable with it, to tell the truth. One day I quote a guest $85 and he books a suite. A month later he calls back to book another and I quote $105. Then the guest asks why the rate went up—what am I supposed to say?"

"Well, there are things you can tell guests who ask that, but we're not going to get into that right now," says Jodie.

Bill, the most experienced front desk agent, speaks up. "I've been using the revenue management program all along, just like you showed me." He turns to his co-workers. "It's really not unreasonable when you look at the big picture of the hotel's revenue. I just tell inquisitive callers that our rates depend on their arrival dates. Some periods are busier for us than others, and that affects rates."

"Bill, it's good to hear that you continued using the revenue management program," Jodie says. "We can get into more detail on applying it in formal training. We've had a lot of changes since the push for volume began—changes in personnel, and even changes in the revenue management program itself. It's clearly time I evaluated the training needs in our department in the area of revenue management program execution. You can be confident, Tracey—and all of you—when you quote rates that they are competitive for what we offer. That reminds me," and here Jodie pauses a moment, "how many of you have actually been inside some of our suites?"

Three of the six employees raise their hands. "How many have seen rooms at the Fairmont or at any of our other competitors?" continues Jodie. Only Bill raises his hand. "So almost none of you have seen the difference between our suites and the single rooms other properties are offering?"

"There hasn't been time to look at what we're selling," protests Jack.

"Much less to look at what anyone else is selling," adds Linda, another reservationist.

"That's what I was afraid of," says Jodie. "In the next two weeks or so, as I'm re-evaluating training needs, I'm going to have each of you spend time gaining an appreciation of the value we offer—especially in comparison with the value of Fairmont's offerings and those of our other competition."

"Are we still going to be offering the $84 supersaver rate?" asks Tracey. "We've had a lot of repeat business because of that rate."

"I've had callers tell me we're the best deal in town," Linda says.

But Bill cautions, "We won't need to use it next week. The Home Builders convention is in and every room in town will be booked. We can afford to charge more next week."

"That's good thinking, Bill," says Jodie. "I know it's nice to be popular with guests and it's easy to use that discount whenever a potential guest shies away from a quoted rate, but the supersaver rate is intended to be used only as a last resort or in other special cases. We shouldn't be offering it too frequently. We also need to adjust our selling strategies when special events come along like this convention."

"Speaking of selling strategies, when are we going to get to go through that training module on selling skills you were talking about?" inquires Linda. "I've heard about it but I haven't gone through it yet."

Discussion Questions

1. How can the management team address the problem of low ADR?

2. What are some ways Jodie could make employees like Jack and Tracey more familiar and comfortable with the revenue management program?

3. What selling skills should training focus on for the Hearthstone Suites Hotel staff?

4. How can the Hearthstone Suites Hotel regain some of the commercial business it has lost?

Case Number: 370CF

This case was developed in cooperation with Lisa Richards of Hospitality Softnet, Inc., a marketing resources and support company (Sixty State Street, Suite 700, Boston, Massachusetts 02109; tel. 617-854-6554).

Chapter 14 Outline

Competencies

1. Describe the advantages and disadvantages of internal and external recruiting methods. (pp. 529–535)

2. Summarize the selection process, including how managers use selection tools, evaluate applicants, and interview applicants. (pp. 535–548)

3. Identify the steps in effective hiring and orientation. (pp. 548–550)

4. Explain the four-step training method. (pp. 551–563)

5. Identify techniques that front office managers can use to schedule and motivate staff members. (pp. 563–570)

14

Managing Human Resources

FRONT OFFICE MANAGERS face much greater challenges than managers of a generation ago. Labor management has always been a significant issue, but the recent past shows that the future is sure to put even more emphasis on this area. Front office managers must be skilled at handling a diverse work force made up of people of varying ages, ethnic backgrounds, cultures, and values. Just as the nature of the work force will change, so will management techniques and strategies. This chapter focuses on some of the basic concepts that front office managers need to know to effectively manage and develop competent staff.

Recruiting

Employee **recruitment** is the process of seeking and screening qualified applicants to fill open positions. The process involves announcing or advertising job vacancies through proper sources, and interviewing and evaluating applicants to determine the best person for the job.

The human resources division often assists the front office manager in finding and hiring qualified individuals. Not all hotels, however, have a human resources division. When they don't, the front office manager may have to seek out qualified recruitment sources, place advertisements, post job openings internally, conduct initial interviews, contact applicants' references, and perform other related tasks. Even when the hotel has a human resources division, it is the front office manager's responsibility to identify the skills and qualities required in the front office job positions and to communicate this information to the human resources division to ensure that it qualifies candidates properly. This generally is done with a job description that identifies the skills, personal qualities, and responsibilities required of the employee filling the position. Regardless of how prospects are identified, the front office manager should personally interview leading candidates for front office positions.

Internal Recruiting

Internal recruiting involves the transfer or promotion of current employees. Through this form of recruiting, managers have access to applicants who are familiar with the hotel (and possibly the front office) and have proven skills. Internal recruiting may also boost employee morale and productivity. Employees tend to show loyalty to hotels that provide opportunities to increase their skills, knowledge, status, and income. Many industry leaders, including company presidents,

Exhibit 1   Advantages and Disadvantages of Internal Recruiting

---

Advantages

- Improves the morale of the promoted employee.
- Improves the morale of other employees who see future opportunities for themselves.
- Managers can better assess the abilities of internal recruits, since their performances have been observed over time.
- Internal recruiting for supervisory and management positions results in a succession of promotions (one to fill each vacated job), which reinforces the "internal career ladder."
- The cost of internal recruitment is lower than the cost of external recruitment.

Disadvantages

- Internal recruiting promotes "inbreeding" and often discourages innovative thinking.
- Internal recruiting can cause morale problems among those employees who were skipped over for promotion.
- Internal recruiting can have political overtones; some employees attribute internal promotions to friendships with managers and supervisors.
- Filling a gap in one department through internal recruiting may create an even more critical gap in another department.

---

vice presidents, and general managers, have risen through the ranks as a result of internal recruiting. Exhibit 1 summarizes the advantages and disadvantages of internal recruiting.

Internal recruiting includes cross-training, succession planning, posting job openings, paying for performance, and maintaining a call-back list.

Cross-Training. Whenever possible, employees should be trained to perform the duties of more than one job. **Cross-training** makes it easier for the front office manager to develop comprehensive employee schedules that include planned employee vacations and absences. Employees find cross-training beneficial since it diversifies their skills, gives them variety, and makes them more valuable to the hotel. Cross-training may also lead to a wider range of promotion opportunities. Registration, cashiering, and reservations employees were cross-trained when front office systems were introduced many years ago. In small properties, reservations, front desk, and telephone duties are often combined into one job. One major hotel company cross-trains front desk agents and bell attendants. In this case, the person who checks the guest in is also the person who transports the guest's bags and escorts the guest to the room. There may be some disadvantages to cross-training, but the overall effects are very positive.

Succession Planning. In succession planning, the front office manager identifies a key position and targets a particular employee to eventually fill that position.

Front office management identifies the employee's training needs and ensures that those needs are met. The manager creates a staffing plan that identifies training dates and times, the trainer or trainers, and the projected date the employee will be qualified to assume the job.

Posting Job Openings. When the front office posts job openings internally, it reaches a known applicant pool. Employees from other departments may want to transfer to the front office, or current front office employees may want to advance within their own department. Whatever the case, front office management must make sure that the employee has the skills for the transfer or promotion, as well as a good work record.

The front office manager should post each available position as soon as it is officially open. The manager can also discuss the openings at department meetings. Some hotel companies open each position to people on staff before it is announced to outside applicants. Job postings are placed in a prominent location, such as the employee lounge. Some hotel properties also find it useful to post entry-level positions. When employees know about these positions, they often encourage qualified friends or acquaintances to apply.

Postings should be comprehensive; they should describe jobs fully and specify minimum qualifications, required skills, and level of pay. The posting should tell applicants whether the job is for a day, night, or weekend shift. In some hotels, employees cannot apply for openings until they have held their current positions for a certain length of time. When this is the case, this restriction should be clearly stated on the job posting.

Paying for Performance. Employees are more likely to be motivated to excel when they know the hotel has a wage program that rewards hard work and productivity. As employees gain more experience and proficiency, they should be paid accordingly. Giving all employees an identical wage increase, regardless of performance, may be discouraging to those employees who exceed expectations.

Maintaining a Call-Back List. While recruiting appears to be an infrequent event, in reality it is ongoing. To assist future staffing efforts, front office management can develop and maintain a call-back list of employees and previous applicants with special skills and interests. Some hotels also maintain a *back-up list,* or waiting list, of former employees who completed their employment in good standing. The front office may hire such individuals as supplemental labor during a peak business period or employee shortage.

External Recruiting

Front office managers may also recruit individuals from outside the hotel to fill open positions. New employees can contribute innovative ideas, unique perspectives, and ideas for creative ways of doing things. **External recruiting** may involve advertising, networking, temporary employment agencies, and employee referral programs. Federal, state, and local government tax credit programs may also provide incentives for management to recruit individuals from designated groups, such as workers with disabilities. Exhibit 2 summarizes the advantages and disadvantages of external recruiting.

Exhibit 2   Advantages and Disadvantages of External Recruiting

Advantages

- External recruiting brings new blood and new ideas into the company.
- Recruits from the outside can often provide not only new ideas but news about how and what competitors are doing.
- External recruits can provide a fresh look at your company, which sometimes reinforces the reasons current employees work for you. Consider, for example, the value of an external recruit saying such things as, "You keep your kitchen much cleaner than they do at XYZ company where I used to work," or "The helpful attitude of employees here certainly makes this a more pleasant place to work than my old job."
- External recruiting sometimes avoids many of the political problems associated with internal recruiting.
- External recruiting serves as a form of advertising for the company (newspaper ads, posters, bulletin board notices, and so on remind the public of your products and services).

Disadvantages

- It is more difficult to find a good fit with the company's culture and management philosophy when recruiting externally.
- Internal morale problems can develop if current employees feel that they have no opportunity to move up in the organization.
- It takes longer to orient external recruits than it does internal recruits.
- External recruiting can lower productivity over the short run because external recruits usually cannot produce as quickly or effectively as internal recruits.
- When employees believe that they could have done the job as well as the external recruit who was hired, political problems and personality conflicts can result.

Advertising. Advertising may involve placing ads in newspapers and on community bulletin boards, hotel signs, the hotel's website, and various Internet job listings. Advertising should indicate the job's requirements, compensation, and benefits, as well as the hotel's work environment or culture. Before placing any advertisements, it is a good idea to review other ads currently appearing in the media outlets under consideration. Identifying the ads that are most appealing and interesting may help managers design their own effective ads.

The hotel can post job openings internally on bulletin boards and in office work stations, or mention them at department meetings. Hotel staff may also post job openings on the hotel's public website (under the heading "Careers" or "Job Openings") and on an employee Intranet. The hotel usually provides various ways to review and apply for open positions, either in writing or online. Hotel staff can review applications manually, review applications online, or apply web-based technology to automatically screen online applications. Online software programs compare an applicant's responses on a web form with a predetermined set of criteria that hotel staff has indicated are minimum job requirements. Screening software can match the staff's criteria to the applicant's responses to produce a preliminary evaluation of the applicant's qualifications and job fitness. Hotel personnel can then review satisfactory applicants and, as appropriate, can contact qualified applicants for in-person interviews. Automated job screening can be an effective, streamlined method of recruiting and applicant qualification as long as the hotel adequately defines proper job descriptions, skill requirements, and applicant screening procedures.

Media outlets. Most newspapers devote sections to local job openings. They may also publish special job-related supplements. Other local publications may specialize in job openings. Community bulletin boards may be located in churches, community centers, shopping malls, and other public places. Bulletin boards usually have space where notices can be posted for a limited time. Some hotels have successfully advertised on hotel signs or hotel vehicles; such ads are very brief, consisting mainly of a simple listing of job opportunities and a contact telephone number or web address. For certain positions, the Internet has become a powerful recruiting tool. Many cities offer electronic job boards on community websites; these often list mainly entry-level positions. Other websites, like hoteljobs.com, monster.com, and hotjobs.com, are geared more for supervisory and managerial positions.

In a reverse use of advertising, some hotel managers look at community bulletin boards that focus on specific types of job advertising and then contact some of the individuals offering their services. For example, individuals may advertise their house-cleaning services on grocery store, church, and community center bulletin boards; these advertisers may be just the right people to contact when a manager wishes to fill positions in the hotel's housekeeping department.

Advertising can be expensive, so it is important to identify which media will generate the most interest among qualified candidates. It is common to use several advertising channels simultaneously. If the hotel has a human resources division, its staff likely knows how to select the most effective advertising media.

Networking. Networking involves developing personal contacts with friends, acquaintances, colleagues, business associates, educators, and school counselors. These personal contacts can often lead to employment referrals. Companies that provide services or supplies to the hotel may also share leads on possible jobs or job candidates. Other network sources may include members of trade or community associations. If a hotel is part of a chain, the front office manager can network with managers of other properties in the area. By working together, they make career advancement better for all employees, and make employment with the chain more desirable.

Temporary Employment Agencies. These agencies can provide staff to fill a wide range of positions. Temporary employee agencies often train a pool of employees in specific employment areas. Such agencies operate for profit and therefore charge a higher hourly rate for temporary employees than the rate generally paid to permanent hourly employees. These higher costs are usually offset in other ways. For example, temporary employment agencies may:

- Reduce overtime, recruitment, and hiring expenses

- Provide already screened and trained employees

- Be able to supply complete work crews

There are some disadvantages to using temporary employees, however. Temporary employees will lack training in property-specific procedures. In addition, they will need time to become acquainted with the hotel layout, amenities, facilities, and departmental hours of operation. As a result, temporary workers may be less productive than the front office's own staff, and may require more supervision. Temporary workers are generally considered short-term additions to the permanent work force.

Employee Referral Programs. Some front offices adopt employee referral programs that encourage employees to recommend friends and acquaintances for open positions. An employee referral program usually rewards current employees who refer qualified staff members to the company. The program works best when front office management establishes the size of the referring employee's reward at the outset. The program must also specify which criteria will be applied and how referrals will be credited to the proper source. Usually, the referred employee must work for a specified trial period before the employee who made the referral can claim the reward. This period often ranges from 90 days to 180 days.

Tax Credits. Some government programs, such as the federal Targeted Jobs Tax Credits Program, provide tax incentives to private employers who hire individuals from specified human resource categories. Anyone hired under a tax credit program *must* be certified as a member of a targeted category by a local office of the state employment commission *before* being hired. To claim the targeted job tax credit, the hotel must certify that the new employee is not a relative or dependent of the property's owner, and that he or she has not worked for the hotel before.

Workers with Disabilities. Some positions in the front office are well-suited to employees with physical handicaps or disabilities. For example, a wheelchair user may be qualified to work as a telephone operator or reservations agent, since such jobs usually do not require standing or a great deal of moving within a work area. Workers with disabilities are usually highly motivated and may perceive their work as important evidence of their ability, skill, and independence.

In general, applicants with disabilities can be recruited through local government job training agencies or through schools that provide training for people with disabilities. Some communities may also offer tax incentives to companies that employ persons with disabilities. Before hiring such individuals, the front office manager must ensure that work areas are compatible with the applicants' needs. A major focus of the Americans with Disabilities Act is to make it easier for people with physical and mental disabilities to find jobs and to advance within their careers. Hotels must take appropriate steps to comply with this legislation, particularly in terms of employment practices and barrier-free design. Since the traditional labor market is shrinking, people with disabilities are becoming an important and growing source of new employees. Job descriptions and specifications must clearly identify any restrictions or requirements that may exclude an employee covered by the ADA. For example, an employee in a wheelchair would not qualify as a bell attendant because of the mobility and heavy lifting requirements of the position.

Selecting

Selecting the right person for a front office position should always involve the front office manager. Depending on the hotel's policy, the front office manager may directly hire an applicant or may be limited to forwarding a hiring recommendation to top management.

Applicants with practical skills, knowledge, and aptitude are likely to become valuable front office employees. Good language, mathematical, and keyboard (typing) skills are frequently required in front office work. Good language skills help employees communicate with guests and other employees; mathematical ability will help employees understand front office accounting and transaction processing; keyboard skills are especially useful for recordkeeping and using a computer.

Since front office work involves a high degree of guest contact, managers usually seek certain personality traits in applicants. These traits include congeniality, flexibility, professional attitude, self-motivation, and a well-groomed appearance. Evaluating applicants in terms of personal qualities is highly subjective. An effective front office selection process usually focuses on a set of skills, attitudes, and personal qualities. In addition, since front office staff members have so much contact with guests, they should reflect the quality of the hotel during that contact. It does not matter whether the contact is by telephone, by letter, or face to face. Guests will form an image of the hotel through employee contact. One hotel company interviews prospective reservations agents by asking a few questions over the telephone. This allows the interviewer to hear the candidate's voice and evaluate how the candidate presents himself or herself over the phone. Proper selection of employees will help ensure that the hotel's image and values are upheld in all guest contacts.

Selection Tools

Job descriptions and **job specifications** are important selection tools. A job description lists all the tasks and related information that make up a work position. A job description may also outline reporting relationships, responsibilities, working conditions, equipment and material used, and other information specific to the position. Job descriptions are especially helpful in recruiting and selecting employees, since they clearly state the duties required of a particular job. Job descriptions may also explain how a work position relates to other work positions in the department.

Although each job is unique, some general statements can apply to work requirements in the front office. A job specification usually lists and describes the personal qualities, skills, traits, educational background, and experience a person needs to successfully perform the tasks outlined by a job description. To develop job specifications, managers may draw on the knowledge of other front office staff and any written material related to the job. For example, managers might describe an employee as demonstrating a professional attitude by reporting to work on time. A professional attitude might further be marked by sensitivity to guests, a sense of humor, congeniality, and good listening habits. A flexible employee might be defined as a team player who is willing to work different positions or shifts as necessary. Job specifications may include terminology that relates to the specific needs of the front office. For example, appropriate dress in a resort might mean casual dress, while it is likely to mean business attire in a commercial hotel. Descriptions of personal qualities must be relevant to each individual property's needs.

Evaluating Applicants

Generally, front office managers evaluate job applicants by reviewing completed job application forms, checking applicant references, and interviewing selected applicants. A hotel with a human resources division may screen applicants on the basis of front office job descriptions and job specifications. In hotels without a human resources division, the front office manager may be responsible for all aspects of screening and evaluating applicants. A job application form should be easy to complete and should require applicants to provide information that helps determine their suitability for the job. Exhibit 3 presents a sample job application form.

Managers should check references to verify an applicant's identity and claims about previous work experiences and skills. Managers should be aware that former employers are often reluctant to provide any information other than the applicant's past job title, dates of employment, and salary. Former employers rarely reveal whether they would rehire the person. Past employer comments, especially if negative, increase the employer's potential liability for charges of libel, slander, or defamation of character brought by the former employee. Front office managers must be familiar with their own property's policy on handling calls regarding the work record of current or past employees. Familiarity with such policy positions will allow managers to better understand the comments of job candidates' previous employers.

It may also be hotel policy to have a police record check and drug test conducted on all job applicants. This may be especially critical for certain positions, such as front office cashier, hotel shuttle van driver, or positions involving close contact with guests or their children. A police background check may help uncover a record of unsafe driving, drug abuse, criminal activity, or fraudulent behavior. A preliminary drug test, administered as a requirement for employment consideration, is intended to detect current or recent usage of unsafe or illicit drugs. As a precautionary note, drug testing should not always be considered conclusive. It may take more than one test before a potential employee is cleared and approved for hiring consideration. In addition, any drug-related policy the hotel adopts must apply to all job applicants, not just some.

Questions asked on a job application form must be carefully structured, since federal, state, and local laws prohibit discriminatory hiring practices. Exhibit 4 lists employment questions that may be discriminatory, and suggests ways to avoid discrimination. Managers may also find this guide helpful when developing interview questions. Since laws, and their interpretation, vary from state to state, a qualified

Exhibit 3   Sample Job Application Form

APPLICATION FOR EMPLOYMENT

GENERAL DATA AND AVAILABILITY

Name _____   Social Security # _____ / ___ / _____
      Last   First   Middle Initial

Address _____   Phone _____
       Street   City   State   Zip

If you are applying for a position which requires you drive, do you have a current Driver's License? Yes ☐ No ☐
If you answered yes, please provide:
                    License Number _____   Class _____

CITIZENSHIP: If you are not a citizen of the United States of America, do you have a permanent resident visa card, I-94
Form or letter from the Immigration Service indicating that you are legally permitted to work in this country?
        Yes ☐   No ☐   If hired, are you able to show proof of status?   Yes ☐   No ☐

If you are under 21 years of age: List Age_____   Date of Birth _____

For employment verification, have you used any other name on a previous job? Yes ☐ No ☐

    List names _____

Positions Desired: 1st Choice_____   2nd Choice_____

Wage or Salary Desired:_____ per_____   Date available to start work_____

For what job status are you applying? Full Time ☐   Part Time ☐ _____ hours per week . Summer ☐

        School Term ☐   Other ☐ Explain:_____

The following conditions may be required at some time in a job assignment. If required would you be willing to work:

A. Shift work? Yes ☐ No ☐   B. Rotational work schedule? Yes ☐ No ☐

C. Work schedule other than Monday through Friday? Yes ☐ No ☐   D. Overtime work ? Yes ☐ No ☐

List any scheduling problems or limitations _____

Is your transportation reliable to meet any work schedule requirement any day of the week? Yes ☐ No ☐

Have you ever been employed at this hotel before? Yes ☐ No ☐ When _____

    Reason for leaving_____ Name of Supervisor _____

How did you happen to apply? ☐ Referred by_____   ☐ Ad in paper_____
                                                                Which paper
                        ☐ Agency _____   ☐ Sign ☐ Passing by

                        ☐ Friend/Current Employee _____
                                                        Name
Do you have any relatives working here? _____
                                    Names
Police Conviction Record: Have you ever been convicted of a felony? Yes ☐ No ☐ If yes, please briefly describe
the circumstances of your conviction, indicating the nature and place of the offense and the disposition of the case. A
felony conviction does not necessarily bar you from employment since this will be looked upon as only one of the factors
considered in the employment decision.
_____

_____

                            Page 1

(continued)

Exhibit 3 *(continued)*

MILITARY EXPERIENCE

Have you ever served in the United States Armed Forces? Yes ☐ No ☐ If so, describe any special training or skills acquired during your service which may be helpful on the job? _____

EDUCATIONAL BACKGROUND

Type of School	Name & Address of School	Years Completed	Graduated	Major Field of Study
High School		9, 10, 11, 12	Yes ☐ No ☐	
College		1, 2, 3, 4	Yes ☐ No ☐	
Other		1, 2, 3, 4	Yes ☐ No ☐	

EMPLOYMENT HISTORY

List the most recent employer first, then follow with the next most recent. We will check all references.

Name and Address of Previous Employer	Dates Worked From Mo Yr — To Mo Yr	Position	Supervisor	Hours Worked Per Week	Rate of Pay
Company					
Address		If currently employed, may we contact this employer for a reference? Yes No			
City State	Why did you leave or are interested in leaving this employer?_____				
Phone					

Name and Address of Next Employer	Dates Worked From Mo Yr — To Mo Yr	Position	Supervisor	Hours Worked Per Week	Rate of Pay
Company					
Address					
City State	Why did you leave this employer?_____				
Phone					

Include any additional employment history on another sheet of paper.

SPECIAL SKILLS

Typing/Word Processing_____ Dictation/Shorthand_____ Telephone_____ Computers_____
Foreign Languages_____ Mechanical_____
                    List   List

PERSONAL REFERENCE
The following person knows me and would be able to give a personal reference:

_____
Name   Address   City   State   Zip   Telephone

APPLICANT, PLEASE READ AND SIGN

I certify that the information contained in this application is correct to the best of my knowledge and understand that falsification of this information is grounds for refusal to hire or, if hired, dismissal. I authorize any of the persons or organizations referenced in this application to give you any and all information concerning my previous employment, education, or any other information they might have, personal or otherwise, with regard to any of the subjects covered by this application and release all such parties from all liability for damage that may result from furnishing such information to you. I authorize you to request and receive such information. I understand this hotel does not discriminate in hiring or employment on the basis of race, color, religious creed, national origin, sex, age, handicap or veteran status.

Signed:_____   Date:_____

Page 2

Courtesy of Renaissance Hotels & Resorts.

Exhibit 4   Pre-Employment Inquiry Guide

SUBJECT	LAWFUL PRE-EMPLOYMENT INQUIRIES	UNLAWFUL PRE-EMPLOYMENT INQUIRIES
NAME:	Applicant's full name. Have you ever worked for this company under a different name? Is any additional information relative to a different name necessary to check work record? If yes, explain.	Original name of an applicant whose name has been changed by court order or otherwise. Applicant's maiden name.
ADDRESS OR DURATION OF RESIDENCE:	How long a resident of this state or city?	
BIRTHPLACE:		Birthplace of applicant. Birthplace of applicant's parents, spouse or other close relatives. Requirement that applicant submit birth certificate, naturalization or baptismal record.
AGE:	*Are you 18 years old or older?	How old are you? What is your date of birth?
RELIGION OR CREED:		Inquiry into an applicant's religious denomination, religious affiliations, church, parish, pastor, or religious holidays observed. An applicant may not be told "This is a Catholic (Protestant or Jewish) organization."
RACE OR COLOR:		Complexion or color of skin.
PHOTOGRAPH:		Requirement that an applicant for employment affix a photograph to an employment application form. Request an applicant, at his or her option, to submit a photograph. Requirement for photograph after interview but before hiring.
HEIGHT:		Inquiry regarding applicant's height.
WEIGHT:		Inquiry regarding applicant's weight.
MARITAL STATUS:		Requirement that an applicant provide any information regarding marital status or children. Are you single or married? Do you have any children? Is your spouse employed? What is your spouse's name?
SEX:		Mr., Miss, Mrs., or an inquiry regarding sex. Inquiry as to the ability to reproduce or advocacy of any form of birth control.
CITIZENSHIP:	Are you a citizen of the United States? If not a citizen of the United States, does applicant intend to become a citizen of the United States? If you are not a United States citizen, have you the legal right to remain permanently in the United States? Do you intend to remain permanently in the United States?	Of what country are you a citizen? Whether an applicant is naturalized or a native-born citizen; the date when the applicant acquired citizenship. Requirement that an applicant produce naturalization papers or first papers. Whether applicant's parents or spouse are naturalized or native born citizens of the United States; the date when such parent or spouse acquired citizenship.
NATIONAL ORIGIN:	Inquiry into languages applicant speaks and writes fluently.	Inquiry into applicant's (a) lineage; (b) ancestry; (c) national origin; (d) descent; (e) parentage, or nationality. Nationality of applicant's parents or spouse. What is your mother tongue? Inquiry into how applicant acquired ability to read, write, or speak a foreign language.
EDUCATION:	Inquiry into the academic vocational or professional education of an applicant and the public and private schools attended.	
EXPERIENCE:	Inquiry into work experience. Inquiry into countries applicant has visited.	
ARRESTS:	Have you ever been convicted of a crime? If so, when, where, and nature of offense? Are there any felony charges pending against you?	Inquiry regarding arrests.
RELATIVES:	Name of applicant's relatives, other than a spouse, already employed by this company.	Address of any relative of applicant, other than address (within the United States) of applicant's father and mother, husband or wife and minor dependent children.
NOTICE IN CASE OF EMERGENCY:	Name and address of person to be notified in case of accident or emergency.	Name and address of nearest relative to be notified in case of accident or emergency.

(continued)

Exhibit 4   *(continued)*

SUBJECT	LAWFUL PRE-EMPLOYMENT INQUIRIES	UNLAWFUL PRE-EMPLOYMENT INQUIRIES
MILITARY EXPERIENCE:	Inquiry into an applicant's military experience in the Armed Forces of the United States or in a State Militia.	Inquiry into an applicant's general military experience.
	Inquiry into applicant's service in particular branch of United States Army, Navy, etc.	
ORGANIZATIONS:	Inquiry into the organizations of which an applicant is a member—excluding organizations, the name or character of which indicates the race, color, religion, national origin or ancestry of its members.	List all clubs, societies, and lodges to which you belong.
REFERENCES:	Who suggested that you apply for a position here?	

*This question may be asked only for the purpose of determining whether applicants are of legal age for employment.

Source: Michigan Department of Civil Rights, Lansing, Michigan.

attorney should review job application forms, related personnel forms, and interview procedures to ensure that there is no violation of anti-discrimination laws.

Interviewing

First impressions do matter. Applicants form impressions of the interviewer, the hotel, the front office, and what it would be like to work there, just as the interviewer forms impressions of how suitable applicants would be for the job. Often, eventual job satisfaction and productivity are the result of the expectations applicants form during an interview.

In large properties, the human resources division usually handles the recruiting (including advertising) and initial screening of all job candidates. Human resources staff will use the job description, job specification, and any instructions provided by the department manager to determine whether the candidate should be referred for the next interview. After that, the head of each department conducts the main, in-depth interview and decides whom to hire. The front office manager may delegate interviewing and hiring responsibilities to an assistant. Regardless of who does the actual hiring, the front office manager is ultimately responsible for hiring and maintaining a qualified front office staff.

Whoever the interviewer is, he or she should be thoroughly familiar with the job and its duties, benefits, wage scale, and other important factors. The interviewer should be an objective judge of people and their qualifications, a positive role model, and a skillful communicator. Exhibit 5 summarizes common problems associated with interviewing. When managers are aware of factors that can distort an interview, they can better prevent them and increase the probability of a successful interview.

The interview should be held in a comfortable, private setting that allows few, if any, interruptions. Focusing on the applicant shows a sincere interest. Applicants tend to be intimidated by business settings in which they sit in front of a desk and the interviewer sits on the other side of the desk. Interviewers often find it workable and more pleasant for the applicant to hold the interview in or near the actual work area. If the work site is too distracting for a sit-down interview, another location should be chosen. Unless there is an emergency, no telephone calls or other interruptions should be allowed during the interview.

Exhibit 5   Common Problems Associated with Interviewing

Similarity Error

Many interviewers are predisposed to react positively to candidates who are similar to themselves (in outside interests, personal background, and even appearance) and react negatively to candidates very different from themselves.

Contrast Error

Candidates should be compared to the standards that the hotel has established for the position, not to each other. Comparing candidates to one another, whether consciously or subconsciously, is particularly troublesome when two poor candidates are followed by a merely average candidate. Because of the contrast between candidates, the average candidate may be viewed as excellent, resulting in a contrast error.

Overweighting Negative Information

It is human nature to notice negative information more than positive information. When we examine a résumé or an application, we tend to look for the negative, not the positive. This also happens in interviews.

First-Impression Error

Many interviewers tend to form a strong first impression of a candidate that they maintain throughout the interview.

Halo Effect

Sometimes an interviewer's favorable impression of a single dimension about a candidate—appearance, background, and so on—can substantially color his or her overall impression. The halo effect occurs when an interviewer views everything that a candidate says or does in this favorable light.

Devil's Horns

The opposite of the halo effect. This phenomenon can often cause interviewers to see everything a candidate says or does in an unfavorable light.

Faulty Listening and Memory

Interviewers do not always hear what is said in the way it was intended, nor do they remember everything that was said.

Recency Errors

An interviewer is likely to remember a candidate's most recent behaviors or responses, rather than behaviors or responses that occurred earlier in the interview.

Nonverbal Factors

Nonverbal factors such as clothing, smiles, speech patterns, and eye contact substantially influence an interviewer's impression of candidates. Some interviewers make up their minds about whom to hire based almost solely on the candidate's attire and demeanor.

Conducting an Interview. The interview process has at least five objectives:

1. To establish a basis for a working relationship
2. To collect enough accurate information to make an informed hiring decision
3. To provide enough information to help the applicant make a decision

4. To promote the company and the work position to the preferred applicant

5. To create goodwill between the hotel and the applicant

Front office managers should speak in a conversational tone while conducting an interview. Care must be taken so that the applicant doesn't perceive the manager as patronizing or condescending. Essentially, managers should treat applicants with the same courtesy and respect they would extend to guests.

Interviewers should allow applicants to set the pace of the interview and should be patient with people who are nervous or shy. Applicants should not be told exactly what the manager is looking for, since some applicants might modify their responses to meet those expectations. Managers should also note the applicant's grooming, since many applicants will have groomed themselves for the job interview according to their highest personal standard.

A well-prepared interviewer has a list of questions already developed before the start of the interview. Interviewers might not ask all the questions, and some questions will evoke answers that lead to additional questions that may not be on the list. Questions should allow applicants to fully express themselves without feeling that they are being interrogated. The use of **closed-ended questions** requiring "Yes" or "No" answers should be limited to verifying information provided on the completed application form or to obtaining additional facts. Asking closed-ended questions such as, "Did you enjoy your previous job?" often do not prompt detailed responses. Also, these types of questions may lead job applicants to respond with answers they feel the interviewer wants to hear. To encourage fuller responses to issues, managers should ask **open-ended questions**, such as, "What did you like most about your previous job?" or "What did you like least about your previous job?"

Generally, an interviewer starts the interview with a period of small talk and perhaps humor to put the applicant at ease. Then, he or she moves into the body of the interview by asking the applicant about job expectations—basically, the kind of work and working conditions the applicant is looking for. Interviewers should then focus on one principal area at a time. For example, the interviewer could thoroughly examine the applicant's work experience before talking about education or other areas.

Good interviewers encourage responses by using appropriate gestures and comments. They also listen carefully, noting the applicant's body language. Sudden changes in position or tone of voice, eye movement, facial expressions, and nervous mannerisms may indicate that the applicant feels uneasy with the discussion. When applicants hesitate before answering a question, managers should follow up with related questions to probe for further information. Moreover, when an applicant responds vaguely or changes the subject, it may mean that he or she wants to avoid the topic. Similarly, interviewers can arouse an applicant's suspicions if they try to conceal or avoid topics. When an applicant asks about the work position or aspects of front office operations, the interviewer should respond as directly and honestly as possible.

Providing the applicant a copy of the job description as part of the interview may be a good idea (although this may have already been done by the human resources department). It will clearly identify what the manager is looking for as well as the requirements of the job. The front office manager can review the job description with applicants, identifying the important duties and responsibilities. This enables applicants to form a clearer picture of the job and an informed opinion as to whether they would like the job. If the interview is going well, there may even be a brief discussion about the actual training the candidate will receive if hired.

In hotels without a human resources division, the interviewer should determine early in the interview whether the applicant meets the position's basic requirements. This is also the time to mention other hiring prerequisites, such as the federal government's requirement that employees prove their legal right to work in the United States (note, however, that an applicant should not actually be required to provide such proof until after a hiring offer has been made). The person conducting the interview should also determine whether the applicant's personal job requirements may be met with respect to working conditions, scheduled hours, pay rate, type of work, and employment benefits. If it appears as though the job will not be satisfactory or workable for either side, the interview should end. Job offers made or accepted under less-than-ideal conditions are likely to lead to higher rates of employee dissatisfaction and turnover.

Interview Questions. A two-step questioning process is the most common technique used in interviewing. First, the interviewer asks for specific information such as who, what, when, or where. The second, or follow-up, question seeks a more in-depth response—one that will tell the interviewer why or how. For instance, the first question might be, "What did you like most about working at your last hotel?" After the applicant answers, the interviewer might ask, "Why was that your favorite?" Other questioning techniques interviewers can use include:

- Asking the applicant for a list rather than a single response, which allows for more spontaneity. Follow-up questions can narrow the field.

- Using direct questions to verify facts and cover a lot of information quickly. A direct question is sometimes called a closed-ended question and usually requires a simple answer, such as yes or no.

- Asking indirect or open-ended questions, or asking the applicant to make comparisons. This technique is useful when the interviewer is seeking more than standard responses. An open-ended question is one that the applicant must elaborate on, such as, "What were your favorite subjects in school?"

- Pursuing a specific subject in depth when a response seems unreasonable or unrealistic.

- Probing for additional information when the applicant gives a partial response. This is usually done by restating the reply as a question, such as, "So you felt that department was just too big, didn't you?"

- Using short affirmative responses to encourage the applicant to continue talking, such as, "I see," or "Please go on." Sometimes, it may also be helpful for the interviewer to nod in agreement.

- Using silence to indicate that the applicant should continue speaking.

- Suggesting sample answers when the applicant does not understand the question.

- Making comments rather than always asking questions in hopes of receiving varying responses.

What to ask. All questions must be based on sound business reasoning. Questions asked during an interview should be relevant to the open position. For example, the front office manager is not likely to ask an applicant for a position as a front desk agent the same questions that he or she would ask a person applying for a job as a front office supervisor. Applicants may be asked about their ability to perform specific job functions. Exhibit 6 presents a collection of sample questions that managers may use during interviews.

What not to ask. Managers must be careful when phrasing interview questions and when deciding what questions to ask. Generally, managers should avoid asking for information that cannot be legally used in a hiring decision. Discussions should not focus on birthplace, national origin, citizenship, age, sex, lifestyle, race, height and weight, marital status, religion or creed, arrest records, disabilities, and membership in clubs or religious or ethnic organizations. Managers may not ask job applicants about the existence, nature, or severity of a disability.

It is also illegal to ask questions of one sex and not the other. For example, interviewers should not ask only female applicants whether they have children or what plans they may have for child care. If such questions are employment-related and if the front office manager can prove they are, they must be asked of both male and female applicants.

Certain types of information must be obtained *after* an applicant is hired, such as proof of age and proof of the legal right to work in the United States. An appropriate time to obtain such information is while a recruit is completing employment papers. Also, a job offer may be conditioned on the results of a medical examination, drug test, criminal record check, or validation of previous employment, but only if the examination or inquiry is required for all entering employees in the job. Medical examinations or inquiries of employees must be job-related and consistent with the employer's business needs.

Interview Evaluation. The sample interview evaluation form presented in Exhibit 7 lists some key traits for front office staff. Portions of this form should be structured according to front office job specifications. The front office manager can use such a form to evaluate an applicant's strengths and weaknesses. After interviewing an applicant, the front office manager may use the form to compile a score based on the following criteria:

- Applicants score zero if they meet an acceptable level of skill in a given area, or if the skill is not directly job-related.

- Applicants score plus one or plus three according to the degree they surpass the acceptable level of skill in a job-related area.

- Applicants score minus one or minus three according to the degree they fail to meet the acceptable level of skill in a job-related area.

Exhibit 6   Sample Interview Questions

Relevant to Job Background

- Did you regularly work forty hours a week? How much overtime did you work?
- What were your gross and take-home wages?
- What benefits did you receive? How much did you pay for them?
- What salary/wage do you desire? What is the lowest amount you are likely to accept?
- Which days of the week are best for working?
- Have you ever worked weekends before? Where? How often?
- Which shift do you enjoy working the most? Which shift can't you work? Why?
- How many hours a week would you like to work?
- How will you get to work?
- Is your means of transportation reliable for the shifts you may be working?
- When you started your last job, what position did you hold? What position do you hold now or did you hold when you left?
- What was the starting salary of your present job or the last job you held?
- How often did you get pay increases on your present job or the last job you held?
- What three things do you want to avoid on your next job?
- What qualities do you expect in a supervisor?
- Why did you choose this line of work?
- Why are you interested in working at this hotel?
- Which work experience most influenced your career decisions?

Education and Intelligence

- When you were in school, what subjects did you like the most? Why?
- When you were in school, what subjects did you like the least? Why?
- Do you think your grades are a good indicator of your overall abilities?
- If you had to make the same educational decisions over again, would you make the same choices? Why or why not?
- What is the most important thing you have learned in the past six months?
- What good qualities did you find in your best teachers? Can these apply to work as well?

Personal Traits

Some of the following may be more suitable for people without much work background:

- What do you like to do in your spare time?
- How many times were you absent or late for your present or last job? Is that normal? What were the reasons?
- What does your family think of your working at this hotel?
- On your last job, were the policies concerning being late or absent without cause clearly explained to you? Were these policies fair?
- What was your first supervisor like?
- How did you get your first job? Your most recent job?

(continued)

Exhibit 6 *(continued)*

For the following questions about personal traits, job titles may be changed to meet the needs of the interview:

- Who has greater responsibilities—a front desk agent or a reservation sales agent? Why?
- Have you ever had to deal with an angry guest who complains about everything? If so, how did you work with the guest to resolve the issues?
- What do you consider the main reason people in the position you are applying for leave their jobs? What would you do to change this?
- What do you consider the most important responsibilities of a good front desk agent?
- Suppose your supervisor insisted you learn a task in a certain way, when you know there is a better way. What would you do?
- Have you ever had a supervisor show favoritism to certain employees? How did you feel about this?
- Of all your job experiences, what did you like the most? Why?
- Of all your job experiences, what did you like the least? Why?
- When you go to a store to purchase something, what qualities do you look for in the salesperson?
- What was your biggest accomplishment on your last job?
- What would you have changed about your last job if you had the opportunity?
- If the opportunity was offered to you, would you return to your last employer? Why or why not?
- How much notice did you give your last employer when you decided to leave (or plan to give your current employer)?
- How would your former supervisor and fellow employees describe you?
- What strengths and weaknesses do you bring to this new position?
- What frustrates you on the job? How do you handle this frustration?
- On your last performance review, what areas did your former supervisor mention need to be improved? Why do you think the comment was made?
- What three areas would you most like to improve about yourself?
- What one thing have you done of which you are the proudest? Why?
- What is the funniest thing that has ever happened to you?
- What is important to you about the job you are applying for? Why?

Questions for Managerial Candidates

- What type of training program did you have for your employees? Who set it up and who implemented it?
- What have you done on your last job to improve the performance of the department you supervised? How was this measured?
- What are the most important attributes of a manager?
- What hotels were your biggest competitors? What were their strengths and weaknesses?
- How would your employees describe you as a supervisor?
- How many people did you have to discipline on your last job? Describe the circumstances. How do you feel about terminating employees?
- What did you do to motivate your employees?

Exhibit 7   Sample Interview Evaluation Form

Applicant
Name _____

Position
Evaluated _____

Date _____

	Poor Match		Acceptable	Strong Match	
RELEVANT JOB BACKGROUND	−3	−1	0	+1	+3
General background					
Work experience					
Similar companies					
Interest in job					
Salary requirements					
Attendance					
Leadership experience					

EDUCATION / INTELLIGENCE

Formal schooling					
Intellectual ability					
Additional training					
Social skills					
Verbal and listening skills					
Writing skills					

PHYSICAL FACTORS

General health					
Physical ability					
Cleanliness, dress, and posture					
Energy level					

PERSONAL TRAITS

First impression					
Interpersonal skills					
Personality					
Teamwork					
Motivation					
Outlook, humor, and optimism					
Values					
Creativity					
Stress tolerance					
Performing skills					
Service attitude					
Independence					
Planning and organizing					
Problem-solving					
Maturity					
Decisiveness					
Self-knowledge					
Flexibility					
Work standards					
Subtotals					

TOTAL POINTS _____

Every applicant possesses strengths and weaknesses. An interview evaluation form ensures that shortcomings in one area do not diminish an applicant's chances for further consideration. After evaluating all applicants, the manager should select and hire the best applicant for the position. Generally, the applicant who scores the highest on the interview evaluation form will probably make the best employee. Once an applicant is selected and has accepted the job offer, the manager should inform other applicants who were interviewed that the position has been filled. Sometimes an unsuccessful applicant for one position may be qualified for an alternative open position. If so, the manager should encourage the applicant to apply or should take the time to notify another department manager of a qualified applicant.

Managers should document all employment interviews, especially interviews for applicants who were not hired. These records should contain only job-related information. The interviewer's personal notes should not become part of a candidate's job application file.

Hiring

The **hiring period** begins when an employer extends an offer to a prospective employee. Hiring involves making all the necessary arrangements to prepare the recruit and current employees for a successful working relationship, including processing personnel records. The hiring period lasts through the recruit's initial on-the-job adjustments. In some cases, job applicants may interview with several managers—including shift supervisors, rooms division managers, and even the general manager—before being hired. Applicants should be told of this process during the initial interview, so that they will understand that more than one visit to the property may be required.

Job Offers

Since hiring requires a degree of skill and knowledge of complex labor laws, most front office managers rely on the human resources division or someone specifically designated by top management. When only one or two people are authorized to make employment offers, the hotel has greater control over how the job is represented and what pre-employment promises are made. The three steps of making and closing employment offers are extending the offer, negotiating the offer, and completing the offer.

Extending the Offer. A carefully worded offer can represent the beginning of a potential employee's commitment to the employer. Successful employment offers depend on timing. The longer a front office manager waits to extend an offer, the less likely a candidate is to accept. In the interim, the applicant may lose enthusiasm or interest, or may accept a job somewhere else. Whenever possible, job offers should be extended in writing (in fact, many hotel companies *require* that job offers be made in writing). Written offers can eliminate misunderstandings about the job title, job requirements, starting pay, or working schedule. A well-written job offer includes a signature line for the applicant to accept the offer. This signature line signifies the applicant's acknowledgment that he or she has read and understands the contents of the offer.

Negotiating the Offer. During the interview process, the front office manager should become familiar with an applicant's background and expectations. Many of the areas that sometimes become obstacles to job offers (such as pay, starting dates, and employment benefits) should be discussed. Management should negotiate a job offer only when it is reasonably certain the offer will be accepted.

Establishing a reasonable starting date informs recruits that the front office expects its employees to give proper notice before leaving a job. Hotel managers cannot expect employees to give proper notice to them when they do not allow potential recruits sufficient time to give proper notice to their current employer.

Completing the Offer. A candidate accepting an offer should sign the written job offer as evidence of his or her agreement with the terms of the offer. Once an applicant accepts a job offer, the front office manager should assure the applicant that he or she has made the right decision. Recruits should be told that they are not expected to know everything about a job at the outset, but that management believes in their ability to handle the job successfully. Supervisors should immediately begin preparations for the recruit's arrival, including informing other front office staff about the new employee. Supervisors should tell current employees the new recruit's name, previous job experience, and starting date. The front office manager should meet with work shift leaders and encourage them to assist with the recruit's training and work relationships.

Processing Personnel Records

Processing new employees' personnel records before they start work helps prepare them for their new positions. Uniforms should be fitted and name tags ordered for the employee's first work day. If the employee needs the hotel to issue a cashier bank or other supplies, this should be arranged before the first day of work, if possible.

The tone of the processing period should be warm, caring, and professional. If it's too light, casual, or hectic, new employees may conclude that the hotel or front office is lax in its policies and procedures. Employees should learn what management expects in the way of service, as well as the goals of the front office and the hotel. Management will find the processing period an excellent time to discuss goals and expectations with new employees.

At this time, the front office manager or human resources division employee should also discuss time cards, pay procedures, house rules, reporting instructions, and uniforms. Use of a checklist can ensure that all the important points are covered. Many of these points will be reinforced during employee orientation.

Orienting

New employees should be given an **orientation** when they arrive for their first day of work. A well-planned and organized orientation helps new employees get off to a good start. Usually, the new employee's first days on a job are filled with anxiety. The front office manager should take full responsibility for orienting new front office employees.

Managers should plan to make the employee's transition into the new job as smooth as possible. Successful orientation programs often include a written agenda that the new employee can use as a reference. The agenda should tell the employee who he or she will meet, where to meet, the time to meet, and what will be discussed. At the least, the orientation should include information about:

- *The hotel*—its history, reputation for service, names of key management personnel, plans for growth, company policies, and chain information.

- *The benefits*—wages, insurance coverage, employee discounts, vacations, and paid holidays.

- *The working conditions*—applicable training schedules, work schedules, breaks, meal periods, overtime, safety, security, employee bulletin boards and log books, and social activities.

- *The job*—the tasks the job entails, how the job fits within the front office, how the front office fits within the hotel, and what performance standards are expected.

- *The front office team*—introductions to fellow employees, overview of the key responsibilities of each employee, and explanation of reporting structures.

- *The rules and regulations*—regarding, for example, smoking, entry and exit, disciplinary action, and parking privileges.

- *The building*—the layout of the building, the location of the employee entrance, locker room, employee dining room, uniform room, front desk, and other important departments. In addition, front desk, reservations, and bell staff should be shown guestrooms, dining rooms, recreation areas, and meeting rooms to begin to understand the layout of guest areas.

Much of this information should appear in the employee manual or handbook. Time should be set aside during an employee's first day of work to complete all proof of citizenship (or work permit), tax withholding, insurance, and similar work-related forms. Uniforms and lockers should be provided if they are part of the job. New employees should also be given a tour of the entire facility, especially the different types of guestrooms and meeting rooms. The tour should include the work area, time clocks, and locations of posted work schedules, supply areas, first aid kits, restrooms, and break areas. A tour of related departments will help reinforce an explanation of the workflow and need for teamwork. During the tour, the front office manager should introduce as many fellow staff members as possible.

Management should ensure that all revenue centers are shown to the recruit. The tour should also point out the locations of housekeeping, laundry, maintenance, accounting, and other important hotel departments. Among the most important features of a tour, however, is the time taken to introduce the new employee to key managers, especially the general manager and the rooms division manager, if they were not part of the interview process. Such introductions can help make the recruit feel part of the team immediately. It also establishes recognition between management and staff.

Skills Training

Ensuring that employees receive proper training is one of the front office manager's major responsibilities. This does not mean that the manager must necessarily be the trainer. The actual training functions may be delegated to trainers, to department supervisors, or even to talented line employees. However, the front office manager is responsible for ongoing training programs in the department.

Most managers and trainers understand that the goal of training is to help staff members develop skills to do their jobs well. Many managers and trainers, however, are not sure of the best way to train. Often, they need a framework for training. The four-step training method provides that framework. The four steps in the method are:

- Prepare to train
- Present the training
- Practice skills
- Follow up

Prepare to Train

Preparation is essential for successful training. Without adequate preparation, the training will lack a logical sequence, and key details of the job may be omitted. Before training begins, the front office manager must analyze the job and assess the training needs of the staff.

Analyze Jobs. The foundation for training and for preventing performance problems is **job analysis,** which is determining what knowledge staff members must have, what tasks they need to perform, and the standards at which they must perform them. Without a complete knowledge of what each staff member is expected to do, a manager can't train properly. Job analysis involves three steps: identifying job knowledge, creating a task list, and developing a job breakdown for each task performed as part of a front office position. The knowledge, lists, and breakdowns also form an efficient system for evaluating performance.

Job knowledge identifies what a staff member needs to know to perform his or her job. Job knowledge can be divided into three categories: knowledge for all hotel employees, knowledge for front office employees, and knowledge specific to a position like a front desk agent. Exhibit 8 lists topics that might be covered with all hotel employees, topics relevant for all front office employees, and knowledge requirements for front desk agents.

A **task list** should reflect the total job responsibility of a position. Exhibit 9 presents a sample task list for a front desk agent. Note that each line on the sample task list begins with a verb. This format stresses action and clearly indicates to a staff member what he or she will be responsible for doing. Wherever possible, tasks should be listed in an order that reflects the logical sequence of daily responsibilities.

A **job breakdown** includes a list of required equipment and supplies, steps, how-to instructions, and tips explaining how to complete a single task. The job

Exhibit 8   Job Knowledge for Front Desk Agents

Knowledge for All Employees	Knowledge for Front Desk Agents
• Quality guest service	• What is a front desk agent?
• Bloodborne pathogens	• Working as a team with co-workers and other departments
• Personal appearance	• Target markets
• Emergency situations	• Using guestroom equipment and amenities
• Lost and found	
• Recycling procedures	• The telephone system
• Safe work habits	• Point-of-sale equipment
• Manager on duty identification	• The front desk computer system
• Property fact sheet	• Front desk printers
• Employee policies	• Room racks
• The Americans with Disabilities Act	• Types of reservations
	• Room inventory and occupancy terms
Knowledge for All Front Office Employees	• Room rate terms
• Telephone courtesy	• Room status terms
• Security	• Frequent guest program
• Guestroom types	• Check-in and check-out guidelines
• Maintenance needs	• Room forecasts
• Property policies	• Payment card approval procedures
• Community information	• Check approval procedures
• Giving directions	• Credit check report
• Airport shuttle services	• Currency exchange
• Elevator courtesy	• Par stock system
• Restaurant menus	• VIPs
• OSHA regulations	

breakdown format can vary to suit the needs and requirements of individual operations. Exhibit 10 presents a sample job breakdown for task 16, "Use effective sales techniques," listed in Exhibit 9.

Each member of the front office staff should know the standards that will be used to measure his or her job performance. Therefore, it is important to break down job tasks and document the standards. In order to serve as a performance standard, each task must be observable and measurable. Exhibit 11 shows a sample training needs evaluation form that can be used as a performance evaluation. The front office manager (or the supervising manager) conducting a performance evaluation should be able to simply check the box matching the staff member's performance. Performance evaluations should be held frequently for new employees. These evaluations should be reinforcing sessions, focusing on areas of success

Exhibit 9　Sample Task List—Front Desk Agent

FRONT DESK AGENT TASK LIST

1. Use the front desk computer system.
2. Use the front desk printers.
3. Use the front desk telephone system.
4. Use the facsimile machine.
5. Use the photocopy machine.
6. Organize the front desk and prepare for check-ins.
7. Use the front office log book.
8. Prepare and use an arrivals list.
9. Block and unblock rooms.
10. Set up preregistrations.
11. Begin guest check-in.
12. Establish the payment method during check-in.
13. Secure authorization for payment cards.
14. Issue and control guestroom keys/key cards.
15. Finish guest check-in.
16. Use effective sales techniques.
17. Preregister and check in group arrivals.
18. Show rooms to potential guests.
19. Use a waiting list when rooms are not ready for check-in.
20. Relocate guests in sold-out situations.
21. Use a manual room rack system.
22. Process room changes.
23. Process safe deposit box transactions for guests.
24. Prepare a cash-only report for outlets.
25. Run and follow up on credit check reports.
26. Process guest mail, packages, telegrams, and faxes.
27. Maintain a guest information directory.
28. Prepare maps and provide directions.
29. Help guests with special requests.
30. Respond to questions about services and events.
31. Handle guest service problems.
32. Cash checks for guests.
33. Pick up, use, and turn in cash bank.
34. Post guest charges and payments.
35. Follow guest privacy and security measures.
36. Process wake-up call requests.
37. Operate the pay movie system.
38. Process guaranteed no-shows.
39. Update room status.
40. Help guests make future reservations.
41. Process guest check-outs.
42. Adjust disputed guest charges.
43. Transfer allowable guest charges.
44. Process automatic check-outs.
45. Handle late guest check-outs.
46. Process late charges.

(continued)

Exhibit 9   *(continued)*

47. Keep the front desk clean and orderly.
48. Reconcile room status with the p.m. housekeeping report.
49. Prepare a current status report.
50. Perform bucket or tub checks.
51. Inventory and requisition front desk supplies.
52. Complete and turn in the shift checklist.
53. Respond to situations requiring first aid.
54. Respond to emergency alarms.

Source: Hospitality Skills Training Series, *Front Desk Employee Guide* (Lansing, Mich.: American Hotel & Lodging Educational Institute).

as well as areas that need improvement. As new employees become more familiar with their jobs, the evaluations can be held less frequently until the employees are fully trained.

Develop Job Breakdowns. If one person in the front office is assigned the responsibility of writing every job breakdown, the job may never get done, unless the operation is a very small one with a limited number of tasks. Those who actually perform the tasks write some of the best job breakdowns. In properties with large staffs, standards groups can be formed to handle the writing tasks. Group members should include department supervisors and several experienced employees. In small properties, experienced staff members might be assigned to write the job breakdowns alone.

Most hotels have a policy and procedures manual. Although this manual rarely includes the detail necessary to set up effective training and evaluation programs, portions of it may be helpful to members of a standards group as they write job breakdowns for each department position. For example, if the procedure sections of the manual include job descriptions and job specifications, they may help a standards group in writing job lists and performance standards. The policy sections may be helpful sources of additional information that can be included in the job breakdowns.

The job breakdowns for tasks that involve the use of equipment may already be written in the operating manuals supplied by vendors. Standards groups should not have to write performance standards for operating the front desk computer system. Instead, the standards group may simply refer to (or even attach) appropriate pages from the operating manual supplied by the system's vendor for in-house training.

Developing job breakdowns involves breaking down each task on each front office job list by writing the **performance standards** that state the specific observable and measurable steps a staff member must take to accomplish the task. The front office manager should assist the standards group in writing performance standards for at least two or three positions. While assisting the group, the manager should stress that each performance standard must be observable and measurable. The value of each performance standard can be tested by asking whether a supervisor or manager can evaluate a staff member's performance by simply

Exhibit 10   Sample Job Breakdown

Use Effective Sales Techniques		
Materials needed: *Promotional programs catalog, promotional materials, brochures, guestroom diagrams, and restaurant and room service menus.*		
STEPS	**HOW-TO'S**	**TIPS**
1. Upsell guestrooms.	❏ Suggest higher-rate guestrooms when guests check in.	*Upselling is a way of selling a more expensive guestroom than the one a guest originally requested.*
	❏ Describe features and benefits of the more expensive rooms.	*It never hurts to offer a guest a better room. You're showing that you want the guest to have a pleasant stay.*
	❏ Show guests room diagrams to help explain features.	
	❏ If guests have children, suggest a larger room to give them extra space.	
	❏ Suggest a room with extra amenities to business travelers, or a larger room so they can hold meetings.	
	❏ If a couple is vacationing, suggest a room with features that will give them a more memorable experience.	
	❏ Be sure to always directly ask guests if they would like to check into a room you describe.	*Don't wait for guests to tell you to book a certain room type. Anticipate what they want and ask if you can book that room type for them.*
2. Suggest the food and beverage outlets.	❏ Suggest ordering from room service if guests say they don't have time to leave their rooms. Tell guests the hours of service.	*Guests usually welcome a positive suggestion.*
	❏ Use good judgment. Don't recommend heavy dishes on the room service menu late at night.	
	❏ Recommend the property's restaurant if guests ask for a good place to eat.	*Remember, you'll be using teamwork when you suggest the property's restaurants.*
	❏ Show guests the menu to help them decide.	

(continued)

Exhibit 10   *(continued)*

Use Effective Sales Techniques (continued)		
STEPS	**HOW-TO'S**	**TIPS**
	❏ Be able to tell guests about reservation and dress code requirements.	
	❏ Listen to guests. If they specifically ask for a restaurant outside the lodging property, suggest local establishments.	
	❏ Suggest the lounge if guests are looking for a place to unwind.	
	❏ Stay informed about changes in menus, hours, and entertainment. Guests expect you to be an expert about your property.	*See "Restaurant Menus" in Knowledge for All Front Office Employees.*
3. Suggest property promotions.	❏ Ask your supervisor which promotions are available at your property.	*Guests like to feel that they are getting "freebies" or "special deals."*
	❏ Study the features and benefits of each promotion.	
	❏ Enthusiastically describe programs that may meet guests' needs.	
	❏ Give guests any brochures and other promotional materials available.	

Source: Hospitality Skills Training Series, *Front Desk Employee Guide* (Lansing, Mich.: American Hotel & Lodging Educational Institute).

checking a "Yes" or "No" in the performance review column. Sometimes measurable performance standards include written tests to verify that employees have the required knowledge. These tests should be easy to administer, using mostly multiple choice, true/false, and fill-in-the-blank questions.

After the standards group has written job breakdowns for two or three tasks, individual members of the group should be called upon to write job breakdowns for the other tasks. Within a specified time, they should submit their work to the front office manager, who then assembles the breakdowns, has them processed into a single format (perhaps similar to that shown in Exhibit 10), and provides copies to all of the group's members. A final meeting can then be held, with the

Exhibit 11   Sample Training Needs Evaluation Form

Training Needs Evaluation for Current Employees

How well are your current employees performing? Use this form to observe and rate their work.

Part 1: Job Knowledge

Rate the employee's knowledge of each of the following topics:	Well Below Standard	Slightly Below Standard	At Standard	Above Standard
Knowledge for All Employees				
Quality Guest Service				
Bloodborne Pathogens				
Personal Appearance				
Emergency Situations				
Lost and Found				
Recycling Procedures				
Safe Work Habits				
Manager on Duty				
Your Property's Fact Sheet				
Employee Policies				
The Americans with Disabilities Act				
Knowledge for All Front Office Employees				
Telephone Courtesy				
Security				
Guestroom Types				
Maintenance Needs				
Property Policies				
Your Community				
Giving Directions				
Transportation to the Airport				
Elevator Courtesy				
Restaurant Menus				
OSHA Regulations				
Knowledge for Front Desk Employees				
What Is a Front Desk Employee?				
Working as a Team With Co-Workers and Other Departments				
Target Markets				

(continued)

standards group carefully analyzing the breakdown for each position. After the job breakdowns have been finalized, they should be used immediately to train the front office staff.

Exhibit 11   *(continued)*

Training Needs Evaluation for Current Employees *(continued)*

Part 1: Job Knowledge *(continued)*

Rate the employee's knowledge of each of the following topics:	Well Below Standard	Slightly Below Standard	At Standard	Above Standard
Knowledge for Front Desk Employees *(continued)*				
Using Guestroom Equipment and Amenities				
The Telephone System				
Point-of-Sale Equipment				
The Front Desk Computer System				
Front Desk Printers				
Room Racks				
Types of Reservations				
Room Inventory and Occupancy Terms				
Room Rate Terms				
Room Status Terms				
Frequent Guest Program				
Check-In and Check-Out Guidelines				
Room Forecasts				
Payment Card Approval Procedures				
Check Approval Procedures				
Credit Check Report				
Currency Exchange				
Par Stock System				
VIPs				

(continued)

Analyze New Employee Training Needs. The task list is an excellent tool with which to plan employee training. Realistically, new staff members cannot be expected to learn all of the tasks before the first day on the job. Before you begin training, study the task list. Then, rate each task according to whether it should be mastered (1) before working alone on the job; (2) within two weeks on the job; or (3) within two months on the job.

Select several of the tasks that you rated as "1" and plan to cover those in the first training session. After the employee understands and can perform these, teach the remaining tasks in subsequent training sessions until the new staff member has learned all of the tasks.

Once you've decided which tasks you'll teach in each training session, turn to the job breakdowns. Think of the job breakdown for each task as a lesson plan for training or as a learning guide for self-directed study. Because the job breakdowns

Exhibit 11 *(continued)*

Training Needs Evaluation for Current Employees *(continued)*

Part 2: Job Skills

Rate the employee's skills in performing each of the following tasks:	Well Below Standard	Slightly Below Standard	At Standard	Above Standard
Use the Front Desk Computer System				
Use the Front Desk Printers				
Use the Front Desk Telephone System				
Use the Facsimile Machine				
Use the Photocopy Machine				
Organize the Front Desk and Prepare for Check-Ins				
Use the Front Office Logbook				
Prepare and Use an Arrivals List				
Block and Unblock Rooms				
Set Up Preregistrations				
Begin Guest Check-In				
Establish the Payment Method During Check-In				
Secure Authorization for Payment Cards				
Issue and Control Guestroom Keys				
Finish Guest Check-In				
Use Effective Sales Techniques				
Preregister and Check In Group Arrivals				
Show Rooms to Potential Guests				
Use a Waiting List When Rooms Are Not Ready for Check-In				
Relocate Guests in Sold-out Situations				
Use a Manual Room Rack System				
Process Room Changes				
Process Safe-Deposit-Box Transactions for Guests				
Prepare a Cash-Only Report for Outlets				
Run and Follow Up on Credit Check Reports				
Process Guest Mail, Packages, Telegrams, and Faxes				
Maintain a Guest Information Directory				

(continued)

list all the steps staff members must perform, they tell exactly what needs to be done during the training. Job breakdowns can direct the instruction and make sure that critical points or steps are not overlooked.

Exhibit 11 *(continued)*

Training Needs Evaluation for Current Employees *(continued)*

Part 2: Job Skills *(continued)*

Rate the employee's skills in performing each of the following tasks:	Well Below Standard	Slightly Below Standard	At Standard	Above Standard
Prepare Maps and Provide Directions				
Help Guests With Special Requests				
Respond to Questions About Services and Events				
Handle Guest Service Problems				
Cash Checks for Guests				
Pick Up, Use, and Turn In Your Cash Bank				
Post Guest Charges and Payments				
Follow Guest Privacy and Security Measures				
Process Wake-Up Calls				
Operate the Pay Movie System				
Process Guaranteed No-Shows				
Update Room Status				
Help Guests Make Reservations				
Process Guest Check-Outs at the Desk				
Adjust Disputed Guest Charges				
Transfer Allowable Guest Charges				
Process Automatic Check-Outs				
Handle Late Guest Check-Outs				
Process Late Charges				
Keep the Front Desk Clean and Orderly				
Reconcile Room Status With the P.M. Housekeeping Report				
Prepare a Current Status Report				
Perform Bucket or Tub Checks				
Inventory and Requisition Front Desk Supplies				
Complete and Turn In the Shift Checklist				
Respond to Situations Requiring First Aid				
Respond to Emergency Alarms				

Source: Hospitality Skills Training Series, *Front Desk Employee Guide* (Lansing, Mich.: American Hotel & Lodging Educational Institute).

The information a staff member must know is usually written on a single page. Assign new employees nine or ten knowledge sections or job breakdowns at a time to study. Do not ask an employee to read all the knowledge sections and all the job breakdowns at once. This would overwhelm the employee, and he or she won't remember enough information to perform the job well.

Analyze Current Employee Training Needs. Front office managers sometimes think that there's a problem with an employee's work or with several employees' work, but they're not exactly sure what it is; or they suspect that something's not quite right with the staff, but don't know where to start making improvements. A training-needs assessment can help uncover a staff member's weaknesses as well as the weaknesses of an entire staff. To conduct a needs assessment of a single employee, observe present performance for two or three days and record it on a form similar to the one in Exhibit 11. Areas in which the employee scores poorly are those you'll want to target when you plan refresher training.

Develop a Department Training Plan. It's a good idea to make a training plan four times a year, every three months or so. And it's best to complete each plan one month before the beginning of each quarter. Follow these steps to prepare for training sessions:

- Carefully review all knowledge sections and job breakdowns that you will use in training.

- Make a copy of each knowledge section and job breakdown for each trainee.

- Establish a training schedule. This will depend on whom you are training and the training method you use. Remember to limit each training session's information to what employees can understand and remember.

- Select a training time and location. When possible, conduct training at the appropriate workstations during slow business hours.

- Notify the employee or employees of the dates and times of the training sessions.

- Practice your presentation.

- Gather all the necessary supplies for demonstrating tasks.

Present the Training

Well-developed job breakdowns provide all the information you need to conduct the "present" step of the four-step training method. Use the job breakdowns as a training guide. Follow the sequence of each step in each job breakdown. For each step, show and tell staff members what to do, how to do it, and why the details are important.

Give them a chance to prepare. Let new employees study the task list to get an overview of all the tasks they will learn to perform. If possible, give the list to them at least one day before the first training session. At least a day before each training session, let new and current employees review the job breakdowns that you plan to cover in that session. Then begin each training session by going over what they will do. Let them know how long activities will take and when their breaks will be.

As you explain the steps, demonstrate them. Make sure staff members can see exactly what you are doing. Encourage them to ask questions whenever they need more information. Be sure to take enough time when presenting your training. Go slowly and carefully. Be patient if staff members don't understand right away. Go over all the steps at least two times. When you show a step a second time, ask employees questions to see if they understand. Repeat the steps as many times as necessary. Avoid jargon. Use words that employees who are new to the hospitality industry or your property can understand. They can pick up the jargon later.

Practice Skills

When the trainer and trainees agree that trainees are familiar with the job and able to complete the steps acceptably, trainees should try to perform the tasks alone. Immediate practice results in good work habits. Have trainees demonstrate each step of the tasks presented during the training session. This tells you whether they really do understand. Resist the urge to do the tasks for the employees.

Coaching will help staff members gain the skill and confidence necessary to perform the job. Compliment employees immediately after correct performance. Gently correct them when you observe problems. Bad habits formed at this stage of the training may be very difficult to break later. Be sure that trainees understand and can explain not only how to perform each step, but also the purpose of each step.

Follow Up

There are a number of things you can do to make it easier for your employees to carry skills over to the workplace after training. Some of these include:

- Provide opportunities to use and demonstrate new skills during and after training.

- Have employees discuss the training with their co-workers.

- Provide ongoing, open communication on progress and concerns.

Continue Coaching on the Job. While training helps employees absorb new knowledge and develop new skills and attitudes, coaching focuses on the actual on-the-job application of what employees learned in the training sessions. As a coach, you challenge, encourage, correct, and positively reinforce the knowledge, skills, and attitudes presented during the training session. On-the-job coaching tips include:

- Observe employees while they work to ensure that they are performing tasks correctly. Let them know when they do something exceptionally well.

- Make casual suggestions to correct minor problems.

- Tactfully correct employees when they make major mistakes. Typically the best way to do this is in a quiet location, when neither of you is busy.

- If an employee uses an unsafe procedure, correct the problem right away.

Give Constant Feedback. Feedback is what you tell employees about how well they are performing. Two types of feedback are positive feedback, which recognizes a job well done, and redirective feedback, which recognizes incorrect performance and reviews how the employee can improve. Some tips for giving both types of feedback include:

- Let employees know what they are doing correctly or incorrectly.

- Tell employees when they perform well after training. This will help them remember what they learn. It will also encourage them to use those behaviors and that information on the job.

- If employees are not meeting performance standards, first compliment them for the tasks they are doing correctly. Then, show them how to correct their bad habits, and explain why it's important that they do so.

- Be specific. Describe behavior by stating exactly what the employee said and did.

- Choose your words carefully; you want to sound helpful, not demanding.

- *Don't say,* "You used quality guest service when you asked the guest who seemed lost if you could help, but you should have known the restaurant's hours of operation. Study your copy of the property's fact sheet."

- *Do say,* "You used quality guest service when you asked the guest who seemed lost if you could help. You could give even better service by learning the restaurant's and other facilities' hours of operation. Let me get you another copy of the property's fact sheet."

- Make sure you understand what the employee is saying. Say something like, "What I'm hearing you say is…"

- Make sure the employee understands your message. Say something like, "I'm not sure I explained everything clearly. Tell me what you think I said."

- Always be sincere and tactful with your comments. Employees appreciate an honest compliment about a specific behavior. And no one likes to be embarrassed or put down by criticism.

- Tell employees where to find help when you are not available.

Evaluate. Evaluate employees' progress. Use the task list as a checklist to confirm that employees have mastered all tasks. Provide further training and practice for tasks that employees have not mastered.

Get Employees' Feedback. Let employees evaluate the training they received. This can help you improve your training efforts for them and other employees. Keep training records for each person who receives training. Track each employee's training history and keep a copy of a training log in his or her personnel file.

Staff Scheduling

Employee scheduling is one of the most challenging tasks a front office manager undertakes. Scheduling can be extremely complex, especially when front office staff has been trained to perform only specific tasks. For example, a front desk agent should not be scheduled as a switchboard operator when he or she has had no switchboard training.

Employee scheduling affects payroll costs, employee productivity, and morale. The more cross-training that occurs within the front office, the fewer staff required to perform front office tasks. Staffing flexibility is the direct result of proper training in several areas. Cross-training provides front office staff with expanded job knowledge and a broader range of skills. Many employees find work more interesting when they are trained to do several tasks. When they see their skills improving and expanding, they feel more confident; the result for the front office is improved employee morale. Good morale has a way of spreading throughout the entire staff.

Front office managers must be sensitive to the scheduling needs of their staff. For example, hourly staff may request a varied schedule to avoid working hours that conflict with school classes. Some front office staff may ask to work varied shifts to learn the unique challenges posed by each shift. Some front office managers base employee scheduling on seniority; others base their schedules on other criteria and preferences. Both methods are fair, but the front office manager must be consistent in applying scheduling criteria and must be attentive to each staff member's needs to determine a workable schedule.

At the same time, the front office manager must keep the needs of the front office in mind. Scheduling employees on days when they are available but not required places an unnecessary financial burden on the hotel.

Front office managers may find the following tips helpful when developing staffing schedules:

- A schedule should cover a full workweek, typically defined as Sunday through Saturday. The schedule should be developed using the hotel's business forecast. Front desk and uniformed service operations usually schedule staff based upon the number of check-ins and check-outs expected each day. The reservations office usually schedules staff based on when reservation traffic is expected. This may take some coordination with the sales department. For example, the sales department may have an advertisement in the Sunday travel section of newspapers. Readers may want to make their reservations immediately, so someone should be scheduled at the hotel to take calls and inquiries.

- Schedules should be posted at least three days before the beginning of the next workweek. Some states require that schedules be posted five days or more before the beginning of the next work period. It is also essential that the front office manager understand laws pertaining to overtime hours and pay.

- Days off, vacation time, and requested days off should be indicated on the posted work schedule. Employees should be familiar with the required lead time to submit a vacation request.

- The work schedule for the current week should be reviewed daily in relation to anticipated business volume and unanticipated changes in staff availability. If necessary, changes to the schedule should be made.

- Any scheduling changes should be noted directly on the posted work schedule.

- A copy of the posted work schedule can be used to monitor the daily attendance of employees. This copy should be retained as part of the department's permanent records.

Alternative Scheduling Techniques

Alternative scheduling involves a staffing schedule that varies from a typical 9 A.M. to 5 P.M. workday. Variations include part-time and flextime hours, compressed schedules, and job sharing.

Part-Time Scheduling. Part-time staff frequently include students, new or young parents, retirees, and other individuals who choose not to work full-time. Employing part-time staff can provide the front office with extra flexibility in scheduling. It can also help reduce labor costs, since expenses attributable to benefits and overtime usually decrease.

Flextime Scheduling. Flextime planning allows employees to vary the time they begin and end work shifts. Each shift has certain hours when all scheduled staff must be present. Staffing needs during the rest of the shift can vary. The front office manager must ensure that each hour of the day is adequately covered. Flextime can enhance staff morale, productivity, and job satisfaction. Moreover, front offices with flextime arrangements can sometimes attract a larger number of high-quality employees. Most front office managers use flextime in one form or another to cover the varying workloads of all shifts. For example, traditional shifts at the front desk are from 7 A.M. to 3 P.M. and 3 P.M. until 11 P.M. Due to heavy check-in traffic, however, it may be more beneficial to schedule one or two employees on a noon to 8 P.M. shift. Airport hotels may have a 6 A.M. to 2 P.M. shift to cover early morning departures.

Compressed Schedules. Compressed schedules offer employees the opportunity to work the equivalent of a standard workweek in fewer than the usual number of days. One popular arrangement condenses the forty-hour workweek into four ten-hour days. Compressed schedules tend to be somewhat inflexible. Front office staff members may prefer inflexible hours within a four-day week to flexible hours within a five-day week. Benefits from the employer's point of view include enhanced employee morale and reduced absenteeism. Front office managers should be cautious when considering the adoption of compressed schedules. In some states, employees qualify for overtime by working more than eight hours a day, even though their total workweek may not exceed forty hours.

Job Sharing. In **job sharing,** the combined efforts of two or more part-time employees fulfill the duties and responsibilities of one full-time job. Usually, the staff members who share a job work different hours and often different shift portions. Some overlap is desired so staff can exchange information, solve problems, or simply ensure a smooth workflow. Job sharing can lessen department turnover and absenteeism, as well as increase staff morale. The front office also benefits, since even if one job-sharing partner terminates employment, the other may be likely to stay and help train a new partner.

Note that all of the scheduling techniques just discussed must be used with certain restrictions. In hotels where the hourly staff is represented by unions, there may be work scheduling rules that limit the flexibility of schedules or require overtime pay after eight hours are worked on any given day. In other cases, state and federal wage and hour laws may place some limitations on scheduling. Before a front office manager begins scheduling employees, he or she should have a thorough knowledge of these union contract rules and government work regulations.

Staff Motivation

Front office managers should strive to create a work environment that fosters the professional development and growth of the staff. To do so, management must provide training, guidance, instruction, discipline, evaluation, direction, and leadership. When the front office lacks these basic elements, staff may become passive, critical, and indifferent to the hotel's objectives. Such feelings may manifest themselves in absenteeism, poor productivity, and high employee turnover.

With the current changes in the labor market and the high cost of employee turnover, the front office must seek ways to retain effective staff. One way to meet this major challenge is to practice strong motivational techniques.

Motivation can mean many different things. For the purpose of this chapter, motivation means the art of stimulating a front office staff member's interest in a particular job, project, or subject to the extent that he or she is challenged to be continuously attentive, observant, concerned, and committed. Motivation is the result of satisfying human needs associated with personal worth, value, and belonging. In the front office, the outcome of motivation should be that a staff member's sense of worth, value, and belonging has improved from taking part in a particular activity. A front office staff member who receives recognition for contributions he or she makes to the front office's success is typically a highly motivated top performer.

A front office manager can motivate front office staff in a number of ways, including training, cross-training, recognition, communication, and incentive programs.

Training

One of the most effective ways to motivate employees is to train them. Training informs employees that management cares enough to provide the necessary instruction and direction to ensure their success. Successful training includes information not only about the job tasks and duties (the "what to do" of a job), but also about the company culture (the "why tasks are done a certain way" on the job). The *what* and *why* must tie together. If the employee does not know why a job is done a certain way, he or she will not really understand the job. This can lead to poor job performance and friction between employees. When employees understand the culture, they become part of it and support it.

Training significantly reduces the frustration front office staff members feel when they do not know what is expected of them. Effective training educates staff about performance expectations, required tasks, and equipment. The investment in training pays off because it makes employees more productive and efficient, as well as easier to manage.

Cross-Training

Cross-training simply means teaching an employee job functions other than those he or she was hired to perform. Cross-training offers many advantages for both front office management and staff. For the employee, cross-training can offer an opportunity to acquire additional work skills. For the manager, cross-training increases flexibility in scheduling. Cross-trained employees are more valuable, since they can perform several job functions. Finally, cross-training can be a valuable motivational tool that removes many of the obstacles associated with professional growth and advancement.

Recognition

When guests make positive comments about a front office staff member or select the hotel for a return stay, it usually reflects guest satisfaction. Front office management should communicate positive feedback to staff as recognition for a job well done. Graphs and charts that depict improvements in revenues, achievements, occupancy, and guest satisfaction can also be effective motivators.

Guest, managerial, and peer recognition are strong staff motivators. Many hotels solicit guest feedback through comment cards. Comment cards may be handed out at the front desk or placed in guestrooms, dining rooms, or other areas. Comment cards frequently ask guests to mention employees who have provided outstanding service. Completed guest comment cards can be posted on an employee bulletin board, especially those complimenting individual staff efforts.

The front office may offer incentives to employees whom guests favorably recognize. For example, a front desk agent who is mentioned through guest comment cards, comments to managers, or letters to the front office may receive dinner in the hotel dining room or a gift certificate.

Another popular form of recognition is an employee-of-the-month program. Front office management or staff may select a front office staff member of the month. Usually, an employee qualifies for this honor by demonstrating extraordinary commitment to the front office, its standards, and its goals. The front office employee of the month usually receives a prize certificate or a plaque.

Communication

Keeping employees informed about front office operations helps produce positive results. Employees who are informed about upcoming events tend to feel a greater sense of belonging and value.

A front office newsletter or bulletin can be an excellent way to establish and maintain formal communications. Articles included in such a newsletter might be job-related or personal, including such topics as:

- Job opening announcements
- Arriving or in-house VIPs and special events in the hotel

- Promotion, transfer, resignation, and retirement announcements
- New recruit announcements
- Performance tips
- Special recognition awards
- Birthday, marriage, engagement, and birth announcements
- Upcoming event information

A front office area bulletin board provides a place to post schedules, memorandums, announcements, VIPs in house or arriving, group functions, regular training reminders, and other pertinent information. Bulletin boards are most effective when they are in an area accessible to all front office staff and when employees regularly review the information. In many hotels, employee bulletin boards may be the only source of day-to-day information employees need to do their job properly.

Incentive Programs

Excellent employees deserve special appreciation for the work they perform. An **incentive program** is one of the most effective ways to acknowledge staff members who excel in their work. Incentive programs vary in structure and design and often are a great way to reward exceptional performance. The front office should develop and establish incentive programs that result in circumstances that are beneficial to guests, the employees, and the front office. An effective incentive program should challenge the staff and create a spirit of friendly competition.

A well-designed front office incentive program should:

- Recognize and reward exceptional staff performance.
- Increase staff productivity.
- Demonstrate commitment to guest satisfaction.
- Promote staff participation in revenue and service improvement through suggestions for improvement.

The following are basic guidelines for developing an incentive program:

- Develop an incentive program that is appropriate and specific to the front office.
- Outline the specific goals and objectives for the program.
- Define the conditions and requirements that front office staff must meet to receive recognition and rewards.
- Brainstorm a variety of rewards and obtain the necessary approvals for any expenditure.
- Determine the date and time the program will begin. Every staff member should participate. Front office managers should be sure to design a program that is fun, realistic, and creative.

- Be sure the program is sustainable. A program might not be carried to completion if it is too complex, or if employees lack interest in it.

Rewards front office managers typically consider include the following:

- Commendation letters

- Certificates of appreciation

- Public photo display (with the staff member and general manager and/or front office manager)

- Recognition dinners or events

- Gift certificates

- Complimentary weekend packages

- Special parking privileges

- Recognition plaques

Successful incentive programs also provide staff with feedback about goal attainment. For example, charts posted on the front office bulletin board that show individual progress may be very motivational for a reward-oriented incentive program. Goals should be challenging, but should not be so unrealistic that they appear unachievable. Unrealistic goals can frustrate employees and destroy the motivational value of the incentive program.

Front office incentive programs usually center on enhanced occupancy, room revenue, average rate, and guest satisfaction. Conducting one incentive program at a time will help staff focus on specific goals. For example, the front office manager may develop an incentive program directed at increasing the average daily rate or occupancy. Staff may work toward achieving a specific occupancy percentage or a specific average daily rate. The incentive program should last for a specific time period, after which the program should end. During a slow season, for instance, the front office manager may want to concentrate on increasing occupancy. During peak periods, the manager may implement an incentive program to maximize the average daily rate through upselling at the front desk.

Performance Appraisals

Front office staff members need to feel secure with respect to their job performance. The interaction between front office staff and management can affect an employee's self-image and job perception. A **performance appraisal** is one of the most effective techniques a manager can use to enhance motivation and morale.

A performance appraisal:

- Provides each front office staff member with formal written feedback on his or her job performance.

- Identifies strengths and weaknesses in performance and provides plans and actions for improvement.

- Gives the manager and each employee the opportunity to develop specific goals and assign progress dates.

- Recognizes and rewards outstanding performance through possible promotions, wage increases, and additional responsibilities.

- Helps identify employee compatibility with a specific work position.

Front office managers will discover there are many methods of and techniques for evaluating staff performance. Although most hotel companies have performance appraisal programs, each front office manager should tailor an appraisal program to meet the department's goals and objectives. Normally, an effective performance appraisal focuses on an employee's job performance and the steps the employee can follow to improve job skills and performance. Performance appraisals should be fair, objective, informative, and positive. When the appraisal process is complete, the employee should clearly understand what he or she is doing well and where he or she needs to improve. Every employee should receive an appraisal at least once a year.

Many front office managers use written performance appraisal forms and procedures. Written appraisals can be very beneficial when employee counseling or termination is necessary. Written job evaluations should be acknowledged and signed by the staff member and placed in the employee's personnel file. The form may also include space for the employee to add his or her own comments and, perhaps, identify what other positions he or she would like to apply for in the future. The supervisor and employee can then develop a plan of action to prepare for the next position. Written appraisal forms are also important because they protect employers from legal action in case an employee feels he or she has been treated unfairly. There is much less chance of a legal problem when a hotel can show the history of work and disciplinary issues with an employee, and what the hotel did to try to correct the situation.

Summary

The nature of the work force has changed, as have the strategies and laws that govern its management. Front office managers must recognize these changes to better manage and direct the efforts of the front office staff.

Employee recruitment is the process of seeking and screening qualified applicants to fill positions. The process involves communicating job vacancies and interviewing and evaluating applicants. Internal recruiting—the promotion of current employees—can enhance front office morale and productivity. Internal recruiting includes cross-training, succession planning, posting job openings on the premises, rewarding employees for job performance, and keeping a call-back list. External recruiting includes advertising, posting job openings on the hotel's website and employee Intranet, networking, contacting temporary employment agencies, and following up on employee referrals. Federal, state, and local government programs encourage properties to recruit individuals from designated groups by offering tax benefits.

Job descriptions and job specifications are important selection tools. A job description lists all the tasks and related information that make up a work position. Job specifications list and describe the personal qualities, skills, traits, educational background, and experience necessary to successfully perform the tasks outlined by a job description.

Job application forms should be simple to fill out and should require applicants to provide only information that can help a manager determine how suitable they may be for the job. Front office managers evaluate job applicants by reviewing completed job application forms, checking applicant references, and interviewing selected applicants. Managers should check references to verify applicant claims.

A job interviewer should be an objective judge of people, a positive role model, a skillful communicator, and a good salesperson. Managers and interviewers should know what to ask and what not to ask; many types of questions are illegal. After an applicant is interviewed, the applicant should be evaluated. Hotel policy may include police record checks and drug tests of applicants. The use of an interview evaluation form will help ensure that shortcomings in one area do not unduly diminish an applicant's chances for further consideration.

Hiring involves making all the necessary arrangements to prepare the new employee and current staff for a successful working relationship. The hiring period lasts throughout the new employee's initial adjustment to the job. Since hiring requires knowledge of complex employment and labor laws, most hotels rely on the human resources division or someone specifically designated by top management to help with the hiring process.

New employees should be given an orientation when they arrive for their first day of work. The front office manager should take full responsibility for orienting new front office employees.

A critical responsibility of the front office manager is ensuring that employees receive proper training. Training can be guided by job lists, which list the tasks that the person in a position must perform. Job breakdowns specify how each task on a job list should be performed. The job breakdown can serve as a training guide and as a tool for evaluating performance. The front office manager can use performance evaluations based on job breakdowns to identify an employee's training needs.

Scheduling employees is one of the most complex and difficult tasks a front office manager faces. Employee scheduling affects payroll costs, productivity, and morale. Staffing flexibility can be achieved by cross-training employees. Cross-training can help lower labor costs and provide employees with expanded job knowledge and a broader range of skills.

Front office management should strive to create a work environment that fosters professional development and growth in employees. To do so, management should provide training, guidance, instruction, discipline, evaluation, direction, and leadership. When an organization lacks these basic elements, employees may become passive, critical, and indifferent to the company's objectives. Such feelings manifest themselves in absenteeism, poor productivity, and high employee turnover.

🔑 Key Terms

closed-ended questions—Job interview questions requiring only "yes" or "no" answers; closed-ended questions should be limited to verifying information provided on the application or to obtaining facts.

compressed schedule—An adaptation of full-time work hours that enables an employee to work the equivalent of a standard workweek in fewer than the traditional five days.

cross-training—Teaching employees to fill the requirements of more than one position.

external recruiting—A process in which managers seek outside applicants to fill open positions, perhaps through community activities, internship programs, advertising, networking, temporary agencies, and employment agencies.

flextime—A program of flexible work hours that allows employees to vary their times of starting and ending work.

hiring period—The time that starts directly after an employment offer has been made and continues through the new-hire's initial adjustments to the job; this period involves all arrangements necessary to prepare the new-hire and current staff for a successful working relationship.

incentive program—A program offering special recognition and rewards to employees based on their ability to meet certain conditions; programs vary in structure and design and are a way to award exceptional performance.

internal recruiting—A process in which managers recruit job candidates from within a department or property; methods include cross-training, succession planning, posting job openings, and keeping a call-back list.

job analysis—Determining what knowledge each position requires, what tasks each position must perform, and the standards at which the employee must perform the tasks.

job breakdown—A written description that details how the technical duties of a job should be performed.

job description—A detailed list identifying all the key duties of a job as well as reporting relationships, additional responsibilities, working conditions, and any necessary equipment and materials.

job knowledge—Information that an employee must understand to perform his or her tasks.

job sharing—An arrangement in which two or more part-time employees share the responsibilities of one full-time position.

job specifications—A list of the personal qualities, skills, and traits required to successfully perform the tasks outlined by a job description.

motivation—Stimulating a person's interest in a particular job, project, or subject so that the individual is challenged to be continually attentive, observant, concerned, and committed.

open-ended questions—Job interview questions requiring more than a "yes" or "no" answer; open-ended questions should lead applicants to provide more detailed responses.

orientation—The period of time devoted to teaching a new employee the basic elements of the job, including the skills and information required to perform the job.

performance appraisal—The process in which an employee is periodically evaluated by his or her manager or supervisor to assess job performance and to discuss steps the employee can take to improve job skills and performance.

performance standard—A required level of performance that establishes the acceptable quality of work.

recruitment—The process in which qualified applicants are sought and screened to fill currently or soon-to-be-vacant positions; involves announcing or advertising job vacancies and evaluating applicants to determine whom to hire.

task list—A list identifying all the key duties of a job in the order of their importance.

Review Questions

1. How are job descriptions and job specifications used in the selection process?

2. Where can a front office manager look for job applicants? What methods can the manager use to find and recruit employees?

3. What are the steps involved in conducting an interview? What techniques and cautions should an interviewer keep in mind when asking interview questions?

4. What points should be covered in an employee orientation?

5. How does a job breakdown expand on the information presented in a job list? What steps are involved in developing job breakdowns?

6. Why is preparing for training important? How can trainers prepare for training? What guidelines can help trainers effectively train?

7. What are several types of alternative scheduling techniques?

8. For what reason(s) are the most effective performance appraisals conducted?

9. What is motivation? What methods can front office managers use to motivate employees? How could an incentive program motivate front office employees?

10. Why is a written performance evaluation important to the hotel and the employee?

Internet Sites

For more information, visit the following Internet sites. Remember that Internet addresses can change without notice. If the site is no longer there, you can use a search engine to look for additional sites.

HR Magazine
http://moss07.shrm.org/publications/
hrmagazine/

Society for Human Resource
  Management (SHRM)
www.shrm.org

Human Resource Executive Online
www.hreonline.com

Case Studies ────────────────────────────────

The General Manager Turns Over Staffing Issues

Bill Miller was the general manager of the Boden Oceanside Resort and Lodge. He was troubled by the turnover at the front office over the past year. During the past five months, the front office had lost Tim, the front office manager; two front office supervisors; and several guest service agents.

Sarah was the guest service agent who had been with the resort the longest—a short one-and-a-half years. Sarah had recently been promoted to supervisor. While she had never been a supervisor before, her work ethic, her demeanor with customers, and her knowledge of the front office procedures and systems seemed to make her an ideal candidate for the position. So, without hesitation, Tim had promoted her. Sarah was now reporting to Bill, since Tim's replacement hadn't been found yet.

Sarah worked well with the rest of the front office staff, including reservations agents, PBX operators, bell attendants, the concierge staff, and the valet staff. Now that there was no front office manager, Sarah and the staff were responsible for organizing their own schedules, managing the cash-outs, and solving most of the day-to-day problems of the front office. This had been going on for more than two weeks now, and Bill was wondering how much longer they could continue to work effectively without oversight from a front office manager. Bill was considering adjusting the structure of the front office so that Sarah and others would have opportunities to move up the ladder and eventually gain the experience necessary to effectively manage the front office.

The new structure he was considering included a new position of assistant front office manager and a reservations manager. The front office already had a bell captain, Sarah the front desk supervisor, and the other line positions necessary to operate the front office effectively.

Bill wondered if this new structure would help alleviate some of the stress that the front office manager might feel, and help to reduce the turnover in this critical position. Bill knew that turnover often occurred within the first thirty to sixty days of employment. This didn't explain the resignations of the front office manager and front office supervisors. They had been with the resort for between two and four years. However, recent turnover in the line staff had been within the first two months of employment.

Bill wondered if the two-week training program dedicated to teaching all of the systems and procedures of the front office was too rigorous for new staff. New hires began with an orientation program that lasted nearly eight hours. Orientation covered general operating procedures, general property information, the mission of the organization, a tour of the property, and a discussion of wages and benefits, federal laws, and company policy. The training that followed the orientation was an intensive two-week program where the new employee rotated through all of the front office and reservation positions, including bell attendant, concierge, and valet. The training was designed to give the new employees an overall picture of the operation at the front office. Often the training regime was punctuated with interruptions due to short staffing or unusually high traffic days, and trainees were asked to pitch in and help at the front desk or bell station. This wasn't too bad, since the trainees were able to practice what they had learned when in that role during one or more of the previous training sessions. However, sometimes the trainees hadn't been introduced to the role and so had to find their way with minimal assistance. Often the trainee would arrive for his or her shift and find that the person that trained them the day before was not on duty and so someone else was assigned the role of trainer for the day. This usually meant that the person asked how it was going and then assumed that the trainee could perform many of the tasks because they were pretty easy. Sometimes trainees had good days and sometimes they had bad days.

Bill also reflected on the hiring process. He was the one who hired the management team, with some assistance from the human resources department. Personnel in the human resources department primarily hired the line staff. They were responsible for recruiting, including advertising for and screening applicants, initial interviews, and finally offering the position. Hiring was pretty routine for the human resources department. The head of human resources was a veteran of many seasons. She commonly remarked to Bill that turnover should be expected in a seasonal business such as the resort industry.

Sarah had been a good hire. She had been attracted to the lodge by an advertisement in her town twenty miles away. She hadn't worked in a hotel before the Boden Resort and Lodge, but was really enjoying the position. She moved up quickly and was looking forward to a possible career in the industry. She was eager to advance and gain whatever skills and knowledge she would need to be successful in management. She was uncertain about how to approach Bill with her career goals or whether she should go directly to the human resources department. After the initial orientation program, Sarah hadn't seen anyone from human resources. She received her paychecks every Thursday at the front desk and never had occasion to visit the human resources department.

Now that the front office manager position was vacant, Sarah wondered if she could fill it. It didn't look very difficult from her perspective. Bill wondered the same thing. It would be so easy to fill the position from within, and Sarah seemed like she would stay around a long time if he could give her a good position. She might be a bit young, he thought, but she was very bright and eager to learn.

As Bill's office phone rang, he was brought back to reality. It was Sarah on the other end. She had a guest who wanted to speak with the manager about a posting that hadn't been adjusted even after the guest requested the adjustment the night before. Bill wondered why the guest hadn't asked Sarah to take care of the situation. He wondered again if she should be promoted to front office manager. Would her promotion have a negative effect on occupancy rates, revenue per available room, and the quality of the guest experience?

Bill determined to set aside some time to assess turnover in other parts of the resort. He pondered what he could do to begin to reduce turnover. He hadn't done the math, but he knew that turnover must cost the hotel tens of thousands of dollars per year. He wasn't quite sure how to calculate the costs of turnover but decided to ask his managers to help solve this problem.

Discussion Questions

1. What recommendations do you have for Bill regarding the hiring process at the Boden?

2. How should Bill review the training process at the Boden?

3. What are some ways Bill could reduce turnover at the Boden?

4. How could Sarah gain the necessary skills for the position of front office manager?

Case number: 608C16

This case also appears in Todd Comen, *Case Studies in Front Office Management* (Lansing, Mich.: American Hotel & Lodging Educational Institute, 2003).

Staffing for Ski Season at the Frozen Penguin Resort

As a winter ski destination, the Frozen Penguin Resort encounters many full occupancy seasonal periods. In fact, the hotel is booked solid for the six weeks in the middle of the ski season (a ten-week season). Anticipating this increase in business, management must develop a plan to staff the resort in both the first two weeks (early) and final two weeks (late) as well as the six-week high point of the season.

Fortunately, Mr. Scott, the newly hired front office manager, used to be responsible for staffing the Seaquestered Summer Resort, a property that experienced similar occupancy cycles. The fact that the Frozen Penguin is located in a wilderness region, however, creates a challenge for Mr. Scott. He always had the luxury of hiring temporary employees from the community college near the Seaquestered Summer Resort, but in the mountains surrounding the Frozen Penguin, there is little availability of temporary staff.

Mr. Scott believes that there are two parts to the solution to the staffing puzzle. First, he figures he must recruit a core staff that will commit itself to working the entire ten weeks. He believes he can pay each staff member a reasonable rate throughout the work period and also offer an incentive bonus, payable at the successful completion of the entire season. Second, Mr. Scott feels that in the past the resort has not sufficiently trained the staff to work at a high level of productivity. He feels that through cross-training and restructuring of front office functions, staff members will be capable of working much more effectively and will maintain good morale.

Discussion Questions

1. What do you think are the strengths and weaknesses of the core staff proposal? Is an incentive bonus for successful completion a sound idea? What else could Mr. Scott do to attract the staff necessary to operate the resort?

2. Provide five questions that Mr. Scott may be wise to ask each candidate during a job interview. Be careful to develop questions that will enable Mr. Scott to evaluate the applicants' potential for the proposed training program.

3. What do you think about Mr. Scott's plan to cross-train and restructure front office functions and responsibilities? What do you believe to be of importance in building morale?

4. How should Mr. Scott communicate the standards to the applicants to ensure that they understand the resort's expectations?

Case Number: 33212CA

The following industry experts helped generate and develop this case: Richard M. Brooks, CHA, Vice President, TWE Group; and Michael L. Kasavana, NAMA Professor in Hospitality Business, *The* School of Hospitality Business, Michigan State University, East Lansing, Michigan.

Memos from the Front Office Manager

Tim Notion, the front office manager of the Boden Oceanside Resort and Lodge, was uncertain about the upcoming summer season. Salary and wages for the front office exceeded $300,000 in the last year, including front desk agents, night auditors, PBX operators, reservations agents, and bell attendants.

Revenue from January to May was reasonably close to budget forecasts, but the bookings for the next few months were perplexing. People seemed to be waiting until the last minute to make plans, causing the major summer season to be booked very slowly. Considering that the property had been dramatically raising rates for the past three years and that the economy had taken a turn for the worse, resort management was hoping that the reservations department would begin peaking soon or they might be looking at a lackluster summer season.

The front office had been hit recently with some turnover of key front desk agents. The new front desk agents, as one would expect, took more attention from the front desk supervisor and assistant front office manager. Tim's assistant had been with the resort for two years but was new to the industry, having come from twenty years working in quick-service restaurants. His newly promoted front desk supervisor was mature, but also new to the hospitality industry, having come from the non-profit sector.

The reservations department had two new supervisors, Robin and Tracy. Robin was promoted to manage the systems and training, while Tracy managed the scheduling, hiring, and communications. Tracy had come to the resort with no prior experience and had worked her way up the ladder over the past three years. Robin had come to the lodge three years ago from a nearby resort. Robin was great at training and had a knack for working with the reservations software program. She worked long hours, but wasn't interested in being fully in charge of reservations because she didn't want to take more time away from her family.

In an effort to manage the front office payroll, Tim was considering some options. He had been trying to hire a reservations manager in hopes that this person could put some discipline into the reservations department. But this had gone unfilled for nearly three months, so the idea of having two supervisors became a reality.

Tracy, the reservations supervisor in charge of hiring, scheduling, motivation, and communications, was having problems with getting her staff together to figure out strategies for making the department more efficient. Since everyone had personal time constraints and no one was willing to come in for a meeting on their day off, she was at her wit's end. She had told everyone that they could clock in for the meeting. On top of all this, Tracy was short-staffed and had no time to do the paperwork and other supervisory duties the general manager and front office manager required. She was supposed to generate the morning report, confirmation letters, quality audits of the reservations process, and special requests for guests.

It wasn't surprising that Tracy couldn't get a meeting together, she confided to Robin. The whole department hadn't had a meeting for over a year. They relied instead on a reservations log that each shift was asked to write in regarding guest issues and other information pertinent to day-to-day operations. Recently, little issues were becoming sore spots among staff members, who tended to complain daily about how they performed certain tasks while others just let them slide. These included tasks such as filing the guest history cards, tidying up the front desk, and highlighting return guest arrivals.

The forecasts for the past three months hadn't been met and therefore the department was under budget for the year. During the recent managers meeting, the marketing director and general manager suggested that the summer months might be slower than anticipated. They told the department managers that they must hold the line on payroll and reduce it if possible. Tim wondered how he could reduce the number of hours even as they headed into the height of the summer season.

After reviewing reports from accounting regarding the front office payroll, Tim decided that marginal reductions in labor expenses could be achieved through more accurate and timely scheduling. He had successfully thwarted any pay increases during the last year by not scheduling any performance reviews. One of the front desk staff members had requested a raise, but Tim had told him that he was close to the top of his pay scale and that they would discuss pay during performance reviews.

Finally, after much thought, Tim generated the following memo to communicate with his staff regarding front office expenses:

Front Office Memo

Date: June 3
To: Front Office Staff
CC: General Manager, Controller
From: Tim Notion
RE: Schedule

I have been reviewing the time punches for the front office in an effort to keep our costs at a reasonable rate. I have determined that many employees are punching in more than ten minutes before their scheduled start times. This must stop immediately! When arriving to work early, you may clock in seven minutes before your shift so that you can get in uniform.

Additionally, all staff must clock out for all meals unless you are in reservations and eat your meal at your workstation. This should happen only when there is one person scheduled for reservations.

Thank you for your help in keeping our costs under control.

The next week, Tim was planning for his summer staffing. His goal was to keep things really tight, using no more labor than necessary to meet the needs of guests. He wasn't going to allow any and all substitutions, as had gone on during his first summer as front office manager. He decided to put his strategy in writing so that his staff would know what he expected during the upcoming busy season:

Front Office Memo

Date:	June 14
To:	Front Office Staff
CC:	General Manager
From:	Tim Notion
RE:	Requests for vacation and time off

We are coming into our busy season and I need to remind everyone about leave requests. Yes, these are requests!

To help with scheduling, I have posted a new calendar in my office. Your request for a leave—once approved—will be recorded on the calendar. Only the assistant front office manager and I may enter names on this calendar. Please do not arrange for a vacation before getting approval for time off. Staffing in the department is limited and we need to work together when planning our summer.

Let's hope for a busy and productive summer season.

Later that month, Tim and the general manager were reviewing expenses for the front office. Bookings were way off for the upcoming and usually busy month of August, and management was feeling the pressure to control unnecessary expenses. The GM and Tim noticed that payroll was still above budget but, frankly, Tim couldn't figure out how to trim any more off his payroll. He returned to his office and took another look at his payroll and schedules for the past month. Finally he wrote the following memo to his reservation staff:

Front Office Memo

Date:	July 4
To:	Reservations Agents
CC:	General Manager
From:	Tim Notion
RE:	Meal breaks

I thought that I had made it quite clear that everyone should take their meal breaks off the clock. It is clear from the payroll report that this is not being followed. Everyone is to take their meal breaks away from the phones. If you choose to take only a twenty-minute break, fine, but clock out. You must take at least fifteen minutes, by LAW. The ONLY exception is for those who are working alone, or for less than a six-hour shift. I am adjusting punches to reflect this policy!

Thanks!

Discussion Questions

1. What suggestions do you have for Tim and Tracy regarding improving communications within the department?

2. Do you think that Tim's memos are effective in achieving his goals? What would you suggest, if anything, to Tim, regarding rewriting these memos?

Case number: 608C14

This case also appears in Todd Comen, *Case Studies in Front Office Management* (Lansing, Mich.: American Hotel & Lodging Educational Institute, 2003).

Appendix

Internet Concepts

The Internet has been the fastest growing area of automation applications affecting the hospitality industry. The popularity of the **World Wide Web (www),** the part of the Internet that supports multimedia, contributes to this growth. The World Wide Web represents one of the more exciting uses of technology, supporting interactive applications, self-service functions, telecommunication options, and video broadcasting. The World Wide Web, also referred to simply as *the web,* is an elaborate distributed database of documents, graphics, and other multimedia elements. It is composed of millions of hypertext documents available at websites around the globe. **Hypertext** is text that is organized so that related items are connected through a network. The web is a system of documents, images, and multimedia that can be easily accessed by any Internet user. One set of hypertext documents can be linked to others to create a large distributed computing network. It is not just a vast library of information resources; it is also a medium for presentation, promotion, and transaction processing.

The web is a menu-based system that organizes Internet resources into a series of menu pages, or screens. Each connected web server maintains pointers, or links, to data on the Internet and is capable of retrieving that data. Data can exist as text files, audio files, video files, graphic image files, or any other data that can be stored in a computer system.

The **Internet,** or simply *the Net,* is larger than the World Wide Web and consists of a large, complex series of computer networks designed to provide global public access to information and communication services. A **network** is a configuration of workstations that enables users to share data, programs, and peripheral devices (such as servers and printers). Data sharing allows system-wide communications, and program sharing enables users to access infrequently used programs without the loss of speed or memory capacity that would result if those programs were installed at each desktop unit (referred to as a *client*). From an economic perspective, device sharing is an important benefit derived from networking. Expensive peripheral devices, such as high-capacity storage devices and color laser printers, can be made available to all clients cabled to a network.

A network environment can be configured as client-server (c/s) or peer-to-peer (p/p). A client-server environment links a powerful computer or several powerful computers (referred to as the *file server* or the *server*) to several (a handful, dozens, or even hundreds) of other, less powerful computers (the clients). Clients may access a variety of programs stored on the server and draw upon the server's processing power to perform tasks more quickly and more efficiently than if they operated in a stand-alone mode. For example, a server might sort through thousands of data items in a matter of a few seconds, whereas it might take much longer for a desktop computer to perform the same task.

An advantage of the client-server environment is that the server can handle multiple client requests simultaneously. Client-server networks also improve system performance by managing communications (e-mail) and providing network administration (monitoring and security). In a peer-to-peer network, each work-station functions as both a client and a server. An example of a simple peer-to-peer network is a home network where two or three computers are connected and may share a printer or communications access to the Internet. Since any client can be a server and any server can be a client, the devices are considered to have equal, or *peer,* status. Peer-to-peer networks, like client-server networks, support communications, database management, and file sharing. Unlike the client-server network, peer-to-peer networks may achieve lower levels of performance and be more prone to security and access control problems.

In reality, the Internet is a network of networks, connecting local and regional computer sites to an expansive electronic grid. The World Wide Web differs from the Internet in that it is the public portion of the Internet. There are many networks connected to the Internet that are private and not for public use.

Internet Operations

The Internet was initially conceived around the same time as the development of interstate highways in the United States. The design of the interstate highway system, which links major cities across the country, was based upon the need to maintain a continuous flow of supplies throughout the country. The roadways were designed with sufficient alternate routing that a steady flow of materials to all parts of the nation could be ensured. These same principles were deemed important in the creation of the Internet. Using the interstate highway system as a model, attention focused on ensuring a continuous movement of data between computers at various strategic locations from coast to coast. Internet planners sought to create a myriad of alternate communication routes across a diversity of computer platforms.

The Internet has produced a technological explosion that continues to affect all aspects of everyday life around the world, including the hospitality industry. While the Internet is technically global, it is estimated that nearly two-thirds of all Internet usage is attributable to the United States. It is for this reason that the Internet tends to be dominated with English-language sites and content directed to U.S. audiences.

The Internet began as a high-speed network created for the U.S. Department of Defense. Military leaders sought a network that could transmit information between agencies at high speeds while also being protected from energy fluctuations or blackouts. It is for this reason that the Internet is an interconnected web of networks without a central hub.

To communicate with each other, the networks use a set of standards called **protocols**. By adopting these same network protocols, government and commercial agencies have been able to connect to the **backbone** of the Internet. The backbone is the component part of the Internet designed to carry a majority of network traffic. When a computer is connected to the backbone it becomes an Internet appliance. In addition, connecting a computer or computer network to a device connected to the backbone provides that device with Internet capability. The backbone forms the main artery of the Internet architecture. Illustration 1 contains a schematic representation of this architecture. In a front office, for example, a local

Illustration 1   Internet Connectivity

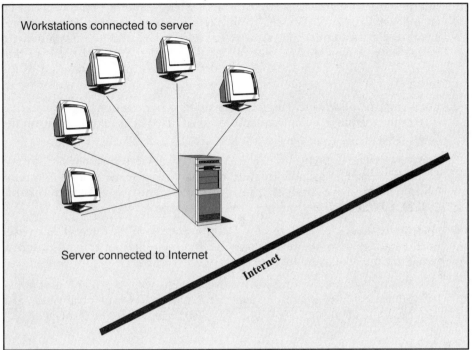

area network (LAN) may be used to connect individual workstation terminals to a server. In turn, the server may also be used to establish a gateway to the Internet. While connected to the Internet, front office staff can share data and information with millions of users worldwide.

Connectivity

The cost of accessing the Internet ranges from complimentary to relatively expensive, with the possibility of a fixed monthly fee and additional usage fees. Few users have direct access to the Internet. Most need to subscribe to an **online service provider (OSP)** or purchase access through an **Internet service provider (ISP)**. Basically, an OSP enables the user to use online services other than the Internet, and, if desired, link to a dedicated server connected to the Internet backbone. America Online and MSN are examples of OSPs because they provide a myriad of services as well as direct access to the Internet. A second (and more common alternative) is an ISP. An ISP provides direct connectivity to the Internet backbone so long as the user is connected to the ISP server. EarthLink, cable television companies, and telephone companies offering Internet access are examples of ISPs. In essence, the ISP provides a channel for the user to participate in the Internet, while an OSP provides other services plus Internet access. Regardless of whether an ISP or OSP link is used, there are five basic component requirements for establishing an Internet connection:

1. *User PC or other computer-based device.* Any device that is connected to the Internet and has programming that understands Internet protocols can be an Internet appliance. Personal computers, printers, servers, scanners, personal digital assistants (PDAs), wireless telephones, and workstations with no memory or data storage capabilities (often called *dumb terminals* or *thin terminals*) are just a few examples of devices that can be connected to the Internet.

2. *Communications software.* This includes all the programming that formats and directs the messages being sent and received, as well as all the traffic on the Internet itself.

3. *Communications equipment.* This includes the devices that physically connect the Internet to an individual PC or an entire network. Communications equipment consists of bridges, gateways, routers, and network interface cards (NICs). The connectivity can be wired or wireless.

4. *An Internet account.* This is required to allow access to the Internet. Each user must have a unique identification on the Internet. Internet accounts are provided through OSPs and ISPs for most Internet users.

5. *Web browser software.* This enables the user to view web pages. The most popular web browsers are Microsoft's Internet Explorer, Netscape's Navigator, and America Online. Without a web browser, web pages cannot be displayed.

Hardware

The Internet is a collection of diverse networks. Data transmitted on the Internet will likely travel through several types of networks, computers, and communication lines before reaching a final destination. Special hardware components of the Internet are designed to move data from network to network in a seamless operation. Such devices as bridges, gateways, routers, and NICs are essential to effective Internet operations.

A **bridge** connects two or more networks that use the same data transfer protocol (the same address format). A bridge makes attached networks appear to operate as a single network. The purposes of a bridge are to extend network capabilities and isolate network traffic.

A **gateway** provides a means for two incompatible networks to communicate. A gateway simply converts the sending computer's request into a format that the receiving computer can understand.

Internet host computers are connected to **routers** that direct messages to different areas of the Internet. A router interprets the protocol used in a data packet (a group of data being sent over the Internet) and translates between sending and receiving protocols. Routers, therefore, can be used to connect networks that use different protocols.

An NIC is basically a communications device that is placed inside a computer that enables it to be connected to a network. The NIC provides a cable connection out of the computer, thereby providing a physical point of connectivity for a wired network or an antenna for wireless access.

Illustration 2   Internet Services

Internet Services

Internet services are generally available to all Internet participants at no cost and do not require special equipment, but may require additional programming in the Internet appliance. There are several services available through the Internet, including: electronic mail for exchanging messages, file transfer protocol for moving files from one location to another, list services for information distribution to subscribers, instant messaging for interactive discussions, newsgroups for focused topic coverage, bulletin boards for electronic postings, and search engines for research. As the Internet evolves, new and unique services will be added to this list. Illustration 2 contains a summary of Internet services.

Electronic Mail

Electronic mail, or **e-mail,** enables users to communicate rapidly whether the receiver resides in the same building, across town, out of state, or elsewhere. E-mail is usually the first application a new Internet user encounters and is the most widely used Internet service. With e-mail, sending a message halfway around the world is as easy as writing a note to the person next door. The only requirement is that the sender must know the intended recipient's e-mail address and have an e-mail software package.

Basically, e-mail is a message or document that is composed, mailed, received, and read through computers. E-mail combines the qualities traditionally attributed to a letter or document sent through the postal service with the speed, efficiency, and dependability of placing a phone call. In addition, sending an e-mail usually costs less than the price of a stamp or phone call.

File Transfer Protocol

File Transfer Protocol (FTP), also referred to as *Telnet transfer,* is a way to access and transfer files, programs, or other services via the Internet. FTP is the oldest and most popular method for transferring files from a remote Internet site to a local computer. FTP sites house programs that are available as **shareware** (which requires a registration fee for use) or freeware (no cost for use). Historically, FTP involved using a complex set of commands to navigate an Internet site and identify files to be transferred. This no longer is the case, as advanced navigational software can be used to access and manage most FTP sites. With the improved ease of downloading files (that is, moving files from a remote site to a local computer) from the Internet, many hospitality software suppliers have begun offering demonstration versions of their products. Although not obvious to the user, FTP provides a means for effectively moving electronic information between dissimilar computers without either the sender or receiver having to modify operating procedures. In essence, FTP is a base for public file sharing.

List Servers

Listserv is short for *list server* and is used to describe an automated information distribution system. A listserv program enables a user to add (subscribe) or delete (unsubscribe) his or her name from an extensive array of active Internet discussion groups. Typically, a user registers for a discussion group and simultaneously subscribes to a listserv mailing list. To subscribe, the user simply sends an e-mail message to the host computer on which the list server is located. Whenever an item is to be distributed to the list, an e-mail is automatically prepared and sent to all subscribers simultaneously.

Instant Messaging

Instant messaging (IM) is a term used to describe any program that allows two or more users to communicate in real-time interactive discussions. It works much like a telephone or teleconference call, only it is text-based and on the Internet. To take part in IM, users must use software called a *client.* After installing the client (most clients are available free via the Internet), a user can gain access (log on) to a host IM server and select among several IM channels, each of which is dedicated to a virtual community of participants (chat group). Selecting a channel allows the user to participate in discussions with other users who are currently connected to the same chat group. After choosing a screen name (chat identity), the user begins communicating by typing text entries. All entered text is instantly passed to the receiver(s) on the same channel. It is for this reason that IM is capable of hosting timely and lively worldwide conversations.

Newsgroups

A **newsgroup** is essentially an online discussion group that focuses narrowly on a particular topic. For example, there are newsgroups dedicated to alternative music, sports teams, alien movies, historical events, political espionage, restaurant reviews, hotel technology, and Burmese Mountain dogs. Newsgroups are organized into various hierarchies by general topic, and within each topic can be many sub-topics. Discussions take place via e-mail, which is sent to the newsgroup's address. A newsgroup may be moderated or unmoderated. If a newsgroup is moderated, e-mail is automatically routed to the moderator, a person who screens all incoming e-mail to ensure it is appropriate before posting it to the newsgroup. In an unmoderated newsgroup, all received messages are immediately posted to all participants.

Newsgroup servers host newsgroups that share information and commentary on predefined topics. The members of each group post and reply to messages, creating message threads. The open nature of newsgroups often encourages broad participation, which may lead to a loss of focus. For this reason, most newsgroups tend to offer a list of **frequently asked questions (FAQs),** which participants must read before engaging in a newsgroup discussion. Presenting a FAQs (often pronounced "faks") section helps maintain focus while guiding the group's ongoing discussions.

Bulletin Boards

Usenet is a network of newsgroups independent of the Internet but with gateway links to the Internet. Usenet was the pioneer of electronic bulletin boards and continues to serve several thousand special interest groups. Usenet is a system outside of, but closely aligned with, the Internet. Usenet relies on e-mail to provide a centralized, text-based news service. For this reason, Usenet participants are referred to as *newsreaders* capable of posting, reading, and responding to online messages. Usenet newsgroups are essentially bulletin boards where users read and post messages about topics of their choice. When a message is posted to a newsgroup, everyone who visits that newsgroup can read the message and respond. The difference between Usenet, newsgroups, and IM is that Usenet and newsgroups are not dedicated to a real-time exchange of information.

Search Engines

A **search engine** enables identification and retrieval of specific Internet resources based upon selected topic or key word searches across selected segments of the Internet. Library materials, archival data, news media, production releases, retail outlets, databases, technical concepts, product searches, and the like can be investigated, discovered, and retrieved. Google, Yahoo!, and Excite are examples of search engines. A search engine is basically a database that contains references to a variety of resources. Users are able to submit queries and interact with databases to determine which, if any, contain resources matching the search criteria. Users can access a search engine, or search service, to try to find Internet sites of interest using specially identifiable words—**keywords** and names. Search engines, for the most part, are available without charge and offer user-friendly features. Once a user enters a query, the search engine responds with a list of possible sites housing the information in question. Search engines tend to offer a variety of search

Illustration 3   Descriptions of Internet Services

E-mail—enables user to send text, graphics, sound, and images across the network

FTP—provides a means for user to copy a file from a remote computer to a local computer

IM—real-time online text-based discussion without the need to post messages to a bulletin board

List Services—channels for information broadcasting via an automated mailing distribution system

Newsgroups—moderated or unmoderated online discussions focused on a specific topic

Search Engine—identification and retrieval of Internet resources based upon key word searches

Telnet—protocol for remote login to another computer and access to its public resources

Usenet—ability to send and receive groups of messages across the network

---

parameters that enable the user to narrow the search query so that the identified resources possess a higher degree of relevance to the item under investigation.

Many search engines provide an index of categories or a directory of topics to assist the user in further qualifying or narrowing the search criteria. In a directory, the user is able to pick a general topic to point toward a specific Internet site—for example, selecting the category "hospitality," then picking the subcategory "hotels," and finally selecting a resort property. Directories are easy to use and can lead to successful outcomes. In addition, some search engines provide reviews and ratings of matching Internet sites. Illustration 3 provides summary descriptions of Internet services.

Social Networking

A **social network** is formed as an online, web-based community of individuals who have common interests, activities, and/or experiences. Active members explore, share, and discuss whatever matters they deem relevant and appropriate, as the network is designed to simplify online communications in real time. It enables the sharing of a wide range of information and opinions posted by people eager for virtual conversation.

A social network is formulated as a free-flowing, unregulated environment that presents both an opportunity and a challenge for hospitality firms. Guests who elect to write about their experiences at the hotel may be helpful or harmful. Non-guests who have an opinion about the business may present a supportive or non-supportive perspective or reaction. In addition, some hotel companies have taken the offensive by regularly providing information to an ongoing dialogue that helps promote the property's image, offerings, and events.

There are numerous social networking websites, including: MySpace, Facebook, Classmates, Bebo, Orkut, PerfSpot, Flickr, LiveJournal, myYearbook,

MSN Spaces, Ravelry, Xanga, and Friendster. Similarly, the list of hospitality-oriented social networking sites is extensive, including TripAdvisor, TravelPost, Gusto!, MyTravelGuide, TravBuddy, Fodors, TripConnect, VirtualTourist, and WAYN. Such technologies as chat sessions, text messaging, e-mail threads, digital media, file sharing, discussion groups, and blogging are popular methods of interactivity.

Internet Addressing

There are two important elements required for effective Internet operations: addressing and communicating. Addressing involves the assignment of unique identification credentials to users and machines. User addresses facilitate an exchange of messages, while computer addresses enable access to Internet resources. The system used to identify people, computers, and resources on the network is called *Internet addressing*. There are two distinct addressing schemes, one dealing specifically with interpersonal communications and the other with machine access. The most common interpersonal communication is e-mail. An e-mail address identifies a person or computer for message exchange. It is read from left to right and uses the format username@domain.name. The domain name describes the organization hosting the e-mail server, and the name portion of the address details the type of organization. For example, consider the e-mail address mikek@ahlei.org. This hypothetical address belongs to Michael Kasavana (user name: mikek), who supposedly works at the American Hotel & Lodging Educational Institute (domain name: ahlei), which is categorized as an *organization* Internet entity (name: org). Unlike e-mail addresses, computer addresses are based on a numerical address on the Internet called an **Internet Protocol (IP) address** and domain name. The IP address is a unique number used to identify every computer connected to the Internet; it is discussed below.

Domain Name System

The **Domain Name System (DNS)** is a method for organizing site names on the Internet. The DNS comprises rules that groups together network computers, called *hosts*, into a hierarchy of authority that allows addressing and other information to be widely distributed and maintained. An advantage of DNS is that it eliminates dependency on a centrally maintained file for tracking host names to addresses.

For example, suppose an Internet sponsor is ready to make a network site available on the Internet. Assuming the site's content and network server are properly configured, the network manager seeks to ensure that the newly created site will be discoverable on the Internet. To reach this destination site, an inquiring user must have a web browser to enter the site's domain name (address). The domain name is the most visible component of Internet identity.

The domain name is formatted as a **uniform resource locator (URL)** specification, such as http://www.ahlei.org. In this example, ahlei.org is the portion of the URL referred to as the parent domain name. Traditional Internet e-mail addresses, like mikek@ahlei.org, also contain the parent domain name. The parent domain name is the common link between e-mail and Internet addresses and is intended

Illustration 4   Web Page Addressing

to designate a group of computers. A host name is the name assigned to a specific computer. The host name is attached to the left of the domain name. The result is the formation of a complete host domain name. If www is the name of a host inside the domain ahlei.org, specifying www.ahlei.org will direct a browser to the host.

Every host on a network requires an Internet Protocol (IP) address. IP addresses consist of a sequence of numbers that identifies a specific location on the Internet. Think of an IP address as a street address. An IP address is tied very closely to the domain name and is primarily used by the network to identify a specific computer's location. The domain name serves as an easily understood human language translation of the IP address. Internet users typically do not have to be concerned with IP addresses, since domain names hide the IP address from the user. Domain names are much easier to remember and share than IP addresses.

The owner of a parent domain can create and administer additional child domains or subdomains. As an example, consider the creation of a subdomain for sales (sales.ahlei.org) and customer service (support.ahlei.org) as extensions of the parent domain name. Domain names reflect a domain's hierarchy by adhering to a set of standards. Domain names are written from left to right, from the most specific (subdomain name) to the least specific (parent domain name) part of the domain name (which is separated by a dot). Illustration 4 provides an example of an IP address compared with its web page address.

Domain Name Extensions

The domain name extension is written to the right of the root domain (after the last dot). This extension is referred to as the *top-level domain* (TLD). Membership in a

TLD category is based on the type of organization to which the user or participating system belongs. Popular top-level domain extensions include:

ARTS—cultural/entertainment entities

BIZ—business reference sites

COM—commercial organizations

EDU—educational institutions

FIRM—business firms

GOV—governmental agencies

INFO—information service entities

MIL—military organizations

NET—network support groups/network providers

NOM—individual or personal nomenclature

ORG—organizations (such as non-profit organizations)

PRO—professional affiliation

REC—recreation/entertainment entities

STORE—businesses offering goods for sale

TV—television affiliation sites

WEB—activities related to the World Wide Web

A domain name extension provides information about the person or organization to which it is assigned. For example, *.com* (pronounced "dot-com") is short for *commercial organizations;* it is probably the most widely used domain naming extension. Sometimes a company seeking to reserve its domain name may face the predicament that the domain name is already taken by another organization and is only available with an alternative extension. For example, the University Inn in East Lansing, Michigan, might find that the URL universityinn.com is already taken by another hotel in another city. The hotel's managers may find that another domain name extension, such as *.net* (pronounced "dot-net"), short for *networks,* is available with the desired domain name. Although once exclusively reserved for Internet service providers, *.net* may be a feasible alternative. In other words, the restrictions previously enforced have been relaxed as Internet activity has grown. Some companies and educational institutions have successfully registered with the *.net* extension.

Domain names must be unique and cannot exceed twenty-four characters. Valid characters are alphabetical letters, numbers, and dash marks. Before a domain name can become active, a thorough search is conducted by the **Inter-NIC** (an agency responsible for administering domain names) to verify its uniqueness. After the InterNIC approves a domain name, it is added to the user's startup file. The computer's IP address corresponds with the domain name and is discoverable by Internet site sponsors.

Internet Acronyms

Three important Internet acronyms are URL, HTML, and HTTP. As mentioned previously, the web is composed of websites with addresses commonly referred to as URLs (pronounced "earls"). URLs typically begin with a prefix that identifies the type of resource being accessed. Typing an URL into a web browser will direct the program to access the website at that address. HTML denotes **Hypertext Markup Language,** which is a text-based generic computer language used for representing the design and contents of documents that can be displayed by a web browser. HTTP (Hypertext Transport Protocol) is an information retrieval technique designed to help users access websites quickly. Addresses for documents on the web typically are preceded by http://. The server's computer name and domain then follow this prefix. When private or proprietary data is requested, the website address likely will automatically change to HTTPS, indicating that the HTTP link is now secure (protected from outside interference). HTTPS provides the user with a heightened comfort level as security measures are engaged prior to data entry.

Internet Communications

There is no central management of the Internet. Instead, it is a collection of thousands of individual networks and organizations, each of which is independently owned and operated. Each network cooperates with other networks to direct network traffic, so that information can continuously pass through the Internet. In order for networks and computers to work effectively, there must be general agreement regarding network communication procedures and standards.

Common communications protocols make network communications possible. Communication protocols, or standards, help ensure communications among computers of different types and from different manufacturers. Data is transferred through the physical paths of a network in various ways. Sometimes transmission involves sending data in different formats or dividing messages into segments. In other cases, data transfer involves coordinating transmissions to make the most efficient use of the media and devices on a network.

The Internet transmits data from one computer to another. If the receiving computer is on the same network as the sending computer, it can send an electronic message directly. If the receiving computer is not on a network to which the sending computer is directly connected, the sending computer sends the message to another computer capable of forwarding it. The forwarding host, which presumably is attached to at least one other network, in turn delivers the message directly if it can, or passes it to yet another forwarding host. It is quite common for a message to pass through a dozen or more forwarders on its way from one part of the Internet to another.

TCP/IP

The various networks that are linked together to form the Internet work basically the same way, in that they pass data around in segments, called *packets*, each of which carries the addresses of its sender and its receiver. The most widely adopted protocol is the **Transport Control Protocol (TCP).** The combination of TCP and IP

Illustration 5   Packet-Switching Process

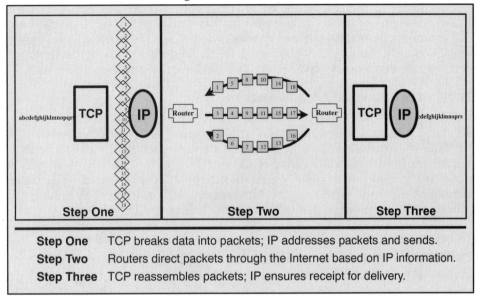

Step One	TCP breaks data into packets; IP addresses packets and sends.
Step Two	Routers direct packets through the Internet based on IP information.
Step Three	TCP reassembles packets; IP ensures receipt for delivery.

is used in nearly all Internet applications. By adhering to the same technical communication standards, Internet users are able to enjoy the services and resources of the network.

The networks connected to the Internet communicate with each other based on two protocols, TCP and IP. Stated simply, TCP/IP creates an envelope in which data resides. TCP is responsible for:

- Breaking documents, files, or messages to be transmitted into packets.

- Reassembling packets at the destination.

- Ensuring that all packets arrive and are in workable form.

The TCP component of TCP/IP assumes responsibility for breaking down the raw data into packets at one end and reassembling everything correctly at the other; the IP part takes care of routing the data packets successfully to their intended destination. The TCP part notifies network-switching devices of the contents of the packet, and the IP part directs where packets are to be sent. TCP simply formats data into packets and addresses each for its destination. Illustration 5 is a schematic representation of the packet-switching process.

A router reads this TCP/IP envelope and then directs the packets through the tangled web of connectivity that composes the Internet. The communicating computers, not the Internet, take responsibility for ensuring the successful transmission and receipt of the packets—the underlining concept being that every computer on the Internet has the capability to communicate with any other as its peer. In a packet-switched network, there is no single unbroken connection between sender and receiver. Instead, when information is sent, it is broken into small packets, sent over many different routes simultaneously, and then reassembled at the receiving end. By contrast, the telephone system is a circuit-switched network. In a circuit-switched network, once a connection is made (for example, a telephone call is connected), that part of the network is dedicated only to that single connection. Obviously, this would not be an efficient means of operation for the Internet, since each transmission would require its own dedicated circuitry.

Local Area and Wide Area Networks

Local area networks (LANs) are networks in a confined geographic area, such as an office building or a campus. Wide area networks (WANs) are combinations of LANs that are connected over large areas. One of the best examples of a WAN is a hotel company's central reservations system, where there are workstations at hotels and at reservations centers, all connected by a network to each other and to a common database. WANs may also be connected to the Internet by linking to a host computer or network that is linked to the Internet backbone.

Information Modes

The Internet helps establish an electronic communications pipeline in a non-traditional way. Internet information is available in either a pull or push mode. An information pull involves a user directing a web browser to a target website and soliciting data or files from the site. In other words, once at the site, the user decides what information or other available resources to review, retrieve, print, or download. As the name implies, an information pull is one in which the user takes desired content from the website. By contrast, an information push involves a site administrator or **webmaster** who distributes information to a user or group of users. An information push resembles the distribution of unsolicited mail by the postal service. When subscribing to a listserv or discussion group, for example, participants are required to provide an e-mail address. This address is likely to be used to distribute periodic communications from the site's webmaster. Typically, it is the webmaster who decides what information to distribute, and when. Similarly, user registration at a website may also lead to unexpected and/or unwanted news, announcements, product specifications, promotional campaigns, junk e-mail, or other information that is pushed to the user. To use a hotel industry example, a potential guest may visit a hotel company's website and request reservation (room and rate availability) information—an example of an information pull. An enrolled frequent guest, however, may be sent periodic electronic messages promoting a variety of hotel packages, features, and special events; these are information pushes.

Web Pages

A website is one or many pages of information linked together in a single package. Related documents residing together on a web host computer make up a website. However, a single server can host multiple websites, each contained in a separate area or directory, much like a hard drive can accommodate multiple directories. Websites can be simply organized in a hierarchy that progresses from general to specific information, or can be complex, with pages that seem to link randomly to other pages on the site. Documents within a site can be linked to any other document in the site, and even to documents on other sites. Most websites, however, are designed in a pyramid or outline structure that gives users a visual model to understand how information is arranged, and indicates how to find and navigate through the site's documents.

A site can be just one page or can comprise dozens or even hundreds of pages. The welcome or home page is the first or top page of a website. Usually, the welcome page acts as an introduction to a website, explaining the purpose of the site and describing the information found on other pages throughout the site. The welcome page can also serve as the table of contents for the rest of the site, providing connections from the top page to other pages throughout the site. Underlined or highlighted hyperlink text is often embedded in the welcome page. The **hyperlinks** serve to connect the top page with other pages throughout the site. Good web design principles suggest that pages throughout the site link back to the welcome page. This approach allows users to always find their way back to the top of a site in order to navigate in other directions.

The term *home page* is also used to describe the default-starting page on a browser. The browser's default home page can be determined and specified by the user. The default home page is retrieved automatically each time the user launches the browser. Browser software companies typically set this default page to be the top or welcome page of its own website, but the user can change this setting to be any preferred page. A browser home page will be the starting place from which the user begins each web session. Most web browsers offer a home icon that will automatically retrieve the starting page, no matter where the browser is currently located or has visited.

Since the web is perceived as a collection of published documents, and a document is composed of pages, elements of a website are typically referred to as web pages. A web page is the single unit of information requested, received, and displayed in a browser. Web pages can be formatted as text, graphics, or both, and should be thought of as units of information rather than as physical pages from a book or magazine.

The size of a web page is defined by embedded codes in the document that signify where a page begins and ends. While web pages can be of any length, a computer screen can show only a limited amount of content. Web pages are not sized to computer-screen dimensions and therefore may be both longer and wider than a standard computer screen. For this reason, viewing a web page may require the use of a vertical or horizontal scroll bar. A scroll bar is used to control which portions of a web page are displayed on the computer screen. Scroll bars usually have directional arrows to guide horizontal and vertical movement. When a web page is displayed in a browser, the user may need to scroll or "page" down through the document to see the entire page. When a web page is printed, it is not only the displayed portion of the page that is printed, but the entire page (which may equate to several printed pages).

A web page can be a hypertext or hypermedia document. A hypertext document contains text hyperlinks to other documents. A hypermedia document contains text, graphics, video, audio, and animation hyperlinks that connect to other documents.

The basic content of a web page can be, and often is, created through a word processor. The word-processed document is then embedded (using special formatting

Illustration 6   Extended URL Address

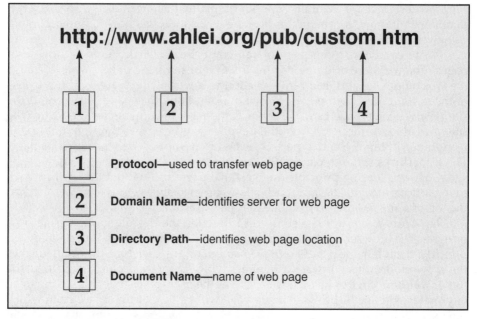

codes) into a web page. The special formatting codes are used to instruct the browser how to display the text. While a word processor can produce documents containing both text and graphics, web pages are usually made more stimulating by combining multimedia with text and graphics. Audio, video, animation, and other forms of active media (including virtual reality) can also be embedded into a web page. Taken together, it is possible to create a three-dimensional space that goes beyond the two-dimensional concept of a page. It is for this reason that the page metaphor is somewhat misleading.

Each page in a website has its own specific address, or URL. URLs are organized similarly to directories on personal computers. Folders and subfolders on personal computers are intended to organize contents for the computer user. In much the same way, URLs allow website contents to be logically organized. URLs that provide for more specific addressing beyond a website's home page are called *extended URL addresses.* Each subsection of an extended URL address is divided by a forward slash: "/." Illustration 6 shows an example of an extended URL web page address. The subsection "pub" represents the publications section of the site, and the specific name of the document to be viewed is "custom.htm."

Hypertext and Hyperlinks

Hypertext creates the foundation for connecting documents or pages on the web and provides the user with a means for rapid information discovery. Rather than reading a document from beginning to end and digesting the material in a sequential order, the user can select a word, phrase, or concept and receive more detailed information on the selected item or topic. Hypertext programming enables document linkage on the same or different Internet server. Hypertext typically consists of a hyperlink that appears on the screen as a highlighted word, phrase, concept, icon, or graphic. By clicking on an item or object, the user is able to navigate across the Internet in search of more information. On the web, that information can be located at any website throughout the world.

There are three types of hyperlinks. *Target hyperlinks* move from one location in a document to another location in the same document. For example, a directory at the top of a web page may contain the equivalent of a table of contents for the site. Selecting an item from the listing will quickly direct the browser to that section of the web document. *Relative hyperlinks* move from one document to another document on the same Internet server. In web terminology, the second document is considered a relative of the first document. *Absolute hyperlinks* move to another document on a different Internet server.

Hypertext and hypermedia allow the user to learn in a non-linear fashion. Reading a book from cover to cover is a linear way of learning. Branching off and investigating related topics as terms are encountered is a non-linear way of learning. For example, while reading an article on hotel front office operations, the reader may want to learn more about reservation systems. Reading about reservation systems might trigger interest in telecommunications technology. Reading about telecommunications technology may prompt interest in wide area networks, and so on. The ability to branch from one related topic to another, in a non-linear fashion, is what makes hyperlinks so powerful and effective. Displaying pages from one website after another is called *web surfing* and is like using a remote control to jump from one television station to another.

Bookmarks

Bookmarks represent an important Internet browser feature. Bookmarks store the addresses of favorite web pages. Bookmarking a favorite site on the web logs the path used to direct the browser to the site, enabling the user to arrive quickly without having to remember and input a long Internet address. Bookmarking is similar to the redial feature on a touch-tone phone. It's not a good idea to randomly bookmark every site visited, because the URLs of those sites will get lost in a long miscellaneous list of favorites. Most browsers allow the user to organize bookmarked sites into specific categories and store them in labeled folders. Sorting and categorizing saved bookmarks through a directory structure creates a virtual bookshelf. Favorite sites and frequently used reference materials are good candidates for bookmarking.

Internet Cookies

Web **cookies** often have a positive purpose but have also created concern among web browser users. A web cookie is the term used to describe a small program that a web server sends to a web browser, often without the approval or awareness of the user. The program captures information from the computer it resides in. The information is stored by the browser and sent back to the server each time the browser makes a request of the server. Many websites use cookies to store login codes. These sites have a security login requirement. Instead of requiring the user to log in every time he or she accesses the site, the cookie sends the login codes to the server every time the user accesses the site. This is often seen as a benefit to users who access many sites and may have many different access codes.

By storing a cookie in the user's browser, the server may be collecting information about the user beyond the login codes, without the user's permission, which is what causes user concern. Depending on the type of cookie used and the browser's capabilities, the browser may accept or not accept the cookie. Accepted cookies may be saved for a short or long time, depending on whether the browser has been programmed to accept and store cookies it receives. Cookies might contain information gained about the user based on recent site visits. This could be abused and result in competitive espionage. Such things as login codes or registration information, online purchasing patterns, browsing routines, user preferences, and the like can be collected by cookies and then forwarded to the web server without the user's permission.

When a server receives a request from a browser that includes a cookie, the server is able to use the information stored in the cookie. For example, the server might customize an HTML document to the user's preferences or create and maintain a log of the user's visits and request patterns. Cookies are usually saved in the user's computer (active memory) until the browser is closed. Upon closing, the cookie may be programmed to lodge itself on the user's hard drive. In any case, cookies normally come with a predetermined expiration date. While in residence on the hard drive, cookies may be capable of gathering some information for later transmission to a web server.

Content-Blocking Software

Some browsers rely upon a content rating system that enables the user to set limits on the kind of material that can be viewed and therefore block certain content, through content-blocking software. There are many reasons users develop interest in content-blocking software. One reason involves the seedier side of cyberspace that allows for the electronic transmission of lewd or obscene materials. Computer obscenity tends to be found in three basic places: dial-in bulletin board systems (BBS), Internet sites, and Usenet newsgroups. Bulletin boards, Internet sites, and newsgroups are not policed and offer uncensored access to anyone who happens upon them. For this reason, there is a need for content-blocking software capable of disallowing access, based on specified criteria and parameters. In addition, many employers desire to limit employees' Internet access to portions of the network that are work-related. Many managers tend to be concerned that the Information Superhighway distracts employees and leads to lower levels of productivity, so they want to limit employee access to business-relevant sites.

Computer Viruses

A computer **virus** is software used to infect a computer program or file. It is intended to disrupt the use of a computer or destroy it. After the virus code is written, it is buried within an existing program. Once that program is executed, the virus code is activated and attaches copies of itself to other programs in the system. Infected programs copy the virus to other programs. Virus programs often are designed to damage computer systems by destroying or corrupting data. If an infected file is transferred to or accessed by another computer system, the virus will spread to the other system. Viruses have become a serious problem, given the increased use of the Internet and other computer networks.

A virus cannot be attached to data; it must be attached to an executable program that is downloaded into or installed onto a computer. The virus-attached program must be executed to activate the virus. Although there are several thousand known computer viruses, the majority are benign and tend to be no more harmful than a creative prank. A benign virus may freeze a screen display or flash a short message. Another may be designed to generate annoying or unusual sounds. In any case, a benign virus typically produces harmless actions that last until the virus is discovered and deleted. Malignant, or harmful, viruses are of four main types:

- Boot sector viruses

- File viruses

- Trojan horse viruses

- Macro viruses

A *boot sector virus* replaces the boot program that is used to start the computer system with a modified, infected version of the boot program. When the infected boot program is executed, it loads the virus into the computer's memory. The most common way for a boot virus to be transferred to a machine is through storage on a floppy disk. If the floppy disk is left in the drive when the computer is turned off and then on again, the machine will become infected because it reads the boot sectors of the floppy disk, expecting to find the operating system there. Once the computer is infected, the boot virus is likely to replicate itself onto all the floppies that are read or written until the virus is eradicated.

A *file virus* inserts virus code into program files. The virus then spreads to any program that accesses the infected program.

A *Trojan horse virus* is a virus that hides within or is designed to look like a legitimate program. A Trojan horse virus normally results in the computer performing an illicit activity during the execution of an application. Trojan horse viruses have traditionally been used to (1) locate password information or make a system vulnerable to future unauthorized entry, or (2) destroy programs, files, or data.

A *macro virus* uses the macro language of an application, such as word processing, to hide the virus code. Even though a macro virus remains hidden within an application, execution of the macro will lead to programs and/or files being damaged. In other words, when a document with an infected macro is opened, the macro virus is loaded into memory. Certain actions, such as saving the document, activate the virus. Macro viruses often attach to word processing or electronic spreadsheet templates so that any document created using the template becomes infected.

Some viruses may also contain logic bombs or time bombs. A *logic bomb* is a program that is activated when a certain condition is detected. A logic bomb is usually used to destroy data, either by reformatting the hard drive or by inserting random bits of data into select files. Logic bombs are typically distributed as public domain software downloaded off the Internet. Once launched, a logic bomb does its damage immediately. A disgruntled worker, for example, could plant a logic bomb designed to destroy reservation or payroll files should he or she be terminated. A *time bomb* is a type of logic bomb that is set to self-activate on a specific date.

Another form of program or file corruption is a *worm*. Although often classified as a virus, a worm, unlike a virus, does not attach itself to another program. Instead, a worm is designed to copy itself repeatedly in memory or on a disk drive until no memory or disk space remains. When this happens, the computer will stop functioning. Some worm programs are designed to copy themselves to other computers on the Internet or intranet.

Antivirus software is designed to detect and remove computer viruses. Antivirus programs search for computer programming code or programs that attempt to modify the boot program, operating system, and other programs that normally are read from but not written to. Antivirus programs also look for specific patterns of known virus code, called a virus signature, which they compare to a virus signature file. Virus signature files need to be updated frequently to include newly discovered viruses, so an antivirus program can protect against viruses written after the antivirus program was released. Another way antivirus programs prevent viruses is by inoculating existing program files. When a program file is inoculated, information such as the file size and file creation date is recorded in a separate inoculation file. Using this information, the antivirus program can detect if a virus program has tampered with the program file. Some sophisticated virus programs, however, take steps to avoid detection. A virus might infect a program, for example, and yet still report the size and creation date of the original, uninfected program. A virus that uses methods to avoid detection is referred to as a *stealth virus*. Its ability to remain free of detection makes the stealth virus one of the most difficult to control. Virus detection software should be updated on a regular basis to ensure the system is safe and fully operational.

Intranet and Extranet Technology

With the enormous growth of the Internet, an increasing number of users have begun using the Internet for interpersonal communications, information gathering, and transacting business. Given the Internet's popularity, it did not take long for companies to recognize that the components that worked for the Internet could be equally valuable internally. When Internet technology is applied and used inside a corporation, organization, or other entity, and available only to its employees, it is referred to as an **intranet**. Most companies construct a **firewall** around their intranets. A firewall is a combination of hardware and software that allows only authorized individuals to access the intranet for specific purposes. Employees can use the firm's intranet to access Internet resources, but a firewall prevents those on the Internet from interacting with the intranet. Often an intranet is composed of a number of different networks inside a corporation that all communicate with one another via TCP/IP. These separate networks are often referred to as subnets. In hotel companies, an intranet may allow employees to access information about company policies, procedures, available job positions, benefits, and other company information.

Most intranet technologies, like those of the Internet, are client/server based. In many instances, however, the way the technology is applied on an intranet differs from its application on the Internet. Applying these same technologies to multiple firms, all of which participate in a private intranet and public Internet applications, leads to the development of an **extranet**.

Creating a system in which internal (intranet), external (Internet), and selective additional (extranet) information and resources can be used seamlessly appears to have many benefits. First, TCP/IP-based networks make it easy for people to have remote access to the network from home or while traveling. Second, accessing an intranet or extranet is much like connecting to the Internet, except that the connection is to a private network or networks, not to a public (Internet) provider. Third, cooperation between an intranet, extranet, and the Internet creates many substantial benefits. Recognizing the power of the Internet and web technologies, companies are developing intranets and extranets designed to enhance communications, productivity, profitability, decision-making, and the like. Intranets and extranets can be used for any purpose other networks are used for, and enable people to work together more easily and effectively.

Extranets are extended intranets connecting not only internal personnel, but also suppliers, business partners, select customers, and other affiliated entities. In both intranets and extranets, the ability to allow high-quality interactions while ensuring confidentiality, security, and controlled access is critical.

An extranet connects multiple remote organizations, with Internet connectivity, in a seamless application. The type and speed of Internet access required to support an extranet is directly related to the number of users and the amount of information that must be served. Extranet applications can provide enhanced interaction with remote facilities, customers, and suppliers. Companies using extranets may no longer need to rely on fax, telephone, and mail communications and should experience savings in phone, paper, and mailing costs. Hotel companies may establish reservations extranets for their best corporate customers, or set up extranets for vendors, to facilitate the ordering, tracking, and billing of food, beverages, and supplies.

Website Design

To attract and retain online visitors, a hotel should focus on the design, quality, and content for its website. Hotel websites, once resembling printed brochures and composed only of text and digitized photos, have become much more sophisticated, presenting visitors with an interactive collection of important business productivity applications designed to enhance the firm's image and complement its strategic plans.

A hotel website should be designed to take advantage of effective graphics and informative content rather than just merely apply sophisticated browser technology. The design of a hotel's website should appeal to the largest possible number of viewers. Many hotel websites now feature online reservations, e-mail feedback, secure transactions, and linked websites. While non-hospitality industry sites may be monetarily supported through subscription and/or advertising revenue, this has not been true for hotel websites. Historically, hotel websites have been designed, developed, financed, and maintained by a hotel company (or its contracted agent).

A well-designed and developed website can be an invaluable resource for a lodging company. The ability to have a worldwide marketing and customer service presence twenty-four hours a day, seven days a week gives lodging companies on the Internet tremendous exposure with minimal risk or expense. It is important to keep the site current and accurate, so the lodging company or hotel should make sure that someone is responsible for the site's contents. This person is usually dubbed the *webmaster*. The webmaster need not be a computer expert but must be familiar with the purposes and operation of the site.

Design Concepts

It is not difficult to create a website; the trick is to design a site that meets the goals and expectations of the hotel and its target markets. Some good questions hotel managers should ask when it comes to their website include:

- Does the hospitality property need to hire a professional consultant to help develop a smart, effective, and finely tuned website?
- How can the site convey the competitive advantages of the hotel?
- What hotel features should the site emphasize?
- Are customized graphics, panoramic pictures, animation, and video clips necessary?
- What parts of the website should be updated regularly, and what parts should be static?
- Should the site be interactive, allowing the user to communicate with the hotel (i.e., make a guestroom reservation, provide feedback on a recent stay, reserve a tee time, order hotel-branded clothing, and so on)?
- What are the keywords and tags that will allow maximum exposure of the website through search engines?

An experienced professional can assist a hotel project team with text layout, graphics, web technologies, animation, and special multimedia features. Illustration 7 presents fundamental website design concepts. Other web design tips include the following:

- *Remove dates from all web pages, unless dates are to be routinely changed as content changes.* There is nothing that immediately informs a visitor of a website's neglect more than a "Last updated" tag that is beyond two to four days old. There simply is no incentive for a visitor to treat the site's content as timely or accurate when it is admittedly out of date.
- *Make site navigation easy (remember the three-click rule).* Failure to provide a user with access to a page on the website in a reasonable time frame can be more detrimental to an effective web design than any other single factor. Special functions, data, or other information on a website should be accessible within

Illustration 7   Fundamentals of Website Design

Text:

- Simple text is the fastest and easiest to comprehend.
- Too much text will clutter the website and make it uninviting.
- Text font size, style, and color can influence the impact of the hospitality property's message.
- Text works best when balanced by graphics, pictures, or illustrations.

Graphics:

- Only those graphics that will get the property's message across should be used.
- Simple graphics are good graphics.
- Graphics should be designed to help visitors interact with the hospitality property's website.
- Consistent graphic design throughout the hospitality property's website is essential in providing the viewer a comfortable visual framework.
- The graphics should be easy and quick to download onto the web page.

Photos:

- Pictures can be most effective in presenting some hospitality property features, especially physical structures or recreational facilities.
- Care must be exercised to ensure that digitized photos are clear, appropriately sized, and displayed quickly.
- Pictures placed in a logical series tend to be most effective.

Animation:

- Animation may be effective in describing sequences and movement.
- Animation can be used to get attention or to highlight website areas.
- Animation should be used to clarify the hospitality property's message; it should not overshadow the message or be used merely to entertain.
- Cartoons should not be mixed with other types of illustrations.
- A controversial cartoon theme or distorted representation can trigger potential adverse reactions.

three mouse clicks. If the guest wishes to make a reservation, for example, the function must be discoverable in three (or fewer) clicks, or the user may leave the site with little likelihood of a return visit.

- *Limit web page length (remember the 22-inch rule).* A web page can become so long that visitors easily get lost or forget what has been presented or where it is located. The "22-inch rule" is designed to make a website easier for a visitor to navigate. A web page 22 inches long is the equivalent of two standard-length typed pages stacked on top of each other, which is a chunk of information that is easy for a reader to handle. Hyperlinked branching to other pages is a better alternative than a single, endless web page.

- *Consider automatically filtering and feeding current items to the website.* Current information stimulates and heightens visitor interest and alerts the user that the site may be different each time it's visited. Many hotel websites feature current weather conditions, unique menu offerings, special overnight packages, contests, click-it rates, and also support cross-promotions of community attractions and special events.

- *Don't think of the website as a big hyperlinks list.* The design feature most overlooked or taken for granted by lodging companies is in the area of hyperlinks. Too often, websites are poorly organized, cluttered, and illogical in content presentation, and few things are more frustrating to visitors than to be confronted with a long list of hyperlinks at a website. The best website designs tend to be the simplest.

- *Remove all counters at the website.* Low visitor frequency indicates a potential problem to those visiting the site. Being the 116th visitor and returning several weeks later to discover you are the 118th visitor does nothing to bolster interest in the site. Statistics for a variety of web activities, including visits, can be obtained in a variety of ways, none of which need to be visible to a site user.

- *Avoid using technology tricks to attract visitors.* Current animation techniques, streaming audio, video players, database displays, and other popular technology applications are likely to become quickly outdated or superseded by enhanced applications. Relying on tricks or gimmicks to attract visitors will not prove as valuable as providing stimulating content or links to relevant sites. Avoid reliance on technology gadgets as a primary web attraction.

Website Strategies

The following list of hotel website strategies is intended to be representative, not exhaustive, of industry practices. Illustration 8 lists popular hotel website features.

Awareness. Attracting new customers is often a primary purpose of website development. A photograph of the property, location maps, a list of contact persons, and information about amenities, restaurants, and the like can be prominently posted at the website to generate consumer interest. In addition, hotel companies may offer real-time reservation capabilities, electronic couponing, and/or frequent browser promotions.

Optimization. Constructing a website does not guarantee visitors. A website sponsor must index the site and reference and promote the site's address whenever possible. Even if the website or brand name is well known, it is common for web designers and webmasters to identify the most popular words used in search engines to find information, and then make sure the site has these words included in the site. This is called *optimization,* since it optimizes the chance that the website will come up when people search for information on the web.

Product Promotion. Providing a display of room types and amenities, floor plans, meeting facilities, recreational facilities, banquet and catering offerings, and other features is relatively common among lodging websites. The ability to describe and show the physical attributes of the hotel and its outlets, focus on awards and testimonials,

Illustration 8   Popular Features of Hotel Websites

Generic Information:
 History/Philosophy/Mission Statement
 Address and Telephone Information
 Weather/Directions/Local Area Map
 Management/Key Staff Contacts (E-Mail Links)
Room Offerings:
 Room Types
 Room Floor Plans
 Room Amenities
 Room Entertainment
 Room ADA Compliance
 Room Availability
Reservations:
 Site Locator/Related Information
 Maps/Vicinity Information
 Online Reservations/Confirmation
 Group and Meeting Planning
 Revenue/Yield Management Applications
 Online/E-Mail RFPs for Special Transactions
Menu Offerings:
 Menu Preview
 Items by Groupings
 Daily Specials/Promotions
 Kids' Menu/Take-Out Menu/Faxback Services
 Home Delivery/Cybermeals
 Banquet and Catering Menus
 Custom Entrées/Private Parties
 Menu Reviews/Critics' Commentary
Other Features:
 Physical Structure/Virtual Tour
 Views/Adjoining Operations
 Meeting/Exhibit/Party Facilities
 Merchandise Sales/Logo Apparel
 Decorations/Ambience Options
 Entertainment/Room Configuration Options
 Employment Opportunities/Applications
 Service Tips/Menus/Entertainment Packages
 Frequent Stayer Program/Preferred Customer Program
 Newsletter/Promotional Programs
 Gift Certificates/E-Couponing
 Guest Testimonials/Photo Album

and present ratings and reviews is essential to effective product promotion. Additionally, some hotels market logo clothing and accessory items via their website.

Customer Pipeline. Websites featuring customer comment sections and correspondence links to property managers are starting to become popular. E-mail establishes a one-to-one communication channel. In addition, a hotel e-newsletter, customer service pledge, employment application, franchise offering, and related documents can be disbursed via the web. By offering current customers special web benefits (such as incentive rewards, frequent-stayer discounts, entry to special events, access to special promotions, etc.), a website can promote customer loyalty while enhancing web value.

News. A website can serve as a medium for rapid distribution of company news, product promotions, special event information, press releases, and other broadcast-worthy information. News items may be company- or industry-specific, or general in nature. For example, lodging industry stock market news, property openings, property updates, staff announcements, and other significant business information can be presented at the hotel's website.

Relationship Building. The web provides a means to cultivate relationships with customers, stockholders, franchisees, purveyors, and personnel at corporate head-quarters. Some hotels reserve website space for franchise and franchisee infor-mation, meeting planner promotions, employee communications, contests and drawings, and the like. Marketing and customer feedback surveys can also be conducted over the web.

Transactions. Online purchasing technology provides a means for customers to conduct secure electronic transactions at the website. Booking a guestroom res-ervation and providing a payment card guarantee is a good example of a secure transaction because it uses a special hypertext transfer protocol with extra security features. Retail sales at websites are conducted through gift shops and merchan-dise centers featuring products bearing the hotel's name and logo. In addition, hotels may offer off-the-premises product delivery services and other transaction-based services. Websites that offer specialty merchandise typically use a *shopping cart* to allow surfers to browse product lines, select products for purchase, and complete payment. Online purchasers are precluded from paying with cash, and therefore must use one of several payment options including credit card, debit card, Google Checkout, PayPal, Paymentech, MoneyZap, and Bill Me Later. As electronic financial formats continue to evolve, the number of payment options available for online transactions will likewise increase.

Employment. A hotel's website can be an effective vehicle for listing job opportu-nities. Attracting job applicants via web-based announcements has proven to be an effective alternative to posting jobs traditionally, since the website can introduce the prospective employee to the company and establish a direct line of commu-nication at the same time. Advanced website designs enable visitors to download and print employment applications or fill out online electronic forms.

Spotlighting. Hotels can use a website to display photos of lobby areas, guest-rooms, dining rooms, and catered events in a calendar-like fashion. Websites can also use spotlighting to highlight special celebrity events or publish personal testi-monials. Such spotlighting can prove important to the website's image while help-ing create the hotel's "virtual personality."

Pointers and Tips. A tip of the day, week, or month can help promote website interest by arousing curiosity and interest through changing web content. This can be especially important to keeping current customers interested in the website. Tips may be directly related to promoting the company (e.g., senior citizen packages, group travel rates, etc.) or general in nature (e.g., how to pack for trips, finding ways to exercise while traveling, selecting the right wine to complement certain foods, and so on).

Intranet Support. Developing a company intranet, or a Virtual Private Network (VPN), provides multi-unit chain operators with unique communication and operations opportunities. For example, chain properties networked together can generate an aggregate purchase order through the chain's intranet. The purchase order file could then be sent to a set of preferred purveyors. The purveyors' websites could then, in turn, send pricing proposals and e-forms for online purchasing. Similarly, a VPN of franchisees could communicate with the parent organization via a link to the corporate web page. Another popular use of a company intranet is to serve as the library of all company information, including policies, procedures, announcements, employee benefit information, job opening postings, and other valuable information. The intranet can be organized in such a way that all employees have access to certain sections of the site, while other portions of the site require special security access. For example, employee benefits might be accessible to everyone, but accounting procedures might be accessible only to those employees with accounting security codes.

Glossary

backbone—Central artery of the Internet carrying a majority of data traffic.

bridge—A connection of two or more networks that use the same data transfer protocol (the same address format). A bridge makes attached networks appear to operate as a single network.

cookies—Information sent from a web server to a web browser that directs the browser to save and transmit collected data whenever requested by the server.

Domain Name System (DNS)—A method for organizing site names on the Internet.

e-mail—Electronic document composed, mailed, received, and read via a computer.

extranet—Privatized website capable of connecting authorized personnel, customers, suppliers, and strategic business partners.

File Transfer Protocol (FTP)—Allows access to files, programs, or other services at a remote Internet site.

firewall—A combination of hardware and software that separates a LAN into two or more parts for security purposes.

frequently asked questions (FAQs)—List of commonly asked questions related to a specific product or discussion topic.

gateway—Allows users on one network to access resources on a different type of network.

hyperlinks—Built-in connectivity to related documents.

hypertext—Web document containing text hyperlinks to related documents.

Hypertext Markup Language (HTML)—A set of special instructions, called tags or markups, used to create, link, and display web pages.

instant messaging (IM)—A term referring to any program that allows two or more users to communicate in real-time interactive discussions.

Internet—A network of networks, connecting local and regional computer sites to an expansive electronic grid.

Internet Protocol (IP) address—An address used by the network to identify a specific computer's location.

Internet service provider (ISP)—Provides connectivity to the Internet through an intermediary computer.

InterNIC—Agency responsible for verifying the uniqueness of IP addresses.

intranet—Internet technology applied and used inside a corporation, organization, or other entity, and available only to its employees.

keywords—A small set of words designed to convey the subject of an article, website, document, etc. on the web.

listserv—Short for *list server,* used to refer to an automated information distribution system.

network—A configuration of workstations that enables users to share data, programs, and peripheral devices (such as servers and printers).

newsgroup—Essentially an online discussion group that focuses narrowly on a particular topic.

online service provider (OSP)—Provides connectivity to online services and the Internet through an intermediary computer.

protocol—Set of rules and procedures for exchanging information between computers. Protocols define how a link is established, how information is transmitted, and how errors are detected and corrected. By using the same protocols, different types of computers can communicate.

router—Device responsible for moving data packets from point to point; an intelligent network connector that directs network traffic.

search engine—A program designed to help users find and retrieve Internet resources.

shareware—Downloadable software requiring payment of a registration fee.

social network—An online, web-based community of individuals who have common interests, activities, and/or experiences.

Transport Control Protocol (TCP)—Transport layer protocol for Internet data transmission.

uniform resource locator (URL)—Formatted Internet domain name.

Usenet—A network of newsgroups independent of the Internet but with gateway links to the Internet.

virus—A program that copies itself into other programs and files and causes damage to those programs and files.

webmaster—A person responsible for administering a website.

World Wide Web (www)—Graphical user interface for the Internet, similar to application software; the portion of the Internet containing websites, where information can be accessed electronically; the collection of hyperlinked documents accessible on the Internet.

Index

Forms for
Night Audit Problem

THE WASHINGTON INN

Name ___Sunshine Master___ Acct. No. _____

Room ___101___ Rate $1330⁰⁰ Arrival Date __3/31__

DATE	3/31	4/1								
Balance Fwd.		(600 -)								
Room	1330 -									
Sales Tax	53 20									
Restaurant										
Bar										
Local										
Long Distance	16 80									
Telegrams										
Laundry-Valet										
Cash Disburse										
Transfer										
TOTAL	1400 -									
Less: Cash	2000 -									
: Allowances										
: Transfer										
Carried Fwd.	(600 -)									

THE WASHINGTON INN

Name BROWN, MR. & MRS. EDWIN Acct. No. _____

Room 245 Rate $48⁰⁰ Arrival Date 3/28

DATE	3/28		3/29		3/30		3/31		4/1					
Balance Fwd.			1	92	65	84	149	76	208	04				
Room	48	-	48	-	48	-	48	-						
Sales Tax	1	92	1	92	1	92	1	92						
Restaurant			14	-	26	-								
Bar					8	-								
Local														
Long Distance							8	36						
Telegrams														
Laundry-Valet														
Cash Disburse														
Transfer														
TOTAL	49	92	65	84	149	76	208	04						
Less: Cash														
: Allowances														
: Transfer	48	-												
Carried Fwd.	1	92	65	84	149	76	208	04						

THE WASHINGTON INN

Name ___JACKSON, LARRY_____ Acct. No. _____

Room ___302_____ Rate $___70_____ Arrival Date ___3/31_____

DATE	3/31		4/1														
Balance Fwd.			72	80													
Room	70	–															
Sales Tax	2	80															
Restaurant																	
Bar																	
Local																	
Long Distance																	
Telegrams																	
Laundry-Valet																	
Cash Disburse																	
Transfer																	
TOTAL	72	80															
Less: Cash																	
: Allowances																	
: Transfer																	
Carried Fwd.	72	80															

THE WASHINGTON INN

Name GREENWOOD, NELSON   Acct. No. _____

Room 324   Rate $24   Arrival Date 3/30

DATE	3/30		3/31		4/1												
Balance Fwd.			21	21	49	92											
Room	24	–	24	–													
Sales Tax		96		96													
Restaurant	13	50															
Bar			3	75													
Local																	
Long Distance	6	75															
Telegrams																	
Laundry-Valet																	
Cash Disburse																	
Transfer																	
TOTAL	45	21	49	92													
Less: Cash																	
: Allowances																	
: Transfer	24	–															
Carried Fwd.	21	21	49	92													

THE WASHINGTON INN

Name FOSTER, MR. & MRS. JACK Acct. No. _____

Room 440 Rate $56⁰⁰ Arrival Date 3/31

DATE	3/31		4/1															
Balance Fwd.			58	24														
Room	56	–																
Sales Tax	2	24																
Restaurant																		
Bar																		
Local																		
Long Distance																		
Telegrams																		
Laundry-Valet																		
Cash Disburse																		
Transfer																		
TOTAL	58	24																
Less: Cash																		
: Allowances																		
: Transfer																		
Carried Fwd.	58	24																

THE WASHINGTON INN

Name __STRAIGHT, MR. & MRS. TOM__ Acct. No. _____

Room __522__ Rate __$56⁰⁰__ Arrival Date __3/31__

DATE	3/31		4/1														
Balance Fwd.			97	34													
Room	56	-															
Sales Tax	2	24															
Restaurant																	
ROOM SERVICE	28	08															
Bar																	
Local																	
Long Distance	6	52															
Telegrams																	
Laundry-Valet																	
Cash Disburse	4	50															
Transfer																	
TOTAL	97	34															
Less: Cash																	
: Allowances																	
: Transfer																	
Carried Fwd.	97	34															

THE WASHINGTON INN

Name **DAVIS, RONALD** _____ Acct. No. _____

Room **100** _____ Rate **INCIDENTALS** Arrival Date **3/31** _____

DATE	3/31	4/1												
Balance Fwd.		—												
Room														
Sales Tax														
Restaurant														
Bar														
Local														
Long Distance														
Telegrams														
Laundry-Valet														
Cash Disburse														
Transfer														
TOTAL														
Less: Cash														
: Allowances														
: Transfer														
Carried Fwd.	—													

THE WASHINGTON INN
CITY LEDGER CONTROL

DATE	4/1													
Balance Fwd.	50000 —													
Restaurant														
Bar														
Miscellaneous														
Transfer Debit														
TOTAL														
Cash														
Allowances														
Transfer Credit														
Carried Fwd.														

THE WASHINGTON INN
ADVANCE PAYMENTS CONTROL

DATE	4/1														
Balance Fwd.	(2930	-)													
Transfer Debit															
Refund															
TOTAL															
Cash															
Carried Fwd.															

THE WASHINGTON INN

Name _____ Acct. No. _____

Room _____ Rate _____ Arrival Date _____

DATE															
Balance Fwd.															
Room															
Sales Tax															
Restaurant															
Bar															
Local															
Long Distance															
Telegrams															
Laundry-Valet															
Cash Disburse															
Transfer															
TOTAL															
Less: Cash															
: Allowances															
: Transfer															
Carried Fwd.															

THE WASHINGTON INN

Name _____ Acct. No. _____

Room _____ Rate _____ Arrival Date _____

DATE														
Balance Fwd.														
Room														
Sales Tax														
Restaurant														
Bar														
Local														
Long Distance														
Telegrams														
Laundry-Valet														
Cash Disburse														
Transfer														
TOTAL														
Less: Cash														
: Allowances														
: Transfer														
Carried Fwd.														

THE WASHINGTON INN

Name _____ Acct. No. _____

Room _____ Rate _____ Arrival Date _____

DATE												
Balance Fwd.												
Room												
Sales Tax												
Restaurant												
Bar												
Local												
Long Distance												
Telegrams												
Laundry-Valet												
Cash Disburse												
Transfer												
TOTAL												
Less: Cash												
: Allowances												
: Transfer												
Carried Fwd.												

THE WASHINGTON INN

Name _____ Acct. No. _____

Room _____ Rate _____ Arrival Date _____

DATE													
Balance Fwd.													
Room													
Sales Tax													
Restaurant													
Bar													
Local													
Long Distance													
Telegrams													
Laundry-Valet													
Cash Disburse													
Transfer													
TOTAL													
Less: Cash													
: Allowances													
: Transfer													
Carried Fwd.													

THE WASHINGTON INN

Name _____ Acct. No. _____

Room _____ Rate _____ Arrival Date _____

DATE																
Balance Fwd.																
Room																
Sales Tax																
Restaurant																
Bar																
Local																
Long Distance																
Telegrams																
Laundry-Valet																
Cash Disburse																
Transfer																
TOTAL																
Less: Cash																
: Allowances																
: Transfer																
Carried Fwd.																

THE WASHINGTON INN

Name _____ Acct. No. _____

Room _____ Rate _____ Arrival Date _____

DATE															
Balance Fwd.															
Room															
Sales Tax															
Restaurant															
Bar															
Local															
Long Distance															
Telegrams															
Laundry-Valet															
Cash Disburse															
Transfer															
TOTAL															
Less: Cash															
: Allowances															
: Transfer															
Carried Fwd.															

TRANSCRIPT OF GUEST LEDGER

Hotel _____   Date _____   Sheet No. _____

Room No.	No. Guests	Name	Balance Brought Forward	Room	Tax	Rest.	Bar	Room Service	Telephone Local	Telephone Long Dist.	Laundry	Cash Disb.	Trans-fers	Total Charges	Cash	Trans-fers	Allow-ances	Balance Carried Forward
		House Total																
		City Ledger																
		Advance Deposits																
		Accts. Receivable Total																